ENCYCLOPEDIA OF

WORLD
MYTHOLOGY

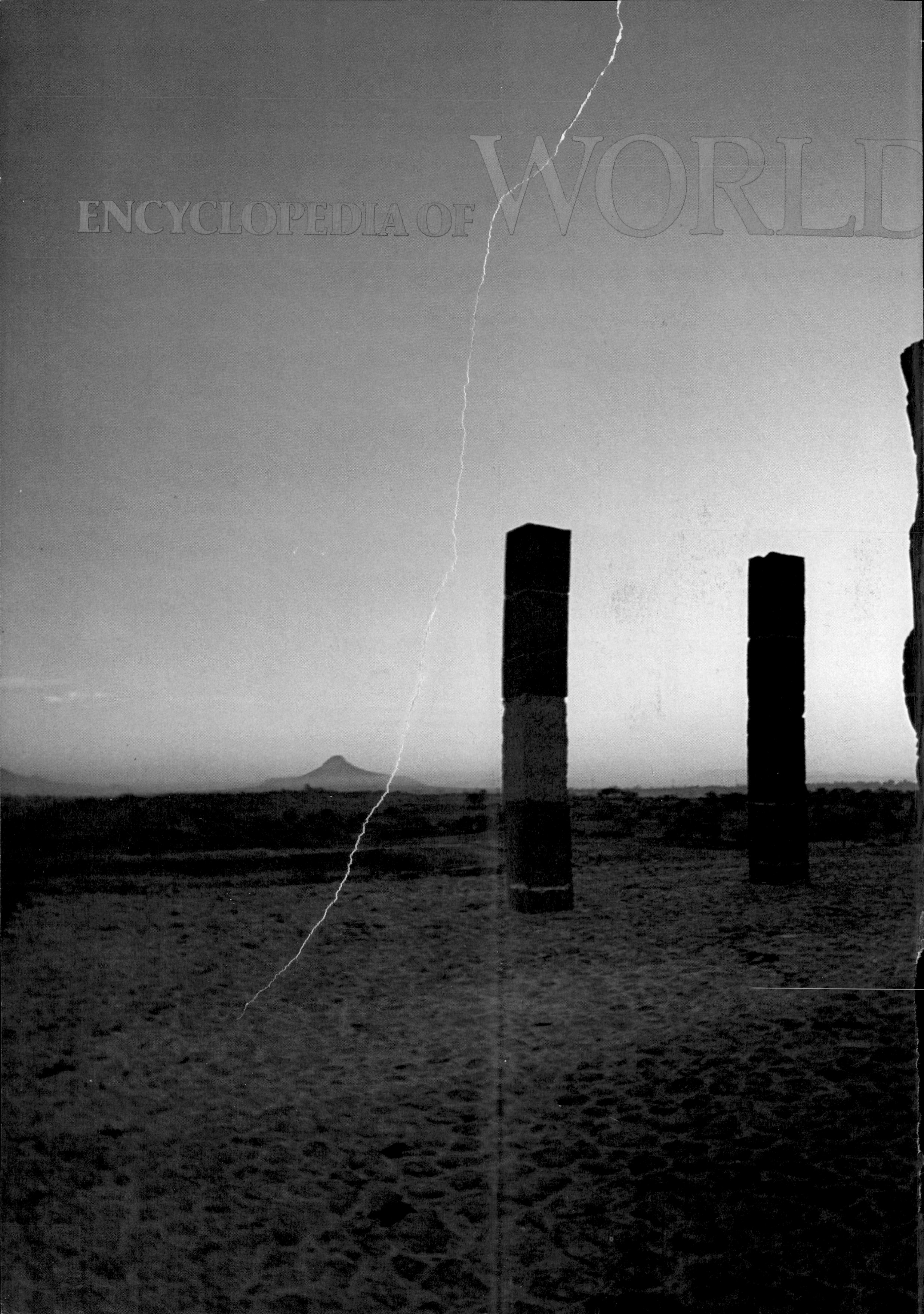
ENCYCLOPEDIA OF WORLD

MYTHOLOGY

Foreword by Rex Warner

octopus
in association with
Phoebus

CONTENTS

First published 1975 by
Octopus Books Limited
59 Grosvenor Street, London W.1

ISBN 0 7064 0397 5

© 1970–1971 BPC Publishing Ltd.
© 1975 BPC Publishing Ltd. This book has
been produced by Phoebus Publishing Company in
cooperation with Octopus Books Limited.

Produced by
Mandarin Publishers Limited
22a Westlands Road, Quarry Bay, Hong Kong
Printed in Hong Kong

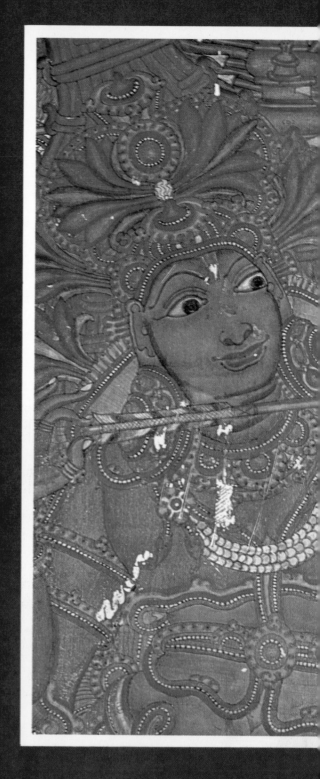

Rama, with bow and arrows,
attempting to retrieve his consort.

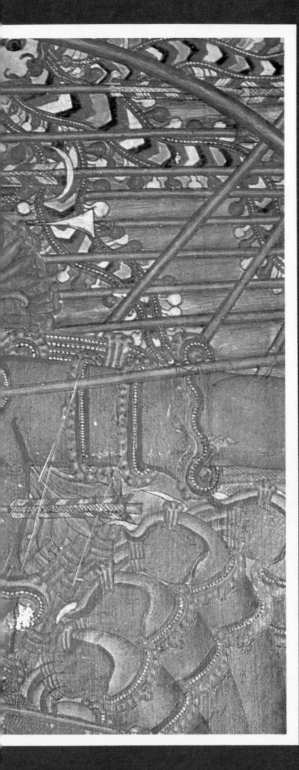

FOREWORD

The words 'myth' and 'story' are both Greek in origin. But the Greek 'historians' were careful to draw distinctions between themselves and the 'mythographers'. The historians claimed to be telling the truth about what really happened and considered that the writers of myths were telling fables, often improbable, often untrue and quite often (or so Plato thought) immoral. On the other hand, these historians never doubted the truth of some of the myths, notably the stories of the Trojan War. It was not till the 19th century of our era that scholars proclaimed that all myths were unhistorical, that the Trojan War never took place and that 'Homer', who did not exist either, supplied us with nothing but something in the nature of a 'solar myth'.

Then, to the fury of the scholars, Schliemann actually dug up Troy and more recent archeologists have confirmed as basically true very many of the 'myths' of Homer and others, including the Biblical stories of the Flood and of the Tower of Babel.

Today it is generally admitted that myth and legend can and often do have a basis in historical fact. Of course there is also very much mythical material which cannot be regarded as historical, except in a very loose sense. Many myths of all countries are attempts to explain the world which to primitive man was even more unpredictable and alarming than it is to us. They also very often express attempts to control or to influence, at least to some extent, this world. In cultures as far apart as the Babylonian and that of the Mayas in Central America, the main preoccupation appears to have been the calendar and the movements of the sun, moon and stars. A theme common to all mythologies is that of the birth, growth and decay and, often, resurrection of all life, animal, vegetable and human.

Every people in the world has its own myths; but it is very obvious that many of these myths are strikingly similar. These similarities may be accounted for by assuming a common racial origin at a very remote period, as, for example, in the case of the Indo-Europeans, who are also linked by language. But sometimes these similarities are found in the stories of peoples who can have had no geographical or racial connections with each other. Human beings it would seem, while unlike each other in many ways, have always still more in common, and their imagination, when confronted with similar events, will react to them in much the same way.

There is, not only in the myths themselves, but in the shaping of them, an infinite variety, even though so many are concerned with the same themes. Some peoples have been peculiarly fortunate in having their myths recorded at a time when a fully formed medium for expression had already been found. Literature in the West has been much more profoundly influenced by Greek mythology than by any other, except that of the Old Testament. It seems to have been just an accident that the first orderers of the material happened to be Homer and Hesiod, both accomplished artists in a long tradition. But, hopeless as it is to analyze the complexity of myths and of their origins and development, it is perhaps better, as it is easier, to emphasize their simplicity, their beauty, their own kind of truth and their lasting power to delight us. This is natural enough, since, in so far as we are human, they are part of us.

Rex Warner

*Ancient hero mythology: Hercules
wrestling with a triton or merman, one of
the numerous adventures in which the
greatest of Greek heroes displayed his
super-human strength.*

INTRODUCTION

The Meaning of Myth

For the Greeks, mythos meant 'fable', 'tale', 'talk', 'speech', but finally came to denote 'what cannot really exist'. The earliest Greek philosophers had criticized and rejected the Homeric myths as fictions and inventions. Xenophanes (6th–5th century BC) rejected the immortality of the gods as described by Homer and Hesiod. He especially criticized picturing the gods in human form (anthropomorphism). 'But if cattle and horses or lions had hands, or were able to draw with their hands and do the works that man can do, horses would draw the forms of gods like horses, and cattle like cattle, and they would make their bodies such as they each had themselves.'

In these critiques of Homeric mythology may be seen an effort to free the concept of divinity from the anthropomorphic expressions of the poets. Nevertheless, the mythology of Homer and Hesiod continued to interest the elite in all parts of the Hellenistic world. But the myths were no longer taken literally; what was now sought was their 'hidden meanings'. The Stoics developed the allegorical interpretation of Homeric mythology and, in general, of all religious traditions. For example, when the myth says that Zeus bound Hera, the episode really signifies that the ether is the limit of the air, and so on. Another very successful interpretation was euhemerism, called after Euhemerus (early 3rd century BC): he tried to prove that gods were ancient kings who had been deified. Consequently, the myths represented the confused memory or an imaginative transfiguration of the exploits of the primitive kings. The Christian apologists borrowed this Hellenistic interpretation of mythology. For them, myths were fictional stories, full of falsehood and absurdities, to be rejected as abominations.

It is only in the past 50 years that Western scholars have discovered the primary and true meaning of myth. But the scientific study of mythology was already popular in the second half of the 19th century, especially through the works of Max Müller, Andrew Lang and Sir James Frazer. According to Müller, mythology was a 'disease of language'. Lang asserted that myths result from a personification of natural forces or phenomena, a mental process characteristic of the animistic stage of culture. Frazer regarded myths as mistaken explanations of human or natural phenomena. At the beginning of the century, Freud and Jung gave a new impetus to the study of myths by pointing out the striking similarities between their contents and the world of the unconscious.

The new and positive approach to myth is greatly indebted to the results of modern ethnology. The scientific study of archaic societies – those societies in which mythology is, or was until recently, 'living' – has revealed that myth, for the 'primitive' man, means a *true story* and, beyond that, a story that is a most precious treasure because it is *sacred*, *exemplary* and *significant*.

This new value given the term 'myth' makes its use in contemporary parlance somehow equivocal. Today the word is employed both in the old sense, inherited from the Greeks, of 'fiction' or 'illusion', and in the sense familiar to historians of religions, the sense of 'sacred tradition, primordial revelation, exemplary model'.

In general, one can say that in every case where we have access to a still living tradition, any myth *tells how something came into being*. The 'something' may be the world, or man, or an animal species, or a social institution. Myth, then, is always an account of a 'creation'; it relates how something was produced, began to be. Myth tells only of that which *really happened*. The actors in myths are supernatural beings. They are known principally by what they did in the times of the beginnings. Hence myths disclose their creative activity and reveal the sacredness (or simply the supernaturalness) of their works. It is this intervention of supernatural beings that made the world what it is today. The myth is regarded as a sacred story and hence a 'true story', because it always deals with realities. The myth which tells how the world was made is 'true' because the existence of the world is there to prove it; the myth of the origin of death is equally true because man's mortality proves it, and so on.

Because myth relates the acts of supernatural beings and the manifestation of their sacred powers, it becomes the exemplary model for all significant human activities. 'We must do what the gods did in the beginning', proclaims a well-known Brahman text. 'It was thus that the (mythical) Ancestors did, and we do likewise', declare the Kai of New Guinea.

What happened in the beginning can be repeated by the power of rites. For this reason it is essential to know the myths. By recollecting the myths, by re-enacting them the man of archaic societies is able to repeat what the Gods, the Heroes or the Ancestors did in the times of the beginnings. To quote only one example: a certain tribe live by fishing – because in mythical times a Supernatural Being taught their ancestors to catch and cook fish. The myth *tells the story* of the first fishery, and in so doing, at once reveals a superhuman act, *teaches* men the way to perform it, and finally *explains why* this particular tribe *must* procure their food in this way. For archaic man, myth is a matter of primary importance, for it concerns him directly, in his existence on earth.

This *existential function of myth* explains why a number of major themes are common to different mythologies. Cosmogonic myths (those describing the creation of the universe) and myths of origin, for example, are to be found everywhere. Destruction of an old world and creation of a new is likewise a largely distributed theme. Myths of the creation of mankind appear to be universal, though the story may vary: the first humans were created by Mother Earth and Father Sky or by a bisexual deity, or were fashioned from earth or from vegetables by a creator, and so on.

But every mythical account of the *origin* of anything presupposes and continues the *cosmogony* – the story of the world's creation. The creation of the world being the preeminent instance of creation, the cosmogony becomes the exemplary model for creation of every kind. This is why the fabulous history of the dynasties in Tibet opens by rehearsing the birth of the cosmos from an egg. The Polynesian genealogical chants begin in the same way. Such ritual genealogical chants are composed by the bards when the princess is pregnant, and they are communicated to the hula dancers to be learned by heart. The dancers, men and women, dance and recite the chant continuously until the child is born. It is as if the embryological development of the future chief were accompanied by a re-capitulation of the cosmogony, the history of the world and the history of the tribe. The gestation of a chief is the occasion for a symbolic re-creation of the world.

The periodic renewal of the world through a symbolic repetition of the cosmogony is found among many primitive and archaic people. In Mesopotamia the creation of the world was ritually reiterated during the New Year festival. A series of rites re-enacted the fight between Marduk and Tiamat (the dragon symbolizing the primordial ocean), the victory of the god, and his world-creating labours. The 'Poem of Creation' (*Enuma elish*) was recited in the temple. But the cosmogony was symbolically repeated also at other important or critical moments; for example (as in Egypt and Fiji) on the accession of a new sovereign.

Myths of cosmic cataclysms are extremely widespread among primitives. They tell how the world was destroyed and mankind annihilated except for a single couple or a few survivors. These myths – implying, as they do in clearer or darker fashion, the re-creation of a new universe – express the archaic and universal idea of the progressive degradation of a cosmos, necessitating its periodical destruction and re-creation in a continuous cycle.

The myth of the end of the world was also popular in ancient India, Mesopotamia, Persia and Greece. In Judaeo-Christian theory, the end of the world will occur only once, just as the cosmogony occurred only once. The cosmos that will reappear after the catastrophe will be the same cosmos that God created at the beginning of time, but purified, regenerated, restored to its original glory. This earthly paradise will not be destroyed again but will last, literally, to all eternity.

It is especially this type of myth that admirably illustrates the relevance and significance of mythology to people today. For the myth of the end of the world is at the centre of countless prophetic movements, of which the best known are the Oceanian Cargo Cults. These movements announce that the world is about to be destroyed and that the tribe will regain a kind of paradise: the dead will rise again and there will be neither death nor sickness. But this new creation – or recovery of paradise – will be preceded by a series of cosmic catastrophes. The earth will shake, there will be rains of fire, the mountains will crumble and fill the valleys, the whites and the natives who have not joined the cult will be annihilated. Thus, in 1923 the prophet Ronovuro, of the island of Espiritu Santo (New Hebrides), predicted a flood to be followed by the return of the dead in cargo ships loaded with rice and other provisions. In 1933, in the valley of Markham in New Guinea, a man named Marafi declared that the return of the dead would be be preceded by a cosmic cataclysm; but the next day it would be found that the dead had already arrived, loaded with gifts, and there would be no need for the people ever again to work.

Similar phenomena occurred in the Congo when the country became independent in 1960. In some villages the inhabitants tore the roofs off their huts to give passage to the gold that their ancestors were to rain down. Elsewhere everything was allowed to go to rack and ruin, except the roads to the cemetery, by which the ancestors would make their way to the village. Even the orgiastic excesses had a meaning, for according to the myth, from the dawn of the New Age all women would be held in common by all men.

Another example of the relevance of mythology today is the extremely widespread myth of the Hero. He is abandoned immediately after his birth because of a prophecy threatening danger to his father, a king. The child is saved by animals or shepherds and is suckled by a female animal or by a humble woman. When fully grown, he embarks on extraordinary adventures (slays monsters, overcomes death on various occasions, and so on).

Later he finds his parents and is revenged on his father (or uncle); finally he is recognized and achieves rank and homage. The dangers and trials of the Hero (encounters with monsters and demons, descents into hell, and the rest) have an initiatory meaning. By overcoming all these ordeals, the young man proves that he has surpassed the human condition and henceforth he belongs to a class of semi-divine beings, which is far superior to ordinary human beings.

Now, many epic legends and folk tales use and readapt the highly dramatic scenarios of a hero's initiation (for example, Siegfried, Arthur, Robin Hood). Furthermore, the myth of the Hero survives in the legends of many medieval kings and in the aureole of the Reformer, the Revolutionary, the political Martyr, the Party Leader. But even in contemporary Western societies one can recognize the nostalgia for Heroes and heroic deeds – for example, the 'Superman', or the immense popularity of detective novels, with the exemplary struggle between Good and Evil, between the Hero (i.e., the Detective) and the criminal, who is the modern incarnation of the Demon.

Below *The outlaw as hero: Zapata, the Robin Hood of modern Mexico, from a mural in a Mexican church.*

Francisco Vives

COMMON MYTHOLOGICAL THEMES

Creation Myths

The creation of the world and the origin of mankind are the themes of many myths. They are found among the primitive peoples of most lands and they can be traced back into remote antiquity. Creation myths are of two kinds: aetiological myths which concern the beginnings of things, and stem from primitive speculation about their origins; and ritual myths, which were essentially connected with various periodic ceremonies, particularly at the New Year, designed to ensure the continuation and well-being of the state or even of the world.

It is interesting to consider how the idea that the world had a beginning or had been created arose in the first place. Although the idea is a familiar one to us, it is not self-evident. The earliest members of our race obviously could not have witnessed the creation of the world – indeed, to them in their brief lives, their physical environment must have seemed eternal, supposing that their minds were sufficiently developed to have reflected on the fact. However, two factors in the experience of the Paleolithic peoples doubtless gave them some idea both of the beginning of life and of creativity. The remains of Paleolithic culture reveal a great concern with the phenomenon of birth, both of humans and animals. The emergence of the child from the womb of its mother must surely have been a most impressive demonstration of the beginning of a new creature, whether human or animal. The earliest creation myths, indeed, instinctively used the imagery of biological birth.

The idea of creativity can also be traced back to the Paleolithic era. As the evidence of their art shows, the Paleolithic peoples must have been aware of the mysterious power of creation when they drew the image of an animal on the blank wall of a cave, or fashioned a piece of stone into the figure of a woman. When pottery was invented in Neolithic times, further stimulus was given to the conception of creativity. In several myths the creator-god is imagined as a divine potter who fashions men out of clay.

It is accordingly not surprising that in the earliest written cosmogonies, or creation myths, we find a mixture of thought and imagery about the beginnings of things which derives both from the new needs of civilized society, and from the cruder concepts of the pre-literary past. Egypt and Sumer provide our earliest examples of creation myths, the texts concerned dating in each instance from about the middle of the 3rd millennium BC.

The earliest evidence of ancient Egyptian thought about the beginnings of things occurs incidentally in the Pyramid Texts. The fact is significant, because these texts

Daylight is created as the morning star is wafted into the heavens by the east wind: Australian bark painting.

Axel Poignant

are not concerned with the creation of the world but with the destiny after death of the kings of Egypt. The priests of Heliopolis, who composed the texts about 2480–2137 BC, drew upon traditions about their god Atum, whose temple at Heliopolis was one of the oldest cult-centres in the land. Atum was a mysterious deity, whose name could mean 'the not-yet-Completed One, who will attain (completion)'. He was identified with the sun god Re, under the composite title of Atum-Re. Various passages in the Pyramid Texts reveal that the priests of Heliopolis believed that originally there had been only a primordial waste of water, without shape or order, called Nun. The 'first time' started when Atum emerged from this primeval deep and began the work of creation.

In order to commence this work, Atum needed a firm place on which to stand, and reference is made in the texts to a primeval hill which also emerged with Atum out of Nun. This primeval hill was identified with the site of Atum's temple at Heliopolis, thus making it the most ancient and sacred place in Egypt, since it was there that the creation of the world began.

The idea of a waste of waters existing from the beginning, called Nun, from which the first land emerged, doubtless reflects the conditions of the Nile Valley. Each year the Egyptians witnessed the inundation of their land by the mysterious rising of the river Nile; then, as the flood subsided, the higher points of land began to emerge from the water. Beyond the delta of the Nile lay the Mediterranean Sea, the 'Great Green', which seemed a limitless expanse of water. Hence came the imagery of Nun and of the primeval hill.

Having conceived of the emergence of their god Atum, the priests of Heliopolis had next to imagine how he could have created the universe. Since they instinctively thought in terms of biological generation, they were, consequently, faced with the problem of accounting for the process of creation from a sole male deity. Their solution was crudely

Above *The sky goddess Nut and her brother Geb, the earth god, were originally locked in a close embrace according to Egyptian belief; scene from the papyrus of Tamenill (c 1000 BC) in the British Museum showing Nut, the vault of heaven, arched over her brother the earth.* **Left** *God created the world in six days, according to the book of Genesis, and rested on the seventh day. Section of an initial letter in a 13th-century illuminated manuscript in the British Museum, showing from top to bottom, the acts of God on the seven days of Creation: the separation of light from darkness; the creation of Heaven; and of of the Earth, the seas and vegetation; the stars, moon and sun; birds and sea creatures; animals, man and woman.*

primitive. According to one passage in the Pyramid Texts, Atum produced two deities, Shu and Tefnut, by masturbation; in another passage, by spitting. These deities were, respectively, personifications of air and moisture.

Since Shu and Tefnut were male and female, the next stage in cosmic creation could be described as an action of procreation. From the union of Shu and Tefnut were born Geb, 'earth', and Nut, 'sky'. In later Egyptian art, Shu, as the personification of air, is represented as lifting up the sky goddess Nut from the recumbent body of the earth god Geb. Evidently the earth and sky were imagined as being at first in close embrace, and thus had to be separated in order to give the universe its shape. In art

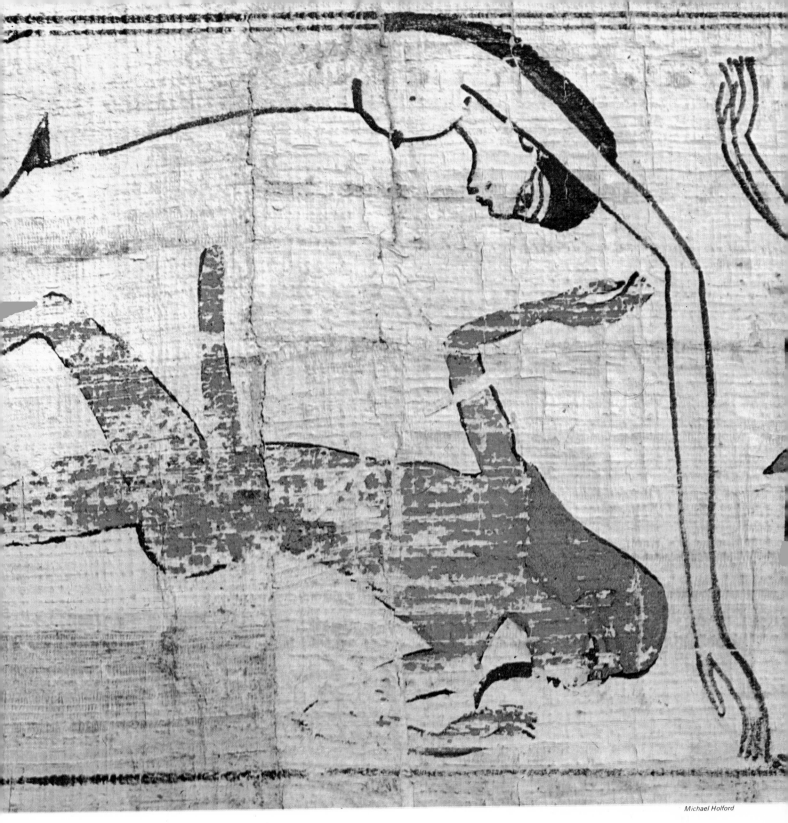

Nut is generally depicted as a gigantic woman, whose body over-arches the earth. The sun, moon and stars are shown as passing over her body, which forms the vault of heaven. It is interesting to note that Egyptian cosmogony differs from most other cosmogonies in making the earth male and the sky female.

The Heliopolitan priests, having thus accounted for the four chief constituents of the cosmic universe, namely air and moisture, earth and sky, did not go on to describe the origin of vegetation, animals or mankind. Instead, they told how from the union of Geb and Nut were born two pairs of deities: Osiris and Isis, Set and Nephthys. This fact significantly reveals the real motive behind their myth of creation. The four

deities mentioned were ancient and important deities who originated from other parts of Egypt. By making these deities the great-grandchildren of Atum, the Heliopolitan priests asserted the precedence of their own god. In other words, this earliest example of a creation myth was designed to exalt Atum as the supreme creator, to whom other gods owed their existence, and his temple at Heliopolis as the most ancient and holy place in the Egyptian world.

This Heliopolitan cosmogony seems to have provided a stimulus to the priesthoods of other great temples in Egypt. At Memphis, as we learn from the famous Shabaka Stone, now in the British Museum, the priests of the local god Ptah neatly rebutted the claims of Heliopolis by claiming that Ptah was the

original creator and that he used Atum as his agent. This Memphite cosmogony is more sophisticated in its imagery, and Ptah is represented as creating by the power of his magical word.

Hermopolis in Upper Egypt was distinguished by the peculiar form of its creation story. There, it was related, eight original beings, represented as frogs or serpents, deposited on an island an egg, out of which the sun god emerged to begin the work of creation. According to the tomb-inscription of a priest of Hermopolis in the 3rd century BC, pilgrims were still being shown the shell of this cosmic egg.

When Thebes became the political capital, about 1580 BC, and its god Amun the chief state god of Egypt, the priests composed a cosmogony which represented Amun as a life-giving wind moving over the inert waters of Nun; this initiated the process of cosmic creation. Thebes, too, claimed to be the first of cities – 'the water and the land were in her at the First Time'. Other temples each had its creation myth, notable examples being those of Esna and Edfu, though of course there were others.

One remarkable feature of the ancient Egyptian creation myths is that they show no concern whatsoever to explain the origin of mankind.

They are literally 'cosmogonies', in that they deal with the beginning of the 'cosmos' or world and the relations of the gods. There are passing references to the creation of men in various other texts; but the Egyptians were

the personification of the sea, is called 'the mother, the ancestress, who gave birth to all the gods'. But it is Enki, the god associated with the fresh waters, who figures most as the creator in the early Sumerian texts. He is depicted as arriving by sea in Sumer, in a kind of golden age at the dawn of time, and impregnating Ninhursag, 'the mother of the land'. Enki's fertilizing activity produces the plants necessary for food. He also invents the pick-axe and brick mould, the two essential implements of Mesopotamian economy.

In one notable Sumerian myth the creation of mankind is described. To relieve the gods from the toil of providing their own food, Enki causes human beings to be fashioned out of clay to act as servants of the gods. At a feast given by the gods to celebrate the crea-

elish. This cosmogony is similar in motive to the Egyptian cosmogonies, in that it was designed to exalt the god of Babylon, Marduk.

This deity was not reckoned initially among the most ancient of the gods of Mesopotamia; in fact, he was regarded as the son of Enki. But when Babylon rose to political supremacy, it was evidently felt by the Babylonian priests that the status of their god had to be raised.

This was done in the *Enuma elish* by telling how Marduk became the leader of the gods and the creator of the world. A primordial chaos is described, when there existed only Tiamat, the personification of the sea, and Apsu, who personified the fresh waters. From the mingling of these two entities the

Ole Woldbye

not so much concerned with the origin and purpose of the human race as were the Mesopotamians and Hebrews. There is evidence, however, of the manner in which the Egyptians believed that human beings were created, as for example in a bas-relief commemorating the birth of the pharaoh Amenhotep III (1405–1370 BC) at Luxor. In this the ram-headed fertility god Khnum is depicted as fashioning the infant king and his *ka* or double on a potter's wheel, while the goddess Hathor endows them with life. According to a text of the 7th century BC, 'man is clay and straw'.

In the creation myths of ancient Sumer attention was focused more upon the beginnings of civilization and mankind than on the origin of the world. The goddess Nammu,

tion of their new servants, the goddess Ninmah challenges Enki to deal with two freaks which she has made. These freaks are a eunuch and a barren woman. Enki adroitly finds a place for them in the Mesopotamian social system. He then challenges Ninmah to find a purpose for the two freaks which he himself has made, a diseased and an aged man. Ninmah can do nothing with them, and she curses Enki because what he has made cannot be unmade. This addition to the myth of the creation of mankind is significant; for it reveals that the Sumerians were concerned with the problems of disease and old age, and that they attributed these ills to the sport of the gods.

The most famous of the Mesopotamian creation myths is the Babylonian *Enuma*

first generation of the gods was born, among whom was Enki, who slew Apsu. Tiamat, imagined as a great monster, sought to avenge Apsu by destroying the gods. Her horrific appearance, and the monsters she creates to aid her, so terrify the older gods that they readily accept the offer of the younger god Marduk to save them on condition that his supremacy is recognized. Marduk meets Tiamat in battle and subsequently kills her.

He then slices up her body and fashions the universe from it. From the blood of Kingu, leader of Tiamat's monstrous host, Marduk makes mankind to serve the gods. The poem ends with an account of how the gods, in gratitude, build for Marduk his great temple at Babylon.

Left '*So God created man in his own image, in the image of God he created him*' *16th-century tapestry in the Accademia del' Arte, Florence, depicting the sixth day of creation.* **Below** *Adam and Eve, tempted by the serpent in the garden of Eden: 15th-century painting by Hugo van der Goes.* **Facing page** *The first living being of Scandinavian mythology was the giant Ymir, born from melting ice and nourished by the cow Audumulla. While licking the blocks of ice in order to obtain salt for herself, Audumulla released the bodies of Buri and his son Bor, the first men. After Ymir's death his body became land, his blood the seas and his skull the heavens: painting of Ymir and Audumulla from the Statens Museum for Kunst, Copenhagen.*

The *Enuma elish* had an important ritual function. It was solemnly recited during the annual New Year festival at Babylon. This festival was especially concerned with the sovereignty of Marduk and with his determining of the destiny of the state for the coming year. One of the themes of the *Enuma elish* is that of Marduk's acquisition of the 'tablets of destiny' after his victory over Tiamat.

The Hebrew creation myths, though later in date than the Egyptian and Mesopotamian, are better known and have exercised a profound influence upon Western thought and culture. They are contained in the first three chapters of the Book of Genesis. Although these chapters in their present form have the appearance of a continuous narrative, careful analysis of the text reveals two distinctive cosmogonies.

The first (Genesis, 1. 1 to 2. 4a) contains an account of the creation of the world in six days, the creation of mankind being the last episode. Scholars generally agree that this cosmogony dates from the 5th century BC, and represents what is known as the Priestly tradition. This account of creation reveals traces of Mesopotamian influence, particularly in the picture of the original watery chaos: 'And the earth was waste and void; and darkness was upon the face of the deep.' The Hebrew word *tehom* 'deep' is akin to the Babylonian Tiamat. What is especially notable about this Priestly cosmogony is that God does not create the world out of nothing, as later theologians maintained; a watery chaos existed before God's acts of creation. Mankind is represented as being created 'in the image of God' and commanded to 'be fruitful, and multiply, and replenish the earth, and subdue it'. God finishes his work of creation in six days and rests on the seventh, thus providing, according to the Priestly writer, the divine example and authority for the observation of the Sabbath.

The other Hebrew creation myth (which starts at Genesis 2. 4b) is recognized by scholars as an older tradition. They designate it the 'Yahwist' tradition, dating it about 900–750 BC. This version does not deal with the creation of the world but concentrates on the creation of mankind, which precedes the creation of the animals, contrary to the Priestly account. God (who is here given his characteristic Hebrew name of Yahweh)

fashions Adam out of the earth (*adamah*) as the Egyptian god Khnum and the Mesopotamian deities made men out of clay. Having animated Adam with the 'breath of life', Yahweh places him in the garden of Eden, imagined as a kind of oasis. In the narrative that follows, the Yahwist writer was primarily concerned to show how mankind became subject to death through Adam's original act of disobedience to his divine creator. This episode involves the mysterious 'Tree of the Knowledge of Good and Evil' and the 'Tree of Life'. The interpretation of this is briefly that by eating of the forbidden fruit, Adam lost his original immortality and became mortal. This mortal nature he passed on to his descendants as the fatal consequence of his first sin. The writer's second motive, to account for the beginning of things, also finds expression in these chapters. He explains the origin of the names of animals, the creation of woman, the wearing of clothes, why the serpent 'goes upon his belly', the origin of the pain of childbirth and the toil of agriculture.

Genesis says that Adam was the father of Cain, Abel, Seth and other children, and died at the age of 930. According to other Jewish traditions, he wrote some of the Psalms (numbers 5, 19, 24, 92, 132) and his grave was in the cave of Machpelah at Hebron, to the south of Jerusalem, where Abraham, Isaac and Jacob were also believed to be buried. Christian tradition placed his grave at Golgotha where Jesus was crucified. This is the origin of the custom of showing a skull at the foot of the cross in paintings and sculp-

ture, and is based on the link which Christians saw between Adam, who alienated man from God, and Christ, the second Adam, who reunited man with God.

Jewish stories said that Adam was originally a man on his right side and a woman on his left (the side of evil), and God separated the two halves. Or Adam and Eve were joined at the shoulders, back to back, and God split them in two with an axe. These tales were probably meant to reconcile the making of man in God's image with the belief that God is beyond sex and incorporates both male and female in himself. If Adam was a copy of God he must have been bisexual. The idea is present in the Genesis story, perhaps for the same reason, Eve being made from Adam's body.

Another story was that the angels were jealous of Adam. Some of them advised God against creating him in the first place but were destroyed by God in a rage. When Adam had been created, the Archangel Michael commanded the host of heaven to fall down and worship him. They all obeyed except Satan, who was too proud and was hurled out of heaven in punishment. Some writers explained that this was why Satan tempted Eve in the form of a serpent, to revenge himself on Adam. The story survives in the Koran.

Egypt, Mesopotamia and Israel provide the earliest and most striking creation myths of the ancient world. Fragments of such myths have been found among Hittite records, and they seem to have exercised some influence on Greek mythology. In ancient

Above *Tloque Nahuaque, the god-above-all of the Mixtecs in Central America, and the original giver of all life including his own: illustration from the Codex Zouche-Nuttal.*

Greece, however, there was no established tradition of creation myths. Certain vague references in Homer suggest some belief that Oceanus was the source of life. The Greek writer Hesiod devoted a whole work, the *Theogony*, to explaining the beginnings of things; but the composition is a strange-mixture of mythical imagery and primitive rationalization. Traces of creation myths are found in other Greek writings. But the naturalistic explanations of the origin of the world advanced by the early Greek philosophers are, doubtless, more characteristic of the Greek mind here; and it is significant that Zeus was not regarded as the creator of the world.

The earliest forms of Iranian cosmogony are difficult to determine. Under the influence of Zoroastrianism a cosmogony recognizing two independent principles was later formulated, in which Ahura Mazdah was responsible for the good aspects of creation, and Ahriman for the evil. Ancient Indian literature contains brief references to speculation about creation but no mythological tradition concerning the actual origin of the world.

China also produced no established creation myth; the alternating cosmic forces of *yin* and *yang* characterize the whole of Chinese cosmogony.

The First Man

Some groups of human beings believe that they are closely related to animals and trace their descent from an ancestor who had both human and animal characteristics. Others say men are descended from the sun, whose light and heat preserve all life in the world. According to an Indian myth, for instance, the first man and woman were the twins Yama and Yima, who were said to be children of the sun.

There is a Maori story that the first human being was made of earth and given life by the sun: 'it was the sunlight fertilizing the Earth Mother.' The Zuni Indians of New Mexico said that men and all living things were the children of the sun and the earth. Elsewhere the sky and the earth are the original ancestors of humanity.

There is a very widespread tendency to give the earth an important role in the creation of the first human beings, sometimes in association with plants, which suggests a poetic parallel between human life and the life of vegetation, both springing from the earth and returning to it again in death. A striking example is a Pawnee story of how Mother Corn led the first men up to the earth's surface.

Below *To the Egyptians man was a complex mixture of physical and spiritual: the soul, shown as a human-headed bird, hovers above the body.*

Before the World was we were all within the Earth.
Mother Corn caused movement. She gave life.
Life being given we moved towards the surface:
    We shall stand erect as men!
The being is become human! He is a person!

Another example is Gayomart, who shone like the sun, the Zoroastrian first man. Gayomart was killed by Ahriman, the evil power, but his seed fell into the earth and from it there grew a rhubarb plant which turned into the first human couple.

A Greek myth says that the first men, the 'golden race', were born from Earth. 'These men ... lived without cares or labour, eating only acorns, wild fruit, and honey that dripped from the trees, drinking the milk of sheep and goats, never growing old, dancing, and laughing much; death, to them, was no more terrible than sleep' (Robert Graves, *The Greek Myths*).

Sometimes the human body is said to be made of earth, fashioned of clay. The Shilluk of the White Nile accounted for differences in skin colour by the differently coloured clay from which the various races of men were made. The Sumerian god Enki caused human beings to be made of clay and the Egyptian god Khnum was believed to fashion men on a potter's wheel.

Some of these themes also appear in the first man myth which has had far and away the greatest influence on the western world, the story of Adam and Eve.

Some Gnostics of the early centuries after Christ identified the god of the Old Testament as the evil being who created the evil world. This naturally involved them in standing the Old Testament stories on their heads. The god who made man was now an evil power and the serpent, the tempter, became a virtuous creature, sent by the good supreme God to teach Adam and Eve the knowledge of good and evil so that they could see for themselves the evil nature of the world which the Jewish god had made.

According to the gnostic 'Secret Book of John', for example, man was created by the god of the Jews, an evil supernatural being named Ialdabaoth (probably a corruption of Jehovah Sabaoth). He seduced Eve after the expulsion from Eden and fathered on her the two sons men call Cain and Abel, but whose real names are Jehovah and Elohim. The one has a face like a bear and the other like a cat. (Elohim, like Jehovah, is a name of God in the Old Testament.)

In Manichean theory, Adam was created by an evil power, begotten of the coupling of two great demons as a receptacle for certain particles of heavenly light, which had been captured by the forces of darkness. The Adam the demons produced was blind,

deaf, fast asleep and unconscious of the divine light within him but the sowers of light sent a redeemer – called Ohrmazd or the Son of God or brilliant Jesus or Jesus the brilliant light – to rescue him. From his demon ancestors man has inherited his physical body and its desires but he also contains the divine light.

The Manichean Adam was spawned by evil as a copy of the heavenly 'primeval man', who had earlier been created by the powers of light. The two different creation stories in Genesis encouraged some Jewish and

Left Man, according to Greek myth, was fashioned from clay by Prometheus the supreme craftsman: this detail from a bas-relief from a Roman marble sarcophagus shows the gods Poseidon, Hermes and Hera in the background as Prometheus prepares to animate his handiwork. **Facing page** *Various episodes from the story of Adam and Eve are depicted in this illustration from the 15th-century* **Bedford Book of Hours:** *within the garden of Eden, Adam names the beasts, God takes Eve from Adam's side, the guilty pair eat fruit from the forbidden Tree of Knowledge and are condemned by God; outside the garden Adam and Eve labour as their son Cain kills his brother Abel.* **Below** *God created man 'in his own image': the idea that man is a miniature replica of God has provided a biblical basis for the theory that man is potentially God and can eventually become God: watercolour by William Blake in the Tate Gallery London.*

Eugen Kusch

John Webb

Gnostic writers to suggest that the first story describes the making of the ideal 'heavenly man', the image of God, a spiritual, non-material being who combined both sexes in himself; and that the second story describes the making of actual earthly man, a being who is part spirit and part matter (his body, made of earth) and who is divided into two sexes. Here again is the theme of the dual nature of man, material and spiritual, animal and divine.

The idea survived in Jacob Boehme's theory (which powerfully influenced William Blake) that there were two Falls. The original Adam was an angelic spiritual being, immortal, bisexual and virgin. He fell for the first time in acquiring a physical body and dividing into male and female. This was followed by the second Fall when the serpent successfully tempted Eve, bringing death and the necessity for reproduction of the species because man was no longer immortal. As in gnostic theory, everything which is physical, material, earthly is regarded as evil, and in particular sex.

The belief that the original Adam was the perfect pattern of humanity, which man had lost but might regain, inspired various medieval heretics to maintain that men and women should go about naked and refrain entirely from work, which would restore them to the state of perfection of Adam and Eve in Eden before the Fall. In 1925 a group of Adamites were discovered in California. Their leader was Eve recreated, her husband was Adam and their farm was the Garden of Eden. They used to danced naked in the farmyard round a bonfire and a lamb was burnt alive on at least one occasion. It is a far cry from the beauty and far-reaching significance of the Old Testament story but the Adamite heresy may perhaps have contributed quite substantially to the notion that nudism is both physically and psychologically healthy.

What may be described as the classical Greek evaluation of human nature and destiny was as pessimistic as the Mesopotamian and early Hebrew views. It first finds expression in the Homeric poems. The most dramatic presentation occurs in the *Odyssey* (book 11), which describes how Odysseus descended into Hades to learn the cause of the misfortunes that prevented his return home after the fall of Troy. In Hades he meets the shade of his dead mother. He tries vainly to embrace her shadowy image, and cries out in frustration and grief. His mother's shade replies: 'this is the way decreed for mortals when they die. The sinews cease to hold the flesh and bones together; for they are destroyed by the power of the blazing fire, as soon as the (conscious) life (*thymos*) leaves the white bones, and the shade (*psyche*), hovers about and then flits away.'

This passage mentions the three constituents of human nature, according to Homer: the body, which was cremated at death; the *thymos*, which was the conscious or rational self; the *psyche*, the life-principle. Death disintegrated the union of these constituent elements: the body was destroyed, the *thymos* ceased to exist, and the *psyche* descended to Hades. The *psyche* was imagined as a shadowy replica (called an *eidolon*) of the

Victoria and Albert Museum

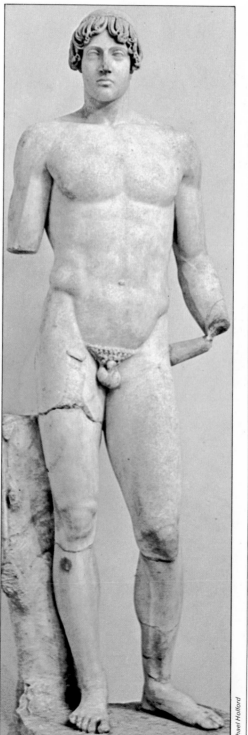

Michael Holford

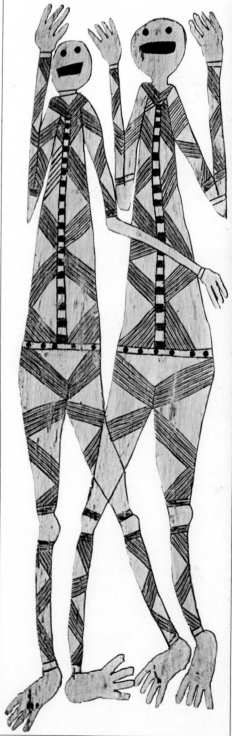

living person, but it had no consciousness. In Hades the shades of the dead are portrayed as being capable only of making chirping noises like birds. However, as this episode in the *Odyssey* shows, they could acquire a momentary consciousness by tasting the blood of a sacrificed animal – an idea derived from the primitive belief that blood is the 'life-substance'.

Several attempts are made in the *Iliad* to account for human fate. In one place Zeus is pictured as arbitrarily handing out mixtures of good and bad lots to individuals from two urns that stood on the floor of Olympus. Other imagery is used elsewhere: that the gods 'bind' men's fates upon them; that 'mighty Fate' spins 'her thread' of destiny at a person's birth; that Zeus weighs the fates of heroes in his golden scales. The fluidity of this imagery suggests that at this early stage in Greek thought, the problem was gradually emerging of relating human destiny to the divine government of the universe. But it was a problem that was never satisfactorily solved, for the Greek concept of deity was essentially based on experience of cosmic power, which is indifferent to human aspirations and values. This is clearly evident in Stoicism, which represented the most sustained effort made in the Graeco-Roman world to produce a philosophy of life in terms of a realistic appraisal of the human situation.

This pessimistic estimate of man's nature and destiny, which can be traced throughout classical culture, from Homeric Greece to Graeco-Roman society, was not accepted by all. Despite its obvious realism, many sought for a more comforting creed. The ancient Eleusinian Mysteries and Orphism promised their respective initiates deliverance from death and a blessed afterlife. Orphism was the more sophisticated cult and it involved the idea of the transmigration of souls, an idea which implied a very different conception of human nature from that of the classical tradition. It presupposed that in each person an immortal ethereal soul (*psyche*) was imprisoned in a material body. Orphic mythology explained that this situation was due to an ancient crime, and that the soul's true destiny was to return to its original divine source. This destiny could be achieved only by the soul's realization of its true nature, and by following a discipline designed to emancipate it from attachment to the world of material things. A favourite Orphic saying was *soma*, *sema*, 'the body, a tomb'.

Since Christianity originated in Judaea and the first Christians were Jews, Jewish ideas about human nature and destiny inevitably formed the basis of the primitive Christian view. As the New Testament shows, belief in the resurrection and judgement of the dead were fundamental tenets of the new faith. The conception of the resurrection reflected the Jewish view of human nature as a psycho-physical organism in a very literal sense. This is most notably seen in the description of the resurrected Jesus. According to St Luke (chapter 24), when the disciples saw Jesus in his resurrected state, they were terrified, supposing 'that they saw a spirit'. But Jesus assured them of his physical reality: 'See my

hands and my feet, that it is I myself: handle me, and see; for a spirit has not flesh and bones as you see that I have.' When some disciples still remained doubtful, he proposed a further test.

The doctrine of Man in Islam has some affinity to those of Judaism and Christianity; the fact constitutes part of the problem of the relation of the Arabian religion to Judaism and Christianity, which predated it. The affinity is especially marked in the eschatology of the Koran. Mohammed regarded himself as sent by Allah to warn his countrymen of the coming of divine judgement. This 'Last Judgement' would involve the resurrection of the dead, and would result in the vindication of the faithful and their reward in paradise, and the eternal damnation of the wicked to the torments of hell.

While these various evaluations of human nature and destiny were being worked out in the ancient Near East and Europe, in India another estimate was gradually established which was destined to affect most of the peoples of eastern Asia. This estimate was similar to that of Orphism in as far as it was based on the idea of the transmigration of souls. But the Indian interpretation dates from about 600 BC, and is undoubtedly older than the Orphic view. Whether the latter derived from India has been much debated, without any agreed conclusion. The idea of the rebirth or transmigration of souls is not necessarily a sophisticated concept, and it occurs among many primitive peoples, so that the Indian and the Orphic views might well have had separate origins.

This Indian interpretation of existence, in its early Upanishadic form, seems to have provided both the basis and point of departure for the Buddhist doctrine of Man. Buddhism concentrated particularly on the miseries of human existence by way of introduction to its own gospel of salvation. It accepted the doctrines of samsara and karma; but it rejected the Hindu concept of a self (*atman*) that was continuously reborn to new forms of incarnated life. Instead, it maintained that the idea of the empirical self stems from a conglomeration of various mental and physical factors (*skandhas*), which produce the sensation of individual existence in a material world. Since this illusory self cherishes its sense of personal being, it takes the world apprehended by its senses for reality and attaches itself to it. Hence, as in Hindu thought, the individual becomes subject to the process of continuous death and rebirth, with all their concomitant pain and suffering.

According to the Buddhist analysis of the human situation, this universal illusion of personal existence is due to a kind of primordial ignorance (*avidya*), which it is the task of the Buddhist teacher to expose.

The spread of Buddhism throughout eastern and south-eastern Asia has meant that the Buddhist view of human nature and destiny has influenced a large part of mankind. It was accepted into China, where it tended to intermingle with or affect the native faiths of Confucianism and Taoism. The native Chinese evaluation of man, however, had certain distinctive features.

The interpretations of man so far des-

'We must all die, we are like water spilt on the ground, which cannot be gathered up again': in the Old Testament death and the other ills of the human condition are the consequences of man's disobedience; Adam and Eve with the Tree of Knowledge, from a 13th-century MS *.*

cribed, although they have varied much in their estimates, have had one feature in common. They all set mankind, as a unique species, over against the rest of creation. Instinctively they assume that man should have a special and unique destiny in the scheme of things.

The Chinese estimate has notably lacked this assumption. On the contrary, it has stressed man's integration with his natural environment. This approach finds characteristic expression in the idea of Yin and Yang. The terms denote two alternating principles which the Chinese, from at least the 5th century BC, discerned as operative in all forms of being throughout the universe. Man was not excepted from their operation, and a Yin-Yang anthropology was elaborated which explained human nature in these terms. The following passage from the *Lu-shih Ch'un Ch'ui* succinctly states this view: 'Heaven, Earth and all things are like the body of one man, and this is what is called the Great Unity (*ta t'ung*).' And it goes on to define the duty of the Sage as that of showing 'how the *yin* and *yang* form the essence of things, and how people, birds and beasts are in a state of peace'.

The original teaching of Zoroaster on the subject of Man is obscure. He uses two terms, *urvan* and *daena*, signifying the non-physical components of human nature that survive death. The urvan seems to approximate to the 'soul', and the daena to denote something akin to 'conscience'. In later Zoroastrianism five constituents of human nature were distinguished and the idea of the daena was also curiously elaborated. The dead were described as meeting their daena after death: to the righteous it appeared as a beauteous maiden; to the wicked as a hideous hag. Zoroastrian eschatology involved a corporeal resurrection, with adults restored to a physical state of 40 years of age, and those who had died as children to the form of 15 years. There was also an Immediate and a Final Judgement of the dead.

The Hero

The Hero God of Thrace: the exact nature of his cult is not known, but more than 1000 memorials to him can still be seen in the Balkans.

Used in everyday speech to mean an outstandingly brave man, or to designate the main character in a literary work, the word 'hero' may also be used in a specialized sense, to refer to figures in so-called 'heroic' literature. Such literature has flourished in many lands in many periods of history, whenever tales and songs are composed about a race of men whose strength and courage are above the ordinary, who accomplish great deeds, have dealings with supernatural beings, and may themselves be of supernatural parentage.

The heroes may occasionally become objects of local cults, with shrines erected to their memory and games held in their honour. Such cults existed among the Greeks, in particular the cult of Hercules, the semi-divine hero of enormous strength who accomplished a series of celebrated deeds, and saved the Greeks from many dangers.

In some cases the traditions of the heroes of the past have produced great epic poetry, as with the Homeric heroes whose exploits are the subjects of the *Iliad* and the *Odyssey*, and the Germanic heroes, who inspired such well known works as the *Nibelungenlied*. Elsewhere there are songs, stories, ballads and more sophisticated written literature which has developed out of the early heroic tales told by people who themselves could neither read nor write. Interest in heroic literature has developed greatly during the present century, since travellers and scholars have collected much material from native poets and reciters who composed their work orally and never attempted to write it down.

Many heroic figures survive from the literature of the past, although countless names once of supreme importance have been lost for ever. The heroic poetry of Gaul, for instance, has disappeared without trace, while the Roman orator Cicero (1st century BC) lamented the disappearance of the old poems telling of the ancient Roman heroes such as Romulus and Horatius, who are remembered only in brief summaries of

their exploits given by later Latin writers. Fragments of the very ancient *Epic of Gilgamesh*, now believed to go back to the 3rd millennium BC, show that the central figure was a human hero of outstanding powers, who defied the goddess Ishtar and went on a hazardous journey to the world's end to search for his comrade Enkidu who had gone down into the land of death, and to find some hope of escape from the mortality to which man is doomed. Already the hero is not content with the limitations of human existence, and his adventures may be seen as a spiritual quest.

The epic poems ascribed to Homer, the finest example of epic poetry known to us, go back to the 8th or 9th centuries BC. The heroes of the *Iliad* and the *Odyssey* are of magnificent stature, living an idealized existence in small independent kingdoms in the eastern Mediterranean, and winning lasting glory by their courage and mighty deeds in times of war and peace. The gods support and oppose them in a very human way, and converse familiarly with one another in the background of the human conflict, while the realities of everyday life are convincingly portrayed. Yet there is nevertheless the sense of boundless possibilities opening out for the human mind and spirit, extending far beyond the limitations of the ordinary world.

There were a host of Greek heroes outside the Homeric stories. Figures like Prometheus the Titan who was imprisoned by Zeus for giving fire to mankind, a legend which has been remembered up to recent times in the folklore of the Caucasus; Theseus who slew the Minotaur, and Jason who sailed to find the Golden Fleece, have remained famous even though their stories have come to us only in fragments. Scenes from their adventures may be seen on many early Greek vases, and in the case of heroes like Theseus and Jason it would seem that fact and fiction have become inextricably intertwined. For many of these heroes, what is important is the journey or the quest which they undertake and their end is often a tragic one.

Another heroic work of epic proportions from the ancient world is the *Mahabharata* of India, which contains much heroic and mythical material, although it has been extensively edited by the Brahmins so that it is difficult to reconstruct its early form. The Jews too had their own heroic age, when they were fighting to establish themselves in Palestine and overthrow the rival tribes which surrounded them. The historical books of the Old Testament contain some fine heroic leaders like Gideon and Samson, while the story of David and his followers is a heroic saga of splendid proportions, with the inner core of seriousness which marks out heroic literature at its best.

There is a wealth of heroic poems and stories from western Europe dating from early medieval times. The contribution of Britain is no small one, for it includes the Anglo-Saxon epic *Beowulf*, the tale of a

northern hero who battled against monsters, established himself as a great king, and died defending his people from a dragon. All this is set against a more human background of wars and family feuds, which has proved of much value to scholars reconstructing the history of early Scandinavia and studying the way of life at this period. The epic has claims to greatness in its own right as fine and moving poetry. The theme of man's struggle against evil powers and the constant threat of mortality at the height of human achievement links it with other heroic works, and once more the pattern is that of the quest of the hero, his fight against great odds, and his tragic end.

Other heroic poems from the Anglo-Saxon period exist only in fragments, but there are so many references to heroes that it is clear that there was a vast body of traditions surrounding them, known to the Anglo-Saxons and to the kindred Germanic nations of north-western Europe. The Vikings continued the heroic tradition, and added to the stock of stories and poems by their own exploits in many parts of Europe and beyond.

One of their greatest heroes was Sigurd the Volsung, who is commemorated on carved stones in both the British Isles and Scandinavia. He slew a dragon and won the gift of secret knowledge together with a mighty treasure, but the gold brought a curse along with it, and he was slain by his brothers-in-law in the course of a feud which he was powerless to prevent. Sigurd was the son of another mighty hero, Sigmund, and the tragic history of this family, many of whom went courageously to their deaths fighting against overwhelming odds, is a stirring one even in the comparatively late form in which it has reached us, in the *Saga of the Volsungs* and a number of poems in Old Icelandic which deal with separate incidents and characters from the extensive *Volsung* cycle of stories.

These tales illustrate the importance of women in heroic tradition. Sigmund's sister Signy dared and suffered much to avenge her father and brothers whom her husband had treacherously killed. Sigurd's ill-fated wife Gudrun and the proud Valkyrie Brynhild, whom he reached by riding through a wall of fire to awaken her from her enchanted sleep, are two unforgettable figures who inspire some of the finest poems in the Icelandic collection.

Brynhild slew herself at Sigurd's funeral, while Gudrun lived on to see tragedy repeated among other members of her family. The story of the Volsungs also inspired the Middle High German epic, the *Nibelungenlied*, in which Sigurd and Gudrun appear as Siegfried and Kriemhild, and which later still won new fame in the operas of Wagner.

Celtic Britain also had its heroes. Early Welsh poems from medieval times have many references to the mysterious King Arthur, whom scholars have subsequently sought to identify with a leader who fought

National Museum of Archaeology, Sofia

John Mills

against the Anglo-Saxon invaders at the close of the Roman period, and whom they have attempted to place in many different areas of Britain. Around King Arthur and his band of famous warriors a rich body of poems and stories developed in Brittany, France and medieval England, in which many of his celebrated followers had links with the otherworld, rode on strange quests and encountered supernatural adversaries. The most haunting and mysterious of these heroic tales are those which are concerned with the quest of the Grail, in which Christian mysticism is mingled with ancient symbols of Celtic mythology.

The heroes of Ireland, of whom Cu Chulainn and Finn are the most famous, are remembered in a large collection of prose stories in early Irish, which extend over a long period and are believed to contain elements from pre-Christian times. In these Irish sagas and in the Welsh tales of the *Mabinogion* about Arthur and other heroes there is a strong element of the fantastic and the marvellous, so that the atmosphere differs from that of the Homeric and Germanic heroic stories.

Later, still, romantic tales about Arthur and his knights developed in the form of the *Chansons de geste* in France, which in turn influenced English medieval literature. Another celebrated band of heroes were the knights of the Emperor Charlemagne, who appears as a warrior-leader, differing considerably from the ruler known in historical records, and whose influence in this guise lingers on in the folk drama of several countries. A short epic in medieval French known as the *Chanson de Roland*, composed in the 11th century, tells of the heroic fight of one of Charlemagne's heroes against the Saracens, and in the next century a group of Spanish poems, the most famous of which is the *Poema de mio Cid*, deals with the heroes of Castile.

From eastern Europe there is a group of narrative poems in Russian, the *byliny*, dealing with the early heroes of Kiev and Novgorod and the later Cossacks. Some of these heroes are kings or warrior-leaders, and some famous outlaws. The poems concerning them were never written down, but were mostly collected from peasant reciters in the 19th century, who still held their audiences enthralled with tales of these old heroes.

Above *St George, traditionally the patron saint of England, probably lived in Palestine in about the 3rd century: his legendary battle with the dragon is probably an allegorical expression of the Christian hero's triumph over evil: illustration from a 17th-century Ethiopian manuscript.* **Left** *Although some heroes are purely mythological figures, others are based on historical characters. Robin Hood, the outlaw of Sherwood Forest, was commemorated in countless ballads.* **Far left** *Greek tradition is rich in heroes; Perseus, who rescued Andromeda from a dragon, is typical of this race of men who accomplished great deeds:* **Perseus and Andromeda,** *painting by Lord Leighton, in the Walker Art Gallery, Liverpool.*

Magic and the supernatural enter constantly into heroic literature, and the heroes have many adventures in the otherworld. Maui, the Polynesian hero, climbs a huge tree which leads him into a world above the clouds; Sigurd rides through a wall of fire to rescue Brynhild; with the help of Hermes, Perseus strikes off the head of the terrible Gorgon in order to rescue Andromeda from the monster.

The end of heroes is often tragic and untimely: Achilles dies in battle, choosing a brief life and lasting glory rather than to live long without great achievements; Samson pulls the pillars of his enemies' hall down upon himself and perishes together with the multitude whom he destroys; Ragnar Lodbrok, the Viking leader, dies in a snakepit defying his enemies with a laugh; Sigurd dies by the swords of his kinsmen because he cannot keep faith with both Gudrun and Brynhild. It is for their deaths above all that the heroes are remembered, and these are in themselves so memorable that the tales remain moving and effective even when retold for children in a style and language far removed from that of the original tradition.

The hero, whether he be king's son, warrior-leader, saint or semi-divine being, blazes a trail for the less adventurous to follow. He is a kind of shadow of the hero-god of the great religions of the world, and such tales should be seen not as an escape into the world of fairy tales but as a source of deep wisdom and inspiration for human kind.

Woman

Goddess, victim, idol, plaything, mother, virgin, harlot, ministering angel, slut, enchantress, hag, 'better half' or 'weaker vessel' – woman plays all these roles in supernatural contexts, partly in reflection of man's frequently professed inability to understand her. Women, in male eyes, are supposed to be contrary and mysterious creatures, bewilderingly combining all sorts of opposite characteristics, as changeable as chameleons, and yet somehow vexingly in touch with reality through intuition, through a secret sympathy with the heart of things.

Among the most powerful strands in the web of the mythical female are that she is man's inferior and that she is essentially evil. In the Jewish, Christian and classical traditions, evil came into the world through woman. In many societies, including our own, women's bodies are hung about with a miasma of impurity and pollution which does not cling to men. In many parts of the world women do not eat with men, they walk a few paces behind their husbands as a sign of their inferiority, and they are often excluded altogether from important masculine activities, including religion.

Orthodox Hindus believe that women cannot attain salvation as women, but only through being reborn as men. Women are evil and unclean, and the virtuous Hindu woman, who must treat her husband as if he was a god, is considered inferior to the worst of men. In the West the more important religious roles are still reserved for men and denied to women, and it is only in the face of stubborn resistance that women have begun to invade male preserves. In religious and magical traditions which classify phenomena in terms of opposites, male is generally classed with good, positive, active, and female with evil, negative, passive. It

is characteristic that one of the dictionary meanings of the word 'female' is 'epithet of various material and immaterial things denoting simplicity, inferiority, weakness, or the like'.

All this has the weight of hundreds of years of tradition and custom behind it: some women welcome it, many accept it, and almost all are brought up to behave in accordance with it and so perpetuate it. But how it began, how hatred, fear and contempt came to be injected into the image of woman – remembering that a child's first love is his mother, that men and women do fall in love and live happily together, and that what may be the oldest known representation of a deity is a figure of a woman – is a question to which there is no certain answer. Psychoanalysts in search of an answer have created new myths of their own, including those of penis envy and the castration complex. Stated in a very brief and over-simplified way, the theory is that the little girl, lacking a penis, feels a sense of inferiority to males which lasts her the rest of her life: and that the little boy fears losing his penis when he sees that little girls have none, and fears that his father will castrate him because he is a rival for the affections of the mother, these fears mingling with desire in his attitude to women, who become both love-objects and hate-objects.

It is true that the theme of castration occurs in mythology and religious practice (in the worship of Cybele, for instance), and the motif of woman as castrator has enjoyed some literary popularity in the wake of Freud, but it seems unlikely that fear of castration is really a crucial element in the myth of woman's evilness. A simpler approach sees the source of this myth in the difference between the sexes itself. Women are different from men, and tolerance of what is different is not a marked feature of human societies. When what is different and 'other' is also desired. it may be resented, hated and feared, as well as loved and idealized.

The fact that it is woman who bears and rears children means that it is first and foremost a child's mother who not only loves and protects him but also thwarts and punishes him. The twin experiences of mother's love and mother's rage seem to implant an ambivalent attitude to women in general, which is reflected in beliefs about the supernatural. For example, Spartan boys were flogged, or ritually 'punished' on the altar of Artemis Orthia, which had a fondness for human blood. In the Cabala the sefirah Din or Geburah, which represents the punishing judgement of God, is on the female pillar of the Tree of Life.

In the Near East, almost always, mother goddesses and love goddesses were also wrathful war goddesses. Kali, the goddess of terror in Hinduism, significantly presides over undeserved retribution as 'the Mother who nourishes but also punishes'. She

typifies 'the deep-seated dread aroused by the unpredictable hazards of man's existence', which in terms of childish experience starts with the bewildering terror of the mother's anger. The age-old assertion that woman is fickle and changeable may have the same root.

The supposed inferiority of woman follows from the fact that human societies have been dominated by men, presumably because men's greater physical strength has enabled them to dominate. The theory that early societies passed through a stage of matriarchy, followed by patriarchy when men seized power from women and enslaved them, is now generally doubted (though there are myths of the reign of women), and even matrilineal societies, where descent is reckoned from the mother, are not usually woman-dominated.

Because women are physically weaker, it is concluded that they must also be inferior mentally and spiritually.

Many attempts have been made, unsuccessfully, to show that woman is biologically inferior to man, and the argument that the emancipation of women would wreck home and family life, and the female character, is old and tenacious. But the pronouncements of Möbius pale into insignificance as a condemnation of woman beside the tirade in the Indian epic, the *Mahabharata*: 'Woman is an all-devouring curse. In her body the evil cycle of life begins afresh, born out of lust engendered by blood and semen. Man emerges mixed with excrement and water, fouled with the impurities of woman. A wise man will avoid the contaminating society of women as he would the touch of bodies infested with vermin.'

This diatribe contains two themes found elsewhere. The first is that when our earthly lives and our earthly bodies are condemned as evil and dangerous, distracting the mind from spiritual things and imprisoning us in ignorance and wrong, then sexual intercourse is considered evil, and so is woman, who tempts man to sex and from whose body yet more imprisoned spirits emerge to earthly life: though in other contexts, of course, woman is deified and revered.

The second theme is that women are unclean. The fact that they bleed at regular intervals has aroused fear and disgust, especially when menstrual blood is regarded as the substance which should have formed the body of a child and is charged with potent and dangerous energy. Contact with this blood and with a menstruating woman has been widely feared as contaminating, and so has contact with a pregnant woman or with childbirth. If women are unclean, then they must be kept at a distance from men's fighting and hunting activities and equipment, and from religious ceremonies, because they might pollute them.

Another physically based reason for masculine fear of woman is that the male organ 'dies' in orgasm, and the emission of sperm has frequently been regarded as a loss to

Corvina, Budapest

Above *Pandora, who raised the lid of a jar containing all evils and allowed them to escape to plague the world, has been described as a typical woman:* **Pandora** *by François Quesnel.* **Facing page** *Relief depicting an Egyptian queen, said to be Cleopatra who 'lost Mark Antony the world'.*

the male of some of his life-energy. H. R. Hays quotes an Australian aborigine as saying, 'The vagina is very hot, it is fire and each time the penis goes in, it dies.' The Roman poet Ovid used the same image in hoping to die making love: 'Let me go in the act of coming to Venus; in more senses than one let my last dying be done.' In *Paradise Lost*, when Adam and Eve make love after the Fall, Adam rises afterwards as Samson rose from Delilah's harlot lap, 'shorn of his strength'.

This motif combines with the fact that women are unlike men in being capable of sex at any time and able to go on longer, to create the myth of woman's insatiable lustfulness and to paint a picture of her as a voracious monster who ensnares a man to devour him, subjecting him to orgasmic 'deaths' until she destroys him.

Greek men were horrified by the worship Dionysus indulged in, partly because it took women away from their 'proper place' in the home, but also because the frenzied rites unleashed all the murderous carnality felt to be inherent in the female nature. In later centuries people were similarly horrified by the cannibalism and orgiastic excesses of witches. It was once customary to refer to women as 'the sex', as though sensuality was a peculiarly female trait.

Jean de Meung, 13th century continuator of the *Roman de la Rose*, put it succinctly: 'Every woman is a whore.' In the book of Revelation (chapter 17) the personification of lust and murder is the great harlot who sits on a scarlet beast, arrayed in purple and scarlet and jewels, holding a golden cup full of abominations and the impurities of her fornication, drunk with the blood of saints and martyrs. The German writer Otto Weininger, who detested both women and Jews, published in 1903 a book called *Sex and Character*, which went through numerous editions, in which he maintained that women are monsters of devouring sexuality: 'Woman wants man sexually because she only succeeds in existing through her sensuality.'

The same stereotype, of woman as a being whose existence depends on draining the life from men, appears in the legends of Lilith, the lamias, the sirens, vampires and demonesses who prey on men sexually. She appears again in modern novels, for instance as the Great Bitch in Norman Mailer's *An American Dream*, who 'delivers extermination to any bucko brave enough to take carnal knowledge of her', and in the fantasy characters, described by Germaine Greer in *The Female Eunuch* as 'those extraordinary springing women with slanting eyes and swirling clouds of hair who prowl through thriller comics on the balls of their feet, wheeling suddenly upon the hero, talons unsheathed for the kill. Their mouths are large, curved and shining like scimitars: the musculature of their shoulders and thighs is incredible, their breasts like grenades, their waists encircled with steel belts as narrow as Cretan bull-dancers'.

The great bitch or cat-woman, the seducer and slayer, is also related to the *femme fatale* or *la belle dame sans merci*, the enchantress for whom men feel an irresistible longing and who pitilessly enslaves and degrades them. She appears in Arthurian legends, she is Delilah, who robbed Samson of his strength and his freedom, or Cleopatra, 'who lost Mark Antony the world'. She is Wilde's Salome and the Dolores, 'Our Lady of Pain', of Swinburne's masochistic fancy.

The *femme fatale* may be essentially passive: her loveliness by itself entraps men and destroys them, as in the case of Helen, whose beauty launched the thousand ships of the avenging Greeks and caused the fall of Troy. Another example is Pandora, whose story was told by Hesiod in his *Works and Days* and *Theogony*. Zeus determined to make men pay for the gift of fire, which Prometheus had stolen, and instructed the divine craftsman Hephaestus to manufacture a 'beautiful evil', a woman, made of soil mixed with water. The goddess Athene taught her to sew, golden Aphrodite 'shed grace upon her head and cruel longing and cares that weary the limbs', and Hermes bestowed on her 'a shameless mind and a deceitful nature'.

Pandora was, in fact, a typical woman as seen by Hesiod, and Zeus presented her to Epimetheus, Prometheus's brother, who foolishly accepted the gift. She then raised the lid of a jar, which contained all evils, and the evils escaped and have been loose in the world ever since. Before this, Hesiod says, 'men lived on earth remote and free from ills and hard toil and heavy sicknesses ...but the woman took off the great lid of the jar with her hands and scattered all these

William MacQuitty

Left *The concept of woman as a passive sexual object or plaything classed on a level with wine and song as a masculine diversion, is ancient and widespread: wall painting in an Egyptian tomb showing women at their toilet.* **Facing page** *In legends of sirens and vampires woman is depicted as a being whose existence depends on draining the life from men; this stereotype is related to the enchantress for whom men feel an irresistible longing, a* **femme fatale** *who may in fact be essentially passive, and whose loveliness by itself entraps and destroys men:* **Left** *Helen's beauty caused the fall of Troy:* **Helen on the Ramparts of Troy** *by Moreau.* **Right** *Head of Nefertiti, wife of the heretic Pharaoh Akhnaten.*

and her thought caused sorrow and mischief to men.' All women are descended from her, 'the deadly race and tribe of women who live amongst mortal men to their great trouble', for Zeus 'made women to be an evil to mortal men, with a nature to do evil'.

Pandora's name may mean 'all-giving' and was perhaps originally a title of the Earth Goddess. Her jar (*pithos*) was turned into a box (*pyxis*) by Erasmus, the 16th-century humanist, and 'Pandora's box' became a phrase for any source of multiple disasters. Early Christian writers likened her to Eve and the Renaissance rediscovered her, though usually not as the source of evil but as the 'all-gifted' one, on whom the gods had bestowed their treasures. However, Jean Olivier, author of *Pandora* (1541), said: 'Eve in Scripture opened the forbidden fruit by her bite, by which death invaded the world. So did Pandora open the box in defiance of a divine injunction, whereby all the evils and infinite calamities broke loose and over-whelmed mortals with countless miseries...'

In the late 18th century, the painter James Barry, who executed an enormous *Creation of Pandora*, called her story 'one of the most splendid of the many specimens of the Heathen manner of adumbrating and allegorizing that introduction of Evil or fall of mankind which is celebrated in Genesis'. Pandora's box was occasionally identified with her genitals, and Paul Klee's drawing of *Pandora's Box* (1920) brings in the menstruation motif, for it shows a goblet shaped like the female genitals, containing some flowers and emitting evil vapours.

The Jewish legend of the Watchers traces the introduction of evil into the world to the angels who descended from heaven, significantly drawn to earth by the sexual attractions of human women, but the story of Adam and Eve has had a greater influence in the West in reinforcing the belief in woman's inherent wickedness. In the account in Genesis it is the woman who succumbs to the serpent's temptation and persuades Adam to eat the forbidden fruit, the action which caused the Fall and implanted the taint of original sin in all human beings. In some paintings of the scene, including Michelangelo's in the Sistine Chapel, the serpent itself is female.

Genesis also stresses the inferiority of woman. She is created after Adam, and fashioned from one of his ribs, and the pangs of childbirth and the subjection of woman to man are among the penalties for the crime, so providing divine authority for the actual situation in patriarchal Hebrew society. The story in Genesis may have been influenced by the Babylonian Epic of Gilgamesh in which Enkidu, the 'noble savage' who is man in his natural primitive state, is seduced by a temple prostitute. She teaches him the delights of sex, instructs him in civilized behaviour, and finally lures him away from his peaceful life with the animals and takes him to the city, and so ultimately to his doom. When he is dying, Enkidu curses her for coaxing him away from his simple life.

If at one end of the scale woman is whore, temptress, murderess, at the other she is a toy or doll, a passive sexual object and plaything, the occupant of a real or psychological harem, classed on a level with wine and song as masculine diversions. The legendary Eve's subordination to Adam, and the numerous representations of her in art as the acme of physical desirability, in styles varying with male tastes of different periods and places, have contributed to this stereotype, which is blisteringly described by Germaine Greer. 'She is more body than soul, more soul than mind ... She is the Sexual Object sought by all men, and by all women. Her value is solely attested by the demand she excites in others. All she must contribute is her existence. She need achieve nothing, for she is the reward of achievement ... Because she is the emblem of spending ability and the chief spender, she is also the most effective seller of this world's goods. Every survey ever held has shown that the image of an attractive woman is the most effective advertising gimmick.'

There is far more to Eve in Genesis, and to woman in supernatural contexts generally than evil and passive inferiority, but the note of wickedness, darkness, danger and death does sound constantly. *Cherchez la femme* men say, if there's trouble there's a woman at the bottom of it.

Many of the mother goddesses of the distant past were deities who gave life but who also gave death, and their worshippers seem to have regarded them with the same mingled emotions of love and terror, trust and fear, admiration and resentment, desire and disgust, which men have blended in their image of woman all through history.

Michael Holford Library

C. M. Dixon/British Museum

The Mother Goddess

'Concerning earth, the mother of all, shall I sing; firm earth, eldest of gods, that nourishes all things in the world ... Thine it is to give or to take life from mortal men.' These words from the Homeric Hymn to Earth typify a religious belief that is as old as history.

From time immemorial man has reflected in wonder and amazement on the earth upon which he lives, and which nourishes himself, his family, his tribe and his animals. As long as man has felt himself dependent on the earth, he has personified it and worshipped or at least reverenced it, in the most potent of all images, the image of the mother.

Today in a Western society which has to a very great extent lost its hold on the realities of agricultural existence, it is said that the earth has become desacralized. Reverence has given way to ruthless exploitation. The mystery has fled, to be replaced by concrete carpets and factory farming. Nevertheless, it is still possible to see shadows and hear distant echoes of what was once an unquestioned item of faith.

Not long ago the suggestion was made that a certain bestseller in the field of religious literature would be a book entitled 'God is a Woman'. The suggestion may have been partly frivolous, but bearing in mind that it is only very recently in the history of mankind that deity has been credited with ex-

clusively masculine attributes, the possibility of depicting supernatural power in feminine terms is far from unreasonable. In the West, God is generally spoken of as 'Our Father which art in heaven', but the naive question 'If God is Father, then who is Mother?' still deserves to be asked. Historically the answer would be: 'The earth on which we live.'

The history of religion reveals a panorama of gods and goddesses, higher and lower spiritual beings, among whom personifications of the earth occupy a prominent place. As a rule these personifications bear all the attributes of female sexuality and motherhood. Sometimes they are paradoxically believed to be virginal. Often, still more paradoxically, they combine within themselves attributes of generosity and grace and also those of horror and destruction. If human love is one of their areas of influence, the senseless urge which leads men into war is another.

Their icons and images may be of the order of the Venus de Milo, an idealized form of female beauty; or, equally, they may suggest a mind diseased – skinny, skull-festooned hags, their fangs dripping with the blood of generations of men. Clearly the mother goddess of human history is no romantic figure, but rather one in which opposites combine, in which the giver of life is clearly seen as the being who also takes

it away, and in which promises are hollow and temporary, and hope a mockery.

The tension and paradox appear to have been almost universal. From Scandinavia to Melanesia, goddesses in which precisely these characteristics predominate have been worshipped, feared and propitiated. This universality has led some scholars to suggest that what we are in fact seeing is the reflection of a human psychological trait which is always and everywhere the same, though clothed in slightly different images and symbols. This psychological interpretation is not without its risks, however. The Paleolithic 'Venuses' for instance cannot simply be equated with medieval figures of the Virgin Mary. The figure of the mother goddess in India is not the same as the Great Mother of the Mediterranean world, however much they may appear to have in common. The hypotheses of Freud and Jung must not be made to carry more weight than they can bear. As well as similarities, there are of course considerable and very significant differences.

Among man's earliest artefacts, dating from the late Paleolithic period, are coarse and crude figurines of pregnant women, their breasts and hips grotesquely enlarged. These, it has been supposed, represent in human form that concern with human reproduction that was a pattern of man's

Facing page *Crude figurines of women with prominent breasts and grotesquely enlarged hips are among man's earliest artefacts and have been found all over the world; it is possible that these represent the fertility that is essential if man is to survive. Figure of a standing woman* (**far left**) *c 6000BC: from Catal Hüyük in Anatolia.* **Centre** *Clay figurine from Assyria.* **Left** *Brazilian figurine made from clay, representing a pregnant woman.* **Right** *The epitome of feminine charm, Venus influenced the fertility of plants and animals: mosaic showing the goddess at her toilet.*

Michael Holford Library

condition of survival. It is not known whether these in any sense represent mother goddesses and there is no way of finding out. The possibility is there but it is only a possibility.

It is interesting, though, that these figurines are seldom more than approximately human. Apart from their lack of proportion, their faces and other personal characteristics are hardly even hinted at. This same characteristic is found in female figurines from Bronze Age peasant cultures and many of the earliest urban cultures, for instance those of north-west India. Excavations made on Indus Valley sites have revealed many such artefacts, often smoke-stained in such a way as to suggest some form of household worship. If this is a continuous line of development, it would seem to suggest something more than merely 'good-luck charms' or magical amulets. The pattern is consistent, at all events: a female figure with rudimentary features, but with prominent breasts and hips, often dressed in a girdle and necklaces, and wearing a head-dress.

Even today the visitor to an Indian village may be surprised to find that the temples of the great gods, Shiva and Vishnu, are regarded by the people as being of less importance than the little shrine of the local goddess, or Grami Devi. She may have many names, most of which are not found in the standard textbooks on Hinduism. But she is 'of the earth', and directly responsible for the fertility of the fields surrounding the village. She may be linked mythologically with the consorts of the great gods, Parvati, a consort of Shiva, Kali his wife, or Lakshmi who was Vishnu's wife, but to all intents and purposes she is the guardian of the village and the one to whom the people turn for everyday purposes. She has her festivals and her particular responsibilities, and it is probable that her nature and function have not changed for more than 5000 years.

However, the most authoritative evidence concerning the worship of mother goddesses comes from the Mediterranean area, from Iran in the east to Rome in the west, and covering Mesopotamia, Egypt and Greece. Indeed, in this area, the names and functions of the great goddesses were so inter-changeable as to make comparative study a highly complex undertaking. The primary identification of the goddess with the fruitful earth is unquestionable, but starting from Mesopotamia there is an involved pattern, in which celestial elements combine with those of the underworld in such a way as to suggest

that the Great Mother may be a composite figure, as complex as the human mind.

The Semitic names for the greatest mother goddess were Inanna in Sumeria, Ishtar in Babylon and Astarte or Anat among the Canaanites. Commonly identified with the planet Venus, her most typical title is 'queen of heaven', though she is also known as 'mistress of all the gods' and 'the lady of the world'. In time, she gathered to herself the attributes of a host of other goddesses, so that in Mesopotamia the word *ishtar* came to mean simply 'goddess'.

She was believed to be the giver of vegetation; a hymn contains the words: 'In the heavens I take my place and send rain, in the earth I take my place and cause the green to spring forth.' She was the creator of animals, and the goddess of sexual love, marriage and maternity. In another hymn it was said: 'I turn the male to the female, I turn the female to the male; I am she who adorneth the male for the female I am she who adorneth the female for the male.' Her worship was frequently connected with the practice of sacred prostitution.

Two other characteristics of the Semitic mother goddess are worth mentioning in this context. The first concerned her connection with a male figure who could be described as son, brother or husband. The best known of these figures was Tammuz (Sumerian Dumu-zi), a god of vegetation and in particular of the growing corn. Every year a festival was held at which his 'death' and 'resurrection' was celebrated.

The vegetation god was believed to die

and rise again annually, and in the myths of the descent of the mother goddess into the land of the dead there is a dramatic image of the search of the mother for her lost son and lover, the search of the earth for the temporarily lost fertility which the new spring restores. A Sumerian version of this myth, *Inanna's Descent to the Nether World*, is one of the earliest examples.

Inanna descends, perhaps in order to free Dumu-zi; she approaches the subterranean temple of Ereshkigal, god of the dead, through seven gates, at each one of which she has to remove part of her clothing, until she finally stands before him naked. An interesting feature of this myth is that on her return, she brings with her all manner of evil and malevolent beings: 'They who preceded her, they who preceded Inanna, were beings who knew not food, who knew not water, who eat not sprinkled flour, who drink not libated wine, who take away the wife from the loins of man, who take away the child from the breast of the nursing mother.' Similar myths were current all over the Semitic world, for instance in Canaan, where the mother goddess Anat attacks and conquers Mot (death) in order to free the fertility god Baal.

The cult of the mother goddess moved westward, perhaps through Cyprus and Crete, into Anatolia and Greece. Significantly, the most popular image of Venus, the Greek Aphrodite, depicts her emerging from the sea on the coast of Cyprus, while her consort, Adonis, is a Semitic figure, with a Semitic name. In her purely Greek form, as

Hamlyn Group/Musée Guimet

Aphrodite, the goddess's cult was fairly decorous, but on the borders of the Greek world, in Corinth, sacred prostitution was practised.

However, on entering the Greek culture, the cult of the mother goddess encountered another similar cult deriving from the Indo-European culture. In Iran, Anahita the goddess who 'purifies the seed of males and the womb and milk of females', described in sculptural terms as 'a beautiful maiden, powerful and tall', was worshipped. Her cult spread through the Persian Empire, and she gradually coalesced in various ways with Athene, Aphrodite, and the Anatolian Cybele. It was Cybele who eventually came to be honoured in the Roman Empire as the Great Mother of the gods, a temple being erected to her honour on the Palatine Hill in Rome in 204 BC.

The cult of Cybele remained, even after its adoption in Rome by the Romans, the responsibility of native Phrygians, who wore their hair long, dressed in female clothes, and celebrated the goddess in wild orgiastic dances to the point of exhaustion. It is believed their consecration to the goddess sometimes involved self-emasculation.

Although this type of worship was not unknown in Greece, particularly in connection with Dionysus, worship of the mother goddess took more decorous forms. The Mysteries of Eleusis incorporated most of the elements already mentioned: a dying and rising pattern linked with the corn, with fertility and with the rhythm of the seasons. The rites of Eleusis were celebrated in honour of the mother goddess Demeter and in honour of her daughter Persephone.

Originally pure fertility rites, they gradually came to be an acted parable of the relationship of man to his surroundings, assuring initiates of the protection of Persephone in the world beyond the grave. The myth is outlined in the Homeric Hymn to Demeter.

Persephone, daughter of Demeter and Zeus (earth mother and sky father) was out gathering flowers. The earth opened and out

leaped Pluto, god of the underworld: 'He caught her up reluctant in his golden car and bore her away lamenting.' For nine days Demeter sought her; on the tenth day she learned the secret from Helios, the sun. Angry, she closed the womb of earth until her daughter was restored to her; however, Pluto made Persephone eat pomegranate seeds, in this way keeping some hold on her. Demeter accepted the arrangement, and before leaving for Olympus, showed the people her mysteries, '... awful mysteries which no one may in any way transgress or pry into or utter, for deep awe of the gods checks the voice'. The secret was well kept, and many details of the Eleusinian Mysteries are unknown, save that the cult became established in Athens.

Another popular form of the worship of the mother goddess in the Roman Empire was that of the Egyptian goddess Isis. Originally the wife of Osiris, identified with the dead pharaoh, she was the mother of Horus, the living pharaoh, who gave birth to her son after having conceived magically on the body of her dead husband. One common representation of Isis is as a mother suckling the infant Horus, thought by some to be a prototype of later Christian images of mother and child.

Indeed, the queen of heaven, the universal mother, was known by many names in the ancient world. For example there is Artemis or Diana, the huntress and mistress of animals: in Acts, chapter 19, there is recorded a celebrated encounter between Paul and devotees of 'Artemis of the Ephesians', a a local many-breasted form of what may have originally been a moon goddess. There

Left *The personification of generosity and grace, the mother goddess also has the power to destroy. Primitive Indian figurine of a fertility goddess; her staring eyes show that she expects sacrifice.* **Facing page** *Durga, one of the aspects of the female side of the great god Shiva, was born to kill demons.*

was the Anatolian goddess Ma, whose priests were known as *fanatici* (servants of the *fanum* or temple) and from whose wild excesses comes the word 'fanatic'. Farther north, there were Celtic and Teutonic tribal goddesses.

Among the latter, the goddess Freya was said to have had sexual relations with all the male members of the pantheon, and as goddess of the dead shared with Odin the custody of warriors slain on the field of battle.

This is much the same kind of ambivalence that is to be observed in most mother goddesses; because the earth receives the dead in corruption and also gives birth and sustenance to crops, men and animals, the connection between the mother goddess and the kingdom of the dead is common. In Greece, for instance, the dead were sometimes called 'Demeter's people', since Demeter was the goddess of earth and the underworld.

Mankind's worship of, and reverence for, the divine figure of the mother, is a religious phenomenon far deeper than creeds, councils and dogmas. It reflects man's profound need for security in a frequently unfriendly world, his own inadequacies and his own fears. In it can be seen the tension between good things and evil, between the gift of life and the fear of death, personified in the goddess who gives and takes away, who creates and destroys, but who is never as aloof and unconcerned as her consort, the sky god. As long as man retains any of his roots in the earth, reverence for the earth – whether personified or not – will remain, and the Great Mother will still have human children, who treat her with reverence.

Many of the attributes of the Great Mother of the Mediterranean countries were transferred to the Virgin Mary and thus to the Christian religion.

William MacQuitty

The Flood

The traditions of many widely separated peoples include legends of a great flood which, at some time in the remote past, overwhelmed vast tracts of land and flourishing cities, and drowned all or nearly all the inhabitants, men and beasts alike. In the more ancient forms of the legend, it is often the whole world that is inundated. One man only, with his family and, usually, a number of animals, manages to escape because, being supernaturally warned of the coming disaster, he is able either to build or acquire a ship that carries him safely through the deluge. Eventually, after a period varying in different traditions from a few days to several months, the anger of the gods is appeased, the floods recede and the dry land reappears. Life is preserved in the midst of universal destruction, and in due course the world is filled again by the descendants of the hero and of the animals that sailed with him.

The most widely known, though not the oldest, of all these ancient tales is that contained in the book of Genesis (chapters 6–9). In it is related how, when ten generations had passed since the time of Adam, Yahweh saw that the world he had created had become corrupt and full of wickedness. He resolved to drown all mankind and everything else that had life in one vast flood, with the exception of Noah, who was a righteous man and worthy to become the ancestor of a new race of human beings in a regenerated world. He commanded Noah to build an ark of gopher wood, giving him directions as to its size and design, and bade him go into it when it was finished, taking with him all his family and male and female creatures of every species known on earth – clean beasts by sevens and unclean beasts by twos.

Noah did as he was told, and Yahweh loosed the deluge. Rain fell without stopping for 40 days and nights, the water rose until even the tops of the mountains were covered, and the ark floated upon it. Every living being perished, except those that were with Noah. After a long time the floods began to subside. The ark came to rest on Mount Ararat in Armenia, and Noah sent out a raven, and then a dove, to discover how far the waters had abated. The raven flew away over the drowned land but the dove, finding no resting place outside, returned to the ark. Again, after seven days, it was sent out and again it came back, but this time it had an olive leaf in its beak. Finally, after a third flight, it did not return and Noah, looking forth, saw that the land was dry. He came out from the ark and built an altar on the mountain, and offered a sacrifice in gratitude for his deliverance. Then Yahweh made a covenant with him, promising that his descendants should multiply and fill the earth, and that never again should the whole world be destroyed by water.

The Mesopotamian legend, from which the Genesis story is clearly derived, is far older. Abraham's people must have known it when they lived in their Chaldean homeland, and probably they carried it with them when they migrated to the land of Canaan. There are several known versions. One was incorporated by a Babylonian named Berosus in a history of his own country written in Greek in the 3rd century BC. According to Berosus's account, the god Cronus appeared to Xisuthros, tenth king of Babylon, in a dream and warned him that there would be a great flood which would destroy the human race. Xisuthros would be saved if he would obey the god's commands which were that, first, he must write a history of the world from its beginnings and bury it in the city of Sippara, and then he must build a ship and fill it with living creatures, men and birds and four-footed beasts.

Xisuthros accordingly buried his history at Sippara and constructed a stout vessel, five furlongs in length and two furlongs broad, on to which he took his family and friends and an unspecified number of animals and birds. The flood came as had been foretold and only those on the ship survived it. When the water began to go down, the vessel was stranded on a hilltop. Like Noah, Xisuthros sent out birds, and when the last of these did not come back, he disembarked with his wife and his daughter and his helmsman to build an altar and offer sacrifice. The other human passengers remained on board, and when their leader did not return they became anxious and went in search of him. They could not find him but presently they heard his voice speaking to them from the air, though he himself was invisible. He told them that he and his three companions had all been taken from this world to dwell with the gods. He went on to say that the mountain on which his hearers stood was in Armenia, and that they must make their way thence to Babylon, and dig up the writings that had been buried at Sippara. This they did, and by them and their descendants many cities were built, ancient sanctuaries restored and all the land repeopled.

An earlier and more interesting variant of the same story forms part of the *Epic of Gilgamesh*. Gilgamesh was not personally involved in the deluge, which took place long before his time, but he heard about it from his immortal ancestor, Utnapishtim.

Long ago, he said, when he lived in the city of Shuruppak on the banks of the Euphrates, the gods sat in council and decided to send a flood whereby all men would be drowned. Ea, Lord of Waters and of Wisdom, was present at this council and contrived, by a subterfuge, to warn Utnapishtim of what was about to happen. Instead of speaking to him directly, as Yahweh did to Noah, he addressed the wall, saying, 'O reed hut, reed hut, O wall, wall, O reed hut hearken, O wall attend', and so conveyed his message without actually revealing the secrets of his fellow gods to a lesser being. He bade him build a ship, well-planned and strong, in which he could save himself and his family. He was to tell no one of the threatened deluge, and if anyone asked him why he was building a ship, he was to reply that he had incurred the wrath of the great god, Enlil, and must therefore seek refuge with Ea upon the ocean.

Utnapishtim made a barge of wood, caulked with pitch within and bitumen without, and set on it a house of six storeys, each storey having nine rooms. Into it he brought his kinsfolk and his handicraftsmen, his cattle and other beasts of the field, and all that he had of living seed and of gold and silver. When the appointed time came, he went in and shut the door. Then the winds blew and the rain fell in torrents, the waters rose and whirlwinds rushed over them, and there was no light anywhere. For six days and nights the tempest raged, and so terrible was it that even the gods were afraid. They drew back, they cowered by the wall, they climbed up into the heaven of Anu for safety; and all but Enlil repented that they had unleashed such destruction.

On the seventh day the storm ceased, the turbulent waters became calm, silence succeeded uproar; but when Utnapishtim looked out he saw nothing but desolation and death. As the flood slowly receded, the hilltops reappeared and the ship grounded on Mount Nisir. Utnapishtim opened a window and loosed a dove, and after an interval, a swallow. Both returned because they could find no dry land, but when a raven was released, it found food to eat and ground on which to alight and it did not return. Then Utnapishtim knew that the water was going down and he came out of the ship, with all his companions, and offered a sacrifice on the mountaintop.

The gods smelt the sweet savour of the offering and gathered round it with delight. Only Enlil was angry when he saw that some human beings had survived, for he still desired the end of mankind. Ea was suspected of having betrayed the secret counsels of the gods, which indeed he had, though in such a way that he was able to deny the charge. He reproached Enlil because it was he who had wished for the deluge. Let it be enough, he said, to diminish the tribes of men by sending a lion, or a leopard, or a famine, or a plague, but let them not all perish together in a flood. Then Enlil relented, and taking Utnapishtim and his wife by the hand, he blessed them and promised that henceforth they should be like gods and live for ever.

The oldest known version of this story is that inscribed upon a tablet unearthed during excavations at Nippur, an ancient city of southern Sumer. It was written, apparently about 2100 BC, in the language of the Sumerians, the ancient people who flourished in Mesopotamia before they were conquered by the invading Semites. The hero in this legend was named Ziusudra. He was a king and also a priest of Enki, the god who, in the Sumerian pantheon, corresponded to the Semitic Ea. When Enlil called upon the assembled gods to destroy the world by a rainstorm, Enki warned his faithful servant. Like Ea, he did so by indirect means, bidding his priest to stand outside a wall and listen to a message addressed to that wall. Ziusudra

built a ship, though because the tablet is broken at that point in the narrative, exactly how he built it and who sailed with him is not known. Then the winds and the rain raged together for seven days and nights, and the

Noah's ark sails past as the rest of humanity drown: detail from an 18th-century Ethiopian manuscript.

flood waters covered the earth. When they had at last abated, Ziusudra offered sacrifice and prostrated himself before Anu and before Enlil. In this version, Enlil's wrath was more quickly appeased than in the Gilgamesh story, and he bestowed upon Ziusudra both immortality and the title of Preserver of the Seed of Mankind.

The deluge is also mentioned in the Sumerian king lists wherein are enumerated their rulers from the country's first beginnings. After some early kings have been listed it is stated: 'Then came the Flood. And after the Flood, kingship again descended from heaven.' Archeologists of the 20th century have proved that the historians of those far-off days were right in supposing that their land had once been devastated by a catastrophic flood. In 1929, during his excavations at Ur, Sir Leonard Woolley found clear evidence of a wide-

spread inundation, greater in extent and magnitude than anything subsequently known in the region, which had occured about 3000 BC. It had been vast enough to cover practically the whole of Lower Mesopotamia and drown most of its inhabitants. For the few who survived, it must have been the end of the world they knew, even if it was not that of the entire earth, as the legend gives it; and it is easy to see how, in the course of time, a mythological tale concerning a universal destruction could have evolved from the orally transmitted memories of so tremendous a disaster.

Flood traditions are very widespread, though they do not exist everywhere. They are found in India, Burma and elsewhere in southern Asia, in Australia and New Zealand, New Guinea and the scattered islands of the Pacific, in North and South America, Mexico and in some European regions. Most of these stories resemble each other in general pattern, as records of a worldwide inundation sent by the gods, from which only one divinely favoured hero and his companions escaped, but they vary, naturally, in their details. India has several versions, of which the earliest known is preserved in an ancient treatise, the *Satapatha Brahmana*. In this it is related that the hero, Manu, was first warned and then helped by a fish. He alone survived the flood. When it was all over, the world was empty, but because he desired children, he practised austerities and offered in sacrifice butter, sour milk, and curds and whey. Out of these substances a woman was miraculously created and from the union sprang a new race of beings – the race of Manu.

Similarly, in the early form of Greek flood legend, as told by Pindar in the 5th century BC, every living creature was destroyed, with the exception of Deucalion and his wife Pyrrha. These two weathered the storm for nine days and nights in an ark which Deucalion had constructed, and which finally came to rest on Mount Parnassus. When the floods had ceased they came down from the mountain and, at the bidding of Zeus, they too created mankind anew, by throwing stones over their own heads. As they struck the ground, the stones thrown by Deucalion became men and those thrown by Pyrrha became women. In this tale it is not recorded how the animals were preserved or re-created, but in a later version, which more closely resembles the Babylonian story and may have been influenced by it, Deucalion is said to have taken into the ark with him two of every kind of land animal, both the harmless and the dangerous, and these, by the power of the gods, lived together in harmony without hurting either the hero or each other.

There was also a Greek tradition that Deucalion's flood was not the only great inundation in the history of the world. There had been two others, one before it in the time of Ogyges, king of Thebes, and one after it, when Dardanus was driven from his homeland by a sudden and terrible, but apparently not a worldwide, flood. He escaped upon a raft, or according to another version upon an inflated skin, and drifting to Mount Ida, he landed there and in due course became the founder of the city of Troy.

In his *Folk-Lore in the Old Testament*, Sir J. G. Frazer has pointed out that the mythologies of Africa and of northern and central Asia contain no stories of a universal deluge, and this appears to be true of western Europe also. With the coming of Christianity, the biblical flood legend was, of course, accepted as divinely revealed truth, and continued to be so accepted for many centuries afterwards, but it does not seem to have superseded any pre-Christian west European myth of the same type. There are, however, several well-known traditions of partial and local floods caused, not by rain storms, but by land subsidence and violent encroachments of the sea. In the form in which we know them today, these are mainly medieval, or later, versions of tales that probably had their origin in a much more distant past and may well have some foundation in fact.

One of these stories is the Welsh legend of the Lowland Hundred. This was a tract of land lying westward of the present west coast of Wales, submerged now under the waters of Cardigan Bay. According to the most familiar variant of the tradition, it was a fertile and prosperous territory, 40 miles long and 20 miles broad, which stretched from Bardsey Island to the River Teifi. It was low-lying and was defended from the sea's encroachments by a system of embankments and sluices. It contained 16 noble cities, of which the chief was called Caer Gwyddno. The site of this vanished town was commonly supposed to be marked by a collection of large underwater boulders at the far end of Sarn Cynfelin, a rocky ridge running some seven or eight miles out to sea. This ridge, and two others like it, are natural formations, but in popular belief they were until fairly recently held to be either man-made causeways or parts of the defensive embankments.

The legend relates that in the early years of the 6th century AD, Gwyddno Garanhir was Lord of the Lowland Hundred, and Seithennin, son of the king of Syved, was keeper of its embankments. One night, when a great feast was held, the latter became exceedingly drunk and either through simple carelessness or as a drunken prank he left the sluices open. In consequence the sea broke through the defences and in a very short time overwhelmed the whole territory. Only a few people managed to escape, including Gwyddno Garanhir, his son Elphin and Seithennin himself.

Another still more dramatic Welsh story – or perhaps a localized variant of the same story – is told of the lost land of Tyno Helig. This was a little kingdom, or chief's territory, which once extended northwards from the Caernarvonshire coast and is now sunk in Conway Bay. Over it, at some rather uncertain period betwen the 5th and the 7th centuries AD, Helig ap Glannawg is said to have reigned, and to have lived in a palace which bore the name of Llys Helig. Tradition said that this palace was situated some two miles out to sea from the present coastline, and that occasionally, when the tide was unusually low, some ruined parts of it could be seen under the water. However, in 1939 F. J. North destroyed this interesting tradition by proving that the 'ruins' were in fact an accumulation of Iron Age boulders.

The catastrophe which destroyed Tyno Helig was popularly supposed to have been caused by the sins of the ruling family, and to have been prophesied by a disembodied voice four generations before it occurred. In one version of the tale, it was the crimes of Helig himself, or of his ancestors, that called down retribution upon the land, though he and his sons saved themselves by swift flight and thereafter led godly lives. In another, it was his daughter and her lover who were responsible. The daughter loved a man of low degree, but she would not marry him because he did not possess that sign of rank, a gold torque. To obtain one, he murdered a nobleman. As he was burying the corpse, he heard a voice crying, 'Vengeance will come!' He fled from that place, but when he told the girl what had happened, she sent him back to find out how soon the vengeance would come. The voice replied, 'In the time of the children, and of the grandchildren, and of the great-grandchildren, and of the great-great-grandchildren.' On hearing this, Helig's daughter said there was nothing to fear, for she and her lover would be dead by then.

They were married and lived to see their own great-great-grandchildren. One day, a great feast was held at Llys Helig, at which their kin of all four generations were present. A maidservant was sent to fetch more wine from the cellar, and found it half-full of water, with fish swimming about in it. She ran back to the hall and told the bard who, according to one variant, was the only person sufficiently sober to appreciate the danger. He, recognizing that the long-prophesied doom had come at last, fled at once, taking the maid with him. These two were the only survivors, for immediately after their flight the sea rushed in and all the land of Tyno Helig was drowned.

Farther south, in Cornwall, we find the tradition of lost Lyonnesse. This legend is perhaps better known than any other British tradition of the same type because, in the course of time, it became involved with the Arthurian romances and the story of Tristan. Lyonnesse, which in Cornish was called Lethowstow, lay between Land's End and the Scilly Isles. Like the Lowland Hundred, it was fertile and prosperous, with many flourishing villages and no less than 140 churches.

This land sank like the others, though here there is no tradition of sin or drunkenness to account for the disaster. The sea must have been encroaching alarmingly for some time before the final calamity, for the legend states that one man, the ancestor of the Trevilion family, took fright at its daily inroads, and sent his wife and family into Cornwall for safety. No one else apparently realized the danger, and Trevilion himself escaped only at the last moment, riding on a swift horse towards the higher ground of the Cornish mainland and reaching it only just in time. Every other dweller in Lyonnesse was drowned.

In western Brittany there is a more elaborate form of this legend which concerns the destruction of the city of Ker-Is. This city once flourished amid fertile lands that are now under the sea. Its site is usually given as in the Bay of Douarnenez, but in some versions of the tale it is said to be submerged off other parts of the Breton coast. It was protected from the sea by a strong dyke and by sluice gates, but it perished in the end because of the wickedness of its inhabitants who, though they were Christians, had fallen into evil ways. The immediate cause of the disaster was the foolish, or perhaps intentionally mischievous, action of a girl whose name was Dahut (or Ahès) and whose father, Gradlon, was ruler of the city.

Like Lyonnesse and the Lowland Hundred, Ker-Is was believed to have vanished at some time in the early 6th century. It is of course obvious that so late a date is impossible. There is no evidence whatever, geological or

Left A Sumerian boat with passenger and boatman appears on the left of a cylinder seal of the third millennium BC: the Sumerian legend of a great flood strongly influenced the Jewish story of Noah.
Facing page *The story of Noah receives a Moslem interpretation in this 16th-century Mogul miniature; the best known of the many flood legends of the world, it has had a great appeal to popular imagination.*

Michael Holford

historical, for the occurrence of floods of such magnitude as recently as the 5th or 6th century AD. The detailed accounts of noble cities, Christian churches, intricate sea defences and sinful human beings with known names and pedigrees are clearly later embellishments of what was probably once a far simpler story. Yet these ancient tales cannot be dismissed entirely as mere products of fantasy and imagination. It is a fact that the coasts of Wales, England and Brittany formerly extended farther than they do now, and that subsidences were still taking place when the lands thus lost were inhabited by our fore-fathers who lived in the Bronze and Early Iron Ages.

Traces of human habitation in regions now well below the high water mark have been discovered by archeologists, such as, for example, the field walls on the submerged sandflats between some of the Scilly Isles, and artefacts in Mount's Bay and round the coast of Gower. If the men who made and used these things were forced by the encroaching waters to abandon their homes, they would have their own exciting tales of disaster to tell, and these, handed down for centuries and gradually becoming more elaborate, would become part of the traditional lore of the regions to which the first tellers migrated.

It is true that the legends take no account of the slowness of geological change, or the fact that the submergence of the lost territories was gradual and intermittent. In all the stories the inundations are swift and sudden. This may be partly due to the telescoping effects of time and repetition and a sense of drama, but here too it is possible that there is considerably more than an element of fact.

Unusually high tides and strong gales together can cause sudden local floods, limited in scope but violent enough, especially in low-lying areas, to do great damage and destroy life and property in a very short time, perhaps even in as little as a single day.

If this happened in the past, as it must have done more than once, it is easy to see how the legend could grow, a few drowned hamlets becoming in retrospect populous cities and their surrounding fields being enlarged into an entire kingdom.

Right Indra, Hindu god of the heavens (mounted on the elephant Airavata), grew jealous of the worship given to Krishna and poured down rain to destroy mankind; but Krishna kept off the floods by holding up the hill Govardhana on his little finger for seven days like a canopy: 18th–19th-century Indian painting.

Death

If man has always felt that the mystery of life must be explained, he seems to have had an equally urgent need to account for the humiliating outrage of death. It is almost as if life, despite its trials, was too good to be true and death, despite its apparent peace, too ghastly to be true. In stories from all over the world, death is an intruder: he was not there at the beginning but made an early entrance. Very frequently he arrives as the result of a mistake, of a message wrongly delivered. Sometimes he is a punishment, visited upon mankind for disobedience, ingratitude or sheer stupidity. In many myths, death comes by agreement, as the outcome of a debate between divinities (one of whom may be malevolent) or among the first men and women themselves.

These three types of myth about the origin of death – the error, the penalty and the decision – are found among many different and widely scattered peoples and it is also quite common for the various features to be combined in a single story. There is a constant recurrence of the idea that death was, in the first days, meant to be temporary and that human beings, but for a tragic and original mischance, would have repeatedly renewed their lives like the moon or like lesser beings such as snakes and crabs which (it was thought) took on a new lease of life when they sloughed their skins or shed

their shells. This concept of lost renewal occurs in all the three main types of myth.

The myth of the mistake, of the message that went wrong, is especially common in Africa. In many versions the chameleon is sent by God to tell the first men that they are to have the gift of immortality; but he dawdles on his way and is overtaken by the lizard, the swifter messenger of death. The Gallas of East Africa tell how God sent a bird with the message that men were to renew their lives by changing their skins. The bird came across a snake feeding on some meat; he was hungry and promised the snake he would tell him 'God's news' if he gave him a share. The serpent finally agreed and the bird told him that men would grow old and die but that all he had to do was cast off his skin to be young again. In his anger, God punished the bird for his treachery and greed by giving it a painful disease which makes it sit on treetops and bleat sorrowfully, whence it is called *holo-waka* or 'the sheep of God'.

In a myth of the Hottentots, the moon sent an insect to tell men that they, like herself, 'would die and dying live'. The insect, going slowly on his way, was met by a hare who asked him his business. The hare said he was quicker and was quite willing to take the message. The insect agreed but the hare (whether through malice or stupidity is not

Above *The Hindu goddess Kali who, in her more horrific aspect, personifies destruction. She is black, often depicted with three eyes and four arms and bloated with the blood of her victims.* Left *William Blake's painting of the Fourth Horseman of the Apocalypse,* Death on a Pale Horse. *'Behold, a pale horse, and its rider's name was Death, and Hades followed him...' In Greek art Thanatos, or Death, was frequently portrayed armed with a sword.*

clear) garbled the message and told men that, unlike the moon, when they died it was the end of them. The moon was angry with the hare and struck him with a stick, splitting his lip. Some say the hare, in the struggle, scratched the moon's face with his claws, which is why her surface is pitted. Others declare it was not the hare's fault. He delivered the message correctly at first but the people refused to believe him, shouted at him and so confused him that he finally told them the opposite of what he should.

The myth of the wrongly transmitted message is also found in South-East Asia and Oceania but in these regions most of the death-origin stories seem to centre on the motif of skin-changing. In part of Polynesia it is said that at the beginning all changed their skins when they grew old and renewed their youth. One day, however, a child cried when he could not recognize his 'new' mother; she was so sorry for him that she put her old skin back on again and later died, as did all other people thereafter. There is a curiously similar African story of a couple who sent their children to fetch water in a basket while they were changing their skins. The children tired of their hopeless task and came back to the hut. The father chased them away but they crept stealthily back and saw their mother half in and half out of her new skin. Whereupon she died and brought death into the world.

The Arawaks of Guyana have a story according to which the benevolent creator visited the earth to see how the first men were faring but they were ungrateful and

The Syndics of the Fitzwilliam Museum, Cambridge

attacked him. So he took away their 'im-mortality' and gave it to the lizards, snakes and beetles.

In the Orinoco basin it is believed that God intended that men should be immortal by changing their skins but that an old woman laughed at such a seemingly ludi-crous idea. God was offended and sentenced mankind to mortality.

The concept of death as penalty or pun-ishment, often for the foolish action of a woman, is found in many parts of the world, besides the story of Adam and Eve as told in the book of Genesis. The aborigines of New South Wales tell how in the beginning God forbade the people to go near a certain hollow tree in which bees had made their nest. The men obeyed but the women wanted the honey. Finally, one of the women hit the tree with an axe and out flew death in the form of a bat which claims all living things by touching them with its wings.

In Baganda legend, Kintu, the first man, is permitted, after many trials and tests, to marry one of the daughters of heaven. God sends the pair to live on earth and gives them gifts, including a hen. He tells them to hurry lest they meet Death (the bride's brother) and not to come back if they have forgotten anything. The woman forgets the hen's feed and goes back for it, at which God, in his displeasure, grants Death's request to accompany them. Death keeps claiming the children as they are born but is prevented from taking them. Kintu appeals to God who relents and sends another of his sons (called 'Digger') to take Death back to heaven. God ordains silence during the pur-suit as Digger chases Death who has hidden in the ground; but the children's cries break the spell and Death is allowed to remain on earth and strike down living things.

The Algonquin tribes of North America say that immortality was granted to men by the Great Hare, himself the source of vital energy. The gift was in a little package which our first ancestor was forbidden to open. But his wife, the Pandora of the New World, could not restrain her curiosity and peeped. As she did so immortality flew away.

There is a very odd African story, told by people living on the shores of Lake Kivu, which shows God trying to save men from death but giving up in exasperation rather than inflicting a punishment. God made man to be immortal and kept a close watch on Death who was always trying to pick quar-rels with men and provoke them to a fight which he knew he would win. One day God was away and Death killed an old woman. She was buried but after a few days her grave began to heave as if she were coming back to life. Her daughter-in-law poured boiling water on the grave and beat it with a pestle, saying 'Die: what is dead should stay dead'. The grave was then quiet and the old woman was really dead. God returned and seeing that the old woman was not there asked what had happened. When he was told, he said he would hunt Death down. Death fled in terror and met another old woman to whom he said, 'Hide me and I shall reward you'. She let him hide under her skirt and he entered her body. God caught them up and decided that, since she was so old, it would be best to kill her and tear out Death and kill him. But Death slipped through his fingers and this time persuaded a young girl to hide him in her belly. God despaired: if human beings kept on thwarting his efforts to save them he might as well give it up as a bad job. So he let Death do as he pleased.

The Upotos of the Congo say that the immortality meant for men was granted to the moon. This happened because in the first days God commanded the inhabitants of the earth and the moon to attend on him. The moon-men came straightaway but the earth-men delayed. In his wrath, God rewarded the moon with ever-renewed life and visited the earth with death. In the Admiralty Islands it is said that the first man, pursued by an evil spirit, was hidden by a tree within itself. The tree asked for two white pigs as a reward but the man brought one white pig and a black one smeared with chalk. The tree, in its anger, said it would help no more, so the spirits catch men and kill them. In the Celebes there is a belief that the sky, at first, was very close to the earth and God used to

lower gifts to the first people on a rope's end. He let down a stone which they refused, and then a banana which they accepted. God therefore decreed that mankind would not be like the stone, immortal, but perishable like the banana.

One of the most imaginative myths of the origin of death is that of the Wintun Indians of the Pacific coast of North America. It is said that Olelbis, being about to create men, sent two buzzards, brothers, to build a stone stairway between earth and heaven, at the top of which there were to be two springs, one for purification and the other for drink-ing – the 'fountain of youth'. As they laboured, Sedit the coyote, the mischievous and clownish creator, came and tempted them. Is all their hard work, he asks, really worth it? Will men and women want to go on ascending and descending the stairway, endlessly repeating their lives? 'Joy at birth', he says, 'and grief for the dead are better, for these mean love.' The brothers are per-suaded and destroy what they have built. But the younger says that Sedit too must take his own advice and die. In frenzied terror, Sedit makes himself wings of sun-flower petals and tries to fly to heaven; but his wings wither and he falls. Olelbis says his own words have condemned him and hereafter all men will die.

The poignancy of this story is reflected in one told by the Eskimos of Greenland. At the beginning, they say, there was no death and no sun. One old woman declared she would be happy without light if there were no death. But another said that if it were not possible to have the one without the other, it were better to have both, for life without light was unbearable.

This brings us to the third type of death-origin myth – mortality as the result of a debate, a theme that has appeared in some of the stories already mentioned. The ten-derness of the last two tales seems to be peculiarly North American: it recurs in a Blackfoot Indian myth of the discussion between the first old man and the first old woman. The man wanted immortality but the woman said there would then be too

Facing page *Detail from an early Peruvian death shroud, embroidered with representations of the grotesque gods of the underworld: Lima Archeological Museum.* Below *Emma-O, in Japanese Buddhist belief, the ferocious ruler of the underground hell and the supreme judge of men. Beside him are two decapitated heads, from which the sinner can conceal nothing; detail from a Japanese scroll painting in the Horniman Museum.*

many people, and, besides, if people died they would be able to feel sorry for one another. They agreed to leave the matter to a sign: they would throw a piece of buffalo bone into the water – if it floated they would opt for immortality, if it sank, for death. The woman, who had magical powers, changed the fragment into a stone and hence we all die.

In Oceania the debate is, it appears, always between two supernatural beings, one of whom proposes life (often by skinchange) and the other death; the second always prevails, since he who has the last word wins. Sometimes one deity is openly malevolent. In the Banks Islands the story is told that Qat, the good god, made wooden images and vivified them by drumming and dancing before them. But he was succeeded by Marawa, the evil and jealous god, who buried his images and killed them.

Some tales are remarkable in that they do not fall into any of these groups. The Aranda aborigines of Australia say that at the beginning first women and then men emerged from the rocks. The leading man was envied and hated by the others because he was nearest to the women, so they pointed a magic bone at him. He fell into a coma, 'died' and was buried. But he was not really dead and his head and neck rose out of the ground; then came Urbura, the evil and enchanted magpie, who stabbed the man in the throat and commanded him to stay dead. The other men and women were turned into lamenting birds. But for Urbura all would have been well.

Perhaps the strangest story of all comes from the Ewe-speakers of West Africa. Yiyi the spider (another example of the cunning and greedy demiurge found in many mythologies) cadged meat from Death during a famine. Death had plenty of meat because he had made a great clearing in the forest and set traps in it. In return for continual supplies, Yiyi gave Death his daughter in marriage. Death told his wife not to go through the clearing when she went to fetch water but one rainy day she did and was caught in a trap. Her husband chopped her up for the larder. When Yiyi discovered what had happened he attacked Death with a knife and ran away in terror to the village with Death in pursuit. Death had never been to the village before and as he lay in wait for Yiyi he amused himself by shooting at the women as they went down to the river for water. He then realized that here was game enough and he had no need to set traps.

One of the earliest known attempts to depict the horror of death was found at Catal Hüyük, a Neolithic settlement in Anatolia dating from the 7th millennium BC. It takes the form of representations of gigantic black birds of vulture-like appearance menacing headless human corpses. The mythologies of ancient Egypt and Mesopotamia provide our earliest written evidence of the personification of death. In the legend of Osiris, this divine hero, who became a type of 'Everyman' in the mortuary ritual, was put to Death by the evil god Seth, who came to be regarded as the personification of evil; in art Seth is depicted as an animal with sharp pointed ears or horns, a long muzzle or snout, and a tail splayed at the end. He is never actually portrayed as the death god, however, nor is such a baleful being ever shown as such in Egyptian art.

Yet, as the following Coffin Text of the Middle Kingdom (c2160–1580 BC) vividly shows, the Egyptians personified death very realistically: 'Save me from the claws of him who takes for himself what he sees: may the glowing breath of his mouth not take me away.' It is possible that, during the Graeco-Roman period in Egypt, the jackal-headed god Anubis, long associated with the Osirian mortuary ritual, became the *psychopompos* (guide of the dead) or even the death god.

In ancient Mesopotamia the Babylonians named the death god Uggae; but he does not figure notably in their mythology under this name. However, death was personified in a horrific manner. Thus in the famous *Epic of Gilgamesh*, Enkidu, the unfortunate friend of Gilgamesh, dreams of his coming death as seizure by an awful being:

Michael Holford

In the story of the Harrowing of Hell, in which Christ descends into Hades to succour the souls of the just, Death is identified with Satan, who is depicted as a skeletal figure in chains, prostrate beneath the triumphant Christ: from a mosaic in St Mark's, Venice.

...he transformed me,
That mine arms were covered with feathers like a bird.
He looks at me (and) leads me to the house of darkness, to the dwelling of Irkalla;
To the house from which he who enters never goes forth.

An Assyrian text of about 650 BC actually describes the dread enemy in an account of the underworld, and pictures a grim figure with the hands of a man and the feet of serpents. There was, however, much fluidity of conception in personifying death; for another Assyrian text gives directions 'For making exchange for a man wanted by the Goddess of Death'. Indeed, Mesopotamian demonology provided a variety of grisly monsters associated with the underworld.

In ancient Hebrew literature, although the origin of death is attributed to the sin of Adam in Genesis (3, 19), God is regarded as ultimately responsible for the individual's death. Hebrew thought tended to separate Yahweh from direct contact with human affairs, and produced the idea of the 'angel of Yahweh' as the agent of death. In later Jewish folklore the angel of death is named 'Sammael', meaning 'the drug of God', since

it was believed that his sword was tipped with gall.

In Iranian mythology death was closely associated with the concept of Time, so that Zurvan, the deification of Time, was regarded as the god of death. Thus an ancient Persian text states: 'For Zurvan there is no remedy. From death there is no escape.' The Persians conceived of two forms of Zurvan: one of them 'Time of the Long Dominion' was the form of Time associated with death, since it brings old age, decay and death to all men. There is some evidence that the idea of this form of Zurvan, with whom Ahriman, the personification of evil, was identified, was incorporated into Mithraism, and found expression in its temples in statues of a lion-headed monster, adorned with various symbols of Time.

In the Vedic literature of ancient India a god of the dead is known under the name of Yama. According to the *Rig-Veda*, he was the son of Vivasvant and 'the first of mortals to die and enter that other world'. In later writings Yama becomes the judge of the dead, and in that role he appears in Tibetan, Chinese and Japanese Buddhism. In Chinese belief, under the name of Yen-lo wang, he presides over the fifth hell. As Emma-O, in popular Japanese art, he is depicted seated at his tribunal, a fearsome figure in the robes of a Chinese judge. Hinduism, however, has other personifications of death. Mara, or Mrtyu, is death personified. The concept has an important role also in Buddhist mythology, but rather as the personification of evil, being *papman*, 'the evil one'. The Hindu

god Shiva, who is conceived as having an ambivalent nature, has on one side of his being Bhairava, 'the terrible destroyer', who haunts cemeteries, and appears wearing serpents about his head and a necklace of skulls. An even stranger conception is the personification of Shiva's destructive energy in the form of the goddess Kali or Durga. This goddess (Kali means Time) is of horrific appearance: her colour is black, she wears a chaplet of severed heads, and her many hands hold symbols of her nature – the exterminating sword, scissors to cut short the thread of life, and the lotus of eternal generation, for existence as an unceasing cycle of birth and death.

Greek mythology personified death in two forms. The more ancient conception is the more grim. Homer refers to the *ker thanatoio* (the fate of death), which was probably imagined as a winged harpy that snatched away its victims. The more sophisticated image of Thanatos (Death) was that of a winged youth, of heroic form, armed with a sword, such as he is shown on a column, now in the British Museum, that once adorned the temple of Artemis at Ephesus. Thanatos was actually portrayed in performances of Euripides' *Alcestis*, described as black-robed, winged and armed with a sword.

In Christianity death has also been personified, although theologically it is regarded as the penalty of sin. St Paul proclaims that 'the last enemy that shall be destroyed is death' (I Corinthians, chapter 15). In the Revelation of St John (chapter 6), Death is depicted as riding on one of the four horses.

The End

The ragged fanatic solemnly carrying his placard announcing that 'The End of the World is at Hand', is an object of ridicule. The image of the mushroom cloud is an ever-present reality to every sensitive person. Between the two – a very real possibility of an end to the world as we know it and the attempt to pinpoint the end and express it in mythological terms – there is much more than an accidental connection. Men have seldom been able to believe wholeheartedly in the permanence of the established order, though they have often poured scorn on the prophet who has dared to remind them of their doubts. It was so in the early centuries of the Christian era: 'Scoffers will come in the last days with scoffing, following their own passions and saying, "Where is the promise of his coming? For ever since the fathers fell asleep, all things have continued as they were from the beginning of creation"' (2 Peter 3.3) and it is so today. The difference now is that the end of the world, if there is to be an end, is seen as coming about through, in some sense, natural causes. In the past, it was held that it would come about through supernatural causes and it was accordingly expressed in mythological terms.

The writer of 2 Peter answered the 'scoffers' by pointing out as a 'fact' that the earth had been created by God out of a watery chaos (as related in Genesis 1.1), that through this same water 'the world that then existed was deluged with water and perished' (Genesis, chapters 6–8), and that by the word of God, 'the heavens and earth that now exist have been stored up for fire, being kept until the day of judgement and destruction of ungodly men' (2 Peter 3.7). Here we have a mythological pattern, repeated in many parts of the world, of creation, destruction and re-creation, and it is in this perspective that practically all end of the world myths must be seen. We may speculate interminably as to the origins of such patterns as these, without ever reaching more than a probable theory. However, it seems likely that in primitive man's experience the succession of day and night, summer and winter, rain and drought, heat and cold; the rising and setting of the sun; the phases of the moon; the wanderings of some, at least, of the stars – all contributed to a sense of insecurity with regard to man's tenure of the face of the earth.

There is no lack of evidence to show that primitive man conceived of the cosmic process not as something stable, but as a great and continuous battle between the forces of creation and destruction, order and chaos. The world had been brought into being by supernatural forces out of chaos; and unless these forces were supported – by prayer, sacrifice and other ritual acts – then the world would inevitably return once more to that same chaos. The cosmic order was, however, maintained by the gods (particularly the High Gods of the sky), and should they so choose, it could be brought to an end. The annual festivals of agricultural peoples, with which cycles of myth are intimately associated, were meant to ensure the continued existence of the earth, particularly the seasonal renewal of its fertility and its life. But in the background was always the fear that at some time, to be appointed by the gods, a return to chaos would take place. Natural phenomena – hurricanes, floods, volcanic eruptions, earthquakes – suggested the means: man's ritual and moral shortcomings suggested the motive.

Common to a surprisingly large number of races was the conviction that all this had, in fact, happened before. The gods had destroyed the world on certain occasions when conditions had become so bad as to be unbearable from the gods' own point of view. But why should they ever become so bad? No simple answer is possible, except that the ancients were evidently under no illusions regarding the perfectibility of mankind.

But even this pessimistic outlook, which placed man's Golden Age in a distant past, and saw his evolution as a development into greater and more sophisticated iniquity, was not the whole of the story.

In ancient Babylon, for instance, where man's position in the cosmos paralleled that of the slave in the city-state, it was up to the gods to decide when the end should come. They had decided before: Sumerian and Babylonian–Assyrian mythology had recorded the legend of the great Deluge, and of the great Ark in which Ziusudra (Utnapishtim) had been saved (compare the Old Testament story of Noah), but had given no cogent moral reasons why this should have been so. Nor were their end of the world myths any the less arbitrary. In Seneca's words: 'Berosus (author of a history of Babylon) says that everything takes place according to the course of the planets, and he maintains this so confidently that he determines the times for the conflagration of the world and for the flood. He asserts that the world will burn when all the planets which now move in different courses come together in the Crab, so that they all stand together in a straight line in the same sign, and that the future flood will take place when the same conjunction occurs in Capricorn.' The astrological aspect is probably to be explained in terms of identification between the stars and the gods themselves, who were ultimately responsible for past and future catastrophes.

The link between past and future is to be seen in a slightly different form in the mythology of the Aztecs of Central America who believed in a series of world ages, each of which had so far ended in a cosmic catastrophe – famine, fire, hurricane and flood respectively. This present age was expected to end on the completion of a 52-year cycle and every 52 years special preparations were made: all fires were extinguished and priests and people ascended a sacred mountain, waiting for the rise of the Pleiades.

Hindu and Buddhist belief similarly looked on the history of the world as consisting in a series of four ages, or *Yugas*, each of enormous length. These have the names *Krita Yuga, Treta Yuga, Dvapara Yuga* and *Kali Yuga*, marked by successive declines in morals, righteousness and piety. By the end of the final age, Kali Yuga, of a Day of Brahma (a thousandfold cycle), Brahmins will have come to neglect their devotions; popular piety will be dead; fire, drought and famine will ravage the earth. Then there will be a century of death, after which the god Vishnu assumes the form of Rudra, the destroyer, and dries up all the moisture on or beneath the earth. There follows a universal conflagration, in which the last vestiges of human occupation disappear from the face of the earth. At last the underworld, earth and heavens disappear also in the vast whirlpool of flame; nothing remains save the eternal and uncreated Brahman. But this is a beginning, as well as an end: the cycle is

In medieval art Death is represented as a skeleton, sometimes armed with a dart with which he strikes the death-blow: 15th-century brass rubbing from the tomb of Richard Notfelde in the Church of St John, Margate.

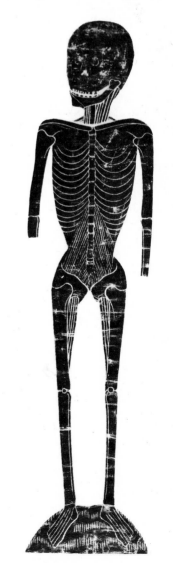

begun again, and a new series of ages ensues, marked by the same stages, the same decline into sin and lawlessness (*adharma*), and earmarked for the same ultimate fate.

This is the myth as found, for example, in the *Vishnu Purana*, and which has left profound traces on classical Hindu thought: Mahayana Buddhist versions are similar in that they retain the theory of the four Yugas, but more elaborate in the characterization of successive ages according to the emergence or otherwise of Buddha-figures in them.

Turning to an entirely different tradition, one of the best known and yet in some ways least understood myths concerning the end of the world is that which is found in the medieval Icelandic sources, and which has to some extent passed into the European consciousness through Wagner's opera *Götterdämmerung* (*The Twilight of the Gods*). The earliest version of this myth ends the first poem in the Poetic (or Verse) Edda, the *Völuspá* (12th century). This is no saga, nor a logically constructed prediction of the 'last times', but rather a poetic apocalypse, perhaps reflecting some of the tension between old and new faiths during the years when Christianity was winning its way into the minds of the Northern peoples.

A far different Indo-European view of the end of the world, and yet one which has marked affinities with Hindu beliefs, is found in ancient Greece. The Greek writer Hesiod, in his *Works and Days*, speaks of the five ages of Gold, Silver, Bronze, Heroes and Iron, in which there is a gradual descent from joy and innocence to guile, misery and corruption. An elaborate theory of cyclical world history was put forward by Heraclitus (c 500 BC) and later developed by Plato; possibly this theory owes much to Babylonian influence, particularly in respect of the idea of the *magnus annus*, or great year, the period during which eight independently revolving planetary spheres return to their point of departure. In Plato's version, a total revolution in one direction is followed by a revolution in the opposite direction; thus the world as it is known is succeeded by an age of 'history in reverse'.

Also from Heraclitus came the notion of a cosmic fire, the *ekpurosis*, into which the world is periodically dissolved, and born anew. This theory was developed in its most elaborate detail by the Stoic preachers of the 2nd century BC and earlier, and passed over into Christianity through the Church Fathers, some of whom even undertook to attempt to prove the doctrine of ekpurosis from the Book of Genesis.

According to the New Testament the end of the present world will be heralded by a multitude of signs such as wars, earthquakes and famines. One of the central symbols in the elaborate imagery of the book of Revelation is a scroll sealed with seven seals, the opening of which lets fearful terrors loose upon the world: Death, the fourth horseman of the Apocalypse, is given power over a quarter of the world when the fourth seal is opened. Detail from **The Triumph of Death,** *a series of frescoes by Francesco Traini.*

Scala

Facing page *In Chinese belief, if the souls of the just were not sent back immediately to a new life on earth they might go to the dwelling place of the Immortals: 18th-century porcelain dish showing Shou-Lao, god of long-life, Fu-Hsing, god of happiness and Lu-Hsing, god of salaries, crossing the seas to their Palace of Immortality; originally human beings, they were deified as a result of merit or good fortune.*

However, the cyclical theories of the Greek philosophers accorded ill with the Judaic tradition out of which Christianity developed, and these were ultimately attempts to reconcile the irreconcilable, so vast were the differences between them.

Turning now to this Judaeo-Christian stream of tradition, the developed Christian view of the end of the world differs in certain important respects from these other mythologies particularly in that it incorporates no trace of a cyclical view of time. It rests on the Old Testament view that in God's good time a new and better world will emerge out of this present order, thus vindicating God's final sovereignty over creation.

Broadly speaking, the Christian Church, while continuing to believe in a vague way in the final summing up of all things in Christ, has long refused to concern itself with the details of the end of the world. There have been exceptions, of course: recurrent periods of biblical orthodoxy have given rise to more or less extravagant claims that the end is in sight. One example of the new mythology which such concerns have brought in their wake is found in the writings of Thomas Burnet (1635?–1715), who reflected in his *Sacred Theory of the Earth* that the destructive fires would be kindled at Rome, the seat of the Antichrist, and would be aided and abetted by all the sources of fire in the world. Since the soil of Britain contains so much coal, it would be preferable to be elsewhere. Happiness was

Each of a series of world ages has ended in cosmic catastrophe, according to Aztec mythology: leaf from the Codex-Fejervary-Mayer depicting five world regions, four of which have already been destroyed. In the centre is the present world.

Paradise

associated with enclosures rather than open spaces in the ancient Middle East, for deserts and hills, the wind and the sun, were generally too harsh to man. When he thought of a pleasant place, he thought of an oasis or garden, where he could relax in the shade with ample water and fruit. Given the resources, he might create such a place for himself.

The word 'paradise' is of Old Persian origin. It means an enclosure, and especially a royal park or hunting ground, a piece of land made more agreeable than its surroundings by cultivation. The Greek translators of the Old Testament, about the middle of the 3rd century BC, employed the word once or twice in that sense, for example in Ecclesiastes 2.5: 'I made myself gardens and parks, and I planted in them all kinds of fruit trees.' But their most momentous use of it was in referring to the garden of Eden, which was to be the divinely appointed home of Adam.

This appears in Genesis, chapter 2. After creating the world, God plants the garden 'in Eden, in the east'. He places Adam in it and creates the first woman, Eve. The name 'Eden' may be Babylonian. Among the luscious vegetation, God's garden contains the Tree of Life, and the Tree of the Knowledge of Good and Evil. A river flows through it and splits up into four streams, which irrigate the then known world.

Life in this earthly paradise is instinctively innocent, with the Lord as a close companion. It is no lazy idyll: Adam must till and keep the garden, with Eve's aid. God forbids them to eat of the Tree of Knowledge. When they disobey, they are expelled. The reason given (Genesis, chapter 3) is that if they stayed, they might eat the fruit of the Tree of Life also, and live for ever. This would have been permissible before; now it is not. Henceforth men must drudge to live. Women must be subject to male dominance and bear children in pain. Meanwhile the garden goes on existing but an armed angel at the gate keeps fallen humanity out.

While the Judaeo-Christian concept of the Fall of Man is in some ways unique, the garden has partial parallels in non-Hebrew mythologies. Two motifs, in particular, connect other 'paradises' with this one. First, Genesis gives the Hebrew version of a widespread idea – the idea of a definite place, an 'otherwhere' or even an 'otherworld', which is part of the universe we know, yet different in quality from the part we live in: a good place, blessed and happy.

Second, Genesis directs attention to the many legends of a lost Golden Age. Long ago, human beings were carefree and guiltless. They were immortal, or at any rate felt no reason to fear death. They lived without sickness in a kindly climate, and never had to work hard. Gods dwelt familiarly among them. For whatever reason, the Golden Age is no more. The gods have withdrawn. Death and disease and wickedness have poisoned life.

But in some mythologies the two themes converge; the paradisal good place not only exists, it is a fragment of the golden world that remains inviolate. If we could reach it we could still find there the delights and divine companionship of the Golden Age.

In classical myth, the Golden Age was when the Titan Cronus, or Saturn, was supreme god. After his son Zeus ousted him, the world declined. Cronus went on reigning in exile, in the regions of sunset. There, for the Greeks, was the 'good place', out over the Atlantic behind a barrier of water. There lay the Isles of the Blest where, in Hesiod's words, 'the bounteous earth beareth honeysweet fruit fresh thrice a year'. There lay the plain of Elysium 'at the world's end' where, according to Homer, 'living is made easiest for mankind, no snow falls, no strong winds blow and there is never any rain'.

Celtic myth looked in the same direction. The Isle of Avalon (before its re-location at Glastonbury) was a warm western Elysium, sometimes described in language borrowed from classical literature. Irish seafaring romances, such as *The Voyage of Bran*, tell of an enchanted archipelago beyond the horizon, including an Island of the Blest which is larger in extent than Erin itself, a place 'without grief, without sorrow, without death'.

Medieval Irish legend drew the pagan and Christian paradises together. The usual Christian belief was that the earthly paradise of Genesis was in a remote part of Asia. Some Irish Christians, however, located it in one of their own legendary lands beyond the Atlantic, and gave it a Celtic atmosphere. The greatest of all their voyage-romances tells how St Brendan sailed in quest of it and finally arrived on its borders. The author of *St Brendan's Voyage* probably knew that the world is round, and he may have harmonized his fancies with orthodoxy by imagining that Brendan reached Asia by sailing west.

Adam's lost abode remains, humanly speaking, empty. Other paradises are variously peopled. The Golden Age dream of freedom from the curse of death is recurrent. The citizens of paradise are, as a rule, immortals. In the Babylonian epic of Gilgamesh, the hero, grief-stricken at human evanescence, goes to an island-otherworld expressly for the secret of immortality. He meets Utnapishtim, the chief survivor of the flood, who is indeed exempt from death. But Gilgamesh achieves nothing by his visit.

In more familiar mythologies, such places as Elysium are likely to be the homes of gods, demigods or fairy-folk, all undying. When human beings do enter, we hear (in the oldest stories) of only a chosen few transported there while alive, and endowed with immortality as a special gift. Homer names Menelaus, husband of Helen of Troy. A better known instance is King Arthur who is said to have gone to Avalon after his last battle and to be still living there.

Classical Greece carried the idea a step farther. Pindar describes the Isles of the Blest as inhabited by a select few of the noble dead, with Cronus as their king. Here the Blest have actually died; the Golden Age motif, though still present in the person of Cronus, has receded somewhat; the Elysian realm is becoming a sort of heaven.

Within the mainstream of Greek religion, this idea remained tentative. But farther afield, similar beliefs are asserted with more conviction. Sometimes the good place, the 'otherwhere', has little or no explicit Golden Age aura and is more essentially a home of the dead. Where admission is a reward of virtue we approach the concept of heaven in its full Judaeo-Christian meaning: the eternal, blissful abode of all those among the dead whose lives have earned such a reward and of no others; the final beatitude; the ultimate goal.

The approach, however, is by degrees. At the more naive mythical levels, the good place may be simply the place of the dead in general. Everybody goes there, to an improved version of earthly life. The spirit realm of the Tumbuka, in Malawi, is an underworld where the departed are always young and never hungry or sad. Such beliefs occur also in New Guinea and New Caledonia. Some American Indians, the Ojibways and Choctaws for example, have

kindred hopes about the region of sunset, or a happy hunting-ground in some secret country. These places are paradises and the homes of the dead, but scarcely heavens, because they are not selective. The goodness of the good place is not therefore in itself a reward.

When selectivity does come in, it may still not take an ethical form. Admission may depend upon social rank. In the Leeward Islands in the Caribbean, aristocratic spirits go to 'sweet-scented Rohutu' and commoners go to 'foul-scented Rohutu'. In Peru, the mansions of the sun were reserved for the Incas and their nobles. Even when conduct is a passport, and the good place has to be earned, the demands are not always moral. Entry may depend on having performed a

Above *In its Mahayana form Buddhism has a graded series of paradises though, because man's ultimate achievement is release from the bondage of personality, existence in these heavens is not regarded as an ultimate goal: the exception, in Chinese and Japanese Buddhism, is the 'Pure Land' or paradise established by the Buddha Amida, where existence is devoid of pain, sadness, hunger or anxiety. 18th-century miniature.* **Facing page** *According to Islam, every Moslem will eventually reach a heaven, and no infidel will: the Koran promises the faithful a paradise of gardens, rivers and shady trees, and unlimited food and wine: 15th-century painting depicting the prophet Mohammed's ascension to heaven.*

Ecstasies become more spiritual as earth is left farther below. The ascent is by way of virtue and holy meditation.

It is important to grasp that these quasi-heavens of Hinduism and Buddhism still belong to a mythological order of ideas. They are not ultimate, nor are they central to the philosophy of either religion. The goal of the highest quest is not personal happiness, but total release from the bondage of personality – otherwise called Nirvana. The celestial realms, therefore, are mere consolation prizes. They appeal to those whose minds are not ready to transcend personal desire and descriptions of them are poetic, not doctrinal. They are also temporary. The soul may dwell in them for aeons, but if it goes there at all, it has not completed its pilgrimage and must eventually leave. The sole exception is in a popular form of Chinese and Japanese Buddhism, the Pure Land sect.

Only in the Mediterranean world does the good place acquire dogmatic status as the final reward of all mankind's spiritual strivings, with salvation consisting in its attainment, damnation in its loss. Heaven in this full sense is associated with Hebrew monotheism and ethical seriousness; with Hellenic firmness of outline and appetite for truth.

As long as Greece had no positive doctrine of immortality, and dismissed the dead as shades, Elysium could survive as a fantasy without raising major issues. But from the 6th century BC onward, the mystics of the Orphic cult (after Orpheus) were asserting such a doctrine and for those who accepted it, the island-paradise would no longer serve. An abode for the blest on the familiar earth was out of keeping with Orphic ideas, which proclaimed salvation as a release from matter as we know it, and from earthly bondage.

A more exotic home was offered to the right-living initiate. The Orphics adopted the word Elysium and altered its meaning, speaking of 'Elysian Fields' in an underworld of strange brightness, a happy resting-place for pure spirits. But besides this – in Orphism apparently and in later Mystery cults undoubtedly – there was also a disposition to look upward. Gradually the good place was transferred to the sky, as in Asia.

The 'heavens' which the teachers of mystical doctrines drew into their systems were at first simply the upper regions. The prevailing astronomy made them concentric spheres, the spheres of the sun, moon, planets and fixed stars, rotating around the earth. Now, by becoming involved with notions about the soul's ascent, 'heaven' acquired a paradisal and more-than-paradisal sense as well as an astronomical one. The Mysteries (with Egyptian influence from the cult of Osiris) and the gnostic schools of the early Christian era envisaged purified souls as rising. Instructed in the right passwords, the adept eluded the planetary demons of middle space. He soared (by grace of his chosen saviour, such as Mithras) to a superior heaven outside the visible system. Here he lived blissfully with the gods and fellow-initiates, for ever.

Meanwhile, in the contemporary Hebrew world of ideas, two trends had emerged.

ritual, or gone through an initiation.

The motif of achieving the good place for one's afterlife through merit appears crudely in the Norse Valhalla, which was reached by martial prowess. Further refinement of selectivity accompanies the development of imaginative power, which tends to locate the good place in the sky rather than on earth. Celestial dwellings for the dead are nearly always selective; the wicked and ignoble seldom go upward. In Egypt during the 3rd millennium BC, the pharaohs hoped to join the sun god and attend him on his journeys through space. While this is another instance of privilege through rank, early texts show that the god's attitude to a deceased ruler could depend partly on his virtues. Later, when similar hopes were extended to lesser

men, this idea of judgement became more prominent.

In the ancient Vedic religion of India the monarch of the dead was called Yama, and he reigned in the outer sky, a realm of light, over all the worthy departed. Their life was an enhancement of earthly life (as in most paradises of myth) with music, sexual fulfilment, and many more pleasures of the same type, and with no pain or care.

Hinduism allots regions above the clouds to Indra, Shiva and other deities. Each is a place of beauty and sensual joy, to be gained by a combination of correct ritual and correct morality. Buddhism inherited such schemes from Hinduism. In its advanced Mahayana form it has a graded series of paradises in a vague, non-astronomical sky.

When most of the Old Testament was composed, Israel's religion had no clear notion
of personal immortality. Its only paradise
was the lost garden. Heaven, as elsewhere,
meant the sky, with the added concept of a
pre-eminent heaven beyond, where God sat
enthroned among his angels.

Judaism, as it grew after the exile in Babylon, slowly came to adopt a more cheerful outlook. Probably under Zoroastrian
influence, it spoke of a future resurrection of
the dead, a last judgement, a world to come.
No unanimity on these matters was reached,
nor has it ever been. Rabbinic tradition,
however, has usually resisted world-spurning
metaphysical speculations. It has its own
place, Gan Eden, where the righteous will
dwell after the resurrection. Gan Eden is,
in effect, Adam's paradise restored. It will
be revealed and opened on earth. Its citizens
will go there as living people, not shades.

The Greek doctrine of a disembodied
existence for souls, between now and the
resurrection, never fitted entirely easily into
Judaism, which is vague about any celestial
heaven; though its teachers and mystics have
sometimes spoken of heaven as a vast celestial
extension of Gan Eden already in existence.
The uncanonical book of Enoch includes a
vision of 'resting-places of the righteous' in
a realm of angels above the sky. Judaism,
today, does teach the soul's immortality.

But it has always shown a tendency to keep
its feet on the ground, and hope for a future
paradise on earth.

In the time of Jesus, such hopes were
bound up with apocalyptic and Messianic
dreams. The Lord's Anointed would appear,
life would be transfigured, the dead would
be raised, the earthly Kingdom of God would
bring paradise regained . . . for the righteous.
Jesus employed apocalyptic language himself, but to convey a message of spiritual
revolution: the kingdom, he declared, is
'within you'. This teaching opened the way
to a fusion of Hebrew and Hellenic motifs.

For the first Christians, the resurrection
of Christ was proof of the coming resurrection of all the dead. When that happened,
the Last Judgement would allot them their
destinies according to their deserts. The book
of Revelation looks ahead not only to the
Judgement, but to a material New Jerusalem
for the resurrected saints. This, like the
Jewish Gan Eden, will be the second paradise;
Christ is the second Adam.

But when the resurrection and judgement
did not come quickly, a question arose as
to what was happening to the dead meanwhile. Christ himself had promised the
penitent thief, one of the two criminals who
were put to death with him, an immediate paradise (Luke, chapter 23), which must
therefore be in existence. In the Christian

apocalypse there is already a heaven apart
from earth. It is, as ever, the celestial dwelling place of God. The New Jerusalem, when
it comes, will come 'down out of heaven'.
Until then the souls of the blessed have their
heavenly places near God, where they await
final reunion with their bodies.

Christianity compiled its heaven from
both Hebraic and Hellenic sources. From
Judaism it adopted the region of the sky
where God and his angels dwelt. From
Greece the Christians took the celestial ma-
chinery, the spheres outside one another,
the spiritual journeyings. The idea of seven
heavens, with the seventh as proverbially
the most exalted, is also Greek. Dante's
Paradiso portrays the souls of the saved ap-

earing in the spheres appropriate to them – hose of the sun, moon, planets and stars. The true home of them all, however, is heaven proper, above the cosmic system.

While it carried the concept of heaven to ts loftiest heights, Christianity never re-olved certain queries. If the souls of the saved went to heaven at once, what would be the point of the future Last Judgement? It could only confirm a destiny already fixed. St Augustine maintained that until the end of the world, spiritual life in heaven was an interim state, a foretaste, an answer which may have owed a debt to a tradition in-herited via Judaism from Zoroastrianism.

Nor have Christians agreed about the qualifications for entry. Even baptism is not universally insisted upon, despite the words of Jesus that: '. . . unless one is born of water and the Spirit, he cannot enter the kingdom of God' (John 3.5). Luther dismissed salvation by works in favour of salvation by faith. Calvin (with a curious reversion to the pagan Elysium) taught salvation by arbitrary divine choice. Islam, in its own version of the Judaeo-Christian scheme, distinguished seven heavens and various hells, temporary or permanent; and it made everything de-pend on faith. Every Moslem, however wicked, would get to a paradise of some kind sooner or later, and no infidel would.

What happens in heaven? The paradises of mythology offer ardent, fairly civilized sensual delights, but Islam is the only major religion which does so. The Koran promises the faithful a reward suited to male Arab tastes. Their home will be a sort of splendid oasis – a true 'paradise' in the ancient sense – with gardens, rivers and trees. Men will wear silken robes and lie on couches, with un-limited fruit and wine, and virtually un-limited harems.

With increasing culture, however, Moslem thinkers have joined Jews and Chris-tians in a more abstract opinion. Heaven is the place where God is; so the final happiness is the beatific vision of God, the source of all good, and therefore completely satisfying to all mankind.

There is no logical flaw in this conception of a Supreme Good from which the soul would never willingly turn away. But in practice it is hard to imagine a convincing heaven, because any perfection that we can specifically think of would pall. The German philosopher Schopenhauer observed that imaginative authors are more successful with hells than with heavens, because their own lives furnish materials for the former, but not the latter.

Copernican astronomy also raised diffi-culties. Heaven could no longer be simply a good place above the sky. However, its re-moval from the visible cosmos – from space and time as known to humans – turned out to bring certain advantages. Disengagement from time meant that such problems as tedium were less forbidding. Life in heaven need not be a monotonous going-on-for-ever. It might be something else, beyond present comprehension, but different, cer-tainly, from all we know.

Abstraction had already gone far in the time of William Blake, who denounced as barren the 'allegoric haven', as he described it, of the Churches.

Progressive thought in and after the 19th century often dismissed it altogether ('pie in the sky' was the classic term of derision) and talked of building a heaven on earth. This, however, could only be taken in the figurative sense.

Aldous Huxley has suggested that para-disal ideas arose from heightened states of consciousness, which can be induced by drugs. On this showing, the religious ap-paratus is valid, but not literally so. It sym-bolized a genuine, transcendent experience, which human beings can rightly pursue.

As Huxley wrote in *Heaven and Hell*:

'The nature of the mind is such that the sinner who repents and makes an act of faith in a higher power is more likely to have a blissful visionary experience than is the self-satisfied pillar of society with his righteous indignations, his anxiety about possessions and pretensions, his ingrained habits of blaming, despising and condemning. Hence the enormous importance attached, in all the great religious traditions, to the state of mind at the moment of death.

'Visionary experience is not the same as mystical experience. Mystical experience is beyond the realm of opposites. Visionary experience is still within the realm. Heaven entails hell, and "going to heaven" is no more liberation than is the descent into horror. Heaven is merely a vantage point from which the divine Ground can be more clearly seen than on the level of ordinary individualized existence.'

Robert Skelton/Victoria & Albert Museum

Robert Skelton/Victoria & Albert Museum

COMPARATIVE MYTHOLOGY

Australasia

Australia

What the aborigines believe about their own origin and their birth from generation to generation, they also believe about animals and birds, reptiles and fish, insects and plants, and indeed also about inanimate things such as rain, wind and fire. Many of the heroic figures who gave the land its features, and from whom men and women arose, were in essence both human and animal or plant. This explains why they could appear and behave now as humans, and now in another form. Indeed, it is often difficult to know whether the mythical exploit is being performed by man or animal.

Through most of the interior of Australia, the mythological heroes, singly, in pairs or in groups, in human or totemic form, journeyed back and forth over vast distances, often criss-crossing each other's tracks. When their courses were finished they sank into the ground or became stones, trees or other objects which have remained to this day as memorials and sources of life.

In Eastern Australia, however, especially along the coast and the great Darling and Murray river system, the leader and culture giver of old, often with his wife and brother or son, or with a group, arose from the earth, or just appeared, origin unknown. In some versions, he landed from the sea. He travelled southward, establishing groups and tribes; furnishing them with implements and weapons; naming natural species; arranging the totemic system and rules of marriage; and teaching the tribes rituals, especially those of initiating young men. And when his work was finished, he went up to the sky.

He was known by different names, of which Biral in the north, Baiame and Goin in New South Wales, Nurundere in the lower Murray River region and Bundjil in Victoria were the most widespread.

Although the cult of the sky-hero is limited to Eastern Australia, all over Australia the sky world is the scene of constant activity of both transformed and translated hu-

man and animal heroes of the Dreaming.

The cycles of the heavenly bodies and the seasons must have contributed to the aboriginal idea of time as a continuing cycle. For them the present is not just the effect of what happened in a past Dreamtime but is that Dreamtime here and now. Time does not go on and on in serial order, but returns on itself. So too, human souls do not arise one from the other in a biological line but appear and reappear from the spirit-homes. In some tribes this is the effect of the moon's success in rising again after regularly waning away into 'death'.

Other stars and groups of stars are subjects of myths and have their own Dreaming explanations. In the region south and east of Broome in Western Australia, two dingos 'arose' out of the ground; they became gigantic men as tall as the sky. They are the *Baga-djimbiri*. As they travelled along the coast, they named animals and plants, and made springs of water by driving sacred pointed boards into the ground; they saw, but avoided, some women in the west who were digging for locusts; they cooked wattle seed, after realizing that trying to eat it uncooked was a mistake; they lost a hitting stick which local men later saw and copied, and which is represented in the sky as the pointer to the Southern Cross; they instituted the initiation rite of circumcision with the stone knife. A large bullroarer which they whirled flew into the sky to become a black patch in the Milky Way. In their travels they also speared a large kangaroo which hopped up to be the Coal Sack beside the Southern Cross. And so the two Baga-djimbiri went on until one day they laughed at a native cat-man. He and his group speared them. Their bodies became watersnakes, and their spirits went up above; they are the Magellan clouds.

This is a typical myth. Gazing upwards and restfully as sleep steals over them, the aborigines retrace the Dreaming in the sky. They see again the deeds and experiences on earth of those early ones who, translated to the sky, hunt and work, dance and sing, or

who may simply shine there forever.

Mythological systems vary in Australia. New sets of beliefs and rituals have been developed here or there, or else introduced from outside. The two most interesting new cults are in the Northern Kimberley area and in Arnhem Land.

In the former region, in the Dreaming, the ancestors of the clans arrived on the coast led by individuals called Wandjina, each with his own name. They moved in groups about this very rugged country, meeting with varied experiences, some of heroic magnitude, until each band or clan settled down in a particular part of the region. In time the Wandjina died, and he, she or they became a painting on a cave or rock shelter in the clan country. The Wandjina was usually represented lying down, bust or head only, but the mouth was (and is) always missing.

Above *Ceremony during the Bangtail Muster at Alice Springs in the Northern Territory. The songs and dances at aboriginal ceremonies frequently enact and re-create the adventures of the tribal ancestors, to strengthen the bond between the ancestors and their descendants.* **Facing page** *Cave-painting of spirits.*

The spirit of the Wandjina went into a nearby water-place, from which it would issue to vitalize its painting. For the Wandjina were and are Dreaming. Associated with rain, the rainbow and the sky, and therefore with the cycle of the seasons, their potency is ever present. Man's duty, clan by clan, is to retouch the paintings with ochres and pipeclay each year as the wet season ap-

proaches, thus ensuring that they are whole; then the power of the Dreaming becomes operative, as in the days when the Wandjina walked on the earth. The rains will fall, vegetation will grow, animal and bird life will abound.

The most striking complex of myth and ritual is in the northern third of the Northern Territory. Elsewhere in Australia male figures are dominant in mythology. Women, when present, usually play subordinate roles: but not so in Arnhem Land. There the myths centre on the Great Mother who arrived from the sea and, moving from place to place, gave birth to groups of human beings in what became the countries of particular clans and tribes, each with its own language. In some myths she also gave rise

either as emanations from her own person or through ritual acts performed by herself, to the life-cells or entities of natural species.

A male consort or companion or brother is sometimes mentioned, but he is well in the background. In spite of this, in the rituals and in some of the myths, a great snake plays an important part. He is the Python, the Rainbow or Lightning Snake. 'When he raises his lengthening body from the springs, billabongs and rivers to the sky, flashing and roaring, the rains and floods come, and with them the wet season and the promise of life and increase for nature and man.' For as the wet season proceeds, the Mother, the Earth, brings forth food for man.

There are local variations of this basic theme. In north-eastern Arnhem Land the

Cave and bark paintings are important in aboriginal religion.
Above *Snakes of an aboriginal fertility cult, painted on board,
from Arnhem Land.* **Right** *Cave-painting of Barramundi fish
found at Nourlangie Rock, south-east of Darwin. One of the
conventions of aboriginal art is that the skeletons are revealed.*

Left *Wandjina spirit who created the
landscape of an area and disappeared
underground, after painting a picture of
himself.*

Mother's role is taken by two sisters, the
Djanggawul, who with their brother came to
the Gulf of Carpentaria coast by canoe from
Beralgu, the island of the dead. In one version
of the story, they are called the Daughters of
the Sun, which left its home to rise up for
them and warmed their backs as they rowed
and rowed on to the Place of the Sun at Port
Bradshaw. And yet they were also the
Daughters of the Morning Star, which
guided them as they paddled their way
across the sea through the night:

> On the sea's surface the light from the Morn-
> ing Star shines as we move, shining on the
> calmness of the sea. Morning Star, sent by the
> dancing Spirit People; those people of the
> rain, calling out as they dance with out-
> stretched arms.

And as each night drew to its end, the rays
of the Star reddened and then paled away
before the rising sun. The epic of the Djanggawul is a great revelation of the poetic
genius of the aborigines.

Another variation is the widespread cult
of the Mother Kunapipi, the ritual of which
has striking parallels to elements in the
the classical mystery religions of Europe.
Coming from across the sea, Kunapipi
landed either in the lower Roper River or
the Victoria River area. She was accompanied by a band of left-handed boomerang

throwers who cleared a road through th
timber, and also by a group of desirab
young women. These were her first-bor
children but she gave birth to many mor
at various places in her travels. She als
performed the now popular Kunapipi secre
ritual, in which those who are to be initiate
at one stage enter a crescent-shaped trenc
which symbolizes Kunapipi's womb, fro
which they emerge ritually reborn. Whi
still in the womb each is given a woode
bullroarer to swing. As he does so, his spir
double enters it, and remains with the bul
roarer in the trench when the initiate
'reborn' once again.

After the bullroarer disintegrates, th
spirit double goes to the place of 'shades
the spirit centre, there to wait until th
individual's death and burial ritual. Th
latter frees the flesh-soul which then join
the double and becomes one with it again
and so awaits reincarnation.

In their mythology and thinking, th
aborigines have not come to grips with th
ultimate problem of the origin of the worl
and of life. The earth and sky exist. Th
Dreaming heroes merely change the outwar
shape of what is. Rivers and valleys, hill
and rocks, anthills and trees, are formed b
their movements and in some cases by th
transformation of their own bodies. Simi
larly, the heroes themselves are not created
They too exist; they appear from the ground
the sea, the sky, and bring with them th
pre-existent life-entities or spirits of all tha
will be, man or animal, bird or fish, insec
or plant. Beyond that, all is mystery.

New Zealand

The Maoris are a Polynesian people whose ancestors arrived in New Zealand from eastern Polynesia, possibly in the 9th century D. These population movements were not planned, rather they were accidental voyages made by adventurous seamen, defeated warriors or wind-blown fishermen. It is known that by the 11th century they had explored much of the east coasts of both main islands of New Zealand, which stretch over 1000 miles from the subtropical North Cape to the temperate southern tip of the South Island.

These early settlers ingeniously adapted their tropically derived culture to the colder and more varied New Zealand environment. Of their familiar plants, only the *kumara* (sweet potato) grew really successfully. The settlers brought with them the dog and the rat. They made their clothing from flax and their more durable tools from suitable local rocks, especially basalt, argillite, nephrite and obsidian. They were expert fishermen and cleverly exploited certain local plants for food, notably fern root, which became a staple ingredient of their diet. By the time Captain Cook first visited New Zealand in 1769, the tribes had evolved a sophisticated seasonal economy within the limited productive areas.

Traditional Maori religion can be seen as the means whereby the people perceived and came to terms with the varied environment of sea coast, forest, swamp, tussock flat and mountain that they encountered in New Zealand. They believed in a pantheon of numerous gods, which some scholars have divided into four groups. It is still sometimes claimed that at the head was a Supreme Being, Io, but the evidence is not very convincing. On the other hand, there were a number of less esoteric gods, the children of Rangi (sky) and Papa (earth), the original parents. These were the gods of the forest, peace and agriculture, war, the ocean, wind and storm, uncultivated food, earthquakes, and also the god of evil. Through myth they provided the ultimate sanctions for human behaviour and attitudes. There were also lesser gods known only within a limited area, and usually restricted to one tribe, such as Maru, a war god. Finally there were tribal ancestral spirits, who were believed to have great influence over the affairs of their living descendants. The ordinary Maori commoner usually felt closest to the members of the last two groups.

Gods were approached by means of ritual offerings and incantations (*karakia*, which is also a generic word for magic). Here, for example, is a translation of part of a karakia used at the kumara harvest:

This is the spade that descends,
This is the spade that reverberates,
This is the spade that resounds,
Penu, Penu, the spade Penu.

Right *Carved wooden panel at the entrance of a Maori assembly house; legend tells that the first carving of a three-fingered motif was brought from the home of Tangaroa, god of fishermen.*

This extract is typical in its reiteration of a particular phrase and in its reference to a phenomenon, in this case the spade, Penu, sacred in tribal tradition.

The major gods were consulted only on more important occasions, such as before war or in the preparations for building a canoe. These rituals were mostly left to priests (*tohunga*), who underwent intensive education during their youth in a *whare wananga* (school of learning). One meaning of the word tohunga is 'skilled', and the influence of the priest was often due as much to his practical as his esoteric knowledge. A tohunga of Tangaroa (god of fishermen) for example, often possessed much information about fishing techniques. As well as obtaining the favour of the god through ritual, he could advise the commoner on the best methods and places for catching different varieties of fish.

Because of his influence over supernatural forces, the priest was considered sacred or *tapu* (taboo). His sanctity was proportionate to his knowledge and to the relative importance of his particular god. When, as was often the case, the tohunga was also of high birth, his power and prestige could become enormous. He might also be skilled in sorcery (*makutu*).

The significance of Maori religion and magic lies in its social context. Kinship was the most important organizing force in prehistoric Maori society. It was the basis for the family group (*whanau*), whose members, ranging through three or four generations, formed a residential unit. A number of whanau, with common ancestry, comprised a *hapu*, which controlled a definite stretch of tribal territory, with its own fishing and forest rights, and owning such valuable objects as canoes. Finally, each individual was a member of one out of about 50 tribes, all of whose members acknowledged descent from a common ancestor, sometimes a mythical hero with supernatural powers. In this way, kinship bound the individual to a series of groups interconnected both socially and symbolically.

Hapu chiefs (*rangatira*) were descended in a direct line from the founding ancestors and were thus tapu. They were believed to possess special inherited powers which endowed them with a strong influence over supernatural forces which was exercised through ritual.

The concept of tapu was thus extremely important. The word can be translated as 'holy' or 'sacred', since the power of tapu was derived from the gods. All free men had such power, to varying degrees, the amount depending on status. Women, unless of high status, were only tapu during menstruation or childbirth. Tapu was regarded with reverence but also with fear, since infringement would result in misfortune, even death, from outraged spirits. It could be transmitted by contact and so, for example, everything a chief touched shared his sacred qualities. It was dangerous, even disastrous, for anyone else to have contact with these things, unless he was equally tapu. A highborn Maori was surrounded by restrictions, lest he should endanger both his own holiness and that of others, and so bring unhappiness and misfortune.

Melanesia, Polynesia and Micronesia

The differences in belief and in social and political structure between Melanesia and Polynesia are reflected in their mythologies. Some resemblances to the Polynesian system can be traced in eastern Melanesia, but Melanesian myths contain nothing similar to the creative activities that are found in the Polynesian pantheon. It is true that certain heroes of the Banks Islands and the New Hebrides – Qat and Tagaro – stand head and shoulders above the minor spirits.

According to one account Qat at first made men and pigs in the same form, but later made pigs go on all fours and men upright to distinguish between them. In another he made men and women of wood and brought them to life by dancing in front of them. But Qat himself had a mother and companions. Tagaro resembles Qat in many ways. He is probably the Polynesian god Tangaroa adapted to a Melanesian cosmogony.

Many stories concern the origin of men. In some New Guinea myths the first people came out of a tree or from the ground. Sometimes the 'first man' finds women on earth, or stories of the 'first people' refer to other people apparently already existing – an inconsistency which does not worry the tellers, for the myths really explain the origin of a clan or a tribe rather than of all mankind, a reflection of the fragmentation and isolation of many Melanesian groups. People living as far apart as central New Guinea and the Solomon Islands have stories of descent from snake-ancestors, or from women who married snakes.

Myths concerning the release of the sea from the ground and the separation of the lands are widely-spread. Often the sea burst out as the result of the foolishness, curiosity or greed of someone who failed to do as instructed.

A number of stories centre round the origin of death, for it is widely believed that at one time people lived for ever. A common group of tales, current as far apart as New Britain and the New Hebrides, tells that once people sloughed their skins when they grew old, and appeared young again. For various reasons a woman re-assumed her old skin, in one version because her child did not recognize her and cried; since then people have died.

It is believed everywhere that the soul or spirit survives after death, though it may be only for a time. Usually there is a land of the dead, on a distant island or mountain or under the ground, and there is often a prescribed route which the dead must follow. Commonly they have to pass a spirit guardian who tests them in various ways. If they fail to satisfy him or outwit him they may be destroyed and cease to exist.

All Polynesians at one time had myths about the beginning of the world. Some feature a deity who is the Creator, others emphasize an evolutionary sequence. In Tonga and Samoa the Creator was Tangaloa (Tangaroa, Ta'aroa), who existed alone above a vast expanse of water. He threw down a stone, which became land, and gave his bird-messenger a vine to plant. The vine withered and rotted, and in the decomposing matter grew a swarm of maggots which became men and women.

Ta'aroa also seems to have been the Creator in the Society Islands. According to Tueira Henry, author of *Ancient Tahiti*, '... Ta'aroa sat in his shell in darkness from eternity. The shell was like an egg revolving in endless space, with no sky, no land, no sea, no moon, no sun, no stars. All was darkness, it was continuous thick darkness ...' The notion of an original void, or chaos, in which there was nothing material or tangible, is common.

Whatever its origin, once created the world evolved. At first the sky father and the earth mother lay embraced, and their offspring, the gods, were born into the darkness between them. Finally one (often Tane) decided to separate them, and thrust the sky up into its present position, allowing light into the world. Evolution often proceeds by a series of procreative acts, pairs of personified abstractions producing offspring unlike themselves, but there is also an idea of continuous growth and development.

Most of the great gods are found throughout Polynesia, but their names and attributes differ in the various groups, and some islands had deities unknown elsewhere. The New Zealand Maori seem to have had a supreme Creator called Io. The name occurs again (as Ihoiho) in Tahiti. One has to

Above Melanesian religion consists basically of making contact with spirits who will help and befriend humans; the approach may be a personal one made by an individual, or ceremonies may be held in which whole communities participate: left to right Ancestral tablet or board found in a men's cult house in the Papuan Gulf region: ghosts of the ancestors are always venerated; New Guinea cult figure: ceremonial dancers hold these in their hands; ornament for a canoe prow, representing a guardian spirit; malanggan, an elaborate carving used in ceremonies held in honour of the recently dead.

distinguish between Io as a true Creator of all things, and the gods who bring order out of chaos. Tangaroa was especially the god of the sea, but in the outlying groups became of minor importance, sometimes a forest god.

Tane was primarily a sky god, of special importance in the Society and Cook Islands and in Hawaii. He was also lord of the forest and, as a result, the patron of woodworkers. In Mangaia, one of the islands in the Cook archipelago, his symbol was a stone-bladed adze, into which he was believed to enter on ceremonial occasions. In some mythologies he created woman and was regarded as the life-giving force.

Tu (Ku in Hawaii) was a war god. In the Society Islands he was associated with Ta'aroa in the creation myths, but his function as war god was usurped by Oro, a son of Ta'aroa who became the supreme deity. But in Hawaii Ku, in various forms, was supreme.

Rongo was widely known in central and eastern Polynesia, alternative forms of his name being Lono in Hawaii, and Ono in the Marquesas Islands. He was an agricultural god, in whose honour harvest festivals were celebrated: he was also patron of singing and music. In a Hawaiian legend he sailed away, overcome with grief at the death of his wife, but promised to return one day in a canoe laden with food. The Hawaiians took Captain Cook for the returning Lono, and their disillusion led to his death.

Goddesses were of less importance. Hina or Hine appears in many forms. According to the Maori tale, Tane created Hine from the sand of the sea-shore as a mate for himself, and took their daughter Hine-Titama, the dawn maiden, as his wife. When she discovered their dual relationship she fled to Po, the underworld, and so originated death. Hine in her different aspects was the goddess of death and the underworld and, as the first woman, a source of fertility. She was also associated with the moon and with women's crafts.

The great gods were too remote to take much interest in the daily affairs of ordinary people, which were the concern of numerous lesser deities: local or family gods, or those who watched over certain crafts or activities. Some were sons or descendants of the great gods, others were deified ancestors. The two classes merged, for chiefs were themselves descended from gods.

Apart from cosmogonic myths, and legends concerning the wanderings and origin of the peoples of the different islands – many of which undoubtedly have historical foundation – there are numerous tales about the adventures of heroes and heroines, about the pranks of tricksters, about ogres and demons. A favourite hero, often regarded as a demigod, is Tahaki. He is the epitome of the great chief: brave, resourceful, handsome, full of mana, gracious and at ease, proud but patient. His adventures do not show him as perfect. That would be dull. He has his faults, he is foolish, and has numerous love affairs.

Tahaki's grandson Rata is a hero of a different kind, a great seaman and adventurer, headstrong, quick-tempered, determined. His mother, Tahiti Tokerau, was abducted by one Puna, who plucked out her eyes to serve as lights and buried her head downwards in the sand so that her feet could be supports for the baskets of Puna's wife. When Rata grew up he determined to rescue his mother. He built a great canoe with the aid of wood spirits, who had at first been

angered by his action in cutting down a tree but relented when they heard of his project. Finally, after numerous adventures, overcoming monstrous guardians and other dangers, he slew Puna and released Tahiti Tokerau. Several chiefly lines claimed descent from Rata.

Probably the most popular hero was Maui. Born prematurely and discarded by his mother, he was rescued and reared by the gods. After learning everything they could teach him he rejoined his mortal family. The stories of his adventures are innumerable. He feared no one and respected no one. No institution or taboo was sacred to him. In a society as rigidly hierarchical and strictly governed by etiquette as the Polynesian, the Maui stories must have provided a welcome safety-valve.

Many of his escapades are simply tricks or jokes, in which he makes the pompous or the great appear ridiculous, or outwits the clever. But some of his greatest feats were of benefit to man. He lassoed the sun which used to race across the sky, and so gave people the day as we know it, with time to work and cook meals. He stole fire, which man had lacked. He fished up islands from the depths of the ocean, according to some accounts with a hook made from his grandmother's jaw-bone (and therefore possessing great mana).

His last adventure, though it led to his death, was his greatest: he tried to save humanity from having to die. Accompanied by his friends the birds he sought out Hina, the goddess of depth. He found her at last, asleep.

Warning his companions to keep silent so as not to wake her, he attempted to kill her by crawling between her thighs into her body and then emerging from her mouth.

When only his legs were still visible the ridiculous sight was too much for the wagtail, which let out an uncontrollable chuckle. Hina awoke, closed her legs together, and Maui was crushed.

The mythology and religious and magical ideas of Micronesia form a less cohesive and clear-cut pattern than those of Polynesia. Cosmogonic myths are relatively unimportant. Certain groups had a Creator being, and the concept of an original chaos or void is present, but many Micronesians seem to have regarded the world as always existing: the task of the Creators was to make it habitable. Stories of the separation of earth and sky are fairly common. As in Polynesia, islands were drawn up from the sea by semi-divine fishermen, whose names are sometimes variants of Maui. There are stories about the snaring of the sun, the obtaining of fire, and other themes popular in Polynesia and other regions.

Many tales concern man-eating monsters or ogres, ferocious but stupid, who are often overcome by children: a theme common in Melanesia. Another group explains the origins of food taboos.

Below *Figures representing gods or spirits are common in Polynesia:* **Left** *this wooden image from the Austral Islands shows Tangaroa, a Creator and sea god, in the act of creating gods and men.* **Centre** *Two-headed figure from Tahiti; images representing ancestral spirits or minor deities were frequently the familiars of sorcerers, who derived their powers from the spirits.* **Right** *Dances celebrating the unity of all creation were a feature of certain Polynesian harvest festivals; wooden figure, from Hawaii, depicting a dancer passing into a trance.*

Africa

These figures stand outside a shrine of the god of thunder in western Nigeria.

The continent of Africa contains some 6,000 different tribes. So complex are African languages, races, cultures and religions that anthropologists cannot yet agree about many of the facts that are available to them.

It follows that where there are so many sorts of men, there are many gods, or concepts of God, and many religious sects with their peculiar rites, magical practices and traditional myths. Some idea of the enormous diversity involved can be seen by comparing the Egyptian Copt, a tall, fair-skinned Christian, with the Bushman of southern Africa, a stunted, black-skinned pagan. Both are Africans, and both are typical in their way of African racial types, cultural groups and religious beliefs.

But there are certain basic concepts which underly all African religions; and these concepts, far from being the mumbo-jumbo popularly associated with medicine-men, witch-doctors, black magic, fetishes, ju-jus and the rest of it, are still a powerful spiritual and social force.

To most Africans. God in one of his many manifestations, or called by one of his many names (there are over 200 principal epithets ranging from 'the Everlasting One of the Forest' to 'He who roars so loud that the nations are struck with terror') is an ever-present being; and his priests (medicine-men and witch-doctors) are recognized leaders of the tribal community.

Estimates give the number of non-Christians and non-Moslems in Africa as 157,031,000, or over half of the total population. In earlier times, before the true character of African traditional beliefs was understood, these people were called simply 'heathens'. They were poor benighted savages who 'bowed down to wood and stone'. The more accurate term used today is 'pagans', from the Latin *paganus*, a word which originally meant a peasant or country-man.

The African pagan (like the pagan everywhere for that matter) believes in a poly-theistic system in which a chief god presides over lesser deities, rather as a king ruled over his domain in ancient times. Nearly all African cults had their Supreme Being, called by a hundred different names which vary from tribe to tribe. But no matter what the chief god is called, he is invariably conceived of as the Maker of the World, the Master of Human Destiny, an omnipotent and omnipresent 'king of kings' and 'lord of lords'. And under the rule of the Supreme Being are all the lesser godlings, each with his special function.

The question that has puzzled observers since white men first arrived in Africa is whether this Supreme Being, whatever his name, is an abstract idea – a sort of creative energy which animates and pervades the universe, but has no direct relationship with man; or whether this god is a personal being, like the Jehovah of the Hebrews, or the 'Our Father' of the Christians. It is, perhaps, typical of the difficulties inherent in a study of African religion that no native has come forward to clarify the question; and that white men can only make their observations from the outside, with no help at all from written scriptures, texts or recorded ecclesiastical history.

Yet all observers who have managed to make contact with pagan Africans agree that the idea of a Supreme Being, though vague, is universal, even among the most primitive of peoples, like the Bushmen of the Kalahari Desert. It is also clear that the worship of this Supreme Being is, on the whole, a lackadaisical affair. The Creator of the Universe is, after all, bound to be somewhat indifferent to a mere human and his problems.

On the other hand, the lesser gods – the spirits of the earth and the ghosts of departed heroes – are thought to be much more sympathetic.

They can be flattered, wheedled and even threatened. A not unusual African prayer will go as follows: 'You are useless, you gods! You give us only trouble! You are a bunch of so-and-so's! What do we get from you? Nothing!'

It is evident that this 'personalized' re-lationship with the deity is not confined to African pagans. Christians, in particular Roman Catholics, often approach God through such intermediaries as the Virgin, the Apostles, local saints, martyrs, and others. And in the Moslem religion, Mohammed and his fellow prophets (including Jesus Christ) are the buffers, as it were, between man and Almighty God.

The African, surrounded from birth by all the wonders and terrors of nature, logically pays more heed to sun, rain, storms, rivers and animals than we do, as these objects are his immediate friends or enemies, and vitally affect his daily life.

Together with all religions, paganism has a collection of myths to explain the Creation of the World and the Fall of Man. While each tribe has its own account, the basic theme is nearly always the same – not unlike the Hebrew version as told in the first chapter of Genesis.

God is said to have made man and woman from clay. These two mortals lived for a time in Paradise, from which they were expelled due to some 'original sin'. A Nigerian legend blames the woman for annoying God by striking the sky with her pounding stick. A Congolese story says that her continual nagging became so intolerable that God lowered her down from heaven in a basket.

Whatever the reason for the expulsion from Paradise, man was alienated from God who, in most African myths, retires into his own domain where he grows older and, it appears, more maudlin. For according to some, his old eyes dribble with tears, which become the rain that falls upon the earth below. According to others, he spends a great deal of his time quarrelling with his wife. Claps of thunder are the Great God shouting.

The underlying notion of nearly all African creation myths seems to be that God and man once lived on earth and con-versed together. Then man – or more fre-quently woman – erred, and the unhappy Fall resulted.

Ever since then, men have tried to climb back into heaven and have even built towers and ladders for that purpose, but without success. Consequently, when Christian mis-sionaries arrived in Africa with the news that man could be saved through Jesus Christ, the appeal of the new religion was enormous, since no African myth explained how man was to ascend into Paradise.

The Ashanti

To the Ashanti the universe is the work of a Creator, Odomankoma. It is he who created the heaven and the earth, men and all creatures of the earth, trees and rivers. As they say on their drums, things that owe their origin to the Creator must be clearly distinguished from the works of man who draws on Nature for his own benefit.

When Odomankoma the Creator created the world, he also created life and death. According to an Ashanti myth, Death became so powerful that he was able to kill the Creator himself. But when the Creator died, the universe continued to be controlled by a Supreme Being, called Nyame. At first this Supreme Being lived very close to earth and was within easy reach of man but he was obliged to move far out into the heavens because women hit the earth continually as they pounded grain in mortars.

From his abode on high Nyame is able to see everything, for he sees even with his eyes turned away. He seems to be everywhere, for the Ashanti say, 'If you have something to say to the Supreme Being, say it to the wind'. He is the giver of rain and sunshine who controls the seasons. He offers protection and help to those who need it. As summarized in Ashanti proverbs: 'It is the Supreme Being that brushes off flies from the tailless animal.' 'It is the Supreme Being that pounds food for the one who has lost his arm.'

The Supreme Being is the source of morality. He does not like men to cheat one another. Man's destiny is in his hands: 'If the Supreme Being does not want you to die and a human being tries to kill you, you will not die.' Men can depend on him, for he is someone on whom one leans and does not fall.

It is not only human beings who owe their lives to the Creator. The Ashanti believe that the supernatural beings which inhabit the universe also owe their existence and power to him.

Of these beings, those who wield the greatest power are the gods (abosom), who may be identified with particular features of Nature. They include river gods, tree gods and mountain gods, as well as gods without any clearly defined habitat. All of them rank below the Supreme Being and are sometimes described as his children. However, within the limits of the powers given to them, they act independently.

The Ashanti believe that a god can enter into a woman's womb and be born into the world. Usually he does not come forth in the form of a human being but as a piece of stone, which is subsequently discovered to be a god. The gods can change their shapes, turning themselves into animals or birds when it suits them, or appearing in human form – in the guise of beautiful women or people who are insane.

The gods also have unlimited mobility. They can stay in and out of their shrines as they like. The fact that shrines are made for some of them in different localities suggests that their worshippers believe that they can be present in many places at the same time.

As well as the gods, the Ashanti recognize the existence of Nature spirits, which find a permanent or temporary home in natural objects and may be beneficial to those who recognize them and harmful to those who ignore them. They are generally not the objects of organized cults. They have no priests, no set form of worship, even though they may occasionally be the focus of rituals.

The most important Nature spirit recognized by the Ashanti is the spirit of the Earth. This is a feminine spirit, for the Earth is like a mother to humanity. Her sacred day is Thursday and in the old days work on the farm was prohibited on this day.

Other Nature spirits are associated with particular trees, especially those used for carving or building. These trees are not the objects of organized cults because they are not personified gods (and so are distinguished from tree gods proper). When an Ashanti wishes to cut down any of them for use, he performs a little ritual so that the spirit enshrined in it may not harm him.

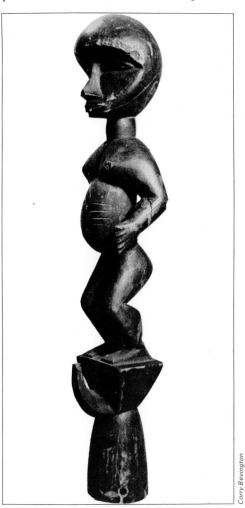

Head-dress worn at an annual ceremony to propitiate the Earth Mother; the custom was abandoned at the end of the 19th century.

Corry Bevington

There is a widespread belief that many spirits inhabit the forest and that it is dangerous for anyone to venture alone into the thick forest unless he knows the lore of the forest. And it is not only Nature spirits that loiter there. Gods may also be met and some of those who become priests discover their gods through being possessed while in the forest.

The Ibo

Before the civil war in Nigeria, the Ibo were estimated at some 7 million and lived on both banks of the Niger.

A myth of origin exists among the Umundri. The following version was narrated by a gathering of their priests. 'The name of our founder is Ndri, the son of Eri: Namuku is his wife. Eri and Namuku were sent down by Chuku (a sky god). All the first things happened at Aguleri where the Umundri group started. When Eri came down from the sky he had to stand on a termite mound as all the earth was then a morass. Eri complained to Chuku who sent a metal worker, Awka, with bellows, charcoal and fire to dry up the land. Awka did so.'

While Eri was alive, the priests continued, he and his dependants were fed by Chuku and their food was sky-substance. Those who ate of it never slept. When Eri died, this food supply ceased and Ndri, Eri's son who had founded Aguleri, complained to Chuku that there was no food. Chuku replied that if Ndri were to slay and bury his eldest son and daughter he could obtain food from their graves. Ndri said this was impossible. Chuku then sent Dioka from the sky to Ndri to carve certain patterns (called *ichi* patterns) on the faces of these two children. Thereafter Ndri was to cut their throats and to bury them in separate graves. Ndri did so. Three Ibo weeks later plant shoots appeared from these graves. From the grave of his son Ndri dug up a yam, cooked and ate it and fell asleep. When he woke up his family were astonished and said they thought he had died. He told them what he had done, and they also ate of the cooked yam and fell asleep.

The next day Ndri dug up *koko* yams from his daughter's grave, ate them and likewise slept. For this reason the yam is called the son of Ndri and the koko yam the daughter of Ndri. When a man takes up the post of *eze* Ndri, that is the kingship, he does not have to slay his first-born son and daughter, though both have the ichi pattern carved on their faces.

Chuku told Ndri to distribute this food to all mankind. Ndri demurred, saying it was obtained by the death of his first-born children. Chuku insisted and stated that in return Ndri and his descendants would have the right of cleansing every Ibo town of abominations or breaches of taboo, of crowning the king at Aguleri, of tying the ankle cords whenever a man took the title of *ozo* or immortality; Dioka's descendants would carve the ichi pattern on their faces.

Ndri and his descendants would also have the right of making the magical yam 'medicine' each year for ensuring a plentiful supply of yams in all surrounding towns. For these and other privileges the surrounding Ibo would pay tribute to Ndri and his descendants. So Ndri distributed the yams and the koko yams and in this way mankind was supplied with food.

Ndri introduced the system of ranking titles. He became the first eze Ndri or divine king while other individuals took and continue to take the title of *eze ozo* after him and in memory of him.

The Congo Tribes

Its religion, myth and magic make the Congo the most striking region of Africa, for here black men lived for thousands of years completely out of touch with outside civilizations. The Congo has always been the heart of Africa both geographically and, to some extent, culturally. Most of the aboriginal population of 15 million people are pure Negroes, racially different from the Semites of North Africa and the Bushmen and Hottentots of South Africa.

Some observers have maintained that these Negroes had no concept of God whatsoever and only worshipped idols called ju-jus and fetishes. They were said to be under the domination of witch-doctors, depicted as masked wizards who performed unmentionable rites, including the sacrifice of living infants. In addition, the Congolese were described as having such a low view of the value of human life that they strangled several of a dead chief's wives and buried them with their feet pointing towards their deceased husband. Cannibalism, too, was rife among certain tribes. Idols, witchcraft, human sacrifice and ritual cannibalism – these were, for many years, considered to be the total scope of Congolese religious beliefs and practices.

It is now known that this picture is only half-true, and is partly due to the difficulties encountered by white men in trying to discover the truth about African myths and magic. It is inevitable that a subject people should be wary of revealing their secrets to their alien masters. This is especially the case where ritual murder, trial by ordeal and similar savage practices are involved, since the European authorities immediately made such customs illegal. Whether the colonial governments were ever able to eradicate such ancient tribal rites in remote areas of the Congo is doubtful.

It is, however, generally agreed that the Congolese have some idea of what civilized people call God, though the principal difference is that whereas Christians, Jews and Moslems believe in a *personal* deity, the African regards God as a vague figure with no particular interest in him as an individual. Yet most natives would readily admit that there must have been a Creator, or Lord of the Universe, a sort of super-king who rules the whole world. They have various proper names for this mysterious and remote deity – Maweja Mulopo, Nzambi, Kalunga, Akongo and so forth, and various honorific titles such as 'Elephant in Strength', 'Tortoise in Patience' and even 'Tomato in Sweetness'.

More specific is a god-chief called Lyangombe, a combination of a folk-hero and a supernatural being of great power. In general, Lyangombe is a beneficent god who is prepared to help his devotees provided he is well treated. As he can protect his worshippers against sickness and calamities, he has a special cult and priests. Lyangombe enters into his chosen people and controls their actions, even deigning to allow his women followers to bear his children. In consequence, missionaries have found him an obstacle to Christian teaching, for his cult is said to lead to considerable licence and promiscuity.

But whatever the Congolese call God, their attitude towards him is inclined to be unceremonious for they neither love nor fear him as Christians are supposed to love and fear their God. This indifference is reflected in the lack of any kind of temple or even of a representation of the Almighty. Congolese folktales which embody a great deal of their religious and social history emphasize the distant, almost hostile attitude towards the Supreme Creator.

At the same time, there is a close, almost personal relationship between men and animals. The legend of why the dog has no hands, for instance, is typical of the animal myths. God denied the dog hands, but told him he could always live close to man, who would be his hands. Thus the dog is the servant of man, and vice-versa. God, however, is depicted as something of a tyrant who drove both men and animals from a pleasant land to a harsh life here below. No particular reason is given for man's expulsion from paradise, except that God was angry over some small misdemeanour. Alternatively, woman is blamed as the prime cause of men's troubles.

Among the Bapende the annual dance, known as **Nioka,** *in which the men are painted to look like snakes, harks back to an old myth which tells how woman tempted man in the form of a serpent, and man turned into a serpent to possess her.*

The Nilotes

The Nilotes or Nilotic peoples of Africa consist of several culturally related tribes and nations. They live south of the Sahara, stretching from the Nile valley of the southern Sudan and Ethiopia, down to Uganda, where some extend west into the Congo, and eastwards into Kenya. The best-known are the Nuer, Dinka, Shilluk, and the Anuak of the Sudan, most of whom, however, are in Ethiopia; the Acholi and Lango of Uganda, the Alur of Uganda and the Congo, and the Luo of Kenya. Their pervading beliefs are markedly spiritual and theistic, Nuer and Dinka in particular giving a central position to a High God associated with the sky and heavenly phenomena, to which ultimately the conditions and vicissitudes of their lives are attributed.

Among the Shilluk, Anuak and Alur variants of a type of divine kingship are generally found. Others follow the religious lead of priests of various kinds, the Nuer and Dinka especially having a well-developed sacrifical priesthood. The roles of both kings and priests are validated by myths which have a profound imaginative appeal to the people, and which serve as the best introduction to their other religious and magical ideas. The widespread association of spiritual forces with the river and the sky, features which dominated the river-plain environment with which all the Nilotes had some original connection, should be noted.

The kings of the Shilluk, who stand in an intermediate position between men and God, are believed to be descended from a culture hero and first leader Nyikango, whose spirit descends on every successor. This first king is represented as descended on the father's side from the sky, and on the mother's side from the crocodile, thus combining in his person the imaginative connotations of the sky and the river upon which Shilluk well-being profoundly depends. Nyikango did not die but disappeared in a whirlwind, according to one widely-received tradition, and can thus in a sense live on in every subsequent king. Shrines to the kings, and priests to serve at them, are distributed over Shillukland. The Shilluk thus have a national cult of the kingship which connects them with a transcendent divinity. A comparable kingship, though in a less-centralized form, is found among the Anuak, whose first king is represented as having been the son of a spirit from the river born of the daughter of a local village ruler. Like the Shilluk royal clan, his descendants have spread themselves and their influence through the land. In these cases the association of the kingship with the sky or the river, or both, suggests that although the kings take part in human society they are also outside and above it.

The pastoral Dinka, who have no centralized kingship, also explain the spiritual primacy of their priestly leaders by a myth which relates them to the river. The first Dinka priest, Ayuel Longar, is represented as having been born of a childless widow who was grieving over her fate on the bank of the river. A spirit of the river told her to wade into the water, raise her skin skirt (the symbol of a married woman) and draw the ripples towards her. She conceived a miraculous child, born with teeth, who as a tiny baby helped himself to gourds of milk, and later during a period of drought found water for the cattle by pulling up by the roots a type of grass which still has sacred connotations. Yet at first the people refused to accept his authority and he left them. They pursued him to a river which he crossed and then, standing on the opposite bank, Ayuel Longar speared them when they in turn tried to cross, as the Dinka themselves spear fish. Eventually by trickery their leaders overpowered him, and wrested his blessing from him. In this way it came about that his descendants and theirs now form clans of priests, whose task it is to pray and offer sacrifice on behalf of the people, and whose symbols of office are sacred fishing spears, which they flourish as they consecrate their sacrificial oxen.

These particular myths are not found among all Nilotes, but it is true to say that their tone and structure are characteristically Nilotic.

The Zulus

The Zulu have a conception of a High God, who broke off the nations from a reed-bed, but he plays little part in their daily life and is not worshipped. Distinct from him is Heaven, a concept of a great power in the sky, barely anthropomorphized, present in storms and particularly in lightning, and manifested in the thunderbolts which are numerous because of the violence of the storms. These thunderbolts are thought to be the excreta of a thunderbird. Heaven is believed to influence certain persons who begin to get drowsy, become ill, and wander far from the habitations of men. They are then initiated as Heaven doctors, and can plant magical substances around villages to protect them from lightning, while during storms they go out on the hilltops and fight the storms with weapons and magic. Several people are killed each year by lightning, and these magicians are much respected.

These beliefs about lightning are not reconciled with the idea that dangerous forked lightning is female, while harmless sheet lightning is male, or with a belief in a goddess who is supposed to make the rain and who is associated with the rainbow, which is believed to be the rafter of her hut in the sky. This goddess is graphically described: '... presenting the appearance of a beautiful landscape with verdant forests on some parts of her body, grass-covered slopes on others, and cultivated slopes on others ... robed with light as a garment ...' The Zulu had few myths of origin or of creation, but they speak of the goddess, who is a maiden, as having come from heaven to teach people to make beer, to plant, to harvest, and all the useful arts.

The most important spiritual beings in Zulu belief are the spirits of their ancestors. These are believed to live below the earth or in the sky, or to appear in the villages in the form of particular kinds of snakes, sometimes dangerous species, but believed to behave peaceably and to be recognizable as their

Keystone

Young man in full ritual clothing prepares to take part in a war dance.

deceased 'inhabitants' by marks on the body. The ancestors are one of the two principal agencies in Zulu belief influencing good and ill fortune: they expect their descendants, those related to them by descent through males, to place all milk and beer in the 'great hut' of the village for them to taste and to pour it into the ground of the cattle corral round which houses are built, in periodic offerings. They also require that sacrifices of cattle be offered to them. Should their descendants neglect to make these offerings, the ancestors will send disease; and they will also do so if their descendants default in their obligations to other kinsmen. They are prayed to at ceremonies for birth, initiation and marriage, and at funerals, and also at sowing first fruits, and harvest, as well as on other occasions. The ancestors of kings and chiefs look after their political dependents.

During illness, diviners of various kinds are consulted to find which ancestor is sending the misfortune so that it can be besought to remove the disease.

It is believed that male ancestors are reasonable and will remove the misfortune if it has been sent for neglect of offerings, or when the breach of obligation which provoked the affliction has been redressed. On the other hand, female ancestral spirits are capricious and are capable of allowing the misfortune to continue for quite extended periods, even after due amends have been made by the descendants.

The Far East

India

The ancient Aryan religion was based upon sky worship, and the early gods were *devas* or 'the shining ones', the father god being known as Dyaus, equivalent to the Greek Zeus and the Latin Jupiter. But when the Aryans reached India this remote Almighty had faded into the background and survived principally as the parent of a more real and active brood. Of these the most prominent was Indra, god of war and the weather, who destroyed his foes with a thunderbolt, drank soma immoderately and bragged freely of his prowess.

Across the sky with him rode the charioted spirits of the storm, singing wild and warlike songs as they sped. Amongst his achievements was that of dragon-slayer. In one way and another he links up with religious ideas of Mesopotamia and as far afield as Germanic Europe. He was pre-eminently the warriors' god, violent and jovial in an age of heroic barbarism.

But though foremost, Indra was not the only Aryan god whose special zone was the sky. There was, for example, Surya or the sun god who drove across the heavens in a flaming chariot, like the Greek Helios or Apollo. The twin husbands of Surya's daughter, the Asvins, also used the sky and

are comparable with the twin Dioscuri of the Greeks, but were specially concerned with shipwrecked mariners and generally with warding off the ills that beset mankind. Vishnu, who was later to become one of the two great gods of the Hindu world, was another frequenter of the Vedic skies. So too was Pusan, though, like the Asvins, occupied with peaceful missions such as protector of herds and herdsmen.

Next in esteem to the boisterous Indra was the somewhat mysterious and complex god or presence, Varuna, who reigned as a heavenly king in a celestial palace and was surrounded by a godly court. Upon Varuna rested responsibility for the order of the universe, for ensuring that day and night and the seasons followed one another in proper succession. Varuna's great quality was that of knowledge. He was present at all human interchange, and he abhorred sin, including the drinking and gambling which characterized Aryan society. He punished wrong-doing and was approached with awe and penitential humility.

In this he was quite unlike Rudra who had no moral sense but was a stormy archer god whose arrows brought disease; grim, though like so many of the ancient gods, capable of occasional beneficence.

By the late Vedic period (middle and latter part of the first millennium BC) – that of

Above *Vishnu is made real to his worshippers through his ten incarnations:* **left** *Vishnu as Rama, hero of the Rama Yana who was cheated of his throne;* **right** *Vishnu as Krishna, the youth whose affairs with the cowherd's daughters are held to be an analogy of the love affair between God and the soul.*

the *Upanishads* – the individual characters and qualities of many of the gods of the *Rig-Veda* had become obscured, or had merged into new complexes: a process which may be ascribed partly to the fusion of Aryan with non-Aryan elements and partly to inevitable changes wrought by time and changing environment. A notable example of this was the gradual exaltation of the fierce Rudra of the *Rig-Veda* into the mighty Shiva of classical Hinduism. *Shiva* meant 'propitious', and was in origin the placatory epithet of Rudra but eventually assumed a separate and independent status as one of the two great cosmic deities of the Hindu world, the other being Vishnu. In character, Shiva was an irreconcilable mingling of the hopes and fears and questionings of his worshippers. He is the destroyer; he haunts battlefields and burning-grounds; he is himself both time and death; he wears a garland of skulls and is surrounded by demons. At the same time he is the creator and is ithyphallic (represented with an erect phallus). Again, on Mount Kailasa in the Himalayas he sits upon a tiger skin in deep meditation. But also he is Lord of the Dance. He wields the trident, and is constantly accompanied by his gracious wife Parvati and his 'vehicle', the Nandi bull. He rules menacingly over his adherents, with whom he nevertheless shares the Hindu urge towards reflection and yogi. He brings together in one stern but ineluctable Being many of the principal strands of Indian religious thought and sensation.

The Hindus are not monotheists, strictly speaking, but they all agree that there is one supreme and eternal Principle, one abiding reality behind the whole phenomenal universe which is in a state of perpetual flux. This 'Being' is the Absolute, and in theology it is called Brahman or simply the 'Self'. Brahman is beyond all attributes and all characterization: but if you conceive of it as possessing attributes such as omnipotence, omniscience, and sovereignty, then it is God.

In the earliest Hindu scripture, the *Rig-Veda*, Vishnu turns up from time to time but he is quite unimportant. He is the faithful companion of Indra who, during the period of the *Rig-Veda*, was the greatest of the gods, the patron of the Aryans as they swept into India and the chastizer of the aboriginal inhabitants, the god of the storm and of war. The only action attributed separately to Vishnu is his striding out three paces. The paces represent the 'measuring out', that is, the creation of the universe; and his highest step seems to be the sky. Later it was to be identified with Being itself, that is, Brahman or the Absolute.

The seed from which Vishnu developed to his full stature as the supreme deity is already here; but it is a very small seed from which so immense a tree should have grown. It was, however, not the only seed, for the full-fledged Vishnu is clearly the result of the coalescence of many gods, none of which belong to the oldest mythology of the *Veda*. In the course of time he coalesced with Narayana, who appears in a rather later Vedic text as a divine sage who offers sacrifice and 'becomes this whole universe'. In the Great Epic, the *Mahabharata*, Narayana dwells, though invisible himself, in a mythical 'White Island' where he is surrounded by his devotees – strange beings by any standards, since their heads are like umbrellas and they each have four testicles – who revere him alone as the one God and thereby partake of his eternal essence. The cult of Narayana in conjunction with Vasudeva is attested by an inscription from the 2nd century BC.

But who was Vasudeva? In the Epic and the *Puranas* (300 BC – 1000 AD) Vasudeva is given as the patronymic of Krishna whose father was Vasudeva; and this adds a new complication, for the origins of the Krishna cult are even more obscure than the cult of Vishnu himself. By the time of the Epic in which the man Krishna plays a leading part, he is already identified with Vishnu and is his incarnation on earth. As such he delivers the most celebrated of all the Hindu scriptures, or holy books, the *Bhagavad Gita*, in which he explains his own nature as God, reveals himself in a quite terrifying vision as all-consuming Time, shows how he is not only identical with Brahman, the Absolute, but actually transcends it, explains the supreme merit and efficacy of loving devotion to the one God, and also explains the purpose of God's incarnation as man. 'Whenever the law of righteousness withers away,' he says, 'and lawlessness arises, then do I generate myself on earth. For the protection of the good, for the destruction of evil-doers, for the setting up of the law of righteousness I come into being age after age.'

In the Great Epic, Krishna is Vishnu incarnate, but Vishnu himself, though he appears in most of this enormous poem as the supreme deity, is not undisputedly so. He is Bhagavan, 'the Lord', but in the background there lurks disconcertingly Mahadeva, otherwise the 'Great God' Shiva, whose supremacy Krishna himself acclaims on occasion. The two gods are still clearly rivals, but a compromise is reached whereby the one true God is invoked as Hari-Hara, *hari*, the 'tawny' or 'he who takes away (sin)', being one of the stock epithets of Vishnu, and *hara* the 'seizer' being one of Shiva's. For from the time of the Great Epic until today God has been worshipped by the Hindus either in the form of Vishnu or of Shiva: for the worshippers of Vishnu, Vishnu (and his incarnations) alone is God, for the worshippers of Shiva the same is true of Shiva. In the so-called Hindu Trinity (the Trimurti or 'three-form' of God, consisting of Brahma, Vishnu and Shiva) Brahma is associated with creation, Vishnu with sustaining, and Shiva with destruction.

The Creation myth associated with Vishnu is rather naive. At the end of each cosmic cycle Vishnu falls asleep on the cosmic serpent Shesha. When he wakes up, a lotus grows out of his navel and in the middle of the flower Brahma is seated, and Brahma then proceeds with the creation of the universe. Meanwhile the wrathful Shiva emerges from his forehead ready to destroy all.

The Nagas

The mountainous border country between India and Burma is inhabited by a group of tribes known as the Nagas. They are of Mongoloid race and speak a variety of Tibeto-Burman languages. The total number of Nagas within the frontiers of India is about half a million, and although divided into a number of tribes, with different languages and customs, they are distinguished from surrounding populations.

Until the middle of the 19th century the Nagas lived in almost complete isolation from the inhabitants of the plains and the higher civilizations developed in India and Burma. Neither Hinduism nor Buddhism has influenced the Nagas and their religious and social practices, but the Nagas have close cultural as well as racial affinities with the hill tribes of the eastern Himalayas.

According to Naga ideas man splits at death into several distinct invisible entities. The 'soul', to which a large portion of the individual's personality is attached, sets out on a long journey to the Land of the Dead. The approach is guarded by a spirit who questions the soul before allowing it entrance. There is a belief that everything on this earth has an exact counterpart in the Land of the Dead.

Another part of the personality remains attached to the skull and is capable of benefiting the living in various ways. The skulls of the dead, both those of kinsmen and those of slain enemies, are periodically fed; this reflects a belief in the power of a spiritual element which remains on this earth while the 'soul' settles down to a new life in the next world.

The religious beliefs of the various Naga tribes are not uniform, but there is throughout a belief in numerous spirits, partly friendly and partly hostile to man, but controllable by the performance of the appropriate rites. Above the host of earthbound spirits stands the figure of a supreme deity, whose name means literally 'Sky-earth', a term which reflects the idea of a universal deity comprising or dominating both spheres. Some Nagas imagine this supreme god as dwelling in the sky and as having existed before all other beings. They attribute to him the creation of the firmament and believe that he causes the thunder to roll and the lightning to flash. He is imagined in the likeness of a human being of immense size. At most important events in the life of a Naga the sky god is invoked, and in innumerable prayers and incantations he is asked to bestow blessings and success on individuals or on the whole community. The sky god is regarded as the guardian of the moral order.

Nagas believe that he can see and hear everything human beings do, and that he is angered by offences against the ethical code. He is thought to punish wrongdoers by an early death or by misfortunes in this life.

Compared to the sky god, the spirits of the earth, the forests and the rivers are not very important in Naga religion, though at times they are placated with offerings of chickens and pigs. Nagas spend a comparatively large part of their time and resources on ritual activities, but do not seem to be open to religious experiences of great emotional impact. Their world view leaves little scope for mysticism, though there are Naga seers and mediums believed to be capable of entering the spirit world while in a state of trance. Some of these seers claim that when their body sleeps, their soul can enter the body of a tiger, and that in the shape of were-tigers they have experiences which they remember in their waking state. According to Naga belief, the bond between such a man and his tiger familiar is very close, and the death of the tiger is invariably followed by that of his human double. In recent decades large numbers of Nagas have been converted to Christianity, and the practice of the old tribal religion is perhaps regrettably, but somewhat inevitably, on the wane.

Tibet and Southeast Asia

Buddhism became gradually established in Tibet from the 7th century AD onwards. The beginnings were slow, rather like the progress of Christianity in the British Isles about the same period, since those who practised the old indigenous religion, often supported by local chieftains, resisted the new faith. The Yarlung line of kings are represented with few exceptions as being its leading early patrons, but it is now historically certain that most of them continued to support the ancestral religion, while sometimes encouraging the founding of Buddhist temples and small monastic foundations.

Little is known with certainty of pre-Buddhist Tibetan religion, but it certainly comprised a cult of the king as a divine being, and special funeral rites involving the immolation of chosen companions together with the deceased king. There is mention of this rite being practised as late as 800 AD. The early religion also included the cult of local gods, especially mountain gods and warrior gods, and rites of sacrifice which were performed when special oaths were taken. This old Tibetan religion is often referred to by Western scholars as 'shamanism', and there were doubtless shamanistic elements, especially in the sense that some priests, through the practice of trance, might 'visit' or identify themselves with the divinities with which they were in special contact.

The assassination of the last of the Yarlung kings in 842 reduced the country to political chaos and so caused a further set-back to the introduction of Buddhism. However, new initiatives were taken in western Tibet by the descendants of the Yarlung dynasty, who established three small kingdoms there. From the 10th until the end of the 12th century trained Tibetan monks and scholars made continuous visits to India and Nepal, collecting and translating all the Indian Buddhist literature they could find. Central and eastern Tibet began to take an interest again, thanks to local aristocratic families who saw political advantage in supporting the new religion. Certainly Buddhism presented itself as a much higher culture than anything the Tibetans had possessed hitherto. Not only was a whole new written style developed in order to make possible the translation of obscure Sanskrit philosophical and religious terms, but this same Buddhist form of literature became the model for all Tibetan literature whatsoever. Thus when the representatives of the pre-Buddhist religion, known as *Bon* (perhaps simply meaning 'indigenous'), came to record their traditions, they inevitably made use of the new Buddhist vocabulary and introduced into their own teachings all kinds of Indian Buddhist doctrines.

Southeast Asia has witnessed a second flowering of several of the great religions of mankind, but unlike India and western Asia it has not been the birthplace of any religious movement powerful enough to shape the ideology of a civilization. Today Buddhism and, in a few regions, Islam dominate the cultural life of the countries of the Southeast Asian mainland, while Hinduism, though no longer practised to any great extent in its original form, has left its imprint on folk belief and ritual traditions.

Throughout Southeast Asia the historic religions introduced by colonists and missionaries from India and other countries have overlaid ancient indigenous religious traditions; but many of these traditions are still alive and are expressed in ritual practices, even among people who consider themselves Buddhists or Moslems. An analysis of the religious pattern peculiar to Southeast Asia must thus focus on the indigenous religious ideas and attitudes rather than on the doctrines imported from the homelands of such historic religions as Buddhism and Islam. These local religious phenomena are found among populations which have remained untouched by external influences, and in their comparative isolation preserve their traditional way of life. Typical of such populations are the hill tribes of Burma, Thailand and Laos as well as some of the simpler indigenous peoples of Malaya. The Lamets, a primitive hill tribe of Laos, for instance, exemplify by their beliefs in a great variety of supernatural beings, and their complex ritual practices, an ideological system unaffected by any of the higher religions. They share with other tribes the firm conviction that the human personality survives after death, and the ancestor cult occupies a central place in their religious thinking and acting.

Many of the religious practices of the Lamets and similar tribes are directed towards the increase of their food supply and specifically towards the prosperity of their crops. The Lamets attribute to the rice a 'soul' which is referred to by the same term as the soul of a human being. The soul of the rice is believed to exist not only in the grains but in the whole plant and indeed in a whole rice field. Numerous rites are concentrated on the rice, and many sacrifices are performed in order to protect the soul, which is the growing power of the rice. Such rites aim not only to increase the crop, but also to keep the harvested rice securely. To a certain degree the 'soul' of the rice is treated like a spirit and equated with the soul which enlivens man: personal spirits attached to individuals, family or house spirits, communal spirits, Nature spirits inhabiting forests, hills, streams and lakes, and the disembodied spirits of the deceased. Buddhist Burmese believe in spirits of the same types, and the Buddhists retained and reinterpreted many of the beliefs in supernatural beings held by their pre-Buddhist forbears.

Most prominent among these spirits are the *nats*. They are the objects of an elaborate cult which forms part of an organized religious system. The cult of the nats rivals Buddhism in its elaboration and ideological systematization. The term nat is used to describe supernatural beings of a great variety of types, but in general they are considered more powerful than humans and able to affect men for good or evil. Most distinctive among the nats is a group referred to as the 'Thirty-Seven Nats', each of whom possesses a distinct, historically or mythologically determined identity. They are conceived as the spirits of outstanding men and women, who suffered a violent death, and on account of this became nats. They are potentially dangerous and easily offended, and some of them personify qualities abhorred by Buddhism, such as sexual profligacy, aggression and drunkenness. The festivals connected with their cult express a general saturnalian spirit, and function as an outlet for the human drives frustrated by the puritanical aspects of Buddhism. The cult of the nats received the support of the ancient Burmese kings, and in modern days political leaders have continued to allocate government resources to the maintenance of nat shrines and the lavish performance of festivals in the honour of these spirits.

Distinct from the nats with malevolent tendencies are benevolent spiritual beings who protect men and accede to their prayers for help. Among them are the gods of the Buddhist pantheon, whose images stand on the platforms of many pagodas, where they enjoy the worship of those visiting the Buddhist sanctuaries. The assistance of these deities is invoked by ritual offerings of food consisting of fruits and vegetarian items.

In Burma and other countries of Southeast Asia, there is also a widespread belief in ghosts and demons. Among the ghosts are the souls of those dead who were denied proper mortuary rites and therefore remain near houses and settlements and haunt the inhabitants. Since any soul is potentially dangerous, certain rites are performed to prevent it from remaining attached to the scene of its previous existence.

Below *Tibetan religion is basically Buddhist, incorporating elements from the indigenous, more primitive religion of Bon; a main feature is belief in Bodhisattvas, who may be devotees on the road to Buddhahood or Great Beings who themselves chose to be reborn into the world to help suffering creation: a lesser Bodhisattva was Vajrapani, wielder of the thunderbolt, gracious to the faithful and terrible to the impious: 5th–6th century.*

Victoria and Albert Museum

China

Religion in China has always been deeply embedded in the social system, and it is not possible to consider the one without the other. It is among the world's richest religions. Intermingled with the strands of Buddhism, Taoism, ancestor worship, folk religion and Confucianism is a deep concern with the fate of society. From this complex background three major interests emerge.

One interest was in man, in his individual relationship to the universe: Taoism has been its important representative. The second was in man as a being important in the future of the world, and has been represented by Buddhism. The third concern was with society rather than with man as an individual or the world at large. This 'social religion', was represented by a set of ideas which had no name of its own (although some of its parts had names) and is of central importance for understanding China.

What one might call the blueprint for social relations in the traditional Chinese system was provided by a group of ideas which has been loosely and popularly termed 'Confucianism', from its connection with the teachings of Kung Fu-tze (550–480 BC). There have been many different interpretations of its precise nature. Some writers have stressed its concern with the things of this world and with ethics. Others, seeking to align it with the 'higher religions', have stressed the semi-personal nature of its concept of heaven. There has been much controversy among scholars over definitions and functions but in outline the theory is as follows.

Originally, there was a single cosmic cell containing 'ether' (*Ch'i*) which was made to pulsate by a creative force known as *Tao*. Tension set up by this activity eventually rent the cell into opposite and complementary halves; twin ethers which encompassed the universe and which are known as *Yin* and *Yang*. The Yin ether is of the earth, dark, female, heavy; while that of Yang is of heaven, bright, male, light. The continuous operation of Tao, which is a sort of natural law, causes these entities to alternate, and by this process five 'elements' are produced: water, fire, wood, metal, and earth. By various combinations of these elements, the multitude of things in this world comes into existence.

The Yin and Yang and the elements were the basis of traditional classifications in China. Colours, parts of the empire, parts of the body, numbers and many other things, were grouped and defined in terms of them. They were thought to determine the natural forces, even the process of history and the fate of dynasties. By their continuous motion all things are formed. Death and decay is the process by which they separate into their original cosmic components. Some liken it

Left *The King of the Seventh Hell, surrounded by obsequious attendants, looks on while hideous dogs and demons drive condemned souls into the river. The Seventh Hell was reserved for those guilty of cannibalism and desecrating graves.*

all to the action of a gigantic pair of bellows, continually sucking in cosmic materials out of heaven and earth, forming them briefly into things as they are now, and then letting them out again to return to nothingness.

If some of this sounds obscure, the Taoist would say it is inevitable. The very adjectives used for Yin, Yang and the elements are attempts to describe the indescribable. The Taoist's task was to achieve an inward appreciation of his own nature, which is the nature of all things, for all things are governed by a single Tao. Only then could he work in true harmony with the universe.

For the Confucian, however, the nature of Tao was known. It consisted of rules of conduct, etiquette and ceremonial. It was a guide for social action. Working through

society, man had the important task of adjusting heaven and earth, and preserving universal balance. Heaven was seen by the Confucian as the source of morality.

The metaphysical significance of Confucianism must have been difficult for ordinary people to appreciate fully. Confucian 'results' were obtained by the use of proverbs and stories of filial piety and by a system of sermons in the rural areas; this had declined in effectiveness by the late 19th century. But a 'basis' had also to be provided. This was done by recourse to the multitude of gods and spirits of Chinese religion and the local cults it absorbed. The system was turned into an animated version of the theory of Yin and Yang.

In the ancient system, gods and spirits

or demons were divided between heaven and earth respectively. Under later influence from Yin-Yang theory, gods became identified with Yang and demons with Yin.

Gods were of different kinds. Some were personified forces of Nature, while others were deified sages, buddhas and bodhisattvas, or saviours of mankind, taken from the more supernatural levels of Taoism and Buddhism. But many were former members of society: a human being contained during life both Yin and Yang or god and demon, both elements surviving as souls. It was believed that a powerful Yang soul, that of a virtuous or powerful person, might become a god; while the Yin soul of a person dying tragically and unexpectedly might be unprepared, and hence resentful, thus becoming a powerful demon.

An ingenious and rather sinister 'takeover' of the pantheon was gradually effected by the State. It took all the good, public-minded gods it could find, added to them by deifying people of noted virtue, and then placed them all in a gigantic celestial bureaucracy. This was an organization paralleling that of the worldly order but going much farther. It stretched into every institution of mankind, into areas beyond the reach of mortal officials.

Significantly, this hierarchy was not only set up but also controlled by the human bureaucracy. The head of the celestial government was the Jade or Pearly Emperor, the counterpart, of course, of the real emperor of China. Under him were boards of administration for controlling the forces of time and of Nature. There was a Ministry of Justice, comprising numerous city gods and presided over by a city god-in-chief. These gods were the counterparts of mortal officials in charge of provinces and districts of China, and individually they were based on temples in the major cities of their territories.

Some gods had dual, even triple roles, which added to the complexity and size of the pantheon. The kitchen god, for instance, was also the patron of professional cooks. The Chinese goddess of mercy is thought to have been an ancient local goddess before the advent of Buddhism, in which her role was to help in the salvation of Buddhist souls. But she is also represented with a baby on her arm and in this form she helped people who desired to have children.

A 3rd-century hero, seen as the embodiment of bravery, loyalty and righteousness, was known under seven names and was the patron of pawn shops, all kinds of friendly societies and sworn brotherhoods; in Hong Kong today he is even patron of the police. He was also a soldier god of wealth and, under another name, god of war. Some civic gods had a role in controlling man after death as well. The earth gods cared for graves. The city gods controlled souls in their districts and had some influence on the fate of Buddhist souls in purgatory.

Michael Holford

Shou-Lao, the god of long-life, holding a peach, a symbol of longevity and immortality, because it was thought that the peaches in the celestial orchard ripened once every 3000 years.

Japan

There is a parallel between the adoption of Christianity in England and that of Buddhism in Japan. Neither religion was indigenous to the country, and in both cases the derivation was not a direct one from source but through an intermediary: in the case of England not directly from Palestine but through Rome; in the case of Japan not directly from India but through China.

The Buddhism that percolated through to Japan in the 6th century of the Christian era was what is called Mahayana Buddhism, which fundamentally is an essentially liberal elaboration of Buddha's teachings with a tendency to compromise with foreign beliefs. On its way through Central Asia and China this Buddhism had absorbed Taoist and Confucian teachings and thus, by the time it reached Japan, contained philosophical modifications and theistic accretions and rituals unknown to Buddhism in its more primitive form.

The early Buddhist sects established in Japan in the Nara Period (623–784 AD) remained strictly Chinese in their use of Chinese styles in temple architecture, Chinese costumes, Chinese rites and even the Chinese language. With the dawn of the Heian Period (784–1185 AD), however, the Japanese founded two sects – *Tendai* and *Shingon* – of their own. While these sects certainly borrowed extensively from parent organizations on the Asian mainland, they nonetheless compromised sufficiently with the indigen-

ous Japanese religions to represent a true departure from a Chinese tradition that, until then, had been wholly dominant. Finally, while Buddhism was waning in India, the land of its origin, Japan produced in the Kamakura Period (1187–1333 AD) forms of Buddhism – Amidaism, Zen Buddhism, Nichiren – that not merely represented a great spiritual awakening but were distinctively Japanese in all their essential elements. Since that time no major developments have taken place.

The modern Japanese take religion calmly even indifferently. Like Christianity in Europe, Buddhism in Japan has left behind a rich heritage of art, architecture, music and literature; but as a vital religious force it is spent. There are new sects that appeal to a vociferous and usually ignorant minority and Zen still exerts an influence over a thinking few. But in general the role of Buddhism in modern Japan is merely to bury the dead and to keep their graves. It may seem paradoxical to say this of a religion that still has a priesthood, possesses scriptures, conducts regular services, maintains magnificent temples and large estates, administers schools and engages in social welfare. But among the intelligent young in Japan it is far more common to find a burning faith in Marxism than in Buddhism. Buddhism has become a matter of rituals; of services and of festivals; it has long since ceased to have an organic life of its own.

Allegiance to sectarian movements has grown steadily in many parts of the world since the end of the Second World War; but

nowhere have sects had quite the dramatic impact that they have had in Japan. The sects that have grown there have not been the Christian splinter movements but indigenous cults, sometimes embracing Shinto and Buddhist elements. Most of them have made very little impact outside Japan except among expatriate Japanese communities in Latin America and among a few American ex-servicemen who have married in Japan and been converted there.

A number of Japanese sects trace their origins to the 19th century or to the 1930s, but their dramatic growth has occurred only since 1945. That year marked the disruption of traditional life-patterns, of political authority and of the nationalist, ethnic and religious myth that had been fostered in Japan in and before the Second World War. To the shock of defeat was added the diffusion of American values by the occupying forces and, in particular, the establishment of official attitudes of tolerance in religious matters. Sects that had emerged earlier and suffered state prohibition revived in a favourable atmosphere for growth: their values were clearly divergent from those of the now discredited government. And new sects also emerged.

The Todaiji Temple at Nara, which contains the magnificent 53-foot-high image of Buddha Vairocana. Built in the 8th century by the Emperor Shomu, the temple testifies to the advance in cultural achievement which accompanied the adoption of Buddhist beliefs by Japan.

The Aztecs

Basically the Aztecs believed that beyond the world and the gods of nature there must be a Supreme Creator, whom they named Ometecuhtli (Omey-te-cu-tli) which means Two-Lord. As Creator he was thought to be two persons in one, for no creation could take place without the co-operation of male and female. Sometimes he is shown as a pair of very old people, and sometimes as a single being dressed half as a woman and half as a man.

It seems that Ometecuhtli was the product of thought by learned philosophers. Most of the Mexicans looked to the central fire-place in their homes as the shrine of the oldest of the gods. They called him Ueueteotl (Old Old God) and saw in him a symbol of the continuous creation of fire (equivalent to life) and the destruction of used-up things. He was a fountain of change at the heart of everything. His place in the heavens was the Pole Star, the pivot of the universe. The oldest image of this god, shown as an aged man seated with a fire-bowl balanced on his head, comes from the ruined pyramid of Cuicuilco, near Mexico City. It dates from more than 2000 years before the Spanish conquest of Mexico.

The Mexicans believed that 13 domed heavens circulated around the pivot of the universe. There was one for each of the visible planets, the sun, the moon, the clouds, the lightnings, the heat, and the rain; all contained within the dome of the fixed stars. Under the flat surface of the earth there were thought to be nine underworlds, the lowest of which were the lands of the dead.

As the central hearth-fire in the house was the pivot of earthly life, so the souls of the dead who eventually entered the fire in the lowest region of the universe ascended to a point where the Creator might send them back to earth. But this again was a philosophic idea. Most people appear to have expected a long stay in the underworld, which was after all a very happy place where people in the form of skeletons enjoyed a normal social life, presided over by the Lord and Lady of the Dead.

To the philosopher this multi-layered universe was like a single drop of water in the hand of the ineffable Creator, Ometecuhtli. But in general the Aztecs believed, much as did their Red Indian forbears, that the world was the back of a gigantic living creature.

The Aztec legends described Mother Earth as a strange monstrous being like a gigantic alligator. Long ago, the black Tezcatlipoca (Tez-caat-li-po-ca) or Smoking Mirror, so named from his symbol, a black obsidian mirror which appeared to smoke when the magicians looked into it to descry the future, had drawn the earth up from the great waters of creation. As he put his foot into the waters, the monstrous alligator snapped at it but the foot was not torn off until the terrible

god of magic and youthful energy had drawn the earth monster from the waters and made her back into the dry land. Since then the god has had but a single foot and his lonely footprint in the heavens is the constellation of the great Bear. According to another story, his foot was cut off when the doors of the underworld closed on his leg.

Tezcatlipoca was lord of the four directions on earth, East, South, West and North. He was also lord of the Nature gods when these other gods were developed.

A popular legend told of a cave in the universe where the Mother of the Gods gave birth to starry offspring. They were the 400 northerners, the 400 southerners, and the planets. Then she became pregnant again. The children were upset and planned to destroy the new child. Only the golden moon girl wanted to protect her mother.

When the new child was born, it proved to be a monstrous sun-before-the-earthly-sun. It was Tezcatlipoca armed as a warrior. He destroyed all the stars. Then, seeing his sister among the slain, he realized that her head might yet live, so he cut it off and cast her into the sky, where the head with golden bells on her cheeks can still be seen as the Moon. Each day when the sun emerges in our real world, we see that the stars of night are slain, but they are reborn as the moon comes among them, grows pregnant and

then meets her ever-recurring end.

Once the earth was established, the gods created men. Three times the human race became too self-opinionated and had to be destroyed, at about 2000-year intervals. They were destroyed by the fire, the waters, the winds. Now the present human race, who were made by the gods from the beloved maize plant which is still the sustenance of mankind, are being tested.

The end of this universe will come from a terrible earthquake. Whether after this fourth sun, the earth will be re-populated by another better race remains to be experienced in the future.

On each re-creation a new sun was made by the gods. At the beginning of the present creation they made a great offering place at Teotihuacan. There they met for four days, waiting for one of them to cast himself into the fire. At last from a distance there came a miserably ill and poverty-stricken god. He had no reason to continue as he was, so he voluntarily cast himself into the fire. Blazing, and blue with magic power, he flew into the heavens as Tonatiyu (Ton-a-tiyu) the Lord of Fate, the sun. The sun appeared every day, and each day had its separate fate for people, so the count of time which the fortune tellers used was based simply on the sun.

The sun was very brave, the source of all brightness and glory. He had his special

C. Reyes-Valerio

Bodleian Library Colour Filmstrip

Above *Coatlicue, the Aztec goddess of the earth, mother of life, death and the gods.* **Right** *The Aztec water goddess tempting Quetzalcoatl, like the earth waiting for fertility from the 'breath of life', the wind which brought the refreshing rains.* **Facing page** *Three times the human race destroyed itself through pride, according to Aztec tradition, and a new sun was made by the gods for each re-creation. A representation of the sun is at the centre of this calendar stone, c1500 AD. Almost 12 feet wide, it was found in Mexico City.*

heaven for brave warriors who had been sacrificed and for women who had died in childbirth. These warriors, dressed as eagles, lifted the sun to the top of the sky every morning; the women lowered him down each evening into the underworld.

All the time the sun was thirsting from the great heat. So he had to be nourished and cooled by offerings of the red cactus-fruit (which meant human hearts and blood). Only a few need be sacrificed to keep the sun moving in the sky, but the sacrifice must never be neglected or the human race would die from the fire which is caused by a motionless sun.

Of all deaths the most glorious was to be sacrificed to the sun. The sun himself sacrificed his victims in the sky as he rose and the stars died. On earth the stars were represented by the spotted quails, which were killed every morning at sunrise. Sometimes people saw at his lucky time the little brother of the sun, Piltzintecuhtli (the Divine Prin-

celing), the planet Mercury.

Sometimes the Great Star was visible in the form of the morning star lifting up the sun. This was a symbol of Quetzalcoatl, the god of the air and of human civilization. Sometimes in the evening they saw the Great Star as the evening star, pushing the sun down into the red sunset. This was the symbol of the evil twin, Xolotl, who was an animal creature, leading people into sin and working black witchcraft against humanity and against the other gods.

The other planets were also gods: and so were the major stars. The groups of stars through which the sun passed were the houses of 13 gods. These were very like our 12 signs of the zodiac, though the Mexicans knew that there were 13 moons in any one year, but that one of them was always incomplete. Thus there was always a relationship between earthly events and the shapes in the sky where the gods had their palaces.

Earth was the domain of the powerful and demonic Tezcatlipoca, who had four forms. He was the yellow Tezcatlipoca as god of the sunrise in the East, of bravery and growing crops. The blue Tezcatlipoca was the fertility spirit and the patron spirit of the Aztec nation. In the West he became the red Tezcatlipoca, who died by being skinned alive so that maize could be given to mankind. In this form he was Xipe Totec, Our Lord the Flayed One. In the North he was the black Tezcatlipoca in the land where the sun never shone, where he became the ruler of all forms of black magic and devilry.

This religion suited warriors and the astro-

nomer-priests but it had little meaning for the farmers who produced the food on which the people lived.

The almost passive centre of the farmers' religion was the maize plant. It had many spirits, but was basically the maize god Sinteotl (Sin-tay-otl). This divine power within the basic foodstuff of ancient America was nurtured by Mother Earth. He loved pretty Chalchihuitlicue, the flirtatious mistress of the rain god Tlaloc, and was cleansed by the winds sent by Quetzalcoatl.

When the first green ears appeared on the maize, the girls took some and danced with their hair thrown loose and with naked breasts, for the maize was now the pretty young goddess Xilonen.

There was also a good deal of interest in the weather and the directions of the winds, which was natural in an agricultural community. The peasant was always aware of the reliance of the community on the powers of nature. But it was realized that these powers might well be capricious. The water goddess, for instance, was described as a brilliant and capricious young woman. She controlled whirlpools as well as the quiet fertilizing rivers. At one of her ceremonies her priests had the right to beat and take clothing and jewellery from any unfortunate passer-by.

In the home of this goddess, where she lived with her husband Tlaloc, the god of all sources of water, there was continuous warm drizzle and brilliant rainbows shone over the masses of flowers and sweet smelling shrubs. They had four servants, the Tlaloques or Little Rains. These were cloud spirits who reclined in the rolling vapours, carrying different kinds of rain. One came from the East and brought the golden spring rains to fertilize the soil; another from the South brought warm blue rains to make all things fruitful; a third from the West brought the red rains which made the plants sleep as winter came; lastly the northern rain was dangerous, for he came from the realm where the sun never shone and so his rains brought destruction and were mostly hailstones.

What would the rain do without the winds? The Aztecs said of Quetzalcoatl that as god of the wind he came to sweep the way for the rains and in this form he was a breath of life which made the vegetation of the earth sway like a serpent covered with green feathers. When his time of power was well advanced, the naughty water goddess decided to tempt him. She stripped naked and sat before him with her beautiful vulva opened, like the earth waiting for fertility from the breath of life which was the wind. The somewhat grotesque painting of this in the Codex Laud also combines the idea that the goddess of whirlpools tempted the wind and so caused the great breakers on the sea in hurricanes.

But Quetzalcoatl was also the morning star and his path, first rising in the heavens and then sinking, was also linked with the fertility myth. And it was the key of the story of the divine King Quetzalcoatl.

The divine king brought blessings to the earth, improved agriculture, made the arts flourish and covered palaces with jewels and precious feather decorations. He taught a philosophy of gentleness and austere asceticism, offering blood from his ears and limbs daily to the gods in the outer heaven. But when the revolutions of time brought the stars into a pattern which meant that his planet was setting, he was tempted. The goddess approached him and visited his court, bringing with her many magicians and enchanters, among whom was the black Tezcatlipoca. At a festival she offered the god-king a bowl of alcoholic pulque prepared from the agave heart. Then as he became intoxicated she offered him magic mushrooms and induced a trance-like ecstasy in which he abandoned his austerity and raped her.

On awakening, appalled at his break with the ascetic code of priestly behaviour, Quetzalcoatl left Mexico. He gave over his power to Tezcatlipoca and sailed into the sun, where his heart burnt up and ascended again as the morning star. Already there was a confusion between the god and the first king of the Toltecs, who was dedicated to the worship of Quetzalcoatl.

In the Quetzalcoatl myth, an account of wind and rain and the passing seasons, which promoted fertility and then passed on, had expanded into a universal parable of the human condition. We all follow this path of development, which ends in loss of energy and eventual death. We also share something of all primitive religion within our own personalities, for the gods of old Mexico, and of many other places, are expressions of images which lie deep in the structure of the human personality.

The Incas

Within four centuries the Inca family expanded from rulers of part of a small town to a semi-divine tribe of which the head, the Sapa Inca, ruled an immense empire which they termed *Tahuantinsuyu*, the Four Quarters, to imply that their father the sun god destined them to rule the entire known earth.

In the mid-11th century, at about the time of the Norman Conquest of Britain, a family of American Indians came from the East and ascended the mountains into a civilized country which had broken up into warring tribal troups. Their legend tells us that they were commanded to find the very centre, the navel or *Cuzco*, of the earth. To ascertain this they carried a wedge of gold, symbol of a sun ray, and at each stopping place they placed the wedge upon the ground to see if it would sink into the earth and disappear. This at last happened when Inca Manco and his sister Mama Occlo, who were the only survivors of the family, came to a little mountain town near the headwaters of the Apurimac river. They were allowed to rule half of the town which they now named The Cuzco, and although they were respected because of the mystery of their origin, it was not until the reign of their great-grandson that the Incas ruled the whole of the town.

In Cuzco the great sun temple was surrounded by smaller buildings which held the lesser gods of all the peoples of the empire, as if they were servants waiting to obey their master. There was only One more powerful than the sun. Inside the sun temple was a wall covered with gold. Upon it there were figures of the sun, moon, thunder, and rainbow. The first humans were there and the first Inca. Then there were the constellations of stars and in their midst an open blank space.

This centrepiece of the golden wall was always empty. It represented the mystery of the Creator, Viracocha, the Breath of Life who was everywhere unseen but eternally giving life, even to father sun.

Below *In honour of their great father the sun, the Incas celebrated elaborate festivals of feasting and rejoicing: wooden beaker showing a ceremonial procession.*

Michael Holford

The Mayas

American Indians speaking dialects of the Maya languages form the greater part of the Mexican states of Yucatan and Chiapas. They are also an important part of the population of British Honduras, Guatemala, Honduras and El Salvador. They are a short, thick set, brown-skinned people with the straight black hair of the American Indians. There is some mystery about them because so little is known about their existence before the early centuries of the Christian era, when they first began to erect stone buildings.

In all probability the Maya had settled in their homeland as groups of small farmers, cultivating maize, peppers, manioc, pumpkins, vanilla, cocoa and cochineal. They collected rubber in the forests, hunted jaguars, peccaries (wild pig) and alligators.

The civilization was based on religion. The high priest of a city ranked equally with the *Halach Uinic* (ruler of men), who in his turn had been previously educated as an adept in religious magic. They worshipped a Creator who lived beyond the sky and who was both male and female. There was Mother Earth, usually depicted as a gigantic monster – alligator, toad and turtle combined – who swam around in the waters of the reedy marsh of Creation. Above her was the sky, with a layer for each of the planets, and spheres of movement for the sun and moon. Below her were the under-worlds where the heavenly bodies passed when out of sight. All around her were the spirits of rain and thunder. She was attended by the deities of the food plants and animals. To the Maya all Nature was alive, constantly dying and being born.

It was an orderly, fatalistic universe. The movements of the heavenly bodies in their regular courses prognosticated the movements of fate. Each day had its fortune, each period of 20 days had an overriding influence. Each year had its agricultural magics. However, when counting long periods of time the Maya used a period they called a *tun* of 360 days. They multiplied the tun by powers of 20 (to 20 tuns, 400, 8000, 160,000 tuns and so on) in order to deal with astronomical calculations which in some way reflected the history of the gods both past and future. When they had to put these long calculations into practical terms of the agricultural year they had to use elaborate 'distance numbers' to find the exact day and season that they were writing about. Venturing into this complicated field it soon becomes clear that the Maya loved numbers and could express ideas through them almost as if they were making computerized poetry. They proved their accuracy by predicting eclipses, transits of Venus, and running a moon calendar.

Facing page *A Maya priest, holding his ceremonial staff, stands over a man who is mutilating his own tongue by passing through it a cord set with thorns: stone relief of the early 8th century* AD. *The Mayans also offered human sacrifices to their gods, especially to the rain gods in an annual ceremony.*

The Maya offered human sacrifices, and the offering of victims to the rain gods was an annual ceremony at Chichen Itza. In the present century two expeditions have searched the great 'well' in the limestone rock. They have recovered bones of the victims together with a great treasure of gold, jade, images of rubber and carvings in bone which had been cast into the well each year, as entreaty for the spring rains which would make the vital maize crop prosper. However although the Maya offered human sacrifices on other occasions they more frequently offered animals and plants to their gods.

Most of the Yucatec temples were decorated with complex representations of Chac, the Lord of the Rains. His mask is easily recognizable with its projecting curled snout. He is often shown carrying his thunder-axe in the paintings on the books. A popular method of calling his attention was to burn 'Pom' incense, balls of raw rubber. The thick smoke rose up like storm clouds, and the god was supposed to see the signal and send his messengers with magical jars of water which they poured through the storm clouds.

People enjoyed the religious festivals which occurred once every 20 days. They came to witness the ceremonies which were mostly dramatic representations of the legends of the gods. It was all very glorious to watch the masked priests dancing in their feathered garments, to sing the chants, and to be present at the sacrificial ceremonies. Of course some of the occasions of human sacrifice were both fearful and exciting, and there were those mysterious moments when the ordinary people were not allowed to witness what the priests were doing in the dark houses on top of the temple platforms.

Carved shell depicting a Maya priest: the Maya survive in large numbers in Central America and their ancient gods have been absorbed into the modern world as kind-hearted saints.

Museum of the American Indian

Brazil

When it was first discovered by Europeans, the coast of Brazil was populated by a number of tribes which nearly all had the same customs and shared the Tupi language. They lived in stockaded villages, several hundred inhabitants to each house, and four houses to each village. They hunted for game in the forest, fished, farmed, and waged war on each other in a systematic way to capture prisoners who were later ritually executed and then eaten.

There are few overt references to cannibalism in their mythology. The main figure is called Maira and is half-way between a god and a hero. He is sometimes called the Walker, in honour of the great journeys the Tupi excelled in, and sometimes the Maker. He did not, however, create the world in its entirety, but transformed what was already in existence into an order in which human beings could live: he was thus a culture hero, giving the main rudiments of their social life to the Indians.

One myth deals with Maira in the shape of a young child who, when wandering in the woods, was met by a poor widow and her children gathering food. Thinking he was about to stop them, the children began to beat him, an act in which he encouraged them – for as the blows fell, it began to rain edible roots, fruit and vegetables, in fact all the food plants the Tupi now grow. Later, when Maira had reassumed adult form, he visited the Indians. Though wanting to give him proper homage for his generosity, the Indians also wished to be quite sure of his identity. They made him jump over three fires, in the second of which he died, his head exploding like thunder.

It is the usual fate of a culture hero to be a stranger, and to die at the hands of those he has befriended. Myths from other tribes show that the theme of the young boy producing food plants when he is beaten is allied to initiation rites, when a youth becomes a man. These rites usually deal with a number of novices at the same time. The Tupi initiation rite, however, was individualistic: a youth proved himself by executing a prisoner, after which he went into seclusion for some months, endured ordeals such as the scarification of his body, took a new name, and was then able to marry.

A jaguar was sometimes dealt with in the same way as a prisoner. An explanatory story from the Tupi-speaking Urubu tribe tells how a man avenged his brother's death by following the cannibalistic murderer to an underground village of jaguars, and killing the chief who was dressed up in his ritual feather regalia. It is this feather regalia which all men now wear, especially for ceremonial occasions, that was originally the property of the jaguar; and other beliefs show us that this jaguar is an aspect of the culture hero himself.

The feather head-dress is an image of the sun, and the hero lives in the house of the sun in the east. At night he has to pass from the west underground, when he puts on a jaguar shape, to go back to his birthplace. Often the souls of the dead are thought to accom-

pany the daytime sun, and anyone dressing up in the feather regalia is imitating this heroic state. Significantly, the Tupi prisoner was dressed up in just this way, and various rites transformed him into something approaching a chief as well, that is, a representative of the village where he was to be executed. More particularly, he was transformed into what became a kind of ritual brother-in-law.

A study of mythology shows that the jaguar is regarded as a brother-in-law throughout South America. Sex always has curious associations with eating and the killing of game, a symbolic equation that has much to do with the operation of the incest taboo. The consequence of this taboo, of course, is to stop a man marrying in his own immediate family, however that is defined. Everyone being in the same position, the simplest solution is to give your sister to another man as his wife in exchange for his sister. When such an exchange is not possible, the husband has to pay for his wife by working for his in-laws. This happened regularly among the Tupi, and such were the antagonisms created by the system that the same word did duty both for brother-in-law and for enemy. The word was 'tobajara', meaning in effect, the rival with whom you have a competition for honour. The jaguar, who rivals man in killing game, is used in myth as the figure to denote the rival in sexuality and marriage.

The enemy captive was a rival of this kind. He was given a wife by his captor and so, like any husband, had to do menial work for him. But he was unlike the usual run of husbands in that he was treated with much affection instead of with the customary disdain and avoidance, and indeed he was called 'the loved one'.

Here we may see an interesting parallel with the vegetation gods of the Middle East, dying yearly amid the laments of the women. However, the Tupi women, even the prisoner's wife herself, made no bones about eating the prisoner. They were even more voracious cannibals than the men, who saw the rite partly as an opportunity to gain prestige for themselves. Throughout the country, the ideal of men is to be hard in body and mind, to be wakeful, abstinent, capable of great physical endurance and of undergoing painful ordeals such as scarification, liquid pepper in the eyes, fasting, or being stung by the largest and most venomous wasps and ants.

This masculine ideal is set against the feminine vice of softness and sleepiness. Several mythologies tell how death came to men because they were too sleepy to answer the call of a tree whose bark regularly comes off in sheets, and which had the gift of immortality.

Masculine virtue is thus aimed at immortality and power. The lethargy, which all are afflicted with, stems from mythological times when it was the women rather than the men who had charge of things. The story is of wide occurrence in South America. Sometimes it describes how the women found what were to be the sacred flutes of the tribe, the representatives of the ancestors, by which means they kept the men in subjection. Nowadays the men, having successfully revolted, have the care of these instruments together with that of the entire religious apparatus and it is death for a woman or an uninitiated youth to see them.

Tupi myth also tells of this reign of women, who did all the work while the men, who had no genitals, lolled in their hammocks like children. The women satisfied their sexuality by calling a giant snake from under the ground, on whose raised head they took their pleasure. This custom continued till a young boy discovered what was happening and cut off the snake's head. The women took offence and left. It was then that Maira took charge by fashioning male members for the men out of the snake's body and sewing them in place, reserving the head for himself. Appeased in this way, the women returned, and the men took command.

This story deals with an adolescent fantasy which often goes with initiation. Tupi youths tied a piece of string around their foreskins to hide their shame, while men wore the penis sheath. The significance of this can be seen among the Bororo, where youths live in their mothers' houses until they are initiated, when they must go to the Men's House at the centre of the village. There they are given a penis sheath and are then ready for marriage. During this lengthy rite, the penis sheath is called the boy's wife, and is a substitute for the sister he cannot marry: instead he marries the daughter of the man who gives him the sheath. The myth of the reign of women quite clearly bears a close relationship to this situation.

Initiation always deals with the separation of a boy from his mother, and his adoption into the society of men. Often one finds the institution of a Men's House or type of club in tribes like the Mundurucu, where men have to live with their wives' families, instead of the wife living with the husband's family: it becomes a 'home from home' where the strains of being a perpetual in-law are not felt. At the same time it is the place where the men celebrate their independence from women in religious form, with the help of masks, dances, songs, musical instruments and mysteries.

Besides the competition for honour between men there is thus a battle between the sexes. The serpent, who is the private lover of women, has to be killed by men whereupon a sound relation between the sexes can be established through marriage. The northwestern tribes tell a story which is a complication of this theme. It deals with a young man suspected of being a cannibal, who is killed by his own people and turns into a palm tree. The sacred flutes, often kept under water when not needed, are carved from the trunk of this tree, and a beer made from its fruit. Whenever an important man dies, his body is burnt and the ashes mixed with the beer, which everyone then drinks in commemoration of him. It is all part of the initiation theme, for the hut where the novices are secluded is often thought of as a cannibalistic monster, serpent or water-demon, which has to be killed for the youths to emerge as newborn men.

The name of the cannibal palm-tree spirit is Jurupari, who has become one of the bogey-men throughout Brazil, for those of European and Negro descent as much as for the Indians. He is the master of the jungle, and is much feared. Among the Cashinawa tribe elements of the Jurupari myth appear in the figure of a Rolling Head, who creates the rainbow – the form taken by the great serpent when it is killed – and the moon.

The Tupi say that the moon was once a man who committed incest with his sister, and the Jurupari stories may have a similar background. In any case, it is this moon man who must be ritually killed, like the Tupi prisoner, in imitation of the moon's monthly birth and death. Among the Bororo people, this moon man is the brother of the sun. Among the Arawak tribes, the sun and moon are also brothers, the sun creating useful animals and the moon harmful ones. Sometimes they are figured as the jaguar and the anteater – a dangerous animal when roused – who quarrel over who is the stronger. The jaguar says that he is, since he eats flesh while the other eats only ants, but the ant-eater replies that this can only be proved by an examination of their faeces. By a trick he exchanges the jaguar's excrement for his own, leaving the jaguar humiliated.

The Tupi also have a story concerning twins. Their mother is the wife of Maira who leaves her when she disbelieves in his magical powers. Already pregnant with his child, she follows him but is seduced by Mikur the opossum, who fathers the other child on her; she then comes to a village of jaguars where she is killed, and the twins are brought up by a jaguar grandmother. When they are adult they avenge their mother by killing all the jaguars but one, who is allowed to escape by Mikur's son, and then go in search of their father. When they find him he puts them through a number of tests and ordeals, such as having to pass through the Clashing Rocks, in which Mikur's son is always killed and has to be brought back to life by his brother.

There are many possible interpretations of such a myth. One certainly deals with the distinction between the mortal body and the immortal soul. The fact that the opossum's son dies and is brought back to life points to the particular manifestation of this belief in shamanism. A shaman is a man (occasionally, in South America, a woman) able to fall into trance and converse with spirits which help him or her to divine the future, diagnose disease and perform cures. The trance is likened to a death, especially that mock death known as 'playing possum', from which comes part of the significance of this animal.

Shamanism is sometimes hereditary, father training son in the techniques of the craft. More often the vocation descends on a man, after a period of psychological disorder or shock, in which he rushes into the woods and returns unable to think or speak clearly and smelling like a corpse – opossums, it should be noted, also have an unpleasant odour. He is then trained to recognize the spirit which confronted him, usually that of a bird or animal.

The Land without Evil was Maira's own land, and several localities were favoured for

Harald Schultz

Man wearing the skins of a jaguar and a wild cat. The jaguar plays an important part in Brazilian Indian beliefs. In some cases the hero who gave a tribe its culture and social organization was a jaguar; others believe that the sun takes the form of a jaguar at night and many of the shamans, or priests, are possessed by the jaguar spirit.

this paradise – in the sky, in the middle of the continent, and on an island in the Atlantic. One group of Tupi searching for it inland wandered all the way up the Amazon, where they were met by Spaniards going in the opposite direction looking for El Dorado.

Tupi myth says that Maira set fire to the world and then flooded it, as a punishment for men's ingratitude. Ge-speaking Indians still believe this may happen; one of their ceremonies, which takes place round a sun-pole, is partly intended to ward off this danger. These Indians originally lived in a part of Brazil plagued by drought and flood, so their belief is understandable. South of Brazil, however, there is the idea that a Celestial Jaguar will one day make an end to the world, and in Brazil proper many tribes think of eclipses as the swallowing of sun or moon by a jaguar, as a punishment for the sins of mankind. Tupi messianism – belief in the coming of a saviour god – is all part of this pattern: it is still concerned with the Jaguar who gave them culture, who made them compete among themselves for honour, and who must be placated if they are not to eat each other up entirely.

North America

The United States

Strangely enough, the wealth of American Indian culture has had little or no effect on the mainstream. It has retreated into a kind of limbo, accessible for ethnological or anthropological study, but no longer an entirely living tradition open to folk borrowings and diffusions. But the other non-white folk culture of the United States is the broadest, most effective and most pervasive tributary of them all.

The Negro contribution is undeniably the greatest single ethnic tributary to the folklore mainstream. But there is also another category that adds further dimensions to the American traditions, because of the nature of the nation's history. This includes the more heroic and romantic of the traditional occupations associated with that epic history.

Farming itself was once such an occupation, in the days of pioneering when a farmer was also hunter, woodsman and fighter of Indians. Eventually these occupations became separated; but they left behind the remarkable lore of the frontiersman. This was mainly a collection of heroic legends telling of Daniel Boone and Davy Crockett on the old frontier, Kit Carson and the mountain men in the far West. But there were also plenty of tall tales about adventures experienced and marvels seen. There is the tale of the 'wonderful hunt', for instance, in which a crack shot manages to kill a huge array of game with only one bullet, thanks to some fortuitous ricochets and other unlikely bits of luck. Variations on this theme crop up in nearly every region, ascribed to different hunters.

Other equally dramatic occupations became prominent. American seamen off the New England coast developed their own lore to add to the British seafaring traditions they had inherited. Inland, on the great commercial freeway of the Mississippi, the river men evolved their special songs, customs, taboos and superstitions, and of course their own heroes. The lumbering industry developed its set of folkways and beliefs, often with traces of Scandinavian lore from the many Swedish and Norwegian lumberjacks. The tales are especially rich, and tell of haunted trees, magical trees and trees that are impossibly high.

Railroading later brought new tales, legends and songs into the mainstream. Songs like 'Casey Jones', for instance, or 'John Henry' which tells of a Negro culture

In Uncle Tom's Cabin (1852), *Harriet Beecher Stowe created an idealistic portrait of a faithful Negro slave, whose acceptance of white beliefs and customs was complete; in fact, during the time of slavery, and afterwards, the Negro created his own tradition from the white materials accessible to him, and has enriched the whole of American folklore by feeding back into it this altered material: illustration to* Uncle Tom's Cabin.

hero who died in competition with a track-laying machine. Coal miners in the East added their own variations to old British and European superstitions about mines, and these were themselves increased, as were mining ghost tales, by gold seekers in mid-19th century California. More recently, the steel industry cast up a quasi-folk hero in Joe Magarac, a Hungarian-American man of steel, who paddled unconcernedly in the molten metal.

Prominent among the special characteristics of mainstream folklore is the American love of story-telling, with the emphasis on particular types of comic stories. One of the favourite kinds is the short 'anecdote' which tells of some brief humorous events or action, and often features an eccentric person, a trickster or a dullard.

A slightly longer story is often called a 'yarn', and may be a straightforward account of an experience of the narrator or someone known to him. Old-timers who had had long and eventful lives were supposed to be great tellers of yarns, whether they had been sailors, buffalo hunters or gold miners. But a well-told yarn may often acquire a little extra dramatic effect and

audience interest by exaggeration and elaboration; if it does it may become a 'windy' or 'tall tale', an American speciality.

American folklore is still developing. As fast as pop culture absorbs folk elements, more is churned out. Some of it is naturally adapted from old motifs; superstitions that were once ascribed to horses and carriages, for instance, now recur in terms of cars, and there are even tales of phantom automobiles. A ghost story involving a real car is told, with innumerable variations, all across the United States. The story is of a young man who picks up a pretty girl hitch-hiker. She directs him to her home, but on the way there she disappears from the car. The driver visits the house, describes the girl, and is told that she was the householder's daughter who died years before. This plot occurs in folktales all over the world, and the modern American versions owe nothing to mass culture.

Equally authentic is the mass of folklore found among modern servicemen. This includes hero tales told among the Marines and stories of phantom ships like the one detected off the West Coast by naval radar. All the old taboos arise again in modern dress.

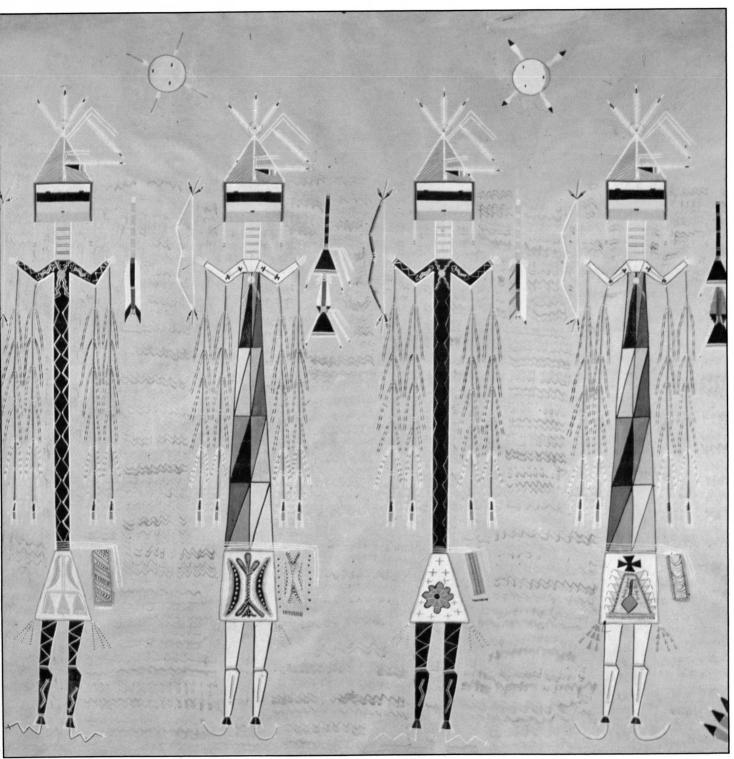

Navaho Indians

America's largest Indian tribe today, the Navaho live on a sizeable reservation that sprawls across the Arizona-New Mexico border. It is poor, eroded, infertile land but like so much of the south-west of the United States it is an area of spectacular natural beauty – magnificently coloured sand and stone, wind-sculpted rock formations, towering hills and high rocky tableland. This visual splendour might be economically useless to an agricultural people but it is fundamentally important to the Navaho. Their religion and their ordinary way of life, which are in any case interrelated, are remarkably attuned to Nature, to the en-

vironment. It is hardly surprising that their religious belief and practice should contain much that is extremely beautiful: the poetry and music of the great ritual chants, the glorious 'sand paintings', the eternal, renewable beauty of Changing Woman, their chief deity.

Changing Woman is an Earth Mother figure, ageing with the seasons, who is restored to girlhood each spring. From her union with the sun, also a major deity, sprang the Twins, hero figures and models of virile warriors. Changing Woman was the Creator who gave life to First Man and First Woman, and taught them all their wisdom and lore, including magic; they in turn created the universe and the Earth Surface People who are mankind.

Navaho myths are illustrated by their sand paintings; the paintings are done to the accompaniment of sacred chants which express the relationship between the spirits and medicine-men: spirits from the 'Shooting Chant' holding sacred objects.

Apart from these major figures, who have wide-ranging powers that involve them in the most important myths, the Navaho mythology includes an immense array of supernatural beings. Some of these, like Changing Woman and the sun, are included among the 'Holy People'. Others are personalized natural forces – Thunder People, Wind People and so on. Several are supernatural helpers, teachers and intermediaries between men and the Holy People.

All the Navaho gods, except Changing Woman, exhibit a share of unpredictability: they are highly humanized, containing elements of both good and evil, although there are a few demonic figures who are almost wholly evil. Hence the gods are accessible to human propitiation and prayer, capable of kindly and protective acts but at other times capable of wilful destruction.

In a sense it is almost wrong to describe these figures as gods. More accurately, they are supernatural beings and powers who exist quite separately from human existence except when summoned by prayer and magic. The myths in which they appear are immensely rich, highly sophisticated in their symbolism and complex interrelationships. But the beings tend generally to be left in the myths, except when called upon to exert their powers for some special purpose, either curative or protective. Moreover, the Navaho have no concept of a life after death in which the dead join the gods in a happy hunting ground. Their afterworld has nothing to do with the Holy People: it is a vaguely defined semi-limbo, far from pleasant. Little attention is given to death in Navaho belief: theirs is a religion of life.

Amulets, protective magic and taboos are highly important to the Navaho. 'Gall medicine' (from animal gall) protects the wearer against witchcraft, as does a wide variety of herbs, shells, carved images of animals and the ever-present pollen, always very powerful to the Navaho. A white shell bead protects the work of a tanner from going wrong; a squirrel's tail tied to a cradle protects a baby.

Finally, there are the taboos which are usually intended to prevent offences against supernatural beings. The Navaho never intentionally kill coyotes, snakes, bears or certain other animals; special rituals must be performed to cleanse someone who has killed one of these creatures by accident. A Navaho will never comb his hair at night, or step over someone sleeping, or go near a tree that has been struck by lightning.

These beliefs and the many other Navaho taboos seem to parallel closely our own society's ancient taboos, which we call superstitions. But for the Navaho, with his all-pervasive religious awareness, they are closely connected with the 'proper way of doing things' – respect for the Holy People, the ceremonies, the natural environment and the rest of the tribe. The Navaho's religious life and worldly life are one and the same. At its best, this unity brings with it an impressive serenity and stability.

Pueblo Indians

Of all American Indians north of the Rio Grande, the Pueblo developed the most impressive civilization. Their culture had matured some time before the Spanish arrived to give them the name we now use (Pueblo means 'village'); and it remained at those heights in spite of later white incursions and ever-shrinking reservations. Indeed, much of the admirable culture of other south-western tribes – the Navaho especially – was borrowed from the Pueblo.

The cult of the *kachina* dancers comes in for much attention, probably because the gorgeous masks and symbolic kachina dolls have been more accessible to anthropologists and tourists than other more secret cult elements. The kachinas impersonate supernatural beings (and the impersonation can reach the level of full ritual possession); ritually disguised, they are important to many tribal ceremonies.

The supernatural beings seem to keep to themselves, until specifically summoned by a ceremony to exercise their power on human behalf. And if they are called properly, if the rites are performed correctly, the spirits cannot refuse to respond.

The spirits themselves occur in large quantities, often in vaguely defined and overlapping groups. The Cloud Beings are prominent, and have criss-crossing ties among various cults and societies, most obviously among the rain-makers. Other spirit groups include the Corn Maidens, the Star Spirits and Dawn Spirits, the rain-bringing Lightning (or Storm) gods who are related to the Cloud Beings.

Out of this welter of supernaturals crowded into the Pueblo environment, a few figures can be separated out as important single deities. Sun Father or Sun Old Man seems to be paramount among the Zuni; Moon and Morning Star are both High Gods (Moon is female to some Pueblo, but male to Hopi and Tewa); Corn Mother holds a dominant position among the Keres. The archetypal Twin Heroes appear among the Zuni as War Brothers, giving power to warrior societies and featuring in hero and trickster myths. Their grandmother, Spider Old Woman, is a powerful deity although she is identified with an actual creature; her power flows towards war, but in myth she is a benevolent healer and intercessor. The ubiquitous trickster Coyote also appears as an intercessor, aiding human development and, like Prometheus, bringing fire. Water Serpent, another individual animal god, is connected with flood and other watery disasters, and also in myth with fertility and sexuality.

The Indians have their share of animistic belief, attributing supernatural power to anything and everything. Stones, mountains, rivers and the like have power; they either have humanized spirits associated with them, or are 'containers' of magical power.

Ancestral worship, or something very like it, occurs as well: the deceased chiefs of cults and medicine societies join the Cloud People and take on supernatural aspects: enemy dead killed in war and scalped are transformed (by a scalp ceremony) into rain-making spirits; for the Hopi, just about all the tribe's dead become Cloud People. Sometimes it is said that wicked Indians will undergo punishment after death: dead witches become mere smoke, without substance, unable to join the Cloud People.

Right *Plumed arms outstretched and bells jingling, the Eagle Dancers of Santa Clara perform at an annual ceremony in July; eagles were kept for a year by Pueblo families and then killed and sent to carry messages to the gods.*

Iroquois Indians

The origins of the Iroquois, the most advanced group of American Indians north of the Pueblos, are lost in the confusion of archeological time. Their legends assume that they were always in their historical homeland of New England.

The Iroquois had many gods, who were essentially the powers of Nature. It was very apparent to the Indians that they were dependent upon the goodwill of powers beyond direct human knowledge; the wind and the rain, the passing seasons, the lightning and the sunshine, the forests and the rivers, all were active and seemingly alive. Thus it was felt that men must act so as to propitiate the living powers of the universe they saw around them.

There were many tricky and dangerous spirits to be charmed away, and they were conjured with in the dances of the False Face society, so called because of the carved wooden masks worn by the performers for them. Unhappily there were cruel and deadly human enemies, and they were weakened by magic and defeated by the young warriors. The overshadowing presence above was felt mostly through the spiritual life-force known as Orenda, coming in varying degrees to human families.

Some families descended from great ladies whose magical powers were greater than most other ancestresses. Some chieftainesses had sons and nephews who were vehicles of the inner wisdom gleaned through contact with ancestral spirits. Some men were given great powers direct from the spirit world. Such men were like lone pines standing high among the forest trees. Such a one was Dekanawida, the law-giver and friend of his fellow philosopher and lawmaker, Hiawatha.

Hiawatha was a Mohawk, but his work began among the Onondaga tribe. The opposition from the Onondaga chief Wathatotaro was so intense that he caused Hiawatha's daughters to be murdered. The teacher then went to the Oneida who persuaded the Mohawk to join them and to invite the Cayuga to the gathering. Then the three nations approached the Onondaga again, and this time Wathatotaro agreed provided that they would bring the Seneca to join them, the Seneca agreed and the whole five nations joined into a league of mutual friendship and protection which they called 'The Extended Lodge', meaning that the Council Lodges of each nation were now joined together.

Dekanawida was traditionally of Huron birth, but his parents tried to drown him because of a prophecy that he would cause trouble to the nation. He survived, and later left home to live among the Iroquois, where he was the great law-giver and was also regarded as a prophet and magician. He is ranked by the Iroquois among the demigods.

Wathatotaro has become also a demigod of a thoroughly terrifying demonic character in more recent Iroquois belief. He was regarded as having strange powers in his own day, and was renowned for pride, sexual prowess and strength, as well as a subtle mind. These qualities made him a very great chief and in spite of his stubborn resistance to the idea of a union of the tribes he was able to gain a predominant position for his Onondaga people within that group. They had 14 hereditary chieftainships in the council of the confederacy whereas each of the other four nations only had ten each. The chief holding Wathatotaro's position was to be the only one empowered to summon a meeting of the confederation.

Thus the three most important chiefs who were concerned with making the league became demigods in tradition and entered the realms of the legendary while still remembered as historical persons.

In the modern world the Iroquois people have become normal citizens, with special treaty rights securing their home reservations from total assimilation into the national states. Many of their younger men earn big wages as steel erectors. In this dangerous trade they have earned a reputation for fearlessness. This appears to have replaced initiation into warrior societies.

An Iroquois philosopher and law-maker, who later became a demigod, Hiawatha lived during the 16th century; in his narrative poem **Hiawatha** *Longfellow used the name of this great Iroquois chieftain, but all other material is Algonquin: in this illustration to the poem, Hiawatha's grandmother Nokomis attempts to dissuade her grandson from setting off on a dangerous quest.*

Eric Cross

In Great Plains Indian mythology, the buffalo were believed to have once been a race of savage, horned human beings, the predecessors and hunters of man. **Left** *The Sioux conception of the happy hunting ground was of a place where warriors were borne through the sky on magnificent steeds; birds were believed to carry messages to heaven: the* **Sky People,** *a modern Indian painting.*

Great Plains Indians

The gods of the Plains Indians were rarely conceived of as a clearly structured, hierarchical pantheon. The gods or spirits were a more or less vague grouping of powers, seldom ranked as lesser or greater, not always with specifically defined attributes or supernatural roles. Some of the tribes did have a definite idea of a supreme deity, who appears in their creation or origin myths. The Dakota Sioux and the Blackfoot tend to give pride of place to the sun, but the Blackfoot complicate matters by ascribing creation to a fairly explicit 'trickster' figure, a god or spirit in temporary animal form. The Pawnee possess myths of the great god Tirawa, meaning father or 'Power Above'; but even in this case the supreme god is little more than a rather cloudy abstraction. He may or may not be identified at times with the sun or some other obtrusive natural phenomenon like thunder or the morning star. But predominantly he tends to be a character in mythological tales rather than an omnipresent god with whom man can come in contact.

Environment plays an important role in Plains myth and most Plains Indians ascribe godhead to the sky, the stars, the moon, the wind and so on. The Pawnee, with a sound if embryonic astronomy, were especially devoted to star gods, and share with other tribes a high regard for the hero-god of the morning star. Water gods are important to the Sioux and others; fire and

thunder, constant companions to the people of the level, dry plains, appear in many tales of mighty spirits. Sometimes the fertility goddess known the world over as the Great Mother or Earth Mother, plays a role in the old tales – probably carried over from the days before the horse, when maize was as economically important as buffalo.

Animal gods occur frequently in the Indian myths, sometimes as one of the great gods temporarily in animal form, more usually as a generalized spirit or power in that form appearing for a specific purpose, and it is in these explicit guises that the Indians make contact with the supernatural in their prayers and worship. In the myths and tales, however, one such animal spirit takes definite precedence: the trickster figure, one of the most complex but fascinating concepts in all mythology.

This god, or hero, is a lesser deity but at the same time he is one of the first gods, who existed before creation. His actions are often heroic, fighting great battles, righting wrongs and punishing evil-doers, and sometimes his role expands into that of the creator of the world or of mankind. Yet many of the trickster stories involve him in the most farcical mischief-making, showing him to be a clever but small-minded practical joker.

The trickster goes by many names among North American tribes: in the Pacific Northwest he is the hero Raven; on the Plains, he is Coyote to the Pawnee. The Cheyenne call him 'Wihio', translatable sometimes as 'white man', sometimes as 'spider'. The Blackfoot trickster is Napi, and has much

in common with the Cheyenne's: his name can mean 'white old man' but is often rendered as just 'old man', especially when his role of creator is implied.

The myths of the trickster as creator often show him bringing about the origin of some natural phenomenon more or less by accident, or as the casual side effect of some joke or piece of mischief. Often the joke is on the gods: the trickster fools and bedevils them into some action that will directly or indirectly benefit the earth and man.

There seems to be little contact, in the sense of direct worship, between the trickster and his believers. He figures in myths that explain Nature and in comic tales, and the Indians seem content to leave it at that. When they wish to make representations to the supernatural world, they direct their prayers and supplications to animal gods or Nature spirits, which can be seen as concentrations of spirit power that have become focused in animal form. So it is not to the buffalo god or the eagle god that the Indian prays – but to the buffalo or eagle power, one area of supernatural power that flows to man through certain animals or natural phenomena, such as thunder power or wind power. These animal or natural powers serve to a great extent as guardian spirits. Tribal spirits are dictated by tradition and the old tales; but individuals can acquire their own direct contact with a specific spirit or power. Some individuals acquired deeper knowledge of the tribal spirits.

The Indian gods can be seen as a grouping of rather abstract supernatural powers less explicitly conceived of in human terms than, say, Greek or Norse divinities. When a vision, engendered by the Sun Dance or other means, illumines an Indian's individual guardian spirit for him it also provides him with some personal magic. Many of the common amulets and talismans in use among Plains Indians were introduced through such visions – for instance, the 'thunder bow', an ornamented bow with a lance-head on one end, partaking of 'thunder power', or what we could call the power of the thunder god. It was a general talisman to bring good luck but also gave protection against lightning and against being wounded in battle.

It might be said that the Plains Indians had little time or energy to spend on working out involved and sophisticated pantheons of gods with neatly arranged aspects and attributes – nor could they concern themselves with too extended and detailed approaches to the craft of magic. Perhaps they obtained most of the magic they needed from their ecstatic and agonized vision quests. And perhaps they found most of the religion they needed in their awareness of their awesome environment.

Algonquin Indians

The original Algonquins or 'fish spearers', lived in a single village in Canada, in the area now covered by the city of Ottawa. Later on the name was used for a group of small tribes who allied themselves with the French settlers in Canada against the Iroquois Indians. But these tribes were in fact only the northern division of a larger group of Indian tribes speaking similar languages called the Algonquin (or Algonkian or Algonquian) linguistic group. They ranged along the eastern seaboard of North America and inland to the prairies. They did not realize that they were probably all related and were in a constant state of inter-tribal warfare, which was later complicated by the arrival of the white man.

It is an element of Algonquin mythology which Longfellow used in his *Song of Hiawatha*; the name Hiawatha is that of a great Iroquois Lone Pine chief, but everything else in the narrative poem is Algonquin.

The Algonquin tribes as a whole, in common with most American Indians, believed that human contact with the unseen powers came through specially selected individuals. These shamans, or medicine-men, were usually marked out in childhood by some unusual psychological features.

In the more recent days of Negro slavery in America, some of the slaves from Ashanti in West Africa mixed with Indians of Algonquin stock, amalgamated their own spirit Anansi, famous as a trickster, with the Algonquin Great Rabbit, and so produced the world of the Brer Rabbit stories.

Important among the Algonquin-speaking tribes were the Cree of the Great Lakes and southern Canada, and their neighbours to the south, the Chippewa (Ojibway). Among these tribes, who to a large extent escaped the colonial wars between the Europeans, the old mythology survived long enough to be recorded by scientific scholars. The survival of the old ideas was greatly helped by the secret society of the shamans known as the Midewiwin. This society had a method of writing in pictorial code. Their pictures scratched on birch-bark or painted on skin recorded the legends of the gods, and also notes on tribal history.

It is from the Cree in particular that we have the most complete form of the myths of the Algonquin-speaking peoples. Before the earth existed, there was water, on which a few floating sticks were placed by two ducks. The animals came along and could find no solid ground to stand on; those who could joined the ducks and dived to find more sticks. They made a raft on which they all lived. Then the Great Manitou placed some sand on the raft. It grew and spread out. In his form of a white hare he is still making the raft which is the earth bigger, and you hear him shaking the raft whenever there is an earthquake.

It came about that Death was sent to earth. As different groups of animals died, the Creator took their bodies and changed them so that the first races of men came into being. There was a daughter of the children of Men and she gave birth to four divine sons. They

'*The Flyer*', an Algonquin medicine-man, by John White. He is acting out the myth of the bird which carries messages between the earth and the world of spirits. He has a dried bird on his head, and the otter skin at his belt contains magic charms.

were Nanabozo, the protector of humanity; Chipiapoos who died to become the protector of the Land of the Dead; Wabosso the maker of white, the magician and guardian of the North; and Chakekenapok, the flint-stone and maker of fire but also the winter. At his birth, the mother died. Thus Nanabozo and Chakekenapok were destined to be enemies.

It was not until Nanabozo had grown up that the two opposed brothers met. Then they stormed around the earth, wrestling and tearing at each other. The magic deer-horn which Nanabozo carried broke pieces off the body of Chakekenapok. These fell to the ground as pieces of flint, and at last Nanabozo won the battle. Chakekenapok was torn to pieces and thrown over the earth. His bones became the ranges of mountains and his intestines turned into the pleasant grapevines.

There was a power granted by the Creator, which the Indians knew as a kind of magic breath called orenda available to all manitous, who were the secret life of every created thing. Seeing that Nanabozo and his most beloved brother Chipiapoos had become so powerful and beautiful, the various manitous planned to kill them. Nanabozo knew all things and was able to elude the spells, but Chipiapoos walked on the thick ice of the Great Lakes and the manitous used their orenda to melt the ice. So Chipiapoos drowned and the manitous hid his body at

the very bottom of the lakes, from which it was impossible that it should ever be recovered.

For six years Nanabozo wept for his brother in seclusion, and sent out his magical powers to destroy the manitous. At last they managed to pacify him by sending their orenda in bags to blow on him like soothing winds. They brought peace to his heart. Four of the greater manitous brought mourning gifts, tobacco and magical medicine pouches made from animal skins. Nanabozo welcomed them as messengers of peace and accepted their invitation to visit their sacred house. There they gave him a drink which brought him wonderful peace and happiness.

Then they combined to form the society of the Midewiwin and Nanabozo was the first initiate. Then they all summoned up the spirit of Chipiapoos and before sending him back to the underworld, they invested him with the powers of Lord of the Land of the Dead and Guardian of Souls.

It was Nanabozo who discovered the magical virtues of the plants which were to be the food of the future human race of our own kind. He stored them in his magical hut, and put the Grandmother of Humanity, Mesakkummikokwi, in charge of them. And so, when the Algonquins picked the food plants, they put a portion of their reaping on the ground as a thank-offering to the ancient lady, 'Our Grandmother'.

Among the Algonquin tribes these and other myths were re-enacted at ceremonies on the anniversary of each event; in other words, at the appropriate seasons for planting maize, hunting deer or reaping the harvest. The timing of the ceremonies was calculated by counting moons and days, so that a practical calendar was linked with the religion. The passage of the stars across the sky marked the great seasons of the year, which were six in number.

The dancing and chanting of the myths at these ceremonies were linked with Nature's progress through the seasons of the year. It was a kind of magical drama. The power summoned up and released in the ceremonies helped the people to enjoy the fruits of earth and protected them from the dangerous powers of manitous.

Agriculture was always a holy thing. The little garden plots which went to make up the village farmland were given magical life by young women silently walking around them on a given night in spring, quite naked and so expressing the fertility of Nature which they were summoning to help them in their task.

The Indians understood well enough that they depended on the powers of Nature for their existence; if there was a poor harvest, a drought, an earthquake – they died. They taught this to the early white settlers but found that the newcomers rewarded good with evil. Though the tribes detested any central authority, the pressure of the white man who seized their lands drove the chiefs to organize large confederations for resistance. On the eastern seaboard the struggle ended with the war of 1675-6 when the Algonquins were decisively defeated, massacred and driven from their heartland.

Pacific North West Indians

'In the beginning there was nothing but water. The Raven was flying over the surface of the water, but could not perch anywhere because there was neither land nor tree. He decided to create the world. He picked up some small pebbles and flew over the sea. Now and then he dropped a pebble into the water and an island came into existence. Thus the dry land appeared in the midst of the water of the ocean. After that the Raven started to create all things. He created trees and grass, fish in the water, and birds in the air, and every kind of beast in the forest. There were now all living creatures except man. He wanted to create man also but could not do it for a long period of time, because he did not know the suitable material to use. He tried to use stone, water, air and many other materials, but in vain. At last he took some clay and wood and created a man and woman.'

So says one of the many creation myths of the Kwakiutl tribes. A supreme god is not recognizable in North-West Coast religion and mythology, although there are a number of dominant characters drawn from the sky, earth, sea and underworld who are credited with, or identified with discoveries and aspects of the way of life.

In effect the legend was a lesson from which man learned and developed a pattern of behaviour based on that of the birds, animals and fish upon which he depended

for food and, therefore, for life itself. Man in fact identified with a particular beast and was that beast in human form, having at some point shed the human form for that of the beast, and returned at a later point in time as a human endowed with the secrets, wisdom and powers of the beast. It was these beasts in addition to the human form that appeared usually in traditional stylized forms in the graphic arts and carvings.

Raven as the creator was a supreme trickster in the true sense; whilst bestowing gifts on man he could at the same time make a fool of man and other mythological characters alike. A Haida myth of the origin of light tells how Raven, seeing the world in darkness and feeling sorry for man hunting for food, set off one day to the Chief of the Sky who kept the ball of daylight hidden to punish the people. To get into the house of the Chief of the Sky, he changed into a spruce needle that fell into the spring, and was swallowed by the Chief's daughter who had come to drink. Soon she became pregnant and a son was born who was Raven in disguise. The Chief was pleased and himself tended the child, who soon learned to crawl, moving from room to room in search of the ball of light. This he found, and began to cry 'Ball, Ball' until eventually the Chief reluctantly and on the insistence of his advisers gave him the ball to play with. Each day he was given the ball, until the Chief and his advisers eventually gave up watching him. At this he rolled it to the door, turned himself back into Raven and flew back to the people, breaking open the ball and allowing the bright light to spread so that the people could see to hunt.

In every society there was a mythical beginning, and on the North-West Coast all living things were thought to be equal and in balance, differing only in their appearance. They were the same in thought, word and deed and taking human form. Man was Salmon, Bear or Raven for example, and conversely Salmon, Bear or Raven was Man. Clan names were claimed through descent from these creatures. The front of the house would be painted with the crest of the ancestral creature, as would be the articles of daily and ceremonial use.

A major ceremony and the most important social event was the potlatch. Invariably associated with status, either of an individual, a clan or a village, it was an occasion for the distribution or re-distribution of the wealth upon which the economy of the Indians was based.

The occasions for such a ceremony were many; the raising of a totem pole for a deceased chief, the introduction of a new chief, the coming of age of a close relative, a marriage, the giving of a new rank or name, the use of a new crest or the raising of a new house.

Today the Indians of the North-West Coast are predominantly Christian. Old practices and beliefs still persist in some places, with a growing awareness and revival, but not as part of their religion so much as a revival of tradition. It will be many generations before they integrate into modern society; environment, cultural heritage and racial background will prevent a rapid transition. It is to be hoped that the emergence will be gentle and allow them to retain their own identity.

Animals played an important part in Indian beliefs, for man modelled his patterns of behaviour on animals, birds and fish, on which he depended for food and so for life itself: shaman's charm in the form of a killer whale.

Museum of the American Indian

NFB-West Baffin Eskimo Co-op

The Eskimo

The religion of the Eskimo, like their entire way of life has been shaped by their environment, and is at one with the harsh, unyielding character of the Arctic in which they live.

The supply of food is controlled by the spirits, and should they be offended in any way, they will withhold the bear, the seal, the whale and the caribou, until recompense is made. In practical terms, this means the observance of a variety of taboos.

It has been pointed out that the supernatural world of the Eskimo is strangely timeless and static. Unlike many primitive peoples, the Eskimo have little conception of a past – least of all an ideal past. Everything is adjusted to the present moment. Significantly, Eskimo mythology is virtually without creation myths, and those that exist, in Alaska, have almost certainly been derived from the North-Western Indians. Nor is there any reasoned account of the creation of man, save as a very incidental by-product of the Sedna myth, which speaks of Eskimo, other men and beasts as having sprung from the union of a goddess and a

dog-man. Man, it seems, has always been as he is; so, too, have the gods.

It is tempting to speak of the Eskimo deities as a hierarchy; tempting, but unjustified, since the Eskimo themselves certainly do not think of them as such. The Eskimo are animists, conceiving the whole world as the abode of spirits, with every natural object inhabited by some spirit. Over and above these are the animal spirits, the air and sea spirits, and other classes of spirits which do not fit neatly into any of these categories. The hierarchical aspect, to the Western theorist, emerges from the fact that the Eskimo conceive of a Supreme Being, Sila (Silap Inua), who has all the characteristics of a High God.

The Eskimo word for 'spirit' is *inua*, which is the third person possessive of *inuk*, 'man', and thus means 'its man' or 'his man'. The inua is in effect a miniature double of the man, animal, or object in which it lives: this is of course a basic idea on which all animism rests. Silap Inua is the inua of the air, who may be male or female, who lives in, or may be identified with, the sky, and controls atmospheric phenomena. To the Polar Eskimo 'Sila' is a synonym for 'weather',

'the universe' or 'the whole' – again a common characteristic of High Gods – but is not normally the recipient of worship, nor the subject of a developed mythology. Sila is the only 'genuine' Supreme Being in Eskimo religion, though other deities can fill something of the same function.

Second in the rank of deities is the moon spirit (with various names of which one is Tarquiup Inua), who controls all land animals and all fertility, human as well as animal, and as such is of incomparably greater practical importance than Sila. A widespread myth tells how the moon and sun were once a brother and sister who lived on earth. The two committed incest, though the girl did not at first know this; when she found out, she fled from her brother into the heavens. He pursued her, and his pursuit is continued for all eternity. A Greenland variation tells how the moon and his sister the sun live in a double house with a single entrance. Not only must the moon spirit be constantly propitiated if he is to grant success in hunting, but since he is the bestower of fertility, he can be entreated on behalf of barren women. It is believed in some areas that the shaman or medicine man can fly o the moon to obtain children for childless women, and may have intercourse with the woman in question as a further (and in all likelihood more effective) measure. The sun, is the moon's sister, is of comparatively little cultic importance.

For Eskimos who rely on sea hunting, the greatest of the spirits is Sedna (also called Nuliajuk, Nerrivik, Arnquagssaq) who 'owns' the seals, whales, walruses and all other sea creatures, and is worshipped (and feared) in Greenland and in the central areas of northern Canada. The most elaborate Eskimo myth tells how a girl named Avilay-oq married a dog, and brought forth off-spring – Eskimo, white men and other crea-tures. The children made so much noise that the couple moved to an island, from which the dog husband had to be sent to the girl's father for food. This was put in a pair of boots, hung round the dog's neck. One day, while he was away, a man came and took the girl away, revealing himself later as a petrel. Her father went to look for her, and took her away from the petrel's country in a boat. But the petrel followed them, called up a storm

Facing page The Eskimo believes himself to be at the mercy of capricious gods and spirits which must be placated if he is to eke out an existence in the harsh, unyielding climate of the Arctic: lithograph of a sea goddess by the Eskimo artist Paulassie: sea spirits in particular are shown respect because they control the main supply of food. Below Spirit charm, part of the shaman's equipment, which enables him to communicate with the forces controlling sea-hunting.

man filled the dog's boots with stones, and he, too, sank. The daughter became one-eyed Sedna, ruler of the sea, who dwells with her father and dog husband in the depths of the ocean. She is both sea goddess and a goddess of the dead.

Sky and sea deities may in some cases 'divide' themselves in such a way as to dele-gate their functions. On Baffin Island, the Kadlu are three sisters who produce thunder and lightning by rubbing skins together – probably an original function of the High God. Other minor deities are connected with the earth. One particularly repulsive speci-men is the 'Disemboweller' of Greenland, a female demon, cousin of the moon spirit, who disembowels anyone she can make laugh. Most local deities in fact are male-volent, and inspire nothing but fear. An interesting group of spirits not quite deities, are the *tornait*, from which the shaman's familiars are recruited. They may be associ-ated with the dead, and one can see in them distorted popular reminiscences of the peo-ple of the Thule culture (the earliest known Eskimo culture), in much the same way as the Celts of Britain are believed by some to have become the 'little people' of folklore. The chief *tornait* is known as Tornarsuk, and treated in some areas as a Supreme Being.

Like other primitive peoples, the Eskimo believes that man has not one, but several 'souls', *inuas*, all of which are associated with the body only temporarily. There are many variations but it is broadly true to say that man can have three types of soul: the 'free-soul', an immortal spirit and source of power which lives on in another world after

what he understood by the soul, answered: 'It is something beyond understanding, that which makes me a human being.'

Most pass after death to a state in which they are at least happy; it is only the few who have had the misfortune to meet death in an unsuitable way who are forced to wander. There is little or no idea of post-mortem judgement on the basis of good and evil deeds involved. What really matters is whether or not the person in question has observed all the taboos, and the manner of his death. So the Eskimo of the Bering Straits believed that the souls of shamans and those who have died by accident (especi-ally in hunting), suicide, violence, starva-tion or in childbirth go to a land of plenty in the sky. Some Eskimos regard the Aurora Borealis as the spirits of the fortunate departed playing football in the heavens. Those who die a natural death descend to the underworld or to the underwater realm of Sedna, a land of gloom and deep darkness, but accessible to the shaman so that he may succeed in releasing the unfortunate soul. The central Eskimo distinguish between a sky heaven (Qudliparmiut) and a subter-ranean hell (Adliparmiut) – again on the basis of the kind of death.

For four or five days – the length of the journey to the land of the dead – the soul remains in the house in which the person has died, and may then stay by the grave until summoned to enter the body of a new-born child. This is actually the 'name-soul', which is passed on as the child receives the name of the deceased, and which represents a kind of transmigration doctrine. The house in which the person has died is abandoned,

and threatened to upset the boat. In terror, the old man threw his daughter overboard, and when she clung to the gunwale, cut off her fingers one by one. The upper joints became the whales, the second joints the seals, and so on. Eventually she sank in the sea, but only after her father had struck out one of her eyes. On his return home, the old

death, or may return as a ghost to plague the living; the 'life-soul' which animates the body and dies with it; and the 'name-soul', which attaches to the name, and which can be passed on to another human being. It must not be thought, however, that these can be sharply distinguished from one another. An Eskimo of the Great Fish River, asked

and his possessions thrown away to avoid contaminating the living. Belief of this kind can lead to terrible consequences: a sick person may be removed from a house, and left to die in isolation; the burial shroud may be put on before the person is actually dead; and in extreme cases, the dying man or woman put in the coffin while still alive.

EGYPT AND THE MIDDLE EAST

Egypt

Two natural features have always dominated life in Egypt, namely, the River Nile and the sun; from them stemmed two of the basic themes of ancient Egyptian religion. Egypt has been aptly described as a land having length but no breadth. The description is not quite accurate, because the Delta area is certainly extensive; but south of Cairo, Egypt really consists of two strips of irrigable land on either bank of the Nile, with the desert stretching away on each side. The land consequently divides into two distinctive parts: Lower Egypt, comprising the Delta area, and Upper Egypt, formed of the long narrow Nile valley. The fertility of the land depends absolutely upon the annual flooding of the Nile and the careful control and conservation of its life-giving waters. This entails the construction and maintenance of elaborate irrigation works. Consequently a strong centralized government, uniting Upper and Lower Egypt under one rule and able to direct the country's labour resources, has always been essential to the economic and social well-being of the people. Such a government was first established about 3000 BC by princes of of This, in Upper Egypt, and the achievement was so important that the Egyptians looked back to this union of Upper and Lower Egypt as the starting point of their national life.

Because the pharaoh (a title derived from *per* meaning 'house' and *aa* meaning 'great') was so essential to the well-being of the land, he came to be regarded as divine. According to a tradition that arose in the Old Kingdom, he was believed to be son of the sun god, and therefore the deity's representative upon earth. The pharaoh was accordingly regarded as the owner of Egypt (in Egyptian *Kemi*, the 'black land'), and the mediator between the people and the sun god. A royal insignia and ritual proclaimed his unique status. When he died, or rather ascended to the sky to join his divine father, his body had to be enshrined in a great tomb, served by a mortuary temple. The pyramids were the distinctive tombs of the pharaohs of the Old Kingdom.

Because the sun so insistently dominates the daily scene in Egypt, it was venerated under the name of Re (Egyptian-Coptic

for 'sun') as the supreme state deity, intimately associated with the monarchy. Known as the 'Great God', Re was conceived under various highly imaginative forms. As Re-Horakhti, an ancient falcon or falcon-headed sky god called 'Horus of the horizon' was associated with the sun god. Re-Horakhti was represented in art as a falcon-headed man, crowned with the solar disc; sometimes this form of the deity was depicted as the solar disc, encircled by two serpents, between the outstretched wings of a falcon. As the sun at dawn, Re was represented as a beetle (*Khepri*) or a beetle-headed man. This strange concept had a subtle significance. 'Khepri' derived from the word *kheper*, meaning 'to become or exist', so that Re-Khepri indicated both the rising sun and the sun as the self-existent creator of the universe. The declining sun was Re-Atum, shown as an aged man of wise counsel; the word 'Atum' conveyed some idea of 'completion'. Atum was the god of Heliopolis, the old centre of sun worship.

Since Re, as the state god, was essentially connected with the kingship of the pharaohs, it was inevitable that his cult should be affected by political changes in Egypt. During the Old Kingdom period, he was worshipped as Re-Atum in his ancient home at Heliopolis, where his temple was supposed to mark the primeval hill where he began the work of creation. When the political capital was moved to Thebes in Upper Egypt, during the Middle Kingdom, Re was associated with the local god of Thebes, Amun. Amun-Re was represented in art as a man wearing a cap, surmounted by two plumes and the solar disc. The great pharaohs of the New Kingdom were zealously devoted to Amun, building at Thebes for his worship huge temples, richly endowed, so that Amun became in effect the sole state god. This exaltation of Amun eventually produced one of the most interesting, though obscure, episodes in the whole of Egyptian history.

It would seem that the priests of Heliopolis, the ancient cult centre of Re-Atum, attempted to combat the exaltation of Amun by promoting the worship of Re untrammelled by association with another god. Accordingly they proclaimed the Aten, the sun's disc, as the symbol of supreme deity.

Michael Holford

Above *Anubis, the jackal-headed god, conducted the souls of the dead to the other world and presided over funerals.* **Facing page** *The goddess Isis spreads out her winged arms in a protective gesture, at the foot of a gold coffin enclosing the mummy of Tutankhamen (detail). Isis was often depicted as a guardian of the dead.*

Meanwhile at Thebes the enormous power acquired by the priesthood of Amun had begun to challenge the royal power. When Amenhotep IV (1372–1354 BC) ascended the throne, he gradually set about supplanting Amun as the supreme deity by the Aten. This king, who soon changed his name to Akhenaten ('Pleasing to the Aten'), was a strange genius whose devotion to the Aten bordered on fanaticism. He moved his capital from Thebes, the stronghold of Amun, to a new city named Akhetaten ('Horizon of the Aten'), where he built a magnificent temple to his god, similar in plan to that at Heliopolis. He expressed his devotion in hymns to the Aten and he had himself frequently portrayed, together with his beautiful wife Nefertiti and their children, worshipping the Aten, whose descending rays, ending in hands, bless the pious family. He took measures to repress the cult of Amun, even to the point of causing the deity's name to be removed from monuments. However, the attempt to reform Egyptian religion did not survive the heretic king, and his successor Tutankhamen (1354–1345 BC) was obliged to submit to Amun's supremacy and bring the court back to Thebes. The memory of Akhenaten was execrated and his monuments destroyed. The ascendency of the Amun priesthood reached its inevitable conclusion in about 1080 BC when Herihor, the 'First Prophet of Amun', took over the royal power at Thebes.

The third main theme of Egyptian religion was constituted by the funerary cult which centred on the god Osiris. This was essentially concerned with the spiritual needs of individuals, which were not served by the state religion. Osiris, the divine hero who died and rose again, had an intimate personal appeal and, since it was believed that resurrection to eternal life could be achieved through ritual assimilation to him, he came increasingly to dominate Egyptian religion; his cult was the longest lived of all those of the Egyptian deities.

The earliest texts record a multiplicity of gods and goddesses. The majority were local deities but some achieved a nation-wide recognition. Amun is a case in point: the political supremacy of Thebes made him the supreme state god. Most local deities, like Bast, the cat goddess of Bubastis, and Sebek, the crocodile god of the Faiyum, had their chief sanctuary in their place of origin, with which they remained essentially associated; sometimes their cult might be accorded a limited observance in one or two other places. The origin of these local deities is unknown. The fact that many of them had animal forms or animal heads has suggested the theory of their derivation from ancient totems; but there is no certain evidence that totemism existed as an institution in early Egypt, and many other local deities cannot be explained in this way.

Of the major deities after Re, Osiris and Amun, whose worship was generally observed through the land, Horus and Isis enjoyed the widest recognition. Horus was a complicated deity who, under certain forms, achieved the status of a state god. His solar aspect as Re-Horakhti, under which he was associated with Re the sun god, was paralleled by another of equal importance but of confusing significance, especially since the two aspects became combined in one single deity. In the Osirian mythology Horus is the posthumous son of Osiris, who avenges his father's death and inherits his kingdom. Since the Egyptians identified a deceased king with Osiris, and his son and successor with Horus, the latter came to be regarded as the divine prototype of the reigning pharaoh.

In the Osirian mythology the god Seth figures as the murderer of Osiris and the opponent of Horus, who finally overthrows him. This god, who seems originally to have been associated with storms and the desert, and so regarded as a strong and fierce being, gradually became the Egyptian god of evil. Seth is generally depicted as an animal-headed man. The animal has never been certainly identified; it has a long curved muzzle, almond eyes and sharp pointed ears. The Greeks later identified Seth with the monster Typhon.

The other chief deity of the Osirian mythology who can claim to have become, with Osiris, one of the two most popular deities of Egyptian religion, and later of Graeco-Roman society, was the goddess Isis, the wife of Osiris and mother of Horus, the daughter of Geb and Nut.

Ptah, the god of Memphis, always enjoyed a position of dignity in the Egyptian pantheon, because Memphis had been the ancient capital of the land and continued an important city. He is represented in art invariably in human form, tightly wrapped in a robe like a mummy; he wears a skull cap and holds a curiously shaped staff or sceptre. The priests of Memphis attributed to him the creation of all things, including the other gods. Memphis was also the cult centre of the Apis bull, a primitive symbol of procreative vitality, which was associated with Ptah as the manifestation of 'his blessed soul'; later the Apis was also associated with Osiris.

Hathor was a widely popular goddess, who manifested herself in various forms. As a beautiful woman, she was the divine patron of music and dancing, symbolizing the joy of life. In a bas relief at Karnak, recording the divine birth of the pharaoh Amenhotep III, Hathor is represented as animating the infant king and his *ka*, or other self, with the *ankh*, the symbol of life. The goddess was also thought of as a cow and was sometimes depicted suckling the king. She personified the sky and is often represented as a cow receiving the setting sun, an office which caused her also to be regarded as a guardian of the dead, whom she transported to the next world. But Hathor had another side to her nature: she was identified with the destructive 'Eye of Re', and as the 'Lady of Punt' she was a divine lioness. She was closely associated with Horus: her name Hathor (*Het Hor*) means 'House of Horus'. Hathor's ambivalence of character is similar to that of the Mesopotamian goddess Ishtar.

The Egyptians deified the earth as a male deity, Geb; but often he was represented as a goose. In the Heliopolitan story of the creation, Geb originally lay in close embrace with Nut, the sky goddess, until separated by Shu, the god of the atmosphere. The Pyramid Texts indicate that Geb was once venerated as the oldest of the gods, and the pharaohs were regarded as his sucessors sitting on the 'throne of Geb'. A very different deity was Thoth, who was associated with the city of Hermopolis but acquired attributes that made him significant to all Egyptians. His appearance is one of the strangest among the many strange Egyptian deities, for on a human body he has the head of an ibis bird. Thoth was regarded as the god of wisdom and the divine scribe; he is generally represented holding the reed pen and colour palette of the Egyptian scribe. He assumed an important role in the judgement of the dead, where he recorded the

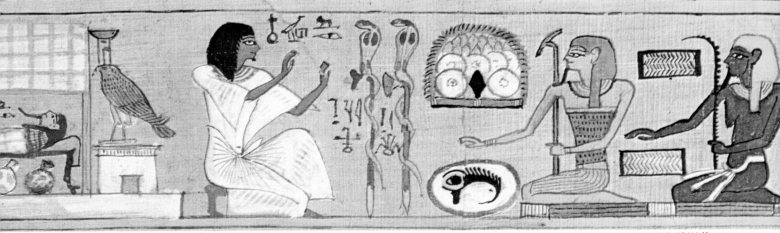

Michael Holford/British Museum

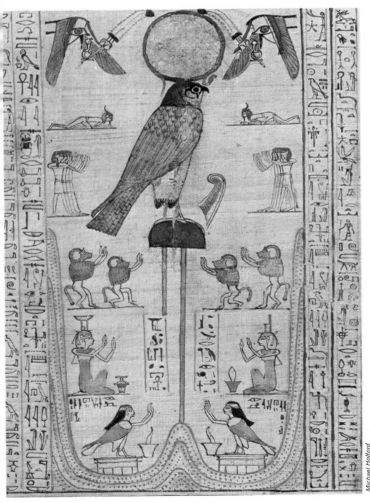

Michael Holford

Michael Holford

Top *The Papyrus of Hunefer shows Osiris on the far left, swathed in white mummy wrappings and holding the crook and flail, emblems of supreme power. In the centre the mummy lies on its catafalque and on either side Hunefer, the royal scribe, offers worship to various divinities.* **Above** *Souls pay homage to the sun god Re, whom the Egyptians conceived under various imaginative forms. As Re-Horakhti he was depicted as a falcon or falcon-headed man crowned with the sun's disc. Detail from the Papyrus of Anhai in the British Museum.* **Above right** *On the same papyrus the sun god is shown as the beetle Khepri with the solar disc; the scarab beetle was thought to be born spontaneously and so an apt symbol for the sun.*

verdict when the heart of the deceased was weighed. The Greeks identified Thoth with Hermes and, as Hermes Trismegistus ('Thrice-great Hermes'), he was the source of the mystic revelation incorporated into the so-called Hermetic literature of the Graeco-Roman period.

A god who deserves special mention, though he was not numbered among the greater gods of Egypt, is Bes. He was represented as a squat, dwarf-like figure with a large grinning face. He may justly be called 'the poor man's god' because of his great popularity, despite his having no cult centre. Bes was the patron of fun and music, and helped women in childbirth. He could be regarded as the god of good luck.

The Egyptians were most obviously poly-

theists; but there is also evidence of a tendency to henotheism, if not monotheism, among them. Most notable is the use of the expression 'the Great God' in their wisdom literature and certain inscriptions. The use of this expression, without further qualification, is significant; it shows that the Egyptians recognized one supreme deity who needed no distinguishing name. It seems certain that in the earlier period the title 'Great God' referred to Re, the sun god; later Osiris may sometimes have been so designated. Akhenaten's concept of the Aten certainly merits the description 'monotheistic'. But it seems likely that the worship of any specific Egyptian deity in its local sanctuary was a kind of henotheism; during the service, the deity concerned was conceived of as the 'one' god, there and at that moment.

Egyptian religion does not appear to have been so rich in mythology as was the religion of the contemporary civilization of Mesopotamia. It had indeed its creation myths and the fundamentally important Osirian myth. Three other myths are known which concerned Re and certain goddesses. One told how Re grew old and mankind rebelled against him. To punish them, Re sent forth his eye in the form of his daughter Hathor. So destructive was the goddess that the sun god had to make her drunk in order to stop her work of slaughter, for otherwise mankind would have been wholly exterminated. A variant version of this myth concerned the fierce goddess Tefnut, who lived as a lioness in the Nubian desert. Re, whose daughter she was, wanted her to return to him and he sent Shu and Thoth, in disguise, to persuade her to come back. On the return journey she transformed herself into a beautiful goddess at Philae, and revealed herself as Hathor at Dendera, which was her chief cult centre. The third myth told how the goddess Isis acquired her magical power. She made a serpent and caused it to bite Re. No god could cure Re in his agony; then Isis appeared and offered to relieve him on condition that he revealed his secret name to her. The tormented sun god was forced to comply and the knowledge she gained gave Isis her great power. There are a number of tales, such as that of the Two Brothers which are full of supernatural details, but they are not true myths.

Egyptian ideas of how and where the dead spent their afterlife are fundamentally confused. This confusion is already present in the Pyramid Texts (c 2400 BC). It doubtless went back to predynastic times and stemmed from different local traditions. Three conceptions of the afterlife can be distinguished. What is probably the most primitive envisaged the dead as living on in their tombs, equipped with various everyday necessities and nourished on daily food offerings made by their relatives. In the Pyramid Texts the existence of a celestial realm of the dead is described. The idea takes two forms: that of ascending to heaven to join the sun god Re in his solar boat on his daily journey across the sky; or of ascending to join the 'Imperishable Ones', the circumpolar stars. The idea of accompanying the sun god became the more generally accepted view. The third conception was associated with Osiris and his realm, which was called the *Duat* or *Ament* (the West).

This realm was subterranean and was situated beneath the western horizon, which in Egypt was constituted by the western desert. The dead had to journey there, encountering many hideous monsters and fearsome obstacles on the way. This land of the dead was imagined as an idealized Egypt, where the blessed dead lived happily the same kind of life as in the Nile valley. Special guidebooks to the next world were provided for the dead: the Book of the Two Ways described alternative land and water routes both equally perilous; the Book of Gates divided the Duat by 12 gates; the Book am Duat told of the 12 time-divisions taken by the sun god on his nightly journey through this underworld. What is particularly significant, in all this complex imagery and practice concerning the dead, is that the Egyptians continued, century after century, to embalm their dead and to furnish their tombs as though the dead really did live in them.

Since most of the extant evidence on Egyptian religion relates to the king and the upper classes of society, little is known of the religion of ordinary folk.

The 'dawn of conscience' has been located, with reason, in ancient Egypt. Already in the Old Kingdom the concept of *maat*, which denoted the qualities of truth and justice, was associated with the 'Great God' as the basic principle of an ordered universe. From this period, too, emerge the beginnings of the belief so important to the evolution of ethics and morality, that the dead would be judged on their conduct in this life as they passed over into the next.

The immense duration of Egyptian religion, and the impressive continuity of its traditional pattern of faith and practice, suggest that the Egyptians unthinkingly accepted an ancient priestly tradition, generation after generation. But there is evidence that this was not wholly so, and that there were those who could look critically at their ancestral faith, especially the elaborate ritual that accompanied the funerary cult.

There exist, inscribed on the walls of some New Kingdom tombs, versions of what is known as the Song of the Harpist, which takes its name from the figure of a corpulent harpist who is depicted singing it. It was probably sung at memorial feasts held by relatives at the tombs of the deceased. In it the futility of the mortuary faith is frankly expressed: 'None cometh from thence that he may tell us how they (the dead) fare, that he may tell us what they need, that he may set our heart at rest, until we also go to the place whither they have gone.' The obvious conclusion is drawn from this scepticism: 'Be glad, that thou mayest cause thine heart to forget that men will (one day) beatify thee. Follow thy desire, so long as thou livest.'

The expression of such sentiments is significant; for it shows that there did exist at least a minority who could doubt the truth of their traditional religion and the effectiveness of its ritual technique for the achievement of a blessed immortality. Yet this faith was able to continue its serene tradition without the suppression of such heretical scepticism.

That it did so thus attests the strength of two things: the spiritual satisfaction which the average Egyptian got from his faith in Osiris, and the practical nature of his philosophy of life. The Greek historian Herodotus, who visited Egypt in the 5th century BC, records an Egyptian custom at banquets of showing the guests a model of a mummy with the admonition: 'Gaze here, and drink and be merry; for when you die, such will you be.' This curious custom was prompted by no spirit of cynicism or levity; it reflected the practical evaluation of life that characterized the Egyptians. They feared death, but they believed that they had the means of reversing its threat of personal extinction

Michael Holford

Above *The Aten, the sun's disc, was elevated to the status of a god by the Pharaoh Amenhotep, who changed his name to Akhenaten, meaning 'pleasing to the Aten', and built a magnificent temple to his god.* **Right** *Akhenaten, who sought to promote the worship of the Aten, the sun's disc, above the worship of Amun, frequently had himself portrayed sitting in the sun's rays. These rays, ending in hands, bless the devout pharaoh.* **Facing page** *An avenue of ram-headed sphinxes led to the great temple of Amun-Re at Karnak near Thebes. The ram was the symbol of Amun and his soul was believed to be enshrined in a ram-headed sphinx, the embodiment of wisdom, mystery and power.*

and they accordingly made provision to secure this immunity: hence the magnificent finds in their tombs.

But such preoccupation with death and the afterlife did not induce pessimism or prompt a this-world-denying attitude. The Egyptians sought to extract the most joy possible from life, while preparing for death and mindful of the judgement that faced them thereafter.

The legacy of Egypt's' ancient religion cannot be accurately assessed. The famous American Egyptologist J. H. Breasted believed that Akhenaten's monotheism influenced Moses and found its fruition in the Hebrew concept of one single God, who is the creator and sustainer of the universe. The connection cannot be proved and the assumption that it did exist has not been generally accepted by scholars. More certain is the influence of Egyptian wisdom literature on the Jewish Book of Proverbs. The elements of Egyptian religion which passed into Coptic Christianity were chiefly related to the world after death; such elements included the idea of a judgement immediately after death and of the assessment as being made by weighing the soul on scales. And the Egyptian elements have yet to be fully evaluated in the Hermetic literature, where the god Thoth figures prominently under the name of Hermes, thus presenting considerable scope for further research.

Gods of Egypt

Horus

As the royal and national god of ancient Egypt, Horus enjoyed a position of such importance that no rite or festival involving the nation or its king could be celebrated without giving him a prominent place. One of the largest of Egyptian temples, that at Edfu, belonged to him. In form he was a falcon – the peregrine falcon, the most fierce and terrifying of all the birds of prey which scoured the Egyptian sky. His name means 'he who is on high' or 'the distant one' and refers to his domain as a sky god.

Horus was identified with the living Pharaoh, just as Osiris was identified with the Pharaoh in death, and from the 1st Dynasty onwards the Pharaoh called himself Horus (with other names). In the Cairo Museum there is a beautifully impressive seated statue of King Chephren of the 5th Dynasty which shows the Horus-falcon stretching out his wings protectively behind the king's head, recalling somewhat the Old Testament phrase 'in the shadow of Thy wings'.

Horus was the leading god of the confederation of clans or tribes which secured sovereignty over the whole of Egypt when the kingdom of Menes was established. The evidence of totemistic systems reveals the striking fact that the totem is identified with the human leader of the clan. Although totemism is not attested in all its features in early Egypt, this particular religious phenomenon can be recognized in the royal status of Horus.

The Horus-confederation was apparently opposed, in the final predynastic struggle for Egypt, by a league under the aegis of the god Seth, who was a deity of canine aspect whose home was in Upper Egypt. It is tempting to connect the political strife which resulted in the enduring unity of Egypt with the early myth concerning the conflict of Horus and Seth, although other explanations have also been offered. According to the myth, Horus and Seth were two feuding brothers, who inflicted frightful wounds on each other. Seth tore out an eye of Horus and devoured it, while Horus deprived Seth of his testicles. A trial ensued before a divine tribunal, in which Horus was vindicated and awarded the legitimate sovereignty of Egypt.

There are suggestions that the god Thoth had tried to intervene in the quarrel in a reconciling role, although he sometimes appears as a helper of Horus, especially as the god who restored to him his lost eye, and more rarely as one who sympathized with Seth. An ambivalence, then, is apparent in the position of Thoth; perhaps it is a two-facedness to which mediators inevitably expose themselves. A tradition of reconciliation is certainly reflected in the symbolism of Egypt's dynastic unity, for whereas Horus is the victorious deity who is permanently incorporated in the personality of the Pharaoh, yet the two gods are shown co-operating for the king's benefit in the ceremony of the 'Baptism of Pharaoh'. The king's jubilee festival (called the *Sed*) used to conclude with a processional visit to the chapels of Horus and Seth, and in the purification or 'baptism' of the king the two gods are shown pouring water over the Pharaoh's head.

Similarly, in the ceremony of 'Uniting the Two Lands', the symbolic plants of Upper and Lower Egypt, the reed and the papyrus, were joined by the two deities; Horus being usually associated here with Lower Egypt. Again, the stolen eye of Horus which was healed and restored was symbolic of the crown. In a royal context, therefore, the ceremony of presenting the eye suggested that the sovereign power of the king had been confirmed.

At a quite early stage the myth of Horus was merged with that of the god Osiris, and the main reason for the merger was the double identification of the king. When he died he became Osiris, but as a living Pharaoh had been Horus. From this divine doubling followed a transfer of the story of the conflict to Osiris. If Seth had been the enemy of Horus, he was now the enemy of Osiris, and the myth maintained that Seth had murdered Osiris. In the early Horus myth the mother of Horus was Hathor, and his father was Geb. Now, in the new Osirian framework, Isis becomes his mother, Osiris his father, and Seth his nephew. In the new framework, similarly, a new Horus is evolved – Horus the child – and the impact of the kingship on this mythic situation is clear: if Horus the king has died and become Osiris, yet the succession in the male line finds a legitimate heir in a young Horus. A further effect of the fusion is that the vendetta against Seth is carried on by the young Horus, who eventually overthrows his father's slayer.

Horus the child (called Harpocrates by the Greeks) gradually assumed an important place in mythology. Many stories were told about his childhood, when he was nursed by Isis or by a foster-mother in the papyrus swamps of the Delta and defended by his mother's magic against the wicked onslaughts of Seth. It will be recalled that Moses too was a babe hidden in the bulrushes, and the legend of Horus may well have influenced the Biblical episode. Among the misfortunes inflicted on Horus the child was the homosexual attack made on him by Seth; the first version of this appears in a Middle Kingdom papyrus, and it tells of the unavailing efforts of Isis to prevent the assault. Seth also attacks Horus in various unpleasant insect and animal forms; Horus may be bitten and injured, but he is healed by the magic of Isis his mother. A curious feature of the childhood legends is that they also tell of a disagreement between Horus and Isis. One version described Horus and Seth fighting in the form of hippopotami in a river. Isis expresses feelings in favour of Seth, whereupon Horus cuts off his mother's head; one source adds that Thoth restored it as a cow-head. According to Spell 113 of the Book of the Dead the hands of Horus were cut off and thrown into the water through a magical curse uttered by his mother. In a few sources the episode takes a sexual form and Horus violates his mother. Mother-incest has indeed been attributed by some to the Egyptian interpretation of kingship, with the suggestion that Isis is regarded as both the mother and the wife, therefore, of the Horus-Pharaoh.

Horus the child on the lap of his mother Isis forms a well-known group in Egyptian art, and the early iconography of the Madonna and Child owes something to the pagan tradition. Christian art was also influenced by representations of Horus the fighter on horseback, although this does not occur till Roman times. Certainly the evolution of St George and the Dragon owes something to the way in which Horus was traditionally shown attacking the Sethian crocodile.

A series of small stelae (tablets) depicted the young Horus dealing triumphantly with snakes, scorpions and crocodiles. These stelae functioned as magical aids against such threatening creatures, the underlying principle, as so often in magic, being that of analogy. Just as Horus triumphed, so will the possessor of the stele. The principle of

Sue Gooders

analogy extended also, of course, to mythical events described in texts. Many medical texts which rely partly on magic use this technique.

A spell contained in the Papyrus Ebers addresses Isis explicitly as the one who healed Horus and pleads for the same treatment in the case of the patient: 'O Isis, great in magic, release me! Free me from every bad, evil and bloody thing ... as you released and freed from (every evil) your son Horus.'

Horus as the ancient god of the sky maintained his status only by a process of assimilation to the cult of another god of heaven, the sun god Re. Egyptian religion teems with theological 'take-over-bids' of this kind. The composite name thus evolved was Re-Horakhti (Re-Horus-of-the-horizon), and the amalgam was expressed in art by means of a falcon that bears a large sun-disc on his head.

Above *A sacred bird to the ancient Egyptians, the falcon was particularly associated with Horus, the sky god; as a terrifying bird of prey that dominated the Egyptian skies, it was an apt living form for Horus, also the royal god: Horus on a plinth from the Tomb of the Nobles, at the ancient city of Thebes.* **Facing page** *The falcon god Horus was identified with the living Pharaoh. Horus the child on the lap of his mother Isis is a common motif in Egyptian art and the early iconography of the Madonna and Child owes something to this pagan tradition: bronze statuette c 600 BC.*

Isis

The great goddess of the ancient Egyptians, Isis was the wife of Osiris, the god who died and was restored to life. He had been king of Egypt, but his evil brother Seth, whom the Greeks later identified with the monster Typhon, had killed and dismembered him and buried the pieces in various places. Isis searched for and found the pieces, put them together and revived him. Osiris became king of the underworld and their son Horus, called Harpocrates by the Greeks, became ruler over Egypt.

As Queen of Egypt, Isis' hieroglyphic symbol is the throne. She is also the exemplary mother who has taken infinite pains to nurse, protect and bring up her son Horus and she is frequently depicted suckling him. With care and incantations she protected him from all diseases, and after the death of Osiris she saved him from Seth who wanted to murder him. When Seth brought a lawsuit against Horus before the court of the gods, intending to become king of Egypt himself, Isis intervened and enabled her son to win the case. Isis therefore did everything that a good woman can do for her husband and child, and became the model for all Egyptian women.

Her sacred animal is the cow, the mother of calves and provider of milk, 'the fruitful image of the all-producing goddess'. For Isis gives life, fertility and prosperity to people, animals and fields.

As man fertilizes woman, and Osiris Isis,

so did the annual flooding of the Nile fertilize the soil of Egypt; coming in the middle of the hot summer, this inundation was looked upon as a miracle and attributed to Isis. When the river dried up in the summer, it meant that Osiris was dead, killed by Seth-Typhon, the hot wind of the desert. But Isis searches for the dead Osiris and finds him on the day of the Nile flood in the river's holy waters. The water, Osiris, flows over the withered earth, Isis, and fertilizes it.

The Nile flood coincides with the first appearance of Sirius, just before sunrise and this was interpreted as a causal event: Sirius (Egyptian Sothis) was seen as the star of the Nile flood and the star of Isis. The day of the rising of Sirius and of the river's flooding became the sacred New Year's Day of the Egyptians.

After the conquest of Egypt by Alexander the Great in 331 BC the country was ruled by Greeks for 300 years, and during this period the cult of Isis became completely Hellenized. When the Romans took over the government in 30 BC they relied on the support of the Greek middle class in Egypt and the language of administration remained Greek; during this era, the goddess's cult spread over the entire area of the Mediterranean basin.

It was only when Constantine the Great, after his victory at the Milvian bridge in 312 AD raised Christianity to the level of the national religion, that the Isis cult lost its importance and was subsequently prohibited. The Greeks identified the Egyptian Isis with their Greek goddesses: Isis, the provider of corn, was the Greek Demeter; Isis, the goddess of love, was Aphrodite; Isis, wife of the king of the gods, was Hera; Isis, the goddess of magic arts, was Hecate, and so on. By depicting Isis as the prototype of the human woman, she was put on a par with the Greek heroine, Io, who was loved by Zeus and had been changed into a cow, the Isis animal. A gad-fly sent by Hera chased poor Io over land and sea until, after a long and frantic flight, she came to Egypt. There, on the banks of the Nile, Zeus changed her back into a woman. This myth was a consolation for everybody who was hunted throughout life as Io was; at the same time it demonstrated the close connection between Greece and Egypt.

Isis was also compared with other goddesses such as Artemis, Persephone and Nemesis, and especially with Tyche, the goddess of fortune (the Roman Fortuna), and with Providence. These various identifications are the expression of living religious feeling. The great goddess appears in many different forms and always reveals new aspects. She is called *myrionymos*, 'the one with ten thousand names', and a Latin inscription is translated as: 'Thou, the one who is all, goddess Isis.' Her whole being is impenetrable, but behind her many faces and names there is one and the same divine Unknown.

Next to Isis are always her husband Osiris and her son Horus and she can never be viewed individually, without her family. However, during the Greek period of Egypt a change set in as other sides of the nature of Osiris were given prominence, and he

Michael Holford/British Museum

was given the name of Osiris-Apis, abbreviated to Serapis. Apis was the sacred bull of Memphis, the old capital of Egypt, and Serapis was the god of this city. However, he also became the god of the new capital Alexandria and of the new Greek dynasty, the Ptolemies.

Isis' ancient role as throne goddess, the Queen of Egypt, was perpetuated among the Greek kings; Cleopatra appeared on official occasions in the costume, one might even say in the guise, of Isis. The Isis religion therefore had a political element, it was the national religion of the Egyptian state: those who worshipped Isis and Serapis acknowledged their loyalty to the reigning royal house.

This fact encouraged the spread of the Isis and Serapis cult in the Greek ruling circles of the Ptolemies, in Cyrene, Cyprus, Crete, the coastal towns of Asia Minor and the Greek islands whose religious centre was Delos. On the other hand, for political reasons, an expansion beyond the sphere of influence of the Ptolemies was not regarded favourably anywhere. There were only branches of the Isis cult in seaports, such as Athens, Salonika and on Euboea. But even in Egypt itself, linking the royal cult with the Isis-Serapis religion was in many respects a disadvantage as pure religious feelings cannot arise when the practice of a religion is welcomed and rewarded so distinctly by those in high places.

The political decline of the Ptolemies, which started in 200 BC, followed by the complete loss of autonomy that resulted from Egypt's incorporation into the Roman Empire, provided a real opportunity for the Isis religion to expand. Having lost its political aspect, it became possible for the religious and ethical aspect to be strengthened.

The transformation of the cult of Isis into a religion of Mysteries first occurred in the Roman Empire. Because there was no longer

a political aspect to worshipping the goddess, the cult now appealed to people as individuals: each one was personally offered salvation, and promised regeneration after death. If a man entered into the service of Isis it was his own personal decision.

The consecration ceremonies of the Isis Mysteries during the Imperial period are described in detail in *The Golden Ass* of Apuleius. There was a wealth of rites: the morning opening of the temple, the vigils, the abstention from wine, meat and love; the rites of cleanliness which included wearing white linen clothes, shaving the head and ablutions. Novices lived for a time within the precincts of the temple; the statue of Isis was contemplated, there was ecstatic prayer and obligatory tears were shed. The worthiness of the candidates was tested at a kind of hearing, and anyone who had sinned gravely was rejected. Sins were confessed and forgiven through immersion in water, and worshippers pledged themselves under oath to the service of the deity and to secrecy. With every new variation the sacred myth of Isis was restated, the seeking and the finding; in each procession Isis sought the dead Osiris, and found him every time the holy water was drawn.

The initiation into the Mysteries was in three stages and consisted of a voluntary ritual death and revival. The initiate stepped on to the 'threshold of Proserpina' (the Greek Persephone) and went on a journey 'through all the elements' for which mechanical appliances were probably used. As in the case of Freemasons, there also seems to have been a coffin ritual, and perhaps a baptism of fire. In all probability, a 'sacred wedding', a sexual union, was an integral part of the initiation. Finally, the initiate received a new name and the mystics then partook of a communal meal, with music and dancing.

There was an entire vocabulary of religious symbols: the life of man was a pilgrimage or a sea journey, the sinful world was the sea, the religion of Isis was the ship and the haven, and Isis herself the mast and the sail. Her priests were the fishermen who rescued the souls from the sea, the evil world, or birdcatchers who caught the souls (birds or butterflies) with their lime-twigs; the mystics were soldiers on holy military service for Isis, or gardeners who laboriously cultivated the garden of religion. The Isis priests were the true philosophers, who attained the perception of God, and the functionaries in the religious organization of the community were the legitimate 'consuls'; the community itself was called Ecclesia, like the Greek general assembly and later the Christian Church.

The wheel was the symbol of Isis, the sponge indicated the purification of the mystics, and the ladder their spiritual advancement. The anchor symbolized the religion that granted security, the bosom the all-providing goddess, the amphora, a two-handled vessel, the holy water; the lamp stood for the night-feast of the goddess, and the yardstick, justice. The winnow, in which the grain is separated from the chaff, represented the cleansing of the soul in the initiation, the palm the 'victory' of the mystic and his rebirth.

Great pilgrimages were undertaken in the service of Isis, from Rome to Egypt, and indeed as far as Syene, now Aswan, where the source of the Nile was said to be, and where the holy water was drawn when the Nile was in spate. Above all, outstanding festival cycles took place in the service of Isis. One of these was the festival of the goddess as mistress of navigation on 5 March. This was a spring festival, when the beginning of the navigation period was ceremonially inaugurated by the 'voyage of Isis'. The goddess's worshippers walked through the town in a long procession, wearing masks, and accompanied by music and choirs, and the first ship was then ceremonially put to sea.

The festival was also called *ploiaphesia*, which can be roughly translated as a 'launching' of the ships.

Isis herself inaugurated the navigation for the year, as according to the myth she had been the first to set sail on a ship. There were two other important festivals, one on 24–25 December and the other on 5–6 January, dates which were also important holy days in the competing Christian religion as Christmas and Epiphany.

The abolition of all frontiers in the Mediterranean area under the *Pax Romana*, with trade and communication among countries restricted less than at any time in history, encouraged the spread of the Isis Mysteries. Like the Jews and the Christians, the Greeks from Egypt formed small communities in all the towns of Asia Minor in order to practise their native cult, and also helped one another in other ways. Anyone who came into an Isis community did not suffer materially; he would have numerous friends and helpers there.

It is clear that the 'chu ch' of Isis had a 'mission' during the Imperial period, and that Memphis and Rome were the holy cities. At four places in Greece and Asia Minor, when Isis sanctuaries were being excavated, identical sacred texts were discovered, depicting Isis proclaiming her power. There is therefore no doubt that propaganda was being spread. It may be assumed that there were Isis sanctuaries or shrines in all the Mediterranean ports, and also in many inland cities and towns as the cult spread.

The cult's growth was partly because of its rather exotic nature: the strange and mysterious rites were an attraction, and at the same time it was Hellenized to such an extent that people quickly became accustomed to it. On the other hand many Egyptian concepts still clung like tiresome and disregarded eggshells to the Isis religion. This was particularly the case with regulations concerning priests. They had to be born into the caste, as they could not be elected.

The exemplary mother of the ancient Egyptians, Isis was later identified with various Greek and Roman goddesses; her cult eventually became a religion of Mysteries: glazed porcelain bust of Isis (above) and (facing page) relief of the goddess; she wears a disc set between cow's horns on her head-dress.

Osiris

The ancient Egyptian god Osiris is one of the most interesting and significant deities known to historians of religions. He is also one of the oldest gods of whom records survive; and he may rightly claim to have been worshipped longer than any other god – his cult was already well established by 2400 BC, and it continued until the forcible suppression of paganism, in favour of Christianity, in the 4th century AD.

Because Osiris was so important to them and they were so familiar with his myth or legend, the Egyptians never seem to have written a formal account of their beliefs about him. Their literature, both sacred and secular, is replete with references and allusions to him, and he is one of the figures most abundantly portrayed in their art. Yet it was left to the Greek writers Diodorus Siculus, in the 1st century BC, and Plutarch, in the following century, to provide posterity with descriptive accounts of this ancient Egyptian god, who was still a potent figure in their day. Their accounts must, inevitably, be treated with much caution; for it is unlikely that they had any direct access to Egyptian records, and they were concerned to rationalize and philosophize what they had learned from their Egyptian guides and interpreters. However, there is reason to think that they did preserve some authentic traditions, and their accounts are significant as evidence of what Osiris had come to mean to Graeco-Roman society more than 2000 years after he first appears in Egyptian records.

In the Pyramid Texts of the Book of the Dead, which are concerned with the afterlife of the pharaohs of the 5th and 6th Dynasties, Osiris plays a strange but vital role in the mortuary ritual. Among its rubrics and spells, reference is made to his murder and the finding of his body: 'Isis comes and Nephthys ... They find Osiris, as his brother Seth laid him low in Nedjet.' Nedjet in historical times was located near Abydos, in Upper Egypt, which was the chief sanctuary of Osiris. In another text of about the same period (2400 BC) there is reference to the drowning of Osiris in the River Nile at Memphis, the ancient capital of Egypt. There are references also in other texts to the casting of Osiris's body into the Nile or to finding it upon its banks. The two traditions are not mutually exclusive; but what is consistently attested throughout all Egyptian records is that Seth murdered Osiris.

The Egyptian evidence is also agreed that the corpse of Osiris was found by Isis and Nephthys, who either prevented its decomposition or restored it when decomposed by various acts of embalment. After effecting the preservation of his body, the dead Osiris was then raised to life again. Various deities are associated in the texts and iconography with this resurrection, namely, Isis and Nephthys, Atum-Re, Anubis and Horus. The means by which it was effected varies considerably. Generally it would seem that magical incantation was envisaged to resurrect the god. Sometimes a more practical

way was imagined, as in depictions showing Isis and Nephthys fanning air into the inanimate Osiris with the falcon wings attached to their arms.

Although he was thus raised to life again, Osiris did not resume his earthly life in Egypt where, as the texts indicate, he had been a king. Instead, his cause against his murderer Seth was tried before a tribunal of the gods of Heliopolis. The verdict was concise 'Guilty is Seth; Osiris is just.' Osiris then became 'the lord of the West', the underworld or realm of the dead.

The legend of Osiris also involves a number of other divine figures. Isis is both the wife and sister of Osiris. Nephthys, her sister, is the consort of Seth, who is represented as both the brother and murderer of Osiris. Horus was regarded as the posthumously begotten son of Osiris. When he had grown to man's estate, he is represented as fighting with Seth to avenge his father and secure his patrimony. He is also described, inconsistently with his posthumous birth, as performing various mortuary offices for his father, including the ceremony of 'Opening the Mouth'.

Such, then is the story of Osiris as it can be reconstructed from Egyptian texts. The versions of Diodorus Siculus and Plutarch are fuller narrative accounts, composed according to contemporary Graeco-Roman taste; but they preserve some outline of the basic pattern of the Egyptian original. Diodorus presents Osiris as an ancient king who taught the Egyptians the arts of civilized living, including agriculture – Isis had discovered the use of wheat and barley, which had hitherto grown wild. He is murdered by his brother Typhon (Seth is here identified with an evil monster of Greek mythology), who divided his body into 26 pieces, which he gave to his followers in order to implicate them in his crime. The death of Osiris is avenged by Isis and Horus, who slay Typhon. Isis recovers the parts of her husband's body, except the phallus, and buries them secretly. In order to promote the worship of Osiris, she then made exact replicas of his body and entrusted them severally to colleges of priests to bury in their local centres – this is obviously an attempt to explain the fact that several places in Egypt claimed to have the tomb or some relic of Osiris. After reigning for many years, Isis died and was deified. Memphis claimed to have her tomb; but many believed that both Osiris and Isis were buried in the island of Philae in Upper Egypt. This account by Diodorus shows no insight into the real nature of the deity or his place in Egyptian religion.

According to Plutarch, Osiris was also a king who civilized both the Egyptians and the rest of mankind; he was identified by the Greeks with their god Dionysus. After the return of Osiris from his world travel, Seth planned his death with the help of 72 fellow-conspirators. Having secretly measured the body of Osiris, Seth made a beautiful chest, richly decorated, exactly to its dimensions. Then, at a banquet to which Osiris was invited, he offered to give the chest to any guest whom it fitted. When Osiris laid himself within it, Seth slammed the lid, and secured it fast. The chest was thrown into the

River Nile, carried to the sea, and drifted to Byblos, on the Phoenician coast. It came to rest on the shore, and a lovely tree grew up and enclosed it. The tree's size and beauty caused the King of Byblos to cut it down and use it as a pillar of his palace.

The sorrowing Isis, who had long been seeking her husband's body, eventually located it, and by a display of magical power, obtained it from the King of Byblos and brought it back to Egypt. There it was discovered by Seth, who cut it into 14 pieces and scattered the parts throughout the land. Isis patiently searched for the parts, burying each where it was found – another explanation of the many burial places of Osiris in Egypt. The phallus was not found; it had been devoured by a fish that became tabu to the Egyptians. Osiris then emerged from the underworld, to train and equip his son Horus to punish Seth. Horus conquered Seth after a hard struggle, and his legitimacy, questioned by Seth, was vindicated by the gods. Isis conceived a son called Harpocrates by her dead husband – Plutarch here mistakes one of the Greek names ('Harpocrates', derived from the Egyptian 'Horus the child') of Horus for another deity.

These Greek versions are evidence of the fascination that Osiris had for Graeco-Roman society. But although Egyptologists today are better placed to evaluate the ancient god than the Greek men of learning, many problems still remain unsolved.

The royal aspect or character of the god is presented in his traditional iconography: besides the white crown, he holds the symbols of Egyptian royalty – the crook and flail. The image, however, is a curious compromise between a living and a dead king. For the body of Osiris is represented in the form of a mummy, yet the face and head are free of mummy wrappings and the hands protrude from the wrappings and firmly grasp the royal insignia.

The association of the pharaoh with Osiris in death, which constitutes one of the most notable themes of the Pyramid Texts, was designed to effect the resurrection of the dead king. It was based on the principle of imitative magic, the dead king being ritually assimilated to Osiris. The whole drama of the mortuary ritual was, in fact, modelled on that of the legend of the death and resurrection of Osiris. In the Pyramid Texts the subject was the dead king; but gradually the royal mortuary ritual was democratized, so that by the New Kingdom all persons who could afford the expense could hope for revivification through ritual assimilation to Osiris.

Because of his connection with the fundamental mysteries of death and the afterlife, Osiris became the most significant of the gods for the Egyptians. At Abydos, the chief centre of his cult, a dramatic presentation of his death and resurrection was periodically performed. Osiris was also connected with the cult of the Apis bull, from which was derived his transformation into Serapis, the great deity of Hellenized Egypt, whose worship was promoted by King Ptolemy I (305–283 BC) as part of his policy to unite his Greek and Egyptian subjects. In the form of a Mystery religion, the cult of Isis and Osiris spread far into the Roman

Empire; and the famous *Golden Ass* of Apuleius (2nd century AD) attests to the power of its appeal – although Isis, as the great compassionate goddess of the universe, tended to dominate the attention of the devotees, leaving Osiris a somewhat background figure invested in deep and shadowy mystery.

The ever-increasing importance of Osiris to the Egyptians resulted in his association with natural phenomena, especially with the growth of corn and the fructifying waters of the Nile. This has led to his identification as a vegetation deity of the dying-rising type by many scholars, pre-eminently by Sir James G. Frazer. The identification appears to be strikingly confirmed by the custom of placing in tombs moist earth shaped in the form of Osiris: the seed sown in it quickly sprouted in the dark warmth, thus symbolizing new life rising from the dead Osiris, and perhaps facilitating the resurrection of the dead person buried in the tomb. However, although a fertility role was certainly assigned to him, Osiris's character of a vegetation god was later and subordinate to his mortuary significance, which was much more firmly established.

Another role which Osiris acquired was that of judge of the dead; but it was not until the New Kingdom that he appears in this guise, and it is not clear how he came to acquire it.

In the Book of the Dead Osiris is clearly presented as exercising his fateful office in two different ways: the dead are directed to make their first 'Declaration of Innocence' to him; and he presides at the weighing of the soul.

The role of judge of the dead logically contradicted that of saviour of the dead which Osiris had in the mortuary ritual. This discrepancy is extremely interesting, because a similar one occurs in Christianity, where Christ is both saviour and judge. The cause, however, is not the same in each case: Osiris probably came to be regarded as the judge of the dead because he ruled the land of the dead; the diverse roles of Christ derived from the Pauline and Jerusalem traditions that were eventually fused together in orthodox Christology.

It is difficult for us today to appreciate what the ancient Egyptians felt when they looked on the image of Osiris. But some insight is perhaps given, if we bear in mind that the image was that of a divine hero who had suffered and died, and then rose from the dead.

Thus Osiris was by no means some remote transcendent deity such as Re, the sun god, but one who had endured the grim ordeal that awaited all men. In his image, moreover, the Egyptian devotees saw also the promise of their own resurrection from death and eternal life in the realm of Osiris. Phenomenologically, if not historically, Osiris was thus a prototype of Christ, and may have prepared the way for him to some extent.

Osiris 'may rightly claim to have been worshipped longer than any other god': this statue shows him wearing the white crown of Egypt and holding the royal symbols of crook and flail.

Serapis

The principal god of Alexandria and the chief deity of Ptolemaic Egypt was Serapis or Sarapis, about whose origin there was much speculation in the ancient world. According to the Roman historian Tacitus, writing in the 2nd century AD, Ptolemy I, the first Greek monarch of Egypt (305–283 BC), was instructed in a dream to send to Sinope, a city on the shores of the Black Sea, for the statue of the god of that place. Ptolemy consulted the Egyptian priests about his dream, but they could not interpret it. It was eventually interpreted by an Athenian named Timotheus who, significantly, was connected with the Eleusinian Mysteries. He identified the god of Ptolemy's dream as Pluto, who was associated with the underworld goddess Persephone at Sinope. After some difficult negotiations, the statue was obtained and brought to Alexandria. Tacitus adds some further explanatory details about Serapis: 'The god, himself, on account of his healing art, is called by many Aesculapius; by others, Osiris, the most ancient deity of the country (Egypt); and many give him the name of Jupiter, as lord of the universe. But the most maintain that he is Pluto – either from tokens which are discernible in the deity himself, or by a circuitous process of probable reasoning.'

This account of the origin of Serapis is not accepted by scholars today. But it is recognized as probable that Ptolemy I did promote the cult of Serapis as a means of uniting his Greek and Egyptian subjects in the worship of a god whom both could appreciate. This god was a hybrid conception of Egyptian origin, venerated already by some Greeks resident in Egypt. The origin and development of the conception provide a curious example of religious syncretism. At Memphis, the ancient capital of Egypt, there had existed from a remote period the cult of the Apis bull as a symbol of divine procreativity. When one of these sacred animals died, it was identified with Osiris, the Egyptian god of the dead and named Oserapis, that is Osiris-Apis. The body of each Apis was mummified and buried, amid public lamentation, with the bodies of its predecessors in the Serapeum, a subterranean labyrinth at Sakkara.

The story which Tacitus tells of the dream-revealed image certainly relates to the form under which Serapis was presented in Alexandria, which was essentially a Greek city. The identification of the Egyptian Serapis with the Greek god Pluto would have been easy; for both Osiris and Pluto were rulers of the underworld. In the magnificent temple, which was built in Alexandria for the new deity and known as the Serapeum, the cult statue showed Serapis as a bearded Greek god, similar in features to Zeus, seated on a throne. His underworld character was symbolized by an accompanying image of Cerberus and by the *kalathos*, 'basket', upon his head, which was a symbol of fertility.

Serapis, through his derivation from Osiris, became associated with the great goddess Isis, and the prescribed oath in law-courts and for legal transactions in Ptolemaic Egypt was, 'by Serapis and Isis and all other gods and goddesses'. He also inherited from Osiris the character of a saviour god connected with the afterlife, and his cult, in some of its forms, constituted a Mystery religion. His association with Asclepios, one of the Healing Gods, which Tacitus mentions, is interesting. But it was not from the Greek healer god that Serapis acquired his reputation as a divine healer but from the ancient Egyptian deified sage, Imhotep, whose sanctuary, at Sakkara, was an Egyptian 'Lourdes', and called an Asklepieion by the Greeks who went there.

From Alexandria the cult of Serapis spread into the Graeco-Roman world, and enjoyed a considerable popularity, doubtless through its combination of the religious traditions of Egypt and Greece. Serapis became identified also with both the time god Aion and the sun as Zeus Helios. The importance of his cult was such that the Christian destruction of the Serapeum in Alexandria dramatically symbolized the victory of Christianity over paganism in the Ancient World.

Facing page Seth had a chequered career in Egyptian mythology; once he was Lord of Upper Egypt, but was later made guilty of the murder of Osiris, and was identified with foreign invaders of Egypt: 19th Dynasty bronze statue of Seth. **Below** *Head of the god Serapis, from Carthage: he was represented as a bearded Greek god, looking like Zeus, but his origins lay in the Egyptian cult of a divine bull.*

Michael Holford

C.M. Dixon/British Museum

Seth

One of the major gods of ancient Egypt, Seth was said to be the son of Geb and Nut and he is conspicuous on the monuments and in texts. In particular he is assigned a prominent role in representations of symbolic rites relating to the pharaonic state. The best known of these is the ceremony of 'Uniting the Two Lands', which is impressively portrayed on the limestone reliefs from Lisht near Memphis, now in the Cairo Museum. Seth is figured here facing the god Horus. Both are animal gods, but here their bodies have human shape; only their heads retain their original form – the falcon head of Horus and the canine head of Seth. The two deities are shown tying the symbolic plants of Upper and Lower Egypt to the sign which connotes unity. In these reliefs Seth is clearly the representative of Upper Egypt.

There is little doubt that the scene mirrors an enacted ritual in which priests impersonated the gods. Seth is depicted too in other related ceremonies, such as those connected with the purification and the coronation of the pharaoh. In an oft-recorded rite which has been called 'the Baptism of Pharaoh' he is shown, together with Horus, pouring water over the king's head in a deeply symbolic act.

Seth's original cult centre was very probably Ombos, the modern Naqada, where a figure of the Seth animal has been found amid vestiges of Naqada's earliest predynastic culture, which derives from the middle of the fourth millennium BC. But what the Seth animal really was still constitutes a problem.

Suggestions made hitherto include the ass, oryx antelope, the fennec (a small fox with huge pointed ears), jerboa (a rodent), camel, okapi, long-snouted mouse, giraffe and various types of hogs or boars. Another view is that the animal is fabulous, like the griffin or dragon. The narrow snout and upraised ears and tail suggest a canine type; perhaps the species was already extinct in Egypt, even in very early times.

In later phases of his development Seth was associated with the ass, the pig and the hippopotamus, and in these cases the interpretation of his character was usually unfavourable.

Indeed a striking fact in the history of the cult of Seth is that after the New Kingdom, from about 1000 BC, the god is involved for the most part in a position of increasing degradation. One reason is that the roles he occupies in mythology are almost inevitably inauspicious.

In the legend about his fierce fight with the falcon god Horus, Seth is said to have been deprived of his testicles, and although he in turn ripped out one of the eyes of Horus, the final victory, including justification in the divine tribunal, went to his opponent. In the myth of Osiris the role of Seth becomes still more sinister: he is the murderer who brought down Osiris in Nedjet. The opposing gods in each case were incorporated in the concept of kingship, Horus being identified with the living pharaoh, Osiris with the deceased one, so that Seth was fated from the start to follow a difficult and inauspicious course.

In relation to the living pharaoh, Seth's place in the official theology was at first protected, as we have seen, by the concept of reconciliation. If Seth represents Upper Egypt in a rite celebrating the unity of Egypt, this means that an early stage of disunity is reflected, when Seth was the patron god of a part of the country, espousing its strife against another part. But the retrospect is now a happy one, and the dominance of Horus in the royal theology does not deny Seth an honoured second place. Later, however, Thoth replaces Seth in some of the symbolic rites, such as the 'Baptism of Pharaoh'. Seth is identified with the victim offered in sacrificial rites, and the slain offering is subsequently equated with the defeated enemy.

The Book of Victory over Seth and the texts of the Temple of Edfu are virulently anti-Sethian, but they derive from sanctuaries of Osiris and Horus. It is true that even in the first millennium BC Seth was specially honoured by the Libyan Dynasty; and if the escalating popularity of Osiris told heavily against him, there were centres of Seth worship which continued to flourish even in the Roman era.

In the legend which describes his conflict with Horus there are some clear pointers to a historical and political substratum. Cosmological explanations become prominent later, and one modern view would interpret the myth as being inherently of this type. Seth, however, is not at all easy to fit into such a scheme.

As a god of heaven, Horus is light, it may be argued; he is eventually equated with the sun god Re, and his eyes are the sun and moon. If so, what does Seth represent? He is not simply a god of darkness; sometimes he is a storm god, a thunderer, while at other times his name is linked with that of the desert.

One recent writer H. te Velde, sees the polarity as that between light and sexuality. Seth is certainly endowed by the Egyptian texts with strong, if somewhat perverse, sexual powers. It is very doubtful, however, whether they are felt to be opposed to the cosmic concept of light. Nephthys, sister and partner of Isis, is usually named as his wife, but the union is not credited with any offspring.

Seth is himself sometimes equated astrally with the Great Bear, and in the texts and representations which portray the fight of Re against Apophis, the serpent demon of darkness, Seth is the champion-in-chief of the sun god. What contributed especially to his decline in status was the tendency to identify him with foreign invaders such as the Assyrians and Persians. In the magical papyri his position remains tremendously influential, even if he is often regarded now as a kind of Satan. By this time he has been identified with the Greek monster Typhon, likewise a challenger of the established divine order.

Seth-Typhon is also sometimes referred to as 'the headless demon', but this term is applied in the papyri to other gods too, including Osiris. Since the magician is anxious to deploy the powers of Seth-Typhon, his attitude to the god may therefore be considered to be ambivalent.

On the one hand he may address him with great respect and declare himself to be his partisan in the struggle against Osiris or Horus; on the other hand, he may call him 'the slayer of his own brother', just to remind him that the magician is acquainted with his crimes and will use his knowledge unfavourably unless the god is prepared to show sympathy in the matter which is the subject of his appeal.

One of the Gnostic sects of later times went by the name of Sethians, paying special honour to Seth, the biblical son of Adam and Eve. Suggestions concerning a second relationship involving the Egyptian god seem to be rather speculative, however, and must be treated with caution, especially if the relationship is retrospective.

Appendix

William MacQuitty

Anubis

Egyptian god of the dead, 'lord of the mummy wrappings' and inventor of embalming, who led the dead to the place of judgement after death and supervised the weighing of the heart; shown as a black jackal or a dog, both of which roamed the cemeteries in Egypt.

Apis

Sacred bull of Memphis in Egypt, connected with the gods Ptah and Osiris, who later became the Graeco-Egyptian deity Serapis, a god of the underworld: Serapis appears on Roman Imperial coins and the famous library of Alexandria was attached to his temple there.

Aten

Or Aton, in Egyptian religion, the disc of the sun; in the 14th century BC Pharaoh Amenophis IV changed

Michael Holford

his name to Ikhnaton (or Akhenaten), 'pleasing to the Aten', denied the old gods and established a short-lived religion of the Aten as the only god.

Dung-beetle

Or scarab, venerated in Egypt because it lays its eggs in a ball of dung which it rolls along the ground: a symbol of the sun, of the creation of life in matter, or resurrection; amulets in the shape of a scarab were worn as good luck charms or placed in the tombs of the dead to ensure eternal life.

Roger Wood London

Falcon

To the ancient Egyptians a sacred bird, identified with the sky and the sun probably because it could fly so high: it was particularly associated with the god Horus who was depicted as a falcon or falcon-headed man and dead falcons were frequently buried in extremely expensive coffins.

Firmament

The vault of the heavens: it was generally viewed in the ancient world as a solid crystal sphere, constantly rotating, to which the stars were fixed; it contained windows through which the waters above the firmament fell as rain; later it was thought of as the eighth sphere surrounding the seven spheres of the planets.

William MacQuitty

Jackal

A cunning animal, like the fox of European folklore which it resembles; as a scavenger and eater of carrion, often associated with death; Anubis, the Egyptian guardian of cemeteries who guided the dead to the judgement of Osiris, was depicted as a jackal or dog: traditionally a timid creature, and Bushmen would not eat the heart of a jackal in case they should become cowardly themselves.

C. M. Dixon

Maat

Egyptian goddess of truth, justice and order, whose symbol was a feather; according to ancient Egyptian belief, in the judgement of the dead the heart of the deceased was weighed against the feather-symbol of Maat and if declared *maa kheru* (true of voice) the deceased was granted entrance into the kingdom of Osiris.

Myrrh

Gum resin used in perfumery and medicine; the three magi or kings brought gold, frankincense and myrrh as gifts to the infant Jesus; used in ancient Egypt for embalming corpses; consequently connected in magic with Saturn, the planet of death, and, as a preservative, with the sun.

Obelisk

Four-sided pillar, usually of stone, tapering to a pyramid at the top, frequently associated with graves and temples in Egypt, where it was a symbol of the sun.

Pyramids

Structures of stone or brick with a rectangular base and four triangular sides which slope inwards and meet at an apex: the most famous are those of ancient Egypt, which were royal tombs; the Great Pyramid at Giza has been described as 'perhaps the greatest single building ever erected by man' and has attracted the speculations of pyramidologists: there are also notable pyramids in Central America.

Pyramid texts

Texts containing myths, burial rituals, hymns, incantations, prayers and magic spells, inscribed on the interior walls of pyramids at Sakkara, near Memphis in Egypt; dating from c 2350 to 2175 BC, they are 'the earliest records we have of Egyptian thought' and 'the earliest body of religious writings we have of mankind as a whole'.

Re

Or Ra, sun god and 'great god' of ancient Egypt, closely connected with the kingship of the pharaohs; as the sun at dawn, represented as a beetle or beetle-headed man: as the declining sun, he was Re-Atum, an old and wise man; linked with the god Amun at Thebes; frequently linked with the falcon-headed sky god Horus, with whom he had affinities.

Sphinx

Hybrid creature combining human and animal parts, typically a lion's body and the head of a man (or sometimes of a hawk or ram): pairs or avenues of sphinxes guarded the entrances to palaces, temples and tombs in Egypt; the Great Sphinx is a colossal image near the pyramids of Giza; in Greek mythology, the woman-headed Sphinx of Thebes strangled passers-by when they failed to solve the riddle she put to them.

Mesopotamia

Ancient man saw the universe in the form of conscious forces, which were conceived of in some specific shape. Such personification was originally not necessarily in human shape, since some of the most primitive concepts of divine powers invested them with animal aspects. Some aspects of the forces active in the world, certainly those thought of as universal gods, must have been personified by the Sumerians before their settlement in Mesopotamia. In addition, each early Sumerian settlement had its own local deity (sometimes identified with a universal deity), with attributed characteristics depending on the dominant features of the locality and community. As society developed, the deities of different settlements were brought into relationship, whilst additionally specific aspects of agriculture and technology (for example, corn or brickmaking) became personified in a deity. Thus arose a considerable pantheon, the names of its members being compiled in god lists before the middle of the third millennium. Genealogies of the gods (theogonies) were developed to explain the relationship between deities.

In one group of theogonies Enlil is the first god, deriving from several generations of vaguely defined primeval beings. In other theogonies, this role falls to An (Akkadian Anum), with Enki (Akkadian Ea) as his son. These two concepts were theologically combined, so that heading the pantheon in its developed form there stood a triad of universal gods: Anum, the sky god and king of the gods; Enlil, 'Lord Wind', originally a wind and mountain god; and Enki (Ea), god of wisdom, originally 'Lord Earth'. Though Anum was nominally king of the gods, executive power was in the hands of Enlil, who often in practice usurped the supremacy. In the mythology of historical times the sphere of Ea's activity was the cosmic sweet waters (Apsu) beneath the earth, probably as a result of the Sumerian Enki absorbing the attributes of a divinity of an earlier stage of religion.

A second group of deities comprised the moon god Nannar (Sin); the sun god Utu (Shamash); Venus, known in Sumerian as Innin or Inanna, 'Lady of Heaven', and in Akkadian as Ishtar; and the weather god, who was of less importance in a purely Sumerian context than to the Semites, amongst whom he was called Adad. These four gods, manifestly related to the diurnal period, are specifically described as sleeping during part of the day. Since in the latitude of Babylonia the crescent of the new moon is seen on a level axis like a boat, Sin was said to ride across the sky in a holy ship. Though, like the other great gods, thought of also anthropomorphically, he bore the epithet 'Brilliant Young Bull', and in a myth took that form to impregnate a cow.

The sun god rode across the heavens in a chariot drawn by mules. It was to him that prayers were addressed by those who lived by the ancient pre-agricultural pursuits of hunting and fishing, although all civilized

The stele of Naram-Sin, c 2300 BC, shows the Akkadian king facing a stylized mountain, his foot resting upon the bodies of his enemies; behind him soldiers climb a mountain path. The gradual infiltration of Babylonia by Semites in the 3rd millennium BC led to modification of the ancient Sumerian religion.

Giraudon

men bowed to him at his rising. Seeing all that happened on earth, he became god of justice and the divine lawgiver, and also controlled omens. He was sometimes thought to pass through the underworld at night.

The importance of Adad, the weather god, increased as one left Babylonia, a region watered almost wholly by irrigation, and moved north-westwards into areas dependent upon rain. Because of the sound of his voice in thunder, Adad was associated with the bull: he was also represented by the lightning symbol.

Inanna-Ishtar, a very complex figure, Queen of Heaven and Earth, the only prominent goddess of historical times, seems to have personified the vital forces of the crises of life. She could be felt as the loving mother who had suckled the king, or as the goddess controlling sexual powers, or as goddess of battle. She was also associated in myth and popular religion with a consort Dumuzi (Tammuz), a fertility deity who was annually lamented when absent in the underworld.

Other deities of major significance included Marduk, originally an aspect of the

scribal profession. The latter function had earlier been attributed to a Sumerian goddess Nisaba, and the conflict between the two concepts was resolved by Nisaba being (by the first millennium) regarded as Nabu's wife. In Assyria it was Ashur, originally the Assyrian tribal god, who ultimately usurped leadership in the pantheon, bearing the title 'the Assyrian Enlil'. Another god who became of particular significance in Assyria was the warrior god Ninurta, son of Enlil.

Though there are indications in mythology that a number of female deities originally held a significant place in Sumerian religion, from the beginning of the second millennium the only goddess of independent significance other than Inanna (Ishtar) was Ereshkigal, Queen of the Underworld, and even in her case a myth describes how she gained a dominant spouse, Nergal. Each of the male deities had a nominal consort, sometimes a pale reflection bearing the feminine form of his own name, sometimes an old Sumerian goddess who originally served an independent function in the pantheon or even existed before the developed pantheon.

might take up residence in an image, which then represented the god's presence and became a focus of the cult, although the god was not theologically thought of as bounded by the visible statue. A considerable wardrobe of clothing, insignia and jewellery would be available to dress and adorn the god's image. Daily food offerings were made and privileged persons, including the king, might be permitted to eat the food remaining from the god's meal table. The deities, in the form of the statues, might upon appropriate occasions make journeys from one shrine to another, either by ship or upon the shoulders of bearers. Their accidental movements on such occasions were of great significance as omens to bystanders.

There is some ambiguity about the relationship felt to exist between Mesopotamian man and the great gods. On the one hand, the great gods were concerned not with the individual but with the maintenance of cosmic and political order and the course of Nature. On the other hand, there are indications that the relationship between a worshipper and a god might be felt as a very

sun god. As god of Babylon, he ultimately achieved supremacy in the Babylonian pantheon, assimilating the characteristics of Enlil; he was also equated with a god Asallukhi, in which context he was, in addition, god of magic. Nabu, god of Borsippa, the nearest city to Babylon, was (probably for this geographical reason) regarded as Marduk's son; he was also patron of the

The great gods, whilst regarded as being concerned with the life of Babylonia and Assyria as a whole, might at the same time be thought of as having their abode particularly in a certain city or cities. Anum lived in Erech or Der, for instance, and Shamash in Sippar or Larsa. The deities were in no sense tied to these places but if the proper rites were performed, an aspect of the deity

Above *The sun god Shamash receives homage from three smaller figures; the sun god's emblem, the solar disc, appears on the altar. The tablet was dedicated by a Babylonian king of the 9th century who restored the temple of Shamash in Sippar. Facing page Imdugud, the sacred lion-headed eagle, spreads his wings protectively over two stags.*

intimate one. In the third millennium Gudea, a city ruler, says to his god: 'You are my father, you are my mother.'

In general, the gulf between the worshipper and the great gods was bridged by the concept of the 'personal god', a minor deity rather like a guardian angel, who could bring the supplication of the ordinary man before the major deities. It seems probable that only a king would have a major deity as his personal god.

Behind the deities prominent in historical times there are traces of an earlier stage of religion, hinted at in the genealogies of the gods, and represented in myths and incantations which mention divine beings thought of as slain, defeated or suppressed. Whilst the deities of historical times are primarily anthropomorphic, some of the divine powers of the earlier stage were conceived in animal form. Anzu (or Zu), a divine being who once challenged the great gods, had the form of a bird, whilst Tiamat, the primeval being from whom in one myth the gods originated, was sometimes represented as a dragon, and another proto-deity whose attributes were absorbed by Ea may have been thought of as an ibex. The supersession of the earlier stage of religion is reflected not only in the various combat myths, but also in the fact that the victor gods bear the characteristics, and sometimes the names or titles, of those they overcome. Thus Ea not only overcame Apsu, the primeval waters, but bore the title 'the Ibex of the Apsu' and is even identified with Apsu. Ninurta not only defeated Anzu, but had applied to him the name Imdugud, elsewhere used of Anzu. Marduk not only subdued Tiamat's marshal Kingu, but could actually be called Kingu.

The number of deities in the pantheon was ultimately much reduced by identifying one deity with another or with aspects of another. For example, one hymn specifically states that a number of great deities are incorporated in the god Ninurta. Such a process would logically have concluded in monotheism. The claim has been made that this

was actually achieved in Babylonia, but this remains questionable.

Myths, either as long literary productions or embedded in fragmentary form in incantations, ritual texts or hymns, are known in both Sumerian and Akkadian. The value of myths for the understanding of Mesopotamian religion has been variously estimated, one extreme view being that they primarily reflect primitive stories from the remote past rather than anything in the religious experience of Mesopotamian man of the second or first millennium. Against this, whilst their origin was certainly (in most instances) very ancient, their use until a late period in incantations indicates that they were still felt to have some relevance to the supernatural forces affecting mankind.

The main themes of myths concern (with variations between Sumerian and Akkadian examples) the creation and organization of the physical universe, the creation of the gods and their functions, the creation of man, the origin and prehistory of the existing order, the origin of disease and healing, and stories of the Flood and the underworld.

A Sumerian myth of creation offers an insight into the concept of the relationship between the gods and mankind. The composition begins with an account of the difficulties confronting the gods in obtaining their food. Their complaint is brought before Enki, god of wisdom, who describes to his mother how to make servants by moulding clay in the image of the gods. Theologically, this reflects the view that mankind exists primarily to serve the gods. When the creation of man has been successfully achieved, Enki and his mother, having become intoxicated in celebration, proceed to make seven abnormal beings, this part of the story being an attempt to explain the occurrence of malformed humans.

The myth of 'Enki and the World Order' described how Enki produced the features of the world as known to the Sumerians. He it was who had given cattle to the nomad 'who builds no city, who builds no house',

and he it was who had decreed for the various lands their characteristic products, and who had instituted the various aspects of agriculture. A typical passage described how in the manner of a bull he impregnated the Tigris, giving it fertility, and making its water available for irrigation.

Like a thrusting bull he stood proudly,
He produced an erection, he ejaculated,
He filled the Tigris with clear water...
The water he produced is clear water...
The grain he produced...the people eat it.

Some Sumerian myths reflect very early cultural advances or changes. The earliest Sumerian settlements were in the extreme south around Eridu, but the cultural centre subsequently moved north to Erech; this situation is reflected in the following myth. Inanna, goddess of Erech, visited Eridu, whose patron Enki, god of wisdom, had in his charge a collection of objects basic to civilization, called in Sumerian *me*, and representing features of civilization which in modern terms would mainly be thought of as abstract concepts, but which the Sumerians, conceiving them as embodied in their symbols, could regard as physical entities. They included such aspects of Sumerian life as kingship and royal insignia, various priestly offices, sexual relations and prostitution, musical instruments, truth and falsehood, various crafts, peace and victory. A feast ensued at which Enki, generous in his wine, made these functions over to Inanna. Subsequently repenting of his generosity, Enki dispatched monsters to intercept Inanna on her voyage home, but failed in his attempt.

One of the most striking myths, centred on Inanna (Ishtar) and extant, with variations, in both Sumerian and Akkadian versions, describes the visit of the goddess to the underworld, for reasons which are not made explicit but which some scholars have suggested (on little evidence) was to gain possession from her older sister Ereshkigal. Inanna's descent took her through seven gates, at each of which the gatekeeper

removed part of her garments and insignia.
Emerging through the final gate naked, she
encountered the deathly glance of Ereshkigal and the judges of the underworld, and
became a corpse.

Anticipating disaster, Inanna had left her
vizier, Ninshubur, with instructions to seek
help from various other deities, if she did
not return within three days. After unsuccessfully visiting Enlil in Nippur, and the
moon god in Ur, Ninshubur went to Enki
in Eridu. Enki created two sexless creatures
(possibly a reflection of the occurrence of
eunuchs in the cult of Inanna) and sent them
to Ereshkigal, from whom after they had
ingratiated themselves, they were to beg the
corpse of Inanna as a gift. The creatures then
restored Inanna to life, but the rules of the
underworld permitted her to leave only if
she provided a substitute. Her return to the
earth was therefore in the company of
ghouls, serving as wardens. At the first two
cities Inanna visited, she found the city god
in mourning for her, and in gratification
exempted them from being taken as substitute. At the third town, a suburb of her
own city Erech, she found the god Dumuzi,
her own spouse, rejoicing instead of lamenting. In chagrin she handed him over to the
representatives of the underworld who,
despite desperate attempts by Dumuzi to
escape, finally took him prisoner, to Inanna's
ultimate grief.

Amongst myths preserved only or primarily in Akkadian the best known is the
relatively sophisticated Creation myth
Enuma elish ('When above'). Recited at
Babylon during the New Year festival,
this began with a description of the origin
of the universal deities Anum and Ea from
a chain of beings descended from the primeval Tiamat and Apsu, the cosmic ocean and
sweet waters. Eventually the bustling activities of the younger gods disturbed the primeval beings, and conflict ensued. After Ea
had overcome Apsu, Tiamat herself entered
into hostilities.

The other gods proving powerless to
challenge her, Ea's virile son Marduk appeared as champion on condition that he
should receive supreme power in the pantheon. With this granted, he fought and
defeated Tiamat, splitting her body like a
shellfish, and spreading it out as heaven and
earth. From the blood of Kingu, leader of the
host of Tiamat, Marduk created man, and
imposed on him the service of the gods. In
gratitude to Marduk the other gods built him
a shrine in Babylon.

This myth reflects theological ideas concerning the origin of man (created to serve
the gods but yet containing a divine element),
and also concerning the reason for the
political supremacy of Babylon.

The myth of 'Adapa', the ending of which
is missing, concerns the limitations of human
beings in the face of the gods. A fisherman,
Adapa, was summoned to heaven for breaking the wing of the south wind. After Anum
had forgiven him, he had immortality within
his grasp when the supreme god offered him
the bread and water of life but – falsely
advised by Ea – Adapa rejected these gifts.

In the relatively late myth of the pestilence
god Erra, datable in origin to the end of the

By 1000 BC political supremacy had shifted from Babylonia to Assyria and northern gods, such as the warlike Ashur, consequently achieved greater prominence: relief from the palace of the Assyrian king Sennacherib, showing a pile of heads of defeated enemies.

second millennium, Erra is represented as offended by mankind's neglect of his cult. He therefore came to Marduk, god of Babylon, to pick a quarrel. By this period Marduk had acquired attributes originally belonging to Anum, and was called 'king of the gods'. For reasons which are not clear, Marduk had to leave his city to go to the underworld, and conciliated Erra by allowing him to take charge during his absence. Breaking trust, Erra proceeded to devastate Babylonia, including the capital itself. Finally Erra's anger was calmed by his vizier, and he confessed himself at fault. This may represent a mythological explanation of an outbreak of plague in Babylon, possibly during the New Year festival, when on the human level the city was dangerously crowded and on the mythic level Marduk was, for part of the period, absent. The epilogue states that the presence of this myth in a house will give protection against plague, and it is known that extracts from this myth served as amulets.

Magic, which in the hands of the exorcist could protect Mesopotamian man from the attack of demons, in the hands of sorcerers (male or female) could be directed against humans. Such anti-social use of magic is widely attested from the beginning of the second millennium, being legislated against by the Laws of Hammurabi. The typical technique in witchcraft was making an image of the victim which was then destroyed, often by burning, but anything closely connected with the intended victim could be used to gain magical power over him.

Not only the deliberate activities of witches and sorcerers but also the commission, even accidentally and unwittingly, of certain tabooed acts, could bring evil supernatural influences upon a man. Curses (not necessarily spoken words) were regarded as physical things which could enter a man's body and be extracted again.

Troubles of this kind were dealt with by another series of incantations, called *Shurpu* (a term also meaning 'Burnings', but in a different sense from *Maqlu*). The victim was diagnosed as suffering from one of an undifferentiated list of offences, including both deeds which would in terms of modern thought be taken as ethical offences and those which were simply accidental breaches of a taboo. Incantations were recited by the exorcist and the patient was then handed an onion, a date, a piece of matting, and tufts of wool. Each of these he had to pull apart and throw into the fire. Accompanying the destruction of each was an incantation of the following type: 'Like this onion which he peels and throws into the fire ... so may oath, curse ... pain, weariness, guilt, sin, wickedness, transgression, the pain which is in my body, my flesh, my sinews, be peeled off like this onion.'

Another procedure used to dispose of evil

influences was to absorb them into some substance or animal. The following simple example describes the method of calming a feverish child by transferring the evil contagion to a dog: 'You shall place a loaf on the child's head; you shall recite a (previously specified) incantation three times; you shall wipe (with the loaf) from the (child's) head to his feet, you shall throw that loaf to a dog. That child will be calm.'

The threat of evil powers, in the form of demons, witchcraft, and other forces released by breach of taboo, came to a climax in relation to the king himself. Many rituals and incantations and a vast corpus of taboo were designed to protect him, and the land whose wellbeing resided in him, from such perils. He might even resign his throne temporarily to a substitute to escape the dire consequences when particularly grave evils were foretold.

The gods were thought to determine in advance the details of a man's life, or events relating to the future of a city or nation. By using proper means, men could obtain a glimpse of these 'destinies'. Many forms of divination developed to this end, some available to the common man, others restricted to the king and matters of statecraft. Amongst the principal techniques were exstispicy, observation of animal behaviour, interpretation of dreams, and astrology.

Exstispicy involved the slaughtering of a lamb and the examination of its internal organs. A question having been previously put to the sun god, his answer could be read by the experts in the configurations and markings of the organs, particularly the lungs and liver.

Omens could be obtained in simpler manner from random events, in particular the behaviour of animals, and there arose large compilations listing these. If ants were seen fighting, this foretold 'approach of the enemy; there will be the downfall of a great army.' If a white dog cocked its leg against a man, hard times would follow.

For the interpretation of dreams, to which much importance was attached in later Assyria, a 'Dream Book' existed, giving the interpretation of some hundreds of dream incidents. Astrology, also important in imperial Assyria, used meteorological or celestial phenomena to predict matters relating to the king or the state. For example: 'During the night Saturn came near the moon. Saturn is the "star" of the sun. This is the solution: it is favourable to the king, (because) the sun is the king's star.' This divination technique was used many centuries before the development of horoscopic astrology, applicable to a particular individual, which, although it also had its origin in Mesopotamian civilization, did not arise until the latest stage, at about 400 BC.

The practical affairs of the Mesopotamians were thought to be controlled by minor deities: these were of two kinds – benevolent guardian spirits and evil demons. One of the former, a winged eagle-headed genie bearing offerings, appears on this alabaster bas-relief of the 9th century from the palace of Assurnasirpal.

98060

British Museum

Syria and Palestine

The fullest contemporary record of religion in Syria is the texts in alphabetic cuneiform from ancient Ugarit, Ras Shamra. From these texts we learn that the senior god was El ('god'), the King Paramount, Father of the Exalted Ones and Father of Men and Creator, depicted as enthroned at the remote 'source of the streams'. His strength and procreative influence is expressed in his title 'the Bull', but he was the principal god in social relationships, and this aspect of his character is expressed by his title, 'the Kindly, the Compassionate'.

El's executive king is Baal, whose proper name was Hadad ('the Thunderer') or Baal Ramman ('the Thunderer'), which Jewish scribes parodied as Rimmon ('pomegranate'). He establishes his kingly power and order in Nature in a primeval conflict with Sea-and-Ocean Currents and associated monsters like Letan (Leviathan of the Old Testament) and Tannin, also known in this connection in the Old Testament, and has his 'house' built as a visible token that he is the reigning king. He is obliged, however, to reassert his kingship in a seasonal conflict against Sterility, or Death (Mot) in a myth which is believed to be related to the chief seasonal crisis in Syria, at the autumn equinox.

Bronze figure of Canaanite god, thought to be El, the paramount deity, father of gods and men, the kindly and compassionate, also associated with the bull.

C. M. Dixon

In this myth Baal is the god of thunder, lightning, and winter rains, 'He who Mounts the Clouds', and is, like the Mesopotamian Tammuz, a dying and rising god, whose fortunes fluctuate with the vegetation he promotes. In his eclipse in the summer season his sister and consort Anat (the north Syrian counterpart of Astarte) is particularly active. Baal, as the vegetation he promotes, succumbs to Mot. His dead body is sought over hill and dale by Anat, called in the Ras Shamra texts 'the Virgin Anat', a rite which had its counterpart in the fertility cult throughout the Near East. There is definite reflection of the mourning of Anat on the recovery and burial of the body of Baal in the Old Testament (Zechariah 12.11) in 'the mourning for Hadad-Rimmon in the plain of Megiddo'. Anat proceeds to avenge Baal. She cuts down Mot, winnows him, parches him with fire, grinds him with a millstone and scatters his remains in the fields for the birds to eat. This obviously relates to the desacralization of the new crop, setting it free for common use, as in the offering of the first sheaf of 'new grain from fresh ears, parched with fire,' in Leviticus 2.14.

In myth related to ritual strict logical consistency is not expected, and Baal revives. His revival is anticipated in a dream by El, who is the final authority in these texts and intervenes at significant junctures to confirm a decision or to foreshadow the future. El's vision is of the skies raining olive oil and the wadis running with honey, which recurs in the liturgies of Israel reflected in Amos 9.13 and Joel 3.18. With similar lack of consistency Mot is introduced in a final 'showdown' with Baal, out of which Baal emerges victor and again vindicates his kingship. This conflict is set 'in the seventh year' and may be related to the seven-year cycle marked in Israel by an artificial famine, when the land lay fallow on the principle that drought must be given full play in order that its force might be exhausted. Thus in the seasonal tension after the long dry summer, pending the coming of the 'early rains', the Syrian peasant relieved his anxiety and predisposed providence by homoeopathic magic, which was the genesis of drama in Greece in the cult of the wine god Dionysus at Athens. In Syria no such dramas are attested, but all the elements of drama are in the Baal myth.

It will be seen that Israel inherited this liturgic theme of the great autumn festival which she developed in the light of her own historical tradition of the great deliverance from Egypt and the Covenant, but the essential features of the seasonal festival survived conflict with the forces of destruction and disorder, the demonstration of the effective kingship of God and the establishment of his government, often by judgement. This is expressed notably in the Enthronement psalms in the Old Testament, in passages in the Prophets which reflect this liturgical theme and in passages on the Day of the Lord in Jewish and Christian apocalyptic books like Revelation. There the sea and certain sea monsters are arch-enemies of

God's ordered government, as in the Baal myth of Ras Shamra in the New Year festival in Canaan.

The role of the king in his sacral function as executive of Baal as the Divine King in his 'passion' and triumph in the great autumn festival cannot be established on the evidence of the Ras Shamra texts, but on the analogy of the corresponding occasion in Mesopotamian religion it is likely. With the necessary changes, it may certainly be demonstrated that in Jerusalem the Davidic king was the temporal guarantee of the effective Kingship of God, which was expressed in the liturgy of the great autumn festival. For Canaan Ezekiel's denunciation of the King of Tyre (chapter 28) expresses the conception of the king as the representative of God, the channel of divine blessings, and, as representative of the community, the royal man in the garden of God. The Legend of King Krt at Ras Shamra speaks of the king as 'the son of El', and the crown prince is 'suckled by the fertility goddesses Anat and Athirat'. The conception of the king as the upholder of the social justice which is the concern of God is expressed in the royal texts from Ras Shamra and, as in Psalm 72 and Isaiah 11.1–9, he is the medium of blessings in Nature. It is not difficult to see here an ideology from which the conception of the Messiah in Israel developed.

The protagonists of this cult are well known through texts, sculpture and figurines. Baal is the active young warrior god, El is an elderly god on his throne and footstool, both being associated with the bull in virtue of procreative interests. Anat, like Astarte in the Old Testament, is the goddess of love, and appears naked in moulded reliefs and pendants, either devoted to shrines or given in return for the payment of a vow and used as amulets to promote childbirth. Sexual rites of imitative magic associated with the Canaanite fertility cult survived in Israel and are constantly denounced by the Prophets. Anat was also the goddess of war, like Ishtar in Mesopotamia, and is involved in what is evidently a bloody massacre in her temple in an episode in the Baal myth at Ras Shamra, which may really describe a blood-letting rite, like the self-laceration of the devotees of Baal at Carmel (1 Kings 18.28), or perhaps circumcision. The mother goddess Athirat (Ashera of the Old Testament) appears as the consort of El, and is probably the goddess represented as the nourisher of life who offers ears of corn to two rampant caprids (goats) on an ivory relief from the seaward quarter of Ugarit. The motif is a development of the rampant caprids reaching up to the fruit of the Tree of Life, which is familiar throughout the Near East. In the references in the Old Testament to the *ashera* as a feature of sanctuaries this is a tree, either natural or stylized, representing the mother goddess Ashera as the receptive element in Nature and as the universal nourisher. The Tree of Life is closely associated in the ancient Near East with the king in his sacral function as

---

mediator of the divine blessing, as in Assyrian sculpture and on the royal couch from the palace of Ras Shamra.

Significant as the fertility cult of Canaan undoubtedly was, it is possible that the dramatic nature of the Baal myth gives an incomplete picture of the actual situation. In royal legends for instance, in dynastic succession and other historical and social situations the predominant deity is not Baal but El, to whom chiefly sacrifice is made in a fast-liturgy on the occasion of a national emergency. This and a certain text from Ras Shamra containing oaths by certain attributes of El indicate a more spiritual conception of El, nearer to the Hebrew God.

Among many other deities in Canaanite religion Dagan, the god of corn (*dagon*), is known at Ras Shamra from offering lists, from Baal's stock epithet 'the Son of Dagan', and from dedication inscriptions on stelae from a temple adjoining that of Baal at Ras Shamra, which dates from c 2000 BC. Reshef was the god who slew men by war and plague. He is known from Egyptian sculpture and may be recognized in bronze figurines of a striding warrior with offensive weapon and shield, well known from archeological sites in Syria and Palestine. In one of the Ras Shamra texts he is called Reshef of the Arrow, and in the Graeco-Roman period he was assimilated to Apollo with his pestilential arrows. From later inscriptions from Sidon, Eshmun is known as the god of healing, assimilated to Asclepius in the Graeco-Roman period, as Baal was to Hercules, by whose labours also order was sustained against the constant menace of chaos. The sun, regarded as a goddess, is a minor figure in the Baal myth of Ras Shamra, and the moon god and his consort Nikkal were also worshipped.

The will of the various gods was consulted and communicated in various ways. In the 2nd century AD, Lucian of Samosata mentions oracles according to the movement of statues of the gods, doubtless at the manipulation of priests in response to specific questions, conveying a simple 'Yes' or 'No', like the sacred lots Urim and Thummim in early Israel. Divination by the entrails of sacrificed animals was also practised, the liver being especially significant, as is indicated by clay models from archeological sites, charted and annotated for consultation or instruction. The medieval Arab writer Ibn an-Nadim mentions divination at Harran by the direction of the gaze or the expression in the eyes of the dying victim as it expired.

At Byblos c 1100 BC there is an instance of the will of the god communicated to the king in an affair of state by an ecstatic of his household and considered authentic by the king. The account of the distress of King Saul before his last battle (1 Samuel 28) mentions prophets and dreams as the media of the communication of the will of God in a crisis, and the patriarchal narratives in the Old Testament and the passage in the Baal myth where El sees the revival of Baal in a dream indicate the significance attached to dreams as communications of the will of God in future events or on the significance of the present situation. People would often resort to shrines in ritual incubation when dreams were taken as sure communications of the purpose of the god.

The temple in Syria varied in form, but the general conception was a large area within the sacred precinct in which the temple proper was the focal feature. This conception is best illustrated in the sanctuary of Bel, or Baal, in the early Roman period at Palmyra in the Syrian desert and the Moslem sacred precinct at Jerusalem. At Ras Shamra and Hazor in the 14th–13th centuries BC, the tripartite temple is known, comprising an outer court with a great altar, shallow vestibule, main nave and inmost shrine, or 'Holy of Holies'. This is the plan of Solomon's Temple at Jerusalem, which was constructed by Phoenician craftsmen. Administrative texts from Ras Shamra attest hereditary office in a large number of professions among temple personnel, priests, votaries both male and female, temple prostitutes, singers, markers of sacred vestments, sculptors, potters, launderers, slaughterers, augurers, or possibly Temple herdsmen, and merchants who traded on account of the Temple. The king of course was the supreme priest, though (except on special occasions) he would delegate his duties.

The myths and legends of Ras Shamra in their fuller context amplify the simple listing of various types of sacrifice in the offering lists. Thus from the description of the duties of the son and heir of the king in the royal legend of Prince Aqhat at Ras Shamra it is known that communion meals were eaten in the sanctuary. The blood and vitals were offered to the god, and the rest was cooked and eaten by the community, thus effecting solidarity of the participants with the god and with one another. The shrine might also house memorials of the ancestors of the community, represented by standing stones, as in the Canaanite sanctuary of Hazor, and probably also at Gezer. By offerings at this tangible token of a favoured ancestor the community hoped to continue to share in the blessing which had been his.

Besides communion sacrifices there were those that were offered wholly to the gods either as food or as an act of total renunciation on the part of the worshipper, being wholly burnt on the altar; and other such offerings were made for purification, as doves were sacrificed in Israel after child-birth, and as firstlings of crop and flock and of game in hunting. In Israel and among the Carthaginians in North Africa animals were sacrificed in redemption of first-born sons, and this was almost certainly done also in Syria.

Archeological evidence has been claimed from Gezer and Tell all-Fara by Nablus for foundation sacrifice of children, but this is disputed. Multiple infant sacrifice, however, is attested by jars full of calcined bones of infants and young animals from the sanctuary of the fertility goddess Tanit at the Tyrian colony of Carthage, in Punic inscriptions and the writings of the African Church father, Tertullian (3rd century AD). Those may have been first-born children dedicated thus as firstlings, but in King Mesha's sacrifice of his eldest son (2 Kings 3), like those in Judah in the latter period of the kingdom, they may have been sacrifices in extremity,

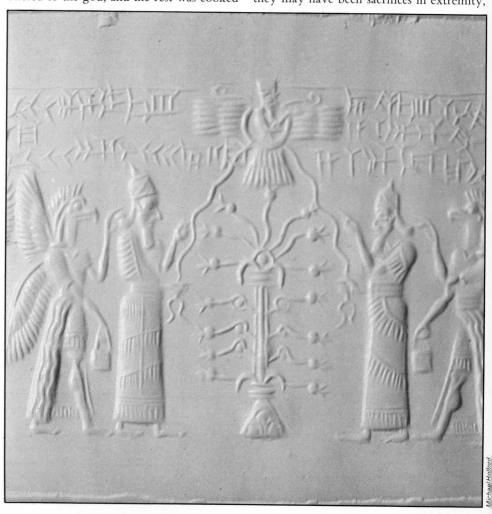

Above *Baal, god of storm and the winter rains, was a dying and rising god, linked with the seasonal death and rebirth of vegetation; both El and Baal were associated with the bull.* **Right** *Statue of Baal Hammon, the principal god of Carthage, the Phoenician colony in North Africa: the name Hammon may derive from Ammon, god of the Siwa oasis in Libya; 1st century AD, from Tunisia.* **Facing page** *The Canaanite mother goddess Athirat or Ashera, was probably a form of the Mesopotamian goddess Ishtar, shown with a palm tree on this Assyrian seal: the fertility rites of Canaan were fiercely denounced by the Old Testament prophets, who strongly disapproved of the moral pollution involved.*

to which Philo of Byblos (64–161 AD) alludes. Other cases, such as that which Diodorus Siculus attributes to the Carthaginians in Sicily after a victory over the Greeks in 307 BC, may be a case of 'death-devotion' (*herem*), a great act of renunciation of the spoils of war, to which King Mesha also refers in his inscription recording his war of liberation from Israel (c 835 BC). The sacrifices would thus correspond to Samuel's 'hewing Agag in pieces before the Lord' (1 Samuel 15.33).

Besides the commemoration of the dead as recipients of the divine favour ritual texts from Ras Shamra refer to the family god ('*il 'ib*), certain of these alluding to 'offerings at the aperture of the divine ancestor'. This is amplified by the discovery of grave-instal-lations of such apertures as pipes of bottomless jars to communicate offerings, especially libations, to the defunct, probably to promote fertility of the earth, over which the dead were believed to have some influence. Such offerings to the dead may be the substance of the ban on offerings of a portion of the harvest to the dead in Deuteronomy 26.14. The dead were termed *repa'im* by the Phoenicians as in Israel, the name for the 'weak' shades in the Old Testament, and were possibly referred to in funerary inscriptions of King Tabnith of Sidon (5th century BC) as 'divine', or at least supernatural, as in the passage on King Saul and the Witch of Endor (1 Samuel 28.13), where the shade of Samuel is described as 'a god'. In this case the king sought revelation of the future.

As recipients of offerings, givers of fertility and revealers of the future, the departed in ancient Syria were regarded as not quite defunct. The Aramaean king Panammu in his inscription (c 750 BC) expects his descendants to invoke him when they make an offering to Baal, so that 'his soul may eat and drink with Baal'. The existence of the shade in the gloomy underworld is familiar in the Old Testament, particularly in Job chapter 3. Though quite undesirable this was apparently still an existence, however insubstantial, and this attenuated life was sustained by offerings, particularly libations, though one of the more recently discovered texts from Ras Shamra refers to animal sacrifice 'for the life of the family god', or the divine ancestor. The belief in this insubstantial life of the dead who require to be revived by libation survives among Arab peasants in Syria and Palestine, who believe that the dead come at dusk to wells, springs and rivers to drink; however, this was but a tenuous existence. In the Legend of Prince Aqhat in the Ras Shamra texts occurs the passage:

> As for mortal man, what does he get as his
>   latter end?
> What does mortal man get as his inheritance?
> Glaze will be poured out on my head,
> Even plaster on my pate,
> And the death of all men will I die,
> Yea I shall surely die.

These lines express the typical view of the afterlife in ancient Canaan.

Apart from the regular cults, men in Syria, as elsewhere and at all times, sought to enlist the powers of the supernatural or to ward off their evil influences by charms and amulets. Prophylactic charms in Aramaic are known, and at least one excerpt from the Baal myth of Ras Shamra was probably used as an aphrodisiac charm. The figurines of the nude fertility goddess were probably also used to promote procreation and child-birth.

Besides these, a great number of amulets have been found in excavations. Those are chiefly Egyptian, the cat and the intelligent ape, the hippopotamus, which was both a sinister force to be placated as the representative of chaos or, in the form of an upright female, a beneficent patroness of mothers, particularly in childbirth.

The grotesque dwarf Bes, the protector of children and pregnant women was also popular.

From the early Egyptian cult of the fertility god Osiris, the goddess Isis and their son Horus, who survived a hazardous infancy to avenge Osiris' untimely death, small images of the infant Horus were favourite amulets, and also the 'Eye of Horus' with its fertilizing tear-drops. Small gold flies and other insects resembling lice, which were found by Sir Flinders Petrie at a site at the mouth of the Wadi Ghazzeh in Palestine, may have had a prophylactic purpose to ward off disease, like the gold mice referred to in 1 Samuel 6.4, which were sent back with the ark by the Philistines when it returned to its homeland.

In describing the religion of Syria the documents of Ras Shamra have been taken as the basis of this account, firstly because they are a contemporary statement, the fullest and most reliable that is available, and secondly because they document the fertility cult, which was the most conspicuous aspect of local religion that impressed Israel as she settled in Palestine. Ugarit, however, was but one city state in Syria, and in the history of the land it is notable that, despite a general community of religion in any given period, there were local variations and different emphases. So too over the long period of paganism until Christianity was established as the faith of the majority (c 500 AD), different variations of the old religion developed through time and in different localities.

In the settled land the old gods were assimilated to the gods of Greece and Rome, as

Baal to Zeus the sky god with his thunderbolt, the fertility goddesses Astarte, Anat, and Ashera to Aphrodite and Juno. Baal in his role as a dying and rising vegetation god was assimilated to Adonis, the lover of Aphrodite, or Venus, but retained his Syrian title Adonis ('lord'); their cult was practised at the source of the River Adonis just south of Beirut.

When the river water ran red, as it did at a certain time in summer, it was considered to be discoloured by the blood of Adonis, who was lamented at that time by the Syrian women. Baal, the divine king who must always struggle to vindicate his kingship and order against the forces of chaos, was assimilated to the labouring Hercules, particularly at Tyre and her colonies in the coastal plain of Palestine south of Jaffa. The god Reshef, with his power of life and death, was assimilated to Apollo with his bow and arrows as plague-shafts, and Anat, the goddess of love and war was assimilated to Athene and Minerva.

The waters of the sea were, in turn, assimilated to Poseidon, who appears as the city god of Beirut on coins from the Graeco-Roman period, and the healing god Eshmun to Asclepius with his serpents. The latter was particularly venerated at Sidon, judging from the name Eshmunazzar, which was borne by two kings of Sidon.

In the caravan city of Palmyra, between Damascus and the Euphrates, the needs of the caravan merchants in the first three centuries of the Christian era are indicated by the cult of the moon, which was also

In the Graeco-Roman period the Canaanite gods were identified with classical deities: coins of the 2nd century AD show Baal (top left) who was assimilated to Hercules; Eshmun (top right) the god of healing, with twin serpents, assimilated to Asclepius; the sea (bottom left) assimilated to Poseidon, the city god of Beirut; the sanctuary of Byblos (bottom right).

venerated at Harran, another great caravan city in north Mesopotamia. The moon had evidently a peculiar significance for those merchants and their distant and protracted enterprises.

The Venus star, known as Athtar, the brightest star in those latitudes, the first to rise at evening and the last to disappear in the morning, was also greatly venerated at Palmyra, where as two gods Arsu and Azizu ('the Gracious and the Fierce') they are represented as mounted respectively on a camel and a horse.

Christianity did not easily oust the Nature religion of Syria, even after it became the official religion of the Roman Empire. Indeed when Porphyry the Bishop Elect of Gaza went to his see at the end of the 4th century AD the lusty heathen impeded his journey; and according to his deacon and biographer, there were eight pagan temples and many private shrines in Gaza and only 280 Christians out of between 50,000 and 60,000 inhabitants, and that after an Imperial edict against paganism had been issued throughout the empire.

The Hittites

German excavations since 1907 within the walls of an ancient city on a hillside near the Turkish village of Boghaz Koi in Asia Minor (Anatolia) have revealed the existence of a kingdom which had that city as its capital and which lasted from about 1700 to about 1200 BC.

The land was called 'the Land of Hattii', its capital was Hattusas, and its people are known as the Hittites, by reason of the un-doubted, though remote, connection of the name Hatti with the Hittites, or sons of Heth, mentioned in the Bible. During those five centuries the rulers of Hattusas extended their dominion over populations speaking lan-guages different from their own. One of these was the Hurrians, whose centre was in upper Mesopotamia and whose name is also reflected in the Bible where it is found in the form 'Horites'.

Our present knowledge of Hittite and Hur-rian religion and mythology is due entirely to the German excavations at Boghaz Koi, which have brought to light thousands of broken clay tablets inscribed in the cuneiform script, once the royal archives of the Hittite kings. The archives of the Hurrians them-selves have not been found, though they may be awaiting discovery.

The Hittite texts present us with a bewil-dering number of divine names. This is mainly because not only each linguistic area within the Hittite empire, but each indivi-dual cult centre had its own names for its deities, though they might have similar attributes to those in other places. For ex-ample, the weather god was Tarhun in Luwian (and probably in Hittite), Taru in Hattic, Teshub in Hurrian; the sun god was Istanu in Hittite, Estan in Hattic, Tiwat in Luwian, Tiyat in Palaic, Shimegi in Hurrian. Some 600 names have actually been counted so far.

The basic type to which a deity belonged is often shown by the word sign with which his name is written, meaning sun god, weather god, moon god and so on. Other-wise it may be deduced from a description of his cult statue or emblem, from his associa-tion with other gods of the same type, or from allusions to his sphere of activity in prayers, myths or other texts. But in many cases the texts give no information about the deity's attributes, so that he or she remains a mere name to us.

The Hittites themselves occasionally recognized an identity, as when we read in a prayer: 'Sun goddess of Arinna, my lady, queen of all countries! In the Land of Hatti thou givest thyself the name "sun goddess of Arinna", but in the country which thou makest a land of cedars (Syria) thou givest thyself the name Hebat.'

It is interesting that when listing divine witnesses to a treaty with a vassal-king they would include not only the sun goddess of Arinna and of Hebat as distinct deities, but also the gods and goddesses of the individual cult centres, even though they might not have distinct names.

The goddess of Arinna (which has not been located) was exalted as patroness of the state. Her name in Hattic was Wurusemu, but the Hittites appear to have addressed her under the epithet Arinnitti. She is always called a sun goddess, but there are indications that in origin she may have been a deity of the underworld, her solar attributes being secondary.

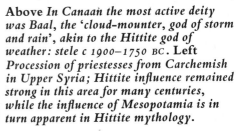

Above *In Canaän the most active deity was Baal, the 'cloud-mounter, god of storm and rain', akin to the Hittite god of weather: stele c 1900–1750 BC.* **Left** *Procession of priestesses from Carchemish in Upper Syria; Hittite influence remained strong in this area for many centuries, while the influence of Mesopotamia is in turn apparent in Hittite mythology.*

The king and queen of the land were her high priest and priestess, and in this state cult her husband was the weather god of Hatti, a great figure who bestowed kingship, brought victory in war and might represent the nation in its dealings with foreign powers: thus a treaty with Egypt is said to be for the purpose of 'making eternal the relations which the sun god of Egypt and the weather god of Hatti have established for the land of Egypt and the land of Hatti.'

This national weather god mentioned here is probably the original sky god of the Indo-Europeans, akin to Zeus and Jupiter, brought in by the immigrants who introduced the Indo-European Hittite language into Anatolia in the 3rd millennium BC, and married to the indigenous mother goddess. The weather god of another city, Nerik, was made their son, and they had daughters named Mezzulla and Hulla and a grand-daughter, Zintuhi.

Among the deities of the state cult must also be numbered the spirits of past kings and queens, who received regular offerings. 'Became a god' is the normal euphemism for 'died' used by the Hittites when referring to kings.

During the later years of the Hittite kingdom the state cult came under strong Hurrian influence. It was at this time that the sun goddess of Arinna and the weather god of Nerik were identified with the Hurrian Hebat and her son Sharruma. Finally, at a holy place near the capital, now named Yazilikaya, a rocky outcrop forming a natural open chamber was adorned with a series of figures in relief representing a national pantheon.

The central group is clearly recognizable as the family of the sun goddess, but the names in Hittite 'hieroglyphs' attached to each deity, including the central group, are those of the Hurrian pantheon. It therefore appears that by the end of the Hittite period, in the late 13th century BC, the Hittites had achieved a measure of unity of worship amongst themselves.

The Hittite mythological texts are, on the whole, poorly preserved, and consequently any account of Hittite mythology must necessarily be incomplete. It seems, however, that in Anatolia itself mythology remained on a rather primitive level. The most elaborate myths preserved in the Hittite archives are either of Hurrian origin or are simply Babylonian myths transmitted to the Hittites by the Hurrians. In the latter class (though it is legend rather than myth) is the Babylonian *Epic of Gilgamesh*, of which there is even a fragment in the Hurrian language.

Even where the gods or heroes mentioned in these myths are ostensibly Hurrian, they can often be recognized as ancient Babylonian or Sumerian deities under a garbled 'Hurrianized' name. These tales appear to be recorded simply as works of literature. They are of considerable interest on account of features in them which reappear in Greek mythology.

The myth 'Kingship in Heaven' tells how the kingship was held by a series of gods for periods of nine years. Alalu is defeated by Anu and sent down to the underworld;

Anu in turn is mutilated and defeated by Kumarbi, who is apparently overthrown by the weather god Teshub. Anu is the Babylonian sky god; the conception of former generations of defeated gods who were banished to the underworld also derives from Babylonia. But Teshub and Kumarbi are Hurrian gods. The myth closely resembles the *Theogony* of Hesiod, where the sequence Uranus-Cronus-Zeus corresponds to Anu-Kumarbi-Teshub.

The longest mythological poem is entitled 'Song of Ullikummi'. It has a similar theme and tells of a plot by Kumarbi to replace Teshub as king of the gods by a stone monster named Ullikummi, whom he begets for the purpose.

> Kumarbi takes wisdom into his mind
> and an evil spirit as enemy he raises...
> At Cool Pond a great Rock is lying;
> her length is three leagues,
> but her width which she has below is one and
> a half leagues.
> His mind sprang forward,
> he slept with the Rock
> and his manhood flowed into her.

After a considerable gap the Rock bore a child, Ullikummi, who was made of stone. The child was taken to earth and placed on the shoulder of Upelluri, a giant like the Greek Atlas, who supported heaven and earth. Here he grew up in the sea, which only came up to his waist. The sun god saw him and went to report the matter to Teshub, who along with his brother Tashmishu, gave battle.

At first they were unsuccessful and the

Stone even came to overshadow Teshub's town Kummiya. Tashmishu reported to Teshub's wife, Hebat, that her husband would have to give up his throne, a message which almost caused her to fall off the roof where she was standing. But Tashmishu and Teshub decided to consult the wise god Ea, who in his turn went first to Enlil and then to the giant Upelluri. Upelluri's reply was as follows:

> When heaven and earth were built on me
> I knew nothing (of it).
> And when they came and cut apart heaven and
> earth with a "cutter"
> that too I knew not.
> Now something is hurting my right shoulder,
> but I know not who he is, that god.

When Ea heard these words, he had only to turn Upelluri's right shoulder and there was the Stone standing on it. But Upelluri's words had given him an idea. He ordered the 'former gods' in the underworld to produce the ancient tool with which heaven and earth had once been cut apart. With this he severed the Stone from Upelluri and so destroyed its power. Teshub went out to battle again, and though the end of the story is lost, we may be sure from the text that survives he emerged victorious.

This tale too has its parallel in the Greek story of Typhon. The reference to the building of heaven and earth in one piece on the shoulder of a giant and their separation by cutting is the only surviving hint in the Hittite records of anything resembling a creation myth.

The myths associated with Anatolian –

Sonia Halliday

The king and queen acted as high priest and priestess to the sun goddess of Arinna, patroness of the state, and were both deified after death: Facing page Hittite king from Malatya in Anatolia. **Above Wife and child of the king leading an animal.**

mainly Hattic – deities are much simpler and more primitive. The 'Slaying of the Dragon' is said to have been recited at a great annual festival called *purulli* and is connected with the Hattian city Nerik. The weather god and the dragon fought together and the weather god was defeated. According to one version, he then appealed to the other gods for help and the goddess Inaras planned a ruse. She invited the dragon to a feast, with barrels of every kind of drink. The dragon came up with his children and they became so drunk that they could not go back to their hole. So the goddess's human assistant was able to tie them up, and the weather god then came on the scene and killed the dragon.

According to another version of this myth, when the dragon and the weather god fought, the dragon not only defeated the weather god but incapacitated him by gaining possession of his heart and of both his eyes.

The weather god then begot a son by the daughter of a poor man. When this son grew up he took as bride the daughter of the dragon, and his father told him to ask for the stolen organs on entering his bride's home. The demand was instantly met, and

the weather god, fully restored, went out to battle again; he succeeded in defeating the dragon on this occasion, but his son took the part of the dragon and was killed with him.

Several myths about Anatolian deities belong to a type which we may call for convenience 'the Myth of the Missing God'. They tell the story of a god who disappears and thereby causes a blight on earth, the search for the missing god, his eventual return, and the restoration of health and vigour to the world. In one such myth the weather god withdraws in anger and the search is conducted by the sun god (whose messenger is an eagle), the father of the weather god, his grandfather and his grandmother Hannahanna.

In another version of this myth it is Telipinu, son of the weather god, who is angry, and the gods who search are the sun god, the weather god and Hannahanna, the grandfather being omitted. In both these versions the missing god is found by a bee sent out by Hannahanna. In another similar story the sun god and Telipinu are missing, not from anger, but because they have been seized by Torpor, a demon who has paralysed all Nature. All these myths are accompanied by a magical ritual, the purpose of which is to attract the god back into his temple and to remove some misfortune or other which his absence is thought to have caused.

They are 'ritual myths', recited to enhance the effect of the ritual. In no case is the ritual connected with the seasons. Such magical

rituals are common in the Hittite archives.

Other fragments of mythology are found embedded in rituals. One text tells how the moon fell down from heaven and how the weather god sent storms and wind after him to frighten him. Another has a passage describing how an eagle found two goddesses of the underworld in a forest holding spindles and spinning long years for the king – forerunners of the Greek *Moirai*, Roman *Parcae* and Germanic *Norn* (Fates).

The underworld contained, beside the dead, an older generation of defeated gods and some others, such as the Fates just mentioned. Its ruler was Lelwanis, whose gender is uncertain and who seems in some way to be identical with 'the sun god of the earth' and even with the sun goddess of Arinna in some passages.

The Hittites regarded their relationship with the gods as one of servant and master. 'If a servant has anything on his mind,' prays King Mursilis, 'he appeals to his master and his master hears him and takes pity on him and puts right what is troubling him.

Moreover if a servant has committed an offence and confesses his guilt before his master, his master may do with him whatever he pleases; but because he has confessed his guilt before his master, his master's spirit is appeased and his master will not call that servant to account.' But a well-intentioned master might still be capricious, and would have his own interests to attend to. 'Now if, honoured Telipinu, thou art up in heaven among the gods, or if thou art gone to the sea or to roam in the mountains, or to battle against an enemy country ... come back again into thy temple.'

A god must be fed, tended, appeased, flattered. His actions, even when attending to his duties, might not always be wise and might entail unforeseen consequences; it would then be the duty of his faithful servant to point this out to him, so that he might correct his mistake and not repeat it in the future.

If, however, misfortune comes as a punishment for sin, it will not be lifted until the sin has been confessed and expiated. Possible causes of divine anger would be brought to light by questioning the priests or by searching the records. It was then necessary to find out by divination which particular offence was the cause of the present misfortune. 'Now, O gods, whatever sin you see ... let the old wives, the seers, or the augurs determine it, or let men see it in a dream.'

The 'old wives' practised a special form of divination by throwing dice; the seers were the experts in the ancient science of haruspicy (inspection of the entrails of the sacrificial victim); the augurs took the omens from the movements of birds. The omens, being either favourable or unfavourable, would give an answer 'yes' or 'no'; in this way, by a lengthy process of elimination, it was possible to discover the precise offence which required expiation. The records of these questions and answers (the latter in technical and barely intelligible language) are among the longest and most numerous tablets in the archives.

The Phoenicians and Carthaginians

A degree of mystery invests both the name and origin of the Phoenicians. *Phoenix* was a Greek word meaning 'purple-red' and 'palm tree'. The Greeks seem originally to have applied the name 'Phoenician' to the inhabitants of the coastal lands of the eastern Mediterranean, between the Nahrel-Kabir and Mount Carmel. It is not certain whether the name referred to the darker complexion of these people in contrast to the lighter colouring of the Greeks, or to the fact that palm trees were a distinctive feature of their land. Phoenicia was also the home of the celebrated purple dye, made from the murex mollusc, which was highly prized in the ancient world. The Roman form of the name was *Poeni*, which was also used to designate the Carthaginians who had originated from Phoenicia. The Phoenicians, however, called themselves 'Canaanites' and their land was 'Canaan', so well known from the Hebrew Bible.

According to Greek writers, the Phoenicians had originally lived in the Persian Gulf area, but had migrated westwards at a remote period and settled on the Mediterranean coast. This account of their origins has not been confirmed by modern archeology. There is, indeed, much evidence of migrations of Semitic peoples from Arabia and the Persian Gulf into Syria and Palestine during the third and second millennia BC. But it would appear also that Semites were living in this area from at least the third millennium, and they cannot be distinguished from any 'Canaanite invaders'. We have, therefore, to consider the Phoenicians as Canaanites, that is, as Semitic inhabitants of the coastal area of the eastern Mediterranean. The term may also be used in a special sense after about 1200 BC, for as a result of the settlement of the Israelites and Philistines about this time in the district later known as Palestine, the area of Canaanite political independence became limited approximately to the territory occupied by the four chief Phoenician cities of Tyre, Sidon, Byblos and Aradus.

Since the Phoenicians were Canaanites, the earlier form of their religion can now be studied from the ritual and mythological texts discovered since 1928 by excavation of the Canaanite city of Ugarit, close to the

modern Ras Shamra. The Ugaritic texts reveal that the Canaanites of the 15th and 14th centuries BC worshipped a number of gods. The presiding deity was El, described as 'the Father of Men', who was regarded as benevolent and merciful. He was 'the Creator of Created Things', and 'the Bull'; the latter title doubtless indicated strength and virility. He is depicted on a stele as a bearded man, seated on a throne, and shown with a tall crown adorned by a pair of bull's horns. A worshipper, probably a king, stands before him, making an offering.

Although El was the supreme deity, the most active god of the Canaanite pantheon was definitely Baal. He was represented as young and vigorous, armed with an axe and a spear, symbolizing lightning. These

weapons indicate his original name and nature – he was Hadad, the weather god. 'Baal' was a title meaning 'lord', and signified ownership or sovereignty of the land. The use of this title denoted the deity's connection with the fertility cult of Canaan; as the weather god he brought the winter rains that fertilized the land. In the mythological texts Baal is described as 'the son of Dagon', the corn god, and at Ugarit their temples were adjacent.

Closely associated with Baal was the fertility goddess Anat, who in later forms of Canaanite-Phoenician religion was called by the name of Astarte. On a stele found at Bethshan, Anat is described in Egyptian hieroglyphs as 'Antit, Queen of Heaven and Mistress of all the gods'. She seems also to

Facing page: Above *The Phoenicians were energetic traders and colonizers who readily adopted foreign gods and foreign art styles. Ivory found at Nimrud, from furniture intended for export to Egypt where the lotus was a sacred plant: 8th century BC.* **Below** *Stele from Carthage, the principal Phoenician colony, showing animal sacrifice and offerings at an altar.* **Below** *Phoenician ivory plaque, 8th century BC, meant for export to Egypt and showing a lion in a lily grove, facing a sacred tree. The lion's head-dress resembles that of the Egyptian goddess Hathor.*

Hittite, Hurrian and Aegean-Mycenean influences were current. A notable memorial of Aegean-Mycenean religion is an ivory carving of the fertility goddess known as the *Potnia Theron* or 'Mistress of the Animals', which was found in a tomb. The stele unearthed at Bethshan, depicting Anat-Astarte, also shows on either side of the goddess the ithyphallic Egyptian god Min and the Canaanite god Reshef, who holds an ankh, the Egyptian symbol of life. In this connection, too, there are the Egyptian mummiform sarcophagi found at Sidon, one of which bears the funerary inscription in Phoenician of Eshmunazzar, a king of Sidon probably in the 6th century BC. This readiness to accept foreign deities was also a feature of Carthaginian life. The acceptance, however, often took the form of identifying the foreign

The Phoenicians themselves worshipped various fertility goddesses, as well as Baal, the weather god, and El, the father of man: Left Terracotta mask found in Sardinia. Below Part of a Phoenician neck-collar, found in a tomb in Sardinia, 4th century BC. Facing page A significant and sinister discovery on the site of Punic Carthage was the 'topheth' in the precinct of the goddess Tanit (left), where small children had been sacrificed by burning, perhaps to appease the gods or for fertility. Their bones were placed in urns and small stelae mark the burying places of these urns in graveyards (right), frequently dedicated to Baal Hammon and Tanit Pene Baal, the chief Carthaginian deities.

G. Tomsich/Spectrum

have been known as *Qodshu*, which could be interpreted as 'sacred prostitute' and refer to the licentious fertility rites which were practised in her sanctuaries. Anat or Astarte was generally depicted in art as nude, with the sexual attributes emphasized.

Among the texts recorded on the tablets found at Ugarit is a long mythological poem which tells of the conflict between Baal and Mot, the personification of drought and sterility. The theme was probably inspired by the annual struggle between vegetation and drought. Baal was apparently conceived of as the spirit of vegetation as well as a fertility god. In the poem, Baal is slain by Mot and descends into the underworld. His death is mourned by El; and Anat seeks for his corpse, which she finds and buries with lamentation and the appropriate funerary rites.

There is without doubt some connection here between the actions of Anat and those of the Egyptian goddess Isis in her quest for Osiris, Anat takes revenge on Mot by killing him and treating his body as grain, winnowing, parching and grinding it. Baal eventually returns from the underworld, and Anat annouces that rain will come again and the parched earth will revive. This mythological text was doubtless related to an annual ritual commemorating the death and resurrection of vegetation.

Evidence found at Ugarit and other sites shows that the Canaanites were attracted to other religions. Ugarit itself was a cosmopolitan port, where many languages were spoken and where Egyptian, Mesopotamian,

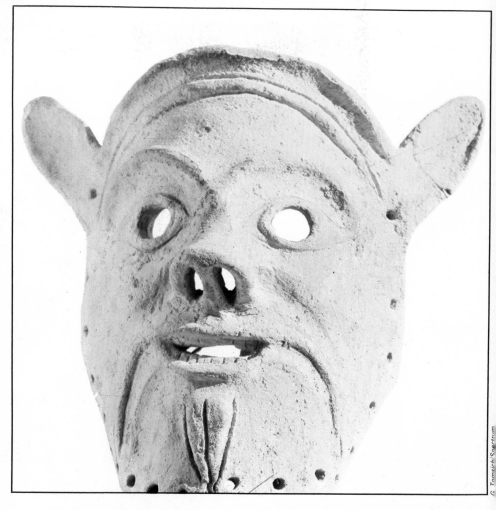

G. Tomsich/Spectrum

Michael Holford

Michael Holford

deity with a Canaanite, Phoenician or Carthaginian deity, which led to confusion of conception: thus the Baalat ('lady') of Byblos was indentified with the Egyptian Isis or Hathor; and Melkart, the patron god of Tyre was assimilated with the Greek Hercules.

As the titles Baal ('lord') and Baalat ('lady') were used in conjunction with some other designations to denote the patron deity of some particular place, so other titles were used. A notable instance is the name Melkart, for the chief god of Tyre: it was composed of two words meaning 'ruler' or 'king', and 'city'. As Baal Melkart, this god became one of the leading deities of Carthage, the daughter city of Tyre. More difficult to explain is the name of Sidon's patron-god, Eshmun. It has been suggested that the name derives from *shem*, 'name', meaning 'the Name' above all others. Eshmun was assimilated to the Greek healing god Asclepios. He appears to have had chthonic (underworld) attributes, which would account for his close association with the fertility goddess Astarte.

Carthage, which was destined to become Rome's great rival in the Mediterranean world, was traditionally founded in 814 BC by colonists from Tyre; it was one of many Phoenician settlements on the western Mediterranean coasts. Its position, in command of the straits between North Africa and Sicily, was one of great strategic opportunity, which it exploited to build up a commercial empire. Carthage steadily outgrew its mother city in size and importance, and

even after its final destruction by Rome in 146 BC, Punic culture lived on and the old Punic gods continued to be worshipped under Roman names.

The Phoenician colonists took their native religion with them to North Africa, and it formed the fundamental pattern of Carthaginian religion. Some differences, however, did develop at Carthage, particularly with regard to the status or character of certain gods. Thus, although Melkart, the patron god of Tyre, was accorded a special position in the daughter city and an annual offering was sent to his temple at Tyre, two other deities had greater prominence at Carthage. They were Baal Hammon and Tanit Pene Baal. The origin of the former is obscure, though it has been suggested that 'Hammon' means 'altars of incense' or more plausibly, that it derives from 'Ammon', the name of the Libyan god of the Siwa oasis, whose oracle Alexander the Great once consulted. This Ammon was identified with the ancient Egyptian god Amun in addition to the Greek Zeus.

The goddess Tanit, although her full title 'Pene Baal' meant '(Tanit) Face of Baal', seems to have had precedence over Baal Hammon, with whom she was often associated. Tanit was undoubtedly the Carthaginian counterpart of the Phoenician fertility goddess Astarte, for the latter does not appear independently of Tanit in the Carthaginian area. In Roman Carthage, Tanit was identified with Juno Caelestis, which indicates that she was also associated with the heavens.

The crescent and the disc naturally suggest

her connection with the moon. The emblem of the hand, with palm turned outwards, probably symbolizes protection and benediction, and anticipates the famous Islamic amulet of the 'Hand of Fatima'. But essentially mysterious is the 'sign of Tanit', which could be interpreted as a schematic figure of the goddess with arms raised in blessing, or as a Carthaginian transformation of the ankh, the Egyptian sign of life.

One of the most significant but sinister discoveries made on the site of Punic Carthage was that of the 'topheth' within the precinct of Tanit. The Hebrew word *topheth* occurs in an account of the reforms carried out by King Josiah at Jerusalem (2 Kings 23.10): 'And he defiled Topheth . . . that no one might burn his son or his daughter as an offering to Molech'. It used to be thought that 'Molech' was a Phoenician god, but recent research suggests that it was a term for child sacrifice practised in Canaanite-Phoenician religion. The topheth of Tanit has provided grim evidence of the longevity of the rite at Carthage, in fact from the 8th century BC to the Roman destruction of the city in 146 BC. Thousands of urns were found there containing the calcined bones of small children and birds and small animals – these latter were possibly intended as substitute sacrifices.

Small stelae, marking the burial places of the urns, mostly had dedications to Tanit Pene Baal and Baal Hammon. The purpose of these child sacrifices was probably either propitiatory or to promote fertility amongst the womenfolk.

Gods, Goddesses and Heroes

Astarte

A great mother goddess was worshipped under various names throughout the Middle East, as Ishtar in Mesopotamia, as Ashtart or Asherah by the Phoenicians and Canaanites. The Greeks called her Astarte and equated her with their own love goddess Aphrodite, who was originally one of her many forms.

Clay plaques representing her have been found in Syria and Palestine, dating from 1700 to 1100 BC and probably worn as charms to promote fertility. She is mentioned frequently and with violent disapproval in the Old Testament and eventually, like many other deities who were rivals of the God of Jews and Christians, she turned into a demon and is one of the fallen angels in Milton's *Paradise Lost*.

> ...Astoreth, whom the Phoenicians called
> Astarte,
> Queen of Heaven, with crescent horns;
> To whose bright image nightly by the moon,
> Sidonian virgins paid their vows and songs.

W. F. Albright has remarked that, 'Goddesses of fertility play a much greater role among the Canaanites than they do among any other ancient people': evidently because of their dread of drought and famine. Though these goddesses had different names and were independent personalities, they had similar functions and were essentially the same goddess. They ruled war as well as fertility, motherhood and sex, and they were frequently represented naked and with the sexual organs emphasized.

Ashtart was chief goddess of the Phoenicians at Tyre and Sidon, and wherever they established colonies they took her with them. She had a temple in their colony at Memphis in Egypt, for instance, and temples at Carthage. A Phoenician statuette of her in alabaster has been found at Galera, near Granada in Spain: she sits on a throne, flanked by sphinxes and with a bowl under her breasts. At some point in her ritual milk was poured into the head of the statuette and flowed into the bowl through holes pierced in the goddess's breasts.

Asherah or Asherat, often called Asherat of the Sea, was the wife of the Canaanite supreme god El, whose name means simply 'the god', and by him was the mother of 70 deities. The same goddess was also worshipped in the south of Arabia and by the Amorites, the Semitic nomads who by 2000 BC had spread northwards from Arabia into Palestine, Syria and Mesopotamia. There is an Amorite inscription to her of the 18th century BC, in which she is called 'the bride of heaven'.

In the Ugaritic texts, dating from c 1400 BC, found at Ras Shamra in northern Syria since 1929, the goddess Anat plays a leading role. The chief god El stays in the background and the most active god is Baal, the storm god who sends the rains which bring fertility to the earth. Anat is his sister and

wife, and she plays the vital part in killing the god of drought and sterility or, in other words, in reviving the life of Nature.

Asherah, the wife of the old supreme god El and the mother of Baal, seems to have been hostile to Baal at first but later joined forces with Anat to help him. Apparently, the followers of both goddesses tried to attach them to the fertility god as the cult of Baal developed.

All these goddesses were imported into Egypt and in the 13th century BC Pharaoh Rameses II called himself 'the companion of Anat'. Ashtart or Asherah appears in an Egyptian sculpture where she is called Qodshu or Qedeshat, 'the sacred prostitute'. She is naked, stands on a lion, and holds a lotus flower, a symbol of life, in her right hand. In her left hand the goddess holds a pair of serpents, which are symbols of life renewed because snakes slough their old skins each year.

In Canaan the symbol of Asherah was a wooden pole, called an *asherah*. It might be a living tree but was more often a tree-trunk with the branches lopped off, standing in a socket on a stone base. The upright pole is again a symbol of life, generation and fertilizing power, and may be the 'tree of life' which appears frequently in Canaanite art.

As goddess of fertility, Astarte typified the reproductive powers of Nature and woman. She was associated with the moon, and often shown with the horns of the crescent moon, because the moon was believed to govern the growth, decay and rebirth of all things as it waxed and waned in the sky. The dove, an amorous bird, belonged to her and at Ascalon in the 1st century AD a visitor saw 'an impossible number of doves' in the streets and houses, because they were sacred and no one ever killed them. Fishes were sacred to her also, perhaps for their numerous offspring.

The Jewish prophets condemned the worship of Astarte, not only because they believed that Yahweh was the one true god but also because of the sexual rituals of the goddess, who was served by sacred prostitutes. Their activities had a practical use, for their earnings financed the goddess's cult, but the sexuality of Astarte's worship was basically imitative magic, intended to sustain the fertility of Nature.

Greek and Roman writers were also repelled by the worship of the Middle Eastern goddesses whose rituals spread westwards, with their phallic symbols, sacred prostitutes and painted priests in women's clothes. In *The Golden Ass* Apuleius (born c 123 AD) describes the priests, 'their faces daubed with rouge and their eye sockets painted to bring out the brightness of their eyes', who carried the image of 'the Syrian goddess' about on on an ass, dancing to the sound of castanets and cymbals, cutting themselves with knives and flagellating themselves for the edification of the spectators before going round with the collecting box. Earlier, in the biblical account of the contest between Elijah and

Astarte in alabaster, a Mesopotamian statue of the goddess of love c 2000 BC. The crescent or horn-shaped head-dress signifies her connection with the moon.

the prophets of Baal, the Canaanite god's priests were said to 'cut themselves after their custom with swords and lances, until the blood gushed out upon them.'

As a result of the denunciations of Ashtoreth in the Old Testament as an 'abomination' and an enemy of God, Jews and Christians decided that she was a demon.

Baal

The west Semitic word *baal* was applied to men and gods to mean ownership. It usually referred to the ownership of a place, so that there were many local gods who were Baals of their own areas, but it could also refer to ownership of a sphere of interest, as in the case of Baal Berith, 'the god of the covenant', who presided over agreements, or even to a god's ownership of those who worshipped him.

From c 3000 BC probably, and certainly by about 2500 BC, the title was applied specifically to a god of the Amorites, a powerful group of Semitic nomads. He was the god of storm and the rain of winter, first found in Palestine and southern Syria, named Adad in Mesopotamian texts and Hadad in texts from Ras Shamra in northern Syria.

The texts found at Ras Shamra since 1929 contain versions, dating from about 1400 BC, of a large number of myths involving Baal, who was the most active deity in the fertility cult of the Canaanites, the early inhabitants of Syria and Palestine. This cult was particularly concerned with the winter rainfall, which was vital to the fruitfulness of flocks and fields. The texts make it possible to reconstruct the Canaanite cult of Baal. They sometimes confirm and sometimes correct the sporadic references in the Old Testament, which are generally criticisms of the abuses and grosser aspects of this Nature cult.

The Baal myth of Ras Shamra describes in dramatic scenes how Baal (or Hadad) champions the gods and the order they sustain against the insults and threatened tyranny of the unruly waters, 'Prince Sea, even River the Ruler'. After a critical struggle Baal overcomes, slays and disperses the waters, distributing them so that they are a good servant rather than a bad master. This conflict is described as a fight for kingship, and the victor Baal is acclaimed as 'king', his kingdom being 'an everlasting kingdom'.

This was the Canaanite declaration of faith in the beneficence of Nature. It was an assurance to the worshippers and a relief to their fears and anxieties, which were expressed and purged by the drama vividly related in the texts. It was also an opportunity to influence the course of Nature by the speaking of words and possibly by an accompanying ritual in which Baal's victory was acted out and so magically recreated each year.

The main motifs of this Baal myth are reproduced in the Old Testament, notably in the psalms which assert or imply the kingship of God and in passages in the Prophets on the theme of the kingship of God and the maintenance of his order against the menace of Chaos in Nature and history. This was the theme of the Hebrew Feast of Tabernacles on the eve of the New Year, adapted from the chief seasonal festival in Canaan when the Israelites settled in Palestine, between c 1225 and 1050 BC.

This same theme is the substance of hope for the future in apocalyptic literature of the New Testament. The imagery of the old Canaanite theme of the kingship of the god and his order in Nature, won in conflict with the unruly waters and certain sea-monsters, such as *ltn* (the Biblical Leviathan), 'the Primeval Serpent, the Tortuous One with Seven Heads' is re-echoed from the Canaanite New Year ceremony.

This is perhaps most familiar to general readers in the vision of the emergence of the reign of God and his saints after the succession of bestial powers, which significantly came up 'from the sea' (in Daniel, chapter 7) and the culmination of the conflict against the bestial powers of evil in the establishment of the kingdom of God and his new creation, when 'sea shall be no more', in Revelation (chapter 21).

Baal's character as the storm god is expressed in a sculptured stele (an upright slab or pillar) found near his temple on the acropolis of Ras Shamra and dating probably from c 2100 BC. He is depicted as a helmeted warrior in a short kilt, striding into action, brandishing a mace (the weapon with which he overcomes Sea-and-River) and a spear, which is grounded, point downwards. The butt of the shaft of the spear is depicted as branching, and this has been taken to simulate forked lightning, which is regularly

Baal, the cloud-mounter, god of the winter rains. Statuette of the 15th–14th centuries BC, now in the Louvre.

noted as the weapon of Baal-Hadad (or Mesopotamian Adad) in texts and in sculpture. However, a seal design from Ras Shamra suggests that the branching spear may depict a cedar tree, expressing Baal's significance as a god of vegetation, particularly associated with the cedars which are the most splendid trees of the mountains of his Canaanite home.

The god's power of fertility is expressed by his association with the bull as his cult animal; he wears the bull's horns on his helmet. His stock epithet in the Baal myth is 'He who mounts the Clouds' (compare Yahweh, God of Israel, 'who makes the clouds his chariot'). The wavy lines shown beneath the feet of the god possibly represent the mountain tops and clouds (and again Yahweh 'treads the high places of the earth'). But they may also represent the waters below, over which he has triumphed.

The essential features of the warrior Baal are reproduced in the figurines of a young active god in bronze, sometimes inlaid in gold and silver, from various sites in Syria and Palestine. They indicate the widespread cult of the god, *the* Baal, the Master or Lord in the Nature worship of Canaan.

Baal was one of the Semitic gods whose cult penetrated to Egypt, possibly carried there by the many Semites deported from Syria and Palestine in the various campaigns of the Pharaohs between the 15th and 13th centuries BC. The Pharaoh Rameses II (d 1224 BC) himself affected Syrian cults.

The most notable cult centre of Baal in Egypt was Baal Saphon near Pelusium, east of the Nile Delta. The name reflects the proper home of the god, Mount Saphon, the modern Jebel al-Aqra, the Mount Kasios of the Greek geographers, a kind of Canaanite Olympus on the northern horizon of Ras Shamra.

Greek authors knew of a temple of Zeus Kasios near Pelusium and an inscription mentioning Zeus Kasios has been found there. The assimilation of Baal, the storm god who 'mounts the clouds', with the supreme sky god Zeus was natural, and equally natural was the worship, on this featureless but dangerous coast, of the god who established his kingship after winning victory over the unruly waters.

As the god of Tyre, whose worship Jezebel is depicted in the Old Testament as striving so hard to promote in Israel, Baal was assimilated in the Greek period (after the 4th century BC) to Hercules, the active young god who also sustained order against Chaos, which was depicted, like one of Baal's adversaries in the struggle, as a many-headed monster of the watery wastes, the Hydra.

A similar theme was known between 2000 and 1000 BC in Asia Minor, as shown by mythological texts from the ancient Hittite capital of Hattusas (modern Boghaz Koi) where the god who successfully overcomes the sea-monster is Teshub, the weather god, who is represented in Hittite sculpture with the familiar features of the bronze figurines of Baal from Syria and Palestine.

The preoccupation with the fertility cult in Syria tended to give Baal-Hadad a predominance even beyond his proper sphere in

Michael Holford

Nature. It is significant that several of the kings of Damascus were called Ben-Hadad ('the son of Hadad'), which may have been a throne-name of them all. It is a fair inference that the name reflects the conception of the king as the earthly guarantee of the kingship of Baal and the stability of order against the menace of Chaos. It was probably a trend to monotheism (the worship of one god) in the conception of Baal of the Heavens (Baal-Shamayim) in Syria between about 1000 and 500 BC which made Baal such a dangerous rival to Yahweh in Israel and prompted Elijah to his famous challenge to the prophets of Baal on Carmel (I Kings, 18).

The bulk of the remainder of the Baal mythology in the Ras Shamra texts concerns Baal's conflict with Mot, the power of drought, sterility and death, where Baal is a dying and rising god, the spirit of vegetation which wilts and dies in summer but revives with the winter rain. These texts relate to the seasonal ritual of the Syrian peasants.

After Baal has succumbed to Mot, the latter suffers the vengeance of Baal's sister, 'the Virgin Anat', who cuts him with a blade, winnows him with a shovel, parches him with fire, grinds him with a millstone and scatters him in a field. Here the rites of desacralization (freeing from holiness) of the first or last sheaves of the grain-harvest underlie the myth; such a rite, in fact, as is described in the Bible in Leviticus (chapter 2) which refers to the offering of the first sheaf, 'green ears of corn, dried by the fire, even corn beaten out of full ears'.

Baal eventually revives, and there is the glad prospect of the skies raining oil and the wadis running with honey (again an aspect of the establishment of the order of God in the Old Testament). Finally, 'after seven years' Baal engages Mot in a great struggle and overcomes him. This may be related to the Hebrew custom of allowing the land to lie fallow in the seventh year, thus simulating a famine, when the sinister power of sterility was allowed to exhaust itself, in the hope that the next six years would be fruitful, and therefore normal.

From the references in the Old Testament to repeated lapses to the cult of Baal and his female associates, we can infer that in settling in Palestine the Hebrews tended to assimilate the Baal cult without adapting it. Official authority was alarmed and the early calendar in Exodus (chapter 23) and the Ritual Code, also in Exodus (chapter 34), insisted that the festivals at the three great seasonal crises of the year be observed 'before Yahweh God of Israel', that is at the central sanctuary of the confederacy of Israel. Owing to this basic experience, Israel was able to transform the theme of the Canaanite New Year festival, the kingship of God was won and sustained against the menace of Chaos, and it was developed as a fundamental element of her own faith.

The popular tendency, however, was to assimilate the grosser elements of Baal worship in the Canaanite fertility cult. To this the prophets are eloquent witnesses, especially Hosea, who inveighed against this materialistic Nature cult and the licentious rites of imitative magic with which it was associated.

Cybele

The cult and myth of Cybele as known in the classical world originated with the Phrygians who entered Anatolia from Thrace in the 13th century BC. It contained elements taken over from the native population, among which was perhaps the figure of Attis. Even in ancient times. Attis was sometimes identified with the Syrian Adonis, so closely did they resemble each other. But Cybele, though she is akin to such other forms of the Great Goddess as Astarte in Syria and Ishtar in Babylonia, Ma in Anatolia and Rhea in Greece, is a distinctive figure because of her special connection with mountains and with wild beasts.

According to some scholars Cybele is the same as Cybebe of the Lydians (who lived in what is now southern Turkey) and certainly little distinction between them is found in classical literature. Cybebe originates from the South Anatolian and North Mesopotamian nature-goddess Kubaba, 'mistress of doves'. But the name Cybele is likely to be Phrygian, since Cybela or Cybelus was a name of her sacred mountain and apparently meant a place of caves or chambers where she dwelt and had her image. In some Phrygian inscriptions from 700 BC onward she is called *matar Kubile* and Attis *Atte papa*, which suggests that Attis was a male consort.

The original centre of her cult was Pessinus near Ankara in Phrygia (now central Turkey) at the foot of Mount Dindyma or Dindymum. The Mountain is now called Gunusu Dagh.

During the 7th century her cult appears to have spread through Anatolia to Lydia and the coast of the Black Sea. From Lydia it reached Greece, where it was little favoured and usually left to Phrygian slaves. In 205 BC at the crisis of the Hannibalic war it was brought direct from Pessinus to Rome. Cybele was accepted there as a goddess who protected cities and maintained life, was established in a temple on the Capitol, and was later honoured with a festival, the *Megalensia*, the Great Mother's Games. Fortune began to favour the Roman armies, and there was even an unprecedented harvest in Italy which repaired the ravages of war. But in spite of its magical efficacy the cult with its rites was found scandalous at Rome, so that it was insulated by special rules. No Roman was permitted to join directly in its rites, still less to serve as a priest. From Rome in the imperial age, when in its train other oriental cults were introduced, it spread to the provinces and lasted until the triumph of Christianity.

The original character of Cybele may be gathered best from the scornful description of the Christian apologist Arnobius who touches on it in a tract written about 300 AD; some of the same details appear in the writings of Pausanias, the Greek geographer of the 2nd century AD, and elsewhere. Cybele was born of the rock Agdus from the seed of Zeus; hence her name Agdistis used in this story. She was at first a bisexual monster of great strength and ferocity. The monster devastated the country and terrified gods

and men until Bacchus tricked it by pouring into its favourite drinking fountain a great quantity of the strongest neat wine as a soporific. As it slept, Bacchus tied its male organs firmly to a tree with a rope of twisted bristles, so that when it woke and sprang up, these organs were torn off with a great flow of blood, and it lost its male sex. From the blood the first almond tree grew. One of the almonds was picked for its beauty and put in her lap by Nana, daughter of the river Sangarius. It disappeared, but Nana became pregnant. She was shut up without food by her father, but fed by the Great Mother until she bore her child Attis. By order of Sangarius, Attis was exposed in the open and left to die, but he was fed by a wild goat.

As he grew up, his beauty attracted the love of Agdistis who hunted with him in the woods and presented him with the game. Midas, King of Pessinus, wishing to deliver Attis from this disgraceful attachment, arranged for him to marry his own daughter, closing the town's gates for the ceremony. But Agdistis burst in, raising the town walls on her head, because she knew that danger threatened Attis if he should marry. Thereupon Attis went mad and castrated himself under a pine tree, scornfully making a gift of his severed organs to Agdistis, who gathered them up and preserved them. Violets grew from them, with which the pine was subsequently decorated.

But Attis himself died from his wounds. In spite of Agdistis's prayers, Zeus would not restore him to life, but merely preserved his body from corruption and kept its little finger in perpetual motion. Agdistis installed the body in a tomb at Pessinus with castrated priests to maintain a cult.

Facing page *Terracotta figure of Gilgamesh from Khorsabad, Iraq.* **Below** *Attis, the consort of Cybele: bronze statue in the Louvre, Paris.*

Giraudon

Gilgamesh

The great hero of Sumerian and Babylonian mythology was Gilgamesh. His deeds are recorded in an epic poem no less adventurous than the *Odyssey*, put into its final written form not more than about a century after the Greek poem. The received text of the Gilgamesh epic was written down on a series of 12 clay tablets inscribed in the cuneiform script used by the Sumerians, the Babylonians and the peoples of Assyria. The fullest version that has come down to us was originally held in the great palace library of the king of Assyria, Ashurbanipal, who made

Michael Holford

a vast collection of contemporary and ancient texts in the course of three decades between about 660–630 BC.

This famous epic became a set book in the scribal schools and has been reconstituted from fragments found not only on many Mesopotamian sites, but also at places as far apart as Megiddo in Palestine and Ugarit in Syria.

Evidence of the poem's existence has been found at Sultantepe and Boghaz Koi, the great Hittite capital in Asia Minor. The Assyrian version ultimately derives from a much older Babylonian text which must have been composed before 1800 BC, for there is no mention of Marduk the god of Babylon, whose cult became the state religion in the reign of Hammurabi. But the earliest versions of all stem from Sumerian

texts of the late third millennium BC, at which time this epic was perhaps not a continuous story, but consisted of a disconnected series of episodes in which Gilgamesh took a prominent place.

The epic itself is enthralling for the insight which it gives into the psychology of the Babylonians and also of their Sumerian forebears.

We also become aware of the historical background and of a heroic age which, though associated with stories about the gods, may be authenticated by historical, or semi-historical, literature such as the Sumerian king lists, and by archeology. The historical position of Gilgamesh is firmly established by an episode in the Sumerian version of the story, which tells of a battle between Gilgamesh and Agga, King of Kish, a name already known from the Sumerian king lists.

Indeed the name of Agga's father has been clearly identified on an alabaster bowl from the Diyala valley, dated about 2700 BC. Thus in the epic we can visualize a real king, Gilgamesh, as well as a world famous historical event, the Sumerian Deluge, the memory of which has been preserved in the book of Genesis.

From this poem we learn that Gilgamesh was a renowned and powerful king who had built the great walls of Erech, one of the most extensive cities of Sumer and Babylonia. Gilgamesh, however, was an arrogant, oppressive and philandering ruler who had exasperated his subjects. In consequence an appeal was made to the gods for a champion who would contend for their rights against the omniscient and headstrong oppressor within their city.

The champion elected to liberate Erech was a hairy hunter named Enkidu, a Sumerian wild man who lived with the animals and protected them. He was seduced by a courtesan, who tempted him with the delights of the city, and Enkidu who had never before partaken of bread developed a taste for strong drink also. On entering Erech he engaged in a wrestling match with Gilgamesh, but after honour was satisfied on both sides the two heroes became firm friends and decided to embark on an adventurous journey together and keep each other company.

In a mountain of cedars, perhaps the Amanus or the Lebanon, they sought out the demon Humbaba and slew him. In this episode we may see a relic of early dynastic Sumerian conquests in Syria recently attested by excavations at Mardikh and Chuera. The two friends returned in triumph to Erech, and the goddess Ishtar became enamoured of Gilgamesh. Unwisely he spurned her advances and accused her of having seduced men and beasts. The goddess, a woman scorned and enraged, induced the high god Anu to send down from heaven an avenging bull to trample on the city of Erech, but Enkidu killed it, thereby sealing his own doom and initiating a long drawn tragedy. After his death, which was foretold in a dream, there follows a lament for Enkidu, for whom an expensive funeral has been thoughtfully and carefully arranged.

Gilgamesh, bereft of his friend, began to

fear for his own life, and resolved to embark on a journey in search of the secret of immortality, although as we are reminded in the ninth tablet of the epic, 'two thirds of him is god, one third is man'. Between twin mountain peaks he penetrated the gate of sunrise which was guarded by the scorpion-man and his wife, and after a long journey through an immense and impenetrable darkness arrived in a garden where the trees bore carnelian and lapis lazuli. He was on his way to find Utnapishtim, the Sumerian Noah who, as he hoped, would reveal the secret of his immortality to him. The sun god warned Gilgamesh that he was on a vain quest and advised him to seek what pleasure he could in life:

> Day and night be thou merry
> Make every day a day of rejoicing.

This part of the narration in Tablet X concludes with a passage worthy of the book of Proverbs in which Gilgamesh reflects on the impermanence of life and its mutability, and man's impotence.

The ensuing Tablet XI is the famous Deluge tablet, which breaks the thread of the narrative. This is thought by many authorities to reflect an identifiable event or events which, according to another Sumerian tablet, may be related to the reign of king Ziusudra who is thought to have lived not more than a century or two after 3000 BC.

The conclusion of the eleventh tablet is that with the advice of a ferryman named Urshanabi, Gilgamesh, his feet weighted by stones, dived deep into the sea and discovered a plant like a thorn, the wondrous plant whose name was perpetual youth. His triumph was short lived, for on his way home, whilst refreshing himself in a pool, a serpent robbed him of his trophy and stole the secret of eternal life.

The last tablet of the series, Tablet XII is an appendix to the whole, for in it Enkidu lives once more. It contains a Semitic version of a Sumerian story. Here we have a remarkable episode concerning a willow tree and its magical properties coveted by Inanna, queen of heaven. Enkidu who has meddled dangerously on her behalf goes to his death, and the story ends with an interview between Gilgamesh and Enkidu's ghost, who gives a woeful account of the underworld. Here we have an unrelieved picture of gloom which, with few exceptions, is typical of Sumerian and Babylonian thought.

The Eyes of Death

In a Sumerian poem, the judges of the underworld pronounce death on Inanna:

The pure Ereshkigal seated herself upon
  her throne,
The Annunaki, the seven judges, pronounced
  judgement before her,
They fastened (their) eyes upon her, the eyes
  of death,
At their word, the word which tortures the
  spirit. . .
The sick woman was turned into a corpse,
The corpse was hung from a stake.

S. N. Kramer *Sumerian Mythology*

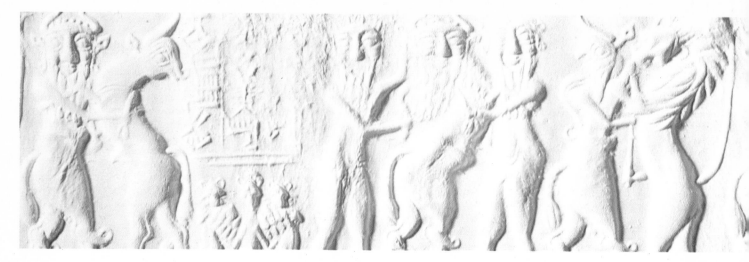

Ishtar

Ishtar was the Semitic name for the old Sumerian goddess Inanna, the most powerful goddess in Mesopotamia. Representing the full potency of womanhood and maidenhood, and possessed of subtle powers in shaping the fortunes of man, she was worshipped for more than 2000 years. Doubtless many facets of her character altered during this period; and different aspects of the goddess were venerated in different cities, some more appealing than others.

For the appraisal of Ishtar there is no more revealing source than the Sumerian hymn, *The Exaltation of Inanna*. Composed in about 2350 BC by Enheduanna, the daughter of King Sargon of Agade in Akkad, in the north of Babylonia, this long poem describes the struggle for her supremacy over Nanna, the moon god in the southern city of Ur, and her final acceptance in the city of Uruk (Erech), also in the south, by the high god, An.

Reading between the lines, we can see how King Sargon, a usurper, set the divine seal to his empire over Sumer and Akkad by equating Sumerian Inanna with Akkadian Ishtar. Here is a glimpse of the kind of political and religious struggle so frequent in the long history of ancient Egypt, but more rarely revealed in the annals of Mesopotamia.

This poem, which begins with the description of Inanna as the lady who possessed all the attributes of divinity, tells of her many accomplishments. Following the description of the dramatic struggle against the older divinities and against the wicked collusion of the older gods in Ur and Uruk, we end in a hymn of praise, through which the high priestess and her goddess emerge triumphant.

Inanna is the radiant lady rapt in beauty, terrifying and tempestuous, but she is also seen as a lady of resplendent light, beloved of heaven and earth. Inanna-Ishtar is also the dread goddess, who can, if she will, accurse vegetation and command fear in mankind. Not only is she possessed of sexual potency, able to control both fertility and sterility, but she is also a mighty goddess in battle, and this martial quality of Ishtar was as pervasive as any in the later development of her character.

In the hymn, she is described as 'the lady mounted on a beast' and as 'lent wings by the storm'; and in art she is frequently shown mounted on a lion or lioness, or leading both together. For example, on the high rock carvings of Maltai in Assyria, she occupied a prominent place in the procession of the gods; she was mounted on a lioness, and no doubt gave her blessing to the Assyrian armies as they marched through the defiles which separated Assyria from Iran, on their campaigns.

The description of her as having been 'lent wings by the storm' recalls the goddess's many sinister images, among which one of the most striking is the great terracotta, known as the Burney relief, in which the naked, winged goddess, usually called 'Lilith', with feathered legs and birds' talons, mounted on lions, appears in the guise of a seductive vamp of terrible aspect. Here she is seen to be of 'terrible countenance', in the words of the poem. In the early poems another side of Inanna-Ishtar's character is revealed, namely, of the goddess who presided over divination, incubation and oneiromancy, the interpretation of dreams. She was invested with all the great powers of womankind, and while possessed of seductive beauty and charm, could, if so moved, turn rivers to blood.

Inanna-Ishtar presided over one of the most important ceremonies of the year – the ritual marriage of the god, in the course of which the king was wedded to the high priestess and in this way induced for his people the promise of agricultural prosperity. Indeed, on the famous stone vase from Uruk, c 3300 BC, Inanna herself may perhaps be recognized, evidently taking part in the spring festival.

There is clearly evidence from later periods of the king's special relationship to Ishtar, the goddess who in the words of A.L. Oppenheim 'becomes the carrier, the fountainhead, of his power and prestige'.

For the people of Agade, Ishtar was an incarnation of the planet Venus, which was known as Dilbat. In military history, Ishtar of Nineveh and Ishtar of Arbela are prominent in battle and ensure victory for the Assyrian armies. A famous war poem of Tukulti-Ninurta I, referring to an event in the 13th century BC, tells how Ishtar intervened at a critical point in the battle as a result of which the Assyrians triumphed over

Gilgamesh and his friend Enkidu subduing wild beasts: plaster cast of an Akkadian seal.

Kashtiliash, King of Babylon and inflicted defeat upon him.

Ishtar was also invoked as a healer; indeed she made a memorable journey in about 1375 BC from Nineveh to Thebes, in Egypt, in order to lay hands on the aged and ailing King Amenophis III. This was not the first occasion her powers had been so used.

But the most sinister episode in the whole mythology concerning this goddess is the account of her descent into Hades, a tale of early Sumerian origin, in which Inanna strives dangerously with her sister, the queen of the underworld, and only narrowly succeeds in escaping from it.

Ishtar, however, is often thought of as an erotic goddess concerned with sexual intercourse, and later in history her hierodules or prostitutes were to earn a licentious and evil reputation, especially in the city of Uruk, where there was an elaborately organized college of priestesses of Ishtar, the head of which was the high priestess herself. This cult enjoyed a considerable expansion elsewhere, and finally emanated in the lewd practices of the Phoenician Astarte, and Hebrew Ashtaroth, so much condemned by the Old Testament prophets.

There is evidence that organizations similar to the one in Uruk existed first in Ashur, and then in Babylon. In Ashur, the religious capital of Assyria, the remains of a temple which belonged to Ishtar *dinitu*, 'the lady of the dawn', or the 'lighting up' have been excavated.

What seems to have happened within the sacred precincts may be deduced from a series of lead discs and tokens found elsewhere in the same city. These plaques showed men, and women who were probably hierodules in the service of the goddess, enjoying sexual intercourse on the brick pillars of the temple. Other figures are also engaged in an erotic dance.

This practice has an interesting counterpart in Herodotus's account of a strange marriage practice in Babylonia, in the course of which eligible women sat in the temple and intending suitors cast a coin in their laps, invoking the name of the goddess in settlement and witness of the marriage contract.

Marduk

Marduk became the high god and patron saint of the city of Babylon, and eventually secured for himself an international prestige which went far beyond the natural confines of the Babylonian Empire.

The name first appears in about 2000 BC, at which time it was of little importance, but it seems possible that originally Marduk was a solar god, for later he was remembered under a Sumerian title, meaning 'the bull-calf of the sun', and indeed throughout his career Marduk was always one of the gods of light.

His ascent to fame, however, was first achieved under the Amorite Dynasty of Babylon which reached its peak in the reign of King Hammurabi, c 1792–1750 BC. On the famous diorite monument discovered at Susa, and inscribed with the text of the Babylonian 'code' of laws, Marduk is twice mentioned in the introduction. He had been allotted 'the divine worship of the multitude of the people', and thus before the end of Hammurabi's reign had become the Babylonian national god and patron, though perhaps not yet supreme. As administrator of justice Marduk was represented on the contemporary cylinder seals with the toothed saw that cuts decisions.

From that time onwards until the Seleucid era, beginning in 312 BC, the fortunes of Babylon were inextricably bound with those of Marduk, who, however, attained his greatest authority during the renaissance of

the Babylonian Empire between the end of the 7th and 6th centuries BC. It is indeed apparent that when Marduk was down, Babylon's fortunes were at their lowest ebb and three historic events illustrate the point.

First, an inscription of the Kassite king, Agum II, recalls that he brought back the statues of Marduk and his wife, Sarpanitum, after they had been in exile in Khana for 30 years.

This banishment referred to had followed the sack of Babylon by the Hittite king, Murshilish I, in 1595 BC. Only with the triumphant restoration of these divinities did Babylon begin to rise again, but it took many centuries for Marduk to recover his prestige.

The renaissance appears to have occurred shortly before 1100 BC when the god's statue was once again recovered, this time from Elam, to the east of Babylon. The reign of Nebuchadrezzar I, who was responsible for the victory over Elam, thus marked a decisive turning point in Mesopotamian religion.

This was indeed a signal triumph, for Elam which had been a deadly menace to Babylonia, was thereafter quiescent for nearly three centuries and, doubtless, the credit went to Marduk.

A third historic event which marks once again a low ebb in the god's fortunes was the devastation of Babylon in the time of Sargon, King of Assyria, and the neglect of the god's sanctuary by Sargon's son, Sennacherib, in the years 705–703 BC. The New Year ceremonies were at that period several

times suspended. But Babylon, which had suffered so much devastation under the early Sargonids, was restored to favour again by the superstitious Assyrian King Esarhaddon. Even after the conquest of Babylon in the 6th century BC by the Persian monarch Cyrus, the fortunes of Marduk waxed strong, though heresies in the form of worship were alleged to have been perpetrated by his predecessor, Nabonidus. Thus, Marduk's fortunes may be followed from historical records and are also attested by his fluctuating popularity as a component of personal names: i.e. how often and at what periods they were given and when neglected in favour of others.

Information about the nature of the god comes to us from religious and magical texts. First comes the famous epic of Creation which was a long poem recited in the god's honour on the fourth night of the Neo-Babylonian New Year's Festival. It was known in antiquity as the *Enuma elish* from the first line which runs, 'when on high the heavens were not named'. There were seven tablets in all which varied in length between about 115–140 lines. They tell us about the creation of the universe, and proclaim the Babylonian belief that in the beginning the

Left Commemorative stele set up in honour of Adad-etir by his son: father and son stand below the symbols of the gods Shamash, Sin and Nergal. Below A boundary stone recording a gift of land in southern Babylonia also bears symbols of the gods, to protect the deed.

British Museum/Michael Holford

Michael Holford/British Museum

Above *The Musrussu dragon, the personal symbol of Marduk, the high god of Babylon. Brick reliefs of the dragon flanked the sacred way along which Marduk and the gods passed after the New Year Festival: from a boundary stone.* **Left** *Ishtar was a radiant goddess rapt in beauty, terrifying and tempestuous, 'lady of resplendent light': eight-pointed star, symbol of Ishtar, from a boundary stone.*

first gods were generated out of the mingling of waters which had preceded the formation of the earliest Mesopotamian slime.

As the gods multiplied there was a schism in the course of which the respectable High Gods such as Anu, Ansar and Ea became divided against the detestable aboriginal dragon Tiamat representing chaos and supported by her evil myrmidons. The good gods, threatened with destruction, were saved from annihilation by the birth of Marduk, son of the magical god Ea, and destined to restore order to the universe. In agreeing to fight Tiamat, Marduk struck a bargain with his superiors and was promised the power to declare fates and work miracles. The magical 'appearing and disappearing' act of Marduk's garment is a notable forerunner of the conjurors Maskelyne and

Devant. The saviour's destruction of Tiamat with the aid of the Seven Winds is a theme frequently illustrated on Babylonian seals, but we cannot recognize in iconography his creation of man out of the blood of Kingu.

Marduk's victory was celebrated by his reorganization of the heavens, by a drunken thank-offering banquet of the gods and by the decision to build Babylon, the shrines of Esagila and the ziggurat, the great temple tower.

It is fortunate that a few tablets written in Babylon and elsewhere have survived to give us a fragmentary account of some of the ritual acts performed during the eleven days devoted to the New Year Festival.

The proceedings may be thought of as a Passion Play in which a ritual marriage between the king and the goddess Ishtar probably took place as well as many other symbolic performances; for example, the king had to give an account of himself before the god through a negative confession, or recitation of uncommitted sins. Most striking was the ceremony in which the king, standing before Marduk, was stripped

of his regalia and had his face slapped by the high priest: it boded ill if the king did not shed tears.

At the end of the festival, Marduk led the great procession of gods which passed along the sacred way, flanked by enamelled brick reliefs of lions, and his personal symbol, the Musrussu dragon, to emerge at the *Akitu* temple where he entertained the divine assembly to a banquet.

The belief that in the course of this festival Marduk was entombed and resurrected is based on a misinterpretation of an Assyrian text and has no foundation. It has been shown that in two late texts the resurrected god was Nergal, king of the underworld, and that this emergence probably represented the victory of the sun after the winter solstice.

The cult of Marduk flourished in Assyria from the 14th century BC onwards, but in the 7th century he was displaced by the national god Assur: a late Assyrian text describing the capture of Marduk and his committal to the ordeal by water is a political tract designed to discredit the god. However, Marduk's popularity was due to his reputation as assistant magician to his father Ea in the rituals for alleviating sickness and misfortune.

The power of the priesthood of Babylon over a dynasty of successful soldiers and notables, not of royal blood, ensured the glorification of Babylon and the rich endowment of the temples. However, the god's fame throughout the ancient world and for posterity derives from the imperial victories of Nabopolassar and Nebuchadrezzar II who rebuilt the city on a magnificent scale.

Appendix

Ashur
Chief god and war god of the Assyrians, often shown firing an arrow from his bow and enclosed in a winged disc; he replaced the god Marduk when the Assyrians dominated Mesopotamia and imposed their religious beliefs.

Giraudon

Attis
Youthful god of Asia Minor, lover of the goddess Cybele; fundamentally a vegetation god who died and was reborn like the crops each year; connected with violets which sprang from his blood and the pine tree into which he was transformed on his death.

Babylonia
The area north of the head of the Persian Gulf, watered by the rivers Tigris and Euphrates, the centre of early civilization and religious development in the Middle East; in early times divided into two parts, the southern called Sumer and the northern Accad or Akkad, the area is rich in mythology.

Dagon
The national god of the Philistines, who may be identified with the early Babylonian god called Dagan. He represents what was probably a primitive Canaanite corn god in his earliest manifestation.

Michael Holford

Ea
Or Enki, the god of the waters, one of the three supreme deities of the Babylonian pantheon, the other two being Enlil, god of storms, and Anu god of the sky: Ea overcame the sweet waters, Apsu, with which he was later identified, and is often depicted in human form with waves about his shoulders: also invoked as the 'Lord of Wisdom', he was the patron of arts and crafts, and was credited with the invention of magic, and the creation of man from clay in the image and after the likeness of the gods.

Michael Holford

El
The supreme deity of the Canaanites and Phoenicians, whose wife Asherah, called Astarte by the Greeks, was the great mother goddess: his name means literally 'the god' and his other titles, 'Father of Men', 'Creator of Created Things' and 'the Bull' indicate his benevolence to man and his strength and virility: he is depicted on a stele as a bearded man, wearing a crown adorned with a pair of bull's horns.

Gilgamesh
As well as being the hero of the Babylonian epic that bears his name, Gilgamesh was thought by some to be the same person as Nimrod, son of Cush, a famous hunter and warrior, who appears in the Old Testament in the Book of Genesis, chapter 10: 'And Cush begat Nimrod: he began to be a mighty one in the earth. He was a mighty hunter before the Lord: wherefore it is said, Even as Nimrod the mighty hunter before the Lord. And the beginning of his kingdom was Babel, and Erech, and Accad, and Calneh, in the land of Shinar. Out of that land went forth Asshur, and builded Nineveh...'

Pomegranate
A symbol of fertility, because of its many seeds; in a Turkish custom, a bride throws one on the ground and the number of seeds scattered when

C. M. Dixon

it breaks shows how many children she will have; the mother of the god Attis conceived him by putting a pomegranate in her bosom; it was a pomegranate seed which Persephone ate in the underworld, committing her to spending a third of each year there: in Christian art, a symbol of hope.

Rivers
Rivers share in the general symbolism of water as the source of life and, like the Nile in Egypt, may be seen primarily as bringers of fertility: to cross a river is symbolically to pass from one spiritual condition to another; in hymns and spirituals to cross over Jordan is to pass the barrier of death.

Sumerians
Early inhabitants of Mesopotamia: they had settled in Babylonia by 3500 BC and 'initiated a cultural revolution which gave the world writing, cities, and a corpus of religious practices and concepts'; each early settlement had its own local deity, so that there was a large pantheon of gods and goddesses, and a complex web of relationships between them.

Taurobolium
A rite in the Mysteries of Cybele and of Attis; the initiate descended into a pit and was then drenched in the blood of a bull which was slaughtered over his head; it was after this had taken place that the initiate was regarded as having been 'reborn'. This rite was also a feature of Mithraism.

Tiamat
Monstrous personification of the sea in Babylonian mythology: from her mingling with the fresh waters the first generation of the gods was born; she threatened to destroy the gods but was killed by Marduk, the god of Babylon, who fashioned the universe from her body and created mankind from the blood of the leader of her army.

THE MYTHS
OF ANCIENT GREECE

The Olympian Pantheon

The abiding mystical concepts derived from Cretan religion are significantly marked by the influence of a mother goddess and a dying god, associated with the bull, who later became worshipped as 'Cretan-born Zeus'. This Zeus, who died and was born again, was different from the Olympian Zeus of the familiar Greek pantheon. He was much more comparable with the Greek Dionysus, also a bull god and a dying god. These two different concepts help us to establish distinctions between the Minoan and the Mycenean phases of earlier Greek religion.

The historian Herodotus records that the poets Homer and Hesiod were the first to compose theogonies, poems dealing with the origin of the gods, and gave the deities their epithets, allotted them their offices and occupations, and described their forms. It is probable that these traditional Greek theogonies derived from the Greek epics which were rooted in the Mycenean period of the late Bronze Age.

Traditional mythology recorded legends about conditions before the Mycenean pantheon of the Olympic gods became paramount. Before this time, the Titans, the children of Uranus and Gaia (Heaven and Earth) held sway. To prevent Cronus, the youngest Titan, from swallowing his baby son Zeus, his wife Rhea bore him secretly in Crete and substituted a stone wrapped in swaddling clothes for the infant, who was reared in hiding. The legends about the birth of Zeus in Crete were responsible for the specific epithet of the supreme god as 'Cretan-born'. This epithet and the oriental connections of his mother Rhea, indicate that he was an old Minoan god, involved in the same basic pattern of oriental ritual which prompted the myths of Ishtar and Tammuz, Isis and Osiris, Venus and Adonis. It is probable that Greek-speaking people who arrived in Crete gave the name of their sky god to an old Minoan deity whose ritual and character can be guessed from the evidence of later times.

The Olympian Zeus was the leader of the traditional Greek pantheon. There is reason to suppose that the hierarchical organization of the gods and goddesses as portrayed in the Homeric epics reflects the actual social conditions of the Mycenean period. The

Above *The mother goddess of Crete held sway over mountain and earth, sea and sky, life and death: figurine of the goddess, her hands in a gesture of blessing.* **Facing page** *The hero Hercules, renowned for his gigantic strength, captures the Cretan bull in the seventh of his 12 labours. The mainland Greeks 'captured the Cretan bull' in a sense, when they conquered the rich and peaceful civilization of Crete.*

Mansell Collection

Homeric Greeks (the Achaeans), burst the bonds of their own ancestral tribal organization and adapted their control of Bronze Age techniques to warfare. The martial character of the Myceneans of the later Bronze Age is exemplified in their fortification of their urban centres, in marked contrast with the unfortified cities of Minoan Crete. Similarly, the Achaean chieftains of the Homeric poems dominate the battlefield.

The heroic age of ancient Greece, as it is portrayed in Homer, represents the violent and ruthless conquest of an older, sophisticated, peaceful and refined civilization by warlike adventurers. Its richest and most important centres were away from the mainland, especially on the island of Crete; so the greatest prizes were out of reach until the Achaeans became sailors.

After 1400 BC the leadership of the Aegean world passed to mainland Mycene; and the Mycenean pantheon presumably spread its influence as the Mycenean social and economic system penetrated widely from its mainland centres. The ensuing social conflict, and fusion of peoples and customs, was paralleled by increasing complexity in cults and in mythology, and in the composition and organization of the pantheon. The most dramatic form of this process was a struggle, never quite resolved, between the old concept of a mother goddess and the newer concept of a dominating male god, Zeus.

Under the monarchical leadership of Olympian Zeus, the gods and goddesses were gathered together in a single heavenly stronghold. Their dwelling-places, built by Hephaestus, surrounded the central palace of Zeus. Although the authority of the supreme male god had become fairly stable, it was not unchallenged. In fact Hera, wife of Zeus, was amongst those who intrigued against his authority.

This Homeric picture of the Olympian hierarchy is paralleled by the Homeric picture of earthly conditions. Even in the midst of war, Agamemnon, the leader of the Greek expedition to Troy, could claim only a loose kind of authority: his control was often disputed by his fellow-chieftains. This instability has its analogy in the inability of the Achaeans to establish a centralized, enduring

Castor and Polydeuces, the divine twins, carrying off the daughters of Leucippus. Raising her hand to her hair is the love goddess Aphrodite and at the far left, wreathed in laurel, is Zeus.

Bronze Age economy similar to the older oriental type.

There is, too, a lack of uniformity in the Homeric accounts of the Olympian system. In two passages of the *Iliad* Zeus is living alone on Olympus. In one passage he hurls a thunderbolt, in the other he sends a violent storm.

It is probable that Olympus itself was a kind of generic term for 'mountain'. However, in a well-known evocative passage of the *Odyssey*, the heavenly Olympus is des-

cribed in a way that is more appropriate to the Minoan Fields of the Blest than to a lofty, mountainous seat of storms, rain and lightning.

The growth of the Olympian pantheon was a process of tribal federation which led to military kingship. The mortal prototype of the weather god who was lord of storms, rain, lightning and thunder, and reigned in a mountain fortress, was the Mycenean overlord. The companions of the god, with their differing functions, at first lived apart from him but eventually, although they kept their traditional functions, they went to live with the Olympian overlord in his stronghold and were subject to his will.

The traditional function, or privileges, or spheres of influence of the gods were the out-

come of heavenly tribal warfare. Legend tells how Zeus made a promise to his supporters before he went to war against the old order represented by Cronus and the Titans. He swore that if he won he would guarantee the rights they already had, and would apportion rights to those who had none; when the conflict was over he became the supreme overlord and bestowed the honours. The traditional province of Hephaestus, for instance, was fire; Atlas held up the skies; Apollo was concerned with music and dancing; Hades with lamentation; the nymphs cared for mortals in the time of their youth, and so on.

The Twelve Gods who were early united into a sort of official Olympian society were normally Zeus, Hera, Poseidon, Demeter,

Apollo, Artemis, Ares, Aphrodite, Hermes, Athene, Hephaestus and Hestia. There were sometimes modifications to the list, as when Dionysus replaced Hestia in the representation of the Twelve on the east frieze of the Parthenon in Athens.

Dionysus has a place of special importance in Greek religion, essentially popular and non-Olympian. However, the cults which he personified and which played such a major role in historical times, had their counterparts elsewhere in much earlier times. Explaining why the cult of Dionysus was conspicuously absent in Crete, M.P. Nilsson observed in *Minoan-Mycenaean Religion*: 'The reason why Dionysus does not appear in Crete can only be that he was not needed there, the religious ideas of which he was the herald having already been applied to the Cretan Zeus.'

The copious amount of legendary material regarding the birth of Zeus in Crete emphasizes its pre-eminence compared with other birth-stories of Zeus. However, the very existence of such a remarkable birth-story, and the cults associated with it, inevitably meant that places other than Crete were also credited with being the site of Zeus's birth. These included Messenia where Zeus was reputed to have been reared by nymphs on Mount Ithome; Arcadia which, apart from Crete, made the strongest claims, with a legend that Cronus had swallowed the stone on Mount Thaumasius and that Zeus was born and reared on Mount Lycaeus; and Olympia, which was said to be Zeus's birthplace in a legend of the founding of the Olympic Games.

It was quite consistent that the dying god, Zeus of Crete, should not only have had his sacred marriage to Hera commemorated in an annual ceremony during which sacrifices were offered with traditional wedding rites but that his death also should have been mourned. This explains why the legend of Zeus's tomb, supposedly located at various places in Crete including Cnossus, Mount Ida and Mount Dicte, has endured from ancient to recent times.

There are a number of versions of the inscription on this legendary tomb, which suggests that 'Zan', the old name for Zeus, was certainly well known in Crete, and also that the cult of Cretan Zeus was involved with, if it did not actually develop from, an earlier cult of Minos. A common link was an annual festival celebrating a god like Adonis or Tammuz, at which this god was eaten in the form of a bull. The evidence for the tomb, relatively late though it may be, indicates that Cretan Zeus was looked upon as a dying god, with the implication that he died annually and was born again.

Initiation, which may well have originated in the Bronze Age, continued to play a major part in various Greek cults and in social life generally. The death and rebirth of an initiate tended to be dramatically represented, often with a contest and some kind of ordeal. It was not only the god, or his animal symbol, who continually died and was born again. A similar pattern persisted in the training of the youth of the Greek city-states in classical times.

The late appearance and subordinate status

of a male Minoan deity served to emphasize the over-riding importance of the Minoan goddess. In Neolithic times there seems to have been no concept of a male divinity in human form. He emerged later, as a secondary deity, but the tendency to raise him to a superior status was clear by the end of Minoan times. With the decline of the mother goddess, the bull became associated with the Minoan kingship, which perhaps had important functions in relation to the governing of the calendar. Hence the bull became a symbol of the sun, and both were fertility symbols. Bull-worship and snake-worship remained associated with traditions of the prehistoric Bronze Age kingship.

The Minoan goddess is a central feature of Minoan religion, just as the palace was a central feature of Minoan social life. In surviving monuments and artefacts she is shown in association with animals, birds and snakes; with the sacred pillar and the sacred tree; with poppies and with lilies; with the sword and the double axe. She appears to have been huntress and goddess of sports, she was armed and also presided over ritual dances; she had male and female attendants, and she held sway over mountain, earth, sky and sea, over life and death. She was household goddess, vegetation goddess, Mother and also Maid.

There are many examples of figurines from Minoan Crete, including votive images from sanctuaries, cult idols from shrines, and statuettes which have been recovered from graves and tombs. The various attitudes assumed by these figurines, which include the 'gesture of benediction' familiar in portrayals of the mother goddess, sometimes recall the postures of a sacred dance. The sitting or squatting position of early specimens could well represent the attitude actually assumed for childbirth. Hence the differing gestures depicted by later statuettes could also have been supposed to have had a beneficial influence on childbirth and on the growth of crops.

As puppets, the images had clear associations with birth and with death, accounting for their presence in graves and tombs. As votive offerings, they represented worshippers appealing for the protection of the goddess in sickness or childbirth, an initiation, marriage or bereavement; or the statuettes could represent the goddess herself. Figurines dating from the earliest times onward have been discovered in Greece, showing that the ancestral idols of magic did not easily yield to the deities of religion as they became more established.

By Minoan times the bull, the dove and the snake had already acquired special prominence. Large numbers of votive offerings included figurines of oxen, goats, rams, swine and dogs. There is no doubt that the birds that are so often portrayed in Minoan religious contexts, perched upon double axes, columns, trees or idols represent divine manifestations. In fact, the birds of the domestic shrines are not mere votive offerings but real representations of deity; and the idea of birds as manifest forms of the

Hera, Zeus's wife, was thought of as woman deified.

Sonia Halliday

spirits of the dead was persistent in later Greek religion.

The most conspicuous Minoan domestic cult was that of the snake, especially in connection with the so-called snake goddess. Snake-worship was quite common in later Greek religion and indeed plays a part in modern Greek folklore.

All these powerful traditions seem to have played their part in the formulation of the mother goddess as an abstract and unifying principle, both one and many. It was perhaps in the Cretan palaces of the Bronze Age that the Neolithic figurine developed most rapidly into a female deity in human form, still attended by magical and totemistic symbols, in the form of trees and stones, animals, birds and flowers. The most sacred Minoan flower was the lily.

Some goddesses of the later conventional pantheon markedly perpetuate the role of the old Minoan mother goddess. Demeter was said to have reached Greece from Crete; she was regarded as divine protectress of agriculture and the fruits of the earth. The myth of Demeter and Persephone recalls the Minoan concept of the mother goddess as both Mother and Maid. The famous Eleusinian Mysteries performed at Eleusis near Athens, were held in both their honour. These mysteries may have originated in the East, but there is little doubt that they were brought to Greece from Crete at some earlier period of history.

The cult of Apollo and his mother Leto originated in Asia Minor. Their association with Crete has long been recognized, together with evidence that the cult of this goddess survived more markedly in Crete than in mainland Greece, where her cults are few and of uncertain age. Other deities and semi-divine heroes were loosely connected with the official Greek pantheon and with traditional Greek mythology. They include Eros ('Love'), Selene ('the Moon'), Hercules, and Asclepius.

The hero of physicians, elevated to divine status, Asclepius had a cult and temple at Lebena in Crete in historical times as a healing god.

The snake, his constant companion and his symbol, indicates his association with earlier phases of religion, recalling the prominence of the snake cult in Minoan belief. He did not really become a god until the end of the 6th century BC; excavations at Epidaurus, the most famous centre of his cult, revealed that the buildings dedicated to him cannot be dated earlier. But the cult, with its combination of superstition, miracle cures and genuine medical lore, enjoyed an increasing respect in the Greek world in later antiquity, which has rightly been contrasted with the growth of scepticism towards the traditional Olympian hierarchy.

By the Christian era the worship of Asclepius had spread widely and was a potent force.

Left *The supreme god of classical Greece, Zeus was descended from the great weather god of the Greek warrior chieftains but his title of 'Cretan-born' connects him with quite a different god and indicates the strong Cretan strands in Greek religion.*

The Great Gods

Aphrodite

Aphrodite was the ancient Greek goddess of love, beauty, generation and fertility. She was, naturally, a popular goddess and her cult was widespread throughout almost all of the Greek world. The Romans identified her with their goddess Venus. She had famous sanctuaries at Corinth and on the island of Cythera, at Paphos and Amathus in Cyprus, and at Eryx located in the west of Sicily.

She figures prominently in Greek mythology, beginning with the *Iliad* and *Odyssey* of Homer (8th century BC) and the poetry of Hesiod (c 700 BC).

Despite her great popularity and important place in Greek religion and culture, Aphrodite was not in origin a native Greek goddess. Her cult came to Greece from Cyprus, where she was known as Kypris (Lady of Cyprus). Aphrodite was probably a local Cypriot version of the great mother goddess, whose worship under various names was almost universal throughout the Near and Middle East in ancient times, and was of great antiquity. The many primitive idols found in Cyprus, depicting a naked female figure with the sexual attributes grossly emphasized, are probably archaic representations of this mother goddess, to whom the ancient inhabitants of Cyprus gave the name of Aphrodite.

There has been much learned but inconclusive discussion about the original meaning of the goddess's name. The Greeks, from the time of Hesiod, tried to explain it as deriving from *aphros*, 'foam', in the sense that Aphrodite was 'foamborn'.

Little, unfortunately, is known of the nature and form of the rites which were performed in the various temples of Aphrodite. At Corinth and in Cyprus she was served by sacred prostitutes; and at Abydos there was a temple of Aphrodite Porne (Aphrodite the Harlot). This connection with ritual prostitution attests Aphrodite's eastern origin; for the custom prevailed at the cult-centres of many eastern goddesses.

Aphrodite, however, was also the divine patron of marriage. At Athens, under the title of Pandemos (of all the people), her cult was dignified and unobjectionable. She had, in fact, many sides to her nature: she was a sea goddess, a goddess of animals, of gardens, and even of death – there was a small statue at Delphi called 'Aphrodite by the Tomb'. This last association is not surprising, for the great mother goddess was also a subterranean deity concerned with the dead.

In mythology Aphrodite was also associated with the three Graces or *Charites* (personifications of charm, grace and beauty) and with the Hours *(Horai)*, goddesses of the seasons. Various animals were connected with her (including doves, sparrows, swans, dolphins and mussels) and forms of vegetation (roses, myrtle, cypress and pomegranates).

Apollo

Apollo, brightest and best of the ancient Greek gods, was the god of music, archery, prophecy, healing, the care of animals and young growing creatures; and from the 5th century BC, at least, he was identified with the sun.

He was the only Greek god to have specific functions in each of the domains allotted separately to the three gods of the sky (Zeus), the sea (Poseidon), and the earth (Hades). His titles bear witness to these functions. He was, for example, Apollo Asgelatas – 'god of radiance'; Embasios – 'favouring embarkation'; and Arotrios – 'god of ploughing'. His titles, of which well over 300 have survived in ancient authors and inscriptions on stone, show that Apollo was a god much loved by people in all walks of life and therefore merited devotion for a particularly wide variety of attributes.

He was the inspiration of a great deal of ancient Greek painting, poetry and music. More than any other figure in Greek mythology or history, he embodied the spirit of Greek civilization. In art he was almost always depicted as the ideal type of young, virile beauty.

In historical times Apollo was worshipped by all the Greeks. He plays a prominent part in the Homeric epics, and in the *Iliad* is the ally of the Trojans. In Homer, he is usually called Phoebus Apollo – 'bright Apollo'. Other epithets associated with him refer to his deadly aim as an archer, or to his silver bow.

But this most typically Greek of gods, if he did not come originally from Asia Minor, certainly incorporated many of the features of a prehistoric non-Greek deity. It is possible that the name Apollo is of Greek origin, although modern scholars are divided as to whether the root-meaning of the word is 'strength', 'sheep-fold' or 'assembly of voters'. But at an early date the original Greek god seems to have been identified

with a Hittite god named Apulunas or Appaliunaas, and the Greeks themselves associated Apollo not only with a legendary northern people, the Hyperboreans, but also with Lycia, a country in what is now southwest Turkey. Apollo's mother's name, Leto, has often been connected by scholars with a Lycian word meaning 'woman'. The Greeks, however, were aware of an ambiguity in the title Lykeios (Lycian) often given to Apollo. Greek poets punned (and in ancient Greek puns had a serious, not a humorous significance) on the associations this title could have with Apollo's fame as a slayer of wolves – *lykos* being the Greek for 'wolf'.

Apollo and his twin sister Armetis were the children of Zeus, king of the gods, and Leto, the Titaness. According to one version of the birth myth, Delos was the only land which would receive Leto as she felt her time to give birth drawing near. Other places feared the power of the god she would give birth to. In historic times, Apollo's birth at Delos was celebrated by an important festival held in that tiny island each spring. According to the historian Herodotus, the Hyperboreans came every year with offerings which they brought from their northern homeland.

Above *The inspiration of ancient Greek painting, poetry and music, Apollo was depicted as the ideal type of young, virile beauty. Head of Apollo in the Rhodes Museum.* **Left** *Bronze head, 2nd century BC, of Aphrodite, goddess of love and the supreme embodiment of feminine beauty, originally a Cypriot mother goddess.*

Athene

According to mythology the goddess was born in full armour from the head of Zeus, which Hephaestus helpfully split with an axe. She thus had no real mother, though one was supplied by the story that Zeus married Metis, 'Resource', and swallowed her before she gave birth (a motif which was borrowed from Zeus's own birth). She had no husband either. Hephaestus, the other god of craftsmen, who was worshipped with her at Athens, might have been the obvious mate for her, but that would have implied divine children.

Athene's warlike qualities made it natural that she should be given a leading part in the overthrow of the Giants, the earthborn rebels who piled up mountains in their attempt to storm Olympus. But as she was responsible for warriors' successes, their disasters were attributed to her anger. Because Ajax the Locrian assaulted her priestess at Troy, she roused a tempest as the Greek fleet sailed home, and Ajax was drowned.

Holy places are very tenacious of the respect in which they are held by the people. The old palaces fell but Athene remained on the citadels where they had stood. From being the goddess of the ruler she became the goddess of the city, and was given this express title in a number of places besides Athens. She was often associated in this function with a 'Zeus of the city'. Already in Homer she is the city goddess of Troy with her temple on the acropolis. So long as her wooden image, given by Zeus to the first king, remained there, the city's safety was assured; the Greeks had to steal it before their victory.

The goddess developed some secondary characteristics in different localities; at Elis, for example, she had the title Mother, and apparently a connection with childbirth. But what appears in many places, and is therefore likely to be an ancient feature, is her association with the crafts, expressed in the title Ergane, 'craftswoman'. At Athens, where ceramics was a major industry, the potters particularly enjoyed her supervision, though she was also the goddess of the whole community. Another important item in the Athenian economy was the production and sale of olive oil, and so the olive too came under the goddess's special care.

Demeter

Demeter was the ancient Greek goddess of corn, and of agriculture and fertility. The second part of her name, *meter*, means 'mother' in Greek and De (or Da) was in ancient times thought to be a word for the earth. The Greeks in historical times had a separate goddess of the Earth (Ge) and Demeter came later in the genealogy of deities, being a grand-daughter of Ge and sister of Zeus. But in origin she is certainly an earth goddess and as such the author of all crops and vegetation, and so the sustainer of the life of animals and men. Her daughter by Zeus, Persephone, was also called simply

Kore, 'the Maiden'. She represented more directly the fruits of the field, but the two were so closely linked that they were often known as 'the Twin Goddesses', and even sometimes as 'the Demeters', a title which shows their original identity.

Because the life of plants between autumn and spring is one of hidden growth under the ground, the story was told how Persephone was carried off by Zeus's brother Hades, lord of the underworld, and compelled to spend each winter with him as his wife. In spring, when the earth was covered in flowers, she would reappear, bringing men joy and happiness. So, as Kore, she was a deity of youth and gaiety, the leader of the nymphs, with whom she was gathering flowers when she was carried off and with

whom she looked after the growth of children and young men and women. But as the wife of Hades, she was also queen of the underworld, governing men's fate after death, and in this aspect a dread goddess.

The most famous of the myths relating to Demeter is that of the Rape of Persephone. This is closely associated with the story of the origins of crops and the art of agriculture, and of the Mysteries. Many legends told how, when Demeter was searching for her daughter, after Hades had carried her off, she received information about the Rape from the local inhabitants of different parts of Greece and was offered their hospitality. In gratitude she gave them her gifts of agriculture and the Mysteries, which she revealed to the rulers of Eleusis.

Top *As goddess of the crops and fertility, Demeter was regarded as an important civilizing influence by the Greeks, drawing men towards a settled life of agriculture and domestic happiness:* **Bodrum Museum. Above** *The owl of Athene, on a 4-drachma piece, Athens, 5th century* BC. **Left** *Athene, who sprang fully armed from the head of Zeus, was the protectress of cities. Detail from a 6th-century* BC *vase, at the Roman Civic Museum, Brescia.*

Hephaestus

The uncouth god of smiths, who was himself a smith, Hephaestus (or Vulcan as he was known to the Romans) was originally a god of fire, in the aspect of flaming gas rising from the earth in certain places. It was only later that he came to be associated with volcanoes in Sicily and Italy. His name was used poetically as a synonym for fire from Homer down to poets who were familiar with Nature-philosophy. He was not in origin a Greek god, his name having no etymology in Greek, but his cult spread from Lycia in southwestern Anatolia to various parts of Greece; there are frequent references to him in Greek literature.

In the *Iliad* he is the son of Hera, who threw him into the sea in shame at having borne such a weakly infant. He was rescued by the nymphs Thetis and Eurynome and remained with them in secret for nine years, making jewels and ornaments, until his talents were discovered by the gods and he was given a smithy on Olympus. Reconciled with his mother, he once tried to protect her from the anger of Zeus, but for this interference Zeus seized him by the foot and hurled him out of heaven. He fell for a whole day before finally striking the island of Lemnos, crushing his legs in the fall: this is only one explanation for his lameness. Hephaestus built the palaces on Olympus and Zeus's golden throne, but is particularly famous as a maker of armour: of Diomedes' breastplate, of the sceptre and also the aegis, or shield held by Zeus, which when shaken produced storms and thunder, and of the arms made for Achilles to replace the armour lost with the slaying of Patroclus. Among his other wonders are mechanical handmaidens of gold, possessed of thought and speech, who support him as he moves, and who assist him at his work. Sometimes he acts as cup-bearer at the feasts of the gods, who laugh at him as he bustles round clumsily on his lame legs. In his elemental character he is called by Hera to drive back the river Xanthus because the river god is furious at his stream being blocked with corpses slain by Achilles, and threatens to overwhelm him. Hephaestus spreads fire everywhere, burning the corpses and the vegetation by the river, and then begins to dry up the river until Xanthus begs Hera to stop him.

In the *Odyssey* Hephaestus, with Athene, is called 'skilled in making gold flow round silver'. He is the maker of a silver mixing bowl with gold edges given by Phaedimus of Sidon to Menelaus; also of the gold and silver hounds that guard the palace of Alcinous, immortal and ageless animals.

Hesiod in the *Theogony* states clearly that Hera bore Hephaestus without any union with Zeus because she had a bitter quarrel with him at the time.

Dionysus

The mythological stories told of Dionysus's birth and his adventurous progresses through the lands of men will of themselves lead us on to the nature of his cult and the historical background of its introduction and acceptance in classical Greece. In origin, Dionysus is no Greek. He plays, for instance, no partisan role in Homer's account of the Trojan War – not even on the side of the Asiatic Trojans. He figures only occasionally, in passing. Homer had heard of his wild rites but clearly knew little about him. Dionysus hails, in fact, from Phrygia and later moves to Thrace, the wild tracts on either side of the Hellespont. His mother, Semele, is associated with the Phrygian earth goddess Zemelo. The Greek mythologists, however, make Semele a mortal, the daughter of Cadmus, King of Thebes – that doom-laden site of so many products of Greek imagination. Semele, needless to say, was beautiful and attracted the attention of the ever-amorous Zeus, the father of the gods. Hera's jealousy, ever fertile of new ways to thwart Zeus, caused her to visit Semele in the guise of an old woman and suggest to the naïve girl that she ask her divine lover to appear to her in his full immortal splendour – not least to impress her sisters Agave, Ino and Antonoe. Zeus, who had promised Semele any favour she might ask, reluctantly consented – whereupon Semele was annihilated by his lightning and thunderbolts. Her unborn son was rescued by Zeus and shut away by him in his own thigh, whence in due time he was born.

But Hera was not to be deceived and on her orders Dionysus was seized by the Titans, who tore him limb from limb and began to cook him up for a meal. Having been restored to life by Rhea (his earth goddess grandmother), he was finally hidden, disguised as a girl, in the household of Athamas, King of Orchomenus in Greece. But Hera made the king demented and he killed his son Learchus, thinking he was hunting a stag. Dionysus was next fostered by nymphs on Mt Nysa where, some say, he invented wine. Grown to manhood, he was himself driven mad by Hera and went wandering about the world, accompanied by Silenus, his tutor, and a rout of satyrs and wild women – the maenads or bacchantes – his former nymph nurses and others. Strange tales are told of these followers and of their extraordinary powers. They caused fountains of milk and wine to spring from the ground; fire could do them no harm – they often carried it in their hands or on their heads; weapons left them unscathed; they had the strength to tear apart live bulls and other fierce beasts, the women no less than the men – yet the women showed great tenderness to young animals and suckled them at their own breasts. Armed with the *thyrsos*, an ivy-twined staff tipped with a pine cone, brandishing swords and enwreathed with serpents, they followed the god as far as India and then eventually retraced their steps to Greece.

Hera

There are definite mythological grounds for the view, maintained by Sir James Frazer and A. B. Cook, that, at Cnossus in Crete there had once existed a ritual marriage of sun god and moon goddess in bovine form. In later cult the ritual became a sacred marriage of Zeus and Hera, which reputedly occurred near the river Theren, where a sanctuary was built and yearly sacrifices were offered with traditional wedding rites. Similarly, at Gortyna, also in Crete, the goddess Europa, possessed by Zeus in the form of a bull, became totally identified with Hera.

Here mention should be made of the view that Hera, described by Homer on many occasions with the traditional epithet *boopis* ('cow-eyed', 'cow-faced') was originally a cow goddess. Her priestess at Argos was Io, who was ravished by Zeus when she had been transformed by him into a cow. The myth of Io also reflects a sacred marriage, the bride being the priestess of Hera, the bridegroom the priest of Zeus disguised as a bull. The ox-herd Argos who watched over Io was *Panoptes* ('all-seeing') – an epithet of Zeus and the sun; and Argos wore a bull's hide.

According to the famous myth, Pasiphae ('She who shines on all', that is, the moon), wife of King Minos, conceived a passion for a bull, sent in answer to the prayers of Minos. Instead of sacrificing this bull, as he had promised, Minos sent it away among his herds and sacrificed another one. His punishment for this piece of deception was the unnatural passion of his wife. Daedalus made for Pasiphae a hollow wooden cow on wheels, sewed it up in the hide of a cow which he had skinned, and put it in the meadow where the bull subsequently went and grazed.

Inside this image he put Pasiphae, and the bull coupled with it. In due course Pasiphae gave birth to Asterios ('Starry One'), who was called the Minotaur ('Minos bull'). The Minotaur had the head of a bull, but the rest of him was human. In obedience to certain oracles, Minos then shut him up under guard in the labyrinth, which had also been made by Daedalus. The labyrinth, in the Greek tradition, was a building whose intricate windings led astray those who sought to escape from it.

The cow and bull became such integral factors in the life of the communities that they figure in mythology as guides in the founding of cities of those who followed the advice of the sun god. The story of Cadmus, who, in obedience to the Delphic oracle, followed a cow until it lay down on the site of Thebes, is familiar. Since the sun was conceived as a bull, it seems likely that the labyrinth at Cnossus was an actual arena of solar pattern designed for the performance of a mimetic dance, in which a dancer may have masqueraded as a bull and represented the movement of the sun. The labyrinth supposedly built by Daedalus was recognized in antiquity as an imitation of the Egyptian labyrinth, which, in turn, was generally believed to be sacred to the sun.

The goddess Hera was possibly an ancient Minoan mother goddess who, with the increasing supremacy of the Greek Zeus, was linked with him in sacred marriage; they were honoured as patrons of lawful marriage despite their own marital irregularities: section from the Parthenon, from the British Museum.

Hermes

In many ways Hermes is the most sympathetic, the most baffling, the most confusing, the most complex and therefore the most Greek of all the Olympian gods. Like the Olympian goddesses, he had a prehistory; he is a very uneasy kind of Olympian, with deep popular roots.

There seems to be little doubt that Hermes signifies 'the god of the stone heap', the spirit immanent in stones set up as cairns or pillars to serve as boundaries, or as landmarks for the wayfarer. Truly a god of the countryside, he was associated with the Minoan pillar cult and there is evidence that the cult of Hermes existed in Crete in historical times.

The *herma* consisted of an upright monumental stone with a heap of smaller stones around its base. Gradually the god, and the pillar which represented him, became more and more human in conception. He was given a phallus to promote fertility, and finally emerged as a fully human figure. Yet the multiplicity of his titles and functions must not be allowed to disguise the fact that he is one of the earliest and most primitive of all the gods of Greece. In the prologue to the *Ion* of Euripides Hermes introduces himself in this way:

> Atlas, who wears on back of bronze the ancient
> Abode of gods in heaven, had a daughter
> Whose name was Maia, born of a goddess:
> She lay with Zeus and bore me, Hermes,
> Servant of the immortals.

This introduction modestly stresses his prehistoric origin and his subordinate status in the Olympian hierarchy. Further insight into the varied functions of this truly popular god is given in the *Plutus* of Aristophanes, and in the Homeric Hymn to Hermes, familiar to English readers in Shelley's translation, and one of the longest and most charming of all the Homeric Hymns. It tells the tale of the infant god's adventures following his birth in a cave on Mt Cyllene in Arcadia, the ancient seat of his worship. From there it was carried to other parts of Greece.

Hermes escaped from his cradle, went to Pieria and carried off some of Apollo's oxen, which he drove to Pylos, in the neighbourhood of Olympia. Returning to Cyllene, he found a tortoise at the entrance to his cave, placed strings across its shell and so invented the lyre on which he promptly played. Apollo discovered the theft, went to Cyllene and charged Hermes with the crime. Hermes's mother Maia showed the god the child in his cradle but Apollo took him to Zeus, who obliged him to restore the oxen. By giving him the lyre Hermes won the friendship of Apollo and also various prerogatives, including a share in divination, lordship over herds and animals, and the office of messenger from the gods to Hades.

As herald of the gods, Hermes was god of eloquence. Prudent and cunning, he was master of fraud, perjury and theft. He was also credited with a variety of inventions apart from the lyre. God of roads, he cared for travellers; and as inventor of sacrifices, he protected sacrificial animals, and was worshipped by shepherds. He was god of commercial transactions and good luck, and patron of gymnastics. The famous sculpture of Hermes by Praxiteles is one of numerous representations of this most versatile of all the Greek gods.

Poseidon

Poseidon starts as the second greatest of the Greek gods. No other male deity ranks as the brother of Zeus, except for Hades, the ruler of the dead: the other important ones are sons of Zeus, and so more certainly subordinated to him. In the *Iliad*, Poseidon is the god whom Zeus has the greatest difficulty in bending to his will. Threatened with physical violence, he protests that his status is equivalent to Zeus'; the universe has been shared out equally among the three sons of Cronus, and Poseidon has the sea, Hades the underworld, and Zeus the sky, the earth being common property.

For Homer, then, Poseidon is the god of the sea. He has a golden palace in the depths of the waters, the sea creatures dance at his passing by, and when he leads the Greeks to battle the waves surge up to their encampment. He causes storms at sea and sailors pray to him for a safe voyage. But he is also the god of the earthquake, and this appears to have been his primary role at the time when the formulaic epic language was taking shape, for his standard epithets all refer to it. Homer never calls him 'marine'.

In Homer his only peer is Zeus, who certainly came with the Hellenes, and afterwards we see Zeus steadily growing in power and universality while Poseidon declines. Perhaps Poseidon had once been the greatest god in Greece.

It is certainly worth considering which of his aspects can be related to his management of earthquakes, and which are extraneous functions such as a supreme god might acquire. It is natural enough that the god who makes the earth heave and toss should be identified as the one who makes the sea heave and toss. It is also possible that the belief that the earth rested on the sea – the starting point of scientific speculation in the 6th century BC – goes back to much earlier times: the god of the sea might then indeed be the 'earth-carrier'. We can understand too why Poseidon should be a builder of walls. (He helped Apollo build the walls of Troy, and he made a prison for the Titans in Tartarus.) The mason would pray to him to uphold his wall; and a god prayed to by masons must soon become a master mason. It is no less natural that he should sometimes be associated with springs and rivers, which are frequently seen to change their courses in earthquakes. On the other hand, the simplest explanation of his special connection with horses is that he was the chief god of a people who depended on horses. And when he appears in genealogies as the first ancestor of a royal line, or in cult as 'Father', 'God of the clan' and so on, he is clearly exceeding the prerogatives of a seismic force.

God of the sky and of storms, Zeus is traditionally depicted carrying a thunderbolt, which was itself regarded as a means of bringing death so that immortality might be conferred: **Right** *Bronze statue of Zeus, c 5th century* BC. **Far right** *Bronze cast for a statue of Jupiter, the Roman god who was identified with the Greek Zeus, 2nd century* AD.

Zeus

Zeus, the god ancestor of Idomeneus, the one member of the Olympian pantheon with an Indo-European name, rose to his eminence with the growing power of the Achaeans. The result was that, in Crete, the name of their sky god was attached to a Minoan deity whose original ritual and character can be discerned from the evidence of later times. It was not until after the Minoan period that this originally secondary deity, this youthful god, pushed his way to the forefront in a variety of forms and under a variety of names. The myth of the Minotaur implies that he was identified with the bull; and the story of the love of Queen Pasiphae for the Minotaur may derive from a form of the sacred marriage, the male partner in the ritual being played by the king masked in the head of a bull. The sacred marriage was closely involved with the fertility of the crops. This association is clearly to be observed – as is also the association with central Crete – in the famous legend of Zeus and Europa, in which Zeus became enamoured of Europa, turned himself into a snow-white bull, then carried her off into the sea.

An archaic kind of Europa, riding on a bull, features in the earliest (5th century BC) coins of the city of Gortyna and also of Phaistus. The type persists on the coins of Gortyna throughout the 5th century. Their pictorial character has plausibly suggested a derivation from local frescoes. This relation is even more conspicuous in the 4th century coins both of Gortyna and of Phaistus. On one type of coin from Phaistus Europa is sitting on a rock and is welcoming with her raised hand the bull who is approaching her. A coin series from contemporary Gortyna tells vividly the story of the marriage of Zeus and Europa, with Zeus changing from a bull into an eagle. Coins of Cnossus, probably struck in 220 BC, when that city was closely allied with Gortyna, are similar to the Gortynian type which features Europa; and Europa on the bull remained as one of the chief coin types of the Roman province of Crete – probably struck at Gortyna between 66 and 31 BC.

It appears to be likely that the final evolution of the male deity from a bull into an anthropomorphic Zeus, the Zeus who later became involved with Europa, must have occured in the Mycenean period. Zeus is featured as the partner of Europa not only in Hesiod, but already in the *Iliad*. Animal sacrifices continued to be conspicuous in the rituals of Zeus, the victims normally being either rams or, as was most frequently the case, oxen. Both of these animals are associated with sky gods in general and with Zeus in particular. They were the most precious victims that pastoral peoples could offer, considered to be most possessed of fertilizing power and most essential to their economic survival. Various traditions combine to associate mainland settlers at Gortyna, or its neighbourhood, with the Arcadian area where the Achaean dialect survived. It is therefore perhaps significant that Gortynian Zeus shared the title of *Hekatombaios* ('to whom hecatombs are offered') with the Arcadian Zeus.

C. M. Dixon

Lesser Gods, Goddesses and Heroes

Achilles

The story of the *Iliad* begins, in the tenth year of the siege of Troy, when the Greek supreme commander, Agamemnon, seized a beautiful slave-girl who had been allotted to Achilles as a prize of battle. Insulted, Achilles refused to fight any more and his absence gravely weakened the Greek resistance to fierce Trojan attacks. Agamemnon tried to make the quarrel up, offering to return the girl to Achilles with many splendid gifts. But Achilles was still nursing his fury and refused to be reconciled.

Lacking Achilles, the situation of the Greeks now became so dangerous that Patroclus, the dearly loved friend of Achilles, went out to fight the Trojans. Patroclus was killed by the best of the Trojan warriors, Hector. When this news was brought to him, Achilles gave a loud and dreadful cry, and his mother, the sea-nymph Thetis, hurried to him from the depths of the ocean. He told her that he was determined to take his revenge by joining the battle and killing Hector. Weeping, Thetis told him that he would seal his own fate.

Berserk with grief and rage, Achilles sounded his terrible warcry. 'The Trojans were utterly confounded. Achilles' cry was as piercing as the trumpet call that rings out when a city is beset by murderous enemies; and their hearts all turned to water when they heard that brazen voice. Even the long-maned horses felt something evil in the wind...'

Next day, Achilles fought in fury, 'like a driving wind that whirls the flames this way and that, when a conflagration rages in the gullies on a sun-baked mountain-side, and the high forest is consumed. He chased his victims with the fury of a fiend, and the earth was dark with blood'. His horses trampled over dead men and fallen shields as he raged on in search of glory, until he found Hector and killed him in single combat, gloating over the Trojan's death agony.

Achilles maltreated Hector's corpse, dragging it in the dust behind his chariot, and he intended to throw it to the dogs to gnaw. But Hector's father persuaded him to return the body to the Trojans so that it could be decently buried.

The *Iliad* ends with the funeral rites for Hector but it is clear that Achilles has not long to live and that he will be killed by Hector's brother Paris and the archer-god Apollo. The *Odyssey* describes his death in battle, with the flower of the Greek and Trojan warriors falling round him in the struggle over his corpse. The sea-nymphs came from the ocean to weep salt tears for him and the nine Muses sang his dirge.

The greatest of the Homeric heroes and the central character of the *Iliad*, Achilles is shown slaying Penthesilea, the queen of the Amazons. From an Attic amphora. He was famed for his savagery in battle.

Charon

This aged and irascible boatman was believed by the Greeks to ferry the souls of the dead across the infernal river (the Acheron or Styx) which separated the land of the living from that of the dead. Charon is thus associated with Hermes Psychopompos, who summoned those appointed to die and led them to Hades. It has been thought that he was originally a death god, as was his Etruscan counterpart Charun. He is mentioned in Greek literature as early as the 5th century BC and is frequently depicted in art, particularly on the white-ground vases called *lecythi*.

Charon had to be paid for performing his sombre office of ferryman of the dead. It was customary to place an obolus, a silver coin, under the tongue or between the teeth of the corpse, to pay the fare. The shades of the dead who had not been properly buried, and thus equipped to cross into Hades, were refused passage by Charon and so left to haunt the living, seeking their release. The Roman poet Virgil draws a grim picture of the grisly ferryman in his *Aeneid* (book 6). 'Charon, on whose chin lies a mass of unkempt, hoary hair; his eyes are staring orbs of flame; his squalid garb hangs by a knot from his shoulders. Unaided, he poles the boat, tends the sails, and in his murky craft convoys the dead.'

Though a pagan concept, the image of the grim boatman and his load of souls deeply affected the minds of many medieval and Renaissance Christians. Dante tells, in his *Divine Comedy*, of his encounter with Charon when he descends, with Virgil as his guide, into the Inferno. 'Charon, demonic form, with eyes of burning coal, collects them all, beckoning, and each that lingers, with his oar strikes.' And Michelangelo, in the stupendous vision of the *Last Judgement* which he painted above the altar of the Sistine Chapel, depicts Charon and his fatal boat with a realism both terrifying and unforgettable. The memory of Charon passed into modern Greek folklore where, under the name of Charos, he carries off the young and old.

The idea that the newly dead have to cross a river to reach the land of the dead is very ancient. It occurs in the Egyptian Pyramid Texts (c 2400 BC) and many means of transport are devised. In the ancient Mesopotamian Epic of Gilgamesh a similar idea occurs.

Circe

The fair-haired sorceress Circe is described in the *Odyssey* as a goddess, although her reputation throughout mythology is rather that of a witch. She was the daughter of Helios, the sun god, and sister of Aeetes, the divine wizard and King of Colchis. Another celebrated witch, Medea, was her niece.

Circe was banished to the isle of Aeaea, after she had poisoned her husband, the King of the Sarmatians, a nomadic people of Persia. Circe's island has been sited as lying at the head of the Adriatic, not far from the mouth of the river Po; according to Hesiod, however, Aeaea lay off the coast of Latium, now a part of Italy, in the promontory called Circaeum, which was once an island.

Circe lived in a marble palace surrounded by woods, practising her magic arts and singing as she sat by her loom. She was attended by nymphs and a troop of wild beasts, whom she had transformed from men she had ensnared. When Odysseus's men landed on her island, they cast lots to decide who should stay to guard the ship and who should go to reconnoitre the land. Odysseus's friend Eurylochus set out with a band of men and, attracted by Circe's singing, they were drawn to the palace. Wild beasts came out to meet them, but instead of attacking the men, they fawned on them and made them welcome. Circe invited them to dine at her table and all entered unsuspecting, except Eurylochus who stayed behind, fearing a trap.

As soon as the sailors had drunk the goddess's drugged wine, she struck them with her wand and turned them into hogs. Eurylochus escaped and told Odysseus what had happened. He set off to rescue his friends and on the way he met the god Hermes who gave him a magic herb named moly, to protect him against Circe's magic. When

Circe attempted to transform Odysseus, she found that her magic was useless. Odysseus forced her to restore his men to human shape.

Circe, who had become enamoured of Odysseus, by her wiles persuaded him to remain for a year on her island. At length Odysseus became restive and was determined to be on his way again. Circe advised him how to navigate the River of Ocean and descend into Hades, and how to deal with the ghosts. When Odysseus returned to Aeaea, having been advised about his own future by the ghost of Tiresias, Circe sent him off on his homeward voyage to Ithaca. She warned him against the Sirens and against Scylla and Charybdis; also of the fatal consequences that would follow if any of his men were to kill and eat the cattle of the Sun on the island of Thrinacia. Circe is an important figure in the *Odyssey* and it is due to her warnings and advice that Odysseus finally reaches home.

Eros

The chubby cherub with his bow and quiver, favourite device of Victorian valentines and rococo art, bears little resemblance to the earliest conceptions of Eros, the Greek god of love. His origins are obscure; some say that he was hatched from a silver egg laid in the womb of darkness, emerging as a monstrous being, four-headed, golden-winged and uttering animal cries. Others hold that he was the son of Iris or of Ilithyia, the goddess of childbirth; while later mythology makes him the son of Aphrodite by Zeus, her father, or by Ares, the god of war, or by Hermes. The Greek writer Hesiod (8th century BC) makes Eros, together with Earth and Tartarus, the oldest of the gods. He represents him as the powerful creative force that attracts together and unites the cosmic couples who created the universe, 'bringing harmony to chaos' and making it possible for life to develop.

Long before Aphrodite appeared among the gods, the ancient Greeks worshipped a god of sexual potency named Eros. That Eros was not only a creative agent but also on occasions a destructive one was already understood: an implicit acceptance of the power of passion to wreck society and threaten law and order. The Latin writer Apuleius (2nd century AD) in later times makes the same point when he speaks of the god 'running from building to building all night long with his torch and his arrows, breaking up respectable homes'. But it is as a cosmic principle that Eros first makes his appearance in Greek myth, a far cry from the petulant boy archer of later tradition.

Although there is no mention of the god in Homer, the passages in which the word *eros* occur illustrate clearly its early meaning. In the *Iliad* and the *Odyssey* eros stands for irresistible physical desire; it is the force which attracts Zeus to Hera, Paris to

Eros presides over a tender scene in which Thetis is reunited with her husband Peleus: detail from the Portland Vase, now in the British Museum.

Helen, an affliction which causes the limbs of Penelope's suitors to tremble uncontrollably. In the later lyric poets of the 6th and 7th centuries BC the conception of this force is broadened to include mind as well as body.

From his birth, Eros's variously imputed parentage signifies several different aspects of his role as the god of passionate love. As the son of Hermes, god of fertility, who was worshipped with phallic images, Eros represents sexual potency and is himself a god of fertility: at his cult centre at Thespiae in Boeotia he was represented by a simple phallic figure. From the devious god Hermes, too, he draws his cunning and his penchant for trickery. With Ares the warrior for his father, Eros reminds us of the fighting man's immemorial attraction for women and the often ambivalent – or, as we would say, 'love-hate' – nature of sexual relationships. As the son of Aphrodite by Zeus, according to Hesiod and the most widely held view, the contrary and perverse element of Eros is symbolized; his parents' union is an incestuous one, signifying that erotic love knows no boundaries and trespasses on forbidden relationships.

Indulged by Aphrodite, he is half god, half spoilt, undisciplined boy. His bow and arrows, first mentioned by Euripides (484–407 BC), are his favourite playthings; the sharp arrows from his quiver producing sometimes love and sometimes disdain in their victims. He takes a malicious pleasure in choosing unlikely targets and delights in the misery he causes. Sometimes Aphrodite, who herself suffers from his archery and is led into all sorts of undignified liaisons in consequence, loses patience with him and confiscates his weapons. The poet Anacreon (6th century BC), while dwelling on Eros's playful side refers also to his cruelty. The god is shown (as also on vase paintings) striking the lovelorn with an axe or wielding a whip. At the same time Eros is the embodiment of the sweetness of youth. He is associated with all beautiful things, he walks on a carpet of flowers and wears a crown of roses. Yet it is not for nothing that the rose is his special emblem, for the rose, though sweetly perfumed, has a sharp thorn. The poet Sappho describes his contradictory qualities as 'bitter sweet'.

The playmates of the god in Aphrodite's train are Pothos and Himeros, representing longing and desire. Eros has a brother, the son of Ares and Aphrodite, named Anteros. Earlier writers show Anteros in opposition to Eros, as the god who avenges slighted love; it is only later that he becomes the brother of Eros, standing for mutual affection and tenderness, yet still constantly at odds with the selfish god of love. Anteros was the younger brother and was conceived on the advice of Themis, Zeus's first wife, when Aphrodite complained to her that Eros remained perpetually a child and never seemed to grow any older. Themis suggested that the remedy was for Eros to have a brother, who would spur him on to outstrip him. As soon as Anteros was born Eros grew stronger and the span of his wings increased. If ever he was separated from Anteros, however, he found himself reduced to his former size.

Hecate

A minor goddess of the Greek pantheon, Hecate was not a true Olympian. But she was the most important representative of the uncanny, a powerful figure in the kind of popular and private belief that is ignored in Homer. Indeed she is not mentioned in the *Iliad* or in the *Odyssey* or in fragments of heroic epic. If her name is Greek, it is the feminine form of the epithet *hekatos*, which as applied to Apollo means 'far shooting' but might in her case mean merely 'distant' or 'remote'. She has connections with Apollo's sister Artemis, also an archer, and she may share with Artemis a common origin in Asia Minor.

Orpheus

Orpheus, like several other legendary singers was held to come from Thrace, the semi-barbarous, semi-mythical country to the north of Greece; or from Mount Olympus, where the Muses themselves were born. And according to an alternative account of his parentage, Orpheus was born from the Muse Calliope and the most musical of gods, Apollo. But he was a mortal, with mortal descendants. Genealogies were constructed which made him the ancestor of other famous minstrels, including Homer. The number of generations inserted in these genealogies implies a belief that Orpheus belonged to a period well before the Trojan War (13th century BC, on our reckoning).

Probably the best known of the stories about him is that he sang so beautifully with his lyre that not only the creatures of the wild came and stood entranced around him, but even the rivers stayed in their courses, and the rocks and trees came sidling down from the mountain.

His other famous exploit was his descent to Hades to recover his wife – usually called Eurydice – after she had been fatally bitten by a snake.

Facing page *Roman relief showing the return of Dionysus from the East; Pan is near the centre: Pashley sarcophagus, 2nd century AD.* **Below** *Animals entranced by Orpheus: mosaic from a villa at Tarsus.*

Sonia Halliday

Fitzwilliam Museum, Cambridge

Pan

Perhaps the most appealing introduction to the worship of Pan, the strange deity of the Greek countryside, is the Homeric Hymn to the god. It is imbued with an idyllic charm, a joyful salute to the folklore god of flocks and herds, whose old home was in remote Peloponnesian Arcadia, surrounded by mountains.

The poet begins by appealing to the Muse to tell him about Pan, son of Hermes, with his goat's feet and his two horns, who is known to be a lover of noise.

This strikes a traditional note at once for, although genealogies vary, Hermes and Pan were both shepherd gods of Arcadia. The god, continues the poem, wanders through the woodland glades with dancing nymphs who tread the sheer hill crests, invoking Pan, the long-haired and shaggy deity whose haunts are the snowy ridges, mountain peaks and rocky ways. He goes through dense thickets, now drawn to gentle streams, now climbing up to the top-most peak from which the flocks can be watched. Often too he darts across the mountain slopes as a keen-eyed hunter.

The next part of the Homeric Hymn goes on to describe how the nymphs sing of the birth of Pan, of how Hermes, the swift messenger of all the gods, came to Arcadia, land of many springs and mother of flocks, to the land where his sacred place is as god of Cyllene. There he fell in love with Dryope, the daughter of Dryops, son of Arcas. Dryope bore him a son, a son who was a marvel to look upon from the time of his birth, with his goat's feet and his two horns and his noisy, merry laughter. But when the nursing mother looked upon his uncouth, bearded face she sprang up and fled in fear, abandoning her child.

Then Hermes took his son in his arms and there was boundless joy in his heart. Carrying him closely wrapped up in the skins of mountain hares, he went swiftly to the abodes of the immortal gods. (The hare, by the way, is a symbol of Pan on some ancient coins.) He set the child down beside Zeus and showed him to the other gods. They were delighted, Dionysus especially; and because the child gave them all such pleasure, they called him Pan which, according to the Homeric Hymn, is derived from the Greek word for 'all', *pas*.

Prometheus

The oldest and fullest account of Prometheus comes from the poems of Hesiod (700 BC). Prometheus was a son of the Titan Iapetus. His brothers Atlas and Menoetius were both punished by Zeus for unruliness, and he too crossed the tyrannical ruler of heaven through his misbehaviour.

Gods and men were settling their affairs at Sicyon (not far from Corinth) prior to living apart. A bull was sacrificed, and Prometheus carved it up for eating. He served Zeus with a good meaty portion, but covered it in skin and paunch to make it look unattractive; while for mankind he set bones dressed up in juicy fat. Zeus complained at the unfair division, whereupon Prometheus, with a cunning smile, invited him to choose his own portion. Zeus promptly seized the better-looking one (the pious poet assures us that he was not really taken in), and ever since then men sacrificing animals have given the bones and other inedible parts to the gods, and divided the meat among themselves.

Angered at the deception, Hesiod continues, Zeus withheld fire from men (perhaps with the idea of preventing them from cooking their meat); he 'would not give it to the ash-trees', the source from which men derive it. But Prometheus stole it in a fennel-stalk and delivered it to us.

Zeus's next move was to send mankind a pernicious commodity to counterbalance the desirable one that they had got. On his instructions the divine craftsman Hephaestus made a beautiful girl, various goddesses adorned her, and Hermes gave her a deceitful disposition. She was named Pandora, and sent to Prometheus's foolish brother Epimetheus. Although Prometheus had warned him not to accept a present from Zeus, he married her, and all mortal women are her descendants. It was she who took the lid off the great jar in which all evils had been confined, letting them loose among us.

To prevent any further roguery, Zeus bound Prometheus in invincible bonds, and secured them by driving them through the thickness of a column. He then sent an eagle to feast on Prometheus's liver. Each night it grew again, and each day the eagle returned to its work, for constant repetition is proper to the torments of sinners. Later, however,

Zeus's wrath abated, and he allowed his son Hercules to win glory by shooting the dutiful bird; yet Prometheus remains in bondage, for there is no forgiveness for thwarting the will of Zeus.

Hesiod probably thought of Prometheus as being bound somewhere at the world's end, where his brother Atlas stands supporting the sky's weight. The column to which he is fastened may have a connection with the idea of pillars of heaven. This conception alternates in Eurasian folklore with that of a world tree or a world mountain which reaches up to the sky. In later versions of the Prometheus myth, the miscreant is shackled to a mountain – Caucasus, from the Greek viewpoint a remote eastern outpost of the earth. The story that the Argonauts saw Prometheus on their legendary Black Sea voyage might go back to a source of Hesiod's time.

There is some evidence that the Caucasus is in fact the original home of the myth. Throughout that region it is related that earthquakes are caused by the struggles of a fierce giant who tried to steal the water of life from the mountain heights, or was otherwise impious, and as a punishment was bound by God to a pillar or in a cavern in the mountain. In many versions a vulture pecks at his heart. He will have to stay there till the end of the world, but when he does break free of his bonds his rage will destroy everything.

Some accounts add that he once found a helper who nearly freed him; we think of Hercules.

Local variants are more reminiscent of the punishments of other Greek sinners. The water of life flows just out of the prisoner's reach: in the same way Tantalus was tormented ('tantalized', as we still say) by food and drink that kept eluding his grasp. Or beside the giant a great wheel turns, day and night; he never takes his eyes off it, for when it stops, he will become free. Ixion was bound on a revolving wheel. Tityus, like Prometheus, was fed on by birds of prey – two vultures.

In the Caucasus, then, we have a straight Nature myth with logical connections (the pecking bird accounts for the prisoner's intermittent wrath); in Greece, a loose group of curious stories. The myth can be traced back to about 400 AD in the Caucasus, and may be much older.

Theseus

Theseus was born in Troezen to Aethra, daughter of King Pittheus. In Athenian legend his father was King Aegeus of Athens, who returned to Athens before he was born, leaving under a hollow rock a sword and a pair of sandals, to be claimed by his son when he was big enough to raise the rock. In the Troezenian legend his father was the god Poseidon, who has an important part even in the Athenian legend. Having lifted the rock, Theseus then made his way to Athens.

However, he did not take the easy way by sea. He went by land, overcoming and killing dangerous robbers. Such were Periphetes, who attacked travellers with his club; Sinis who bent down pine trees, tied his victims to the tops and then let the trees spring up and apart to tear them limb from limb; Cercyon who forced men to wrestle with him until he killed them; Sciron who made travellers wash his feet on the top of a precipice so that he could kick them over; and Procrustes who forced them to fit one of his two beds, stretching out the shorter travellers to fit the longer bed and lopping the taller to fit the shorter. He also killed the ravaging sow of Crommyon. On being welcomed by Aegeus at Athens, he was very nearly poisoned by a drink offered by the witch Medea, then married to Aegeus; but Aegeus recognized him and cried out in time.

Aegeus then told Theseus of the affliction that the Athenians suffered at the hands of Minos of Crete. In vengeance for the killing of his son Androgeus in Attica, Minos every year carried off a band of Athenian youths and maidens to be given as victims to the Minotaur. This was a monster with a human body and a bull's head, usually said to have been kept in the labyrinth of Cnossus, a building designed in the form of an intricate maze, from which no one who entered could find his way out.

Theseus went voluntarily as one of the victims. When he arrived on Crete, he won the help of Ariadne, daughter of Minos. She gave him a ball of thread to unwind as he made his way into the labyrinth and follow so that he could find his way out again. He killed the Minotaur with his sword and then set off homeward in triumph with the captives, who were no longer needed as food for the Minotaur. He took Ariadne with him, but left her behind on the island of Dia off the coast near Cnossus or, as was more commonly said, on the island of Naxos, where the god Dionysus found her and took her as his wife.

As Theseus approached Athens, he forgot to change the black sail of the ship, a sign of mourning for the young Athenians, for a white one which would be a sign of deliverance. This he had promised to do if he came home safe. Aegeus, who was looking out for him, concluded that he had perished and hurled himself from a cliff.

Theseus thus became king of Athens. He had to fight rivals, the sons of Pallas, brother of Aegeus, but prevailed over them. He subdued the wild bull of Marathon, being sheltered on his way by an old peasant woman, Hecale. On an expedition with Hercules and others to Themiscyra, where the Amazons lived on the south coast of the Black Sea he carried off an Amazon, Antiope or, according to others, Hippolyta, and made her his wife; he later repudiated her and married Phaedra, daughter of Minos. The Amazons made war on him, invaded Attica and were with a great effort defeated. By his Amazon wife he had a son, Hippolytus.

Theseus was in Hades at the time with his friend Pirithous the Lapith, who was attempting to carry off Persephone, queen of the underworld. Pluto, however, cunningly persuaded Theseus and Pirithous to sit on seats, to which their flesh grew. Theseus was rescued by Hercules, who could not free Pirithous.

When Theseus eventually returned to Athens he found that the people were disaffected. He left for the island of Scyros, where the king Lycomedes, fearing that he meant to annex the island, treacherously thrust him over a cliff. A skeleton of great size, said to be his, was found on Scyros centuries later and carried to Athens.

Bulls occur frequently in the history of Theseus, adventurer, ravisher of women and subduer of robbers and monsters: he slew the bull-headed Minotaur and subdued the wild bull of Marathon, and his son Hippolytus was killed by a bull from the sea: black-figured Greek vase of the 6th century BC, showing Theseus killing the Minotaur.

Michael Holford/British Museum

Mythical Beings

The Amazons

The Amazons were a mythical race of warrior women, whose battles with a number of Greek heroes were recorded in various local legends. Their original home was in the gorges and forests of the Thermodon valley in Pontus in Asia Minor, and their capital city was Themiscyra on the coast of the Euxine (modern Terme, on the Black Sea coast of Turkey). According to one tradition, men were excluded altogether from their country, but for purposes of propagating the race the Amazons made an annual visit to the Gargareans in the Caucasus. Girls born of these unions were then brought up by the Amazons, each one having her right breast either burnt or cut off to make it easier to hurl a javelin or stretch a bow. Boys were either put to death or sent back to their fathers. Another version has it that a number of men were kept for mating purposes, but had the status of slaves, and were allowed to perform only those tasks executed in other countries by women.

Legend also has it that the legs and arms of these men were mutilated to prevent their challenging the Amazons' power.

Whether men were or were not included in the Amazon state, only women bore arms, not only defending their own country, but making expeditions of conquest into neighbouring territories. They fought both on foot and on horseback, carrying crescent shields and wielding spears, bows and battle-axes. Their life consisted mainly in hunting and war-like exercises and the training of the girl Amazons. They were ruled by a queen, and they worshipped Ares, the god of war, from whom they were believed to be descended, and Artemis, goddess of the hunt.

Two of their queens, Hippolyta and Penthesilea, figure in widely told Greek myths. The ninth labour imposed on Hercules by his master Eurystheus was to take from Hippolyta her girdle, symbol of her royal power, which had been given to her by the god Ares. According to one version of the myth, Hercules withstood a cavalry charge of Amazons single-handed and routed their whole army, killing Hippolyta at the same time.

Later legends linked the name of Theseus, mythical King of Athens, with Hercules' expedition against the Amazons. Theseus carried off Antiope whose sister Oreithyia, sworn to vengeance, led an invading army into Attica. The Amazons were defeated by the Athenians after four months fighting. Some say that Antiope was killed in the fighting, but others that she survived to make a scene at Theseus' wedding (she being the mother of Theseus' son Hippolytus, though not his lawful wife), where she threatened to murder all the guests. Theseus killed her, to prevent her.

In another legend, Hippolyta brought yet another Amazon force against Theseus after this wedding, and in the ensuing battle was killed accidentally by her sister Penthesilea. Pursued by the Furies of her dead sister, Penthesilea sought refuge in Troy, where she obtained purification from her blood-guilt at the hands of the aged King Priam. In gratitude she enrolled in the Trojan army, where, as the war-god Ares' daughter, she fought bravely until Achilles killed her. Achilles then wept for the lost beauty, youth and courage of the dead queen and made love to her corpse. Thersites, reputed to be the ugliest Greek at Troy, jeered at Achilles' grief and accused him of unnatural lust, whereupon Achilles killed him. This enraged some of the Greeks and Diomedes, a cousin of Thersites, threw Penthesilea's corpse into the River Scamander.

Various explanations of the origins of the legends about the Amazons have been put forward. Some writers trace them to the armed slave-girls who were dedicated to the service of certain Asian deities, and the association of the Amazons with Artemis supports this theory.

Centaurs

Centaurs were monsters in the classical sense, in that these legendary creatures combined two species in one skin. They had human heads and arms and torsos, merging into the bodies of horses. Centaurs were often savage and unbridled, according to report. Yet they had much mysterious wisdom and virtues far surpassing those of ordinary men.

The ancient Greeks regarded the centaurs as fanciful celebrants who danced in the train of Dionysus, the wine god, but also believed that their own forefathers had both befriended and fought against centaurs in the days of old. The latter conviction probably had some basis in fact, for the name centaurs signifies 'those who round up bulls' and the idea of the centaur may well have sprung from the cattle-breeders of Thessaly in northern Greece, who spent much of their time on horseback and whose manners were rough and barbarous. Alternatively, it has been suggested that the original centaurs were Cimmerian and Scythian raiders, rough-riding nomads from the north, who often invaded Thrace in the north-east.

In mythology the origin of the centaur was more poetic. It was said that a most reprehensible mortal man named Ixion had founded the race. This Ixion committed the outrageous offence of daring to attempt to seduce Hera, wife to Zeus and queen of heaven itself. To see how far Ixion's impudence would go, Zeus formed a cloud image of Hera and substituted it for the goddess. A monster, Centaurus, was born of this strange union, and when grown to maturity, himself united with the mares of Mount Pelion and in so doing produced the centaurs.

Another, more austere legend has it that Chiron was the first centaur. Chiron had begun life as a Titan. He fought against the young gods of Olympus but they defeated him. Apollo, the god of light and reason, punished Chiron by making him half-horse.

He had been educated by the gods and in turn undertook the instruction of hero after hero: Actaeon, Jason, Castor and Polydeuces, and Achilles, each served an apprenticeship with Chiron in the wilderness.

But Chiron's own fate was an unhappy one. He fell wounded by a poisoned arrow in a tragic accident. The arrow came from the quiver of a good friend, the best of men, impetuous Hercules. There was no antidote to its poison. To escape the wound's unending agony, Chiron renounced immortality in favour of his fellow-Titan, Prometheus. Zeus then generously set the kindly centaur's image in the heavens as the constellation Sagittarius, the Archer.

Caeneus, in trying to prevent the half-human, half-horse centaurs from raping the women of the Lapith tribe, was mercilessly hammered into the ground by these monsters: stone relief from Olympia.

Mansell Collection

141

The Furies

In their original and best remembered form the Furies are among the most fearsome products of the Greek imagination. They are the avengers, three loathsome and implacable female beings, fulfillers of curses and especially of curses called down upon those who murder their elder kith and kin. Born of blood, roused from hell by the shedding of blood, they are satisfied only by the blood of their quarry.

In the dreadful beginnings of the gods, Uranus, lord of the sky, fathered the Titans upon Gaia, the earth. Uranus was afraid of his children and hid them away in the body of their mother. At length she could bear it no longer and persuaded Cronus, her youngest son, to attack her husband. Cronus thereupon took a sickle and castrated his father, and when the blood from Uranus's genitals fell upon the earth, his wife, she conceived and bore the Furies. It seems strange that they, whose chief task was to hunt down the betrayers of blood kinship, should themselves have been born of their father's blood, shed by their brother. But they came into being out of an act of revenge that was done in defence of their mother; and it is the rights of mothers, even when they are unjust, that they uphold with particular ferocity.

The ancient authors describe the Furies with relish. They are horrifying in appearance and they stink. With snakes in their hair, they brandish torches and metal studded whips. They bark like bitches, virgin hell-hounds. They have suitably ominous names: Alecto, 'the Endless'; Tisiphone, 'the Retaliator'; Megaera, 'the Envious Rager'. Although their main duty was to avenge those murdered by their kin, they also sometimes took it upon themselves to right the established order in other ways.

The Gorgons

In the common versions of the myth, at least in those which became accepted by such writers as Apollodorus, there were three Gorgon sisters, daughters of the ancient sea gods, Phorcys and Ceto, namely Stheno and Euryale, who were immortal, and Medusa who was mortal. According to most writers, they lived on the Atlantic shores of Africa, which seems to link them with the underworld, which was likewise placed in the far west. According to the philologists, the name Gorgons should once have denoted a terrible roaring or bellowing. But in Greek usage the name always suggests their glaring eyes.

Perseus, son of Zeus and Danae, grew up on the island of Seriphos, whose king Polydectes conceived a passion for Danae, while Perseus protected her. To get Perseus out of the way, Polydectes sent him to fetch the Gorgon's head, an enterprise which would, he hoped, lead him to his death. But Perseus was helped by Hermes and Athena. The nymphs gave Perseus the winged sandals of Hermes, the *kibisis*, apparently a large sack or wallet, and the cap of Hades which made its wearer invisible. Hermes also gave him the sickle (*harpe*), a special curved sword with which he was able to cut off the head of Medusa.

Perseus flew to the home of the monsters where he found the three Gorgons asleep, their heads covered with snakes instead of hair, and their mouths armed with great tusks like those of boars. Their gaze turned to stone all who beheld them. As they slept, Perseus stood over them, Athena guiding his hand, and looked away at a polished shield while he cut off the head of Medusa. From her as she died sprang forth the winged horse Pegasus. Perseus put the head into the sack and set off homeward, pursued by the other two Gorgons, who could not see him but tracked him by smell. They failed to catch him. On his way back he made use of the Gorgon's head against his enemies, and when he arrived at Seriphos he turned Polydectes and his followers to stone. He returned the sandals and other gifts to the nymphs and finally gave the head of Medusa to Athena to adorn her goatskin shield.

If the origins of the Gorgons are sought outside Greece, the most likely source is the Near East, Anatolia, Phoenicia or Mesopotamia, where religious art abounds with monsters.

'And over the terrible heads of the Gorgons, a great Dread quivered'; it seems likely that such fearsome creatures had a special connection with the underworld: Greek head of a Gorgon, from Syracuse in Sicily.

The Harpies

Like the Sirens, the Furies and the Gorgons, the Harpies were female monsters of Greek legend. They were depicted in art and literature as winged women, or as birds with women's faces and long, hooked claws, and their peculiar activity was to swoop upon human beings, or at least upon their food; their victims were carried off to unknown places. The origin and nature of the Harpies are in dispute, but they seem to have a definite connection with the underworld, having some ghost characteristics.

Wind and spirit were closely allied in ancient thought, as was breath, and the Harpies are linked in literature with storms, whirlwinds or sudden squalls such as are particularly dangerous at sea and damaging on land. They appear first in Homer, where the Harpy Podarge (swift-foot) is mentioned in the *Iliad* as mating with the wind Zephyrus, and giving birth to the two supernatural horses of Achilles, Xanthus and Balius. In the *Odyssey* (book I) Telemachus says that Odysseus has been away so long that he must have been carried off by the Harpies 'with no tidings, out of sight'. So too, in her grief, Odysseus's wife Penelope wishes that she had been carried away to the mouths of Ocean by a storm such as swept off the orphan daughters of Pandareus. A legend relates that the goddess Aphrodite, who had been protecting these girls, left them unattended for a period while she interceded for them on Olympus. The Harpies

then swept them off and 'gave them as servants to the hateful Erinyes'. Since the Erinyes or Furies belonged to the underworld, the Harpies must have brought the maidens alive to dwell among the dead. This was the fate which Odysseus's family and friends imagined had overtaken the hero.

The Harpies belong particularly to the Argonautic legend, in which the Argonauts visit Phineus on their way eastward to Colchis to find the Golden Fleece, and the fullest account of them, which has become traditional, appears in the *Argonautica* of Apollonius Rhodius, written in the 3rd century BC. The Argonauts arrive at the palace of Phineus on the west coast of the Black Sea and are welcomed by him because they will deliver him from the Harpies. Phineus had accepted the gift of prophecy even at the price of blindness and a long old age, but had misused it and offended the gods. As his punishment, the Harpies were sent to swoop down upon his table at every meal, carrying off nearly all the food but leaving enough to keep him alive and miserable, and leaving also a disgusting stench which could be smelt for some distance.

C. M. Dixon

Above *Harpies are commonly described as birds with the faces of women, as they are depicted on the Tomb of the Harpies in Asia Minor.* **Right** *Originally goddesses who inspired poetry and song, the Muses presided over the arts and sciences generally: Terpsichore, the Muse of choral dance and song; Greek vase, 440 BC.*

The Muses

Apparently the Muses were once three in number, but were later thought of as a company of nine. They were: Calliope or Calliopeia, 'the beautiful voiced', the epic Muse, who was represented with a tablet and stylus and sometimes with a roll of paper or a book; Clio, the Muse of history, who was depicted either sitting or standing, with an open roll of paper or chest of books; Erato, 'the lovely', Muse of erotic poetry and of mime, who was sometimes shown with the lyre; Euterpe, 'the well-pleasing', Muse of lyric poetry, was represented with a flute; Melpomene, 'the singer', was portrayed with a tragic mask, the club of Hercules, or a sword; Polyhymnia or Polymnia, 'Muse of the many hymns', was depicted in attitudes of meditation, normally without any characteristic symbol or object; Terpsichore, 'delighting in dance', was shown with lyre and plectrum, an instrument used for plucking stringed instruments, as Muse of choral dance and song; Thalia, or Thaleia, 'the festive one', Muse of comedy, of playful and idyllic poetry, was portrayed with a

Michael Holford

comic mask, shepherd's staff or ivy wreath; Urania, the heavenly Muse of astronomy, was represented with a staff pointing at a globe. These neat distinctions were developed in later antiquity, however, and names and functions tend to differ according to the sources.

The traditional association of the god Apollo and the Muses is as familiar in Greek mythology as is their joint patronage of poetry, dancing and music. This association appears to derive from prehistoric times and is comparable with actual choral performances by a female chorus under a male leader. The poet Pindar (5th century BC), in one of his odes, describes how the Muses danced in a chorus led by Apollo with his seven-stringed lyre at the marriage of Peleus and Thetis, the parents of Achilles.

In Homer's *Iliad*, after the Olympian deities have feasted, Apollo plays his lyre as the wine goes round and the Muses sing, 'answering one another'. In one of the Homeric Hymns the Muses sing, again antiphonally, of the immortal gifts of gods and the trials of mankind, while the *Horai* (Hours) and *Charites* (Graces) dance hand-in-hand to Apollo's music, and the god himself actually takes part in the dancing.

The old bards derived their inspiration and usually their real knowledge of things from the Muses who were, for the epic poet Hesiod, 'the daughters of Memory'. The epics begin with invocations to the Muses. Odysseus, for instance, in Homer's *Odyssey*, compliments a minstrel by saying he must be inspired by Apollo or the Muses.

Although Apollo's association with these goddesses is clearly attested in the early epics, and can reasonably be assumed to have derived from prehistoric times, the Greek traditions also suggest that the Muse goddesses and the god Apollo were brought by different routes to form their association on the Greek mainland, perhaps in Boeotia in central Greece. For the Muses were originally mountain goddesses from the north, from Pieria and Olympus, whose later cult extended southwards to Helicon and Parnassus. In historical times in antiquity their main centre was at Thespiae, an ancient town in Boeotia, where they were worshipped by a society named after Hesiod.

The origin of Apollo is more controversial, some scholars favouring a northern, and some an eastern origin, while others suggest a compromise twofold origin from north and east.

However that may be, those who argue for the more primitive and separate role of the Muses, before their association with Apollo, emphasize that the god was absent at the funeral of Achilles, as Homer describes it. For the poet says that the Nereids stood around the body, weeping bitterly as they wrapped it in the winding-sheet, while the nine Muses, answering one another, sang the dirge. A male would have had no part in an old traditional dirge such as this, performed exclusively by women.

The Muses have exercised great influence on the European cultural tradition. This is natural, as they were deeply embedded, from the earliest times, in the most basic cultural impulses of social life.

Nymphs

The Nereids were the daughters of Nereus, the wise old man of the sea. Traditionally, there were 50 of these marine nymphs of the Mediterranean, dwelling with their father in the depths of the sea, lovely young goddesses, kindly to sailors. One of their number was Thetis, the mother of Achilles, who also befriended both Dionysus and Hephaestus. Brought up by Hera, she was obliged by Zeus and Hera to marry Peleus, a mortal. The story of the marriage illustrates a common folktale motif of the fairy or nymph won through guile and struggle, at least for a period of time. Thetis, like other sea creatures, had the power of self-transformation, but Peleus, instructed by Chiron, the wise old centaur, held her fast until she promised to marry him.

After the birth of Achilles, Thetis returned to the sea, but emerged again from time to time to give him comfort and succour. At the end of the *Odyssey*, the ghost of Agamemnon tells how Thetis came up from the sea with the other Nereids to join in the mourning at the funeral of Achilles, and brought a golden urn for his bones, a gift from Dionysus, made by the smith god, Hephaestus.

Different from the nymphs of the broad ocean and the sea were the Naiads, the nymphs of running water, of rivers and springs. These are the divine counterparts of the human girls who regularly purified themselves at such places before religious ceremonies or who, as brides, bathed before their weddings in rivers or in water brought from them. There were also the Oreads or Orestiads, special mountain nymphs, and the Dryads and Hamadryads, who were closely involved with trees and tree cults.

As M. P. Nilsson pointed out (in *Greek Popular Religion*), Artemis is a great goddess very similar to the nymphs and is traditionally accompanied by nymphs. She haunts mountains and meadows, and is connected with the tree cult, with springs and rivers. She protects women in childbirth and watches over little children. She was leader of the nymphs; small wonder that she was a popular goddess, nymph incarnate. She took the young of all creatures under her care and a choral passage in the *Agamemnon* of Aeschylus portrays her anger at the sight of two eagles tearing a hare with her unborn litter in the womb.

Artemis was known as a bear goddess in various parts of the ancient world in a ritual associated with initiation and marriage. In Arcadia, the mother of Arcas, after whom the district was named, was changed into a bear shortly before he was born. The mother's name was that of the nymph Callisto, properly an epithet of Artemis. Artemis Brauronia had her temple at Brauron in Attica. Here girls, dressed in saffron, performed a bear dance before they were married.

It has been reasonably argued that the bear goddess belonged to the ancient Pelasgians, who brought her to Arcadia from Attica, to Attica from Lemnos, and ultimately from the shores of the Black Sea.

Satyrs

Partly human, partly bestial, the satyrs were minor rustic gods or demons, traditional companions of the god Dionysus, lewd and lascivious by nature. Their ultimate origin is puzzling and it may be that their association with Dionysus began in Attica and Ionia. They were commonly represented with bristly hair, round and upturned noses, and pointed animal-like ears, with small horns growing from the tops of their foreheads and with tails like those of horses. Dressed in animal skins, wearing wreaths of ivy, vine or fir, bibulous, sensual and pleasure-loving, they lie sleeping, play musical instruments or join in wild dances with the nymphs.

Above *Some nymphs were connected with the sea, others with mountains or trees. The nymphs of rivers and springs were divine counterparts of human girls who purified themselves there. As spirits of the pulsing life of Nature, the nymphs were the companions of the lustful satyrs: medallion of a sleeping nymph with satyrs.* **Facing page** *The sirens appear in the Odyssey as beautiful maidens who enchant passing sailors with their song so that they swim ashore and perish; Odysseus escaped this fate by commanding his men to bind him to the mast: Odysseus and the Sirens, 3rd century mosaic from Dougga.*

Their chief prototype is Silenus himself, that ancient Falstaff, bald, jovial and rotund, carrying a wine bag, usually so tipsy that he rides around on an ass or has to be propped up by other satyrs. A dancer and flute player, he was also regarded as a prophet, and therefore to be taken seriously.

To make any sense of this odd jumble of characteristics we must bear in mind the nature of the god with whom the satyrs were closely associated. As E. R. Dodds has pointed out, in the introduction to his edition of the *Bacchae* of Euripides, to the Greeks of the classical age Dionysus was not solely, or even mainly, the god of wine. His cult titles identify him as the power in the tree, the blossom-bringer, the abundance of life, his domain the liquid fire in the grape, the sap thrusting in a young tree, the blood pounding in the veins of a young animal, all the mysterious and uncontrollable tides that ebb and flow in the life of Nature. It may well be that his association with certain wild plants, such as the fir and ivy, and with certain animals, is in fact older than his association with the vine.

'It was the Alexandrines,' adds Dodds, 'and above all the Romans – with their tidy functionalism and their cheerful obtuseness in matters of the spirit – who departmentalized Dionysos as "jolly Bacchus" the wine-god with his riotous crew of nymphs and satyrs. As such he was taken over from the Romans by Renaissance painters and poets; and it was they in turn who shaped the image in which the world pictures him.'

The Greeks in the time of Euripides were beginning to bring other Nature spirits of other cults into association with the satyrs. Thus the chorus in the *Bacchae* tells the myth of the origin of the kettledrum; how it was invented in a Cretan cave by Curetes to drown the cries of the baby Zeus, then presented to Rhea, his mother; and how the satyrs introduced it into Dionysiac ritual.

C. M. Dixon/Victoria & Albert Museum

Bardo Museum/Sonia Halliday

Sirens

Female beings connected with the underworld, the Sirens were particularly dangerous to men; it is hard to find any story in which women suffered at their hands. They first appear in the *Odyssey* (book 12) as beautiful females who sit in a meadow by the sea, enchanting passing sailors with their song so that they swim ashore, or land, and perish miserably. Round them is a great heap of bones which come from the rotting corpses of men.

Odysseus was advised by the enchantress Circe at the time when she warned him of the Sirens, to stop the ears of his rowers with wax as the ship passed them; and she told him that, if he wished to hear their song himself, he should make his men bind him to the mast and not release him however much he might implore them. A mysterious calm fell as the ship passed their island, so that it depended entirely on rowing to make headway. The Sirens sang to Odysseus that they knew of all his deeds and sufferings at Troy. In Homer they are mentioned in the dual number, so that he recognized no more than two. Their names are not given, and their physical form is not described. Like other such beings in the *Odyssey* they are not located in known or normal geography.

For the historical period corresponding to the heroic age, it is of some interest that tablets inscribed in the script known as Linear B from Mycenean Pylos seem to refer to decorations on furniture as *seremokaraoi* and *seremokaraapi* which has been interpreted as 'siren-headed'. If this is so, the word *serem*, in that form with M not yet changed to N, already existed in Mycenean Greek, and the Sirens were known in myth in some form. What form the Mycenean 'siren-headed' decorations had is not known.

In later periods poets and mythographers continued to write of Sirens, revealing more of their nature. Hesiod in a fragment of his *Eoiai* called their island Anthemoessa and named them Thelxiope, Molpe and Aglaophonus, daughters of Phorcys the sea god, saying also that they frequently calmed the winds.

In the 7th century BC the lyric poet Alcman spoke of the Muse 'the clear-voiced Siren' as if Siren and Muse were the same, and elsewhere mentions the Sirenides, but only for their music. A fragment of Sophocles makes them daughters of Phorcys and 'singers of songs of Hades'. The comic poet Epicharmus makes the Sirens try to attract Odysseus by descriptions of the food and drink that they enjoyed and which he might share; plump anchovies, sucking pigs, cuttle-fish and sweet wine. When they begin to speak of their evening meal Odysseus cries 'Alas for my miseries'. Other comic poets, Theopompus and Nicophon, mention the abundant feasting of the Sirens and their unkind taunting of the hungry wanderer Odysseus.

This association with fabulous plenty is difficult to explain, even given the food-loving conventions of comedy. A certain similarity to Harpies comes to mind in this connection.

Appendix

Artemis
Greek goddess of the hunt and wild animals, 'lady of wild things', sister of Apollo: probably of Cretan origin; later identified with the Roman Diana. Famous for her temple at Ephesus.

Ate
Greek word for 'ruin, disaster': personified as a power which so disorders a man's mind that he cannot tell right from wrong; in the *Iliad* she is the daughter of Zeus, an early example of the problem of how far God is responsible for evil; some later European writers thought of her as a demoness as a result of this, though with small justification.

Atlas
In Greek mythology, the giant who held up the sky to prevent it from falling on the earth; he was identified with the Atlas Mountains in Africa and legend said that he was turned to stone when Perseus showed him the Gorgon's head; his name was first used for a collection of maps by Mercator in 1595, with a picture of him holding up the globe of the earth on his enormous shoulders. Some of his attributes give him affinities with Hercules.

Autolycus
The son of Hermes and grandfather of Odysseus; one of the Argonauts. He had the gift of making anything he touched invisible and became, like his father, an accomplished thief. Trying to steal the cattle of Sisyphus he met his match, for the beasts had been marked secretly under their feet, so Sisyphus was able to identify them, and despite his protestations, Autolycus was unmasked as a robber and a thief.

Bacchus
A name of Dionysus, the Greek god of fertility, wine and ecstatic frenzy, whose worshippers were called Bacchae or Bacchantes; Bacchanalia was the Latin name for the mysteries celebrated in the god's honour, originally confined to women, banned at Rome in 186 BC but reintroduced during the 1st century AD, and the source of much revelry.

Cyclops
Or 'circle-eye' (plural Cyclopes), name given to the one-eyed giants of Greek myth; divine craftsmen, they were the forgers of Zeus's thunderbolt: best known is Polyphemus who, in Homer's *Odyssey* imprisons Odysseus and his men, but is outwitted by the hero: generally depicted in classical literature as a figure of burlesque and fun.

Dioscuri
'Sons of Zeus', the twin heroes Castor and Polydeuces of Greek myths (Castor and Pollux of Roman): they protected sailors, and were believed to have come to the aid of the Roman army at the battle of Lake Regillus, c 496 BC; they sailed with the Argonauts to fetch the Golden Fleece; they were worshipped in Sparta, where their symbol was two upright pieces of wood joined by two cross-pieces, hence the astrological symbol for Gemini, with which they were associated.

Dryads
In Greek mythology, female spirits who guarded oak trees and are shown dancing around them: they were later connected with groves and woods in general; mortal daughters of Zeus, they were long-lived and generally benevolent to men: a hamadryad was the life-spirit which lived in each tree and which died when the tree decayed: tree spirits are also known in many other parts of the world.

Echo
Repetition of sound which can often be heard in high mountains: in Greek mythology the name of a mountain nymph, vainly loved by the god Pan, who in his wrath had her torn to pieces by mad shepherds, only her voice remaining: in another story Echo was doomed by Hera to repeat only what others say because she had distracted Hera's attention from Zeus's amorous affairs with her idle chatter; she was, therefore, unable to declare her love for Narcissus and sadly pined away until only her voice was left.

Elysium
In Greek mythology a land of perfect happiness and perpetual spring where those favoured by the gods lived exempt from death; according to Homer the Elysian Fields were located at the end of the earth, on the banks of the river Oceanus, and were ruled by Rhadamanthus; later classical writers identified it as the part of the underworld to which the righteous went after death and from there it was a short step to identification with Paradise and, eventually, the Christian heaven.

Euhemerism

The theory that mythology has its origins in history; propounded by the Greek scholar Euhemerus in the 3rd century BC, who tried to prove that the gods were in fact ancient kings who had been deified: in an account of a fabulous journey to islands in the Indian Ocean, he claimed to have discovered inscriptions commemorating great kings and heroes, whose names corresponded with those of the Greek gods.

Golden Fleece

In Greek mythology, the object of the voyage of Jason and the Argonauts, who, helped by the enchantress Medea, stole it from Colchis on the Black Sea, where it hung on a tree guarded by a dragon: it was the fleece of a ram which could think, speak and fly, sent by Hermes to save two children whose lives were threatened by their cruel stepmother.

Graces

The three *Charites* (plural of *charis*) of Greek mythology, Aglaia (the radiant), Thalia (the flowering) and Euphrosyne (joy), personifications of grace and charm, companions of the love goddess; originally there were more than three of them and they stood for the joy and beauty of fertile Nature; associated with flowers, especially the rose and the myrtle; later, they conferred on human beings not only beauty and charm but also wisdom, intellectual power and artistic ability, somewhat similar to the Muses.

Bibliotheque Nationale, Paris

Hades

'The unseen', the Greek god of death, later the name of the underworld which he ruled, the home of the dead, later still, another word for hell. Feared as pitiless and unyielding, Hades had little cult and was not often represented in art; his queen was Persephone, who spent the winter with him in the underworld.

Picturepoint, London

Halcyon

Fabulous bird, supposed to breed at midwinter in a nest which floats on the sea; the wind and waves remain calm for seven 'halcyon days' to make this possible; from the Greek word for 'kingfisher'.

Villa Giulia Museum

Helen of Troy

According to Greek mythology, the most beautiful woman in the world, daughter of the mortal Leda and the god Zeus in the guise of a swan, her beauty attracted all the princes of Greece and to avoid strife her foster-father made the suitors vow to defend the chosen husband against anyone who resented his good fortune; she married Menelaus, and on her abduction by Paris, the former suitors stood by their oaths and besieged Troy. Helen reappears in some of the Faust stories of the Middle Ages.

Mansell Collection

Hermes

Hermes was the son of Zeus by Maia, and when he was born on Mount Cyllene, his mother laid him in swaddling bands on a fan, but he grew so quickly that the moment her back was turned he went off in search of adventure. He then became adept as a thief, and there may well be early connections with inter-tribal cattle raids behind the legend. Zeus made him his ambassador and messenger, and he became the god of eloquence and good fortune as a consequence.

Hestia

Greek goddess of the hearth, both the household hearth as the focal point of the family and the public hearth of a community as the centre of its life; daughter of Cronus and Rhea, and a virgin, she has little mythology. Her Roman counterpart was Vesta, whose sacred flame was tended by the Vestal Virgins.

Hierophant

One who reveals sacred things, from the title of the chief priest of Eleusis who displayed the holy objects in the main ceremonies of the Mysteries; in occult societies often the title of the official who presides over initiation ceremonies.

Invocation

Appealing to a god or spirit by prayer or incantation; summoning up a god or spirit; the poets of antiquity invoked the Muse for inspiration; invocation, 'calling on' a good supernatural being or force, is sometimes distinguished from evocation, 'calling out' an evil one, but the two words are frequently used interchangeably.

Michael Holford/British Museum

Iris

Greek goddess of, and personification of, the rainbow; sister of the Harpies in Hesiod, in the *Iliad* she is a golden-winged messenger of the gods; she seems to have had no cult.

Statliche Museum

Keres

In Greek mythology, malignant spirits who brought all kinds of misfortune and trouble including disease, old age and death; some believed them to be the executors of the will of the Fates and others that they were the souls of the dead.

Kiss

Gesture of love, respect, worship; the Greeks and Romans kissed images of the gods.

Labyrinth

Or maze, a complex arrangement of buildings or intricate network of enclosed paths, from whose centre it is difficult to find a way out; to penetrate it and then return sym-

Academia Nazionale

bolized spiritual death and resurrection. To the ancients the labyrinth was linked with the idea of a sacred centre of ritual, reserved only for the initiated; there were labyrinths in Egypt, as indeed elsewhere, thus testifying to the great antiquity and widespread occurence of labyrinths. The most famous, however, was no doubt the Labyrinth of Cnossus, in Crete, which was said to have been built by Daedalus on the orders of King Minos, to house or hide the Minotaur.

Michael Holford

Maenads
Or Bacchae, frenzied women devotees of the Greek god Dionysus; armed with ivy-twined staffs tipped with a pine cone, and clothed in animal skins, they roamed the mountains celebrating the cult of Dionysus with ecstatic dance and song; they tore live beasts apart and devoured the flesh, probably as a rite of communion with the god.

Medea
In Greek mythology, a witch who fell in love with Jason and used magic to enable him to steal the Golden Fleece; she escaped with him and murdered her young brother to delay the pursuers; when Jason deserted her she killed the children she had borne him; her name means 'the cunning one' and she was the niece of Circe.

Metamorphosis
Change of form or shape, a common occurrence in myths, legends and folktales; the gods may adopt temporary human or animal forms; witches turn their victims into loathsome forms; Lot's wife was punished by being turned into a pillar of salt, and Actaeon by being transformed into a stag; werewolves are human beings who turn into wolves at night; there are many stories in which rival magicians in combat change rapidly from one shape to another.

Metempsychosis
Or transmigration, the passage of a human or animal soul into a new body after death; the new body may be of the same species or a different one; in India and Greece the belief developed that souls pass from one form of life to a higher or lower one.

Tate Gallery/John Webb

Minotaur
In Greek mythology, the monster with a human body and a bull's head who was the offspring of Queen Pasiphae of Crete by a bull; he was kept in the labyrinth at Cnossus and,

every nine years, seven young men and seven maidens were sent from Athens to be his prey; he was killed by the hero Theseus.

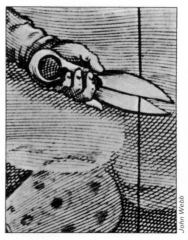

John Webb

Moira
The three Fates of Greek mythology, Clotho, Lachesis and Atropos, first named in Hesiod's *Theogony*; *moira* originally meant a person's 'lot' or 'rightful portion' in life. The Fates were sometimes said to be present at birth because that is when an individual's lot is decided; in modern Greek folklore they appear on the third night of a child's life and fix the course of his life.

Moly
In Greek mythology, a magic herb given by Hermes to Odysseus to protect him against the enchantments of Circe (*Odyssey*, book 10); it is described as having a black root, a flower like milk, and being hard to uproot; it has not been convincingly identified with any real herb, though mandrake, garlic and rue have been suggested.

Muses
In Greek mythology nine divinities who presided over the liberal arts. They were the daughters of Zeus, and companions of Apollo. Their names are Clio, the muse of history; Euterpe, muse of lyric poetry; Thalia, muse of comedy and pastoral poetry; Melpomene, of tragedy; Terpsichore, of dancing; Erato, of songs of love; Polyhymnia, of sacred song; Urania, of astronomy; and Calliope, of epic poetry.

Nectar
The sweet liquid produced by plants: in Greek mythology, the drink of the Gods which with ambrosia, their food, kept them immortal; it may originally have been a drink made of honey, possibly mead, though it has alternatively been connected with mushrooms; more generally, used for any supremely delicious drink.

Nereids
Nymphs of the Mediterranean Sea, as opposed to the Oceanides, who were nymphs of the Ocean, and Naiads, who were the nymphs of the lakes, rivers and fountains. There were also Oreads who were nymphs of the mountains and Dryads and Hamadryads who were the nymphs of trees. They had some divine gifts, such as that of prophecy and long life, but were not immortal.

Net
Symbol of a snare or trap, of entanglement and involvement; Aphrodite and Ares were caught in guilty passion in the net of Hephaestus.

Odysseus
Or Ulysses (from the Latin form of his name), King of Ithaca who was one of the Greek leaders at the siege of Troy; prominent in the *Iliad* and the central character of the *Odyssey*, which describes his adventures on his ten years' journey home after Troy had fallen; later writers tended to depict him as a crafty rogue; he may well have been a real chieftain around whom legends gathered.

Oedipus

In Greek mythology, a king of Thebes who was fated to kill his father and commit incest with his mother; to prevent this, as a baby he was abandoned in the hills with a spike driven through his feet, hence his name, 'swell-foot'; he grew up unaware of his true parentage, killed his father, Laius, solved the riddle of the Sphinx, and married his mother, Jocasta; when the truth was discovered, he blinded himself, and went into exile; Freud named the 'Oedipus complex' after him.

Oenone

A nymph of Mount Ida who fell in love with the beautiful shepherd Paris before it was realized that he was the son of King Priam. They lived together very happily, but since she could prophesy, she foresaw the disaster if he went to Greece, and that her knowledge of medicine would be useful at the hour of death. All this came true, but Paris left her. At his death she took her own life.

Olympic Games

Athletic contests in honour of Olympian Zeus, founded in 776 BC and held every four years at Olympia, the principal sanctuary of the god in Greece; the games were abolished in the 4th century AD and re-founded in the 19th century; the first in the modern series of games was held at Athens in 1896.

Olympus

Mountain on the borders of Thessaly and Macedonia, close to 10,000 feet in height, the highest peak in the Greek peninsula and the home of the Greek gods; also the name of several other mountains in Greece and Asia Minor.

Omphale

Queen of Lydia. Hercules had become mad, and whilst in a fit, he had murdered Iphitus. The oracle said that he was to go into slavery for a period of three years. He was thereupon sold to Queen Omphale, who took over his club and lion's skin, whilst he carried out women's work. Another version of the story was that they merely exchanged clothes for amusement before going to sleep in a grotto. At midnight Pan crept into the grotto and thought that he was climbing into Omphale's bed, but to his amazement he was literally kicked out by an irate Hercules. Pan therefore spread the rumour as revenge.

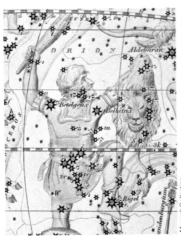

Orion

Constellation which resembles a man with belt and sword; named for a gigantic and beautiful hunter of Greek mythology who was killed by the goddess Artemis and despatched to the sky; revered by the Egyptians, who saw in it the figure of the god Osiris.

Pagan

Derived from Latin *paganus*, 'countryman', implying belief in a variety of Nature gods and spirits, and sometimes implying delight in Nature, the senses, the things of this world; generally refers to a believer in the polytheism of the ancient world.

Pandora

In Greek mythology, the first woman, created by Zeus to punish men after Prometheus had brought them the gift of fire; she opened the great jar or box in which all evils had been confined, so letting them loose to plague the world; her name, which means 'All-giving', suggests that she was originally an earth goddess in all probability.

Pantheism

From Greek *pan*, 'all', and *theos*, 'god', the belief that all is God and God is All, the sum total of everything that exists.

Psyche

Greek word for 'breath', used to mean life, soul, spirit or mind, as distinct from body: in classical mythology, a beautiful girl with whom Cupid, the love god, fell in love; she eventually became immortal herself and the lovers were united; the story, told in *The Golden Ass* of Apuleius, was taken as a parable of the union between the human soul and divine love.

Scylla and Charybdis

In classical mythology, Scylla was a monster with six heads, 18 rows of teeth, 12 feet, and a voice like the yelping of dogs, who lived in a cave and snatched seamen from passing ships; nearby lurked Charybdis, a whirlpool; Odysseus sailed between the two, which were later located in the Straits of Messina between mainland Italy and the island of Sicily or Trinacria, as it was called.

Selene

Greek moon goddess, of little importance in myth or cult; said to have been the sister or daughter of the sun; she fell in love with Endymion, who fathered on her 50 children, the 50 months between each celebration of the Olympic Games; other, more important goddesses connected with the moon were Hera, Artemis and Hecate.

Silenus

In classical mythology, one of the Sileni, woodland spirits who became associated with Dionysus and the satyrs is represented as an elderly, fat, hairy but bald-headed man with the ears of a horse, riding an ass or a wineskin; he is profoundly wise and constantly drunk; sometimes said to have been the teacher of the young Dionysus or the father of the satyrs; Socrates was compared with him for wisdom and ugliness.

Snake

Appears in the myths and religious beliefs of almost all societies, playing many different roles: associated with rejuvenation, immortality, longevity and wisdom.

Thyrsos

Ivy-twined staff tipped with a pine cone, or sometimes with a bunch of grapes and vine leaves, which was an attribute of the Greek god Dionysus and was carried by his worshippers; ivy was the plant of Dionysus and the phallic pine cone an emblem of fertility and immortality; the god was also linked with wine.

THE MYTHS OF ANCIENT ROME

The Founding of Rome

The name of Aeneas, the Trojan warrior who is first mentioned in Homer's *Iliad*, is linked in legend with the foundation of Rome. In the *Iliad* Aeneas's mother, the goddess Aphrodite, and the god Poseidon predicted that his heirs would rule over the Trojans in great glory; thus of all the Trojans only Aeneas was assured of survival after the Greek conquest. The figure of Aeneas also belonged to the series of legends on the wanderings of heroic warriors after the Trojan War. Because of the incidence of towns and other coastal landmarks which anciently bore names similar to his, Aeneas became the archetype of the wandering refugee who founded cities. The most remarkable of his postwar exploits were his visit to Carthage and a contribution to the beginnings of Rome, whose Italian empire was destined to fulfil Aphrodite's prophecy of the Trojan's enduring dominion. The legend of Aeneas's activities in the western Mediterranean is far older than Virgil's epic poem the *Aeneid*, which was published after the poet's death in 19 BC.

In this poem Aeneas flees from the sacked city of Troy in the company of his son Ascanius and his aged father Anchises. After many adventures Aeneas reached Italy where various sites were connected with his visits and dedications. Aeneas strengthened his band of Trojan followers by a dynastic marriage with the native princess Lavinia, whose father Latinus offered land to the Trojan and shared his kingship with Aeneas.

In some accounts Aeneas is represented visiting the place which would later hold the city of Rome founded by his descendants. However, Aeneas himself never played an actual role in the foundation. Before the Romans began to investigate and record their origins there already existed two reports of the relationship between Aeneas and his descendant Romulus, who according to the older reckoning was the grandson of Aeneas. The accepted date of the destruction of Troy as around 1200 BC and the tradition of the foundation of Rome as c 753 involved both Greek and Roman scholars in a chronological discrepancy. This they solved by creating a dynasty of kings, usually named *Silvii*, who ruled over the people of the ancient Latian city of Alba Longa.

According to the literary tradition of the Silvian dynasty, Amulius deposed his brother, the rightful king Numitor, and consecrated his niece, Rhea Silvia, to the goddess Vesta so that she would remain forever childless. The maiden was loved by Mars and she conceived and gave birth to twins who were exposed to die. They were borne along by the Tiber and brought to land near the site of an archaic Roman shrine, the Lupercal and its neighbouring holy fig tree, the *Ficus ruminalis*: both landmarks play an important role in the legend of the twins. Although the literary devices of the tale bear the marks of a Greek legend, it also bears unmistakable traces of Roman invention by its attention to well-known local landmarks. The names of both Romulus and Remus refer to places: Rome itself and Remoria or Remona, evidently an old name of the Aventine Hill. Indeed Romulus itself means no more than 'Roman'.

The Lupercal was a grotto at the foot of the Palatine Hill attached to the cult and ceremonies of the two old religious fraternities of *Luperci*, the *Fabiani* and *Quinctiales*, who annually purified persons and places during the festival of *Lupercalia* on 15 February. In consequence of the linguistic derivation of Lupercus from *lupus*, 'wolf', the Romans believed that a she-wolf had suckled the newborn twins. The suckling itself was suggested by the *Ficus ruminalis*, the name of which was thought to have come from an obsolete word for teat and the verb *ruminare*, 'to chew'. In fact, the manifest sense of the fig tree's variant names, Romula and Romularis, and the obsolete name of the Tiber river, Rumo, demonstrate that the sense of ruminalis was 'Roman'. In any event, the story of the wolf and the twins was already well established in 296 BC when two Roman magistrates dedicated a statue group of the three at the Lupercal.

A later rationalization of the tale attempted to suppress the unlikely animal by reinterpreting the wolf as a *lupa*, the common Latin designation of a whore. In this account the twins are discovered by the shepherd Faustulus who entrusted them to his wanton wife, Acca Larentia. A minor goddess, she was worshipped at her shrine in the place called Velabrum, also situated at the foot of the Palatine Hill.

Reaching manhood among Faustulus and his fellow shepherds, Romulus and Remus assumed the leadership of a band of cattle-rustlers who plundered the territory of the usurper Amulius. Caught and brought before the deposed Numitor, Romulus and Remus pleaded so eloquently and regally that their identity became known to their own grandfather. Thus reunited and aware of their rightful inheritance, the twins overthrew the usurper and restored their grandfather. Yearning for their old haunts and impatient of waiting their turn at the Alban kingship, they returned to the place where the waters of the Tiber had once set them down. In the tradition of Alba Longa as the mother-city of Latian towns, they led a proper Alban colony to found a new city on the site. The brothers quarrelled over the colony's location and name and decided to seek a sign from the gods to settle the matter (known as augury). Remus took his place upon the Aventine Hill and Romulus upon the Palatine, and both watched the heavens for a sign. To Remus first appeared six vultures, but twelve vultures flew into Romulus's line of vision. In this fashion the god Jupiter indicated to the colonists the site and name of Rome.

Romulus himself drew the sacred boundary of the city which the Romans called a *pomerium*. The manner of marking the boundary was to plough a furrow with a team of a cow and a bullock. The plough had to be lifted over the place of each gate. The cow was yoked on the inside of the boundary, apparently to invite fertility within the city, and the bullock on the outside, to keep sterility beyond the town's boundary. Romulus forbade his brother to leap the boundary, a magical act evidently bringing ill-luck and in the most frequent version, himself slew Remus who taunted the founder by leaping over it.

Romulus reigned long and well, leaving a much larger kingdom than he had founded. One day while performing some public act in the Campus Martius – the field of Mars – he ascended into heaven and joined the gods. Later a certain Julius Proculus announced that he had seen Romulus, who

told him that he had become the god Quirinus. This apotheosis of Romulus is closely connected with the cult of Mars.

The gods of the Romans may be divided into groups of natural forces and their phenomena, physical activity, single abstract conceptions, deities of a given place and, finally, divinities of unknown origins. Among the gods of Nature stand Jupiter, Mars and Ceres. Jupiter was once the sky and the day. So he might be worshipped as a god of the sky and be called Thunderer or the like after some heavenly appearance. Mars belongs to the forces of springtime, and so his cult was concentrated in March.

Ceres ruled the growth of crops and vegetation in general. Her origin leads naturally to the next group, the type of physical activity. At an earlier stage Ceres was no goddess. *Ceres* or *cerus* was a verbal noun from the root 'to make grow' (*creare*) or 'to grow' (*crescere*). It was Growth itself. By the classical period Ceres had acquired all the attributes of a fertile lady and had narrowed her attentions upon agriculture, with the notable exception of her invocation at a wedding. She was identified with the Greek grain goddess, Demeter, as early as the 5th century. Indeed her oldest Roman temple may have been totally the result of Greek influence. Be that as it may, Ceres in cult and in story rarely exhibits a purely Roman background.

Venus represents the same type of deity. She began as the physical activity of coaxing and luring, but was early assigned a role in keeping watch over vegetable gardens. In some parts of central Italy the same priestess served both Ceres and Venus. A third such deity was Juno, whose name must be related to the word 'youth', a period of animal life which she as a goddess preserved and prolonged. In many instances the Romans forgot the origin of such 'gods'.

These divine types differ in origin very little from the manifest abstraction which never, or only occasionally, assumed a human form that could overwhelm the deity's beginnings to such a degree that a Roman could not understand its principal function. In this category are Tellus, Dis, Fides and Salus. Tellus signifies the earth, which is anything but an abstraction. However, *tellus* was most certainly the state or essence of earth, 'earthness', rather than a natural power such as growth or physical activity such as coaxing. The sole major festival of Tellus was named for the slaughter of pregnant cows, which were cremated so that the bountiful ash might be employed in fertilization. Tellus was enriched and was not in itself a force or deity. However, under Greek influence the 'earth' became a mother goddess.

Dis shows affinities with Tellus and also influence from a Greek quarter. Dis belonged to the underworld. His name means 'rich', which was thought a suitable translation of

Cupid, the Roman god of love, identified with the Greek Eros, embraces the mortal Psyche. Roman religion is full of instances of borrowing, and sometimes modifying, the gods and cults of the many peoples within the Empire.

R. Schoder SJ

the Greek Pluto. Whereas Tellus received annual sacrifices, the underworld's Dis received sacrifice every century (*saeculum*) at the splendid and gorgeous Secular Games. Tellus had one Roman temple which had been vowed in wartime on account of an earthquake. Her old cult was performed in the open away from temples. Dis had the one altar, buried except for a few hours every century. Evidently neither deity was represented by a man-like statue, although the Romans considered one a goddess and the other a god. Tellus remained quite Roman in cult in spite of learned attempts to equate her with the Earth of Greek mythology. Dis, on the other hand, was an integrated foreigner.

The many deities invoked at the Secular Games exhibit a miscellany of Roman, Italic and Greek gods, worshipped by prayers and with utensils emanating from equally diverse quarters. The core of the ritual went back to the middle of the 4th century BC. The Games were controlled by the Fifteen Men (formerly Ten Men) For Sacrificing, a powerful priesthood in charge of imported state cults. The cult of Tellus, however, was carried on by the chief pontiff and the Vestal Virgins, the oldest civil priests of Rome. Yet Tellus, 'Earth', and Dis, 'Rich', share similar beginnings and interest in the soil's goodness.

Of the same type are Fides Publica and Salus. The former, 'the People's Trust', had a very old cult and precinct. The latter, 'Welfare' or 'Safety', received a temple very late although the notion of the people's well-being dominated many areas of the civil religion. Both were acknowledged as gods to the extent that they were given temples, but neither had a human representation and, so far as we know, they were female only because of their grammatical gender. Ceres, Venus, and probably Tellus, originally, had a neuter grammatical gender and became 'feminine' in the process of becoming deities with functions seemingly appropriate to women.

Ops offers herself as an example. The grammatically feminine word means 'abundance', 'resource' and 'provender'. On 25 August she received worship from the Vestal Virgins at the King's House. On 19 December fell her oldest civil festival, which the Romans recognized as a ceremony for a deity generous in the bestowal of natural resources. Hence, she was honoured after the harvest and in the dead of winter. Yet this 'goddess' could not withstand the tendency to anthropomorphism and became in the popular mind the wife of Saturn, for no better reason than the occurrence of his great festival on 17 December, two days before hers. The one temple Ops certainly had was probably not very old. Sacrifice at the King's House suggests that originally the cult was domestic and later raised to a public status.

Most Romans left the celebration of civil gods to the state priests. At home and within the tradition-bound clans private worship continued unabated for centuries. Indeed, the extent, variety and tenacity of private cult demonstrates how gods were so deeply rooted in pagan hearts. The primitive centre of the household cult was the hearth. The name of the goddess Vesta means no more

then the hearth-fire. Vesta's public cult of the City's fire kept by her virgins grew as her domestic cult declined.

Other domestic deities were the Penates, Lares and Genius. The Penates were gods of the food cupboard (*penus*). The Lares occupied the hearth but were also capable of functioning elsewhere. The Genius typifies the house cult and the Roman mentality. The word signifies the procreative force of the male householder. It was honoured at least on every birthday by libations of wine. The Genius joined the Lares in a small shrine with an artificial hearth set in every dining-room and was often portrayed between the two Lares. He was a model householder, wearing a toga and holding in one hand a horn of plenty, or cornucopia, and in the other a wine-saucer.

Although some ancient authors give the impression that the domestic gods received little more than perfunctory attention, the physical remains, especially those of Pompeii, eloquently counter such an impression with their evidence.

Every household had its altar. Besides the painted or sculptured Lares and Genius are found a variety of statuettes of other gods, coins left in safekeeping, and ceremonial utensils, not the least important of which was the candelabrum or oil-lamp that reminds us of the candle which the electric bulb has replaced before the madonnas in Italian kitchens and on Italian street corners. The latter devotion also descends from ancient pagan practices.

The humble cults flourished on the streets and in the countryside. When the Emperor Augustus encouraged some form of worship of the ruler, he allowed the imperial Genius to join the neighbourhood Lares so that his family's pre-eminence came daily to the attention of the Roman lower classes. Another typical and widespread deity of the lower class was Spes, 'Hope'. Innumerable tablets, statues, reliefs, paintings, altars, shrines and chapels which have come to light in Italy and throughout the Roman Empire attest the religious depth and sincerity of untold thousands.

Although the old popular enthusiasm for the great state cults declined, no one can assert that religious apathy prevailed among the Romans. Indeed, Christianity's 'victory' was truly a victory, the often bloody finale to a long battle. The imperial cult, worship of the dead emperors as gods and the live one as a divine Genius or Divine Will (*numen*), was by no means so superficial as might be believed.

The early Christian emperors of the 4th century allowed it to continue in some areas though at the same time they for-

bade the actual sacrifice that went with it.

Although Roman religion welcomed cults and gods from many foreign and conquered areas, it did not freely digest all ancient manifestations known elsewhere. For instance, magic and astrology never figure in Roman religion. Prophets and oracles might be heeded but they remained peculiar or alien. Visions were not uncommon, but divine epiphanies (appearances of the gods) were rare.

The Romans often sought knowledge of the future from either haruspicy or the lots.

The latter were usually wooden tokens or strips inscribed with some ambiguous phrase with the divinity of a place issued. Although men hawking lots or fortunes could be found in Rome, the great centres of prediction by lots were at a little distance from Rome. Near Etruscan Caere, modern Cerveteri, the lots rose spontaneously from hot springs. The most famous of all such shrines was the magnificent temple complex set atop the citadel hill of Praeneste, modern Palestrina. The deity of this place, appropriately called Fortuna Primigenia, issued lots to the high and the low for centuries. We possess many records of thank-offerings made to Fortuna whose predictions had proved beneficent not only to individuals but also to guilds of skilled workers.

Romans and Italians reported to the pontiffs unnatural occurrences which, if they happened in grave times, might cause mass hysteria and required expiation – androgynous babies, animals with too many limbs or

heads, rains of bloody meat, mice gnawing gold, bulls mounting brazen cows, and like phenomena. On rare occasions such prodigies could even prompt human sacrifice. Thus what was contrary to Nature could cause acts contrary to the norms of Roman religion.

The religious beliefs of the Roman people remained without the slightest moral tone. Spiritual communication and fulfilment do not enter our discussion. The Romans wanted to be in good standing with the forces of Nature. In most instances, the observances were left in the hands of well-born priests whom the state recognized. The Roman's attitude toward his gods somewhat resembles the situation in early Israel. Romans expected the deity to act generously on their behalf or not to act at all. If the deity acted in the manner expected, he was rewarded with a gift of an offering or a sacrifice. If he failed too often or acted too badly, he was abandoned for another. The Romans believed that certain deities watched over them and supposed that others took care of their neighbours in like manner. To this end, they felt it necessary to deprive their enemies of their gods, their sacred utensils and all means of worship.

The modern mind may tend to find this mode of religion criminally selfish but the Romans seldom questioned the efficacy of a religion which had grown outward from a bend on an Italian river to embrace the greater part of Europe, North Africa and the Near East.

The Etruscans

Our sources of knowledge of Etruscan religious thought and practice fall into three groups. Firstly, a few Etruscan inscriptions, secondly the archeological remains which are numerous but cannot speak and are subject to varying interpretation, and thirdly the writings of later Greeks and Romans.

In Macaulay's poem, *Lays of Ancient Rome*, he speaks of the 'nine gods' by which Lars Porsena of Clusium swore 'that the great house of Tarquin' (the Etruscan king) 'should suffer wrong no more'. We know the names of more than Macaulay's nine gods worshipped by the Etruscans, but little about their functions and relationships, and while many have Etruscan names, they were early affected by Greek and oriental influences and equated with the names of Greek and Roman deities. Such equation of names does not of course always involve complete identity of function.

The chief god Tinia or Tin, a thunder-god, was identified with Zeus and Jupiter. Voltumna (Vertumnus) was also very highly honoured. Tinia was worshipped alongside Uni (Juno) and Menrva (Minerva) in tripartite temples of which the most famous is that on the Capitol at Rome, built by the Etruscan kings, in the 6th century BC. The god Sethlans was identified with Hephaestus-Vulcan, Fufluns with Dionysus-Bacchus, Turms with Hermes-Mercury, Turan with Aphrodite-Venus. The Greek Apollo, Artemis and Hercules appear as Aplu, Aritimi

and Hercle. No doubt many of the gods had mythologies of their own before they were identified with Greek counterparts.

The Greek Charon and other lesser deities of the underworld gained increasing importance as this aspect of the future loomed larger in Etruscan thought. Other deities had local or family names, and the city of Populonia near Piombino may have been named after Fufluns. The process by which alien deities might be welcomed into the Etruscan pantheon is illustrated by the Pyrgi inscriptions which record the introduction of the Punic Astarte into the Sanctuary of Uni with the name Uni-Astarte. In addition, there were many groupings of gods and a host of minor deities. Beside the triad of Tinia, Uni and Menrva, there were the 'nine' gods who hurled lightning, *Dei Superiores* who counselled Tinia about when to throw his worst thunderbolt, other advisers named *Dii Consentes*, the Penates, the Lares and others, many of whom were perhaps regarded as gods of fate.

The gods were worshipped in temples, the earliest known dating to 600 BC. It may be that open air sanctuaries with altars were used in more primitive times. The temples were set in sacred precincts, usually against the rear wall, with an altar standing in the space in front. They contained the cult statue of the god: the most famous surviving one is the terracotta statue of Apollo at Veii near Rome.

The tomb frescoes, with their scenes of feasting and dancing and their more sinister glimpses of torturing demons, suggest the

prospect of paradise or hell in an afterlife in which the individuality of the dead survives. Since the wealthy were buried with great riches – shields, weapons and chariots for the warriors and jewellery and toilet articles for the women – the fortunate may have hoped for a continuation of the joys of earthly life. The horrors of hell prefigure the demons of Michelangelo and Dante. The gruesome figures of Charun with his hammer and the vulture-beaked Tuchulcha with donkey ears and armed with serpents, carry off the dead. The parting, when the dead man starts on his long journey, either on foot, horseback, chariot or boat, is vividly shown on many sarcophagi.

Livy described the Etruscans as 'a nation more than any other dedicated to religion, the more so as they excelled in practising it', while the Christian writer Arnobius later described Etruria as the 'creator and mother of superstitions'. The general impression is that unlike the Greeks, the Etruscans felt the insignificance of man dominated by fate and the divine will. Heaven and earth were closely linked, the vault of heaven being orientated and divided up into sections where lived the various deities; sacred areas on earth were correspondingly orientated and divided.

Much of Roman religion and ritual was concerned with appeasement of natural forces: three Etruscan musicians with pipes and zither on a tomb fresco in Tarquinia; Roman ceremonial practice required constant flute music to avoid ominous sounds.

Gods and Goddesses

Diana

The classical mythology of Artemis tells that she was the daughter of Zeus and Leto and the sister of Apollo. In some of the stories Artemis was born first, with no pain, and immediately acted as midwife to her mother for the birth of Apollo, thus prefiguring her later care for mortal women. The evolution of her character is a good example of the transition from the pre-Hellenic to the Hellenic world in Greek mythology and of the resulting confusion. Artemis's name is apparently not Greek. In Homer she is a rather ineffective partisan of the Trojans and is called *agrotera* (she of the wild) and *potnia theron* (mistress of wild beasts). She is the huntress, leading the life (as remarked by Charles Seltman in *The Twelve Olympians*) of an unmarried daughter of Homer's 'gay and brilliant feudal families', the goddess of 'energetic women' such as Atalanta, the better of men in hunting and wrestling yet 'unwilling to wed any of them'. The analogy with the sports-mad young ladies found among the New England rich is not too far-fetched, given changes in space, temperament and time.

Although the later Greeks and the Romans certainly regarded Artemis as a virgin, this was not the view of the earlier Greeks. To them, she was celibate but above all independent – if she wanted a man, she would have one but she would not be bound to him. However, as the comparatively uncomplicated, guilt-free Homeric past slid away, Artemis changed from the attractively open-air girl, perhaps sometimes accompanied by an attendant lover, to the more forbidding character of the austerely chaste huntress.

It is in this role that the goddess is most familiar. This is the Artemis of Hippolytus, her virgin and, to most contemporary minds, priggish acolyte who repulsed the advances of his stepmother Phaedra and was destroyed (as was she) by Aphrodite; of Actaeon who, having by no fault of his own seen the goddess bathing naked in a spring, was by her changed into a stag and done to death by his own hounds; and of the later European imagination.

In the oldest, pre-Hellenic, stage and particularly in Asia, Artemis, though concerned with the wild, was one of the many manifestations of the mother-goddess, the source of life and fertility. In the mainstream of the purely Greek tradition, this maternal aspect was transmuted into a role almost that of the maiden aunt, the busy attendant at births, a companion of the young. On the periphery, and especially in the cult at Ephesus, the more overtly female, life-generating aspect remains to the fore.

But this concern and love for young things may also be connected with the boisterous side of Artemis's character. In the famous hymn by the Greek poet Callimachus (c 305–240 BC) the goddess asks Zeus her father to give her only nine-year-old girls as her companions: she appears as a kind of tomboy goddess. At Athens, for instance, girls of this age were dressed in bearskins to take part in a festival of Artemis.

The image of the bear (like that of the stag) runs through several of the Artemis legends. One of the best known concerns Callisto (the name means 'loveliest'), originally a Minoan forerunner of Artemis but in classical mythology a nymph in her train. There are many versions of the story. In one, Zeus seduced her in the form of a bear; in another, Hera, enraged (yet again), turned Callisto into a bear and tricked Artemis into

Statue of Diana; as a pagan deity, goddess of the moon and patroness of witches, she was regarded as a demon by the early Christians.

killing her; in a third, Artemis discovered Callisto to be pregnant and herself turned her into a bear and shot her. The victim was transported to the skies as the constellation of the Great Bear (the Plough) and her son was Arcas, the ancestor of the Arcadians. Some say Arcas had a twin brother, none other than Pan.

In one of the stranger versions of the Callisto story, Zeus had his way with her after assuming the form of Artemis herself. This is an example of the strand of what we would call lesbianism in the legends of Artemis. It would be a mistake to put too

much emphasis on this; but her liking for exclusively female society, her savagery towards certain men and towards her female attendants if they involved themselves with men, all point in this direction. Some of her folk cults, indeed, were decidedly ambivalent, with male dancers impersonating women and girls sporting phalluses.

The link between Artemis and the moon, so evocative to later generations, did not emerge until the 5th century BC. It probably sprang from her concern with woman and from her brother Apollo's identification with the sun; but the connection is nowhere recognized in any cult, as far as we know at the present.

Much the same goes for her frequent confusion with the witch-goddess Hecate who, like her cousin Artemis, was also connected with the guardianship of women and the young in general. Nonetheless, these identifications gave rise to the eerily romantic image of the triple goddess, potent in the night sky, in the wilds of the earth and at accursed crossroads, where Hecate was worshipped and grim happenings occurred. On this darker side, Artemis was also credited with the power (and inclination) to send plagues and sudden death.

Although essentially a goddess of hill and heath, Artemis was revered as the chief divinity in three famous Greek maritime cities – Syracuse, Marseilles and Ephesus. It was in the last of these that her cult became particularly renowned. Tradition has it that the city of Ephesus was founded about 900 BC by Ionian Greeks who brought with them the worship of Artemis. These Ionians mingled freely with the local inhabitants and assimilated many Asiatic customs. Tradition also relates that the Amazons built a temple at Ephesus to house a primitive image of a goddess (later identified with Artemis), probably made of a palm trunk. This temple was destroyed by barbarians around the middle of the 7th century. About 100 years later the great king Croesus erected a magnificent temple which in time became one of the Seven Wonders of the World. The chief object of veneration, mentioned in the Acts of the Apostles, was a wooden statue of Artemis.

The temple was the recipient, over a very long period, of rich gifts, which often took the strange form of gold and silver panoplies and garments for the statue. These would be changed at intervals, rather as a child dresses a doll.

The most curious of these odd accoutrements were vestments to which were attached large golden representations of dates, giving the appearance of clusters of ample breasts. But oddest of all, on the head of the goddess was set a small shrine which probably contained the *diopet*, the most ancient and sacred thing in the temple. This was a small stone (possibly, in fact, a neolithic implement) which had been venerated in Ephesus since long before the Ionians came and which was believed to have fallen from Zeus in heaven.

Janus

The precise origin and earliest character of Janus eluded even Roman savants. His name denotes any passageway, usually the classical arch, and yields the common Latin word for 'door' *(ianua)*. The god was considered present in every door or gate. Nevertheless he remains best known for his function in certain public arched gateways which did not belong to a fortification system. It is not clear whether *ianus* primarily meant the passageway itself or its god. Equally unclear was Janus's function within the passageway.

The month of January and invocation of Janus by the Salian Brothers, an ancient priestly group, authenticate Janus's long-standing worship. The Salian Brothers, serving the god Mars, and the month were traditionally instituted by Numa Pompilius, Rome's second king, around 700 BC. Although over five centuries later it became the first month of the civil year, January was reckoned the eleventh month of the liturgical year. The reasons for making January the first month were entirely secular but the Romans interpreted the choice as a sign of Janus's protection of all beginnings, which had developed from his supervision of entrances. On 9 January Janus received his only regular state sacrifice, which took place in the Regia, the chief pontiff's house in the Forum, where Rome's priest-king offered a ram. Ceremonies on his behalf must have been observed at the famous arched gateways and his few temples on diverse occasions. Scraps of the very old Salian Hymns contained special prayer-songs to Janus. These were sung in March at planting time when Janus seems to have aided vegetation: rather curiously, since a god particularly concerned with passage-ways seems to have little relationship with a vegetation deity.

In the 2nd century BC, Janus appears in connection with two private sacrifices. One was made to Ceres, goddess of the growth of crops, and took place before the harvest. This association recalls the Salians' invocation of Janus as 'the good creator', for Ceres meant no more than 'growth' before her apotheosis. In the harvest ceremony Janus was invoked as deity, with Jupiter and Juno.

The second ceremony was an agricultural rite of Mars which required preliminary invocation of Janus and Jupiter. Preliminary invocation of Janus in these and a few other ceremonies is assumed to derive from his function as protector and promoter of beginnings. However, his name does not stand first in most prayers and rites. In the oldest surviving records the god belongs to a group of vegetation deities and deserves the name of good creator. The passageway does not occur in such invocations.

According to Roman belief Janus was exclusively Roman. Early in the 2nd century Rome's first specialist in the calendar stated that the name January came from Latium, a region surrounding Rome, and had not originated at Rome itself. The Romans also recognized Janus in a cult image taken in 241 BC from Falerii, a town of the middle Tiber valley. The Faliscans were related by language to the Latins and by culture to the Etruscans and Sabines. Rome remained the paramount centre of Janus's cult. Some of her oldest coins carry the usual and famous representation of Janus *bifrons*, 'two-faced'. Occasionally a four-faced Janus, *quadrifrons*, is mentioned. The former anthropomorphic Janus belonged to the simple passageway and the latter to the gateways comprising two intersecting paths, where Janus faced in the direction of each of the four ways.

Some of the god's epithets were thought

to indicate his divine functions; Patulcius and Clusivius (or Clusius) pointed to Janus being open or closed (from *patere* and *claudere*), while Consivius was related to the root of the word for sowing seed, which is *conserere*.

These old interpretations are subject to the linguist's doubt. Both Patulcius and Consivius seem to be found in Janus' Salian song. Other epithets are Junonius Curiatius and Quirinus. The first recalled Janus's association with Juno in the harvest ceremony. The altar of Janus Curiatius was paired with an altar of Juno Sororia. Curiatius must be referred to the *curiae*, primitive divisions of Rome. His rites may have comprised purification of adolescents on their coming of age and entrance to their ancestral curia. Quirinus belonged to the same civil system and his name also derived from this word. However, Janus Quirinus was worshipped by all the curiae and was a state god.

Janus Quirinus possessed the most famous 'temple' of Janus, situated off the Forum.

The origin of the shrine is clouded in antiquity overlaid by folktale. The small rectangular building had double doors at each end, which caused this Janus to be called *geminus*, 'twin'. The side walls did not reach right up to the roof, but were surmounted by grates.

A statue of the two-faced god was within this bronze enclosure that was presumably a monumental gateway on the street leading from the civic centre. This unusual temple stood as a symbol of war or peace to the

Roman coin with a double-headed Janus: the god facing both ways was believed to be present in every gate, door and passageway.

Romans. Many Latin writers confirm how the open Janus betokened war and the closed Janus peace, the opposite of what might be expected. In explanation of this anomaly, students in modern times have argued that Janus was imbued with the vigour of war and therefore was closed in peace and open in time of war. Except for the connection with Mars, who was also an ancient god of vegetation and fertility, Janus shows few signs of belligerence. Moreover, when Augustus Caesar closed Janus Quirinus to herald a new era free from civil war, he mentioned only one closing in 235 BC, some six years after the first war with Carthage. There is very little truly old evidence for understanding the occasion of opening and closing Janus, when one normally expects a gate or passage to be closed during war as a gesture of defence.

Jupiter

Rome's most important and powerful god, Jupiter came to Italy with the migrations of Indo-European speaking people. His name's first element, giving us 'Jove', is related to the Greek Zeus and to the Latin and Germanic words for 'day'. Its second element is simply 'father', bestowed on him and a few other Roman gods, just as Zeus was often so addressed. In their own literature the Romans transferred the many tales of Zeus to his Latin counterpart. Jupiter's cult was found in most parts of Italy and his functions readily became fused with those of Etruscan, oriental and north European gods of like character.

In Italy Jupiter was revered as lord of sky and daylight. Rain and its consequences were owed to him. Thunder and lightning were sent by this god whom Romans majestically represented with the thunderbolt and eagle which otherwise adorned every military standard. Because the ancient Italians trusted to natural phenomena in ascertaining the divine will, both thunder and lightning, together with the flights of certain birds were scrupulously observed as sent from Jupiter. All important public business could be validly transacted only if and when such heavenly signs were propitious. The Romans developed the interpretation of the signs into a fine art, the 'auspices'.

Official consultation of Jupiter probably led the Romans to accord him pride of place among the political gods of the state religion. Since Zeus, too, enjoyed a comparable position in many Greek city states, the Romans and others may have imported into Italy the idea of the god as a defender of the people.

Jupiter's religion exhibits a number of cult practices. On the Aventine Hill, for instance, Jupiter Elicius had an altar, or a mere stone, by which the Romans could summon heaven's gift of rain. Smaller stones might be employed to solemnize oaths, for Jupiter also stood as guarantor of man's good faith. This aspect of his worship strengthened Roman political reliance on Jupiter because he sanctified the many treaties which played a fundamental part in ancient warfare and diplomacy. Besides stones, some trees such as the beech and certain oaks were sacred to Jupiter; this attachment apparently arose from their relative susceptibility to his lightning. Thanks to his control of the rain, the god was beneficial to Mediterranean farming, and one of Jupiter's many festivals concerned successful grape harvesting.

Not only Rome's chief magistrates but also a priest and his priestess wife, the *flamen Dialis* and *flaminica*, ministered to Jupiter. No priesthood supplies a better index to the primitive quality which marks Rome's old religion. The flamen was compelled by law to observe and eschew many practices to which no other priest was bound, with the object of protecting him from pollution. Jupiter's flamen was forbidden to mount a horse, gaze upon the army, swear an oath, touch a corpse or enter a sepulchre; he must not wear a ring unless perforated and without a stone, lend fire from his hearth unless for prescribed rites, knot his clothing or hair, or walk under grape bowers; he was not permitted to touch or speak of female goats, uncooked meat, ivy or beans, or to eat leavened bread, or to uncover himself out-of-doors where he was seen by his god. On the other hand, he was required to have his hair trimmed only by a free-born barber, and the hair trimmings and nail parings were buried under a fruitful tree; to sleep on a bedstead whose legs were smeared with clay; to sleep no more than three nights away from home; to allow no one to sleep in his bed and to keep sacrificial cakes at its foot; and at all times to wear his special white pointed cap (*apex*). By an outmoded ceremony he wed only a lady of his patrician caste whom he might not divorce; if she died, he quit the priesthood.

His priestess wife, the flaminica, was bound by her husband's restrictions and by a few of her own. For instance, she wore specially dyed clothing, kept a twig from a fruitful tree in her elaborate head-dress, and did not ascend a ladder beyond the third rung. On certain days, she might not comb or arrange her hair although she apparently still wore the head-dress. Some of these restrictions obviously belong to the priest of a sky god; others are simple taboos against flatulence or corruption by the dead. It is little wonder that towards 200 BC the flamen botched a sacrifice, thereby forfeiting his office and that thereafter eligible candidates for the priesthood rarely came forward. Ceremonial limitations left many priestly functions to the chief magistrates, the consuls.

In matters of war and government the Romans ever looked to Jupiter for help and advice. His major shrine on the Capitol gave him the name *Capitolinus* although the official style was *optimus maximus* 'best and greatest'. This temple had three chambers, one each for Jupiter, Juno and Minerva. In the central chamber stood his statue garbed like a triumphant general in resplendent toga. Every fifth year the statue's complexion was reddened with lead paint.

The god it seems, as well as his triumphant model, had once been smeared with the blood of a fallen foeman. Founded by Rome's last Etruscan king, its liturgy was partly inspired by the Etruscans although the temple was dedicated by the new republican government in 509 BC. The god's puissance among the Romans encouraged them frequently to convene voting assemblies in its precinct. On the same height was situated the small temple of Jupiter Feretrius, a god of oaths. On its walls hung three sets of armour taken by Roman chief magistrates from enemy chieftains whom they had slain in battle with their own hands and dedicated to the god.

Jupiter enjoyed cult through public games that began as religious ceremonies and developed into those gorgeous spectacles for which the Romans were renowned. Feretrius's games included boxing matches and foot races held on oiled animal skins. Others comprised chariot races and, later, stage-plays produced under Etruscan and Greek influence. Like the triumphal games to which they are related, Jupiter's festivals were preceded by a lavishly-mounted parade of statues of almost every deity installed at Rome, of state priests and the magistrates. The statues were borne upon platforms which also held paintings and religious paraphernalia. His games fell in September, October and November and at one time totalled 29 days. On 13 September, he received a banquet in return for the rain which had made possible the harvest.

Of equal historical importance was the festival of Jupiter Latiaris on the Alban Mount. Since time immemorial the Latins foregathered to offer annual sacrifice under a rotating presidency from the several constituent peoples of Latin stock. In later republican times the sovereign Roman consuls presided over this religious remnant of a Latin league. A truce of the god secured the sharing of the meat of sacrificial victims by the assembled Latins or, later, by their representatives. From an imperial point of view the Roman consul could no more omit this ceremony than he could fail to greet Capitoline Jupiter before and after his military expeditions.

While in late pagan times Jupiter's divinity attracted astrological and philosophical speculation and quickened religious syncretism (or intermingling), his Roman cult retained the savour of its simple beginnings and propagated veneration of the Empire's greatness. From first to last the Romans acknowledged him as their patron and lord.

Jupiter, or Zeus, as an eagle, bearing off Ganymede: statue by Cellini.

Scala

The Lares

As tutelary deities the Lares usually protected a given place which supplied them with their distinguishing epithet. Far and away the most frequent, if not oldest, manifestation is met within the household *(familia)*, where the single Lar Familiaris (Household Lar) received regular monthly offerings of garlands on the hearth as well as daily observance at mealtimes. This Lar protected the household and its wealth, no matter how small, and was invoked on important family occasions: sometimes he also gave oracular signs to the householder. The Lar in fact came to symbolize the home.

In the oldest fully surviving Latin prayer, however, the Lares, together with Mars and certain 'seed gods', are invoked by the Arval Brothers (an ancient Roman college of priests) at the boundaries of the cultivated land *(arvum)*. Where two fields joined, the Lar of each boundary line was honoured by the farmer and his slaves; both the convergence of boundaries and its marker were called *compita*. The compital shrine was a small tower with niches for every Lar thought to be present; here the Lares Compitales were found. Because the boundaries of property were usually marked by a path or a road, the Lares Compitales are best known from worship at rural crossroads and busy urban intersections. Sometimes they were the only or chief deities at country junctions where a hamlet comprised a few huts. At a normal junction, made by two roads, two Lares would be jointly worshipped; the practice became established, so that no matter how many lines converged, only two Lares were thought present. Even the Lar Familiaris was depicted in duplicate, although each household had only one Lar. The Lares Semitales were venerated for their protection of paths *(semitae)* and the Viales for their protection of highways *(viae)*.

The great annual festival of the Lares was the movable feast of Compitalia, which fell soon after the winter solstice. Like other winter festivals Compitalia called for artificial light, and the liturgical use of candles first appears here. Indeed, not a few aspects of Compitalia became an integral part of the Western Christmastide. The Lares' victim was the pig, which remained traditional Christmas fare until challenged by fowls.

Very early the Lares enjoyed the veneration of the humble and came to be the most important gods of society's lowest stratum, slaves and freedmen. Such people were of alien extraction, and the Lares exercised a strong force in their assimilation into Roman society. Slaves and freedmen especially observed Compitalia, for it was one of the few state cults to which all persons were admitted, regardless of condition. Much merrymaking accompanied performances of crude, extemporaneous farces. As early as the 5th century BC the Roman government expressed concern over the intrusion of foreign rites at the urban compita. It is highly likely that its first importation of foreign drama was by foreign slaves and freedmen into the winter festival.

Rome and her colonies were officially di-

vided into neighbourhoods *(vici)*, and the countryside into villages (also *vici*), to which belonged a public cult of Lares Vicinales or Compitales. Because the greater population often consisted of slaves and freedmen, the freedmen mayors and slave attendants of each neighbourhood and village supervised regular worship. Shortly after 12 BC, Augustus Caesar converted this cult into the worship of the Lares Augusti, Lares of 'increase' associated with the worship of his *genius*, his personal 'procreative force'.

Every householder's genius had been propitiated beside his Lar Familiaris; in this way Augustus successfully adapted a long established cult to the new Imperial religion without imposing his direct worship in Italy (though outside Italy he was directly worshipped). On compital altars portraits and symbols honoured the emperor and his family; sometimes Augustus donated statues of neighbourhood gods, who acquired the epithet *Augustus*. In the months of May and August the altars were strewn with flowers on his behalf.

At many Roman intersections the Lares' marble altars stood before a small temple housing statues of two Lares and a genius. At most compita in Italy stood a simple altar of stuccoed brick, built against a wall on which were painted the three figures. Lares were represented as Greeks wearing tunics and holding a wine bucket and Greek goblet; usually they appeared to dance while their faces betrayed tipsiness. In contrast, a Roman toga clothed the genius, who held a sacrificial saucer and cornucopia.

Above *Two Lares, depicted as young men wearing short tunics and holding wine buckets and goblets, are painted in dancing posture on either side of a genius, or guardian spirit, dressed in a Roman toga; this shrine is typical of the altars which stood at many Italian boundaries and crossroads. Lares, who were usually shown in duplicate, were particularly venerated by the lower classes of Roman society.* **Facing page** *Mars was concerned with both agriculture and war, and the Roman infantry always met on the 'Field of Mars'. He was equated with the brutal Greek war god, Ares, from whom most of his mythology was borrowed, including the story of his liaison with the love goddess. Effigy of Mars on a Roman coin of the 2nd century* AD.

Lares rarely enjoyed grand worship in state temples. Among the exceptions were the Lares Praestites, 'protectors' of the Roman people. The 'grunting' Lares Grundules, called after the pig victim, numbered 30 and probably protected the 30 civil divisions. The title 'Lar' could also be applied to other gods, such as Silvanus, lord of the forest.

Aeneas, the legendary Trojan ancestor of the Roman people, is addressed as a Lar on a dedication of around 300 BC. This designation very probably reflects the custom of adding the appellation Lar to foreign deities or heroes after their cult had been appropriated to themselves by slaves and freedmen.

Mars

Among the ancient Italians there was no greater god than Mars, after Jupiter. He was known by an unusual variety of cult names: Mars, Mavors, Maurs, Mamers, Marmar, Marmor, Mamurius, and the honorific compound Marspiter. Many Latin and neighbouring communities named a month after him, and our month of March preserves the memory of his veneration. The Roman month *Martius* embraced the spring equinox and by its season reinforced the god's oldest functions in agriculture. March marked the first month of the oldest known liturgical year at Rome. Certain state priests promoted the growth of crops at the onset of the year, prepared for the new year by cleansings and otherwise marked what we today keep as the New Year. For a time 15 March opened the official year but later yielded to 1 January, which acquired from 1 March such customs as decoration with evergreens. However, March retained many ceremonies of the new year as well as the constant cult of Mars which mainly entrusted to the Salians, priests whose title seems to be derived from *salire* 'to dance, leap'.

On fixed days in March the Salians proceeded along an established route where they would stop at certain points and perform rites that included the chanting of some of the oldest hymns in the Latin

British Museum/Michael Holford

language, beating time on the ground according to the ritual three-step, and carrying outmoded spears in which Mars lurked, and shields, one of which was sent from heaven. Their dancing and beating of spear on shield was probably thought to advance the growth of the crops. However, the priests' military accoutrements and the regular resumption of warfare in March always underlined the god's martial aspects. The surviving scraps of the Salian Hymns mention many Roman gods, and Mars himself in the form *Mamurius Veturius*, evidently the Mars of the old year. The hymns certify the Salians' concern for agricultural growth and the welfare of the infantry (armed with spears of a kind different from those which the priests themselves carried). Much of the Salians' intervention with their god was directed toward cleansing the community and its utensils.

Peculiar to Mars in Roman religion is the use of the horse. On 14 March a racing festival, *Equirria*, was kept for Mars on the Campus Martius, 'Field of Mars'. On the same ground every 15 October another race was run, after which a horse of the winning chariot team was sacrificed to Mars. The blood of its tail was dripped onto the hearth in the king's former residence, the Regia. The ashes were later compounded with the cremated remains of unborn calves sacrificed on 15 April and applied in the cleansing held on 21 April, Rome's birthday. The horse's blood may have been intended to ward off barrenness, while the cremated calves were sacrificed to invite fertility into the community.

A third race came in late February and presumably marked the end of the old year. The last month of the liturgical year was crammed with cleansing rites. The *Quirinalia* in February honoured Quirinus, an epithet sometimes applied to Mars. Both Mars and Quirinus had Salian priesthoods as well as their own *flamen*, a Roman priest peculiarly bound by a set of religious restrictions. Quirinus as a distinct god was an offshoot of Mars who acquired considerable prestige of his own. As a promoter of peace, Quirinus represents the willingness of Mars to cease warring and to accept terms from the enemy.

At the end of May another priesthood, the Arval Brothers, annually kept their agricultural cult by invoking the name of Mars thrice in three different forms, by thrice repeating the petitions and by dancing the ritual three-step (*tripudium*). No older prayer than the Arval Hymn fully survives to us. After having invoked the help of the Lares and before and after inviting the seed gods, the Brothers begged Mars to prevent the invasion of blight and the collapse of growing grain, to leap the boundary and to remain on the land. This prayer was sung five miles from Rome, apparently at the border. The god's arrival by avoiding contact with the boundary itself demonstrates an irrational fear which still survives: brides are carried over the threshold lest their stumbling bring barrenness. Mars was expected to remain on the land, but not to import barrenness. His protection of Roman ploughland (*arvum*) is paralleled by old evidence from one Umbrian town where, like the Campus Martius, two fields belonged to the Martial woodpecker, where Martial Growth (*Cerfus Martius*) was hailed for cleansing the community and for damning foreigners, and where this Martial Growth controlled two divine powers, Protection and Fright.

Just as old but less clear at the outset is the Mars who was the god of war. The Salian priests certainly observed in part a cult of war. After it became a formal republican assembly of all citizens, the Roman infantry always met on the Campus Martius and never within the city's sacred boundary (*pomerium*). The Field of Mars held the oldest known altar to Roman Mars. At the only archaic temple to Mars, which stood over one mile from the city on the Appian Way, the cavalry formed for its annual parade into the town, and the infantry rallied at the out-

set of a campaign. Consequently it is often asserted that Mars was purposely kept from the city because he was bellicose. Indeed he was worshipped outside where the Romans expected him to promote growth. However, the Salians worshipped him only in the city and there, too, kept their shields and spears, which they addressed 'Mars, awake!' The early lack of urban temples does not prove, however, that Mars was solely a war god in origin.

Some of the Martial temples may be of relatively late construction on sites where he did the greatest good, on the land. The Emperor Augustus greatly enhanced the god's material condition at the end of the last century before Christ. In 53 BC, the political and financial magnate Licinius Crassus had gone to Parthia (modern Iran) to seek military glory. Instead, Crassus was slain, his army routed and massacred, and his standards captured. Julius Caesar and Mark Antony vainly hoped to recover the first standards lost to an enemy within memory, but the former succumbed to death and the latter to Cleopatra. It was left to Augustus to recover the standards by diplomacy.

Not only did he choose to represent his success as a military victory by depicting a kneeling Parthia and a triumphal arch on his coins, but he also lodged the standards in one of the two urban temples he built for Mars Ultor, 'the Avenger'. Thus Augustus made Mars responsible for a real military victory over Caesar's murderers at Philippi, as well as for a revenge upon the invincible Parthians. The Avenger's temple in Augustus's forum attained such importance that the grand plaza gradually exchanged the Emperor's name for the god's. Until some 40 years ago the street of Christian Rome which ran above the Forum Augustum was still called Via Marforio.

The early equation of Italic Mars with the Greek Ares lent great emphasis to the literary role of Mars as war god. Ares appears in Greek poetry mainly as a divine personification of war and violence. Some argue that *Ares* means 'destroyer', which if true would explain his relative lack of cult. Ares enjoyed prestigious family connections in mythology, where he is represented as a most unpleasant god. In terms of divinity Ares cannot compare with Mars, but most of the mythology of Mars was borrowed from Greek poets. Two peculiarly Roman tales show the difference.

One explains why the month of Mars comes at the year's beginning. The god sought Minerva in marriage. The withered hag of a matchmaker, Anna Perenna, pretended to have gained Minerva's consent, but herself wed Mars. The festival of Anna Perenna (which means little more than the 'everlasting year') fell on 15 March when a riotous and promiscuous mob kept her holiday.

In another Roman legend Mars figures in the foundation of Rome, whose story abounds in Martial religion. Mars fathered the founder of the city on an unwitting virgin. The Romans believed this paternity foreordained Rome's unsurpassed glory in arms.

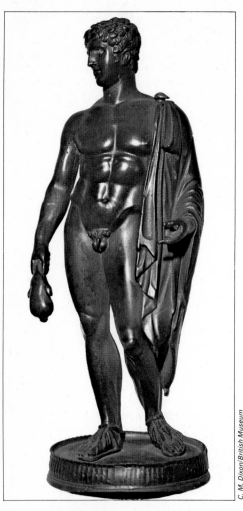

C. M. Dixon/British Museum

Mercury

The name of the Roman god of trade derives from the Latin words for 'goods' and 'payment'. His worship thrived at the meanest level among tradesmen and shopkeepers. Unlike many Roman deities, he enjoyed no great state cult and priesthood. From first to last Mercury quickened business and fostered general prosperity. The Roman god of commerce was likened to the Greek Hermes who made him a literary gift of many attributes unknown to the Mercury of the true cult.

Rome's only temple for Mercury was dedicated in 495 BC on the Aventine Hill; its foundation accords with the major religious event at the beginning of the Roman republic. The Aventine region and its cults were especially important to plebeian politics. A famine in 496 was followed by the dedication of a temple on the Aventine to Ceres, Liber and Libera in 493. Although the trinity bear Latin names, they are in fact the Greek Demeter, Dionysus and Kore honoured with a temple built by Greeks and paid for with Roman money at the instance of the Sibylline Books of Destiny which contained the ecstatic utterances of the Sibyl, and which were a constant source and inspiration of Greek and Etruscan religion to the Romans.

Sometimes it is assumed, perhaps correctly, that Mercury's temple belongs to the influx of Greek religion and that it rose before the others in hopes that trade rather than

growth itself, Ceres, might have alleviated the dearth of grain. Whereas the temple to the trinity was destined to become an important religious and political centre for plebeian political aspirations in the face of patrician exclusion, Mercury's solitary temple never acquired great glamour despite its obvious popularity.

Every May, on the anniversary of its founding, the temple became a meeting place for Roman merchants. Like many another club this guild met the businessmen's need for a religious association and for an expression of solidarity. (Craftsmen met under the protection of Minerva and had their own guilds.) The month of the dedication and the annual meeting seem purposely chosen to honour the Greek Hermes' mother, Maia. Since the Roman Mercury had no such mother, the Roman state and its merchants were apparently influenced in worship by Greeks, even down to mythological details.

The temple and its cult were entrusted to a board of *Mercuriales* who were drawn from the second rank of society, in contrast with the social eminence of other Roman priests. In two cases membership on this board was combined with membership on the board of *Capitolini*, who were in charge of the Capitoline Games held in honour of the great god Jupiter. One man boasted that he was the elected leader of the Capitolini, Mercuriales, and the residents of the Aventine district; this priest had made his career first in the Roman army and later in the lower rungs of the civil administration under Augustus.

Clubs of Mercury sprang up wherever Latin-speakers went. These businessmen's associations sometimes styled Mercury *Felix* and thus retained the older sense of the word, 'productive, prosperous'. Despite the paucity of temples, Mercury was frequently honoured in Rome and other business centres with altars, statues, murals and even small roofed shrines set especially at urban intersections.

The neighbourhoods worshipped him alongside their ubiquitous, guardian spirits called Lares. Augustus took a keen interest in fostering his lowly cult; accordingly, Mercury assumed the epithet Augustus which recalled not merely the Emperor's devotion and benefaction but equally that title's derivation from the verb *augere*, 'to increase'. Before the time of Augustus, neighbourhood Mercuries acquired such peculiar titles as *Malevolus*, 'Ill-willing', in the case of one who faced no shop, and *Sobrius* where he was honoured by a milk libation in a district without a tavern. In contrast to the latter is a guild of wine merchants who were incorporated as the Club of Father Liber and Mercury. Liber was the Roman god of vine and wine.

In poetry Mercury always reflects the Greek Hermes. In one Roman poem he is made to sire the Roman Lares, who earned this prestigious parent through the humble association of neighbourhood religion.

As far as astrology is concerned, simplicity was never a characteristic of this planet, for it was thought to influence the entire field of education, including all types of learning. Intellectual brilliance, quick-wittedness and

scholastic ability are therefore typical of people born strongly under Mercury.

Mercury rules trade and commerce and those born under this planet are always intrigued by technical skills, and are often knowledgeable about trades such as carpentry and engineering. A Mercurian will always have an answer for any question; and although it may not always be correct, it will at least be glib and convincing. Although not all Mercurians are plausible rogues, the plausible rogue will almost always be a Mercurian.

The shy, timid and tongue-tied people of this world need the Mercurians to speak up for them, and a discussion about whether or not the time is ripe for wages to be raised often turns out to be an argument between two Mercurians. It is likely that neither of them will become heated, for Mercury often appears to be rather cold and aloof, even in sexual affairs; unlike many people, Mercurians think of these as just a part of the glorious game of life. When they marry, many of them do not really take their partners 'for better for worse, for richer for poorer . . . till death do us part' as they think that if necessary the game can be played with a different partner.

The Roman god of commerce, Mercury was the patron of businessmen, and was frequently honoured in the trade centres of the Roman world. **Below** *Pottery urn in the shape of a face, with a dedication to the god around the base, 1st century AD.* **Left** *Bronze statue of Mercury holding a purse.*

Louvre/C. M. Dixon

Mithras

During the period between 1400 BC and
400 AD Persians, Indians, Romans and Greeks
worshipped the god Mithras. The god was
particularly important in the old polytheistic
religion of the Persians between the 8th and
6th centuries BC and again in the Roman
Empire in the 2nd and 3rd centuries AD. No
direct evidence remains of Persian paganism,
and if we wish to get an idea of this poly-
theistic religion we must fall back on re-
construction from texts of a later period.
Plenty of material is available, however, and
many points can be discovered which are
very probably accurate.

There are four important sources for
Mithraism. The first is a cuneiform script
tablet from Boghaz Koi in Turkey which
contains a contract between the Hittites and
the Mitanni, an Iranian-speaking tribe in
Mesopotamia c 1400 BC. In this contract,
Mithras is invoked as a god before whom an
oath may be sworn. Secondly, there are some
Indian texts in which the god Mitra appears
as a 'friend' and as a 'contract', and has connections with the sun. Unwillingly, he par-
ticipates in the sacrifice of the god Soma,
who frequently appears in the form of a bull
or as the moon. Thirdly, great hymns of
praise (*yashts*) were written, probably in the
5th century, in honour of Mithra and the
goddess Anahita. The Mithraic yasht ex-
tolled the god as the Lord of Contract, who in
war grants victory and in peace prosperity.

*Roman relief of the 3rd century AD, from
one of the Mithraic sanctuaries, which were
constructed underground, showing the god
sacrificing the bull. It was this act which
created the world, for all living things on
earth arose from the body, blood and seed
of the bull.*

Sacrifice of bulls was part of the cult. It is closely connected with Mithras as god of contracts, as in ancient times contracts were sanctioned through common sacrifice and a common feast. According to Plutarch, Mithras was the 'mediator'. This corresponds to what we know about the old Persian Mithras. The contract as a bond between humans, friendship and feasting after the sacrifice which was a unifying force, and the sacrifice itself linking men with the gods are all examples of Mithras's role as a mediator. Mithras, the sun, was in old Persian times also closely connected with kingship. People swore oaths by the king and by the sun. Kingship also incorporated above all else the idea of law and order at a time when the abstract concept of the state was still unknown and there were no written laws. Order was visibly present in the person of the king; the king was the law, and when he died chaos erupted, as law and order were gone.

The Persian social system was feudal, in the sense that there were no abstract legal rights and duties but only reciprocal personal obligations between man and woman, parents and children, lord and peasant, and so on. Mithras, who represented law and order, was the divine exponent of the Persian system as god of contracts and of all reciprocal relationships.

After the destruction of the Persian Empire by Alexander the Great nothing more is heard about the Persian worship of Mithras. Yet over three centuries later Mithras was worshipped in the states between the Parthian Empire and the Graeco-Roman world, for example in Armenia, where Mithras was again god of kings and feudalism. In a Mithraic ceremony, King Tiridates I submitted to the Roman Emperor Nero in the 1st century AD and made his kingdom a fief under Nero's control. Mithras was also the god of the kings of Commagene, to the south of Armenia. It is likely that Mithridates of Pontus (1st century BC), the great enemy of the Romans, worshipped Mithras; his kingdom included the northern coast of modern Turkey, and the Crimea. Finally, we know from Plutarch that the pirates of Cilicia, the south coast of Turkey, also worshipped Mithras during this period. On the other hand, Mithras was of no importance in the Greek-populated areas of Asia Minor. The Persians were the national enemies of the Greeks and consequently their god Mithras had no chance of success with the Greeks.

It is an open question whether the Roman Mithras mysteries were the same religion as the Persian Mithraic cult. The Persian religion changed to accommodate the different conditions of the Roman Empire. Certainly, many elements of the old religion were retained, but at the same time the Roman theology contained elements unknown to the Persians. For example, the Romans took their doctrine of the fate of the soul from Plato's philosophy. One could say that the Roman mysteries were a completely new religion. It may be that there were one or more founders of the new cult.

The sacrifice of the bull had been the great holy deed of Mithraism. The sun god, through his messenger, the raven, had commanded Mithras to sacrifice the bull; on some reliefs the raven flies to Mithras on a sunbeam. The god carried out the sacrifice with great reluctance: in many representations he is sadly averting his gaze, he is innocent of the animal's suffering. But when the bull died, a great miracle occurred – the world began: the cloak of Mithras was changed into a celestial globe on which planets, the zodiac and fixed stars were shining; the white bull, now a crescent, was moved into the heavens. (Luna, the moon goddess, is seen in the reliefs frequently averting her eyes from the sacrifice.) From the tail and from the blood of the bull arose ears of corn and the vine. Then came all the trees and plants, the four elements, the winds and the seasons; from the seed which issued from the bull there arose the good animals and all living things. This Mithraic deed was a blessing: 'Thou hast saved us also by pouring out the blood eternal', according to one of the few verses we have obtained from a Mithraic hymn. The power of evil wanted to prevent the creation; the scorpion, snake and lion try to drink the seed of the bull. Evil will not be destroyed until the end of time; as long as he is on earth man must always struggle for good and against evil.

Particularly instructive is a relief in London on which Mithras is sacrificing the bull not in the cavern but in the celestial sphere, which is indicated by the zodiac: the heavens arose following the sacrifice of the bull. Each sunrise signifies a repetition of this cosmogony. The stars began to revolve in the sky, and this was the birth of time. The sun circling around the earth caused the day, the orbit of the moon the months, and the path of the sun through the zodiac (the ecliptic) the years.

There are numerous other Mithraic myths to be seen in the reliefs, often in the small pictures near the main scene: the birth of Mithras from a tree; Mithras shooting at the cloud with an arrow (bringing the rain), or at the rock (causing a spring to gush forth); cutting the corn; taming the bull; his contract with the sun god; the holy meal; the ascent to heaven on the chariot of the sun god. The myth of the birth of Mithras from the rock has the same significance as the sun rising over the mountains on the horizon and the cosmogony in the sacrifice of the bull. The birth of Mithras from an egg depicted on the relief at Newcastle-upon-Tyne shows the egg turning into a celestial globe, represented by the zodiac; here Mithras is equated with the Orphic primeval god Phanes (Eros) who arose out of the egg.

The beautiful Mithraic statues of Venus, Mercury and Jupiter show that, as well as Mithras and Cronus, the god of time, the gods of the planets were worshipped.

Roman statue of Mithras: the god's cult was converted into a mystery religion, under the influence of ideas drawn from Plato. He made a powerful appeal to soldiers and imperial officials and was probably introduced into the legions by high-ranking officers from Rome.

G. Drury/Guildhall Museum

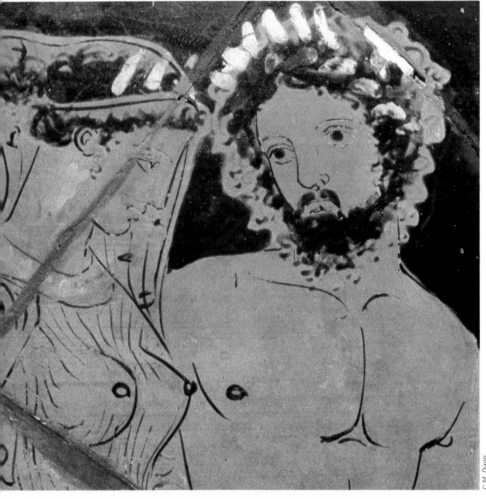

C M Dixon

The one celebrated action of Hades, or Pluto, in classical mythology was the rape of Persephone, whom he carried off in his chariot to his grim underworld kingdom, the home of the dead and common destination of mankind.

underworld as a warden of the dead, which would suit one of his titles, *pylartes*, 'fastener of the gates'. But this pitiless guardian of the dead was simply strict and rigorous; he was not any kind of devil, and his realm, except for some places where notorious offenders were punished, was not a hell, but the common destination of mankind.

A mythical object which by its name was connected with Hades was the helm or cap of Hades, *Aidos kynee*. The name has the general sense of 'cap of darkness' or 'cap of invisibility'. The cap is worn by Athene in battle against Ares in the *Iliad* (book 5), by Hermes in battle against the giants and by Perseus in his attack on the Gorgons. In myth it is not worn by Hades, nor in Greek art is it shown on his head, nor is it certain that he really owned it or lent it. The connection of the cap with Hades therefore remains obscure.

Hades or Pluto as one of the chthonic or underground powers has not simply the gloomy aspect which he wears in the epic tradition. He is not solely the lord of the underworld. This is obvious from the name Pluto, connected with *ploutos*, 'wealth', a word which originally meant particularly the wealth of crops which grow out of the ground and of precious minerals which lie beneath it. In this aspect he is thought worthy of cult by Hesiod: 'pray to Zeus beneath the ground', that is to Hades, as well as to Demeter. It was in this aspect again that Hades was associated in cult with goddesses Demeter and Persephone at Eleusis.

Hades is called 'another Zeus' by Aeschylus in his *Suppliants* and as Zeus *katachthonios* he is mentioned in Homer with Persephone as enforcer of a father's curse. He is in this sense a power supporting life and the family. He has also a title Euboulos or Eubouleus, which in translation means 'giver of good counsel'.

The entrance to the realm of Hades was seen in many caves and clefts to be found about Greece and also in parts of Italy settled by Greeks. The most famous in Greece were the cave of Taenarum in southern Laconia and a whole region of Thesprotia in the north-west. Thesprotia had rivers called Acheron and Cocytus and a lake called Acherusian, all of them names belonging to the mythical Hades, and also an oracle of the dead which in some traditions Ulysses visited when he had come to Ithaca and had to travel further on the Greek mainland. Pausanias remarks that Theseus and Pirithous invaded Thesprotia to carry off the king's wife. This looks like a version of their descent into Hades to carry off Persephone. The suspicion is confirmed by Plutarch, who says that the heroes went to Epirus to steal the daughter of Aidoneus, king of the Molossians, who had a wife called Phersephone and a dog called Cerberus.

Pluto

The god commonly known as Pluto in Roman times, and later, was also and more often in earlier times called Hades (*Aides*), though that name has come to be used in modern languages for the underworld where he lived as lord of the dead. In Greek there is also the form Aidoneus, used by Homer in the *Iliad* and in the Homeric Hymn to Demeter; in Latin he is called Dis, a translation of the Greek Plouton which means 'wealthy', and Orcus, commonly derived from the Greek *horkos*, 'oath', because his name was used in oaths. He is also called the subterranean Zeus (Zeus *katachthonios*) as in the *Iliad* (book 9). Among the gods he is the most hated by men, who rarely honour him with cult, and the most separate from other gods. He remains nearly always in his own realm, the House of Hades. The name Hades is generally agreed to mean 'the unseen one'. Hades is the son of Cronus along with Poseidon and Zeus, but he is very little active in Greek myth.

According to Homer, when Zeus and the other Olympians had overthrown Cronus and his Titans, Zeus divided the world between himself, Poseidon and Hades: Zeus had the sky, Poseidon the sea and Hades the misty darkness, while the earth and Olympus were common to all (*Iliad*, book 15). In the *Odyssey* Hades as a person is mentioned in Book 11 but always along with Persephone, and he does not appear. In the *Theogony* of Hesiod the underworld, including Tartarus

is described. It is a vast abyss and the prison of the overthrown Titans. Its entrance in the far west is reached by Day and Night in turn as they travel across the sky to 'the awful home of murky Night' which never holds both at once. Somewhere near the entrance, 'there in front', stand the echoing halls of Hades, god of the lower world, where he dwells with Persephone. A fearful hound guards the house. Fawning with his tail and ears on all who enter, he never lets them go out again; he devours whoever he catches attempting to leave. He is evidently Cerberus.

There is only one famous action of Hades or Aidoneus in Greek myth: his breaking through the earth with chariot and horses to carry off Persephone. The narcissus, which Persephone tried to pluck, had special links with the underworld. Horses, too, had a connection with it in its most alarming aspects, and Hades is often called *klytopolos*, 'owner of renowned horses' – an attribute which calls to mind the word 'nightmare'.

Hades is active once more in a curious myth told in the *Iliad* (book 5). Hercules wounded him with an arrow 'at Pylos among the dead' and caused him so much pain that he went up to Olympus to have the arrow drawn out of his shoulder by the healer god Paieon and the wound treated with pain-killing drugs. The commentator Eustathius explains that Pylos here is not the town mentioned in Homer but the gate of the underworld. This passage again suggests that Hades was often believed to have his dwelling near the entrance of the

Saturn

In literary presentations of classical mythology from Roman times onward, the figure named Saturn has been filled with the content of the Greek Cronus, one of the Titans who were sons of Mother Earth and who ruled before the Olympians and were overthrown by them eventually. Scholars have therefore tried to discover what kind of deity the Roman Saturnus was in origin, and why and when he was selected to be a Roman Cronus. It is a matter of some importance that in classical times the Greek Cronus seems to have been confined to myth, and hardly to have received any cult. This would be natural for a figure driven

from power by his son and therefore no longer important for human destinies.

The name of Saturnus was connected by such ancient writers as Festus and Varro with the sowing of crops (*Satus*) but this derivation is doubtful. It may be Etruscan, as F. Altheim has argued: he regards it as connected with the place-name Satrium and the Etruscan clan called *Satre*. This would mean that Saturnus was the god of this clan, but that fact alone would not show what kind of god he was. Festus mentions that Saturnus's name occurs in the very ancient song of the Salii, an archaic priesthood of the city of Rome. His festival the Saturnalia is recorded in the earliest form of the Roman calendar of festivals. He is connected with another deity – the goddess

Lua, to whom captured weapons were dedicated.

On an Etruscan bronze from Piacenza, which is in the form of a liver used in divination, the name occurs on the left or ill-omened side. But even this Etruscan origin does not exclude a close and very early connection with the Greek Cronus. Greek influence in south Italian and Etruscan religion goes back nearly to the days of the earliest Greek settlements of the 8th century BC. Why an Etruscan clan should adopt Cronus from the Greeks and rename him after itself is a question hard to answer, given his faded and mostly sinister character in Greek myth. But Greek religion of earlier stages than the Olympian mythology of Homer continued to survive in many parts of the Greek world. Its divine figures are little known, but Cronus may have been important among them.

The temple of Saturn was on the slope of the Capitoline Hill in Rome. There is little evidence from inscriptions outside the city for his cult in Italy. The festival of the Saturnalia was famous for the temporary suspension of the authority of the higher classes over the lower and of masters over slaves. Saturn, who as an exile saw the world upside-down, was the natural patron of slaves on such an occasion.

Saturn was also, rather oddly, connected with weights and measures, and the minting of coins: he was even guardian of the treasury. The Saturnian metre of older Roman poetry was a rhythm originally Greek but apparently adapted to a language of stress rather than quantity, as Latin was in earlier times. The adjective *Saturnius* had sometimes a special quality. *Saturnia Juno* means simply Juno as daughter of Saturn, as Hera was daughter of Cronus in Greek myth. *Saturnia tellus* in Virgil means Italy as a rich land reserved for the finest breed of men. But in *Saturnia regna*, 'Saturn's reign', there is much more of the Greek content of 'life under Cronus' when human life had been easier and gentler, before Zeus made it hard.

This is the usual character of Saturn in classical Latin literature. But his sinister aspect never disappeared, and in later astrological belief it became predominant.

The cruelty and crimes of the reigning Cronus, his exile at the hands of Zeus, and the gloom and despair in which he spent the rest of his days were well-known features of Greek myth, which reappeared in stories told of Saturn under classical Greek influence. To Greek myth, by the date when classical Latin literature arose, there had been added another element, the Babylonian lore connecting various gods with various planets. The influence of these planets on human destiny was the influence of these gods transmitted by a particular channel, and portioned out according to their predictable movements in the heavens.

Although the phrase 'Saturn's reign' was used to describe a time when life was easy and gentle, Saturn's connection with the Greek Cronus also makes him a god of melancholy character, full of gloom and despair: statue of Saturn, 3rd century AD.

Venus

The word *Venus* is related to English 'wish' and, more remotely, 'win'. The Latin common noun means 'charm', 'attraction', 'delight'. Its derivative verb *venerari*, which in antiquity also meant 'venerate', primitively signified the sacral act of alluring or enticing something from beyond mankind's power. Thus a famous literary echo of an old prayer reports the formal enticement of willingness from the god Quirinus (*veneror horam Quirini*). The goddess who sprang from the abstract *venus* forever retained the skill of wheedling.

Rome's foremost expert in religious history, Varro, was struck by the absence of Venus's name in the oldest records. Indeed Venus could not boast an old priesthood or festival or shrine at Rome. Further, Venus was unique in Italy. Etruscans spoke of Turan, 'Lady'. In the Oscan dialect the comparable goddess was Herentas, very similar in concept because the name is related to the aforementioned Latin 'willingness' and to English 'yearn'. There is reason to believe that Venus had not even been universal to the Latins of central Italy. She seems especially Roman and thus contrasts with Jupiter whom all the Indo-European speakers knew, or with Mars who, though native to Italy, was shared by all peninsular inhabitants.

Most of Venus's cult remains unknown to us. Some Romans insisted that the month of April was named after Aphrodite, her Greek equivalent. However, this folk etymology was based on the cult of Venus on behalf of vegetable gardens. As early as the late 3rd century her name signified the garden produce itself. The Romans consecrated gardens to Venus on 19 August, and vegetable gardeners kept the day holy.

There is no certain answer as to why Venus was related to the Vinalia, two wine ceremonies in the civil calendar on 23 April and 19 August. These festivals belonged to the sky god Jupiter. Aside from the coincidence of their worship on days of the Roman Vinalia, there is some Campanian evidence of a state cult of Venus Jovia. This worship can be construed in one of two ways. Either Venus is already identified as Aphrodite whom Zeus (Jupiter) fathered, or the goddess originated as the sky god's *venus* or, to use the local term, *herentas*. Of course, vineyards do not greatly differ from gardens. Also, in a sense, all plants need to be coaxed or wheedled to put forth their fruits. Such coaxing may be enacted by sexual representation. Be that as it may, no clear and direct evidence of such religious practice emerges from the ancient evidence on Venus.

At least as early as 290 BC, Venus was somehow associated with the August Vinalia because her first temple was dedicated on that day by a patrician, Fabius, who had built it with fines exacted for ladies' debauchery. Although it stood at least 600 years, this temple's activities are rarely mentioned. Venus's epithet Obsequens, 'compliant', and the source of the building funds point to an already existing identification of the goddess with the Greek Aphrodite and the Etruscan Turan, who were definitely goddesses of

female sexuality. Despite the sexual aspects of both the cult title and the ladies' misbehaviour, Fabius had a personal reason for the choice of his piety. He claimed that Venus had submitted to the wishes (*obsequi*) of his father and himself. The two Fabii had fought together in several campaigns against the Samnites and after the last Samnite war Venus Obsequens received her temple. Unfortunately, we do not know whether the Samnite Venus was worth conciliating in war.

Venus perhaps exercised some political sway among the Latins, for there existed two large precincts a few miles south-west of Rome where Aphrodite or Frutis, sometimes called Venus, were annually worshipped by all the Latins. One or both shrines, purportedly of great age, may have actually been related in cult to the widely renowned goddess of Mt Eryx on the western tip of Sicily. The Erycine sexual goddess was variously identified with Aphrodite and the Phoenician Ishtar. The Latin Frutis was said to have received her cult statue from Erycina.

One tradition explicitly equated Venus Erycina to the Aphrodite who bore Aeneas. Accordingly, the Trojan hero gratefully transported her cult to Cyprus, to Sicily and to Latium. Aphrodite occasionally had the epithet *Aineia*, which was interpreted to commemorate her maternity. The maritime route of Aeneas's legendary wanderings can be traced from one to another of Aphrodite's shrines. Some place-names of the western Italian coast preserved indications of Aphrodite in her role as protector of seafarers. Venus inherited these places as Roman rule spread.

After successive humiliations from Carthage's great general Hannibal, a direct descendant of the two Fabii observed what seems a family tradition and dedicated a temple to the true Venus Erycina in 215 BC. By this gift Fabius and the Romans placated a deity who had protected Carthage during the earlier Punic war and who was also an ancestress of the Roman people, through Aeneas who came to Latium and founded Romulus's line.

Venus Obsequens had received her temple at roughly the same time as the Romans first reared a statue group of Romulus and Remus being suckled by the she-wolf. Venus Erycina had been integrated into the Roman tradition of their non-Italian ancestry. Consequently Rome's Capitoline Hill, reserved for truly Roman gods, allowed a site for Venus of Eryx.

Venus is certainly connected with the month of April by the dedication in 181 BC of a third temple on the earlier Vinalia of 23 April. This Venus, another Erycina, had been promised a temple during a war with the Ligurians of northern Italy, whom the Romans reckoned distant relatives of the Sicilians. Situated just outside the city, the new shrine reproduced the very temple on Mt Eryx where temple prostitution still thrived. Rome's Erycine precinct attracted the city's less savoury residents. On 23 and 25 April prostitutes and the offspring of prostitution and pimping kept their holy days here. Late April and early May had become

The Italian Venus was identified with the Greek goddess of love, Aphrodite, who was the mother of Aeneas and so an ancestress of the Roman people: the 'Venus of Rhodes', Greek sculpture of the 1st century BC.

holidays given over to sexual promiscuity and stage plays. Since the 3rd century such rites, introduced under the influence of the Greek Sibylline Books, had been consecrated to Flora, spirit of blossoming. They had their likely model in the cult of Aphrodite Antheia (Flora in Latin). For centuries the Floral Games provided notorious spectacles of sexual licence. Venus herself was not directly worshipped with Flora; nevertheless as divinity of produce and prostitution Venus belongs to the same kind of religious mentality.

The Sibylline Books reinforced the association in 114 BC, when the Romans were prompted to dedicate a temple to Venus Verticordia, 'Turner of Hearts'. Her name was intended to commemorate the acquittal of two Vestal Virgins charged with breaking their vows. Whatever the intent of the title, which is supposed to suggest the conversion from lust to chastity, Venus clearly retained her latent power of coaxing.

Through Cornelius Sulla, who briefly engrossed the Republican government by his dictatorship of 82–79 BC, Venus entered the realm of personal politics. Sulla, also her devotee in other ways, adopted the style *Epaphroditos*, 'Aphrodite's darling', which he rendered *Felix* in Latin. The latter style, which he may also have applied to a Roman Venus, comprised all notions of fertility, prosperity, success and good luck. At Pompeii a coastal colony of Sulla's veterans accorded Venus unusual prominence. The Pompeian cult perhaps combined Sulla's patroness with the town's continuing adoration of Venus Physica, Venus of Nature (*physis*), which preserved the Greek idea of growth.

In 55 BC Pompey the Great dedicated a temple to Venus Victrix 'the Winner', atop his theatre, which was the first permanent theatre in Rome. Opposition to its construction was probably blunted by the consecration to Venus. At about the same time, Rome's great poet Lucretius published his philosophical poem on Nature, in which he invoked for poetic inspiration Venus, ancestress of the Aenead race, and which he dedicated to Memmius whose clan corporately worshipped Venus.

The patrician clan of Julii asserted even stronger proprietary rights of ancestral cult for Venus since they claimed direct descent from Iulus, the Trojan son of Aeneas. Julius Caesar surprised no one by emphasizing his clan's rise to power in his own person by vowing a temple to Venus Genetrix during the battle of Pharsalus, at which Pompey was defeated. Caesar raised the temple (perhaps the first built entirely of marble at Rome) in his new forum and dedicated it in 46 BC, although his adopted son Augustus completed the work. Beside the statue of his ancestress Caesar set a golden statue of Cleopatra.

In the Greek East subject provincials joined Aphrodite with deified Rome in a religious demonstration of loyalty to the Empire and to the imperial house which Caesar had generated. Ultimate expression of the catholic loyalty of the Empire is met during the reign of Hadrian (117–128 AD). This emperor of Spanish birth devoted himself to the adornment of Rome, Italy and the Empire, whose ideal he generously cultivated with lovely and magnificent buildings. Hadrian did much to accord the provincials a sense of merit for their role in the Empire's government. To amplify his notion of imperial unity Hadrian built Rome's largest and handsomest temple to Venus and Roma, which he situated beside the Colosseum. Adoration of Roma, a provincial concept, remained unique to this temple. Each goddess had her own precinct, placed back to back. By universal usage this double temple was referred to as the City's Shrine. Hadrian chose to dedicate the temple on 21 April, the feast of Parilia, in order to honour Venus in her month and Roma on her birthday in the city's 888th year.

At Rome Venus was worshipped under other cult names. Most of these are easily understandable; Placida, 'pleasing'; Alma, 'nurturing'; Pudica, 'demure'. A few are most obscure, for instance Calva, 'bald'. The goddess's popularity extended throughout Italy and the Latin-speaking western Empire. She invited identification with lesser local divinities and found herself acquainted with universal notions. Thus she provides other examples of the Roman capacity to enlarge the concept and identity of their gods.

Near the great cemetery on the Esquiline Hill once stood a holy grove called Libitina where corpses were prepared for burial. The profession of undertaker was also *libitina*. Cult for and in groves was quite common but a grove cult for the dead was extraordinary. By the Imperial age the Grove of Libitina was no more than an address, and very probably just the name of a street. From the name of the grove, or from that of its tutelary deity, the Romans thought up a goddess Libitina. At some later point

they could not intellectually tolerate the plethora of insignificant divinities. Perhaps the very distaste for the subject of funerals had prepared the Romans to believe Libitina governed sexual desire (*libido*); thence the easy next step carried them to apply Libitina to Venus and to rear a temple to this goddess of lust. The word Libitina seems to have entered Latin from Etruscan, where it meant 'dead'. Libitina was not necessarily an Etruscan goddess, but a euphemism for death and its sequel.

Another example of a latterday Venus can be derived from a known locality. In early times the Romans knew the Little Aventine Hill as Mt Murcus. The valley between the

Gold votive figure of a Mycenean love goddess, with birds; doves were sacred to Venus.

Aventine and Palatine Hills was named the Murcia and was ultimately given over to the construction of the enormous Circus Maximus; this embraced a number of old religious sites, among which was an altar to Murcia. Murcia shared her name with the turning posts at that end of the racecourse. Being overwhelmed physically by the affairs and structures of the Circus and her link with the locality having been forgotten, Murcia became the subject of learned speculation. Her name was derived from the Greek *myrtea*, 'myrtle'. Since this shrub was sacred to Aphrodite, Murcia came to be another name for Venus. With the discovery of her new identity Murcia's cult seems to have perished.

Next and more perplexing is the case of Venus Cloacina. *Cloaca* is the Latin word for sewer. In uniformity with the need for

a deity to oversee every place and structure, a shrine to Cloacina was put up in the Forum over the Cloaca Maxima, the town's main sewer. The Romans fancied that cloaca was derived from a verb of cleansing. Further, they supposed that the goddess of cleansing must be Venus, because the local plant used for sacral cleansing was the same as the myrtle. Finally, both Cloacina's shrine and Murcia's altar were situated over running water. This Venus was humanly represented and her statue held a flower of some kind. By involutions peculiar to the ancient mind Venus became mistress of funerals, racecourse turning posts and sewers.

A last instance of Venus's acquisition of alien functions illustrates another Roman religious peculiarity. When the Romans entered Carthaginian Africa, they readily acknowledged the native goddess Venus Caelestis, 'heavenly' Venus. The existence of an obscure Greek deity, Aphrodite Ourania, perhaps promoted the Romans' acceptance of Caelestis. At any rate the ground was soon prepared for the introduction of the planetary week and the convictions of astrology. In the wake of these innovations Venus lent her name to the sixth day of the new week which still keeps alive Mesopotamian astrology in Italy, France and Spain, where Ishtar's planet is commemorated in Venus's day.

Appendix

Aesculapius
Roman name of the Greek god Asclepios, whose province was healing; patients came to sleep at his shrines and were cured by dreams.

Ceres
Roman goddess of corn and of the creative powers of the earth, the equivalent of the Greek Demeter; guardian of marriage, and associated with the dead under the earth and with the wine god; her name still survives in our word 'cereal'.

Cupid
The Roman god of love, identified with the Greek Eros: son of Venus or Aphrodite, the love goddess; frequently depicted as a beautiful winged boy with his bow and arrows, which arouse love in those they strike: like love itself, he is erratic and mischievous: the delightful story of how Cupid woos the mortal Psyche is told in *The Golden Ass* of Apuleius.

Ivy
Powerful magical plant, associated with holly and with Christmas; as an evergreen, connected with the Roman Saturnalia and other winter festivals to mark life's continuance and coming rebirth in the spring; plant of the Greek god Dionysus and the Roman Bacchus; the god was often depicted wearing an ivy wreath and his worshippers, the Bacchae, were said to chew ivy as an aid to attaining frenzy; also connected with inspiration and poetry, and believed to diminish drunkenness.

Juno
In Roman mythology, the wife and sister of Jupiter, identified with the Greek goddess Hera; she was the queen of heaven and protectress of females; she was particularly associated with childbirth and with the month of June, which was considered a favourable month in which to marry; at Roman weddings the bride's girdle was consecrated to Juno.

Left
Traditionally the side of evil; probably because the left hand is normally the weaker; black magic is 'the left-hand path' and to move deliberately to the left in magic is to appeal to evil influences; the Latin word *sinister* meant both 'left' and 'evil': in palmistry the left hand represents what you are born with, while the right what you make of yourself.

Libation
A drink offered to a deity, or the pouring out of the drink: the offering might be poured on the ground or floor, on an altar, on the body of a sacrificed animal, or on the fire; the Greeks and Romans poured a libation to the household god.

Manes
In Roman religion, the spirits of the dead; the name may be euphemistically derived from the Latin for 'good'; it came to be used for the spirit of an individual dead person but had earlier meant the dead as a collective group of divine beings, *Di Manes*; the dead had a festival in February, when they returned from the underworld to haunt the world of the living.

Minerva
Roman goddess, identified with the Greek Athene; patron of arts and crafts, and the inspirer of wit and resource, she was a protector of cities among the Etruscans.

Orgy
Sexual revel, usually assisted by dancing, drink or drugs, in which conventional restraints are thrown aside; in religious and magical contexts, based on the belief that release of the animal and irrational impulses of human nature brings an ecstasy in which man is raised to the level of the divine; the word is derived from *orgia*, the rites of the worship made to the Greek god Dionysus.

Penates
As a feature of Roman religion, the household spirits who were the 'gods of the food cupboard', in other words guardians of the family larder; they were worshipped in close association with another set of spirits known as the Lares and the hearth; food was offered to them at meal-times, and on special occasions, such as birthdays, they would be given cakes, honey, wine, incense, or sometimes a pig.

Saturnalia
The festival of Saturnus, to whom the people who lived in Latium attributed the introduction of agriculture and the arts of civilized life. It fell towards the end of December, at a time when the agricultural labours of the year were over, and in very ancient times it had something of the nature of a harvest-home of more recent times. It had much in common with the modern Christmas, and indeed many of the modern customs stem from it.

Vesta
The Roman goddess of the hearth, and the equivalent of the Greek goddess Hestia. She was worshipped at home as the deity of the family and her public cult was conducted in a circular shrine, which was looked upon as the 'hearth' of the whole community, and it was there that a perpetual fire burned, tended by the Vestal Virgins. For a long time matches were known as vestas since they provided fire.

Vestal Virgins
The priestesses of the sacred fire of Vesta in Rome; they were most probably the successors of the King's daughters who originally tended the fire on the royal hearth; from this function they became the national guardians of the nation's fire. If they let the fire go out they were beaten; chosen when they were small girls, they served for 30 years, during which time they had to remain chaste. This was often the cause of considerable scandals.

Villa of the Mysteries
A miraculously preserved villa which was excavated at Pompeii, the town which was overwhelmed by eruptions of Vesuvius in 63 and 79 AD; murals depict the rituals of the cult of Dionysus, of which this was the centre.

THE MYTHS OF NORTHERN AND CENTRAL EUROPE

Scandinavian Mythology

The three main gods who stand out in the myths of northern Europe, and of whom we learn also from carved stones and figures and scenes in metalwork, are Odin, god of inspiration, magic and the dead; Thor, god of the hammer, who preserved gods and men from giants and monsters; and Freyr with his twin Freyja, the best known of the fertility deities, the Vanir.

Odin was the ancestor of Scandinavian kings, and was worshipped by those who lived by their weapons and went out to plunder and conquer in many lands in the Viking Age; war captives and animals might be sacrificed to him and their bodies hung from trees.

Thor was the sky god and the god of the community, who supported law and order; the Assembly opened on his day, Thursday, and men took oaths on his sacred ring. The fertility gods were worshipped by men and women of all ranks, for all wished for health and prosperity for their families, their animals and their crops, and humble offerings of locks of hair and neck rings and pots of butter made to them have been found in the holy places.

Other divinities appear in the literature: Heimdall, watchman of the gods, sometimes called the father of mankind; Tyr who bound the Fenris wolf; Loki, the eternal mischief-maker; Balder, the fair son of Odin, who perished unfortunately by his brother's hand; Njord, the god of ships; Bragi, god of poetry; Hoenir, the mysterious silent deity, and Mimir, the wisest one, whose head was kept and consulted by Odin. All these occur in the tales and were known to the poets. They have varied and controversial origins; some perhaps, like Tyr, were once powerful gods whose names were replaced by others until they faded into legend; some were variants of the fertility gods Freyr and Freyja, like Njord and Idun who kept the apples of youth; some, like Bragi, may have been created by literary men out of the titles of the great powers. In his *Prose Edda* Snorri strove to bring these varied figures together into some kind of harmony, but even he found many problems in the way.

Besides the gods, there was a host of lesser supernatural beings who were said to inhabit mountains and rocks, forests, marshes and rivers, and who could both help men and do them harm. They might be called elves, land spirits, giants or trolls, and they were closely linked to special localities; they are probably as old as human habitation in Scandinavia, and after the conversion one of the fates of the old gods was to be relegated to this company.

There was much lore about the gods and their world. At the end of the Viking Age this was clearly pictured as Asgard, where the gods dwelt in their halls under the leadership of Odin. There were two other regions beside Asgard, Jotunheim, the abode of giants, and Hel, the realm of the dead, and these three kingdoms were said to lie under the three roots of the World Tree, Yggdrasill, which stood in the very centre of the universe. Middle Earth, the home of mankind, was joined to the realm of the gods by the rainbow bridge, which was called Bifrost. This picture must not, however, be taken too literally; tremendous distances divided these worlds, as appears from the impressive descriptions of journeys made from one to another through darkness, cold and vast spaces.

The creation of this universe is told in poems and stories. One tradition is that it was formed from the body of the giant Ymir, created in the beginning when heat and cold came together in the primeval abyss and life was brought into being.

There is reference made to a primeval cow who nourished Ymir, and also of the sons of Bor who slew him and created the worlds from his flesh and bones, eyes and hair. The first men and giants are said to have sprung from his body, although there is also a tale of the gods creating man and woman from trees on the shore. As all things had a beginning, so also they were of necessity brought to an end, and the myth of Ragnarok, the end of the world and its recreation, is among the most justly famous of the northern myths.

The account of Ragnarok in *Völuspá* is one of great vigour and imaginative power. Just as in the beginning life was created, according to a tradition recorded by Snorri in the *Prose Edda*, from the coming together of cold and heat, so these finally combine to destroy it, and the earth like a burning ship is consumed by fire as it sinks beneath the waves.

The gods are awakened to their peril by the horn of Heimdall, the watcher by the bridge, and by the crowing of the cock on the World Tree. Odin, who knew when Balder perished that the time of doom was approaching, rides swiftly to Mimir's pool to learn what is to come. Then he calls out his huge army of heroes through the many doors of Valhalla to advance against the enemy. He himself goes forward to meet the wolf, and is devoured. Thor meets his ancient adversary, the World Serpent, and strikes it down with his hammer, but is overcome by its poison and eventually falls beside it.

Tyr encounters the hound Garm, and each slays the other. Heimdall and Loki do battle together and both are destroyed. Freyr meets Surt, but has no sword to match the dazzling weapon of the fire giant. At the end Surt flings fire over the earth, and men perish with the gods as the land is engulfed by the encroaching sea.

Yet in this universal holocaust, some survive. The young sons of the gods do not perish; Odin's son Vidar slays the wolf by setting a foot on its lower jaw and tearing it apart; the sons of Thor inherit their father's hammer, which once more will defend the world from chaos. The mysterious power Hoenir survives, and Balder returns from the dead to live in peace beside his slayer Hoder.

It would seem therefore that these gods who are to rule the new universe have been sheltered in the World Tree, for from the Tree emerge the man and woman who are to repeople the world of men. Earth now rises anew from the sea, green and fresh and fair, and a new sun, fairer than her mother, journeys over the heavens.

Facing page '*The wolf Fenris shatters the magic cord which holds him and advances against Asgard, his gaping jaws filling the whole heaven. He devours the sun, and darkness comes upon the world.*' **The god Odin, summoning his army of heroes, goes out against the wolf and is devoured: Norwegian choir stall, 13th century.**

Gods and Goddesses

Balder

Balder is one of the most puzzling figures in the company of the Scandinavian gods. He is said to be a son of the great god Odin and is one of the inhabitants of Asgard, the home of Odin and his attendant gods, but we know little about him except for his death. There is no reliable evidence for a cult of Balder, no ancient cult centres associated with his name, no recognizable figures or carvings of him, no symbols associated with his worship. His name occurs in an early German spell (the Second Merseburg Charm) and the name *Baldaeg* is found in genealogies of the early Anglo-Saxon kings as the son of Woden (Odin), but these do not prove that Balder was ever known as a god to the heathen Germans.

Balder has received so much attention because of the moving story of his death, told by Snorri Sturluson, a great master of Icelandic prose, in his *Prose Edda* of the 13th century. A little earlier, in the 12th century, another learned but less gifted writer, Saxo Grammaticus of Denmark, wrote a long Latin history of the kings of his country, and included in the early books many stories of the old gods, among them the death of Balder.

According to Saxo, Balder was a human hero, although it is implied that he was the son of a god, and he was assisted by supernatural women who gave him a special food, prepared from snakes, which made him impervious to wounds. Balder wished to marry the maiden Nanna but he had a rival in another warrior called Hoder (Hotherus) who also went to the supernatural women for help. Following their advice, Hoder travelled to a land of cold and darkness and won a magic sword from its guardian, Mimingus. This was the only weapon by which Balder could be slain. There were battles between Balder and Hoder, in some of which the gods themselves took part, but in the end Hoder won the maiden Nanna, and wounded Balder with the magic sword. Balder was carried into battle on a litter, and died three days later from his wound. Odin went to great lengths to avenge Balder, disguising himself as a smith in order to woo a princess called Rind, by whom he had a son who grew up to slay Hoder.

In the better-known version of the story as told by Snorri, Balder was the son of Odin and Frigg, and was of radiant beauty, a youth beloved by all. He had ominous dreams threatening some calamity, and in order to protect her son Frigg asked all living creatures and inanimate things to give her a solemn oath never to do Balder harm. After this the gods found it amusing to fling darts and weapons at Balder, knowing that he could not be hurt. But the god Loki desired Balder's death. He discovered that Frigg had neglected to take an oath from a tiny plant which grows on the oak, the mistletoe, since it seemed too young to matter.

From it Loki made a dart which he gave to the blind god Hoder, suggesting that he fling it at Balder in sport. The dart pierced Balder, and he fell dead.

There was bitter grief among the gods, and they held a great funeral for Balder and burned him on his ship, together with Nanna his wife who had died of grief.

Odin sent a messenger on his own horse Sleipnir down the dark and perilous road to the kingdom of death and over the bridge of the dead, to bring Balder back. Hel, goddess of the realm bearing her name, agreed to release Balder on one condition: all things,

Ny Carlsberg Glyptotek, Copenhagen

Statue by H. E. Freund in Copenhagen of the god Loki, who caused the death of Balder. Balder was mortally wounded by a dart made of mistletoe, which had been overlooked when all created things swore never to harm Balder.

on earth, living or dead, must weep him out of Hel. At Frigg's summons all created things, men and beasts, plants, stones and metals, did indeed weep, as they may be seen to do after frost when the air grows warm. But there was one old giantess in a cave, called Thokk, who churlishly refused to join in the mourning for Balder. She was really Loki in disguise, thwarting the desire of the gods, so that Balder remained in Hel.

Other references to Balder in the Norse poems are brief but there are allusions to Odin's attempts to save Balder from death, to Loki's part in his slaying and to the

funeral of Balder attended by all the gods, a representation of which is said to have been carved in an Icelandic hall of the 10th century.

There are two separate ideas which appear to be deeply rooted in pre-Christian thought. First, Balder was either a son or a follower of the god Odin who, although god of the dead, was unable to save him from death. Odin's failure to do so brought about his own doom and that of all the gods at Ragnarok (the destruction of the gods). There are implications that a hostile power in the underworld struck at the gods through Balder, represented in Snorri's tale by the malice of Loki.

Secondly, the radiant god struck down by death and mourned by all creation strongly suggests a memory of a fertility cult, in which men lamented the death of their god. Their lament brought him back from the dead, so that spring returned to the world. The dying Balder carried round in a litter recalls similar traditions concerning Freyr and Balder's name, like that of Freyr, is thought by some to mean 'Lord'. Some have seen in this a likeness to the custom of weeping for the dead god in the Near East although it should be noted that there is no resurrection or rebirth in the story of Balder.

The connection with mistletoe, of which Frazer made so much in *The Golden Bough*, is itself problematical. There are traditions of a sword called Mistletoe elsewhere in Norse tradition, and there is also a very famous sword called Mimming, the same name as that of the sword's guardian in Saxo's story. Mistletoe does not grow in Iceland or western Norway, and this may be a foreign element imported into the North, replacing an earlier motif of a sword and a tree in the otherworld. The motif of a plant, not included in a general pact, which is used to slay a hero is one found in folktales of the Near East, and in a medieval Jewish legend about the cross of Christ.

The Balder story has reached us in relatively late literary sources, and the possibility of outside literary influences has to be borne in mind. There are certain striking resemblances in Snorri's version to legends about the crucifixion of Christ.

The Anglo-Saxon poem on Christ's cross, known as *The Dream of the Rood*, has a reference to all creation weeping for its king when Christ was on the cross. There are also folklore elements in the story, in the idea that the moisture of a thaw is Nature weeping for Balder, and in references by Snorri to a flower called Balder's brow and by Saxo to a burial mound in Denmark where Balder was said to be buried, out of which a stream flowed when men tried to break into it.

Indeed the whole subject of Balder is an extremely complex one but while scholars argue as to the earliest form of the tale of his death, there is no doubt that elements of this story at least formed an important part of the pagan lore of early Scandinavia.

Freyr, Freyja, Frigg

Archeological remains give us little help in visualizing these members of the Scandinavian community of gods and goddesses, since the only recognizable image surviving from the Viking Age is a little phallic figure in a pointed cap from Rallinge in Sweden, presumably an amulet, which is thought to represent the god Freyr. The goddesses go unrepresented, although their influence permeates the myths, and their symbols and those of Freyr are found continuously in pagan art. There is no doubt of the importance of these deities, and the medieval Icelandic historian Snorri Sturluson who collected many of the surviving myths, declared that Freyja alone of the gods still remained alive.

Freyr and Freyja were said to be the twin children of the Njörd, the god associated with fertility and the sea. They belonged to the group known as the Vanir, the deities of fertility, who were distinguished from the Aesir, the group to which Odin and Thor belonged. Frigg was the wife of Odin, occupying in the late myths the position of Queen of Heaven. It is not very easy however to differentiate her from Freyja. Both goddesses were invoked in child-bearing, both could fly in bird form, both were called weeping goddesses, and both were renowned as givers of good gifts to mankind. It seems as if they may represent different aspects of the ancient, ambivalent goddess of the earth who gave fruitfulness, and who ruled the realm of the dead. She was worshipped in Scandinavia from the Neolithic period, and small figurines of a woman with bare breasts, clad in a short skirt and neck-ring and with her hair in a plait, survive from the late Bronze Age, about a thousand years before Christ. In the myths of the Viking Age – from about the 9th century AD – Frigg appears primarily as wife and mother, while Freyja is the mistress of gods and men alike, accused of taking lovers everywhere and greatly desired by the giants. Possibly the older, Germanic Frija, wife of Wodan, who has given her name to Friday, was the predecessor of both goddesses.

Although we know little of Frija, one interesting myth about her has survived from an early chronicle of the Lombards, the *Origo Gentis Langobardum*, used by Paul the Deacon in the 8th century AD. Here Frija persuades her husband by a trick to give a name to the tribe who sought her help. She turned Wodan's bed to face the east, and then told the people to come out at sunrise, the women with their long hair hanging over the faces. 'Who are these Longbeards?' asked Wodan in surprise, and since he had bestowed a name on them, he was bound to give them the gift of victory that went along with it. There are similar stories of Frigg persuading Odin to support her suppliants, and it was said that she sent an apple to King Rerir, the founder of the Volsung race, when he sat upon a burial mound and besought her for a son: he shared the apple with his wife and the hero Volsung was born. The most important myth involving Frigg concerns the death of her son Balder. At his birth she sought to

protect him from harm by extracting a pledge from all created things not to hurt him but she overlooked the humble mistletoe that was finally instrumental in killing him. After his death she called on all the world to weep for him so that he might return from the realm of the dead. This is perfectly in accord with the widespread and ancient pattern of the Earth-Mother Goddess lamenting over her dead son found in many parts of the ancient Mediterranean world.

In the late Viking age however Frigg is overshadowed in the myths by the more vivid character of Freyja, called the bride of Vanir. Her name means 'Lady' while that of

Historiska Museet, Stockholm

In Norse mythology, Freyr was the god of peace, prosperity and fruitfulness, and there was a close link between the god and the king of the pagan community: grotesque Viking statue thought to represent Freyr.

her twin brother and consort Freyr means 'Lord', and it is made clear that she was worshipped under many different names. Some, like Gefn, emphasize her as a Goddess of Giving and others suggest an association with crops or with the sea. The giantess Gefion, who turned her sons into giant oxen to plough round the peninsula of Swedish Zealand and make it into an island to give to her Danish people, probably represents another aspect of the same goddess of fertility, associated with the sea as well as the underworld. Idun, guardian of the apples of eternal youth which kept old age away from the

gods, and which were once stolen by the giants with fearful results, may well be yet another personification of the same deity.

Freyja's famous treasure was her necklace (thought by some to have been a girdle) named Brishingamen, and this has been an attribute of the goddess since the Bronze Age. There is a story of how she obtained it from the four cunning dwarfs who made it, paying for her acquisition by sleeping a night with each in turn, and of how Loki stole it from her by entering her bower in the form of a fly, so that Odin could make use of it to strike a bargain with Freyja.

Freyr had his own ship, Skipbladnir, said to be large enough to hold all the gods, but small enough to fold away into a pouch when not in use. Tales of a supernatural boat which could travel with incredible speed may be linked with this magic vessel of the gods. There is a widespread tradition also of a boat which carries a divine child across the sea to become the founder of a kingdom, found in the opening section of the Anglo-Saxon poem *Beowulf*, and this tradition too seems to be associated with the Vanir. The practice of ship-burial, when the dead man or woman was laid on a boat in the grave, or burnt in one on the funeral pyre, seems to have been part of the Vanir cult.

Horses, pigs and birds, in fact all creatures associated with the fertility deities, were slain at the great ship funerals in Norway and Sweden in the Viking Age, while the seed-corn, hazel nuts and apples found in the Oseberg burial ship of the late 9th century are typical symbols of fruitfulness. It has indeed been suggested that the young woman buried with great pomp at Oseberg may have been a priestess of the Vanir. A beautiful little carved wagon was found buried with her, recalling the famous description by Tacitus of the journey of the goddess of fertility through parts of Denmark in the 1st century AD. He calls her Nerthus or Mother Earth, and describes her journey in a wagon unseen by men, bringing prosperity and respite from war and welcomed everywhere by the people. The resemblance between the name Nerthus and that of Njörd, father of Freyja, provides us with what may have been an earlier pair of deities of the fertility cult.

Freyr and Freyja owned a golden boar, named Gollinborsti or Goldbristles, reckoned among the treasures of the gods. The boar was a widespread symbol of the pagan period, especially on helmets, since it was thought to protect the worshippers of the Vanir in battle. One such helmet, surmounted by a gilded boar with gold studs for bristles and ruby eyes, has survived from the Anglo-Saxon burial mound at Benty Grange in Derbyshire, and similar helmets are pictured on metal plates from 6th century Sweden. The early kings of Sweden possessed helmets with names like 'Battle Boar', and these may have been used as boar masks in ceremonies connected with the Vanir.

The horse was also sacred to the Vanir, and there are references to horses sacrificed to Freyr, and of a horse dedicated to the god by its owner, which no man was allowed to ride. This forms the theme of one of the famous Icelandic sagas, that of Hrafnkel, priest of

Freyr, and while this is not a historical account, it probably preserves partly remembered traditions of earlier customs. There is every indication that the horse sacrifice, a regular ritual for centuries over a large stretch of Europe and Asia where horse-rearing played an important part in men's lives, was an essential rite in the cult of the Vanir. We have an account of Hakon the Good, the first Christian king of Norway, attempting to avoid the ceremony but being forced to conform by the people, and this describes the king presiding at the sacrifice, eating the flesh and drinking the blood of the slaughtered animal. The custom of horse-fighting, described in the sagas and also shown on early memorial stones, may have formed an essential part of the sacrificial ritual.

There was a close link between Freyr and the king of the pagan community, and ancestor kings in their burial mounds, like those at the sacred place at Old Uppsala in Sweden, appear at times to be identified with the god. Freyr was said to have been carried round the land to bring blessing to his people after death, before he was laid in a mound and the same is told of King Frod of Denmark, an early ruler whose reign was represented as a golden age. The name Frod was apparently borne by many Danish kings, and seems to have been another title of the Vanir god, possibly bearing the meaning 'fruitful'.

The main emphasis in the Vanir cult was on the maintaining of the existing order, and in particular of the seasonal round which brought new life and food to sustain it. Men turned to the Vanir for help by divination and Freyja's name is associated with one particular divination rite, that of *seidr*, which she was said to have taught to the gods. This was usually performed by a woman known as a *völva* or seeress, who sat on a high platform and fell into a trance induced by the singing of spells, after which she answered questions on certain aspects of the future, particularly about the coming season or the destinies of children. *Seidr* could also be a dangerous activity, used to bring harm and even death to others. There was one type of horse sacrifice too, when the skull and sometimes the whole carcass of the horse was raised on a pole and used as a hostile rite against an enemy. Such practices as these no doubt belong to the darker side of the Vanir cult, hinted at but seldom clearly defined in the literature, which led to bitter condemnation by the Church. The Vanir were indeed amoral deities, concerned not with justice nor morality nor the keeping of oaths, but essentially with the bringing of new life and power into the world. This power might be put to good or evil purposes, and such life-bringing deities are always worshipped in strange, even revolting forms, with orgies, ecstasies and sacrificial rites.

To some extent the cult would appear to rival that of Odin, god of magic, ecstasy and the dead, and the myth of the war between the Aesir and the Vanir, which ended in a truce may be based on this. Thus it was that Freyr and Njörd came to Asgard to join the Aesir, while both sides spat into a bowl to symbolize their agreement, and with its

Frigg, the Norse mother goddess and protectress, appears with the gods Thor and Wotan on a detail from the 12th-century Swedish tapestry of Skog in Hälsingland, in the Stockholm Historical Museum.

contents fashioned the wise giant Kvasir, from whose blood was formed one of the greatest treasures of gods and men, the mead of inspiration. Indeed the three main cults, those of Odin, Thor and the Vanir, between them covered the main needs and concerns of men, and while there was some overlapping and occasionally enmity between them, the picture as a whole is one of acceptance, and of the gods dwelling peaceably side by side, in accordance with the substance of the myth.

Loki

The ambivalent character of Loki – god or giant, jester or demon – presents one of the most tantalizing problems in Scandinavian mythology. Loki plays an important part in the myths. He carries out pranks which bring the gods into danger and then by his cunning rescues them again. He accompanies the great gods, Odin and Thor, on many enterprises and proves himself an accomplished shape-changer and master of duplicity. Finally, out of seemingly inexplicable malice, he causes the death of Balder and so opens the way to the catastrophe of the Twilight of the Gods.

In the myths Loki is closely associated with the treasure of the gods. One story tells how he mischievously cut off the hair of Thor's wife Sif, and Thor would have killed him had he not found two cunning dwarfs to fashion new hair from real gold. The dwarfs also made a magic ship for Freyr and a spear for Odin. Then Loki set two other dwarfish craftsmen to compete with these smiths, wagering his head that such treasures could not be equalled. The second pair made the golden boar of Freyr and Odin's magic ring Draupnir, and finally began to forge a hammer for Thor.

Fearing that he might lose his wager, Loki turned himself into a fly and tried to spoil the work, and as he stung the smith on the eyelid at a crucial moment, the hammer was left with too short a handle. Nevertheless the gods pronounced it the finest of all the treasures, and Loki only kept his head because he insisted his neck was not included in the wager and might not be touched; in the end they sewed his lips together instead.

When the giants try to steal the treasures of the gods, Loki is always involved. Once the giant Thjazi bore him off to the land of giants and only released him on condition that he brought him the golden apples which ensured the gods perpetual youth. Loki lured Idun, who guarded the fruit, out of Asgard and Thjazi bore her off with her apples, leaving the gods to grow old and wrinkled. Loki was threatened with death if he did not bring the apples back, so he flew to giantland in the form of a falcon, turned Idun into a nut and flew back, pursued by Thjazi in the form of an eagle. He reached the walls of Asgard just in time, and the gods set fire to a heap of shavings and singed Thjazi's wings, so that he fell into Asgard and was slain.

Another giant, Geirrod, captured Loki while he was journeying in falcon shape and starved him for three months until he promised to entice Thor to his abode without his hammer or belt of strength. Loki managed this but Thor was helped by a giantess who lent him her staff, another belt and iron gloves. Possibly Loki was also responsible for the theft of Thor's hammer by the giant Thrym. If so, he made amends, for he accompanied Thor, who was disguised as Freyja, on an expedition to retrieve the hammer and managed to allay all suspicions by his quick answers. There is also a tale of how Loki stole Freyja's necklace for Odin, turning himself into a flea and biting her as she slept so that it was possible for him to unclasp and steal away the treasure.

On another occasion Loki brought Odin and Hoenir into danger when, with a well-aimed stone, he killed an otter eating a salmon by a waterfall. The otter was the son of Hreidmar in animal form, and Hreidmar seized and bound the gods and demanded as payment for his son's life sufficient gold to cover the otterskin completely. Loki was sent to find the gold, caught the dwarf Andvari swimming as a fish in the river, and forced him to surrender a great golden treasure in exchange for his release.

Loki helped the gods once more when a giant was building a marvellous horse, Svafil-fari. The giant had been promised the goddess Freyja as his wife, with the sun and moon thrown in as extra payment, if he could finish the work in the course of one winter, and the gods became afraid that he would succeed and claim his reward. Then Loki turned himself into a mare and lured away the stallion, so that the giant could not fulfil the conditions and fell a victim to Thor's hammer. The result of Loki's encounter with Svafilfari was a wonderful foal with eight legs, and this became Odin's horse Sleipnir, who carried him on his journeys to the land of the dead.

Most of the Loki stories ended happily for the gods, with one important exception, which was the death of Balder. When the gods realized Loki's guilt, they resolved to kill him. He evaded them for a while in the form of a salmon, but Kvasir the wise found the shape of a burnt net among the ashes of Loki's hearth, reconstructed it and caught the salmon by its tail. The gods then bound him with the entrails of his son, beneath three flat stones. Above his head a snake dropped poison but his faithful wife Sigyn caught it in a bowl, and it is only when she goes to empty this that the writhings of Loki cause the earth to quake. He is doomed to lie thus until the end of the world, and in the account of what will happen at the destruction of the world Loki reappears to fight beside the giants and help to encompass the final overthrow of Asgard. A panel which seems to represent Loki in his bonds and Sigyn beside him with her bowl may be seen on the Gosforth Cross in Cumberland, which is a Viking monument of the 10th century.

Behind the merry tales of Loki's pranks, there are more sombre associations with death and evil. He appears as a bitter-tongued troublemaker in the mythological poem *Lokasenna*, when he reviles all the gods and goddesses in turn, accusing them of stupidity, cowardice and every kind of scandalous behaviour.

Sometimes he appears as a terrible and evil giant in the underworld, and his children are said to be the wolf who finally swallows up the sun, the world serpent who lurks in the depths of the sea, and Hel, the corpse-like queen of the realm of death. The picture of the bound Loki struggling in the depths of the earth resembles that of the bound giant in a series of myths and folk beliefs from the Caucasus, and possibly this particular myth may have been influenced by tales brought back by the Vikings from Russia and the Near East.

Odin

The god Odin stands out as a dominant figure in Scandinavian myth and legend, and scenes and symbols associated with him abound in the pre-Christian art of the Viking Age. He has a double heritage from the Germanic past, taking over from the war god and sky god Tiwaz on the one hand and from Wodan, ruler of the underworld and ancestor of kings, on the other. The wealth of traditions concerning him may be partly due to new influences from Eastern Europe in the Viking Age, imparting fresh vigour to his cult at a time when contacts between Sweden and the East were well established. It is noteworthy that the figure of the god on his eight-legged horse Sleipnir first appears in Scandinavian art on memorial stones of Viking Age date on the Baltic island of Gotland, on the direct route to Russia.

Certainly the cult of Odin as reflected in literature and art is a rich and many-sided one. Odin is the god of the dead, the guide who conducts them to the otherworld, either in his own form or represented by his messengers, the Valkyries. He is also the

This statue of Odin emphasizes the god's majestic aspect as All-Father and leader of the Norse gods. At his shoulders are the two ravens which every day flew round the world and reported to Odin what they had seen. The two wolves which accompanied the god symbolized, like the ravens, Odin's association with the battlefield, for these creatures fed on the corpses of the slain.

National Museum, Copenhagen

god of inspiration and ecstasy, who brought mankind the gifts of poetry, oratory and learning. He is the god of battle, inspiring his worshippers, the warrior princes and leaders, with fanatic loyalty. Sometimes, in spite of his association with the dead, he is seen as All-Father, the leader of the gods, and he possesses some of the powers and symbols of the god of the sky. He is a shape-shifter and expert on magic, and he is a travelling god, moving up and down the world and taking an active interest in the affairs of men, while he also journeys beyond it and visits the realm of the dead in order to learn hidden secrets.

Men and animals were sacrificed to Odin, and he himself claimed to have been sacrificed by his own special rites, pierced by a spear as he hung from a tree, that he might win knowledge for gods and men. He moved among the heroes as an old man with one eye, dressed in a cloak and a broad-brimmed hat. It was said that he had given up his other eye in return for wisdom and that it was hidden in the well of Mimir, the ancient guardian of the underworld.

One of the myths tells how Odin won the mead of inspiration for gods and men by his magic powers. This mead had been brewed from the blood of the all-wise giant Kvasir, mixed with honey. The dwarfs who slew him filled three vessels with the magic drink, but it was taken from them by a giant, Suttung, and he shut it firmly within his stone mountain.

Odin set off to achieve it by cunning, and in disguise he went among the men of Suttung's brother Baugi as they were cutting hay.

He sharpened their scythes with a great whetstone, so effectively that they began to quarrel over it and ended by cutting each other's throats. Odin took the place of all nine of them, asking no wages except a drink of the magic mead. Baugi agreed but his brother was unwilling, so with Baugi's help Odin bored a hole in the mountain wall, crawled in in the form of a serpent and slept three nights with the giant's daughter, who agreed to give him three drinks of the precious liquid. In three draughts Odin emptied the vessels and then flew away in eagle form to Asgard, where the gods were waiting with a row of vessels to receive it; he spat it into them, and from that time the gift of poetic inspiration and oratory has been his to give to men. Knowledge of the runes, which were bound up with magic spells, was also due to Odin, since he won them by his endurance on the World Tree.

Odin, like Wodan before him, was the ancestor of kings, and he would appear to young warrior princes, encouraging them by gifts of special weapons, horses or armour, and instructing them in battle magic and the art of warfare. One of his treasures was the great spear Gungnir, the flight of which decided victory when armies met. There was a tradition that it was a lucky omen to be the first to hurl a spear over the advancing enemy, for this dedicated them to Odin and so ensured victory. But though the god gave aid to his warriors, he was bound to play them false in the end when their time came to fall in battle. The splendid sword given by Odin to the young hero Sigmund the Volsung was shattered by the spear of the god on the battlefield in the end, and Odin himself hurled down Harald War-tooth of Denmark from his chariot, when he had withdrawn his favour and given it to Harald's opponent. Thus the capricious nature of Odin's generosity and his treachery to those who have served him faithfully is stressed in both poetry and prose. The god Loki taunted him with giving victory to cowards who did not merit it, while in a 10th-century Norwegian poem King Hakon of Norway, entering Valhalla after death in battle, refused to lay down his weapons since no trust could be placed in Odin. The reason given in the poetry for his faithlessness is his need for great champions in his own realm, against the day when he must lead out his army to do battle with monsters and the enemies of the gods.

Those who died in sacrifice to Odin, either in battle or by some terrible end like that of the old hero Ragnar Lodbrok, who perished in a snakepit with a song of triumph to Odin on his lips, were said to be welcomed in the hall of Valhalla after death. The Valkyries, the fierce battle-maids of the god who rode to do his will on the battlefield and conduct dead princes back to his realm, welcomed them there with horns of mead, and this scene is pictured many times over on the Gotland memorial stones. It is said in the poems that in Valhalla, the hall of the slain, men fought all day and those who fell were restored again in the evening, when they all feasted sumptuously on pork and drank mead.

To a large extent Valhalla appears to be a symbol of death and the grave, in which an everlasting battle is said to take place, rather than any bright palace in the heavens, and it must not be taken to indicate a literal belief in a special kind of immortality. But the idea of kings and high-born warriors joining their ancestors after death and being welcomed by the god they had served is a tradition deeply established in the lore associated with Odin's cult.

Odin was the great magician, the god with the power to bind and loose by means of spells which he laid upon the minds of men. Such spells could cause panic and paralysis at a moment of crisis, or could free the mind from fear and hesitation so that Odin's men emerged triumphant at the time of testing. His symbols are in keeping with his many-sided reputation: the spear, the raven and the wolf because of his connections with battle; the horse and the eagle because of his power to travel between the worlds and over the sky; the three-way knot to signify his power to bind, no doubt associated also with the sinister knot which dispatched his victims; the maiden with a horn or cup in her hand to welcome the dead because of the joyous entry into Odin's realm – a link also with the mead of inspiration.

The hammer of Thor, the Scandinavian thunder god, as a talisman: in the North the sign of the hammer rivalled the cross as a sacred symbol and was a protective amulet against lightning, fire and calamities of all kinds.

John Moss

Thor

The god of thunder among the Germanic peoples, Donar, developed in the Scandinavian North into a vigorous, dynamic figure of mighty strength, with a red beard, a voracious appetite, and a great axe-hammer to protect gods and men from the evil forces of chaos and destruction. Thor remained a dominant influence until the end of the heathen period, and in the 10th century his silver hammer symbol was worn in opposition to the Christian cross, while his famous fishing exploit when he hauled up the World Serpent from the sea was carved on crosses and memorial stones in Scandinavia and the British Isles and celebrated in a number of Icelandic poems. He is presented in the literature as a god of considerable popular appeal, worshipped by the landowners of Norway in particular, and carried by them to Iceland.

Thor was a suitable god for a farming community, for he was closely linked with the earth. As the 11th-century chronicler Adam of Bremen observed, he ruled not only thunder and lightning but winds and showers, fair weather and crops; while his wife Sif, famous for her bright hair might be a variant of the ancient fertility goddess, typifying the golden corn. It was said that Thor's mother was Earth itself, so that the link between sky god and earth goddess is still reflected in the traditions concerning him.

Thus it is not surprising that Norwegians leaving for Iceland used sometimes to take with them earth from under the family shrine to the god, and also the two main pillars supporting the building, the 'high-seat pillars', which were sometimes said to have Thor's image carved on them. These could be thrown overboard as the ship drew near Iceland, so that Thor himself might lead his worshippers to the place where he desired them to dwell. The ancient thunder god was associated with oak forests and in Iceland, where forests were unknown, the wooden pillars sacred to the god served as an echo of he earlier tradition. Once a settler who had no wood for high-seat pillars prayed to Thor, and in answer a great tree was washed up on the shore, which provided pillars not only for him but for his neighbours also, to their manifest joy.

Whether indeed Thor had special temples built for him, as described in the sagas, is a matter for controversy. It may have been that he presided over the living quarters, and that the high-seat pillars were those of the

Small bronze statuette of Thor, of c 1000 AD, seated in a chair and holding the hammer; it was found in Iceland where Thor, who controlled rain and storms, was highly regarded by farmers and seafarers.

Hamlyn Group

hall itself, where the ritual feasts were probably held.

In the myths Thor is an active figure, frequently said to be off fighting trolls, and continually engaged in struggle and adventure. He does not ride on horseback like Odin, but is said to walk to the assembly of the gods, wading through rivers. In his passage across the sky, however, he is said to travel in a wagon drawn by goats, and the noise of its rattling wheels is heard as thunder in the world of men. When he hurled his hammer at giants, rocks split and boulders were shattered.

This was a magic weapon of potency, held to be the greatest treasure of the gods; it was used as a throwing hammer and was said always to return to the hand. It is pictured on carvings with a long thong, as if the thrower whirled it round his head before letting it fly at his opponent. The hammer symbol long lived on in folklore, and was a protective amulet not only against lightning and fire, but against theft and flood and all kinds of calamities, while the sign of

the hammer made with the hand, like that of the cross, conveyed a blessing and gave protection.

Sometimes in the myths Thor hurled glowing fragments of red-hot metal at his enemies, but his favourite technique was to smash their skulls with his hammer. The association with fire is suggested by the strange story of Thor's duel with the giant Hrungnir.

Thor flung his hammer, violently, and the giant, who was armed with a stone shield, threw a whetstone at Thor. Hammer and whetstone met in mid air; the hammer went on to shatter Hrungnir's head, but one piece of the stone lodged in Thor's forehead. A possible explanation of this myth might be sought in Lapp custom: the image of the thunder god of the Lapps had an iron nail in the head on which fire could be kindled with flint, in a ritual which re-enacted the lightning.

Thor plays a large part in the myths, and from these much of our knowledge of his powers and importance is drawn. Sometimes he appears as a figure of comedy, the bluff, simple fellow who trusts in his strong arm and has no time for the tortuous wiles of Loki and Odin. But the humorous tales do not indicate hostility towards the god, but rather testify to the affection felt for him by his worshippers. One of the most famous myths was that of his struggle with the World Serpent, of which several accounts survive. He went out in the boat of the sea giant Hymir, who did not recognize his divine passenger, and he had with him the head of Hymir's largest ox. The giant was alarmed by the speed with which the boat moved when Thor took the oars, and utterly terrified when the ox-head was thrown out as bait for the serpent which encircles the world, and the monster was hooked on Thor's line. As the struggle continued Thor took on his divine strength, pushing his feet through the boat and bracing himself against the sea bottom. The serpent's terrible head appeared and the two stared fiercely into each other's eyes; then according to one version Hymir cut the line, and the serpent fell back into the depths, there to await the world's end. Thor in wrath knocked the giant into the sea and waded back to shore. The struggle between the sky god and a monster of the deep is a pattern familiar in many mythologies. Originally Thor may have slain the serpent, although at the end of the pagan period the episode was set in the account of Ragnarok, the last battle between gods and monsters, and Thor, after slaying the serpent, himself perished from its poisonous breath.

The fishing story is linked with a visit to Hymir's hall and a battle with the giants. Hymir's wife assisted Thor, who had been challenged to break the giant's precious cup, by prompting him to hurl it at Hymir's head, against which it was shattered. Thor then marched away with the giant's cauldron, which was to be used to brew ale for a banquet of the gods. This is one of a series of tales in which Thor enters the realm of the giants and finally overcomes them, although the odds at first are against him. Once he visited the kingdom of Geirrod, who had forced the god Loki to bring Thor

out without his hammer or his belt of might. Thor was again helped by a giantess, who lent him another belt, gloves of iron and her magic staff, so that he was able to survive the ordeals prepared for him. First he was beset by the swelling waters of the River Vimur, because one of Geirrod's daughters stood astride the river and was adding to the waters by her own efforts. He struck her with a well-directed rock and reached the shore with the help of a rowan tree. Next he sat down in the goatshed, and found his seat being forced up to the roof by two other daughters of the giant, but he pushed it down with his magic staff and broke their backs. Finally Geirrod himself flung a ball of hot iron at him, but Thor caught it in the gloves and sent it back to lay Geirrod low.

Another famous story reads like a satiric version of the myths, and is told with much wit by the antiquarian writer of the 12th century, the Icelander Snorri Sturluson. Thor set out with Loki and two servants to visit the realm of Utgard-Loki, a giant expert in magic. On the way, they encountered an enormous giant, who gave his name as Skrymir and offered to accompany them. Thor was continually frustrated, since he was unable to unfasten the giant's bag of provisions, and when he finally lost patience and struck Skrymir on the head, the giant only asked if a leaf had fallen, or a bird dropped something from the tree above. Finally he left them and they went on to Utgard, a stronghold of such size that they were able to creep through the bars of the gate. The king was rather contemptuous of such puny figures, but asked if they had any special skills.

In the trials of strength that followed Thor and his companions suffered further humiliation. Loki had an eating contest with a man called Logi, but although he devoured all the meat he was given his opponent ate the bones and the trough as well. Thialfi ran a race with a lad called Hugi, and was utterly outstripped. Thor himself undertook a drinking contest, but to his shame was unable to empty the horn offered him in three draughts: the liquid only fell a little below the rim. Next he tried to raise the king's grey cat from the floor, but could only get one paw off the ground. Finally he was asked to wrestle with the king's old foster-mother, but found himself unable to throw her. The king feasted them well after their defeat, and next morning they took their leave. Once outside the gates, the truth was revealed to them. The blows aimed at Skrymir, really Utgard-Loki in disguise, had been diverted by magic and had fallen on three mountains, leaving deep pits where the hammer had struck. The bag which Thor could not undo was fastened by iron bands; Loki's opponent in the contest was Fire, which can consume more than any god or man, while Thialfi had raced against Thought, swifter than any in its flight. The horn offered to Thor had its tip in the ocean, and his great gulps had lowered the sea, as if the tide had ebbed; while the cat was in reality the World Serpent, and all had trembled when Thor raised it so far by his strength, lest the universe should perish; his last opponent was Old Age, able to overcome the mightiest.

Finnish Mythology

For most people, the music of Sibelius is the only window into the world of Finno-Ugrian religion (a linguistic term meaning a family of languages spoken from Lapland and the Baltic in the west to the Urals in the east). In Sibelius's tone-poems, such as 'Pohjola's Daughter', 'The Return of Lemminkäinen' and above all 'The Swan of Tuonela', a romantic picture is evoked of dark forests, long nights and mystery. Knowing that the composer drew his inspiration from the Finnish national epic the *Kalevala*, we might suppose that if we knew his work we should have the key to the Finnish religious mind. In fact, the picture is much more complicated.

The peoples who speak the Finno-Ugrian languages belong today to Sweden (most of the Lapps), Finland, Hungary and Russia; they are widely scattered, and have been subject to many different religious influences. In some areas traditional religious beliefs survive only as half-remembered folklore.

The earliest written sources date from the coming of Christianity. In 1551, Michael Agricola, the great reformer of the Finnish Church, included a list of the old gods in the preface to his translation of the Psalter. Needless to say, his purpose was to be theologically controversial rather than scholarly, and these sources have to be used with care, and backed up wherever possible by folklore

and anthropology. The same applies to the *Kalevala*, which in its present form is a 19th-century compilation by Elias Lönnrot, the Finnish scholar, on the basis of popular traditional material.

The setting of the *Kalevala* is the struggle between life and death, light and darkness, represented by the kingdoms of Kalevala and Pohjola. Its heroes, especially Väinämöinen (a figure who has some affinities with Orpheus) and Lemminkäinen, meet death, but emerge victorious. Their quest is a quest for power; and the *Kalevala* is shot through and through with magic, in the sense of power over both the material world and the world of the spirits. For the people of the North, magic was the goal of all knowledge and all wisdom, and both Väinämöinen and Lemminkäinen, like the Scandinavian Odin, were great magicians.

In this respect the *Kalevala* is a microcosm of circumpolar religion, from Lapland to Labrador, and the object of all its religious practices was to secure man's place in a dangerous world by means of magical techniques. Of trusting dependence on the great supernatural powers there is little or nothing; of fear, wisdom and cunning a great deal. Its typical figure is not the priest or prophet, but the shaman, with his power over the spirits and the capacity to project his own spirit through the air to the dwelling-place

of the dead, as Väinämöinen does. In this, the Finno-Ugrians were at one with all the Northern hunters.

But for more than 3000 years most Finno-Ugrians have been agriculturalists and like all agricultural peoples, their religious beliefs and practices must be seen in the context of the need for fertility – of man, animal and plant – and within the framework of heaven and earth, wood and stream, life and death.

At the head of the Finno-Ugrian pantheon stand the figures of the Sky Father and the Earth Mother, the primeval pair who are the joint sources and guarantors of fertility, to whom sacrifices are made in order that the fields may be fruitful. The Sky Father (either the sky personified or a personal living god in the sky) was called by various names: Jumala, Ilmarinen and Ukko ('grandfather') being the most common among the Baltic Finns. Jumala means 'sky', and Ilmarinen contains the word *ilma*, 'air, sky'. Similar words are found among the Cheremis of the Volga basin and the Votyaks in the Urals region. Jumala seems originally to have been a god of the sky; Ilmarinen a god of the atmosphere, wind, and weather (in the *Kalevala* he is a blacksmith, perhaps indicating an original connection with lightning); Ukko was a god of thunder, similar to the Scandinavian Thor, and, like him, was worshipped with spring sacrifices, liba-

Above *Painting of the episode showing (left) Väinämöinen's meeting with Aino; the maiden preparing to enter the water (right) and (centre) the hero attempting to seize Aino, who has become a water divinity.* **Facing page** *Lemminkäinen, one of the main characters in the* **Kalevala,** *the great epic poem of Finland, was torn to pieces by the son of Tuoni, Lord of the Dead, when he attempted to kill the swan that swam on the dark river surrounding the underworld. He was magically restored to life by his mother: this and subsequent paintings depicting episodes in the* **Kalevala** *are by A. Gallen-Kallela.*

tions, the consumption of intoxicants and sexual indulgence. After the coming of Christianity all three came to be identified in various ways with God, Jesus and saints such as St George, St Nicholas, and many more.

The Earth Mother, as the consort of the Sky Father, was known in Finland as Maan-Emoinen or Rauni (a word derived from the Swedish name of the sacred tree, *rönn*, or mountain ash), in Estonia as Maa-ema and among the Votyaks as Muzjem-mumi.

The omnipresent forest was sacred to the Earth Mother, but was also thought of as possessing a life, will and power of its own; as such, it might well be personified as a spirit (*haltija*) or spirits in human form. By and large, the forest spirit (*metsänhaltija*) was benevolent if treated with respect. He or she would provide game for the hunters, and guide the lost traveller; and to this end small symbolical offerings were made, perhaps on a tree stump. Michael Agricola recorded the forest spirit's name as Tapio, and his kingdom as Tapiola; but the spirit might be female, or even a family of spirits.

Of the animals of the forest, the bear was the incomparable monarch. The first drops of blood from any game animal had to be poured on the ground in order to propitiate the spirits, but the skulls of bears were accorded special reverence and were mounted on a sacred tree, looking in the direction of the rising sun: a rite that was probably nearly as old as the forest itself. Both bear and wolf might be identified with the spirit of the forest, and animals generally were known as 'Tapio's flock'. Each species was also believed to have its 'owner', or guardian spirit, the bear mother, fox mother, and so on. It is interesting that in Christian times, saints such as St Anne and St George have taken over from the haltija of the forest some of their functions as protectors of hunters. There were many lesser vegetation deities outside the forest, whose functions were also taken over by Christian saints.

The country east of Finland is a region not only of forests and fields, but also of lakes and rivers, and water spirits played an important role in popular belief. Just as the forest spirit owns the animals, so the water spirit, often pictured as a woman with long hair, is the owner of the fishes, and has to be propitiated when a good catch is desired.

In their houses, too, the Finno-Ugrians lived close to the world of the spirits. Each home had its own proper guardian spirit, who looked after the house and its inhabitants in return for small regular offerings of food and drink.

Finno-Ugrian beliefs and practices concerning the nature and destiny of man show remarkable similarities with those of Siberia and the northern parts of the North American continent. Common to all is the belief that man has more than one soul: he has a life-soul which is identified with the breath, and which animates the body, disappearing on death; and a free-soul, thought of as a man's 'double' (Doppelgänger), and which continues to enjoy independent existence after death, either in some land of the departed, or as a wandering and often mischievous ghost. It was believed that the dead themselves did not walk, and it was their haltijas, or spirits, that appeared as ghosts. In addition, there are vestiges of belief in the name-soul, in so far as a name was thought to carry with it qualities and attributes that could be passed on to a child.

In transactions involving the soul and the shaman, it is always the free-soul which is meant: sickness is believed to be caused by 'loss of soul', and a cure can only be effected if the lost soul can be caught and brought back by the shaman. Alternatively, cases of 'demon' possession would be treated by some form of exorcism. It was thought that death could occur when the soul of an afflicted person had passed entirely into the sphere of influence of some malevolent power. Death was never by 'natural causes'; always by supernatural.

The land of the dead, Tuonela or Manala, as pictured in the *Kalevala*, is beneath the earth, approached by a long and difficult path, and surrounded by a dark river, on which a swan swims (the 'Swan of Tuonela', in Sibelius's tone-poem). The Lord of the Dead is Tuoni, and his consort is Tuonetar; their daughters are evil spirits, bringers of disease. The dead live more or less the kind of life they have lived on earth, even marrying and having children, but there are traces in folklore of the belief that the land of the dead was a 'mirror-land' in which the sun rose in the west and set in the east, in which everything was upside-down, and in which the dead gradually regained their youth. Some Finno-Ugrians also believed in a celestial 'heaven', peopled by heroes killed in battle or by lightning. Otherwise there is little indication of any kind of moral distinction being drawn between people after death.

Finnish folklore is generally associated with the *Kalevala*, the great epic poem compiled by Elias Lönnrot (1802–84) from oral traditions he collected while practising

medicine in North Karelia, now part o
Soviet Russia. 'Kalevala' means 'land o
Kalevala', the great national hero of Finnish
and Estonian folk poetry, and is generally
thought to signify the 'fatherland of heroes'
The final version of the *Kalevala* was published in 1849, and consisted of 50 canto
containing 22,795 verses.

Elias Lönnrot's motive in collecting ora
literature stemmed from nationalist senti-
ment: he wanted to show that the Finns had
a cultural heritage comparable to that o
other peoples. The desire to create an artistic
whole explains why he arranged his materia
in a sequence unknown to the unlettered
singers of folksong, why he often united
several characters into one and why he even
made up passages. Nonetheless the *Kalevala*
clearly reflects the main themes of Finnish
folklore. Although the basic plot is heroic,
Lönnrot wove into his work every type of
Finnish oral tradition ranging from legends,
tales and epic poetry to lyric 'bird' poems,
riddles and magic charms.

The action of the *Kalevala* centres on seven
distinct episodes. It begins with the creation
of the world from an egg and the birth of
Väinämöinen, an ancient hero sage, whose
mother was the Virgin of the Air, but who
was born in the water. Väinämöinen uses
his magic powers to prepare the primeval
wilderness as a home for the people of
Kalevala. This is followed by Väinämöinen's
wooing of Aino who prefers death by
drowning rather than marriage to the old
man. Then follows a description of the
relations between the people of Kalevala
and their northern neighbours in Pohjola,
identified by most scholars as Lapland.
Väinämöinen, Lemminkäinen the wild adventurer, and the hero-smith Ilmarinen all
in turn undertake the hazardous journey to
woo the daughter of Louhi, the Mistress of
Pohjola. It is Ilmarinen who finally wins her,
but only after accomplishing various tasks
including the forging of the *sampo*, a magic
mill that provided unlimited amounts of
grain, salt and money.

Five cantos known as the *Kullervo*-cycle
follow. Kullervo is a hapless youth separated
from his family by a feud between his father,
Kalervo, and his uncle, Untamo. While he is
still a boy his uncle makes several unsuccessful attempts to murder him. Kullervo is
finally sold as a slave to Ilmarinen, whose
wife torments him beyond endurance; he
takes his revenge by causing her to be torn
to pieces by a pack of bears and wolves.
Kullervo flees and by chance is reunited
with his family. Fate still pursues him,
however, and returning home one day he
meets and seduces a girl only to discover
that she is his long-lost sister. The girl com-
mits suicide and in despair Kullervo sets

In the **Kullervo-cycle,** *part of the*
Kalevala, *Kullervo revenges himself upon
the wicked wife of Ilmarinen by turning
her cows into bears and wolves which then
devour her:* **The Curse of Kullervo.**
*Väinämöinen, an ancient sage and the
chief hero of the epic poem, was frustrated
in his desire to marry Aino, who flung
herself into the sea to escape marriage
with him.*

out to slay his uncle Untamo. The cycle concludes with Kullervo taking his own life.

The death of Ilmarinen's wife provides the link back to the main narrative. Ilmarinen decides to return to Pohjola and woo his sister-in-law. Unsuccessful in winning her affection and angered by the ease of life that the sampo, the magic mill, has provided for the inhabitants of Pohjola, he persuades Väinämöinen and Lemminkäinen to accompany him on an expedition to seize it. There follows a series of struggles during which the sampo is smashed and most of it lost in the sea; Louhi the Protectress of Pohjola sends diseases to Kalevala, and hides the sun and moon, but is finally forced to leave the people of Kalevala in peace.

Finally, Marjatta, a virgin, conceives by swallowing a whortleberry, and gives birth to a son. Väinämöinen wants to have the baby killed; but when the two-week-old boy reproaches him, he is forced to acknowledge a greater power. The boy is christened King of Karelia and Väinämöinen departs to a place between heaven and earth to await a day when his people will need him again.

Finnish folklore, typified by the *Kalevala*, embraces elements from many ages and sources. For the purposes of a general analysis there are four major strata. The oldest stratum of Finnish folklore is represented by the pervading atmosphere of magic which owes much to the shamanistic cults of northern Eurasia. The same stratum also includes legends concerning the creation of the universe, struggles between men and animals, the worship of animals, and laments. Scholars are not entirely agreed on the date of this stratum, but it probably goes back to several centuries BC, before the ancestors of the Finns had emerged from Russia, when they were still in contact with other Finno-Ugrian peoples.

The second stratum dates from just before the birth of Christ, when the ancient Finns began to reach the east Baltic area and came into close contact with the ancient Balts and Germans. This period saw the distinctive *Kalevala*-type metre, and the 'origin' poems or spells. This is a form of magic which is rarely found beyond the Finnic area. By describing the origin of an object, displaying one's knowledge of its nature, the object could be created, in the case of fire or iron; overcome, in the case of the bear or other enemies; or warded off, in the case of illness. It is interesting that the actions of these spells were brought about by the power of knowledge, without appeal to a supernatural force. It is also thought that the poems about Väinämöinen, Joukahainen, who is also featured in the *Kalevala*, and Ilmarinen began to evolve during this era.

The third stratum dates from the early Middle Ages when contacts with Scandinavian peoples became more frequent. Evidence of these contacts is found in the borrowing of the Scandinavian ballad form and thematic concepts. The sampo-episode is reminiscent of a Viking raid and comparison with the Icelandic sagas shows that there can be no doubt of the sampo-cycle's Scandinavian origin.

The fourth stratum coincides with the introduction of Christianity in the 12th

Ateneum, Helsinki

century, and the subsequent spread of medieval tales and legends, which often underwent considerable local modification both before and after reaching Finland. Among the themes dating from this period are the *Kullervo*-cycle, related by some scholars to the medieval *Amleth* or Hamlet tale; and Väinämöinen's playing of the zither-like *kantele*, which recalls the medieval versions of the Orpheus legend. The impact of Christianity on Finland's pagan culture is pleasingly symbolized by the episode in which Väinämöinen relinquishes his power to the child born of the virgin Marjatta. The same period is also characterized by a marked increase in folk literature forms with especial proliferation of spells, ballads, proverbs and riddles.

For centuries Finns have been reputed to possess demonic powers, but the practice of devil-worship within Finland itself does not seem to have been widespread. It is clear that the ecclesiastical authorities never had cause to fear witchcraft as it was feared in England and on the Continent, for in the whole of Finland's history less than 60 people were sentenced to death for this crime. The practice of magic, however was a central feature of Finnish life (and still is, in a few remote areas); it is also an essential feature of Finnish folklore and the *Kalevala* contains some 4,200 verses of spell poetry. Magic was used to ensure success, and sometimes protection, in hunting, fishing, farming and raising livestock; and spells were used to cure or ward off illness, to protect against evil and to foretell the future. In fact there

The sampo, *a mill that provided unlimited amounts of salt, grain and money, was magically forged by the smith Ilmarinen; but in one of the climactic episodes in the* Kalevala *it is destroyed, and Väinämöinen is able to rescue only its scattered fragments:* **The Forging of the Sampo.**

was a magic formula to accompany almost every aspect of life.

There were various ways in which magic could be worked: the supplicant could make offerings to spirits of the forest, field and so on; he himself could recite spells; or he could have them recited by a recognized worker of magic, who generally performed the spell alone or only in the presence of the supplicant. He rarely performed before groups of people for fear of weakening the magic. The spell was often in verse, and the wizard would move his body to the rhythm of the chant. Sometimes this induced a state of trance which may be seen as a survival of ancient shamanistic practice. This state was much sought after, for it was believed to give greater effect to the spell.

Finnish magic has much in common with that practised throughout Europe and Asia, where much of it originated. The influence of the ancient spells of India and Egypt reached the Finns through the ancient Germans and easily took root in minds that regarded shamanistic magic as the driving force of life. The majority of surviving Finnish spells, however, spring from the Christian beliefs and legends.

Germanic Mythology

In the Iron Age (from 600 BC onwards) we find the earliest evidence for a specifically Germanic religion. There are again indications of the worship of a supreme god of the sky, whose name is thought to have been Tiwaz. This was the god whom the Anglo-Saxons in the 5th and 6th centuries worshipped as Tiw in England, while he was remembered in Scandinavia as Tyr. The third day of the week, Tuesday, was called after him throughout the Germanic world. The name Tiwaz is related to the Greek Zeus and to an earlier form of the Roman name for Jupiter, and these names are all thought to be derived from the Indo-Germanic word for god, probably associated with the light of the shining heavens. The Anglo-Saxon Tiw is remembered in a number of place names: Tuesley in Surrey, Tewin in Hertfordshire and Tysoe in Warwickshire.

Tiwaz was equated by the Romans with the god Mars, also a god of the third day of the week, and so must have been seen by them primarily as a god of battle. One of his titles however was Mars Thingsus, which associates him with the *Thing*, the local assembly where free men met to deliberate together. This aspect of Tiwaz was taken over by Thor in the Viking Age.

The swearing of oaths on weapons and the sacrifice of weapons in thanksgiving for victory are both known to have been part of the cult of the Germanic gods. Tacitus states that the Germans sacrificed for victory to Mars and Mercury, that is, to Tiwaz and Wodan (or Wotan). One form which this took was the slaying of captives taken in war, and there is also archeological evidence for the plunder won in battle being deliberately damaged and then thrown into pools or left lying in heaps on the ground. Such offerings have been recovered from the peat bogs of Denmark and North Germany, and the great finds like those of Vimose and Nydam have added considerably to our knowledge of Germanic weapons and craftsmanship from the 2nd to the 6th century AD, as well as emphasizing the religious awe and stern discipline which demanded such costly sacrifices. Tacitus records that the Hermundari and the Chatti both vowed to sacrifice everything which they won in return for victory, and that the Hermundari, who were successful, carried out their vow.

Such practices began in Roman times, and may be due to the increasing influence of the cult of the god Wodan among the Germanic peoples. It had become customary a little earlier, in the Celtic Iron Age in Denmark, to bury weapons in the graves of the wealthy dead, and to leave in their graves dishes of roasted meat, with cups, jugs and horns of wine and mead, the equipment for a feast. Since in the Viking Age both weapons and feasting were consistently associated with the kingdom of Odin in the other world, such practices may indicate the spread of the cult of his predecessor Wodan among the Germans. Wodan was the god who ruled the land of the dead and was

Above *The eagle was the bird of Wodan, probably partly in imitation of the Roman eagle of Jupiter. Small eagle brooches and figures of eagles on shields, like this one from Sutton Hoo, were used by the Germans as amulets to ward off danger.* Facing page *Battle scene from a memorial stone in Gotland, showing a woman holding a horn who may be a Valkyrie, the welcomer of dead heroes to a happy life in paradise. Battle spirits of this kind were known to the Germanic peoples from early times.*

also associated with inspiration and magic. He was a god of cruel sacrifices, and his human and animal victims are said to have been suspended from trees. References to such sacrifices come from Greek and Roman writers and are in general corroborated by what we know of the worship of the god Odin in later times in Sweden.

Another aspect of Wodan may be represented by traditions of the Wild Hunt, a host passing through the sky on stormy nights. The riders were on black horses and were followed by wolflike hounds, which could be heard baying in the air, and in some parts of Sweden, Denmark and Germany the leader was said to be the god Odin or a spirit called Wode. Since Wodan was a wandering, restless god, the leader of spirits of the dead, who was associated with the horse and the wolf, this may well be a genuine pagan tradition going back to pre-Christian times.

Wodan's name is probably connected with the Gothic *wut*, which signifies fury or extreme mental excitement. The name Odin (Othinn) in Old Norse appears to have had a similar basis, coming from an adjective applied to a violent storm or fire but also used for poetic genius or furious rage. Odin was the god of magic, inspiration, ecstasy and intoxication, and the Germanic Wodan and Anglo-Saxon Woden may be assumed to have had the same general character.

Odin, as god of battle, was followed by his Valkyries, the battle spirits who went out to choose the slain, sometimes described as dignified women on horseback and sometimes as bloodthirsty creatures revelling in slaughter. Such battle spirits were known earlier to the Germanic people, and female spirits called the Alaisiagae, with various symbolic names associated with battle, are mentioned along with Mars on stones at Housesteads on Hadrian's Wall.

The raven and wolf, creatures of the battlefield, are also closely linked with Odin. These are the vultures of the north, feeding on corpses of men and beasts, and as such would seem to belong to the sinister cult of

the dark power Wodan rather than to Tiwaz, the god of the sky. They were not viewed solely as scavengers, since Odin was attended constantly by two ravens which flew round the world to bring him tidings and came to tell them in his ears. The symbol of a figure or a human head between two birds, which seem to be pecking it from either side, was known both to the Germans and the Celts. It might be seen as a grim pun in the German heroic style, representing the birds which peck at the corpse and the hanged man, and at the same time serve as the messengers bringing tidings to the god of death.

The eagle also was a symbol of the god, partly imitated no doubt from the Roman eagle which stood for the divine Emperor and which was carried by Roman armies. Small eagle brooches and fine eagle figures on shields, like those on the great ceremonial shield from Sutton Hoo, were used by the Germans as protective amulets. Another widespread symbol of the god was the spear, which in Norse literature is called Gungnir; one of the great treasures of the gods, it was flung over the host which Odin had doomed to defeat. The spear was an important symbol in the Bronze Age, and may have been originally the weapon of Tiwaz as god of battle. Little silhouettes in bronze, dating from the 6th and 7th centuries, of a warrior riding a horse and carrying a spear – often a weapon of exaggerated size – are often found.

While there is a considerable amount of evidence for the cult of Wodan among the Germanic peoples, there is far less for that of the third of the main deities whom they worshipped, the god Donar (Thunor to the Anglo-Saxons), whose name connects him with thunder and after whom the fifth day of the week, Thursday, was named.

Donar was identified by the Romans with both Jupiter and Hercules; the first association was evidently based on the power of the god over the storm and the thunderbolt, while he was linked with Hercules because he was seen as the protector of men against giants and monsters.

Clearly the functions of Donar must have overlapped considerably with those of the sky god Tiwaz, and his cult may have belonged to the tribes who lived in the thickly forested areas of Germany. It was linked with the oak forests of England, and places named after him are found in Saxon rather than Anglian districts. They are often formed from the element *leah*, meaning a forest clearing, like Thunderley and Thundersley in Essex. The name Thunaer is included in an early Saxon renunciation formula as a heathen god to be renounced by the Christian convert. Donar may have been represented by the oak tree or the axe before figures of the gods in human form became known among the Germans owing to Roman influence.

Donar's thunderbolt was symbolized by the axe, a sign of divine power from Neolithic times onwards. At some stage in the north it came to be pictured as a hammer, and tiny hammer-shaped amulets have been found in Anglo-Saxon graves. Prehistoric stone axes and fossil stones known as 'thunder weapons' were treasured in Denmark, Germany and England up to modern times; they were held to protect the house against lightning, fire and other calamities, and they were carried by German soldiers as protection against bullets in the Franco-Prussian war. A case was recorded from northern Germany in this century of a farmer who kept three prehistoric stone axes in the house and laid them in the first holes made by the drill at sowing time, and there is no doubt that the thunder god was associated with the fertility of the earth as well as the control of storms and the well-being of the community.

The deities known in Scandinavia as the Vanir, gods and goddesses connected with fertility, are the hardest to trace in early Germanic mythology. Clearly the worship of the Earth Goddess continued throughout northern Europe from the Neolithic period onwards. In the Viking Age this goddess had many names, of which Freyja is best known, and the sixth day of the week, Friday, was called after her predecessor, Frija, throughout the Germanic world. No convincing evidence of cult places called after her has survived in England, although some of those called 'Friday' may have been associated with the goddess.

German goddesses of bounty are known from Roman times, and stones of this period from England and Germany show two or three seated goddesses with fruit, bread or horns of plenty, or sometimes one figure alone. The sacred place of one of these goddesses, Nehalennia, has been found under the sand on the Island of Walcheren in the Netherlands, and it is clear that travellers appealed to her for a safe crossing over the North Sea.

Evidence for a male god like the Swedish Freyr, Freyja's brother, is harder to find. However, naked phallic male figures in wood and metal, roughly shaped with bearded faces, have been found in Denmark and North Germany, dating from the Roman period. A male and a female figure in wood from Braak in Schleswig-Holstein might well represent twin fertility deities; they are simple but impressive shapes, larger than human, which have by chance been preserved in the peat. Freyja's symbol, the boar, which she shared with the male fertility god, is well represented in Anglo-Saxon England.

Tacitus mentions twin gods called the Alcis who were worshipped along the North Sea coasts in the 1st century AD. They could have developed from the twin deities of the Bronze Age, and would correspond with the protective brothers known to the Greeks as the Dioscuri, the sons of the sky god himself.

There are what might be twin gods on the gold horn from Gallehus, dated about AD 500, and twin dancing figures on helmets of the 6th century. There is little sign of such twin figures in the literature of the period except for pairs of brother kings in early Swedish tradition, and the Anglo-Saxon pair Hengest and Horsa, whose names mean Stallion and Horse, and who are said to have led an invasion of England in the 5th century; the Dioscuri were consistently associated with horses.

Other myths concerning the gods and their world may be dimly glimpsed in Germanic tradition. The myth of the creation of the world from the body of a giant may have been associated with Tuisto, who according to Tacitus was the father of Mannus, the ancestor of the German race; he would be equivalent to Ymir, for example, in Norse mythology.

A belief in the ultimate destruction of the world, an important element of Norse mythology, was probably also known to the pagan Germans.

There are indeed many isolated clues to the lost mythology of the Germanic peoples in the pagan period, and the study of their rich symbolism, constantly coming to light in fresh finds of decorated cremation urns and brooches and weapons of the Roman and later periods, will doubtless help us in due course to integrate these, and to gain a fuller knowledge of early religion among the Germanic tribes.

Detail from 8th-century Northumbrian casket, showing the revenge of Wayland the Smith on King Nithhad. Wayland, on the left, holds in his tongs the head of the king's son, whose body lies beneath the anvil; the female figure is the king's daughter, whom Wayland dishonoured; Wayland's brother Eigil killed birds to make the feather cloak used by the smith in his subsequent escape.

Slavonic Mythology

Geographically, the Slavonic tribes came to be divided into southern, eastern and western Slavs. All three groups are now distinguished by their different dialects and their own folklore but, as far as is known, the mythology was, in the main, similar among all Slavs. Information about the customs, religion and myths of the ancient Slavs has come down to us almost exclusively through their neighbours. Apart from written sources, of which there are few that are reliable, there is some rather imaginative information to be found in Arabian travellers' accounts. The western sources are by far the most precise, but allowance must be made for their obvious Christian bias. These accounts tend to contain sweeping parallels to the Greek and Roman pantheon of gods. Russian chroniclers, who wrote their accounts when the Slavonic gods had long been dethroned, stress the inferiority of the old religion in comparison with the Christian faith.

More valuable is the archeological evidence and that of the existing folklore, such as the customs connected with the seasons, as well as Church records that deal with those pagan practices that have passed into Christian ritual. Folklore, songs, sayings, epics, sculpture, dances and games provide material that yields much reliable information. Slavonic folklore is abundantly rich and has survived well into the 20th century: in Russia major changes in the social structure and the way of life occurred only with the Revolution.

The pagan Slav felt himself to be part of Nature and his feelings for it were of a religious kind – he worshipped all its manifestations. From these very close ties his gods were created and can be seen to be personifications of the life he experienced around him. He worshipped individual aspects of Nature, from an oak tree to a large stone, a swamp or a ravine. In an equal measure everything was endowed with an all-pervading life force with which he felt an affinity. From this intimate connection with Nature arose the knowledge of how to make use of its gifts and powers, such as were latent in springs and herbs, for example. The pagan Slav personified those powerful manifestations of Nature on which he felt most dependent, and these personifications entered the upper ranks of his mythology as gods. He also believed that each domain of Nature was inhabited by all kinds of spirits and demons. Whereas the ancient gods came to be forgotten soon after Russia became converted to Christianity, this lower order of beings survived in popular belief and magical practices and in folk customs, many of which merged with the Christian folk tradition.

Although many names of Slavonic gods and spirits have come down to us, in many cases their individual functions are not clear. Often it is not even known whether, perhaps, they originated in another people's mythology, or where exactly they were worshipped. The attempt has been made to

Giraudon

Volkh, a mythical being of Slav mythology depicted as a hawk. He had the ability to assume a number of forms, such as a grey wolf or a tiny ant, and was renowned for his sorcery.

establish their geographical distribution through an etymological analysis of place names. As there is no written evidence of the gods of the Poles, Czechs, Serbians or Bulgarians, the information available covers mainly the areas of the eastern Slavs and the Baltic or western Slavs.

Opinions are divided as to whether a basic dualism underlies the Slavs' mythological concepts. According to the 12th-century chronicler Helmold, whose evidence is confirmed by recent Soviet research, the Elbe Slavs used to offer prayers to the divinity of good and evil; these were personified in Chernobog and Byelbog, gods of darkness and light. Chernobog was regarded as very powerful, being the cause of all calamities, and prayers were offered to him at banquets

to avert misfortune. 'The Slavs have a remarkable superstition, for on the occasion of banquets and festivities they carry about a round vessel, over which they speak words which are not a blessing but rather a curse, which they utter in the name of the gods of good and evil, for from the good god they expect good fortune, but from the evil god misfortune.' No other specific evidence concerning these two divinities has been preserved. Helmold testifies further that in spite of a fundamental dualism, the Slavs wor-

shipped one god, ruler of all the other divine powers to whom they used to attribute parts of Nature, as fields or forests, as well as the human emotions of sorrow and joy. This god, he says, cared only for things celestial, whereas the rest, who sprang from his blood, obeyed the duties assigned to them, enjoying distinction in proportion to their nearness to the chief god. The name of this Supreme Being is not known.

The names of a number of gods and spirits that were worshipped at one time have been established with some degree of certainty. The sites of some of the statues of the principal east Slavonic gods were the hill before the palace in Kiev and by the River Volkhov in Novgorod. According to manuscripts dating from the 12th to the 16th century, these statues represented the gods Perun, Khors, Volos and Dazhbog. Perun's statue was erected by Vladimir, who later became the first Russian prince to accept Christianity. The idol is described as having been made of wood, with a silver head and a golden beard. Vladimir's uncle Dobrynya, a celebrated semi-legendary hero of many

Facing page *Slav mythology abounds with stories of heroes and their legendary feats; Ilya-Muromyets tries to release Svyatogor from the coffin in which he has shut himself. Drawing by I. Bilibine.* **Below** *Baltic Slavs pay homage to an image of the god Svetovit; he was famous for his prophecies, especially those to do with the success or failure of the harvest. Drawing by I. Bilibine.*

historical songs, was responsible for setting up a similar image of Perun in Novgorod. As no remains of temples dedicated to their gods have been found among the eastern Slavs, it is assumed that they used to erect their statues in the open. We are told that they were commonly placed on hills, facing east and the direction of water, a nearby river or lake.

When Prince Vladimir received baptism in 988 AD, he ordered all idols in Kiev to be destroyed. The statues of Perun in Kiev and Novgorod were dragged down to the river. The Novgorod idol was tied with ropes, pulled through the mire down to the river, where it was beaten with rods so as to cast out the demons that were thought to inhabit it. Perun appears to have been perhaps the most important east Slavonic god, being a solar deity, a god of lightning and of fire. His worship was widespread among the Slavs, judging by the many place-names in Slovenia, Bohemia, Bulgaria and Poland which are connected with his name. Worship of this god disappeared in about the 11th century. In the Christian era his worship was transferred to St Ilya. Nestor, the medieval Russian chronicler, tells that when Prince Igor was about to conclude a treaty with the Byzantines, the Christian Russians took oath in the church of St Ilya, while the pagans swore to Perun.

Dazhbog's statue also stood on the hill in the courtyard of the castle at Kiev. In old manuscripts this god is referred to as 'Tsar Sun'. According to the 12th-century Russian prose epic *Slovo o polku Igoreve*, Vladimir

and the Russians call themselves the grandchildren of Dazhbog; however, it is a common tendency of all people to explain their origins as having links with divine beings. Dazhbog also seems to have been known among the southern Slavs. A Serbian fairy tale relates that 'Dabog, the Tsar, was on earth and the Lord God was in heaven.' Dazhbog is here contrasted with God and is regarded as an evil being, for in early Christian times the memory of the previous pagan gods was linked with the Christian concept of evil and its personification, the Devil or Satanael. Dazhbog, who probably took over the role of sun god from Perun, played a significant part till long after Christianization because of his connection with fire and the Slavs' worship of the hearth as a sacred place in the house. The Christian clergy fought a long and difficult battle against this worship of fire. In a sermon we read that even 'priests do not scorn the company of the idol-worshippers, they eat and drink with them ... they pray to the fire which they call Svarozhich' (another name of Dazhbog). As Christianity was introduced to the Slavs by their rulers, the common folk clung to their pagan beliefs for a long time, but gradually the old gods of the sun and the fire were replaced by Christian angels and saints.

The worship of fire and the hearth dates back to the days of nomads and hunters of Paleolithic times, to whom the fireplace and the spirit of the ancestors which lived in it constituted the central point of their religious worship.

The names Ovinnik, Yarilo and Kupala,

Giraudon

which were later used in folk ritual in connection with the worship of fire, stand for basically the same idea, since all are part of the customs of the sacred fire and its purifying power. Fire worship was frequently condemned by the Church, as in a sermon of the 12th century by the Bishop of Turov, Cyril, who wrote: 'We do not worship fire. Now neither the forces of Nature, nor the sun, nor the fire ... are called by the name of God ... for idol-worship has come to an end and the devilish violence has been overcome by the sacrament of the cross.'

Many magical rites stemmed from belief in the capacity of fire to cleanse and heal. Until the 20th century, for example, Russian peasants believed that the most effective means of healing and protecting was the so-called 'new fire', which was obtained by rubbing together two pieces of dry wood. In the event of an epidemic, frightened superstitious villagers would put out all fires in their houses and then, after having said special prayers, would go out together to fetch this 'new fire' for their homes. The holy fire became part of Christian belief. It would be brought home from church on particular feast days, especially at Easter, and was regarded as a protection against unclean powers.

On the whole, though, Christianity succeeded in banishing the old gods from the consciousness of the Slavonic tribes, but it did not succeed in suppressing the religious customs connected with them; these customs remained very closely connected with Nature.

Another major Slavonic deity was Volos or Veles, the god who protected cattle. What appear to be remnants of the worship of this god were still to be found until recently as part of the harvest festival customs in southern Russia. The peasants would tie the last handful of ears into a knot, which used to be called 'plaiting the beard of Veles'; in some districts a piece of bread was put among the ears. Veles was also known among the ancient Bohemians. Later his worship came to be transferred to St Blaise, a shepherd and martyr of Caesarea in Cappadocia whom the Byzantines called the guardian of flocks.

Some Church records give an interesting indication of the Slavs' worship of the heavenly bodies. A sermon of John Chrysostom admonishes those who worship the sun, the moon and the stars to repent of their sins. Similarly, in a sermon, Cyril of Turov regrets that even now, in the 12th century, the Devil tempts people to believe in God's creatures, in the sun, the moon and the stars. In his 'Hymn of the Mother of God' he says: 'They have forgotten God and believe in the creatures that God has given us for work, and so they have called everything gods.'

Thracian Rider God

Over a wide area of the Balkans, especially in the territory known as Thrace in ancient times (now Bulgaria), great numbers of monuments have been found of what is called the 'Thracian Rider'. These monuments generally take the form of stone stelae,

upon which the figure of a horseman is carved, together with other attendant figures or symbols. They date from the Roman Imperial period, mostly from the 2nd and 3rd centuries AD. Some specimens have been found further afield, in Anatolia and Western Europe. The identity of the 'Rider', and what he meant to those who carved his figure on these stones, remain uncertain despite much research into the matter.

There are a few deductions which can be made about the significance of this mysterious figure. First, it must be noted that the figures of a horse and rider frequently occur on classical Greek and Etruscan funerary monuments. Such representations had a mortuary significance – the deceased was departing from this world to the next. But the Thracian Rider does not appear on tombstones, and so cannot be reckoned as having a sepulchral character. Instead, his monuments were located in sanctuaries, and from this it can be deduced that he was a divinity of some kind.

Here the mystery of his identity becomes very puzzling. Although the monuments often bear inscriptions in Greek and Latin, and name the divine Rider to whom they are dedicated, the mystery is only deepened by what they record. The name most frequently given is 'Heros' or 'Heron'. This could be the designation of a dead man, for the dead were sometimes 'heroized' in Greek funerary inscriptions. But this is unlikely to have been the case here, since the monuments were not tombstones; some inscriptions read *theo Heroti*, 'to the god Hero'.

In other inscriptions, the Rider is named Phoebus, that is, Apollo, or Asclepios, the Greek god of healing. Such names suggest that the mysterious Rider was being equated with well-known Greek gods, though himself remaining unnamed.

Clues to what the divine Rider meant to his devotees seem to be provided by various iconographic features visible on the monuments.

The Rider was generally depicted with his cloak streaming out behind him, suggesting vigour and speed of movement. He frequently flourishes a club or double-axe, the latter being a symbol of many Near Eastern weather or sky gods. But more significant is the fact that a number of monuments show the deity with three heads. Such multiplication of physical features is usually a primitive way of suggesting superhuman ability. Three heads, so arranged that one looks forward, one backwards, and one full-face, would seem to indicate a deity who was all-seeing and all-knowing. Since these powers were usually attributes of a sun god, the Thracian Rider probably had solar associations, even if he was not actually a sun god. Then the fact that he is sometimes shown as hunting a great wild boar, often a symbol of evil, may mean that the deity was regarded as a divine saviour, who hunted and subdued the forces of evil and disorder.

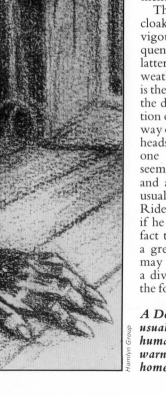

A Domovoy or Slav domestic spirit; usually conceived of as a hairy creature in human form he protected the family and warned them of impending disaster in the home.

Hamlyn Group

Appendix

Bards
Poets and story-tellers, regarded in northern Europe as possessing magical powers and closely associated with the Druids.

Draupnir
The magic ring of the Germanic god Odin; also the name of a dwarf who may originally have been the maker of the ring; Odin placed it on the funeral pyre of Balder.

Det Kongelige Bibliotek

Edda
The title given to two separate books, the *Elder* or *Poetic Edda*, and the *Younger* or *Prose Edda* of Snorri, which together provide a major source of information about the beliefs and culture of the Scandinavians before the advent of Christianity. Probably composed in Iceland in the early 13th century, they contain myths and legends associated with the principal northern gods and heroes.

John Webb

Elf
In northern European mythology elves were originally small supernatural beings of two kinds, the light elves who lived in Alfheim, and the dark elves who lived in Swartheim; they later became the fairy people of Germanic folklore and were often thought of as mischievous and malignant, having the power to harm people with their 'elf-arrows'; children born with deformities were said to be 'elf-marked'.

Karin Hoddle

Elm
In Teutonic mythology the first woman, Embla, was created from an elm by the three gods Odin, Hoenir and Loki who gave the tree breath, soul and warmth; in England the elm was also known as 'elven' because of its association with the elves, and in Devon it was believed that lightning would not strike an elm. According to country lore, when the leaves of the elm were as big as a mouse's ear it was time to plant barley, while the shedding of its leaves before the autumn foretold disease among the cattle, with consequent disaster as a possibility.

Holda
Germanic sky goddess, sometimes also a fertility goddess or goddess of the hearth; she was commonly the leader of the Wild Hunt which rode

on stormy nights; snow was caused by Holda shaking her feather bed, while rain fell when she washed her veil; in Germanic folklore she became identified with the Queen of the Elves and was also associated with witches, herself appearing as an old, witch-like woman; Grimm's fairly tale *Frau Holle* (an alternative name for Holda) repeats many of the motifs of earlier legend, and weaves them into a somewhat frightening children's story.

Ignis fatuus
'Foolish Fire', the pale flickering light sometimes seen hovering over marshy ground or graveyards; it is thought to be caused by the spontaneous combustion of gases from decaying matter; also called will-o-the-wisp, jack-o-lantern, fox-fire, corpse light, friar's lantern, fairy fire; in folk belief it is ascribed to a mischievous spirit which misleads night travellers, or to fairies or witches; in Germany it is said to be a wandering soul, in Russia the soul of an unbaptized child; sometimes taken as an evil omen.

Kraken
It seems likely that the kraken was a kind of giant polyp or cuttle-fish, perhaps a survival of some almost extinct prehistoric sea creature. Bishop Pontoppidan, who wrote quite extensively about this inhabitant of Norwegian waters, had a theory that the floating islands, which suddenly appeared or disappeared in Northern seas, were in fact kraken; and also that the medusa or jelly-fish might be its ovum.

Lapps
The ancient Norwegians, believing that the Lapps were skilled in sorcery, were in the habit of visiting them secretly to learn their art; indeed their medieval kings were obliged to prohibit journeys to Finnmark for the purpose. Finnmark is the most northerly province of Norway, where many Lapps live. They were converted to Christianity at the end of the 17th century.

Leaping and Jumping
A way of expressing religious fervour and of inducing ecstatic excitement: high leaps in Basque, Russian, Balkan, British and other folk dances may be rooted in imitative magic, in the form of jumping to make the crops grow tall and the herds increase, as in the hymn of the Curetes of ancient Greece, 'leap for fleecy flocks, and leap for fields of fruit'.

Ragnarok
The 'Doom of the Gods', or 'Twilight of the Gods' in Scandinavian mythology, the destruction of the

Engay Kusch

gods and the world by evil monsters, the forces of chaos; afterwards a new heaven and a new earth will appear,

Troll
This elemental spirit of northern European mythology belongs to that supernatural fairy community which was once assumed to exercise dominion over Nature, a class of spirit regarded with considerable apprehension since all elementals were known to be capricious, treacherous and frequently hostile.

Tyr
Scandinavian sky god, worshipped as Tiw in Anglo-Saxon England; his early Germanic name was probably Tiwaz, related to Greek Zeus and Roman Jupiter; he had only one hand; the other having been bitten off by the Fenris wolf; he gave his name to Tuesday, but had declined in importance by the Viking Age.

Valhalla
The hall of the slain, the paradise ruled by Odin in Norse mythology, to which heroes and distinguished warriors went after death, conducted there by the Valkyries, Odin's battle-maidens; there they fought all day and those who fell were restored again in the evening, to feast on pork and mead.

Yggdrasil
In Scandinavian mythology, the world ash tree; standing at the centre of the universe, it connects together the heavens, the earth and the underworld; after the doom of the gods

at the end of the world the man and woman who will repopulate the earth emerge from the world tree.

Yule
Old-fashioned term for the Christmas season, from the Norse winter fire festival over which the god Odin presided; the Yule-log should be brought into the house with ceremony on Christmas Eve and should be lighted from a piece of the previous year's log, which has been kept all year to preserve the luck of the household.

THE CELTIC REALMS

King Arthur and the Knights of the Round Table

The hero of a famous cycle of legends and romances, Arthur was said to have been born at Tintagel in Cornwall. He became King of Britain and held court at Camelot as the leader of a band of noble warriors, the Knights of the Round Table. The knights rode out to seek adventure and great deeds, notably in the quest of the Grail – in Christian legend the holy cup used by Christ at the Last Supper. Arthur was betrayed by his wife Guinevere and his nephew, or son, Mordred. Wounded in battle against Mordred, he was carried away by three fairy queens to Avalon, the land of immortal heroes, from which he will return to lead his countrymen in the time of their greatest peril.

The rest of our information about Arthur comes from romantic stories which may or may not be founded partly on fact. In Celtic legend he became a great hero, violent and boisterous, who rid the land of giants, monsters and witches. He seems to have resembled the Greek hero Hercules in performing superhuman feats or 'labours'. He slaughtered the Demon Cat of Losanne, he hunted the fabulous boar Twrch Trwyth and drove him into the sea. A Welsh poem called *The Spoils of Annwn*, probably written in the 10th century, refers to Arthur's raid on the land of the dead, the isle of Annwn. He sailed there in his ship Prydwen and although he took three times Prydwen's normal complement with him, only seven men returned from the expedition alive.

The object of the raid was to seize the magic cauldron of Annwn, from which only the brave and the true could eat – 'It will not boil the food of a coward or one forsworn.' This cauldron may be the original Grail and if it supplied the food of immortal heroes, Arthur may have gained immortality by seizing it.

In the early Celtic stories Arthur has a large band of heroic comrades, including Cei Wynn (who became Sir Kay in the later romances), Bedwyr (Sir Bedivere), Gereint (Sir Gareth), Gwalchmai (Sir Gawain),

Llenlleawc (Sir Lancelot) and Drwst Iron-Fist (probably Tristan). His wife is Gwenhwyfar (Guinevere). Some of the old Celtic gods are with him, now turned into men – Manawydan, Teyrnon and Gwynn son of Nudd, the master of hell. Also in his retinue are personifications of superhuman qualities, like Drem son of Dremidydd (Sight son of Seer) who could see a fly in Scotland from as far away as Cornwall, and Clust son of Clustfeinad (Ear son of Hearer) who could hear an ant getting up in the morning 50 miles off.

An English chronicler named William of Malmesbury, writing in 1125, said that the Britons (or possibly Bretons) told many fables about Arthur, though he was 'a man worthy to be celebrated, not by idle fictions but by authentic history'; and that in 1087 the tomb of Walwin (Gawain) had been discovered in Wales on the sea coast, but no one knew where Arthur was buried and so 'ancient ballads fable that he will return'.

William's implied call for an authentic history of Arthur was never answered but a few years later, c 1135, the first full and connected account of the hero appeared in Geoffrey of Monmouth's *History of the Kings of Britain*.

Geoffrey's book begins with the supposed first King of Britain – Brute (Brutus), great-grandson of Aeneas, who was one of the survivors of the Trojan War and the hero of Virgil's *Aeneid*. Brute and his Trojan retinue came to Albion (Britain), which was inhabited only by a few giants, and founded the city of New Troy (London). The island came to be called Britain, from Brute, and subsequent British kings were descended from him, down to Uther Pendragon, who succeeded to the throne when the Britons were hard pressed by the Saxons. Uther Pendragon does not seem to have ever existed in reality, and his name may come from a mistranslation of the Welsh phrase *Arthur mab Uthr*, 'Arthur the terrible', as Arthur son of Uther.

According to Geoffrey, Uther Pendragon

British Museum

Above *When Arthur lay dying, Sir Bedivere took the sword Excalibur and threw it into the water, from which a hand rose and caught it. Early 14th-century manuscript.* **Facing page** *King Arthur, from a late 14th-century French tapestry. The real Arthur was probably a war-chief who fought against the Saxons invading Britain c 500 AD.*

fell violently in love with Igerna, the beautiful wife of the Duke of Cornwall. Her husband snatched her away from court and shut her up in Tintagel castle while he went to gather troops. Uther was furious and led an army into Cornwall to punish the duke. He also appealed to Merlin, the great magician, who by magic art made Uther look exactly like the duke. Disguised as Igerna's husband, Uther had no difficulty in entering both Tintagel castle and Igerna's bed, and consequently Arthur was conceived at Tintagel.

Arthur was 15 when Uther Pendragon died and was buried at Stonehenge. He was crowned king at Silchester. He defeated and harried the Saxons, plundering them of much treasure with which he rewarded his fighting men. He won a great victory in Somerset, in a battle probably intended to be Mount Badon though Geoffrey does not say so. Arthur wore 'a helm of gold graven with the semblance of a dragon.' His shield was called Pridwen (formerly his ship in *The Spoils of Annwn*). His sword was called Caliburn (later Excalibur) and had been forged in Avalon.

Arthur went on to subdue the Scots and to marry the beautiful Guinevere. His sister married Loth, Duke of Lothian, and by him had two sons, Gawain and Mordred. Kay and Bedivere were also prominent among Arthur's knights.

Foreign rulers were alarmed by Arthur's successes and when he discovered this, 'his heart was uplifted for that he was a terror unto them all, and he set his desire upon subduing the whole of Europe unto himself.'

Annoyed by a demand for tribute from the Roman Emperor, Arthur and his barons led an army to the continent, leaving Guinevere and Mordred, Arthur's nephew, to govern Britain. The Roman Emperor, Lucius Hiberius, brought levies from Byzantium, Africa, Spain, Persia, Egypt, Syria and Babylon in an army of over 40,000 men against Arthur. The armies met in France and Arthur was victorious in a tremendous battle of 'thrust of spear and stroke of swords and fling of javelin.' Bedivere was killed and Kay died of the wounds he received. After 'a most unconscionable slaughter', the Romans were driven from the field.

Arthur intended to march on Rome but meanwhile in Britain Mordred 'had tyrannously and traitorously set the crown of the kingdom upon his own head, and had linked him in unhallowed union with Guinevere the Queen.'

Arthur returned at once to Britain with his army. The gallant Gawain was killed in battle against his evil brother Mordred, who was driven back to the river Camel in Cornwall, while Guinevere fled to a nunnery. In a final battle at the Camel (Geoffrey's interpretation of the *Cambrian Annals'* battle of Camlann), the traitor Mordred fell 'and many thousands along with him'. But 'the renowned King Arthur himself was wounded deadly and was borne thence unto the Isle of Avalon for the healing of his wounds, where he gave up the crown of Britain unto his kinsman Constantine...in the year of the Incarnation of Our Lord five hundred and forty-two.'

In the year of Geoffrey's death, 1155, Robert Wace translated Geoffrey's *History* from Latin into French under the title of *Roman de Brut* (The Story of Brute). He remarked that the Bretons of his day told many stories of the Round Table, and this is the first reference to the Round Table which has survived. By 1200 an English cleric named Layamon had turned Wace's *Brut* into English, adding to it the story that after the final battle with Mordred, the fairy queen Morgan took Arthur in a boat to Avalon. He also said that Arthur had the Round Table specially built so as to avoid disputes about precedence among his knights: it seated 1600 men.

Meanwhile in France, another able writer, Chrétien de Troyes, had turned his attention to the Arthurian legends.

In Geoffrey of Monmouth Arthur is the central figure and hero; in Chrétien and the later French legends Arthur recedes into the background. Chrétien's poems are about the adventures of individual knights of Arthur's court: Gawain, Yvain, Erec, Lancelot and Perceval. Geoffrey as an Englishman was pleased to imagine Arthur conquering most of western Europe, including France; Chrétien and other Frenchmen imagined no such thing and their Arthur is not a great conqueror. Geoffrey placed Arthur and his court in real surroundings; in the French legends, though a few names of real places are used, Arthur and his knights live in a country that never was, a timeless fairyland beyond reality. Geoffrey never mentions the Grail; Chrétien began a poem about the Grail but did not live to finish it. Geoffrey has comparatively little to offer in the way of marvels and magic: Chrétien and his successors have far more. This element of the marvellous and the supernatural probably came to French writers from the travelling story-tellers, and originally from Celtic sources.

Chrétien portrayed Arthur's court in a way which suited his own surroundings and his own ideals. He was heavily influenced by the code of chivalry which affected the polite society of courts and castles in France in his time.

Quests are the chief feature of Chrétien's stories and of the later romances. A knight rides out to seek adventure and to preserve, or re-establish, his honour and reputation as a ferocious but courteous fighting man. During the quest he does battle against enemy knights, who may be chivalrous warriors like himself or evil, crafty and treacherous oppressors of the poor and weak. He rescues beautiful women from wicked knights and wizards. He is often captured and escapes death or dishonour by a hair's breadth at the last moment. He encounters savage beasts and monsters, glamorous seducers and witches, enchanted castles and spell-bound forests.

In the 15th century the Arthurian legend reached its finest expression in Sir Thomas Malory's *Morte D'Arthur* (written in English despite its French title). The book is a reworking of much of the earlier Arthurian and Grail material and although there are inconsistencies and confusions because so many different tales are combined together, the result glows with the charm and splendour of Malory's style.

The story of Arthur has attracted many writers and artists since Malory, including Spenser, Tennyson, the Pre-Raphaelites and Masefield. Whether Arthur was originally a sacred king has been hotly disputed by scholars.

An old Welsh poem says that he had three wives, all named Guinevere, which might suggest that he was regarded as a sacred king married to the Triple Goddess. Mordred's attempt to seize both the throne and Guinevere suggests the combat between the sacred king and his rival and attempted successor, who tries to oust him as consort of the Goddess. The evidence is inadequate to prove the theory but it may be that this ancient theme, lying beneath the surface of the legend, has helped to give it a deep and timeless appeal.

Camelot

Camelot was the capital of King Arthur where, according to legend, he reigned over the Britons before the Saxon conquest.

The oldest known stories of Arthur never refer to Camelot, as such. The King first holds court there explicitly in the romance *Lancelot*, written by Chrétien de Troyes between 1160 and 1180. Three centuries later Malory makes it the chief city of the realm, where the Round Table is housed. He sometimes equates it with Winchester, yet in one passage of his work it seems to be north of Carlisle. Tennyson never attempts to localize Camelot: in the *Idylls of the King*, it is symbolic, in the poet's own words 'of

Facing page: **Above** *An oak table in Winchester Castle, once believed to be the original Round Table. Henry VIII showed it proudly to royal visitors. The Tudors based their claim to the English throne partly on their supposed descent from Arthur.* **Below** *Arthur feasting in Camelot, where the Round Table was housed.* **This page** *Arthur's knights constantly set out in search of adventure. The supreme quest was the Holy Grail – the cup used by Christ at the Last Supper.* **The Knights Swear the Quest for the Grail.**

the gradual growth of human beliefs and institutions, and of the spiritual development of man.' The name in fact has tended to become evocative rather than geographical. Thus the conversion of T. H. White's Arthur cycle into a musical involved an almost inevitable change of title from *The Once and Future King* to *Camelot*.

Local legends and antiquarian guesswork have proposed several sites for this elusive city. One is Colchester, the Roman Camulodunum. Another theory places it near Tintagel, Arthur's reputed Cornish birthplace, in a district which contains the River Camel and Camelford. However, the candidate with the strongest claim to a genuine underlying tradition is Cadbury Castle in Somerset.

The 'Castle' is an earthwork fort of the pre-Roman Iron Age on an isolated hill 500 feet high, which looks over the Vale of Avalon to Glastonbury Tor in the distance. The ramparts surround an enclosure of 18 acres on top of the hill. The village of Queen Camel – once simply Camel – is fairly close, as is the River Cam. The antiquary John Leland, in the reign of Henry VIII, speaks of local people referring to the hill-fort as 'Camalat' and as the home of Arthur. Folklore of immemorial age has clustered round it. A well inside the ramparts is called King Arthur's Well, and the summit plateau King Arthur's Palace. The King is said to lie asleep in a cave and at midsummer the ghostly hoof-beats of his knights can be heard riding forth.

Cadbury Castle, easily the largest and most formidable of the known British strongholds of that period, fits logically into the picture as the headquarters of the greatest British leader. In that sense it could be the 'real Camelot' of the 'real Arthur', as archeological investigation may one day show.

Furthermore, its archeological context includes other places that figure in the Arthurian legend. Thus at Tintagel in Cornwall, while there is no sign of the pre-Norman castle where Arthur was allegedly born, the famous headland is now known to have been inhabited in his time. Its occupants were British monks, and the imported pottery used by their community has supplied key clues to the dating and interpretation of other sites, including Cadbury itself.

Glastonbury

The small town of Glastonbury in Somerset, famed for its ruined Abbey, is dominated by the Tor, a hill rising about 500 feet above sea level and commanding a wide expanse of low-lying country. The abbey is the centre of a vast complex of legends as it is traditionally the oldest Christian foundation in Britain, and in some sense a repository of pre-Christian mysteries.

At the start of the Christian era, Glastonbury was virtually an island encircled by lagoons and rivers. To the British Celts it was a place of great religious awe, the enchanted Isle of Avalon, consecrated to the shades of the dead. An alternative name for it was Ynys-witrin, the Isle of Glass and

'Glastonbury' is a corrupt Anglo-Saxon rendering of this.

The legend recounts how in the 1st century AD Joseph of Arimathea, the rich man who buried Christ, brought the Holy Grail to Avalon. In obedience to a vision, he and his companions built a wattle chapel, the 'Old Church'; this was still standing in the early Middle Ages, dedicated to the Virgin and deeply venerated.

By the 5th century, Christian hermits were living on the spot and worshipping in the Old Church and St Patrick reorganized the little community and gave it a monastic rule. King Arthur, after receiving mortal wounds in his famous last battle, was reputedly buried in the Abbey graveyard.

When the Saxon conquerors took Glastonbury they were no longer heathens them-

selves: hence, this is the one place in Britain with Christian continuity stretching backward without a break to King Arthur, to the Romans, in fact to the apostolic age. It is a national shrine, with a spiritual character which has always set Britain apart from the rest of Christendom.

The first known story that connects Arthur with Glastonbury is told by Caradoc of Llancarfan. About 1150 Caradoc wrote a Life of the 6th-century British monk and historian Gildas. In this he says that Gildas lived for a time with the Glastonbury community. Meanwhile Arthur (portrayed by Caradoc as a somewhat dubious upstart) was trying to extend his power over Britain. Somerset was independent under its king Melwas, who had a stronghold close to the monastery. He carried off Arthur's wife

'Guennuvar' and kept her there. Arthur arrived with troops from Devon and Cornwall, but the marshes hindered his advance. Gildas and the Abbot mediated and, meeting under the sacred roof of the Old Church, the kings agreed on a pact and the lady was restored.

In the Round Table romances the story reappears, but the geography becomes vaguer and the characters change. Melwas turns into 'Meleagant' and Lancelot takes Arthur's place as the rescuer. The abduction of the Queen looks like a Celtic fairy tale motif. However, the recent discovery of what may be interpreted as a Dark Age citadel on the Tor suggests that Melwas may have been a real local king, in which case a war and treaty involving Arthur become more plausible.

The better-known story of Arthur's grave is confused by the doubts over the name Avalon and its application to Glastonbury. The island of Avalon, the otherworldly apple orchard, may have been originally the island of Avallach, an unlocalized hero of Celtic legend. Geoffrey of Monmouth's *History of the Kings of Britain*, composed between 1135 and 1140, says that Arthur's sword was forged in the Isle of Avalon, and that he was taken there after his last battle for his wounds to be healed. However, Geoffrey's Avalon is no definite place, and in a later work he makes it a sort of Isle of the Blest in the Atlantic.

Glastonbury may have been a pagan centre and a supposed gateway to Annwn, the realm of shades and fairy folk – which indeed is sometimes equated with Avalon in Welsh folklore. Its pagan aura may even account for the monastery, if the founders' motive was exorcism and purification. But all this is conjecture. If Arthur was buried there, the reason was simply that the monks' graveyard, with its relics of saints, was an honourable burial place.

Left Glastonbury was well qualified to possess a sacred aura for the Celts. A Welsh legend preserves the belief that Glastonbury Tor was an entrance to the otherworld, and the chapel on top of the hill was dedicated to St Michael, the vanquisher of evil powers. **Below *The Holy Thorn, which blooms near Christmas time, may have been brought to the Abbey by a medieval pilgrim.***

The Holy Grail

Shorn for the moment of most of their enticing details, the Grail legends are basically about a knight who comes to an eerie and magnificent castle which is the home of a crippled king, the Fisher King or Maimed King. In the castle the hero sees a magic sword and a lance which is dripping blood. During a lavish feast he sees the Grail itself, variously described as a dish, a cup, a ciborium (the vessel in which the sacred host is kept, a cup with an arched cover surmounted by a cross), or even as a stone. The Grail is carried in procession during the feast, or sometimes itself serves the feast. The hero is supposed to ask a question. If he fails to ask it, he has failed in his quest and calamities follow. If he asks the right question, the Fisher King is healed and, in some versions, the Waste Land which he rules is once again restored to fertility.

Looming dimly in the background behind the medieval legends are older Irish and Welsh stories in which a hero visits the otherworld, sees its marvels and mysteries, and sometimes seizes one of its treasures. The close connection between the Grail and feasting is one of the clues to its origins in Celtic mythology, which is rich in 'vessels of plenty', magic vessels which provide limitless quantities of food and drink. Feasting was one of the great Celtic pleasures and naturally the feasting in the otherworld was beyond anything to be found in this one. The smith god Goibniu, for instance, brewed beer in a cauldron for an otherworld feast which made everyone who took part in it immortal. In many mythologies it is the food and drink of the otherworld which keeps its inhabitants forever young.

The magic vessel of plenty is not always a cauldron. It may be a dish, like the platter of Rhydderch the Generous which instantly provided the food anyone wanted, according to a 16th-century list of the Thirteen Treasures of the Island of Britain. In *Culhwch and Olwen* (one of the stories in the Welsh collection called the *Mabinogion*) four magic vessels have to be obtained for Culhwch's wedding feast: a cup in which is the best of all drink; a platter or table on which everyone would find the meat that he wanted; a horn for pouring out the drink; and the cauldron of Diwrnach the Irishman, for boiling the meat. The variety of Celtic vessels of plenty may be one reason for the later variations in the shape of the Grail.

The cauldron of Diwrnach was stolen from Ireland by Arthur and his men. It was probably an otherworld cauldron originally, for the same list of the Thirteen Treasures includes the Cauldron of Tyrnoc (or Dyrnawg) the Giant, which would boil food for a brave man but not for a coward. A similar otherworld cauldron was seized by Arthur in a Welsh poem called *The Spoils of Annwn*. 'The cauldron of the Chief of Annwn, what is its nature? Blue round its rim and pearls; it will not boil the food of a coward....'

Another celebrated cauldron is the one which belonged to Bran the Blessed. According to the story of *Branwen* (also in the *Mabinogion*) this cauldron restored the dead to life: 'a man of thine slain today, cast him into the cauldron, and by tomorrow he will be as well as he was at the best, save only that he will not have power of speech.' This cauldron's failure to restore speech may have something to do with the failure of some of the Grail heroes to speak at the crucial moment of the quest.

Bran was probably the prototype of the Fisher King, whose name in some of the medieval romances is Bron. The son of a sea god, he died from a poisoned spear wound in the foot, which might be the origin of the Fisher King's crippling wound in the thighs. His head was cut off and taken by his companions to a great hall, where they passed a joyous 80 years in its company, never seeming to grow any older. This scene seems to reappear in the French romance *Perlesvaus*, written c 1225, in which Gawain sits down to feast in the Fisher King's hall with 12 knights, each of whom was 100 years old but none of them looked more than 40.

The oldest extant romance of the Grail is the unfinished *Conte del Graal* (or *Roman de Perceval*), written c 1180 by the French poet Chrétien de Troyes, who says that he based it on a book his noble patron had given him. The principal hero is Perceval, an uncouth young man who was brought up in seclusion by his widowed mother in the remote wilds of Wales, from which he made his way to Arthur's court. He knew nothing of the ways of the world but was advised by an older knight not to talk too much or pester people with questions.

Trying to find his way home again, worried by the fact that his mother had fainted when he left her, Perceval came to a river and saw a man fishing from a boat. The fisherman invited Perceval to his castle nearby. At the castle, a squire came in, carrying a white lance which dripped blood from its point. Curious but mindful of advice, Perceval asked no questions. Next a beautiful girl came in, carrying in her hands 'a grail', made of gold, set with jewels and giving off an intensely brilliant light. The company sat down to eat and with each course the Grail passed before them but Perceval reined in his curiosity and 'did not ask concerning the grail, whom one served with it.'

Perceval was shown politely to bed but next morning the castle was completely deserted. He rode out over the drawbridge, which was promptly raised behind him. He shouted to whoever had raised it but there was no answer. Riding away into the forest, he met a maiden who told him that the castle belonged to the rich Fisher King, who had been wounded in battle by a javelin which pierced both his thighs. He was now crippled and fishing was his only pastime. Perceval had done ill by not asking about the lance, and worse by not asking about the Grail, for his questions would have cured the Fisher King 'and much good would have come of it'. What held his tongue was his sin against his mother, who had died of grief for him.

Perceval returned to Arthur's court, where a hideously ugly damsel – 'never was there creature so loathly save in hell' – rode in on a mule to reproach him. 'Fortune is bald behind, but has a forelock in front . . . you did not seize Fortune when you met her.' He should have asked why the lance bled and who was 'the rich man whom one served with the grail.' If the Fisher King is not healed, 'Ladies will lose their husbands, lands will be laid waste . . . and many knights will die.'

Perceval was determined to discover the answers to the two questions. For five years he rode out, proving his mettle in many a strange adventure, but in all this time he never went into a church or worshipped God. One Good Friday he met a knight who reproached him for bearing arms on the day Christ died. Perceval went to a holy hermit to confess his sins. The hermit told him that the one who was served with the Grail was the father of the Fisher King. What it served him with, and all that he lived on, was the sacred host. On this diet he had lived 15 years without ever quitting his room. The hermit told Perceval to 'believe in God, love God, worship God', to go to church and to serve his fellow men. At this point the story breaks off.

Partly because it is unfinished, the story raises more difficulties than it solves. The lance is not explained, nor why the question should heal the Fisher King. Confusingly, there are two kings in the castle (as in many of the later romances). There are three different explanations of Perceval's silence. The Grail is described at the end as a large dish on which the sacred host is served to the Fisher King's father, but most uncanonically by a woman instead of a priest. All the

same, it is a hauntingly powerful story.

Some authorities doubt whether Chrétien himself wrote the last part of the tale but as we have it, at any rate, it is clearly not a pagan story, even though it uses motifs which were originally pagan. This is driven home by the sound Christian advice which the hermit gives Perceval at the end.

After Chrétien's death, others turned their attention to the Grail legends and the old pagan themes were increasingly Christianized. Chrétien's *Conte* itself was continued in four different sequels. In the First Continuation (probably before 1200) Gawain sees the 'rich grail', which moves about by itself at the feast, serving each course and filling the wine-cups. The lord of the castle explains that the lance which bleeds is the Holy Lance with which a Roman soldier pierced Christ on the cross, 'and at once there came out blood and water' (John 19.34).

Both the Lance and the Grail have now been connected with the blood of Jesus, the blood which was spilled to save men from death and the Devil. The Grail itself has been identified as the cup of the first Mass, containing the wine which was not merely figuratively but in all reality the life-blood of God.

Most of the great relics relating to the life and death of Jesus had been found, or at least it was believed they had been found, and the idea that the cup of the Last Supper was still in existence and was guarded somewhere in secret was an immensely exciting one in an age which believed in the miraculous power of relics to sustain and save.

Above *Unlike the other Arthurian heroes, Galahad's history does not go back into the pagan past. He was a character deliberately invented to contrast the ideal of the perfect Christian knight with the brave but essentially worldly ideals of chivalry.* **Facing page** *Gawain was one of the greatest heroes of the Round Table, famed for courage and courtesy. Setting out on a quest he takes leave of Arthur and Guinevere* **(left)** *and rides through a forest* **(right).** **Below** *The Grail appears to the knights of the Round Table and provides each man with the food he most desires: it is shown in this 14th-century French* MS *as a ciborium, containing the host.*

Bodleian Library Colour Filmstrip

Bodleian Library Colour Filmstrip

Galahad

'But in the Siege Perilous there shall no man sit therein but one, and if there be any so hardy to do it he shall be destroyed, and he that shall sit there shall have no fellow.' These are Merlin's words in Malory's *Morte D'Arthur* and the knight who had no equal and who took his appointed place in the Siege Perilous, the empty seat at the Round Table, was Galahad.

The coming of Galahad to Camelot, one year at Pentecost, marked the beginning of the quest of the Grail and the end of the fellowship of Arthur's knights. A sword had been found, embedded in a great stone and with lettering on the pommel which said that only the best knight in the world could draw it out. Lancelot refused the attempt but Gawain and Perceval tried and failed. When the knights sat down to eat at the Round Table, an old man came in, leading the young Galahad without sword or shield but with an empty scabbard. The old man led Galahad to his place at the Siege Perilous. The other knights marvelled and showed Galahad the sword in the stone. He drew it lightly out and settled it in his scabbard.

A greater portent was in store, for after a tournament in which Galahad proved his prowess as a fighter, when they all went to supper they heard a terrible roll of thunder, a ray of bright sunlight shone into the hall, 'and all they were alighted of the grace of the Holy Ghost.' Unlike Christ's disciples who spoke in tongues at the first Pentecost, with which a parallel and a contrast are being drawn here, the knights sat as silent as if they had been struck dumb. 'Then there entered into the hall the Holy Grail covered with white samite, but there was none might see it, nor who bare it.'

Awestruck, Gawain and most of the other knights vowed to go in search of the Grail. King Arthur sadly lamented that he had been bereft of 'the fairest fellowship and the truest of knighthood that ever were seen together in any realm of the world: for when they depart from hence I am sure they shall never meet more in this world, for they shall die many in the quest.'

Galahad rides many journeys and finds many adventures. With Perceval and Bors he comes to a miraculous ship (the ship of Faith) in which is the sword that struck what Malory called 'the dolorous stroke', the blow that killed King Lambar and turned his kingdom into the Waste Land.

Galahad took this sword and eventually, after years of search, the three knights came to the castle of Corbenic, the home of the Maimed King and the Grail. Here they saw the Grail itself.

Galahad no longer desired to live, for the Grail had revealed to him 'those things that the heart of man cannot conceive nor tongue relate'. He had been 'translated from the earthly plane to the celestial, to the joy of the glorious martyrs and the beloved of Our Lord'. After further adventures Perceval became a hermit and Bors made his way back to Camelot. But Galahad, who had seen the supreme vision of heaven, could not return to the world of men. His prayer to die was granted and his soul was borne to heaven by rejoicing angels. A hand came down from the sky and took the Grail and the Lance, and carried them to heaven also, and no man has ever seen them since.

Gawain

The first of King Arthur's knights to dedicate himself to the search for the Grail was the one whose spiritual bankruptcy was most clearly demonstrated in the quest. Originally a hero of pagan legend, Gawain became the very model of a chivalrous knight, famous for courage, loyalty, generosity and courtesy. But in the later stories he is overshadowed, first by Lancelot and then by Galahad.

In Geoffrey of Monmouth's account Gawain is Arthur's nephew, a hothead and a notable warrior. In the campaign against the Romans he starts a skirmish when greatly outnumbered, because he is infuriated by the sneers of the enemy, and he strikes one opponent such a terrible blow with his sword that he splits him through helmet and skull down to the breast. He is killed in battle at Richborough when Arthur's army lands to settle accounts with Mordred.

William of Malmesbury, writing a few years before Geoffrey, said that in 1087 the tomb of Arthur's noble nephew Walwin had been discovered on the Welsh coast. It was 14 feet long. In a sculpture of c 1100 at Modena Cathedral in Italy, Gawain is helping-helping Arthur to rescue Guinevere.

Chrétien de Troyes portrayed Gawain as the pattern of chivalry. No lady in distress ever appealed in vain to 'the good and gentle lord Gawain', and to equal or outdo him was the final test of heroic valour. The early 13th-century German poet Wolfram von Eschenbach said of him in *Parzival* that: 'on the battlefield his heart was a fortress, towering so against sharp attacks that he could always be seen in the thick of the fray. Friend and foe acknowledged that his battlecry rang loud in pursuit of fame...'

In the Austrian Grail romance *Diu Krône* Gawain is successful, but generally he loses stature when the story-tellers take him out of his native element of courts and fair ladies, jousts and battles, and send him in search of the Grail. The first sequel added to Chrétien's *Conte del Graal* in the late 12th century contains a haunting account of Gawain's experiences at the Grail castle.

When the Round Table is finally brought to disaster, he is given back something of his old high quality. Opposing his half-brother Mordred and his brother Agravaine, he remains loyal to Arthur. Wounded in combat with Lancelot, his last actions are attempts to heal the breach between Lancelot and Arthur. He dies, and is buried in a chapel in Dover Castle and, Malory says, 'there yet all men may see the skull of him, and the same wound is seen that Sir Lancelot gave him in battle.'

Lancelot

'No knight was ever born of man and woman, and no knight ever sat in a saddle, who was the equal of this man.' The earliest surviving romance of Lancelot of the Lake, greatest and most tragic of the heroes of the Round Table, is the *Lancelot* (or *Le Chevalier de la Charrette* – the Knight of the Cart) of Chrétien de Troyes. The story tells how Queen Guinevere was kidnapped by the wicked Meleagant, son of the king of an enchanted land from which no prisoner could escape. Lancelot, who was passionately in love with Guinevere, and she with him, drove his way through all dangers, obstacles and enemies to rescue her, so breaking the enchantment and setting free all the other prisoners held captive there.

Chrétien may have been the first author to exploit the theme of the love of Lancelot and Guinevere, which plays such a crucial role in the later Arthurian legends. It is significant that the poem, which exalts the lovers' passion almost to the level of religious rapture, gives them an excuse by showing Arthur himself as a weakling and coward who is taunted and defied by the evil Meleagant.

The story that Guinevere was kidnapped, however, is older than Chrétien. The famous carving at Modena Cathedral apparently shows her being rescued from an enemy castle, and Caradoc of Llancarfan's *Vita Gildae* (possibly c 1100) says that Melwas, the king of the Summer Country, carried Guinevere off to his stronghold at Glastonbury and Arthur had to come to her rescue.

Lancelot himself is also older than Chrétien. In the Welsh tale of *Culhwch and Olwen* he is Llenlleawc the Irishman, who may originally have been the Irish god Lug. Later, he has strong ties with the land of Brittany. He takes his title 'of the Lake' from the tradition that he was brought up by a lake fairy. Chrétien mentions that he owned a magic ring which freed anyone who gazed on it from the power of enchantment, given him by the fairy. In the late 12th-century German *Lanzelet* the infant Lancelot is stolen from his mother by a fairy who takes him to her castle on a crystal mountain, in a magic island of 10,000 maidens where flowers and trees bloom all the year round. When he grows up, she sends him to Arthur's court to be knighted.

In the French prose tale of *Lancelot* (early 13th century, part of what is called the Prose *Lancelot* or Vulgate cycle) the fairy is called the Lady of the Lake. Before sending Lancelot to Arthur's court, she gives him arms and the magic ring, and instructs him in the duties of chivalry and the importance of protecting the weak and defending the Church. He becomes the best knight in the world, the indomitable hero of innumerable battles, jousts and quests. As Malory puts it, 'in all tournaments and jousts and deeds of arms, both for life and death, he passed all other knights, and at no time he was ever overcome but it were by treason or enchantment.' But Lancelot and Guinevere fall helplessly in love and because of their sinful liaison Lancelot fails in some of his adventures. He is told that a better knight will appear and will win the Grail.

This proves to be no less than Galahad, Lancelot's own son, begotten on the daughter of the keeper of the Grail castle while Lancelot is under an enchantment and thinks himself in the arms of Guinevere.

In the next work in the cycle, the *Queste del Saint Graal*, Lancelot fails in the Grail quest because he is a sinner. He has always kept sternly silent about his affair with his royal mistress but now, bitterly disappointed, he breaks down and confesses to a hermit: 'I have sinned unto death with my lady, she whom I have loved all my life, Queen Guinevere, the wife of King Arthur... For her love alone I accomplished the exploits with which the whole world rings. She it is who raised me from poverty to riches and from hardship to the sum of earthly bliss. But I know full well that this bond is the sin that has earned me Our Lord's dire wrath...' He promises to renounce her and because of his repentance he eventually reaches the Grail castle and is granted a partial and passing experience of the Grail.

The search for the Grail has destroyed the old fellowship of the Round Table by devaluing its aims and standards, and by revealing human weakness.

Scenes from a French MS showing: the birth of Lancelot; Lancelot with his mother and the Lady of the Lake; his knighting at Arthur's court; and his vision of the Holy Grail.

Morgan le Fay

Among the weirder figures in Arthurian legend is Arthur's sister Morgan le Fay. Her English name comes from the French Morgain la Fée, the 'fay' or fairy. In Italian she is Fata Morgana.

Her family background, in her earliest literary guise, is quite different. She is a daughter of Avallach, king of the enchanted island best known as Avalon. Morgan is thus placed in an otherworldly setting, derived from pagan mythology. Besides Avallach, tradition mentions a second lord of the island.

The romancer Chrétien de Troyes names him as Guingamor and says Morgan was his mistress. But both male rulers fade out. In Arthurian lore generally, Morgan is lady of Avalon in her own right, with another parentage.

As a literary character, she seems to have taken shape during the early 12th century in the Arthurian lays of Breton minstrels, racially akin to the Welsh. When they adopted her she was a water nymph of Breton folklore. But Welsh legend furnished a similar figure called Modron, said to have been Avallach's daughter, and her attributes were annexed to Morgan.

The Welsh lady Modron, whose attributes she acquired, is known to have been the river goddess Matrona. Morgan herself may have been the Breton form of a goddess whom the Irish called Morrigan.

In a bewildering variety of stories Parsifal, who is a beautiful but uncouth young man when he first arrives at Arthur's court, becomes one of the chief figures in the legend of the quest for the Holy Grail: Illustrations from a 13th-century manuscript show Parsifal with Hector (above) after the two knights have exhausted each other in combat and (right) praying with Galahad, the best knight in the world. In the French Queste del Saint Graal *Galahad alone penetrated the mystery of the Grail.*

Bodleian Library Colour Filmstrip

Bodleian Library Colour Filmstrip

Parsifal

Parsifal is one of the leading characters of Arthurian romance. His name appears as variants of Perceval in French and English, Parzival in German. In the basic story Perceval's father has been killed about the time of his birth and his mother takes refuge with her son in the mountains of Wales. Perceval grows up to be strong and handsome but quite ignorant of the ways of the world and of the rank to which his parentage entitles him. One day he meets a band of Arthur's knights and goes off with them. At Arthur's court he astonishes everyone by both his personal beauty and his uncouth manners. After many perils, he learns all the skills and courtesies of chivalry.

In a bewildering variety of stories, not all of which are mentioned here, the rude and rustic youth becomes the hero of the quest for the Holy Grail. The earliest version is the *Conte del Graal*, a poem by Chrétien de Troyes written c 1180, which tells the story of Perceval's adventures at the castle of the Fisher King, his failure to ask the right question about the Grail, and his return to Arthur's court, where he is reproached by the Loathly Damsel. Perceval subsequently swears the Quest: he will search till he finds the castle again, he will ask the question, he will not spend two nights in the same place till all is accomplished.

Chrétien then breaks off to recount the adventures of Gawain. When we next meet Perceval, five years later, he is in a sorry state.

He has done many deeds of prowess, has sent 60 knights as prisoners to Arthur; but he has failed in the quest and has forgotten God and never been to church. It is Good Friday and he does not know it. A group of penitents chide him for being in arms on a holy day. On their advice, he goes to a hermit who lives nearby. Very repentant, he confesses he has done 'nothing but evil' for five years, and has done nothing to obtain pardon. The hermit, who turns out to be his uncle, tells Perceval his sin lies in his unwittingly having caused his mother to die of sadness. From this came his failure to ask the question and all the trouble thereafter. The hermit explains that the Fisher King's father is he who is served with the grail, sustained for 15 years on the sacred host alone carried in the vessel. He enjoins the good knightly life on Perceval who does penance and receives communion.

Here Chrétien's unfinished story ends. Various authors attempted 'continuations'. In one, Perceval comes a second time to the castle and succeeds in mending, save for one small crack, a broken sword. The Fisher King had wounded himself while trying to repair this sword, which had belonged to the evil Lord of the Red Tower, the slayer of the Fisher's brother. Perceval undertakes a mission of vengeance, finds a smith who repairs the remaining crack and kills the Lord of the Red Tower. On his return, the Fisher King is cured and reveals himself as Perceval's uncle. The young hero is crowned as his successor and when at length he dies the Grail is carried up to heaven.

The French prose romance *Perlesvaus* (c 1200) has a remarkable ending which tells of Perceval's visit to an enchanted island, a Christianized version of a pagan Welsh 'otherworld'. Here dwell men of incredible age, with hair and beard 'whiter than new fallen snow (and yet) young of face... they all seemed to be of the age of thirty-two years'.

Astounding things tend to occur in this monastery-like community: an armed knight lives in a cask of glass, a golden chain and crown descend from the ceiling, a pit opens in the floor and 'the greatest and most dolorous cries that anyone ever heard' issue from it. The two 'masters', who know all about Perceval and the Grail, tell him that he cannot leave unless he promises to return as soon as he sees a ship with a sail bearing a red cross. If he does, he will have the crown and be king of a nearby island, 'very abundant in all good things'; if he does not rule as well as the present king, who has been 'chosen to reign in a greater realm', he will be sent to the Island of Suffering, the cries from which he has just heard. Perceval agrees and – the· Fisher King having died in the meantime – returns to the Grail castle where a voice tells him that 'the Holy Grail shall appear here no longer but within a short time you will know well where it will be'. One day the ship of the red cross appears and Perceval sets sail. In the words of the American scholar R. S. Loomis: 'The author declares that never did earthly man know what became of Perceval and that the history speaks of him no more.'

Tristan

Tristan was the son of Blancheflor, sister of Mark, king of Cornwall, and Rivalin, the lord of a part of Brittany. Rivalin was killed in battle before Tristan's birth and Blancheflor died in childbed. Brought up by his father's loyal marshal, Tristan grew to be strong and handsome, skilled in hunting, literature and music. Stranded by misadventure in Cornwall, he made a favourable impression at Mark's court, and was recognized as the king's nephew and knighted.

At that time one of the great sorrows of Cornwall was the tribute exacted by the Irish. Every year Morold, champion of the king of Ireland, would appear and demand the handing over of a party of noble youths for service in Ireland. So fearsome was he, no Cornish knight dared oppose him, but Tristan challenged him to combat. After a long and savage duel, Tristan slew Morold by cleaving his skull, a splinter of his sword remaining in the bone when the body was taken back to Ireland. But Morold had wounded Tristan with a poisoned spear: the wound would not heal and his life was feared for. It was known that the only person skilled enough to cure him was, of all people, Morold's sister Ysolt, the queen of Ireland. Tristan therefore made a typically bold plan. He sailed to Ireland and, off Dublin, his friends set him adrift alone in a small boat disguised as a minstrel named Tantris. The locals pitied him and took him to court, where the queen did indeed cure his wound. Tantris became a great favourite and was engaged as tutor in literature and music to the young princess, also called Ysolt.

When he finally returned to Cornwall, some of the courtiers began to be jealous of this young paragon who was the king's heir. They persuaded Mark that he should marry and have sons; and who better for bride than the young Ysolt, whom Tristan had praised so vividly for her beauty and intelligence and whose hand would bring peace between the two nations? Mark agreed and Tristan was sent to put the proposal.

Tristan landed in Ireland and found the country ravaged by a dragon so terrible that the king had promised his daughter in marriage to any knight who slew it. Tristan killed it and cut off a large piece of its tongue which he kept under his shirt. Now the king's steward (a cowardly man who was the princess's unwelcome suitor) happened to be riding past and could not believe his luck when he saw the reptile dead and nobody about – for Tristan, sorely wounded and overcome by the foul fumes exhaled by the monster, had fainted in a nearby wood. The steward lopped off the dragon's head and hurried to court to claim Ysolt's hand, to the dismay of the princess. But her wily mother knew the steward was incapable of this heroic deed. She and her daughter, accompanied by her niece Brangane, searched in the neighbourhood and found a stricken man whom to their astonishment they recognized as 'Tantris'. Under the queen's care, Tristan speedily recovered. But the young Ysolt noticed to her horror that a nick in the blade of his magnificent sword

Tristan arrives at a castle below the sea: from a Flemish MS *, c 1500.*

exactly matched the splinter she had taken from the skull of her beloved uncle Morold, whom she had sworn to avenge.

In a scene of high comedy, as Tristan sits helpless in his bath, Ysolt rails at him and tries to kill him with his own sword. Her mother, to whom Tristan confesses all and discloses the object of his present mission, calms her down and declares that bygones should be bygones – and that if the truth is not brought out before the king, Ysolt will have to marry the hateful steward. The princess agrees but remains implacable in her hostility to Tristan. When, at court, the steward is humiliated by Tristan producing the dragon's tongue, the king agrees to the alliance. Tristan sets sail for Cornwall with Ysolt, Brangane and all the youths who had been taken in tribute.

Now begins the passion. During the voyage, Tristan and Ysolt, still barely on speaking terms, call for a drink. By a fatal error, a lady-in-waiting gives them the flask containing a love potion brewed by the queen for Ysolt to give to Mark. It has an immediate and catastrophic effect, and by the time they make port Tristan and Ysolt have consummated their love. Terrified, Ysolt persuades her virgin cousin Brangane to lie in the dark with her husband the king at the beginning of the wedding night. The stratagem is successful: Ysolt comes to bed before wine and lights are brought. Later, she orders Brangane to be secretly murdered, lest the truth come out. But her assassins have not the heart to kill the girl who protests her innocence so eloquently.

Ysolt and Brangane are then reconciled.

Tristan and Ysolt then begin a long period of hidden tortured love. Rumours begin to go about of an attachment between them. They will both be killed if the witnesses see them and now they can never be happy together. 'Keep me in your heart; for whatever happens to mine, you shall never leave it.' Ysolt gives him a ring as a token of their love and to use to confirm any message he might ever have to send. She passionately bids him an agonized farewell.

Eventually, in a battle, as so many years before, Tristan is wounded by a poisoned spear and the wound will not heal. He suffers atrociously and knows that only Ysolt who learned her mother's skills can cure him. He sends Kaedin with the ring, to beg Ysolt to come.

Overheard thereupon by Ysolt of the White Hands, Tristan asks that the ship, when it returns, should carry a white sail if Ysolt is on board and a black if she is not. Kaedin sets out, finds Ysolt and has little trouble in persuading her to come.

At last the ship comes into view and Tristan, rousing himself on his bed, asks his wife the colour of its sail. 'Black,' she replies. 'At this,' in the words of Thomas, 'Tristan feels such pain that he has never had greater nor ever will, and he turns his face to the wall and says: "God save Ysolt and me! Since you will not come to me I must die for your love."'

Appendix

Avalon
Paradise of Celtic legends, an island of apple trees situated in the far west, to which King Arthur was taken after being wounded to death; first mentioned in the 12th century by Geoffrey of Monmouth, who said that the fairy queen Morgan ruled there; later thought to be the area round Glastonbury.

Brut
Or Brute, or Brutus, legendary descendant of Aeneas; expelled from Rome with his followers, he conquered the island of Albion, which took its name of Britain from him, and subsequent British kings were descended from him; the story was told in Geoffrey of Monmouth's *History of the Kings of Britain*, c 1135, and was generally accepted as true until the 17th century.

Excalibur
The enchanted sword of King Arthur. As a youth Arthur proved his right to kingship by drawing Excalibur out of a great stone; in later stories Arthur obtained his magic sword from the Lady of the Lake, and at his death ordered Sir Bedivere to return the sword by throwing it into the water; also called Caliburnus, Excalibur is probably connected with another magic sword, *Caladbolg*, which belonged to the Irish hero Fergus.

Fairy Rings
Circles of grass of different colour or texture from that of the rest of the field, where fairies are traditionally supposed to hold their dances: any-

one running nine times round a fairy ring during a full moon was thought to be able to hear them talking and laughing, but it was dangerous to sit in the ring on May Eve or All Hallows' Eve as the fairies might spirit the offender away.

Fisher King
In legends of the holy Grail, the lord of the Grail castle and keeper of the Grail and the bleeding lance, he was crippled and fishing was his only pastime; his infirmity was bound up with the desolation of his land and people, and he could only be cured by a question asked by the Grail hero; the story combines Christian elements with earlier pagan themes. Failure to ask the question meant that the hero failed in his mission.

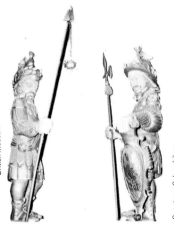

Gog and Magog
The names of two mythical giants, statues of which now stand in the Guildhall, London. According to legend, Gog and Magog were the last survivors of a race of British giants overcome by Brutus, who had them taken to London where they were compelled to work as porters at the gate of the royal palace. In the Bible, Gog is described as a terrible ruler living in the north, and in the Apocalypse the terms Gog and Magog stand for all the enemies of the kingdom of God. Their names have also been given to two hills.

Guinevere
In the Arthurian legends, the wife of Arthur and mistress of Lancelot; in early Welsh stories she was Gwenhwyfar, and there were said to be three of her; there was an old theme of her abduction and rescue; in the later legends, she brought Arthur the Round Table as her dowry, and the traitor Mordred seized her, or tried to, when he usurped Arthur's crown; the monks of Glastonbury said that she was buried there, with Arthur.

Guy of Warwick
Hero of a popular early 14th-century English prose romance, named after him; his legendary feats included the slaughter of a destructive dragon in Northumberland; he went on pilgrimage to the Holy land where, among other adventures, he killed a Saracen giant; he came back to England to rescue King Athelstan from the Danes by killing another giant who was the Danish champion.

Hereward the Wake
Anglo-Saxon outlaw and resistance leader against the Normans, who became the hero of popular legends; he and his followers helped the Danes to sack Peterborough Abbey in 1070; his stronghold on the Isle of Ely was besieged and taken by William the Conqueror; Hereward escaped but nothing more is known of him; there

is no evidence that he was called 'the Wake' in his own day, and the name probably comes from his supposed connection with the Wake family from Bourne in Lincolnshire.

Isles of the Blest
Or Fortunate Isles, a happy otherworld of lovely flowers and trees, music, feasting and beautiful women, to which souls go after death; usually located in the far west where the sun sets; St Brendan voyaged to the Isles of the Blest or Earthly Paradise; shown on medieval maps, somewhere in the Atlantic.

Kelpies
Water spirits or fairies of Scottish folklore, who often took the form of a horse; usually mischievous, they were thought to graze on the banks of rivers and lakes; having enticed travellers to mount them, they tossed them into the water and devoured them; to see a kelpie was said to be a sure portent of drowning.

Leprechauns
Fairy shoemakers of Irish folklore; they own buried hoards of gold which are much coveted by human beings; if caught, a leprechaun can be forced to reveal where his treasure is hidden but he will vanish if you take your eyes off him; leprechauns live alone and vary in stature from a height of a few inches to the size of of a three-year-old child.

Little People
Respectful and often affectionate term for fairies: believers in fairies frequently preferred not to name them directly for fear of summoning them, and instead used vague, preferably complimentary, terms like 'the little people' or 'the people of peace'.

Robin Goodfellow
Capricious but not always unfriendly hobgoblin, apparently Puck under another name; said to be the child of a fairy king and a mortal woman, and to have the power of changing shape; in origin probably a minor fertility god or spirit.

The Celts

The Celts themselves did not commit their religious traditions to writing and it is necessary to use a variety of sources of information to discover the nature of the religion and mythology of the pagan Celtic peoples. They were not illiterate, for we know that some of them used Greek for their business transactions. However, they regarded their laws, their genealogies and their history in the same sacred light as their religion. All these disciplines were required to be handed down orally from master to pupil, from priest to acolyte. It took some 20 years of intensive application to assimilate and master the secrets of Druidic lore. The oral tradition is fundamental to the Celtic temperament; a deep respect for it has continued down to the present day in the Celtic-speaking areas of Europe (Brittany, Wales, Ireland, Scotland, the Isle of Man).

For information about Celtic religion on the continent of Europe, and to a lesser extent in Britain, there are the written comments of Greek and Roman authors, interested in noting the habits and customs of the barbarian peoples of Europe. From Roman times there are the sculptured monuments on which native gods, goddesses and cult symbols are figured, often in Roman guise, accompanied by a dedication to a native deity. There are inscriptions and native coins which often bear Celtic names and magical symbols, and there is the evidence of place-names.

Over and above this, the native literatures of Wales and Ireland, the oldest in Europe outside the classical world, form a great repository of mythology and pre-Christian practices. Although written down only in Christian times, the persistence and longevity of the oral tradition was such that we can be quite confident that there is a genuine core of true mythology to be found underneath the embellishments of the storytellers, the censorship of the Church, and the motifs borrowed from classical and Scandinavian sources.

All the evidence for pagan Celtic religion, fragmentary and varied as it is, emphasizes the fact that the Celts were deeply conscious of religion. The inhabitants of the physical world and those of the otherworld – that gay land beyond the grave – were in constant communication with each other. There is nothing to show that the virtuous attained the otherworld after death for ethical reasons; nor is there any hint of a gloomy otherworld. The land of the gods could be entered in life by the clever, aggressive hero, by means of treachery or force. Or it could be attained by mortals through the invitation of an immortal being, who usually had amorous intentions. But for the Celt there was, and could be, no rigid division between the two territories.

At times, as on *Samain*, (1 November) the great religious feast of the Celts, which was a season of gloom and portent and sacrifice, the inhabitants of the otherworld became hostile and dangerous. They played tricks on mankind and caused panic and destruction. They had then to be appeased, and their powers turned once more in a direction favourable to mortals.

Their feasts, and other more local celebrations, were held at the main sacred site of each tribe or region. The priests who officiated at these gatherings, the intercessors between the mortal and the divine, were extremely powerful. Some of them at least were known as Druids. There is evidence that there were priests other than Druids but we know little about them. The name Druid seems to mean 'knowledge of the oak', and this would be appropriate in a society which held the oak in special awe. Maximus of Tyre, a philosopher of the 2nd century AD, reports that the Celts worshipped Zeus in the form of a tall oak tree.

Our knowledge of the Druids is scrappy and of unequal value. Modern lore about these priests stems only from antiquarianism, not from ancient testimony. In spite of the fragmentary nature of the real evidence it is clear that the Druids constituted a powerful and influential priesthood in some Celtic regions at least. They performed the sacrifices, read the omens, and appeased the gods by performing the rites correctly.

The Irish Druids figure as magicians, teachers, shape-shifters (those with the ability to change form) and even buffoons, but whether this reflects their true role in early Irish society, or merely the fancies of later Christian writers, must remain in question. Their origins are shrouded in antiquity and there is no reason at all to suppose that they were newcomers, originating with the Celts themselves. Their order may have had a longer ancestry elsewhere in Europe.

The Celts practised human sacrifice. The Romans considered this ritual to be barbarous and caused it to be discontinued. They also struck a lethal blow at the Druids, whose power and political influence was a threat to the success of Roman campaigns in the Celtic areas. Caesar, referring to the practice of human sacrifice, describes the great images of interwoven branches which were filled with men and set alight, 'and the men die in a sea of flame'.

Three fierce Celtic gods, Teutates, Esus and Taranis, are mentioned by the Roman poet Lucan. A commentator on Lucan says that people sacrificed to Teutates were drowned or suffocated in a vat; those sacrificed to Esus were stabbed and then hung up in a tree; Taranis apparently favoured burning.

There is little definite in the Irish texts to demonstrate the nature of human sacrifices in that country, but it is certain that they were practised there also.

There are many dark hints and allusions which suggest that the motif of the triple death (by drowning, stabbing and burning) was more than a literary convention, and echoed the tradition of sacrifices of the three great Gaulish gods. Several stories contain the motif of the tricking of the hero and his company into a house, the door of which is secured while they are feasted and made drunk. The building is then set on fire, and all perish in the conflagration or escape through the heroism and supernatural strength of the hero. There are hints of ritual drowning in tubs or wells, numerous examples of foundation sacrifices, even in Christian contexts, and episodes in the early stories which point to the sacrifice of infants.

Animals were certainly ritually killed and the bull-sacrifice (*tarb-feis*) was an integral feature of the inauguration of a new king, a ceremony of deep religious significance in early Irish society. Bull-hides were used by the Druids to sleep on while they had their omen-giving dreams, having first chewed some of the flesh of a cat, a dog and a red pig, and consulted their 'idol gods'.

It is extremely difficult to find any orderly pantheon in the Celtic gods and goddesses known to us, or any clear-cut division into deities of specific functions or departments. However, the knowledge that the structure of Celtic society was of a semi-sacred nature, that the king was regarded as the visible agent of the god – sometimes his son, sometimes allegedly the mortal mate of the tribal goddess, the Earth Mother – suggests that the Celts thought of the world of the gods as being organized in a similar way; and there are hints of this in the Irish tradition.

C. M. Dixon

Above *Many pagan Celtic monuments were later Christianized: stone figures of the 8th or 9th century, possibly hidden in the structure of a 12th-century church because of their pagan affiliations: in Co Fermanagh, Ireland.* **Facing page** *Christian cross obscuring the earlier Celtic inscriptions on an Irish memorial stone: the old inscriptions give the name and descent of the dead man, probably to help keep him alive in the afterworld.* **Right** *The 'Bishop's Stone' at Killadeas: the south side of the stone shows a Christian abbot with bell and crozier; the west is probably a representation of a pagan Celtic head.* **Below** *Hunting the ferocious wild boar was a popular and dangerous pastime, for it demanded great skill, and there are many legends of supernatural boars and their adventures in early Irish and Welsh literature.*

National Museum of Ireland

C. M. Dixon

Over and above the numerous tribal and local divinities, we hear of such powerful shadowy beings as Anu, or Danu, mother of the gods. Anu is referred to as 'she who nurtures well the gods'. Danu, from whom the Irish gods called the Tuatha De Danann ('Tribes of the Goddess Danu') are named, has Don as her equivalent in British mythology. Danu's three sons are the gods Brian, Iuchar and Iucharba, known to tradition as *fir tri ndea*, 'men of the three gods'. Brigit the goddess is elsewhere allegedly the mother of this powerful trio, and it may be that she is in fact Danu, known by another name.

One of the most difficult factors in any attempt to get a realistic idea of the nature of Celtic deities and their individual qualities is this custom of giving a single divinity a multiplicity of names, many of them merely descriptive epithets. As a result, much that is confusing in Celtic mythology may become

desired, their leader in war, their ultimate judge in legal matters, lord of the otherworld feast, mate of the tribal goddess.

It seems that the god himself tended to move with the tribe when it set out for new conquests and territories. But the goddess, who was much concerned with the actual geographical region over which she presided, remained behind to be overcome by the nextcomers, and to be killed or used for their own purposes, or mated with their own tribal god. Celtic gods and goddesses were not believed to be inviolable.

Over and above the basic pair, so well attested by representation in art, by inscriptions on stone and by the legends of the Celtic world, there were other gods and goddesses of lesser and limited importance but more specific functions. These deities were concerned primarily with the arts, with crafts such as that of the smith, with medicine and healing; or they presided over important

Facing page *In addition to the more powerful deities the Celts worshipped a host of minor spirits, demons and fabulous creatures, many of whom could change shape at will. Stone carving of a monster holding severed human heads: the Celts were head hunters and worshipped the head.* **Below** *Head of a Celtic god surrounded by various animals which were sacred to the Celts, including the fabulous beaked, winged horse. The torc round his neck and the wheels on either side of him were often deposited with the dead: a detail from the Gundestrup cauldron in the Danish National Museum.*

clear if it can be convincingly demonstrated that certain major deities, though seemingly different, are in fact a single deity with a number of names, functions and manifestations. The undoubted power of Brigantia, goddess of the Brigantes, for example, suggests a high position in some supernatural hierarchy.

At present the evidence all points to a huge number of named gods and goddesses, with a comparably large assortment of attributes and symbols, but with a markedly limited range of functions. The tribal god was an all-purpose figure and, despite the differences in his name, he was basically the same throughout the Celtic lands. He was a 'good' god, like the Dagda of Ireland, protector of the tribe, giver of all that was good and

A Magic Kiss

One day Niall, son of Eochu Muigmedon King of Ireland, went hunting with his four brothers. They came across a hideous old woman guarding a well. 'She was as black as coal. Her hair was like a wild horse's tail. Her foul teeth were visible from ear to ear and were such as would sever a branch of green oak. Her eyes were black, her nose crooked and spread. Her body was scrawny, spotted and diseased. Her shins were bent. Her knees and ankles were thick, her shoulders broad, her nails were green.' As a price for the water in her well, the loathsome hag demanded a kiss from each of the brothers in turn; but only Niall overcame his revulsion and embraced her. Thereupon she was

transformed into a beautiful woman: 'She was as white as the last snow in a hollow. Her arms were fully and queenly, her fingers long and slender, her legs straight and gleaming . . .'

Reading these old tales, one has the impression that the Irish of past centuries lived on easy terms with the supernatural. If we can judge by the reactions of the characters themselves, no surprise was occasioned by the intervention of folk from the Otherworld, or by spells cast and shapes shifted. The natural order of things was something vaster and more flexible than we envisage today.

D.D.R. Owen
The Evolution of the Grail Legend

people swear'. This is understood and sufficient to make the oath binding.

The number three was sacred to the Celts. Sometimes they portrayed their deities in groups of three, or as having three heads or three faces. In the tales the deities or semi-divine heroes are described as being one of three people of the same name and birth, or as having been born three times in succession.

In addition to the powerful gods and goddesses with their many names and symbols, there are other and lesser supernatural beings – spirits and guardians of certain places, godlings and nymphs, sprites and demons. There were animals and birds which were sacred to the Celts, and many of the deities are represented as having bird or animal parts, or bird or animal servants and messengers. There were sacrificial beasts, and birds of good or evil omen, the companions of the gods, and their visible form on occasion.

The boar was held in high esteem by the Celts, its flesh being their choicest food; while the boar hunt was a favourite pastime. Several of the deities have names which link them with boar cults. There are many legends of supernatural boars and their adventures in the Irish and Welsh literary traditions. The otherworld feast is alleged to be sustained by magical pigs which, no matter how often they are cooked and eaten, are whole and alive again next day, ready for the next feast.

The bull also played an important role in mythology, while the horse, the stag (attribute of the Celtic stag god Cernunnos, 'the Horned One') the dog and the ram all figure in the world of Celtic mythology. The ram-headed serpent seems to have occupied a foremost place among the sacred animals, and various other fantastic beasts are figured or referred to in different contexts.

Shape-shifting or changing of form was allegedly much indulged in by the Druids and also by the deities, and several of the semi-mythological characters in the early legends take the form of an animal, some meeting their deaths while in this shape. Birds, too, were regarded as playing a very distinctive and individual role, the crane being sinister and ominous, an idea which has continued on into modern folk belief. The swan was invariably the form taken by benevolent deities, often when engaged in amorous exploits, and sometimes wearing chains of gold or silver, their magical badge which set them apart from other birds.

The otherworld of the Celts was a world of magic rather than a world of formal doctrine and inflexible deities; a world which mattered in everyday life rather than at religious feasts and periodical rituals alone; a world not of gloom but of gaiety. Its inhabitants were conceived to be gods and goddesses whose attitude to human beings was not always beneficent, but who could be propitiated by those who knew the correct form. It was a world which could on occasion be entered by mortals; and the deities were likewise believed to be capable of appearing at will in the world of men – not always to the benefit of mankind.

Jean Roubier

local features such as sacred wells and rivers. But there must have been a good deal of overlapping, and the all-purpose god could, according to tradition, turn his hand to any skill or craft when the occasion demanded it.

Certain gods, such as Lugus (Irish Lugh, Welsh Lleu), Sucellos, Camulos, Esus, Teutates, have a fairly wide distribution in stone inscriptions and place-names, and some are known from the literary traditions. It is not clear whether these represent deities of a greater and more universal power than the local tribal gods, fathers of the gods themselves in fact, or whether their wider distribution is due to population movement and conquest. Or again, it may be that they were official gods of the Druids themselves, more concerned with 'national' than tribal concerns.

The mother goddess of the Celts was often conceived of as a warrior, fighting with weapons and instructing the hero in superior secrets of warfare. She was also believed to be capable of influencing the outcome of battle, not by her weapons but by magic and incantation, sometimes taking the form of a sinister bird (crow or raven) and flying over the hosts, causing frenzy and confusion, foretelling the future, and rejoicing over the carnage.

The Celts believed it was undesirable and positively dangerous to name a sacred thing by its correct name. As a result the gods are often referred to in a roundabout way, as were other sacred matters. The Ulstermen, for example, do not swear by a named god but by 'the god by whom my

Gods, Saints and Heroes

Bran

Bran the blessed plays a major role in one of the 'Four Branches' of the collection of medieval Welsh tales known as the *Mabinogion*, probably to be dated to the second part of the 11th century, but containing material that is much older. In the story of *Branwen daughter of Llyr* Bran figures as King of Britain, but his divine origins are clearly discernible. He is described as being so huge that no house could ever be built big enough to contain him. He is just and generous, the possessor of a magic cauldron which could restore the dead to life, a patron of the arts and a true and good king.

Bran's sister is Branwen, and her unfortunate marriage to the King of Ireland touches off a story of tragedy and magic.

The name Bran means 'raven' and because of this attempts have been made to identify Bran as a raven god. There is in fact insufficient evidence in the surviving mythology to support this theory.

Roman statue of Brigantia, the northern English equivalent of the Irish goddess Brigit. She holds the spear of the Roman Minerva and the globe of rulership, with wings of victory sprouting from her shoulders: 3rd century AD, from Birrens, Dumfriesshire.

National Museum of Antiquities of Scotland, Edinburgh

Brigit

Brigit was the daughter of the powerful tribal god, the Dagda, according to early Irish literary tales. Her name, meaning 'the Powerful One' or 'Queen', links her with the North British Brigantia, 'the High One', with whom she may originally have been identical. Brigantia was goddess of the Celtic tribe of the Brigantes, who occupied what are now roughly the six northern counties of England. Dedications to this deity are also known from the Continent, and it seems probable that her spheres of influence must have been closely similar to those of her Irish counterpart.

The evidence suggests that the two goddesses are in fact fundamentally the same deity, but venerated according to local preferences and requirements in different Celtic regions. In Brigit and Brigantia we are dealing with powerful pagan Celtic religious ideas: the influence of these deities was widespread in Celtic areas, and their cult enduring. In British art Brigantia is associated with Minerva.

Caesar, in his observations about certain Celtic divinities, remarks: 'About these gods they hold nearly the same views as other people do...that Minerva first instituted the arts and crafts.'

Brigit of Ireland is essentially a patroness of craftsmen and their crafts. Brigantia is not only likened to Minerva but figures also in Roman times as a nymph goddess, who presided over springs to which healing powers were probably attributed. Brigit was similarly concerned with medicine and healing of all kinds, and many wells of different virtues were named after her successor in Christian times, St Brigit of Kildare. It thus seems very probable that Brigantia of North Britain and Brigit of pagan Ireland shared the same origins.

Brigit also shows a close affinity with certain Celtic goddesses portrayed in groups of three which are found in the art of Roman Gaul and Britain.

She figures in Irish traditions as one of three sisters all named Brigit. It is almost certain that this is a purely literary attempt to explain the pagan Celtic idea of a single god or goddess depicted in triple form in order to emphasize his or her divine powers. This threefold character would then link Brigit with the portrayals of the triple goddesses of Gaul and Britain; these mother goddesses were worshipped in the Roman Empire by men of all nations. The Celts regarded the number three as being especially magical and powerful, and for this reason they often gave their deities attributes or characteristics with this number, such as three heads.

Brigit of Ireland is also deeply concerned with fertility and childbirth and this further links her with the groups of three mother goddesses with their symbols of plenty and maternity. In the literature of early Ireland, Brigit was the goddess of poetry and wisdom.

Cu Chulainn

The stories of the *Ulster Cycle* were written down in the form in which we now have them c 1100 AD, but their manuscript origins were much earlier. They are concerned with the *Ulaid*, the people of Ulster, in northern Ireland, about the turn of the Christian era. The main story in the cycle is that of the cattle raid of Cualnge (*Tain Bo Cualnge*), the splendid epic which deals with the rivalry between the provinces of Connaught and Ulster, and with Cu Chulainn's heroic defence of the Ulstermen.

Cu Chulainn knew the secret language of the poets, for the great *fili* or poet, Amairgin, had been his foster-father, and had instructed him in the poetic and juridical arts. He first outraged, then pacified, the society into which he entered, in true heroic fashion. He had physical beauty of a kind that was extraordinary because it differed from the physical ideal of his tribal background and yet it was striking enough to impress favourably all who saw him. He was small, in a society in which height was revered; dark, where fairness was in vogue; a beardless boy, not a mature bearded warrior. He was called a *sirite*, 'sprite', a law unto himself, nevertheless upholding the honour of his people against impossible odds. He was known as *siabartha*, 'distorted one', because of the terrible change in his appearance when his battle ardour was aroused. He was the fear of every warrior, the beloved of all women who looked upon him in his full beauty. He was the son of the great god Lugh, the lover and subjugator of the goddesses, arousing the desire even of the terrible Morrigan, the war goddess, with her dark bird-form and her terrifying magical and prognostic powers.

The *Ulster Cycle* contains some historical material, but the main characters and episodes are of a manifestly mythological nature.

Cu Chulainn epitomizes the concept of the Hero for Ireland. We must suppose it to have been a concept common to the early Celtic world, where magical powers and superhuman battle feats were believed to be accompanied by fierce physical distortions and strange emanations such as the 'hero's light'.

In the *Tain* it is said about Cu Chulainn: 'The hero's light rose from his forehead, so that it was as long and as thick as a hero's whetstone. As high, as thick, as strong, as powerful and as long as the mast of a great ship was the straight beam of dark blood which rose up from the very top of his head and became a dark magical mist, like the smoke of a palace when a king comes to be attended in the evening of a wintry day.'

Right *Statue of the Irish hero Cu Chulainn in Dublin's General Post Office. His legendary exploits, aggressiveness and great physical beauty commanded the highest respect in pagan Celtic society.*

Finn

The two most renowned heroes of early Irish tradition are Finn and Cu Chulainn. The latter is alleged to have lived about the turn of the Christian era, while Finn was reputed to have died in the second half of the 3rd century AD, aged 230 years – a sure indication of his superhuman nature. Each of these two warriors has attracted the interest of the Irish story-tellers, and each in his own way has stimulated their imagination and inspired their talent, in a country where such talent is by no means rare.

Similar though they were in many ways and, in the earliest tales, both operating in a heroic milieu, there are marked differences between their individual characters and their roles in their own society. Cu Chulainn never gained the hold on popular tradition that Finn and his followers obtained; and it seems that in the case of Finn there was a strong oral tradition concerning him amongst the common people at the time of the earliest manuscript records, and that this tradition was to persist, even down to the present time.

A triad of deities are Finn's enemies in an 8th-century story: these were the Fothads, known as *Aendia*, 'Single God', *Trendia*, 'Strong God' and *Caendia*, 'Fair God'. Another divine opponent of Finn in another story of the same period, 'Finn and the Man in the Tree', is Dercc Corra mac hui Daighre:

> One day as Finn was in the wood seeking him he saw a man in the top of a tree, a black bird on his right shoulder and in his left hand a white vessel of bronze, filled with water in which was a skittish trout and a stag at the foot of the tree. And this was the practice of the man, cracking nuts; and he would give half the kernel of the nut to the black bird that was on his right shoulder while he himself would eat the other half; and he would take an apple out of the bronze vessel that was in his left hand, divide it in two, throw one half to the stag that was at the foot of the tree, and then eat the other half himself. And on it he would drink a sip of the bronze vessel that was in his hand, so that he and the trout and the stag and the black bird drank together. And then his followers asked Finn who he in the tree was, for they did not recognize him on account of the hood of disguise which he wore.

The most famous prose tale of the *Fenian Cycle* is the 'Pursuit of Diarmaid and Grainne', a version of which goes back to the 10th century. Finn is married to Grainne, a daughter of Cormac the king. She prefers his son Ossian, but he refuses her for the sake of his father. She then falls in love with Diarmaid, and thereupon forces him to elope with her.

The story is concerned with their adventures in escaping from the vengeance of Finn and his men, and Finn's ultimate revenge when Diarmaid is slain some years later hunting the great supernatural boar of Ben Gulban. Finn has many adventures with the inhabitants of the pagan otherworld, and a number of the modern folktales and ballads are concerned with these, testifying to the continuing power of myth and legend.

Gwydion

Gwydion is mentioned frequently in early Welsh literature and is one of the principal characters in the story of *Math, son of Mathonwy* in the *Mabinogion*. Gwydion and his brother Gilfaethwy are nephews of Math, a renowned magician who has instructed Gwydion in enchantment and sorcery. Math was forbidden to be without a virgin in whose lap his feet were held, except in time of war. This virgin is Goewin, a girl of exceptional beauty and virtue. Gilfaethwy falls in love with her and Gwydion, detecting this, determines to help him. Extreme care is necessary, for as Gilfaethwy says to his brother: 'Thou knowest the peculiarity of Math son of Mathonwy; whatever the whispering, however low, there be between men, once the wind has met it he will know of it.' But Gwydion uses his powers of sorcery to outwit his uncle.

He promises to fetch the wonderful pigs which belonged to Pryderi, ruler of Dyfed. With 11 others disguised as bards, he goes to Pryderi's court and is made welcome there, for Gwydion is 'the best teller of tales in the world' – an essential requisite for a Celtic deity. In exchange for the swine he gives Pryderi 12 stallions, 12 greyhounds and 12 golden shields. These he has made by magic but the spell will last only for a day, and Gwydion and his men hurry away with the swine. Pryderi and his men overtake them, and Math joins in the battle. This leaves the virgin Goewin on her own: Gwydion and his brother return to Math's court where both rape the girl in Math's own bed. Then they return to the battle.

Gwydion finally defeats Pryderi in single combat.

Lleu

The episodes concerning Lleu Llaw Gyffes begin here. Aranrhod, Gwydion's sister, is proved not to be a virgin when she undergoes Math's chastity test. When she runs from the room she drops a boy-child, and also a 'small something else'. Gwydion snatches this up before anyone has seen it properly, and hides it in a chest. It is another boy, clearly the result of his incestuous union with his sister. Gwydion looks after the boy himself.

One day Gwydion and his son set out for Caer Aranrhod, his sister's home. She welcomes him but refuses to give the boy a name, and Gwydion vows she will do this in spite of herself. Next day he walks with his son along the sea-shore where he forms a magical ship. 'And they began to fashion shoes, and to stitch them.' When they are seen from the fortress, 'he took away their own semblance, and put another semblance upon them, so that they would not be recognized'. Aranrhod asks for a pair of golden shoes, but Gwydion will not make a pair of the correct size until she comes to have her foot measured. This she does, and a wren alights upon the ship while she is there.

Her son aims at it and hits it perfectly. 'Faith,' says she, 'with a deft hand has the fair one hit it.' Gwydion says: 'He has now got a name and good enough is his name. Lleu Llaw Gyffes is he from now on.' (*Lleu* means 'fair', *llaw* 'hand' and *gyffes* 'deft, skilful'.) Everything magical now vanishes and the son is changed back into his own shape. Gwydion's sister swears a destiny on her son, that he will never bear arms until she herself equips him with them.

In due course, Gwydion and Lleu, who is now a young man, go once again to Aranrhod's dwelling in the guise of two youths, claiming to be bards. They are welcomed, for 'Gwydion was a good teller of tales'. They go to bed and 'at early cock-crow Gwydion arose. And then he summoned to him his magic and his power'.

By daylight the countryside was in a state of uproar and Aranrhod bursts into the room crying, 'We cannot see the colour of the deep for all the ships thronging together.' She goes to get arms for the two men and Gwydion tricks her into arming her son completely herself. All the turmoil then ceases and she realizes that Gwydion has got the better of her yet again. She swears Lleu shall never have a wife 'of the race now on earth'. Gwydion goes to get Math's aid, and together they make a wife for Lleu from the flowers of the oak and of the broom, and of meadowsweet.

Lleu is given land by Math and settles down to rule prosperously. However, on one occasion when he is away from home, his wife Blodeuwedd is unfaithful to him; she and her lover, Gronw Bebyr, plot his death. Although Lleu is practically invincible, his wife persuades him to tell her the one way in which he can be killed, and the lovers make their preparations. Lleu is struck by Gronw with the fatal, poisoned spear in the manner which he has divulged. He screams and flies away in the form of an eagle.

Math and Gwydion are deeply distressed when the news reaches them; and Gwydion sets out to find his son. Eventually he comes to an oak tree, to which he has been led by a sow which has been feeding on Lleu's rotting flesh and maggots, and sees him emaciated in the tree. He persuades him to come down to his lap and turns him back into human form. Lleu is only skin and bone but skilful physicians nurse him back to health in less than a year. Gwydion finds Blodeuwedd and says to her: 'I will not slay thee. I will do to thee that which is worse; that is' said he, 'I will let thee go in the form of a bird.' He turns her into an owl and she flies away. Lleu then slays Gronw.

Facing page *According to legend, the standing stones of Carnac were an army of pagans who pursued St Cornely; to escape them he turned them to stone. In fact they are part of a huge burial ground, probably dating from c 2000 BC, and including stone tombs, stone circles and grave mounds.*
Below *The guardian saints of Brittany are a curious collection, numbering over 500 in all. Some are minor local gods or early Breton chiefs. Some, who have lasted for centuries and are still acknowledged, are barely tolerated by the Roman Catholic Church. Included among them is St Gwenole who founded the abbey at Landévennec, now in ruins.*

Brittany

The Bretons played an important part in the formation and spread of the Arthurian legends through Europe. Their travelling entertainers had a high reputation in the Middle Ages; the poetess Marie de France, who borrowed from them the themes of her lays, wrote in the 12th century: 'Brittany is poetry'. Many heroes of the stories of the Round Table were Bretons. Lancelot of the Lake, who was brought up by the fairy Vivien, spent his childhood in the forest of Broceliande near Paimpont which still exists today. He took his name from the nearby lake where the fairy had her palace. The Bridge of the Secret, where Lancelot and Queen Guinevere pledged their love, can also still be seen.

In the same forest is the Fountain of Youth, whose waters are believed to have powers of rejuvenation, and the Fountain of Barenton, sacred to the Druids and still the symbol of Celtic poetry. It was there that Merlin the Wizard met Vivien and fell in love with her. The Garden of Joy, not far away, was their trysting-place. The water of Barenton also possesses allegedly miraculous powers: when it is poured on the Stone of Merlin nearby it lets loose storms and causes other natural phenomena. At one time the population of the neighbouring town of Concoret (Morbihan) used to go there in procession and the priest would dip the foot of the cross in the spring, to bring rain in dry years.

It was also in Brittany that part of the story of Tristan and Isolde took place. The hero's uncle, King Mark of Cornwall, took his name from that of an ancient Celtic horse god (horse in Breton is *marc'h*). Strange legends are still current about Mark in the region of Douarnenez and in Penmarc'h. The latter place name means 'the horse's head'.

Tristan of Leon after his love affair with Mark's wife, the Irish Isolde, retired to Brittany. There he married another Isolde, the daughter of the king of Carhaix in western Finistère. When mortally wounded, he asked to be taken to await the boat which was bringing his first love back to him. It was to the headland of Penmarc'h that he was taken; it was there that the two lovers died, facing the sea which unites all Celts.

The major theme which constantly recurs is that of death and the afterlife. It is a theme which permeates the peninsula completely. A seemingly divine person known as Ankou is at one and the same time the provider and the master. Awe-inspiring, omnipotent, Ankou is the true ruler of the world. In popular imagination he appears supreme, since everyone eventually obeys him.

Ankou has various guises. Each parish has its own version, which changes moreover, because the last person to die in the year has to play the role of Ankou during the whole of the following year. He is represented as a skeleton, or as a man without a nose and with empty eye-sockets. He often has a hat with a wide brim which hides his face and prevents people from recognizing him at first.

In pictures he usually carries a scythe handled the wrong way up. Ankou uses it to kill those people he has marked out, but instead of using it in the normal way of reapers, he throws it in front of him, cutting edge first.

To travel along the muddy and potholed roads, he rides on a cart with creaking axles. Two acolytes escort him; one holding the horse's bridle, and the other opening the gates and doors.

This funeral carriage, called *Karrig an Ankou*, Ankou's Chariot, often appears in the narratives. To hear it is a bad omen: it means that there will be a death in the parish.

For the tired, homecoming reveller who encounters it around midnight, it is a terrifying experience. Ankou inspires dread and it is rare ever to escape him. The unfortunate man will only have a short space of time to put his affairs in order.

THE MYTHOLOGY OF ANIMALS

Divine and Legendary Creatures

Bear

The ancient Greeks told of a bear-goddess named Callisto, who was transformed by Zeus into the constellation called the Great Bear. But behind this pretty story lay a darker fact: the cult of Zeus Lycaeus, which some authorities connect with were-wolfism and others with bear worship, but which definitely involved human sacrifice. Lycaon himself, in legend, was the father of Callisto; and the cult grew out of his sacrifice of a boy (in most versions, his bearish grandson Arcas) to Zeus.

Callisto herself came to be closely associated with the virginal goddess and huntress Artemis. There are accounts of a bear cult from Brauron in Attica that centred on the worship of Artemis in bear form. But here only traces of ritual sacrifice remain in the mock-sacrificial presentation of young girls, dressed bear-like in brown robes, as initiates.

The Great Bear is a powerful god in the mythologies of peoples linked by a basic language form, 'Finno-Ugric', including the Finns, Lapps, Estonians and Lithuanians, and also a variety of primitive nomadic tribes across the north of Russia. In these religions, as in those of some North American Indians, the shaman or priest identified himself with the bear god. He wore bear garb and he was believed to turn into a bear.

Naturally, bears are important in the myths of North American Indians. In a way, the bear was the Indian's greatest competitor, for it is as omnivorous as man. So bears ate the salmon caught by Pacific Northwest tribes, the buffalo meat stored by Plains tribes, the maize grown by tribes in the southwest – and, sometimes, members of the tribes. Indian myths and customs show a great respect for the creature.

Boar

From antiquity to the Middle Ages and later, the boar was first of all a symbol of the fertility of the earth. In Germany when the corn waved, it was once said, 'The Boar is rushing through the corn' and children were warned, 'Don't go through the corn, there's a boar in there.'

The last sheaf to be gathered at harvest (sometimes called 'the Sow') was saved, and from it was made a loaf in the form of a boar; this was placed on the Yule table until the end of the festive season. It was then kept until the spring sowing, when part would be eaten, and part mixed with the seed-corn to ensure a healthy crop. A comparison may be drawn with the Scandinavian Yule custom of drinking and eating to a good agricultural year and to peace.

The idea of sacrifice in the dead of winter to the fertility deities was not far off, though it must be admitted that there is little direct evidence on this point.

The boar was the sacred animal of the fertility god Freyr in Scandinavian mythology. Snorri's *Edda* tells how Freyr rode to the unfortunate Balder's funeral behind the boar Gollinborsti (golden bristles), also known as 'the one with terrible tusks'. Another boar mentioned in the Eddic literature (the source books of Scandinavian mythology) is Saehrimnir, the boar which was killed and eaten afresh every day by the dead heroes in Valhalla.

Legends of gods slain by boars, or while boar-hunting, are numerous. Adonis, consort of Aphrodite and Attis, consort of Cybele, both met their end in this way. The same may be true of the Egyptian god Osiris, though the evidence here is undoubtedly scanty.

The Cretans held that Zeus himself was a prince ripped up by a wild boar and buried in their midst. This assertion is supposed to have earned them their reputation as liars.

Thus the boar came to be the incarnation of the enemy of the gods; in Egypt, for example, the evil god Seth was porcine in form. Traces of a similar conception in the West can be found in traditions of Odin's wild hunt.

Battle of the bear and the unicorn; from a 14th-century MS in the British Museum.

Bull

Throughout ancient Sumeria, a bull god called Enlil was worshipped as god of the storm and supreme god of fertility. It was through his power that there was water, the fields were green, and all things grew. Mankind itself drew life and sustenance from him. Praising Enlil as their father, the 'exalted overpowering ox', 'Lord of the world of life', 'powerful chief of the gods', the Sumerians of about 3000 BC addressed him with stirring invocations.

Naram-Sin, who wore the horns of bulls into battle, presented captive kings to Enlil in recognition of the bull god's sovereignty. This close association between king and god in Sumeria had many interesting facets. Both bull god and king came to share the title 'Wild Bull'. Sargon was so called, and the seal of his servant shows a man watering a bull. Kings wore bull-horned head-dresses as a symbol of their divine appointment and power. And to make the interrelation complete, there arose the custom of placing long, curled beards upon images of the bull god. This practice, probably ritualistic in origin, was rooted in the conception common in Mesopotamia that the beard was a sign of strength and masculinity.

The relationship in Egypt between kings and bull gods was even closer. Narmer-Menes, the king who forcibly united Upper and Lower Egypt into a single kingdom not long before 3000 BC, worshipped Apis and spread the gospel of the bull god throughout the land. Moreover, it was either his adroitness or his simplicity which led him

Right *The cat was sacred to the Egyptian goddess Bast. Cemeteries containing the bodies of mummified sacred cats have been discovered with bronze statues of cats, like this one which is dated to c 600 BC.* **Below** *'A boar is a sovereign beast', an emblem of courage and ferocity, the most dangerous of animals for the hunter, and the slayer of men and even of gods. It is sometimes an incarnation of evil, sometimes an embodiment of the dead, sometimes a symbol of the fertility of the earth. A fiercely tusked boar, from a manuscript in the British Museum, with a wyvern, a dragon with barbed tail and wings.*

actually to conceive of himself as a bull.

In Crete, for example, while the bull god was primarily connected with the sun and fertility, he was likewise linked with the force, the deep-throated roar, and the destructiveness of earthquakes, which were common to the island. Crete also developed the first public, ritualized bullfights as we know them.

In Greece, the bull was the focus for socially approved rites of sexual abandon which evolved directly into Greek theatre. And in Rome, as the foremost rival of Christianity for centuries, Mithraism introduced the ritualistic washing away of sins and purification of the body with a bath in the blood dripping from a dying bull.

Cat

During the thousands of years in which the cat has lived among human beings it has been venerated at one period as a deity, and at other times cursed as a demon. In parts of ancient Egypt where the cat was regarded as sacred to the cat-headed goddess Bast, spiritual ruler of the city of Bubastis (now Tell Basta) to the east of the Nile Delta, to be so foolish as to kill one might be punishable by death.

Diodorus Siculus, the Greek historian, described how a Roman who committed this crime was murdered by a mob despite the pleadings of high Egyptian officials. If a cat died, from any cause whatever, its owner went into mourning, shaving his eyebrows and performing elaborate funeral rites. Cat cemeteries were established on the banks of the Nile, where the sacred animals were mummified and then laid to rest, together with vast quantities of cat mascots and bronze cat effigies.

The cat was invested with this aura of holiness elsewhere in the ancient world. The Roman goddess Diana sometimes assumed the shape of a cat, and the chariot of Freyja, the Scandinavian fertility goddess, was drawn by cats. This reverence was due not so much to the animal's importance as the guardian of the granaries against mice (as in ancient Egypt) or to its role as the traditional enemy of the serpent, but to the beauty of its eyes which were strangely reminiscent of the moon.

From the magic of their eyes arose the belief that cats were filled with strong mediumistic powers. In the East the cat is said to bear away the souls of the dead, and in some parts of West Africa negroes accept that the human soul passes into the body of a cat at death.

An Italian legend tells of a cat that gave birth to her kittens beneath the very manger in which Christ was born. But the cat was not to be venerated in Christian Europe.

William MacQuitty

British Museum

Chimaera

The Chimaera was a monster compounded of parts from three creatures: lion, goat and serpent. It appears in Homer's *Iliad* (books 6 and 16) as located in Lycia, in Asia Minor, where it is killed by the hero Bellerophon.

The Chimaera was of divine, not human origin, being 'a lion at the front, a serpent at the rear and in the middle a *chimaera*'. This word, which seems to leave part of its body unexplained, meant 'goat'. 'The Chimaera breathed flashing fire. But Bellerophon killed it, relying on marvels from the gods.' He fought his way through other perils to marry the king's daughter.

The fiery breath of the Chimaera may be a mythical rendering of the flaming gas that rises from the ground here and there in the south-west of Anatolia.

Alternatively, it has been suggested that the Chimaera was a personification of the storm-cloud. Nowadays the word is used to describe any fantastic or horrible imaginary creature, and is also the term applied by biologists to plants and animals having hybrid characteristics.

Cock

There was a Greek story that when Mars spent a night with Venus in the absence of her husband, Vulcan, he commissioned Alektraon (the Greek for 'cock') to watch at the door. He fell asleep and Mars, surprised by the returning husband, punished Alektraon by transforming him into a cock. He has been vigilant at dawn ever since, therefore. The Greeks believed that the cock was sacred to Apollo, god of the sun, and it became associated with Asclepius, the god of healing, Apollo's son by the nymph Coronis. This association with Asclepius and healing is an outcome of the bird's connection with the sun and the life-giving powers, and its opposition to the powers of darkness. In the *Phaedo* Plato records Socrates's request before drinking the hemlock that a cock should be offered to Asclepius on his behalf.

Sonia Halliday

Michael Holford

Above *The cock is part of folklore and tradition in many parts of the world; in both Asia and Europe the crowing of a cock was believed to drive away ghosts: mosaic at Misis, Turkey.* **Right** *The complicated and impressive dance performed by cranes during their mating season was at one time believed to be a magic ritual, and its movements were imitated in human dances: the sinister climax to an ancient Chinese crane dance was the burying alive of the dancers. Chinese watercolour in the Victoria and Albert Museum.* **Facing page** *Etruscan bronze of the Chimaera in the Archeological Museum, Florence. The name of this mythical monster has come to be used for any hybrid animal or in a metaphorical sense for fear.*

Cow

The cow for centuries has been looked upon as a tangible symbol of life and fertility by nomadic and pastoral peoples, who depend on this uncomplaining beast for nourishment and prosperity. In mythology the cow has come to be associated in particular with the divine givers of life, the mother goddesses, either of the sky or of the earth.

In ancient Egypt the goddess Hathor, mother of the sun god, was frequently represented either as a cow, or as having a human face, with cow's horns and ears. It was believed that every night she engulfed the sun god, only to give birth to him afresh every morning. Similarly Nut, another Egyptian sky goddess, was depicted as a cow, supported by the other gods, and with the stars on her underbelly.

In many ancient religions, however, the cow as a source of fecundity took second place as an object of worship to the bull as a source of generative power. The male symbol thus took precedence over the female. This is true of ancient Near Eastern religion generally. In Greece and Crete, too, the bull-cult of Minoan-Mycenean religion was far more important than any corresponding veneration of the cow, though in some traditions the sky god Zeus was said to have been nursed by a cow. His consort, Hera, is described by Homer as *boopis*, 'cow-eyed'.

This idea of divine nourishment is also to be found in ancient Scandinavian myth-

ology. Snorri's *Edda* tells of the primeval giant, Ymir, who was nourished by four rivers of milk from a cow. The beast, Audumulla, was herself created out of condensing frost. Being thirsty, she licked the blocks of salty ice around her and as the ice melted under her warm tongue, the head and then the body of a man appeared. This was Buri, grandfather of Odin, who was the greatest of the gods.

It is in India and in Hinduism that the cow plays the most striking role, both in mythology and in the day-to-day practice of religion. In practice, Indian cow-worship is restricted to one species of the animal, the East Indian humped zebu. The roots of this worship are certainly Indo-European, and have much in common with features already mentioned. The cow is thought of as a symbol of the divine bounty of the earth, and as the 'mother' of gods and men. The high god Varuna is called 'son of Aditi' in the oldest of the four chief Hindu collections of prayers and hymns, the *Rig Veda*, while the goddess Aditi is called 'the Cow, the sinless'.

The myth of the earth taking the form of a cow receives its first detailed expression in the *Vishnu Purana*, an ancient Sanskrit collection of legendary lore. In this, Prithu, the monarch of all, approached the earth in order to make her yield plants. The earth assumed the form of a cow and ran away, but was finally caught and persuaded to nourish the earth with her milk. Then Prithu milked the earth into his own hand, and there grew up all manner of corn and vegetables for man's food.

Crane

As happened not infrequently in the bird lore of antiquity, accurate observation merged into myth. Aristotle noted that cranes when sleeping stand first on one leg, then on the other. Aelian, the Roman writer of the 3rd century AD, improved on this; he stated that they posted sentinels and that these birds held a stone in the raised foot to help themselves to stay awake. Horapollo, a Greek grammarian living in the 4th century AD, referred to the crane as a symbol of vigilance. Thus the stone-grasping belief is probably an addition to much earlier tradition, based on the fact that the crane is indeed a wary bird.

There was also a mythological or symbolic association between cranes and trees. On a Celtic altar of the 1st century AD, found in Paris, the god Tarvos Trigaranus is shown felling a willow tree in company with three cranes and a bull. In Eastern symbolism the crane and the pine tree, signifying long life, are often depicted together. In Irish legends there are indications that the crane was once regarded as being possessed of supernatural qualities.

St Columba, who was called 'crane cleric' was said to have turned some women into cranes. In the West the lofty 'alphabetical' flight of the birds connected them with Apollo, the god of sun and poetry, and with Hermes, the patron of communications. But the association between long-necked birds and the sun is indeed a very ancient one.

Crow

Black, the colour of the crow, has long been associated with death and disaster; and because large birds of this colouring are relatively uncommon, a need was felt to explain their dark hue. A number of legends purport to explain how they acquired it. Thus, according to the Greek geographer Pausanias (2nd century AD) and other writers, when Apollo became the lover of Coronis, the mother of Asclepius, he commissioned a snow-white crow to mount guard while he went to Delphi; despite this, Coronis, although already pregnant by him, became unfaithful with Ischys. Before the crow set out with the news Apollo divined what had happened and, infuriated that the crow had not picked out Ischys's eyes, turned the bird black.

Another story relates that the gods were sacrificing and the raven was sent to bring water from a fountain for a libation but he dallied, waiting until some figs were ripe. So the bird was condemned to suffer from thirst in summer – and that is why the raven croaks so hoarsely.

The frequent allusions in folklore to the association between the raven or crow and water might seem unaccountable, for these birds are not especially partial to damp habitats and, indeed, sometimes frequent rocky outcrops and ruins in desert country. The association has apparently arisen through ravens being frequently seen circling among black storm clouds. Thus the species was credited with some of the qualities of a storm bird such as were attributed to large high-flying, and sometimes mythical, birds in Asia and elsewhere. Among the Greeks and Romans the crow was likewise considered to be a weather prophet. Many Greek writers refer to the raven as presaging tempests, though some characteristics of its behaviour were interpreted as prognosticating good weather. The raven's association with clouds and rain meant that it was often regarded as a thunderbird.

Perhaps the most familiar episode in which the raven is associated with water is the account in Genesis of the sending forth of a raven by Noah from the Ark to search for land. This is derived from an older myth of the Deluge originating in the ancient city of Acre in Israel, in which the dove, swallow and raven are sent forth in turn to discover whether the waters had subsided. It is recorded that at Krannon in Thessaly there were two ravens and never more – a detail perhaps based on observations that the birds pair for life – but at Krannon the ravens were connected with a magical rain-making ceremony. Coins of the 4th century BC depict two ravens on a small wagon containing a jar of water with pieces of metal suspended from it. By jolting this contrivance the jangling sounds and splashing water simulated a miniature thunderstorm. It was believed that in this manner rain could be induced to fall on earth.

As a wise bird flying hither and thither and at times reputedly in touch with the gods the raven was said to act as messenger, informant and guide.

Cuckoo

Augury and ornithomancy are based on notions that bird behaviour has ulterior and sometimes supernatural significance. Thus in Cornwall to hear the cuckoo on the right presaged good fortune, while to hear it on the left boded ill. In Norway more elaborate prognostications were made according to the point of the compass from which the bird was heard calling. As bird augury was practised on a considerable scale by the Romans, some of the associated notions may have been carried north and have influenced regard for the cuckoo, though it is possible that interpretations of its call as prophetic arose independently, influenced by the human timbre of its notes.

The similarity of the cuckoo's two syllable call to words in various languages has formed a basis for a considerable variety of traditions. A Bohemian legend relates that the cuckoo is a metamorphosed girl calling for her lost brother or, alternatively, if the words are interpreted differently, announcing that he has been found. The theme of a Serbian song is that the spirit of a dead man could not find release because his sister wept so incessantly at his grave. So she transformed herself into a cuckoo and cries continually, 'Ku ku, Ku ku', having the meaning 'Where are you?'

There may be some connection between these two stories and a belief that the cuckoo goes to a mysterious realm, the land of the dead, in winter. This is supported by an odd Estonian legend according to which Christ came to a cottage after a wicked stepmother had murdered two children and told the father that they would appear in spring as two living creatures. When spring came they emerged as a cuckoo and a swallow respectively.

The cuckoo has often been associated in the past with cuckoldry: Shakespeare speaks of the cuckoo who 'mocks married men'. In the *Asinaria* of the Latin dramatist Plautus (c 250–189 BC), a man's wife, finding him in adultery, shouts at him: 'What? is the cuckoo lying there? Get up, gallant, and go home.' The connection between the cuckoo and cuckoldry appears to have arisen from its nesting behaviour and its consequent reputation as a usurper.

A belief dating from the time of Aristotle or earlier, and still lingering in the countryside today, is that the cuckoo turns into a hawk in winter; this arose, no doubt, to explain the bird's disappearance. Plausibility was given to the notion by the similarity between the cuckoo and the merlin, a kind of falcon, together with the disappearance of the merlin from much of its winter range to its breeding haunts about the time the cuckoo arrives.

There was a widespread belief in England and on the Continent that on hearing the first cuckoo of the year one should wish, and there are still people who make a ritual event of the occasion by turning the coins in a pocket, for luck. It is said that if you have money in your pocket on hearing the bird, you will not want for it throughout the year.

Above *According to one legend, the downfall of Britain will follow swiftly if the ravens in the Tower of London are harmed in any way.* **Facing page: Above** *The similarity of the cuckoo's two syllable call to words in various languages has led some people to regard it as a bird endowed with the gift of prophecy: from the title page of Andrew Borde's* **Merry Tales of the Madmen of Gotam. Below** *The modern use of the dove as a symbol of peace derives from the story of Noah and the Ark. When the bird returned with an olive leaf in its beak, Noah knew that the flood waters had subsided.*

Dove

The Greeks explained in a myth how the dove became associated with Aphrodite, the goddess of love. The goddess and her son Eros were playfully competing in picking flowers and as Aphrodite was winning because she had the help of a nymph named Peristera (Dove), so Eros turned the nymph into a dove and henceforth she remained under the protection of Aphrodite. A Greek writer mentions that as Adonis had been honoured by Aphrodite, the Cyprians cast doves into a pyre to him. The mythology of the goddess, whose names Aphrodite Anadyomene signify Sea Foam, Rising from the Sea, and especially the story that she was born from an egg brooded by a dove and pushed ashore by a fish, suggest that her cult came from across the sea to Greece.

Dragon

Where there are myths, there are usually dragons. But although it would be easy to recognize a dragon, and descriptions and artistic representations of dragons abound, it is not so easy to define the beast. Like other fabulous monsters, such as the chimaera and griffin, the dragon is a mixture of several creatures. One of the earliest dragons to leave a permanent mark in the world (he is depicted in white glaze against a blue background on a gate in ancient Babylon) appears to have the head and horns of a ram, the forelegs of a lion, a scaly, reptilian body and tail, and the hind legs of an eagle. Each race has naturally drawn on the part of the animal world with which it is familiar in putting this composite beast together. The dragon of the ancient Egyptians is a close relation of the crocodile, while elephant dragons appear in Indian myths, and stag dragons in Chinese.

The dragon is even more dangerously equipped than any of his mythical rivals. The forked tongue and tail, the glaring eyes and ominously flared nostrils, the scorching breath, the sharp teeth and talons, and the armour-plating of the body add up to a formidable array of weapons. But strangely enough, the dragon is by no means always hostile to man. In the East, particularly, he is often a symbol or a portent of prosperity, and there are many tales of individual acts of kindness performed by dragons for the benefit of men.

Though most people nowadays would associate the dragon with fire, his primeval element is water, whether the sea, rivers, lakes, water-spouts or rain-clouds, and this watery connection is what chiefly distinguishes the dragon from other mythical hybrids. Even desert-dwelling people insist on it, and their dragons spend a lot of time lurking at the bottom of wells. Indeed, the bottom of the well is often identified with the dragon's eye, and this is a link with another distinguishing characteristic of the dragon: its baleful and searching gaze. There is little doubt that the very word 'dragon' is derived ultimately from an ancient Greek word meaning 'to see'. In the Old Testament the dragon is mentioned several times in the same breath as the owl, another creature with large, bleak eyes.

The dragon is known in many other parts of the world: in Hanoi, which was once known as the Dragon City; in Iceland, where the god Loki has associations with a female dragon; in the British Isles, where there are dragon caves and dragon-haunted lochs; and in Hawaii, where all the dragons are descended from the mother goddess Mo-o-inanea, the 'self-reliant dragon'.

According to some modern psychologists, the dragon is still with us, representing, says Jung, the 'negative mother-imago, and thus expressing resistance to incest, or the fear of it'. The dragon's guardianship of treasure represents, according to the same author, the mother's apparent possession of the son's libido: the treasure which is hard to attain lies hidden in the unconscious.

Like a number of other birds with religious associations the dove came to be regarded as oracular. According to Virgil, two doves guided Aeneas to the gloomy valley where the Golden Bough grew on a holm oak. There was a tradition at Dodona in Greece that the oracle was founded by a dove, and the oracle in the oasis of Siwa (Ammon) which Alexander the Great sought out was similarly reputed to have owed its origin to a dove. The Romans sacrificed doves to Venus, goddess of love, whom Ovid and other writers represented as riding in a dove-drawn chariot.

The Roman worship of Venus was to a large extent derived from a Phoenician sanctuary (Eryx), where the dove was revered as the companion of Astarte.

Eagle

In antiquity the eagle had a more significant role in Mesopotamia than in Egypt, where Horus, the falcon god, was of considerable importance. This is understandable when we take into consideration the differences in climate and topography between the two regions: such geographical factors had much influence on religion. Ancient Egypt was a land of sunshine dependent on the annual rise of the Nile whereas the Mesopotamian city states came into being in a region fringed by mountains and menaced by storms and floods. As far back as the 3rd millennium BC a double-headed eagle was associated with Ningursu of Lagash, the Babylonian god of fertility, storm and war. These associations are explicable when we remember the eagle's habit of soaring powerfully among the clouds, which were regarded with the greatest concern in such an area as they brought fertility to the fields but might also be responsible for disastrous flooding. The double-headed eagle was adopted by the Hittites and later cultures down the centuries. Evidence of the prolonged continuity of tradition is apparent in its becoming the emblem of Austria.

Another example is provided by the eagle-and-serpent motif. It appeared among the Hittites in the myth of the strife between the weather god and the serpent Illuyankas and has continued throughout many centuries and cultures; it appears today in the lectern of Peterborough cathedral and also in the arms of Mexico. In nature, it is not uncommon to see an eagle carrying a snake in its talons in regions where the snake-eating, short-toed species of this bird are found. In antiquity the conflict between the bird which soars high and the reptile which creeps into holes in the earth impressed people who looked on it as expressing the tension between the forces at war in the universe. Interpretations varied but the motif remained a portrayal of life's warring opposites.

In Indo-Iranian mythology, the eagle had an important role. It was associated with two themes, both of which had wide ramifications; in the Hindu text, the *Rig Veda*, it figures as the bringer of the sacred *soma*, an intoxicating spirit distilled from a plant of this name. In the *Avesta*, the holy book of the Parsees, it is said to dwell on the 'All-healing Tree Light' which in religion and art is related to the Tree of Life. From the cults in which these large symbolic birds were involved emerged beliefs in monstrous mythical winged creatures, such as the Arabian Anka, the Persian Simurgh and the Roc which carried off Sinbad the Sailor, as well as composite part-bird beings like the Indian Garuda. There are reminiscences of these strange creatures in the Book of Daniel where we read of a lion with eagle's wings and in Revelation in which other composite creatures are mentioned. Underlying such concepts is the attempt to symbolize supernatural power.

Asian influence may be detected in the exalted status of the eagle in Greek mythology, as the attribute or associate of Zeus.

His eagle-surmounted sceptre at Olympia was in the tradition of Babylonian processional sceptres and such signs of authority continued into the Middle Ages.

In the Old Testament the eagle typifies swift and high flight and is noted as frequenting battlefields, but in most contexts the vulture is not clearly distinguished from the eagle. Through inadequate observation and the misunderstanding or deliberate embroidery of texts, eagle lore became increasingly divorced from natural history.

Frog

In mythology the frog appears comparatively rarely but, when he does, he seems to evoke either extreme repulsion or respect. The ancient Jews, for instance, regarded him with abhorrence. In the book of Revelation, seven angels 'pour out on the earth the seven bowls of the wrath of God'; when the sixth does so, 'three foul spirits like frogs' appear; 'demonic spirits, performing signs'.

The Jewish attitude to frogs doubtless goes back to the early days of their culture, when these creatures were called up by Moses and Aaron as the second plague of Egypt (Exodus, chapter 8). The Egyptians themselves, on the other hand, clearly regarded the frog in quite a different light: Heket, their gentle goddess of childbirth, had the head (and sometimes the entire form) of a frog and, in a variant of the Egyptian myth of the creation of the world, she and her ram-headed husband Khnum were the first to 'build men and make gods'.

The frog also plays an important part in a central Asian creation myth, in which Otshirvani the creator and his assistant Chagan-Shukuty came down from heaven and saw a frog playing in the primeval waters. Chagan-Shukuty picked it up and put it on its back on the surface. Otshirvani sat on the frog's stomach and told his assistant to dive and see what he could find beneath the waters. After repeated attempts, Chagan-Shukuty brought up some earth. At Otshirvani's behest he sprinkled it on the frog which sank, leaving the little earth, just big enough for the divine pair to rest on, afloat on the deep. As they slept, Shulmus the devil came and saw his opportunity to destroy the gods and the still tiny earth by flinging them into the waters. But when he picked up 'the earth'

it grew so that he could not see around him; he ran, but the more he ran the bigger grew the earth. Finally, he gave up and dropped the now enormous earth just as Otshirvani awoke. Shulmus escaped to continue his evil work in new ways. In other Asian myths the frog supports the world.

The frog is also connected with the deluge myths found in many parts of the world. In Queensland, Australia, the aborigines say that a great frog once swallowed all the water in the world, causing great drought and suffering. It occurred to the people that if only they could make the frog laugh, he would bring up the water and all would be well again. Several animals did comic turns and dances for him; but he remained unamused until the eel, by squirming and wriggling about, made him roar with laughter. As he laughed the waters burst out.

The Huron Indians of North America have a similar story saying that all water was in the belly of a huge frog until Ioskeha, the great hero of creation, stabbed him and returned the waters to the lakes and rivers. In other North American legends animals brought order to the world, which was then destroyed by monsters bearing fire and flood; according to the Alaskan tribes, one of these demons was a monstrous frog-woman.

Naturally enough, for many peoples the frog is associated with rain. This is especially so, it seems, in India and South America. Orinoco tribes in Venezuela have kept frogs captive and beat them in time of drought. A hymn in the Hindu *Rig Veda* seems to show that frogs were worshipped for bringing rain or that, awakened themselves by showers, they brought long life and prosperity; the gods granted rain when the frogs croaked but the moon killed them with the dew. It was also thought that the much-needed moisture could be summoned from the skies by pouring water over a frog or by hanging it up. In Malaya the same result could be achieved by swinging it on the end of a cord. Some Chinese tales say the dew brings frog spawn down from the moon; the frog is called the 'celestial chicken'. By contrast, the Shan and the Karen tribes of Burma regard the frog as the enemy of the moon.

The frog is generally respected in Japan, where he is one of the animals of the zodiac: 19th-century statuette or netsuke in the Victoria & Albert Museum.

Goat

The goat is sometimes a symbol of agility and sometimes of an obstinate insistence on having one's own way (and so its Latin name is enshrined in the word 'caprice'). In popular traditional astrology those born under Capricorn are assigned the goatish characteristics of leaping over difficulties and butting away obstacles.

The scapegoat ritual tended to connect the goat with evil and, through the link with Azazel, with the fallen angels and the Devil. This association was hammered home by St Matthew's gospel (chapter 25) in which Jesus likens the righteous to sheep and the wicked to goats.

The copulation of women with a divine goat is reported in antiquity from Egypt. In the 5th century BC, Herodotus (book 2) says that the people of Mendes in the Nile Delta venerate all goats, and in particular the male ones.

'One of them is held in particular reverence, and when he dies the whole province goes into mourning ... In this province not long ago a goat tupped a woman, in full view of everybody – a most surprising incident.'

Herodotus identified the divine he-goat as Pan. Much later, Plutarch (died c 120 AD) says that the most beautiful women were selected to lie with the divine goat of Mendes.

Drawing from southern India of the god Brahma, riding on a cosmic gander.

Goose

In many parts of Europe and Asia the goose has played an important role in local folklore, custom and mythology, and in the British Isles it is one of the few birds still involved in ritual observances. The preservation of such folk rites in a sophisticated society usually indicates the very great antiquity of the beliefs that are originally associated with them.

Beliefs and ceremonies associated with the goose used to be characteristic of most northern countries. In pagan Sweden the goose figured as a grave offering; in Germany geese were sacrificed to Odin at the autumnal equinox and there was apparently a goose goddess at Cologne. During the 13th century the inhabitants of Friesland were accused of a form of witchcraft in which a goose was involved.

Goose beliefs and cults were not confined to Europe. Among Siberian tribes the bird figured in various ceremonies. One tribe sacrificed it to the river or sky god while another made a 'nest' for the goose god of skin, fur and cloth. Further south, in India, the wild goose is considered of great significance and the god Brahma is frequently depicted riding on a gander. Aphrodite, the Greek goddess of love, was also shown being borne through the air by a goose. In China a goose was carried at the head of processions and a pair of geese or duck might be presented to a newly married couple; the mandarin duck is taken as a symbol of marital fidelity.

All these beliefs and rituals appear to have originated in an association between the goose and the sun, and consequently with fertility. In early times people were greatly impressed by the spectacle of huge flocks passing overhead in spring and they connected the birds with the lengthening of the days, greater warmth, growth or vegetation and the mating of birds and beasts. Wild geese thus came to represent the power which wrought these changes – meaning either the sun or sun god.

Goose feasts may be a dying tradition in the British Isles but another ritual, derived from goose beliefs, is still widely observed though without realization of its origin – the custom of 'breaking the wishbone' when a chicken is served for dinner.

Chris Barker

Hare

As a figure from the unconscious the hare constantly recurs in dreams, and in world mythology it is closely associated with the moon. It has performed the role of deity and devil, of witch and witch's imp, and for reasons hard to comprehend this most timid of creatures has been regarded by mankind with a mixture of horror and awe.

The Algonquin Indians worshipped the Great Hare, who was credited with forming the earth.

In Greece and China it was associated with the moon; in the former country it was connected with the lunar goddess Hecate and in the latter with the powers of augury. Buddha in one of his reincarnations took the form of a hare, which leaped into a fire and implanted its image upon the moon.

In pre-Christian Europe the hare was regarded as a symbol of fertility and therefore of the spring. The Romans divined the future from its movements and its sacred flesh was denied to ordinary mortals.

Many people feel an aversion to eating the meat of the hare and there is a suggestion of totemism underlying this objection. But it is possible that it was also based on the rules of magic; it would be extremely dangerous to consume the flesh of so timid an animal for fear that this same timidity would be transmitted to the eater.

The hare was reverenced in Europe as the spirit of the corn, particularly in Germany, Holland, France and Ireland, where the reaping of the last of the corn was known as 'cutting the hare'. Reapers were urged on at harvest end with the cry, 'We'll put the hare out of it today.'

Horse

As a symbol of terrestrial, or earthly power, the horse was projected into the heavens in the form of the divine horses of the ancient religions, and in this manner became integrated with sky gods. In classical mythology, Poseidon or Neptune is said to have created the horse which became sacred to him, and he is also said to have invented horse racing.

Among other myths concerning the origins of the horse is that which declared the horse to have been created out of an egg, the symbol of creation.

In Christian art the horse is represented as the symbol of the three saints Anastasius, Hippolytus and Quirinus, who are shown being torn asunder by wild horses. However, to horse-users everywhere, the horse has always symbolized the qualities of power, speed and pride.

In its role as a divinity the horse has played many parts, of which the divine horses of King Diomedes and the Celtic goddess Epona are prominent examples. Epona, a divinity of the Gauls, was both a goddess and protectress of horses, a tribute to the valour of the Celtic warriors.

Many gods, goddesses and demi-gods were closely associated with the horse in antiquity and Demeter, the Greek fertility goddess, was sometimes represented with the head of a horse. In almost all of the ancient civilizations the sun was believed to have been drawn across the sky in his chariot by celestial horses. It was in this august fashion that Dag, the Norse god of day, was conveyed through the heavens by the white steed 'Shining Mane' which spread its light across the whole living world. According to Norse mythology Mani, the moon goddess, travelled across the sky in a car drawn by Alsvidur, 'the All Swift'. Diana, goddess of the moon, travelled likewise in a horse-drawn chariot. The gods Thor and Helios drove their cosmic chariots through the heavens, while the mighty Odin was borne through the clouds on the back of his eight-footed steed.

In sacrifice we submit our most precious possessions to the gods, and the horse, the symbol of social power in ancient societies, was accorded this dreadful honour. In Imperial Rome, the October Horse was sacrificed as an offering to Mars. In some of these barbaric rites, horses were driven over precipices as offerings to the sea deities.

Part of the funeral rites of the warlord of old was the obligatory killing of the war horse in order that it might continue to serve its dead master in the afterlife, a custom which continued until as late as the 14th century. The traditional military funeral with its riderless horse, carrying its dead master's boots reversed on either side, is a last surviving relic of this form of sacrifice. The nomadic tribes of the Altai Mountains of Central Asia continued the sacrifice of horses until well into the 20th century, despite attempts to suppress the custom by the Soviet government. In a government poster of the 1920s the skins of flayed horses are displayed on poles above the legend: 'There are no gods. No sacrifices of horses will deliver you from your need.'

In Western Europe horses were burned alive in rural districts as late as the 18th century as a magical device, intended to remove disease from the remainder of the herd, or were burned alive in order to prevent the death or theft of the other animals.

To ancient man the drama of the heavens was performed by demi-gods, animals and men, the gigantic reflections of their pale selves on earth. The hooves of the divine horses pulling the celestial chariots accounted for the thunder; the whip-lash was the lightning that flashed terrifyingly across the sky; and there were the famous Wind Horses among whom were Pegasus and Hofvarpnir, steed of Gna, messenger of the divine Frigg. Sometimes the heavens would be agitated into a fury of terrifying commotion, as if an army was marching through the clouds. Out of this was born the legend of the Wild Huntsman with his diabolical horse and baying hounds, searching for human souls.

Allusions to mystical, allegorical and cosmic horses find a place in many religions including Christianity. In both the Old and New Testaments occur supernatural horses. Elijah and Elisha saw visions of fiery horses and in Revelation, St John describes the terrible horses that harry mankind, having 'tails like serpents'.

Hyena and Jackal

In Europe a very wide variety of magical properties were attributed to the hyena. Greek writers recounted the Arab belief that if one of these animals stepped on a man's shadow it deprived him of the powers of speech and movement. They also reported that if a dog, standing on a roof in the moonlight, cast its shadow where a hyena could step on it the dog would fall to the ground. The statement by the 16th-century writer, Bartholomew, that the hyena by circling an animal three times, could charm it into immobility may be a later elaboration of these notions.

Christian hermits living in the Egyptian desert in the 4th century were on familiar terms with hyenas and did not attribute magical properties to them. Stories are told of a hyena who led a hermit far into the desert to the cave where another was living; of another which on finding a hermit lost in the wilderness guided him to safety; and of St Macarius of Alexandria who, when a hyena brought her blind whelp to him, cured it by applying saliva to its eyes.

In a number of biblical contexts the word translated as fox refers to the jackal, an animal that appears in folklore and folktales as crafty and shrewd rather than malicious. As a scavenger and eater of carrion it acquired in some areas an association with death: in ancient Egypt Anubis, the jackal-headed guardian of cemeteries guided the dead to the judgement of Osiris. According to the ancient Indian laws of Manu a faithless wife would be a jackal in her next incarnation. The animal's apparent timidity is the reason why the Bushmen of southern Africa protect their children against becoming timorous by forbidding them to eat the animal's heart.

In Indian folktales the jackal has a role rather similar to that of the cunning fox in Europe. In one story a crocodile seizes a jackal's leg but the jackal talks the reptile into believing he is holding a tree root. In another a Brahmin who compassionately releases a tiger from a trap is about to be eaten when a jackal persuades the tiger to re-enter the trap. In yet another, an elephant swallows a jackal but dies when it is eaten by the animal inside it. The jackal finds himself trapped in the elephant's dried-up skin but calls for rain and escapes when rain falls and softens the hide.

Facing page *The jackal was associated with death in some areas; in Egypt the jackal-headed Anubis was thought to guide the dead to the place of judgement: wall painting showing Anubis with Nefertiti, the wife of Ikhnaten.* **Right** *The kraken was said to surface only on summer days when the sea was calm, and because of its enormous size its entire body was never visible; at first sight the monster could be mistaken for an island, or a group of islands: 16th-century* **Carta Marina,** *a map of the North Sea showing a ship anchored to one of these gigantic creatures; two sailors have disembarked and are cooking a meal on the monster's back.*

Kraken

It seems likely that the kraken was a kind of giant polyp or cuttle-fish, perhaps a survival of some almost extinct prehistoric sea creature. Bishop Pontoppidan, who wrote quite extensively about this inhabitant of Norwegian waters, had a theory that the floating islands which suddenly appeared or disappeared in Northern seas, were in fact kraken; and also that the medusa or jelly-fish might be its ovum.

Another bishop, cited by Pontoppidan as a reliable witness, claimed that in 1680 the remains of a young kraken were found putrefying when the creature got wedged among some rocks in a fiord. Apparently, the monster was not particularly dangerous, except because of its size. Any ship, even one as large as a man-of-war, that was caught up in the swell of a submerging or surfacing kraken would be wrecked because of its huge displacement.

The creature only appeared on hot summer days when the sea was calm. Norwegian fishermen, who rowed out several miles to where they reckoned the sea should be at least 480 to 600 feet deep, would suddenly find a depth of only 120 to 150 feet, and the water at that point teeming with shoals of cod and ling.

This they took to be a sign that a kraken was present. If the water began growing shallower they stopped fishing immediately, and rowed some distance away, for it meant that the monster was about to emerge.

Owing to its enormous size, the whole body was never visible; an entire kraken could be observed only when it was young.

The back of a fully grown monster was estimated to be 1½ miles in circumference, and at first sight the creature looked like a number of small bumpy islands, surrounded by fronds of floating seaweed, with fish leaping about the shallows. After a time, huge tentacles were said to appear, with which the kraken propelled itself along, and gathered food.

The kraken only remained on the surface for a short while. Its descent into the ocean was a treacherous time, for it churned the waters around it into a whirlpool and drew everything into its depths.

The creature lived according to a definite rhythm. For some months it was seen only to eat, and at others solely to excrete. During the latter period the sea's surface became thick and disturbed and gave off a pungent aroma. The smell and muddiness attracted the shoals which gathered to feed and the kraken then opened up its tentacles and drew in all the fish, which were converted into bait for the creature's next feeding period when it became due.

Whether the kraken was merely a legendary sea monster, or the remains of some primeval sea creature, or the much dramatized account given by lonely sailors of an extremely large cuttle-fish, Bishop Pontoppidan's own words seem particularly apt in describing all those monsters which the modern world has not glimpsed: 'In the ocean many things are hidden.'

ANGLI

Lion

The size, strength and magnificent appearance of the lion caused it to be associated in ancient times with divinity and hence with royalty; leonine qualities were attributed to gods and goddesses and this animal is still referred to as the 'King of Beasts'. The Egyptian goddess Sekhmet was represented as lion-headed. At Syracuse in Sicily a lion was led in procession in honour of the Greek huntress goddess Artemis and at Baalbek (in modern Lebanon) chants were sung to a lion apparently regarded as divine, while it ate a calf.

The mythology of the lion differs in various regions, according to the extent to which people are familiar with it. Among those who know the beast only by hearsay or in captivity its characteristics have been exaggerated and embellished, whereas in the lore of African tribesfolk accustomed to living among lions, they may be revered or regarded, as in some folktales, as rather stupid and ridiculous animals.

Among many primitive peoples the distinction between man and animal is blurred; some African tribesfolk believe that a sorcerer can transform himself into a lion and the Bushmen think that a lion can become a man. The Dinka of Sudan regard lions as their totemic ancestors, sleep out in the wilderness without fear and leave portions of the animals they kill for them. On the Congo and Zambesi Rivers the souls of dead chiefs are believed to pass into lions but among the Ngonis of Central Africa this was not thought of as a privilege reserved for chiefs. Some tribes treated a dead lion with ceremonial respect.

In contrast, the lion of folktales may be depicted as easily outwitted by smaller and weaker animals, as in versions of the widespread and universal motif in which the downtrodden get the better of the mighty (as in Cinderella). In the *Panchatantra* (a Sanskrit book of fables), a Tibetan folktale and some African stories the lion is tricked by the jackal or the hare. One of these relates that a lion one day found a hare leaning against a rock. In answer to the lion's inquiry the hare said that the rock was liable to fall. Would the lion kindly help to support it? The lion obligingly put its weight against it while the hare sneaked away, leaving the lion pushing against the perfectly stable rock. This story illustrates the diffusion of folktales for versions of it are told in Georgia and Puerto Rico, as a part of the cultural heritage brought to the New World by slaves. In contrast to this story, the lion in Aesop's fable, 'The Lion's Share', outwits the other animals.

There are many tales of the magnanimity of the lion, in which the beast spares or befriends human beings. One of the earliest is the story of 'Daniel in the Lion's Den', and the 'Androcles and the Lion' motif is also ancient. A similar story is told of St Jerome.

Facing page *15th-century Greek mural showing St Mamas riding a lion; in legends the lion often appears as a friend and helper of man.*

Lizard

The sun-loving behaviour of many lizards has inspired various beliefs that they are associated with the sun. In the ancient Near East they symbolized overpowering heat, and in Egypt they were associated with fecundity, probably because of their increased activity when the Nile floods stimulated the resurgence of life. In Dahomey, the lizard is said to have fetched fire from the sun. The reappearance of lizards after hibernation seemed mysterious and in Europe it was believed that during this period they became blind. It was said that in spring these creatures climb up an eastward-facing wall and look to the east; when the sun rises their sight is restored. European lizards are mostly keen-sighted and so the belief arose as long ago as the time of Pliny (1st century AD) that a lizard talisman restored sight to the blind. Lizards appear carved on corbels in medieval cathedrals, such as Southwell and Wells; they symbolize the life-giving and enlightening power of the gospel.

The idea of the lizard as a god, kin to the gods or their messenger, appears to have been due mainly to its associations with the sun. Such beliefs are particularly characteristic of Polynesia, where lizard cults were observed. The Samoans revered several gods in lizard form. The Maoris considered the green lizard to be an incarnation of Tangaloa, the heaven god, and for the Hervey islanders of Polynesia, Tongaiti, the night heaven god, was a nocturnal spotted lizard. In Africa the Shilluk had a tribal lizard god. The Australian Aranda connected the lizard with their sky and earth myths and believed that the sky would fall if they killed one.

Magpie and Rook

The magpie's contrasting plumage contributed to its being regarded as a mysterious, sinister and oracular bird. According to a North of England legend, it was a hybrid between the raven and the dove, the two birds released by Noah from the ark, and therefore had not been baptized in the waters of the Flood. In Germany witches were said to ride on magpies or to appear as these birds, and in Sweden there was a saying that in August the magpies go off to draw the Devil's waggons of hay, hence their neck feathers can be seen to have been rubbed by the yoke. In north-east Scotland the magpie was the 'De'il's bird' and was believed to have a drop of Satan's blood on its tongue. It could acquire human speech if its tongue were scratched and a drop of blood from a human tongue inserted.

Such beliefs probably arose from the calls uttered by a party of magpies which sounded, to the imaginative, like human chatter; and from the fact that it had been observed that magpies in captivity are able to imitate words. In Brittany it was said to have seven of the Devil's hairs on its head. Because of the bird's sinister and Satanic associations in many areas, it was considered unlucky to kill a magpie, or thought advisable to do so only during certain periods.

Nightingale

The song of the nightingale has been more generally admired and praised than the song of any other European bird. The male sings by night as well as by day, so that even those with little interest in birds cannot fail to notice its characteristic song.

Among Greek and Roman writers who commented on the bird's song were Aristophanes, who tried to reproduce the sound verbally in his play *The Birds*, and Pliny, who departed from his usual matter of fact style to describe it enthusiastically. It was the Greek myth of Philomela, however, which was responsible for the prominence of the bird in Latin literature and eventually in our own. According to the story, Procne, the wife of Tereus, king of Thrace, asked him to bring her sister Philomela to stay with her but when Tereus laid eyes on his sister-in-law, he fell violently in love with her. On the journey home, he ravished her and cut out her tongue so that his crime might not be known. He kept her hidden but Philomela was able to inform her sister by weaving an account of what had happened into a cloak which she sent to her. Procne took terrible revenge on Tereus, killing their son Itys, and serving him to her husband for dinner. The sisters fled from the tyrant king, and when he pursued them, Zeus turned Procne into a nightingale, Philomela into a swallow and Tereus into a hoopoe. Latin poets misread the story and made Philomela the nightingale, so that English poets, following them, wrote of Philomela as the nightingale.

The nightingale's song has not always been admired. A hermit in a Sussex forest was so disturbed by their singing that, so it was said, he laid a curse upon them so that they never again appeared in the neighbourhood. St Francis, on the other hand, is said to have competed with a nightingale in singing praise to God – and to have admitted himself defeated.

A nightingale in full song can indeed sing around the clock with a few intermissions. Country people, noticing this, associated the bird with insomnia and drew the conclusion that organs of the nightingale could be used to produce sleeplessness, on the magical principle of 'like producing like'. The eyes and heart, if placed close to a person in bed, would keep him awake – and if they were dissolved surreptitiously in his drink he would certainly die of insomnia.

Ostrich

The widespread notion that the ostrich did not brood, which dates from at least as far back as the 2nd century, led to the belief that it hatched its eggs by gazing at them intently. This belief was repeated by writers down the centuries, including Vincent of Beauvais and Montaigne, and the ostrich egg thus became a symbol of single-minded devotion. In present-day Greek churches an ostrich egg suspended in a conspicuous position is a reminder to the worshipper to focus his thoughts and prayers. The moral was drawn that as the ostrich leaves the eggs so the hermit retires from worldly involvements.

The belief that the bird consumes hard, inedible objects is also of long standing. Pliny said the ostrich could digest anything, but Aelian, who was better informed, stated that it kept pebbles in its gizzard. Rabbinic writers commented that it ate glass. An early Christian document (*Physiologus*) remarks that the ostrich eats glowing iron because 'his nature is very cold'.

Among the fanciful ideas about ostriches given currency by writers of the 15th and 16th centuries were that these birds terrified horses by flapping their wings, and that underneath the wings there was a small bone with which they pricked themselves when provoked to anger. Such ideas may have arisen from observations of these strange birds flapping their short wings as they ran away.

For some reason the idea arose that the ostrich is deaf as well as silly. In Philemon Holland's translation of Pliny, *Historia Naturalis* (1602), we read: 'But the veriest fools they be of all others; – for as high as the rest of their body is, yet if they thrust their head and neck once into any shrub or bush, and get it hidden, they think then they are safe enough, and that no man seeth them.' Hence the proverbial ostrich, symbolical of stupidity and an inability to face realities. No doubt the belief arose from ostriches being seen with heads down feeding before they became alarmed.

The belief, mentioned by Aristotle, that ostriches lay more eggs than any other bird was based on the finding of large clutches. As many as 60 have been recorded but the ostrich is polygamous and several may lay in one nest.

Owl

As early as the Old Stone Age we have evidence of the interest aroused by this bird, for a pair of nesting snowy owls with their chick is engraved on a rock face in a cave in southern France. On a Sumerian tablet dating from 2300–2000 BC a nude goddess is depicted flanked on either side by an owl. She is believed to be the goddess of death. A number of biblical references associate the owl with misery and desolation, and the bird is mentioned in connection with 'dragons' and wild beasts and also with mourning. Greek and Latin writers refer to the owl as a bird of ill omen. Ovid, Pliny and other authors associate the birds with death and their calls are mentioned as sinister. When an owl appeared in the Capitol at Rome it occasioned such alarm that the place was cleansed with water and sulphur to expel any evil influences it might have brought.

As is not uncommon with creatures or objects regarded as mysterious and arousing a strong emotional response, owls may sometimes be regarded as having properties contrary to those generally attributed to them. Something which is apt to frighten people may come to be considered effective as a deterrent against that which they fear; the evil thing may be enlisted as an ally. In ancient China, where owl sacrifices were offered, ornaments called 'owl corners' were placed on buildings in the belief that they protected them from fire. In Semitic countries the owl is usually regarded as ominous and in Persia is spoken of as 'the angel of death', yet in Israel little grey owls are considered good omens when they appear near the crops. Perhaps the belief originated from the observation that these birds prey on birds and mammals which damage crops. In ancient Athens the little owl was associated with Athene, probably as goddess of night, but being a common bird it was regarded in a friendly way and became the emblem of the city. 'There goes an owl' was the Athenian saying indicating signs of victory.

Latin writers early in our era alluded to the custom of hanging up owls in order to deflect storms and it was believed that an owl nailed up with wings outspread would avert hail and lightning. The custom of nailing owls to barn doors persisted into the 19th century in England. The Romans used representations of owls to combat the Evil Eye. Among the tribes of northern Asia owls were regarded as able to counteract evil powers. An owl might be placed over a child's cot to frighten away evil spirits. In India owl feathers were placed under the pillow of a restless child in order to induce sleep. The Ainu people of Japan made wooden images of owls and nailed them to their houses at times of famine or pestilence.

In Africa owls are commonly associated with sorcery. When an owl perched on a dwelling in Bechuanaland the witch-doctor was called in to perform purificatory rites. The souls of sorcerers were called 'owls' in Madagascar. The Yoruba of Nigeria believe that wizards send out owls as their emissaries to kill people. In certain regions of Nigeria the natives avoid naming the

Above *Although it often has strongly evil associations, by contrast the owl is sometimes regarded as a wise and benevolent bird: North American Indian effigy jar in the shape of an owl.* **Facing page** *In medieval times the pelican was believed to peck its own breast to supply its young with blood: illustration from a 13th-century English bestiary incorporates this popular motif.* **Left** *The ostrich became a symbol of single-minded devotion because it was believed that it hatched its eggs by gazing at them: mosaic from Thurburbo Majus in Tunisia.*

owl, referring to it as 'the bird that makes you afraid'.

In North America notions concerning owls varied. While the Pawnees thought of them as giving protection, the Ojibwas believed in an evil spirit which appeared in the guise of an owl. In California the white owl was thought to be an evil spirit and its feathers were worn as a counter-charm.

Since owls were regarded as embodying weird powers they were associated in Germany and elsewhere with witchcraft. The witches in *Macbeth* (Act IV Sc. 1) included in their brew 'Lizard's leg and howlet's wing': Pliny stated that an owl's heart placed on a woman's breast would force her to divulge secrets. This was repeated by Albertus Magnus and reappeared as recently as 1863 in a book published in Pennsylvania. Among the Greeks magical and medicinal virtues were attributed to owls' eggs. Given to a child they would ensure his life-long temperance. Owl-egg soup was a remedy for epilepsy and treatment of grey hair with the contents of an owl's egg would darken it. As the egg had to be one from which a male chick would have emerged, any failures could be easily explained.

The owl figures in a number of fables and legends. The story of 'The War of the Owls and Crows' may have symbolized the opposition between the moon and the sun.

Peacock

The peacock is native to southern Asia and beliefs about in are widespread in that region, especially in India where, since 1963, it has been recognized as the national bird. As far back as the *Rig Veda*, the Hindu collection of sacred writings dated c 1200 BC, it was recorded that the steeds of the god Indra possessed hair like peacock's feathers. The peacock has an important place in Hinduism and the national epic, the *Ramayana*, relates that when the gods transformed themselves into animal forms in order to escape the demon Ravana, Indra, the god of thunder, rains and war, became a peacock. In recompense the bird was endowed with a thousand eyes in its feathers, the capacity to rejoice when the rains came and the power to kill snakes; obviously it had been observed that the bird attacks serpents, and displays and calls at the beginning of the rainy season.

Various names signify that the peacock dances joyfully on seeing clouds or hearing thunder. The term for one of the 108

Bodleian Library Filmstrip

postures of the classical Hindu dance signifies 'sportive like the peacock'. A number of divinities are portrayed mounted on the bird – in India Brahma and his wife Sarasvati, in Indo-China the warrior god Skanda and in Japan Kujaku-myoo (Mahamayuri), who protects from calamity and is besought to send rain.

The association of the peacock with rain also spread throughout Europe, where as far west as Ireland its calls are believed to forecast rain. The 15th-century *Hortus Sanitatis* declares that it is a sign of rain when the peacock 'mounts on high' and Michael Drayton (1563–1631) wrote of the strutting peacock yawling 'gainst the rain'.

From the knowledge that the peacock kills snakes there developed in India the belief that its bile and blood acted as an antidote against poison; smoke from its burning plumes was held to dispel venom and, in the Punjab, those bitten by snakes smoked its feathers. Travellers were recommended to carry a peacock to ward off snakes. In England during the 15th century the Eastern notion of the antipathy between the peacock and snakes became elaborated into the assumption that the bird's raucous call frightens away serpents.

Besides providing antidotes to poison,

various part of the bird were regarded as effective in curing many diseases and disabilities ranging from tuberculosis, forms of paralysis, asthma, catarrh and headaches to barrenness. Among Hindus and Moslems peacock feathers are believed to ward off evil, especially evil spirits. Umbrellas of the plumes were carried by persons associated with royalty and one was held over the pope on important occasions. In India the mere sight of the bird is believed to bring good luck and to bestow peace of mind.

In Chinese and Japanese art the peacock has decorative and symbolical significance; it is often depicted together with the peony. A defeated Chinese general of the Chin dynasty who took refuge from his enemies in a forest is said to have been so grateful to the peacocks for not betraying him that he conferred peacock feathers on those showing special bravery in battle.

The reference in the Old Testament to 'apes and peacocks' sent to Solomon (I Kings 10.22) cannot be taken seriously, as the translation is guesswork. However, peacocks are known to have been kept and reared in Babylon.

Aristotle mentions the peacock which, like the cock, was called 'the Persian bird', and a reference in a play by Aristophanes may imply that a Persian ambassador brought a gift of peacocks. Alexander the Great imposed heavy penalties on those who killed Indian peacocks.

The birds were depicted on Greek coins. They were sacred to Hera, and a myth relates how the goddess set the hundred-eyed giant Argus to guard her husband's mistress, Io; when Zeus sent Hermes to charm and kill Argus, Hera used the giant's eyes to ornament the peacock's tail.

Although through its connection with rain, and hence fertility, the peacock was generally regarded as auspicious, there were exceptions to this view. In Java it was associated with the Devil and in Mosul in northern Iraq the Yezidis, who held that the Devil was not evil, called him the Peacock Angel. According to a Persian poet, the bird's 'hideous feet' remind it that it can never attain paradise. There is a somewhat similar anecdote in the *Physiologus*, which contains stories collected in Egypt in early Christian times. It states that the peacock, on seeing his feet and realizing how they contrast with his beautiful plumage, screams: so the Christian should avoid pride and lament his sins. In the medieval bestiaries this theme was elaborated: it was stated that as the peacock on awakening cries out because it has dreamed it has lost its beauty, so the Christian should fear lest he lose his virtues.

The peacock was taken over from pagan into Christian art and appears very commonly in Christian iconography. It was early adopted as the symbol of the Resurrection, possibly because after moulting it was seen to become clothed again in splendour; there are examples in the Roman catacombs. St Augustine stated that its flesh was incorruptible. From this may have arisen the belief that peacock feathers preserved objects from decay if placed with them. In many medieval paintings angels' wings are composed of peacocks' plumes.

Pelican

The lore of the pelican has so little relevance to the actual behaviour of the bird that it might refer to a mythical species. Its chief interest is in illustrating the origin of an important symbol from confused ideas. The pelican was familiar in Egypt as a large bird opening its wide gape to enable the young to feed from the fish brought in its pouch; but the symbolical pelican's significance was mainly borrowed from the vulture. In the Bible vultures are not clearly distinguished from eagles. Thus in Exodus 19.4 we should read: 'I bore you on vultures' wings' rather than 'on eagles' wings' and in Deuteronomy 32.11: 'Like a vulture...that flutters over its young, spreading out its wings.' As the Hebrew words for 'vulture' and 'compassion' are very similar, an association was established between large birds and parental care which was transferred to the pelican.

The notion that the pelican feeds or even revives its young with its own blood may perhaps be traced to vultures being seen to bring bloody morsels to their chicks.

The *Physiologus*, an early Christian compilation which wove together biblical ideas with Egyptian mythology concerning animals, contained two stories elaborated from these notions. One relates that the pelican loves its young very much but these, when they are large enough, strike ungratefully at their parents.

The old birds then retaliate and kill the chicks; but soon they are overcome with compassion and the mother comes on the third day, opens her side and sheds blood on them, restoring them to life. It is also stated that in order to foil the snake the pelican makes its nest in a lofty situation and builds a hedge around it. The snake, representing the Devil, puffs his venom on the nest and kills the young. When the pelican returns she flaps her wings against her sides, drawing blood which rains down on the chicks and resuscitates them.

Christian writers used these stories to illustrate their teaching. St Jerome interpreted them as showing how those dead in sin were made alive through Christ's blood shed on the cross, and down the centuries emphasis was laid on the parental affection of the pelican. The representation in carved wood or stone and in stained glass windows of the bird pecking her breast to supply her young with blood became frequent in the Middle Ages as a symbol of Christ and the Eucharist. Such symbolism had special importance during centuries when few could read but the pelican also acquired considerable prominence in literature.

Shakespeare could assume that his audiences would understand allusions to the symbolic pelican. King Lear, for instance, recalling the story of the bird's ungrateful young, refers to Regan and Goneril as 'pelican daughters'. But for centuries the 'pelican in her piety', as the heraldic representation of the bird was called, continued to be a symbol of the noble virtue of heroic self-sacrifice and often appeared in heraldry, as in the arms of Corpus Christi College, Cambridge.

Phoenix

For a mythical creature, the phoenix is familiar enough; it is used in everyday life as a trademark, it rises from stylized flames on heraldic bearings, it enriches the poet's language, and appears briefly in history. What its legend is and means, on the other hand, has largely been forgotten as the symbol gains wider and wider currency in the modern world.

The phoenix, according to the most developed forms of the story, is a bird about the size of an eagle, brilliantly coloured in plumage; it is either purple with a golden collar, or a dazzling mixture of red, gold and blue.

The bird is the only one of its kind, and lives in Arabia; at the end of an epoch, as it feels death drawing near, it builds a pyre of the sweetest spices, on which it then sits, singing a song of rare beauty. The rays of the sun ignite the nest, and both this and the bird are consumed to ashes. From the ashes there arises a worm, which eventually grows into a new phoenix. The bird's first task is to gather the remains of its parent and, accompanied by a throng of other birds, to fly to Heliopolis (the City of the Sun) on the Nile. Here the priests of the sun receive it with great ceremony; it buries its parent in the temple, and returns to Arabia, its mission accomplished.

The roots of this story first appear in ancient Greek literature, in Herodotus's account of Egypt (c 430 BC). When he was at Heliopolis, he was shown the bird in pictures; and its very name may be due to his confusing it with the date palm on which it is often depicted, which is also *phoenix* in Greek. It was a red-gold bird about the size of an eagle, and the priests said that it arrived there every 500 years bearing its predecessor embalmed in a ball of myrrh, which it buried in the temple of the sun.

Later writers have recounted other details, such as the bird's rebirth as a worm from its dead parent's body, and the accompanying flight of birds. There was, however, some doubt as to the length of the true interval between the arrival of two phoenixes: Aelian (c 170–235 AD) mocks the priests who do not know when it will arrive and 'have to confess that they devote their time "to putting the sun to rest with their talk", but do not know as much as birds'. Tacitus reports: 'Regarding the length of its life, accounts vary. The commonest view favours 500 years. But some estimate that it appears every 1461 years . . .' The particular phoenix which had come to his attention as a historian was that said to have arrived in the reign of Tiberius; but since the previous one had been welcomed at Heliopolis under Ptolemy III, and 'as between Ptolemy and Tiberius there were less than 250 years some have denied the authenticity of the Tiberian phoenix, which did not, they say, come from Arabia or perform the traditionally attested actions.' Pliny rejects it out of hand; although it was displayed in public, 'nobody would doubt that this phoenix is a fabrication'.

It is only in the 4th century AD that the idea of a fiery death is to be found, in two complete poems on the phoenix, by Claudian and Lactantius.

Above *The priests of Heliopolis maintained that the phoenix arrived from Arabia every 500 years, bearing its predecessor embalmed in a ball of myrrh: phoenix on a Sicilian mosaic.* **Right** *Egyptian green glazed model of a sow and her piglets: the pig is an uncanny animal and often the subject of taboos. In northern Europe pork was the food of kingly hospitality and the otherworld feast but Jews and Arabs consider it unclean meat, for reasons lost in the past.* **Facing page** *The seal's semi-human appearance, cries and gestures lie behind the numerous legends of families said to be descended from seal ancestors, and the stories of seal maidens who married humans but eventually returned to the sea.*

Pig

The domestic pig has never ranked very highly in popular esteem, for not only is it the Buddhist symbol of indolence and the European symbol of licence, but to the ordinary mind it represents gluttony and obstinacy. Yet the pig is undoubtedly a noble animal and was deservedly an object of worship in Crete, while in Greece it was sacrificed to the gods at the time of the planting of the corn.

In ancient Egypt the pig represented the spirit of Osiris at sowing time and the spirit of Seth at the harvest. It was regarded as unclean, and the swineherds who attended it were not allowed to enter a temple and not permitted to marry anyone outside their own ranks.

Pig meat was eaten by Egyptians only at the Midwinter feast, and the pig could only be sacrificed at the full moon. As a possible relic of this tradition there are those who still believe that a pig must be slaughtered when the moon is waxing or otherwise it will shrink in the pot.

The eating of pig is taboo to both Jew and Arab and it was also long out of favour in Scotland and in parts of northern Ireland. One possible explanation for this custom is that the pig had originally been the symbol of a social group – its totem – and was regarded as the tribal ancestor: thus to eat a sacred pig could be fatal to the interests of the tribe. A further reason for the prohibition of certain kinds of food is the belief that one becomes what one eats. The fastidious individual who accepts the doctrine that one assimilates the habits of the pig by eating pork is naturally disinclined to adopt this type of diet.

In the past, both Hebrew and Arab have been prepared to accept martyrdom rather than eat pork and in 16th-century Spain anyone with a distaste for this meat stood in permanent danger of arrest by the Spanish Inquisition as a secret and recalcitrant adherent of Judaism.

In China and in Europe the pig is a good luck talisman, yet among many fishing communities the animal itself is regarded as extremely unlucky, and even the use of its name is taboo. There are occasional reports of fairy pigs emanating from the Isle of Man, and at Andover in Hampshire a spectral pig is said to be seen on New Year's Eve.

Robin

The robin's red breast often inspired associations with fire and blood. According to a Welsh legend, the robin flies to a land of woe and fire with a drop of water and tries to quench the flames, but gets its feathers scorched so that it is called Bronrhuddyn, 'scorched breast'. When it returns it feels the cold more than other birds and should be given crumbs. In France, where it is said that the wren fetched fire from heaven, the robin went too close to it when its feathers were in flames and so its own breast was singed.

What would appear to be a degraded version of these stories is told in Guernsey. The robin brought fire to the island but scorched its plumage on the way. According to a legend current in the Inner Hebrides, when the Christ child was born the fire in the stable almost went out but the robin fanned the embers into flame, burning its breast feathers. Mary blessed it and when the feathers grew again they were red instead of brown. In western France on Candlemas Day a peculiar ritual was performed. A robin's body was spitted on a hazel twig and set before the fire. As the hazel was a magical tree among the Celts, this hints at some pre-Christian belief. In Germany it was commonly held that the presence of a robin averted lightning.

The similarity between the colour of the robin's breast and bloodstains linked the bird with death and religious beliefs, especially with Christ's blood at the Crucifixion.

Roc

The behaviour of this mythical bird is described in the *Arabian Nights*. It dwells on an island and feeds on elephant calves. When it alights to brood on its egg, which is like a huge dome, it stretches out its legs behind it. Sinbad waited until it was sitting, crept up, unrolled his turban and used it to tie himself to the protruding legs. At dawn the monstrous bird soared away, carrying him with it, and when it alighted he freed himself. As he watched, he saw the Roc seize and carry off a gigantic serpent. He made his way into a ravine where the soil was strewn with diamonds but the snakes there, which issued forth at night, could swallow an elephant at one gulp. Sinbad was startled when the carcass of a horse thudded down. He discovered that merchants made a practice of hurling such carcasses into the ravine, so that when the eagles and vultures bore them up they could secure the diamonds adhering to them.

Sinbad resorted to a stratagem, first collecting a quantity of diamonds, then fastening himself to a carcass and waiting till a giant bird carried him with it out of the ravine.

The story bears evidence of being composite, as it seems that several kinds of monstrous birds are involved. Facts have been exaggerated to fantastic lengths. Various species of birds of prey do feed to some extent on snakes and in eastern lands vultures devouring dead bodies are a familiar sight.

Seal

The seal legends in the British Isles have such affinities with those of the Scandinavian countries that it is tempting to believe they were introduced by Norse invaders, though some elements seem to belong to earlier modes of thought. Similarities between stories of seal maidens and of mermaids, both of whom were credited with prophetic gifts, suggest that the traditions fused. The seal maiden may have contributed to the northern mermaid legends.

In the west of Ireland, the islands north of the Scottish mainland, and the Faroes, certain clans, families or persons are said to be descended from seals. The sept (division of a clan) of the Mackays in Sutherland are known as 'the descendants of the seal'. The laird of Borgie in Sutherland saw a mermaid seeking a place to land. He stole her cowl (or cap), which gave him power over her, and she became his wife. She told him her life was bound up with the cowl. The laird hid it in the middle of a haystack, but eventually his servants found it and showed it to the mermaid. She took it and, leaving her baby son in his cot, plunged into the sea. From time to time she came close inshore to see her son, weeping that she could not take him with her. He and his descendants became famous swimmers and it was said that they could not drown.

A similar story is told of the MacCodrums of North Uist. In Colonsay in Argyllshire, the McPhees were held to be descendants

of a drowned maiden whose sealskin the clan chief had found by the shore. It is said that people belonging to such families must not kill seals. The Coneelys in the West of Ireland were said to have been seals – hence their name, which has that meaning. According to the tale it became changed to Connelly. Comparable stories were told of the O'Sullivans and O'Flahertys of Kerry, the Macnamaras of Clare, and the Achill Islanders. In them we have the vestiges of very ancient beliefs in which a clear distinction between men and animals was not recognized.

It is debatable whether these beliefs have been influenced by notions once prevalent in the Arctic and sub-Arctic where men, by means of mimetic performances and wearing or wielding skins or parts of animals, identified themselves with seals. They must be viewed in relation to the widespread swan maiden theme, according to which birds are seen to alight, doff their feather garments and reveal themselves as women to a watching man who, stealing a robe, makes one of the maidens his wife. The basic motif is obviously very similar and is certainly of great antiquity.

The earliest literary references to seal people are by Greek writers, Hesiod, Pindar and Apollodorus, but oral traditions may date from much earlier. The Phocians of Central Greece were said to be descended from seals. According to myth, Phocus (the name still used in the scientific classifications of seals) was a son of the nereid or sea nymph Psamathe, who had been pursued by Aeacus and in spite of transforming herself into a seal was forced to submit to his embraces. If, as has been suggested by Robert Graves, the dance of the 50 nereids on the shore at the wedding of Thetis and her return to the sea after the birth of Achilles, was a fragment of the same myth, this would increase the story's resemblance to northern versions.

One such story told in the Faroes is about a young man who stole a seal maiden's skin while the seal people danced on the shore. This legend has a tragic ending as, in spite of the warning given by the seal maiden in a dream, men kill her seal husband and children and a curse comes upon the islanders so that many are killed on the cliffs or drowned at sea.

The theme of kinship with mankind which underlies many of the seal traditions has not prevented their ruthless exploitation; five species are thought in danger of becoming extinct.

In 1616 a Scottish woman was brought before a court on a charge of offering a man's fingerbone to be used in order to cause butter to come more readily in the churn. She was convicted although she said that the bone came from a seal. It is doubtful, however, whether seals have ever been connected with witchcraft.

A story said to have been current in 19th-century Greece seems to be a recent fabrication. A swimmer, venturing too far out to sea, might be seized and strangled by a seal. The creature would then carry the corpse to the shore and weep over it. Thus arose a saying that when a woman wept false tears she 'cried like a seal'.

Serpent

There is probably no creature which is found more widely distributed in the mythologies of the world than the serpent. Snakes occur even in the myths of lands where there are no snakes – such as among the Eskimo of the far north, perhaps recalling long-past days in warmer regions. St Patrick may have driven the snakes out of Ireland but could not cleanse the isle of snake legends, including his own.

At the dawn of history, or at least in its early morning, the age-old chthonic religions faced invasions by new cultures worshipping sky gods, gods of light. As the two groups of people met and fought, so their religions came into conflict as well. In India one outcome of such a conflict was that prehistoric snake cults were not entirely lost but were assimilated into the religion of the invading Aryans and survived in the later Hindu myths of semi-divine beings with serpent bodies, called the Nagas.

In many folktales the Nagas are not evil but act beneficently, and a female Naga or Nagini may often marry a mortal. But they are vengeful and terrible if harmed, and so exhibit a considerable share of demonic aspects. Hindu gods and heroes, including Krishna, often come into conflict with them; but elsewhere, Nagas play valuable parts in the mythic structure. Much outright snake worship remains in parts of India, including that of the snake goddess Manasa in Bengal, who is identified as a most high-ranking Nagini.

In Western myth, the clash between old chthonic gods and incoming sky gods appears, predictably, as a straightforward battle. It is especially so in Greek mythology where in two crucial instances the serpent motif appears on the side of the old gods. Apollo, the brilliant new sky god of the Hellenes, displaces a pre-Hellenic worship (probably a snake cult) in the myth of his combat with Python, a serpent monster. The god killed the serpent on the slopes of Parnassus, in its lair at Delphi. There his temple was established; there the Delphic oracle under his patronage grew to its later position of considerable power in the Greek world. And the priestess who delivered the oracles when possessed with the god was called the Pythia.

In Egypt the god Seth at a late stage of development took on the attributes of an evil god and was identified with another serpent monster of Greek myth, Typhon, who was defeated in a great battle by Zeus. This creature was the last of the fearsome old gods, children of Mother Earth, who resisted the incursion of the gods of Olympus. In some versions of the myth of Apollo's battle the consonants of his enemy's name are reversed, and Python is called Typhaon. The etymological similarities are clear. Typhon, in the Zeus myth, was formed of coiled serpents from the thighs down, with arms and hands composed of hundreds of snakes. Zeus, the supreme sky god, fought this chthonic horror and was finally victorious.

The Nagas of India show that the confrontation of dark against light, earth against

sky, need not always mean total war and the triumph of the latter. It can lead to a peaceful blending or assimilation, a reconciliation of opposites. And this notion even managed to creep into Greek mythology. There, as elsewhere, its usual symbolism makes use of a remarkable combination of the bird and snake motifs.

The combining of earth and sky motifs occurs in the myth of the Olympian god Hermes; often depicted with his winged sandals and snake-entwined caduceus, he was the intermediary between heaven and the underworld, and acted as guide to the souls of the dead.

Similarly, it occurs in the myth of the Graeco-Roman god Asclepius, the healing god, and founder of medicine; as the son of Apollo he shared the god's association with the sky, yet his symbol was the snake. The symbol may have come from another pre-Hellenic snake cult and oracle (a minor version of Delphi) taken over by the Asclepian cult.

It would thus be reinforced by the symbolism of renewal in the snake, which casts its skin each year. Of more importance, the priests of Asclepius performed diagnoses and cures by a technique that began with dreaming.

The Greeks usually saw dreams as issuing from the underworld (a concept not unlike that of the unconscious mind) and so the snake, as inhabitant and symbol of that region, naturally became the symbol of the god who healed by dreams. And the snake still appears as the chief emblem of the medical profession today.

One of the most remarkable of the world's serpent deities is the god Da or Dan of Dahomey in West Africa. He is usually seen as a snake with tail in mouth and therefore resembling a cosmic snake.

Spider

'Will you come into my parlour, said the spider to the fly?' The spider inevitably suggests an evil arch-intriguer, weaving a web of duplicity in which fragile innocence is entrapped, or a blood-sucking money-lender who entangles the unwary borrower in his toils. In fact, the spider is as much preyed on as predator, providing food for lizards, wasps and other foes, and it is ironic that the fly, a creature of dirt and disease, should be equated with the innocent victim.

Some people have a deep loathing of spiders and could not bear to touch one, but, although the spider can be a type of evil and betrayal, and so of Satan, it has also been seen as a model of industry and wisdom, and a spider motif engraved on a precious stone makes a talisman which is supposed to confer foresight on the wearer.

Attitudes to spiders vary considerably, in fact. In West African and West Indian folk-lore, there is a great body of stories about Ananse, or Anansi, a spider who is a hero and trickster of infinite cunning and resource, and in some cases the Creator of the world. In European lore the spider spun a web to conceal the child Jesus from his enemies, and spiders also saved the lives of Mohammed and Frederick the Great. The famous story of Robert the Bruce and the spider points the moral that faith and persistence can bring victory out of defeat. Or the spider's web can be regarded as the home of the eternal weaver of illusions, and the spider which spins and kills, creates and destroys, can symbolize the perpetual alternation of forces on which life depends.

The cross on the back of the common garden spider has helped to preserve it from the hostility of mankind, and the spider, like the toad, has played an important part in the folklore of medicine, since both creatures were believed to contain within their bodies a powerful health-giving stone. The 17th-century antiquarian Elias Ashmole claimed to have cured himself of the ague by sus-pending three spiders around his neck. To relieve whooping cough it was once custom-ary to wrap a spider in raisin or butter, or shut one in a walnut shell, the malady fading away as the spider died. Spider's web was used as a bandage for wounds and was sup-posed to cure warts.

The golden money spider, the living sym-bol of a gold coin, confers riches on anyone upon whose body it runs, and if caught and put in the pocket ensures plenty of ready cash, or a new suit of clothes. The superstition is current in Norfolk that a money spider suspended over the head is a charm for winning the football pools.

Facing page In Hindu mythology, Nagas were semi-divine beings with serpent bodies; sometimes they were beneficent but if they were harmed they were vengeful and terrible; 12th-century bronze statuette of a Naga, Angkor Wat, Cambodia. Right There are many tales of people being transformed into deer; in Greek mythology Diana turned Actaeon into a stag because he saw her bathing: Italian dish.

Stag

Animals with horns or antlers are depicted in paintings and carvings executed by men of the Old Stone Age; and the 'Horned Sorcerer', a painting of a man wearing antlers, in the cave of Les Trois Frères in southern France, suggests that such beasts were of ritual importance. Among the Hittites a god whose sacred animal was the stag was worshipped. His cult, which dates back to the third millennium BC, was wide-spread, and models of stags have been re-covered from tombs. A god of the country-side, he is represented standing on a stag, holding a falcon and a hare, and it is possible that, before the Hittite city states arose, he may have presided over the chase and was therefore important.

The Celtic divinity Cernunnos was de-picted wearing antlers and, usually, in a squatting posture, as on the Gundestrup cauldron found in Jutland, where he is shown surrounded by animals and may have been regarded as a Lord of Beasts. A rock carving in Val Canonica in northern Italy shows a phallic figure apparently worshipping before a horned god who wears a torque (metal ornament).

The god was probably frequently regarded as a source of fertility and power. Evidence from the Near East indicates that horns represented supernatural power.

At Syracuse in Sicily women singers wore garlands, and antlers on their heads, and at a festival in honour of Artemis men were similarly adorned. In another such ritual men postured like women. There was yet another ceremony in which men wore phalluses, and one in which women wore imitations of the male organ. There were evidently ambiva-lent ideas concerning Artemis, the huntress goddess, who was represented in art with one or more stags. Animals, and even human beings, were sacrificed to her. Actaeon, the young hunter who inadvertently interrupted her bathing, was transformed into a stag and torn to pieces by his own hounds.

There is a curious connection between the stag and precious metals. The hinds captured by Artemis and harnessed to her golden chariot bore horns. Hercules's third labour involved capturing the Ceryneian hind which had brazen hooves and golden horns, and which was sacred to Artemis, and bringing it to Mycene.

The *Rama Yana*, an Indian epic, mentions a golden-antlered stag whose coat was flecked with silver, and in China deer are associated with places where precious metals are mined. Silver models of deer were placed in Chris-tian sanctuaries because the stag was regarded as a symbol of Christ; when confronted with a serpent it represented the Christian over-coming evil.

A ritual stag-hunt took place on Mt Ly-caeum at the beginning of the Christian era, and as late as the 5th century AD stag mum-mers danced in the south of France. In North America deer dances were performed by antlered dancers to increase fertility by causing rain to fall, and to encourage the growth of wild crops.

Stork

Legends tell of storks being transformed into human beings, possibly because the large size and upright posture suggest an affinity with mankind. Typical versions occur in Germany, where it is also said that a wounded stork weeps human tears, and there are modern Greek and Arab stories relating that in the distant lands to which the birds go in autumn they live as men. As early as the 13th century, Gervase of Tilbury mentioned people who at times became transformed into storks. There is an Eastern legend of a man who managed to turn himself into a stork, and who found the birds' conversation so amusing that he forgot the formula by which to regain human form.

During the Middle Ages writers quoted Aristotle to the effect that the male stork kills his mate if she is unfaithful, and Chaucer referred to it as 'the avenger of adultery'. In the 3rd century AD Aelian embroidered on this belief in a story about a stork who blinded a human adulterer in gratitude to the husband who had allowed it to nest on his house. From classical times the stork has had a reputation for filial piety. The young were in fact said to care for their parents in old age.

The English poet Michael Drayton (1563–1631) referred to 'the careful stork . . . in filial duty as instructing man'. In a Russian folk-tale an old man pleads with a stork to be his son.

The fable that the stork brings babies seems to be a fairly recent one and is most detailed in Germany. Bavarians say that baby boys of good disposition ride on the bird's back while naughty boys are carried in its bill. In some localities, if a Christmas mummer dressed as a stork nudges a woman or girl it is said that she will soon be pregnant. In Holland and Germany children sing to the stork to bring them a little brother or sister.

A number of ancient ideas may have contributed to the development of the baby-bringing theme. Its association with water connects the stork with fertility, it was the messenger of Athene, who in some places was associated with childbirth, and its old Germanic name, *Adebar*, means 'luck-bringer'.

The stork appears in Aesop's *Fables*, where we are told that the wolf swallowed a bone which stuck in its throat. He roamed around howling with pain and offering a generous reward to anyone who would help him. At last the stork undertook the task. Poking his long bill into the wolf's throat he extracted the bone. When he asked for the promised reward the wolf laughed and said: 'You should count yourself lucky that I did not bite your head off when it was in my mouth.' The moral is that kindness is not always requited.

In another fable a farmer catches a stork in a net with cranes and geese. The stork pleads that he only happened to be in the company of the other birds and was not stealing grain as they were, but the farmer tells him that as he was with thieves he must suffer the same punishment.

Swallow

When man began to erect solid buildings the swallows found that the eaves provided sheltered niches for their nests. An ancient Egyptian papyrus refers to a lovesick girl hearing the swallows early in the morning inviting her into the countryside. Greek writers often mentioned the bird which, in common with other European peoples, they looked upon as a harbinger of spring. And it was a Greek writer, Aristotle, who first wrote: 'One swallow does not make a summer.' A black-figured Greek vase now in the Vatican depicts an elderly man, a youth and a boy greeting the first swallow to appear in spring. The youth shouts 'Look, there's a swallow!', the man cries 'By Heracles, so there is'. The boy exclaims 'There she goes,' and then, 'Spring has come.' In the 2nd century AD boys went from house to house on Rhodes singing:

> The swallow is here and a new year he brings,
> As he lengthens the days with the beats of his
>   wings,
> White and black
> Are his belly and back.
>
> Pay his tribute once more
> With cheese in its basket,
> And pork from your store,
> And wine from its flasket,
> And eggs from your casket, and bread
>   when we ask it.

A springtime swallow song is still sung in some areas of Greece. The Greeks had a low opinion of the swallow's song which they likened to a chattering in barbarous tongues. In spite of its joyous spring associations, the swallow became associated with wretchedness in the story of Philomela and Procne. As the story goes, in this myth, Tereus cut out the tongue of his sister-in-law Philomela lest she should divulge to her sister Procne that he had violated her. Whereupon the gods transformed all three into birds: Tereus was turned into a hoopoe, Philomela into a nightingale and Procne into a swallow. Ever since, the swallow has only been able to utter incoherent twitterings.

Augurs claimed that they could interpret the bird's call, and inferences were drawn from its behaviour. The fluttering of a swallow around the head of Alexander the Great was regarded as a portent of tragedy, but returning swallows were considered to predict the safe return of Dionysus. Greek and Latin writers mention that weather was forecast from the swallow's flight; and throughout Europe low-flying swallows are regarded as an indication of bad weather that is on its way.

Observations of swallows flying low over lakes and rivers may have inspired the Chinese to throw swallows into water when they prayed for rain. The associations between swallows, rain and springtime growth were responsible for offerings being made to the genius of the house on the day when the swallows returned. According to one poem, heaven decreed that the swallow should give birth to the Shang Dynasty. Its egg was said to have caused the pregnancy of the ancestress of the Shang line.

Swan

Since myths in which people are transformed into swans are ancient and widespread, they evidently hark back to primitive modes of thought in which the distinctions between gods, men and animals were often vague and blurred.

Aeschylus, the Greek playwright, mentions swan maidens; Aphrodite was represented in art riding on a swan or goose, and Ovid tells of Cycnus being turned into a swan by his father Apollo. Both Apollo and Venus rode in chariots drawn by swans. Zeus was said to have turned himself into a swan to couple with Leda. The sacred character of the swan is indicated by the belief held in areas as far apart as Siberia and Ireland that to kill a swan brings misfortune or death. In County Mayo the souls of virtuous maidens were said to dwell in swans.

The most widespread swan transformation myth tells of a man who sees a flock of swans alight by the water, and watches them discard their feather garments, revealing themselves as beautiful maidens. He steals the robes of one of the swan maidens and lives happily with her until one day she finds the garments, puts them on and disappears.

In an Irish account that dates from the 8th century, Angus, the son of the Dagda, 'the good god', falls in love with the swan maiden Caer who appears to him in a dream. On visiting Loch Bel Dracon at the time of the great Celtic festival of *Samain* (1 November) he sees a flock of 150 swans, each pair linked with a silver chain, and among them his beloved Caer wearing a golden chain and coronet. When he calls to her she leaves the flock and he, too, takes swan form. Together they circle the loch three times and, chanting magical music which puts to sleep all who hear it for three days and nights, they fly to the royal palace. Among the Buriats of Siberia who regard the eagle as their paternal forbear and the swan as the mother of their race, a swan maiden tale is told which has close affinities with Irish stories. There are also Indian versions, and in Malaya and Siam the theme forms the basis of a dramatic performance.

The belief that the swan sings while dying has a long history. Although Pliny contradicted this tradition it has been transmitted down the ages, and has been endorsed by poets almost up to our own times. This story may also have originated in the North. Although dying swans do not sing, a flock of bewick swans in full cry produces a resonant, mysterious, melodious tumult which seems to pervade the whole landscape. Chaucer refers in *The Parliament of Fowles* to 'swan-song'. Shakespeare wrote in *Othello* 'I will play the swan, and die in music', and in *The Merchant of Venice* 'He makes a swan-like end, fading in music'.

Facing page *The size of the swan and its flight high in the sky implies power, and its association with water implies fertility: Zeus turned himself into a swan to father children on Leda;* **Leda and the Swan,** *school of Leonardo.*

Unicorn

A fabulous beast born of man's imagination, the unicorn plays a leading role in some of his most ancient myths and legends. Its form and function are as variable as the minds and religions of men; but whatever its shape – and it has been described as an ox, ram, goat, bull, antelope, wild ass, horse, rhinoceros, serpent or fish, and as a monster in which the characteristics of several of these animals are combined – a one-horned beast was always a symbol of supreme power, connected with gods and kings. It concentrates into a single horn the vigour and virility associated with the two horns of real animals.

An early distinction was made between the caprine unicorn, a gigantic one-horned goat, and the equine unicorn, in the form of a horse. The latter, the unicorn *par excellence*, was gracefully adapted by the College of Heralds as a symbol of 'the very parfit gentil knight'.

The first to mention the unicorn in the West was Ctesias of Cnidos, a Greek historian and doctor who was court physician to the kings of Persia for some 17 years. A fragment of his book on India, written about 398 BC, is the most important Western document concerning the unicorn: 'There are in India,' wrote Ctesias, 'certain wild asses, which are as large as horses, and larger. Their bodies are white, their heads dark red, and their eyes dark blue. They have a horn on the forehead which is about a foot and a half in length. The dust filed from this horn is administered in a potion as a protection against deadly drugs. The base of this horn is pure white, the upper part is sharp and of a vivid crimson; and the remainder or middle portion is black. Those who drink out of these horns made into drinking vessels are not subject, they say, to convulsions or the holy disease.'

16th-century French tapestry illustrating the belief that only a virgin holding a mirror can tame a unicorn; the sexual symbolism, which includes the flagstaff, the crescent motif on the flag, rabbits, holly berries and oak leaves, suggests that the tapestry depicts the traditions of courtly love.

Whale

The whale was once worshipped as Mamacocha, or 'Mother Sea', among the Indians on the east coast of Central America. The Arabians believed that a fabulous whale, Bahamut, provided the base upon which the whole world rested, and that earthquakes were the result of its movements. (The beast referred to in Job 40.15, by the similar name of Behemoth, is now considered to have been the hippopotamus.) The whale that swallowed shipwrecked Jonah, and in whose belly the prophet spent three days and three nights, is one of the ten animals that have been allowed to enter paradise, according to Mohammedan legend.

In Christian thought the whale became an allegory of evil, the emblem of the Devil, the archetypal snare, baited with sweet aromas, which lured the unwary to eternal damnation. The whale's mouth has often been depicted as the gateway to the otherworld, while its belly has been said to symbolize the infernal regions.

Among some Indian tribes on the western coast of America, the whale was regarded as a totem animal, and was thought to have the power to sink enemy canoes. Whales' teeth and whalebone are both supposed to be extremely effective as amulets; in fact, the teeth have been used for that purpose since Neolithic times. Chieftains of Tonga, Samoa and Fiji wore necklaces of whales' teeth, shaped like curved claws, as signs of high rank. Pieces of whalebone were highly valued as charms since they were supposed to confer some of the physical powers of the whale upon the owners.

Ambergris, a grey waxy substance found in the intestines of the sperm-whale, is supposed to be a powerful aphrodisiac.

Shape-shifting between the whale and other creatures of land and sea was not unknown. An Icelandic myth tells of a godless youth who was condemned to assume the shape of a whale as a punishment, and who was killed when he attempted to swim up a waterfall. North American Indians have legends of a terrible killer whale which approaches the shore and assumes the shape of a ravening wolf.

Wolf

Few European mammals equal or surpass the wolf in the richness of its folklore, though in the British Isles wolf lore is much scantier than on the Continent, where in some mountainous forested regions the animals are still to be found. By the mid-13th century there can have been few wolves left in England but not until the 18th were the last wolves killed in Ireland and Scotland.

Much European wolf lore is pervaded by a fearsome awe, less apparent in North American wolf traditions. But although fear of wolves is a natural human reaction, the friendly wolf appears fairly frequently in myths and legends, indicating that the animal awakens ambivalent responses. The *Rig Veda* tells of Rijrasva, whom his father blinded because with misplaced generosity

National Gallery

he gave 101 sheep to a bitch wolf: the wolf prayed for her benefactor, to the Asvins, benevolent deities, and they restored his sight. On the other hand, according to ancient Iranian doctrines the wolf was created by the evil spirit Ahriman. A similar belief is still current among the Voguls of Siberia.

The associations of Greek gods and goddesses with wolves hint at older traditions beneath the mythology of the anthropomorphic divinities. It was said that the priest of Zeus could take the form of a wolf. The goddess Hecate could also take wolf shape. Leto, the mother of Apollo and Artemis, appeared as a she-wolf and a wolf was emblazoned on the shield of Artemis, the huntress. The god Apollo was said to have expelled wolves from Athens and any citizen who killed one had to bury it by public subscription. Sophocles called Apollo 'the wolf-slayer', yet a number of myths describe how

A famous legend tells how St Francis of Assisi tamed the ferocious wolf of Gubbio: a painting by Sassetta shows the saint arbitrating between the citizens of Gubbio and the wolf.

his children by mortal girls were fostered by wolves. This motif of children tended by a she-wolf reappears in the story of Romulus and Remus and in later legends. Despite this myth of the kindly wolf the Romans associated the animal with Mars, the god of war.

In Scandinavian mythology the Fenris wolf is one of the three children of Loki, the others being the Midgard serpent and Hel (Death). Fenris, whose jaws stretched from heaven to earth, created much trouble among the gods until they managed to bind him with a magic cord. However, as the representative of Fate he waits, until at the end of the world, he swallows up the sun.

Woodpecker

Perhaps the first hint in literature that the woodpecker was considered a rain-maker and thunderbird is its name in Babylonian, meaning 'the axe of Ishtar', for Ishtar was a fertility goddess. The earliest written evidence of the bird's exalted status is a reference by Aristophanes: 'Zeus won't in a hurry the sceptre restore to the woodpecker tapping the oak.' There appears to have been a belief that the bird once occupied the throne of the High God and received reverence such as Zeus received in Aristophanes's time.

There is definite evidence that the woodpecker was consulted as an oracle, if not actually worshipped. An account survives of an oracle connected with Mars in the Apennine Mountains, where an image of a woodpecker was placed on a wooden pillar; engraved gems show a warrior consulting such an oracle. Mars was originally associated with fertility as much as with war, which perhaps explains his association with the fertility-bringing woodpecker.

There is further evidence that the woodpecker is a bird of fertility. Greek myth relates that Celeus, whose name means 'green woodpecker', attempted to steal the honey which nourished Zeus while he was an infant. As a punishment the angry god turned Celeus into a green woodpecker. Celeus was the father of Triptolemus, the inventor of the plough – a king or chieftain instructed by Demeter, the Earth Mother, in the ritual which procured the fertility of the soil.

The significance of all this is obscure until we realize that the green woodpecker often feeds on the ground, picking up ants, and that its beak could be regarded as serving the same purpose as the primitive plough, which was not much more than a single prong drawn through the soil. The story says in effect that the green woodpecker was the first ploughman.

More recent legends confirm the woodpecker's connection with ploughing. According to a tale of the Letts, a people of the eastern Baltic, God and the Devil engaged in a ploughing match. God had a woodpecker to draw his plough, but the Devil had horses and quickly ploughed a whole field, while the woodpecker was making little progress. During the night God borrowed the horses and ploughed a field. The Devil was so impressed next day that he stupidly exchanged his horses for the woodpecker. When the bird lagged behind he angrily struck it on the head and this is why the woodpecker has a blood-coloured crown. In a veiled way this story tells of the suppression of ancient beliefs.

There are plenty of other indications of the association between the woodpecker, rain and fertility. In France, Germany, Austria and Denmark it is given names equivalent to the English local name 'rain bird'. In Italy there is a saying, 'When the woodpecker pecks, expect rain or storm.' In France the story goes that at the Creation, when God had made the earth, he called on the birds to help by hollowing out places which could be filled with water and so become seas, lakes and ponds. Only the woodpecker refused to join in. A German version says that it was because she would not dirty her fine plumage. So the bird was condemned to peck wood and to drink nothing but rain. That is why she clings to the tree trunk calling 'Rain, Rain'.

It was at one time believed, or half-believed, that the mysterious herb springwort, with which doors and locks could be opened, could be obtained by blocking the woodpecker's nesting hole. The bird would fetch the herb and apply it to the blocked entrance. If a strip of red cloth was placed below the nest, the bird, mistaking it for fire, would drop the sprig on it. Another plan was to watch where the woodpecker went to fetch the plant.

Bodleian Library Colour Filmstrip

Wren

French wren ceremonies were enacted in an area stretching from Marseilles north-westwards up to Brittany. They were more elaborate than in Ireland, probably indicating that the cult was carried to the British Isles from France and lost some of its characteristics on the way.

The ceremonies are certainly very ancient and probably date from the Bronze Age. Unfortunately, documentary evidence earlier than the 19th century is practically non-existent, so we have to piece together an interpretation from a variety of scattered clues.

The actual geographical distribution of the ritual is significant. It would seem that the people amongst whom wren ceremonies were important reached southern France from elsewhere in the Mediterranean and carried elements of their culture north-westwards, eventually reaching the British Isles. There are grounds for believing that these same folk may have been the builders of some of the megalithic monuments which are found in areas where wren ritual was practised.

The date of the custom provides a valuable clue to its meaning. Midwinter was for our ancestors a crucial turning-point of the year and many ceremonies performed at this time were intended to combat or chase away the powers of darkness and co-operate with the sun in restoring light, warmth and growth to the world. The wren frequents thickets and penetrates holes, crevices and other dark places, as its scientific name *Troglodytes troglodytes*, 'dweller in caves', indicates. It was therefore a suitable representative of the powers opposed to or complementary to the sun.

This view is borne out by the well-known fable of the competition between the eagle and the wren to decide which could fly highest. The wren defeated the eagle – the bird of the sun – by trickery. In many languages the wren is called 'king', suggesting that long ago it was regarded as allied with mysterious powers; these may have been the dark potencies believed to reside in the earth. An ancient Irish document refers to the wren as a bird with oracular powers, and therefore of even greater significance.

As heat proceeds from the sun, it was natural that birds, being creatures of the sky, should be regarded as fire-bringers. Such birds were commonly identified by the red badge of fire on their plumage. The robin was another one of these and in France the wren was also a fire-bringer, perhaps because when it is in its full spring plumage some of its feathers have a ruddy tinge. It was said that when the wren fetched fire from heaven most of its plumage was scorched away. The other birds compassionately donated some of their feathers, but the robin came too close and its breast feathers were burnt. Another French version relates that as the wren was flying to earth with the fire its wings burst into flame; it passed the brand to the robin whose breast feathers also became alight. The high-flying lark then came to the rescue and brought the precious burden down to mankind.

The Bretons explain that the wren fetched fire, not from heaven but from hell. Her plumage became scorched as she escaped the infernal regions through the keyhole.

So closely were the robin and wren associated in folklore that they were regarded as male and female of the same species – a notion which has lingered to the present time in some localities.

Although in many localities the wren was hunted and killed at the winter solstice, this does not imply that it was generally regarded as in any sense an evil creature. On the contrary, it was usual for birds and beasts held in high respect to be sacrificed on some special occasion during the year. In France it was said that the crime of robbing a wren's nest would entail the destruction by fire of the culprit's house, or that his fingers would shrivel and drop off.

An indication of the affection in which the wren was held in France is provided by its appearance in legends connected with various saints. A delightful story records that St Malo, finding that a wren had built a nest in his habit, which he had laid on a bush while working in the monastery vineyard, went without the garment until the bird had reared its young. St Dol, noticing that the monks at his monastery were distracted during their devotions by the calls of the birds in the neighbouring woods, ordered the birds to depart. He made an exception of the wren, because its sparkling song cheered the brethren without interfering with their concentration on prayer and praise.

Appendix

Bee
Symbol of industry and orderly government, frequently a messenger of the gods; according to a Breton story, bees sprang from the tears shed by Christ on the Cross, and in Europe it was always considered wise to tell the bees of a death in the family, or they would desert the hive.

Bestiary
Collection of moral tales about real or fabulous animals, very popular in medieval Europe and providing artists with a guide to animal symbolism in Christian art and architecture; the whale, for example, is a form of the Devil because he lures seamen to their deaths, while the panther's sweetness of breath makes him an emblem of Christ.

Buffalo
The American bison, on whom Plains Indians depended for survival; a major supernatural power in their myths, such as Buffalo Old Man and Old Woman in Kiowa or Apache tales; great buffalo dances as of Mandans, with full head-dresses from buffalo heads and mime of herd movement, used to lure herds for hunters; associated with rain, buffalo was prayed to by Sioux and others when rain was needed.

Butterfly
Symbol of the soul and of attraction to the light: in Europe, North America and the Pacific it was widely believed that the soul has the form of a butterfly, which gave the creature uncanny and sometimes ominous connotations; in northern Europe to see one flying at night was a warning of death, and some said that the soul-butterfly's ability to leave the body in sleep accounts for dreams; medieval angels were sometimes depicted with butterfly's wings and fairies are often shown with them.

Buzzard
Scavenger bird, associated in much mythology with cleanliness and so with curative powers; Pueblo Indians used its feathers in curing rituals, and to 'sweep away' evil; American superstition says a buzzard feather worn behind the ear will prevent rheumatism, buzzard grease will cure smallpox; also associated with death in the Old South, where beliefs say that witches sometimes take buzzard form, and that a buzzard shadow will do harm if it passes over you.

Crab
Sometimes a symbol of the union of opposites, because it is at home both on land and in the water: in the Tarot card called the Moon a crab crawls up onto land from a pool, a symbol of the depths of the mind revealing themselves; in some of the Pacific islands crabs are gods, or the shadows or messengers of gods: the fourth sign of the zodiac is Cancer, the Crab.

Elephant
Revered in the East for its strength and stability, it was also held to be a symbol of wisdom, moderation and pity, and was associated with kings and royal authority. In Hindu legend Indra, the king of the heavens, rides an elephant called Airavata, and the elephant-headed Ganesha, god of worldly wisdom, is often petitioned for success before any enterprise; the universe was also thought to be supported on the backs of elephants: in Siam, sacred white elephants were reared by human nurses.

Hawk
Like the eagle and falcon, hawks are frequently connected with the sun in symbolism, because of their flight, dominating ferocity and yellow eyes. The sparrowhawk belonged to Horus in Egypt and was a solar bird in Greece and Rome; the kite was sacred to Apollo as lord of the Delphic oracle, because circling in the sky it sees everything; in Japan there was a divine golden kite, Nihongi.

Jaguar
An animal which plays an important part in South American Indian myths, being regarded as a brother-in-law, as man's rival in killing game, and as a rival in sexuality; some tribes believe that the hero who gave them their culture was a jaguar and that a Celestial Jaguar will one day make an end of the world; in Brazil it is thought that the sun takes the form of a jaguar at night and shamans are possessed by the jaguar spirit, sometimes turning into were-jaguars at death.

Lamb
Often the victim of sacrifice in early times because it stood for unblemished purity and innocence: in Christian tradition it is a symbol of Christ.

Petrel
Sea bird, named for St Peter because it flutters across the waves with its feet touching them, as if it was trying to walk on the water; this may account for the belief that it is unlucky to kill a stormy petrel, from which

the same belief may have spread to its larger relative, the albatross; the petrel is also related to the shearwater, sometimes called 'damned soul' because it flies to and fro over the sea, apparently never resting.

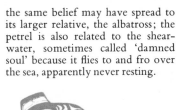

Raven
Large black bird of the crow family, possessed of a harsh croaking voice and an appetite for carrion, and generally of disturbing and sinister character in folk belief; frequently associated with battlefields, corpses and death; two ravens acted as the spies of the god Odin; Raven is an important figure in the mythology of American Indians, especially of the North Pacific coast.

Snail
Used for magical healing in the past, especially in wart cures; one method was to rub the warts with a snail and then impale the snail on a thorn, so that as it slowly died the warts would fade away: snail slime was considered effective against consumption and other diseases.

Snake
Appears in the myths and religious beliefs of almost all societies, playing many different roles: associated with rejuvenation, immortality, longevity and wisdom, because it sloughs its skin, and with sexuality because of its phallic shape. Snakes which live under rocks or in holes in the ground are connected with the underworld, the dead, fertility, the unconscious mind. In Christianity, linked with evil and sex, because of its role in tempting Eve.

THE MYTHOLOGY OF PLANTS

Trees

In the faith of ancient Egypt, the numerous deities were frequently supposed to inhabit trees, chiefly the sacred sycomores (*Ficus sycomorus*, not to be confused with our sycamore). These sycomores were thought to exist on the borders of the great desert that lay between this world and the next, and the souls of the departed, on reaching these trees, would receive from the deities supplies of food and water. Paintings in the Book of the Dead, and in tombs, depict such meetings on the soul's travels.

In the Old Testament there are many references to sacred groves and to the setting up of altars in these groves and under trees, notably oaks; the history of Old Testament religion is of a struggle between the worship of a unique, omnipresent deity and that of a great many lesser ones, such as the Canaanites held in regard. Similarly, the earliest Christian missionaries often had to contend, as in ancient Germany, with sacred groves, trying to destroy them or to build their churches within them.

Even when lesser deities had been overthrown, the need to placate the tree, or to use its magic power, was such that temples carried representations of them, as in the temple of Ezekiel's version where, echoing Assyrian and Babylonian motifs, the decoration included 'cherubim and palm trees, a palm tree between cherub and cherub. Every cherub had two faces; the face of a man toward the palm tree on the one side, and the face of a young lion toward the palm tree on the other side' (Ezekiel, chapter 41).

The concept of the tree as a god's dwelling place appears in Persian mythology: the cypress was considered especially sacred, symbol of Ahura Mazda or Ohrmazd, chief of the pantheon. Tree worship was widespread in India; Gautama Buddha was reputedly incarnated as a tree spirit some 43 times, and he received spiritual illumination while meditating under the bo-tree. Many ancient Indian sculptures show a stylized sacred tree, surrounded by devotees and often hung with garlands. On the Stupa of Barhut there is

one showing elephants paying homage to a banyan. There were not dissimilar decorations in Mexico.

The original object of veneration was doubtless the tree itself, as continued to be the case until very recently, with primitive peoples in Africa, Malaya, Sumatra and elsewhere. Later an erect tree-trunk might suffice, and an altar might be placed before the tree or trunk for offerings. The next logical step is to transform the trunk into a pillar which, like a cut trunk, can be erected in a suitable place. Standing stones in Britain and menhirs in Brittany are examples. The upright stones which represented gods in ancient Phoenicia may well derive from such pillars.

Later comes the combination of pillar and sacred animal foreshadowed by Ezekiel: the ancient world was full of representations of a pair of animals facing each other on either side of a stone pillar, such as the lionesses over the famous gate at Mycene, or the antique slabs within St Mark's, Venice, which show a stylized tree between pairs of monsters. A further stage in the stylization of the worshipped tree is the placing on it of a mask or cloak to represent the god, and finally the carving of the trunk into a statue.

The statue treatment is, of course, very familiar to us in the religions of ancient Greece and Rome, where personified deities abounded. In both countries gods were worshipped in connection with individual trees or groves. The symbolized tree is frequently seen on Greek paintings, vases and tablets. Many of the deities had particular trees: Artemis was in different places goddess of the cedar, hazel, laurel, myrtle and willow. Pausanias (2nd century AD) records the cult of the 'hanging Artemis' in Arcadia, presumably in reference to a mask hung on a sacred tree. The laurel, sacred to Apollo, became very important both in religious and lay ceremony, as did the olive, Athene's tree. Could the impressive pillars of Greek temples – as indeed of Egyptian ones before them – have derived from tree trunks; like the Byblos obelisks, a formal statement of the

sacred grove? They were certainly decorated with vegetation motifs, while in many places they were combined with a sacred grove planted outside the temple.

In his form of Jupiter Feretrius, the chief god of Rome appears to have been a sacred tree, and Rome was reputedly founded where the floating cradle of Romulus and Remus became entangled in the roots of a fig tree, the *ficus Ruminalis*. The 'King of the Wood', the priest of the sacred grove of Diana at Nemi, was the king of the trees, 'the incarnation of the spirit of all vegetation' in person. Maximus of Tyre, writing during the 2nd century AD, refers to the continuing worship of individual trees, notably at the festival of Dionysus, when anyone with a tree in his garden dressed it up to represent the god.

Among the sacred groves of the ancient world one of the most notable was that of the oaks of Zeus at Dodona, which apparently flourished for at least 2000 years. The laurel at Delphi has perhaps achieved more notoriety. The tree oracle was thought to be connected by its roots with the underworld and hence to the wisdom and foreknowledge of the dead. In Mesopotamia the cedar was both deity and oracle; it was sacred to the god Ea, whose name was supposedly engraved on its innermost core.

Many oracular trees are mentioned in the Old Testament, such as the 'tree of the diviners' at Shechem, mentioned in the book of Judges (9.37); 'the tree of the revealer' in Genesis (12.6); and the mulberry trees which gave David the signal to attack the Philistines (2 Samuel, chapter 5). Tree oracles are recorded from Armenia, Arabia and Persia, while in Rome there was a prophetic ilex grove on the Aventine hill. Tree omens remained important to the Romans, among many other types of augury; major examples are the withering of laurels which foretold Nero's death, and the fall of a cypress which did the same for Domitian.

In many societies, people have believed in lesser spirits who inhabit trees. They were

C. M. Dixon

responsible for the well-being of their trees, and sometimes of other plants and animals, and if not propitiated might be hostile to humans. Those most similar to man were likely to be least hostile.

The jinn of ancient Arabia, for example, inhabited trees and thickets among other places, and were monstrous creatures capable of assuming different forms. Unfriendly or evil Egyptian monsters of similar type inhabited trees or posts and were likely to way-lay the spirits of the dead on their difficult journey. Similar monsters appear in the Bible, translated as 'satyrs' or 'devils', but in the original they are 'hairy monsters', and similar to jinn.

Greek and Roman mythology has a wide range of wood-inhabiting creatures, including the centaur and cyclops, haunters of forests, and the man-goat combinations of pans and dryads. Pans had many human attributes; protectors of herds, they were generally friendly to man, but by no means beyond playing unkind tricks on him. Satyrs and sileni, and their Roman counterparts, fauns and silvani, were more bestial; Hesiod described these wood spirits as 'a useless and crafty tribe'. Within the last century Greek peasants believed in malicious demons which were half human and half goat. Many of these creatures later became specific: Pan, Silenus and Silvanus became particular spirits.

The concept of the tree as the universe is best known in its Scandinavian form, where the ash, Yggdrasil, represented the world tree; in India it was the fig, Asvattha. But the idea is found in many other parts of the globe.

Above *The Naga Kalika and his wife comfort Buddha as he takes his seat under the bo-tree.* **Right** *Adam and Eve with the serpent and the tree of knowledge, from a late 13th-century manuscript.* **Below** *A tree of immortality, like other conifers, the yew was planted in graveyards: 15th-century illustration.*

Radio Times Hulton Picture Library

British Museum

With this tree the world of man rises in a mountain, where the gods live; the tree's trunk springs from this mountain, its outspread branches forming or supporting the sky, and the stars and planets, while its roots reach into the abyss or underworld, forerunner of hell. The fact that the branches held the stars may account for the Eastern jeweller's frequent conception of golden trees hung with jewels. An infinity of symbolic detail accompanies the different parts of the world-tree. Metal world-trees were conceived in China and Russia. Charlemagne destroyed the Saxon 'Irmensul' or World-pillar, which was in fact a tree-trunk representation of this belief.

The cosmic tree often bore fruits which the gods ate to ensure their immortality: and so it became a tree of life. The Persian *haoma* and Indian *soma* are examples of such life-giving trees; and so of course are the mystical trees of the paradise from which Adam and Eve were expelled – the tree of life and the tree of knowledge of good and evil. Man was created within this paradise and, if he spent a righteous life, would return to another.

Indian, Chinese and South American legends mention the souls of the dead climbing into heaven up the trunk of a tree.

In India the tree of life and knowledge was, yet again, the fig. In the Koran, paradise – the 'seventh heaven' – contains the enormous Tooba tree, covered with many kinds of fruit, and from which rivers spring flowing with water, milk, honey and wine.

In Greek myth the garden of the Hesperides is supported on Mount Atlas, which

Herodotus describes as the Pillar of Heaven Hercules overcame the multi-headed dragor that guarded the sacred tree and snatched it golden apples, the fruits of knowledge.

These stories show how deeply the sense o sacred trees was fixed in man's mind. H came to regard the tree as embodying earth heaven and hell, as the paradise of the departed and even as the origin of the humar species, as well as a symbol of immortality Many widely separated mythologies describe the origin of the human race from trees In the Norse *Edda*, Odin and his brother change two trees on the seashore into male and female humans who become the parent of mankind. One Greek story was that mer had germinated from tree seeds: Hesioc gave ash, but in the *Odyssey* it was the oak

These stories link up with such myths a the story of the birth of Adonis, who appeared when the tree into which his mother Myrrha had been transformed was struck b a sword. Attis originated in an almond, and was later imprisoned by Cybele in a pine tree from which every spring he was reborn Parallel with Attis is Osiris, whose image wa annually imprisoned in a hollowed pine log which was burned a year later. From these legends came the pine cone as a symbol o resurrection. Many Greek and Roman god may have been born under a tree.

Left *Tree of life, from the church of St Dominic in Oaxaca, Mexico.* **Above** *The tree of Jesse, showing the descent of David's line in the form of a tree: from Cyprus 15th century.*

Flowers and Other Plants

Doubtless the Neolithic people who lived in the early township at Catal Hüyük in Anatolia knew much about plants; certainly the Egyptians worshipped and enjoyed the Nile water lily or lotus before 3000 BC and the Sumerians knew a great deal about herbs by 2200 BC. In these early civilizations plants not only provided food but were almost the only known medicines and provided almost all cosmetics and dyes. Trees, outspanning human lives, were very early objects of veneration; indeed, like the oak, they might be the seat of deity itself, while evergreens such as fir were obvious symbols of immorality.

Curiously, many useful or beautiful plants have little or no links with myth and magic; while some insignificant plants such as vervain, for instance, are important. Few food plants are magical, although corn is the chief plant representing the annual return of summer, the defeat of winter, and the successful production of food. It was used in the rites of Osiris and Adonis whose death was symbolized by the blood-red anemone.

Many herbs with real or supposed healing qualities inevitably have magical attributes and rituals attached to them to canalize their power. Apart from the genuine herbalists, those wishing for power encouraged the belief that they possessed it supernaturally, by working up rituals and giving an elaborate range of attributes to their materials of whatever origin.

Some plants were specially suitable for magic. The notorious mandrake, for example, the shape of whose root often resembled a human figure, was perfect for associative magic; it also possessed genuine anodyne qualities and, taken in excess, the ability to make people mad. Laurel was early discovered to produce frenzy if chewed, or its smoke inhaled, and hence became the chosen plant of many Greek oracles.

The rose is an important item in the 'language of flowers', where its basic meaning is 'love'. Meanings have been given to flowers since ancient times. By the 18th century the language of flowers was well developed, as this quotation from Lady Mary Wortley Montagu (1690–1762) demonstrates: 'There is no colour, no flower, no weed, no fruit, herb, pebble or feather that has not a verse belonging to it; and you may quarrel, reproach, or send letters of passion, friendship or civility, or even of news, without even inking your fingers.'

The Victorians, in an age which Osbert Sitwell has described as 'repressed but always respectable', kept up the language of flowers: it was necessary for a posy to speak volumes at times when the presence of the inevitable chaperone prevented the expression of romantic thoughts. Victorian books have interminable lists of the hidden meanings of flowers – not by any means consistent with one another.

By choosing, for example, various kinds of rose the lover could indicate some 40 different sentiments, such as 'Thou art all that is lovely', 'If you love me you will find it out', 'I am worthy of you', and even 'Beauty is your only attraction'. Among the flowers which had specific meanings were anemone, for refusal; apricot, for timid love or doubt; azaleas, for ephemeral passion. Bramble conveyed envy, the foxglove insincerity, the gardenia, secret love, while grass stood for submission and phlox for a proposal. Combinations of flowers added complexity to the language.

The shift in importance from the god in the oak to the magic of the mandrake, and eventually to the sentimental floral dictionary of the Victorians, is a clear index of man's changing values. The disappearance of plant lore and magic, except among country folk and the less educated, is an indication of the advance of scientific knowledge in the 19th century and its destruction of the credibility of earlier beliefs. What little is left is often almost subconscious and apparently irrational.

Thus hospital nurses will still try to prevent visitors from bringing a bunch of red and white flowers into a hospital ward, not so much because they are aware of the symbolism of red standing for blood and white for death, as from a vague feeling that 'it's unlucky'. Superstition is still with us without the folklore behind it.

Our earliest ancestors plucked and ate all kinds of plants, and came to realize that some had thorns or stings, while others appeared to soothe; some were good to eat, others unpleasant or deadly, and a few had curious effects if swallowed. And as man began to develop ideas about gods and spirits, about good luck and bad luck, he connected many of these ideas with plants – for if a plant could kill, intoxicate or soothe, it must have an inner power.

Below *Some plants and flowers have been thought peculiarly sacred. Ivy (left) belonged to Dionysus and Bacchus, and is the plant of poetry, inspiration and ecstasy; as an evergreen, it is a symbol of life's continuance through the winter and, with holly, is connected with Christmas. The lotus (centre) is one of the great sacred plants of the East, associated with woman and fertility, and with immortality. Laurel (right) was the plant of Apollo, and poets, athletes and heroes were crowned with laurel wreaths.*

Royal Botanic Gardens Kew/Michael Holford

Apple

Felling an apple tree is unlucky because the apple stands for immortality, for eternal youth and happiness in the life after death. The Scandinavian gods kept themselves forever young by eating the golden apples of Idun, goddess of youth and spring. In Welsh legends kings and heroes go after earthly death to live happily in a paradise of apple trees called Avalon (the name possibly coming from the Welsh word for an apple, *afal*).

This link with the sun comes out strongly in the Greek story of the golden apples which were kept by the Hesperides or 'nymphs of the evening', the daughters of Night, in their garden in the farthest west, where the sun goes down to its death in the evening. A dragon with 100 heads guarded the apples but Hercules managed to kill the dragon and steal them. He took the apples to his master King Eurystheus, who gave them to the goddess Athene. She returned them to the Hesperides again, which makes this labour of Hercules seem singularly pointless. But it is likely that in the original story Hercules won immortality by stealing the apples.

As an emblem of renewed life and youth, and because of its appearance when cut in half, the apple also stood for desire and belonged to love goddesses in Celtic and Greek mythology. This is its role in the story of the Judgement of Paris. A golden apple marked 'for the fairest' was thrown down at a wedding feast on Olympus, the home of the Greek gods. Three goddesses – Hera, Athene and Aphrodite – each claimed to be the most beautiful, and Zeus decided that the contest should be judged by Paris, one of the sons of the King of Troy and the handsomest man alive.

The goddesses stripped naked so that Paris could judge them properly and each of them tried to bribe him to give her the apple. Aphrodite, the goddess of desire, promised him the love of Helen, the most beautiful of mortal women. Paris gave the apple to Aphrodite, which the other goddesses bitterly resented. She kept her promise and Helen ran away with Paris; which was the immediate cause of the TrojanWar.

This story, intended to account for the origin of the war, appears only in the later legends about it and has an odd ring, as it explains no religious ritual or custom and does not seem to be connected with any particular religious belief, except that the apple belongs to Aphrodite as a love goddess. It may be an elaboration of a brief reference in Homer's *Iliad* to Paris humiliating Hera and Athene at a meeting in his shepherd's hut by his preference for Aphrodite, 'who offered him the pleasures and the penalties of love'.

Ash

Various Greek myths link the birth of mankind with a universal ash tree. The poet Hesiod's fable of Zeus creating a race of brazen men from ashes accounts for the reference in Homer, when Penelope says to Ulysses, 'Tell me thy family from whence thou art; for thou art not sprung from the olden tree...'

Nordic myths also suggest that man was created from the wood of the ash by the god Odin; and the word itself derives from the Norse *aska*, meaning 'man'. In the *Edda*, the sacred book of the Northmen, the ash becomes the World Tree, Yggdrasil. Its branches overspread the world and reached the heavens, while its roots penetrated the abyss known as Hel, from which our modern word 'hell' is derived. Halfway up the trunk was Midgard, the disc-shaped earth, surrounded by ocean, with the serpent of eternity and a final mountain boundary on its outer rim. Asgard, the mountain of the gods at the base of Valhalla, reared up immediately around the trunk.

The association of the ash and snakes is widespread. In the 1st century AD Pliny wrote on ash's magical efficacy against snakes, how a snake would rather perish in a fire than crawl over an ash twig, and that they even avoid the shade cast by an ash tree; regarding which the 16th-century writer Gerard remarks: 'It is a wonderful courtesie in nature, that the Ash should floure before

Above *The apple's connection with the sun is shown in the story of the apples of the Hesperides, the nymphs who lived in the west where the sun sets. From a 19th-century triptych by Hans von Marées.*
Below *Yggdrasil, the world tree in Nordic myth, was an ash-tree: its roots reached to hell and its uppermost branches touched heaven. It was also believed that the disc-shaped earth was situated half-way up the trunk*

the serpents appear, and not cast his leave before they be gon againe.' To carry an as twig or wear ash leaves in your hat woul protect you against being bitten by snakes if you were, drinking ash sap would cure th bite. An ash stick was guaranteed to kill snake outright.

Witches were also repelled by the ash, bunch of ash keys being considered particu larly useful against them. Ash sap was fed t new-born babies to protect them from ev spirits, and a baby's first bath should b before a fire of ash wood. A bunch of as leaves would guard a bed and its occupan

Elder

Scandinavian mythology makes much of Hydle-moer, the elder mother, a relation of Hulda, goddess of marriage. It was she rather than witches who was responsible for disasters following injury to an elder, but this was a matter of revenge, and could be averted by asking permission before cutting an elder or making use of it. Forms of this belief have been recorded from Huntingdonshire and Lincolnshire. A Danish legend suggests that if one stands under an elder at midnight on Midsummer Eve, the King of the Elves will be seen passing by. It was, however, widely considered unwise to sleep beneath an elder and to dream of it betokened illness that was to occur.

Epitomizing all the minor myths and the general distaste for this often crooked, ugly, ill-smelling tree, a major myth grew up about the elder. In Jacobus de Voragine's medieval *Golden Legend* we find the first account of the elder's use for gallows and as an appropriate graveyard plant, and further, although the elder does not grow naturally in Palestine, the statement that it was both the tree on which Christ was crucified and that on which Judas killed himself. William Langland, in his poem *Piers Plowman*, repeats the latter legend:

Judas he japed with Jewen silver
And sithen an eller hanged hymselve.

Sir John Mandeville in his *Travels* (1355) claims to have seen Judas's very elder by the Pool of Siloam near Jerusalem.

Elder has been used in medicine since Egyptian times, not just as a charm but for making curative lotions. The dwarf elder was even more valuable than the tree in ancient medicine, being recommended against bites of mad dogs and snakes, for dropsy and gout, to cure piles, and especially as a purge. It could also be used to dye hair black and cloth blue. While it was, in France, one of the herbs dedicated to St John, its main claim in mythology is its reputation of growing only where the blood of a Dane has been spilt.

The way this myth grew up has been demonstrated by Geoffrey Grigson. The plant was anciently called walwort, probably derived from Old English *wealhwyrt* meaning 'foreigner plant', referring to the dwarf elder's introduction to Great Britain. In 1538 the name danewort is given (by William Turner) as an equivalent, and as late as 1640 we find Parkinson repeating older herbalists in explaining that this referred to the plant's purgative qualities in producing 'the danes', namely diarrhoea. 'Danes' may derive from *dain*, an old word meaning 'a stink'. *Historia Regum Angliae*, written by John Rous in the 15th century, contains an account of 'ebulus' (the old Latin name) growing freely where the British people – the Mercians – died when the Danes overran the country. In his *Britannia*, William Camden puts this story together with the name danewort and concludes that the truth must be that the plant thrives where Danes have died. After this the tale becomes ever more widely repeated.

British Museum

Fig

The first plant mentioned in the Bible, where it occurs 57 times, is the fig, *Ficus carica*: 'Then the eyes of both of them were opened and they knew that they were naked; and sewed fig leaves together, and made themselves aprons.' Many Biblical references testify to the importance of the fig (as much a symbol of security as a producer of food) such as 'a land of wheat, and barley, and vines and fig trees' and 'every man under his vine and under his fig tree.' Its attractions as a fruit were praised by Mohammed, 'If I should wish a fruit brought to Paradise it would certainly be the fig.'

Besides being man's first garment – an attribute sometimes adopted by sculptors to conceal the private parts of their nude figures – there are legends which suggest that the fig (which belongs to the same family as the mulberry, hop, breadfruit and Indian hemp) was in fact the Forbidden Fruit rather than the apple which is traditionally associated with Eve. This would be in keeping with the mysterious and slightly suggestive appearance of the pear-shaped receptacle commonly referred to as the fruit, inside which are numerous tiny flowers, the only access for pollinating insects being a small opening at the end.

Another fig tree with Biblical associations was one, for centuries pointed out to visitors, under which the Holy Family was supposed to have rested on their flight into Egypt. This gave rise to a legend of a fig opening its trunk as a refuge to Mary and the infant Jesus when pursued by Herod's soldiers. The fig is also one of the many trees on which

Above *Medieval legend identified the elder as the tree on which Judas Iscariot killed himself. The guilt-stricken Judas is shown first contemplating suicide, then hanging from the tree of ill omen.*

Judas is supposed to have hanged himself and hence a plant of ill omen.

Roman mythology brings in the fig several times, although in widely differing contexts. In one legend the Titan Lyceus, pursued by Jupiter, was transformed into a fig tree by Rhea, mother of the gods. Rhea's husband Saturn is elsewhere associated with the fig's creation, and for this reason the inhabitants of Cyrene crowned Saturn's statue with fig-wreaths. Bacchus is credited with creating the fig, which was therefore sacred to him; and certainly, during Bacchanalian festivities, the fig shared the honours with the vine, and Bacchus's virility was credited to it. Female votaries on these occasions wore necklets made from dried figs, while men carried statues of the phallic god Priapus carved from fig wood.

The Romans believed a fig tree to be responsible for the siting of Rome, as the cradle in which Romulus and Remus arrived became lodged in the roots of a fig on the banks of the Tiber. The resulting veneration for the fig can be traced over the space of four centuries.

This sacred tree became known as *Ficus ruminalis*. Ruminus was the surname of Jupiter, provider of mankind's food, while Rumina was goddess of the female breast. This strengthened the Bacchic connection in making the fig symbolic of fecundity and procreation, and it was sacred to Juno as goddess presiding over marriages.

Fir

In mythology references to the fir include not only the true firs but any kind of cone-bearing tree or conifer, and many of these are undoubtedly kinds of pine. The word 'fir' is used in the same way in the Bible. As one of the first timbers to be used for boatbuilding, the pine was sacred to the sea god in classical times.

In Phrygia the pine was sacred to Cybele, 'Mother of the Gods' and the goddess of fertility. Legend tells of her love for Attis, a young shepherd, whom she charged with looking after her temple, making him vow to remain celibate. In one version he fell in love with a nymph and, mad with remorse for neglecting his vow, castrated himself and bled to death beneath a pine. In a Roman version the goddess – now Rhea – prevented his death by turning him into a pine and was only consoled when Jupiter assured her the tree would remain evergreen.

The spring festival of Cybele involved cutting down a pine and carrying it, shrouded corpse-like and decorated with the violets believed to have sprung from Attis's blood, into the sanctuary.

Right *Hazel wands were used for royal sceptres, and traditionally the rods of Moses and Aaron, like those of other priests and magicians, were made of hazel. Illustration from a late 15th-century Book of Hours, showing the miraculous blossoming of Aaron's rod which has grown a lily, symbol of purity.* **Below** *Because of its longevity, and because it is evergreen, the Japanese regard the pine as a symbol of constancy and long life; this concept is reflected in the aged couple, Jo and Uba, the spirits of the pine tree, who are depicted in this Japanese print: Victoria and Albert Museum.*

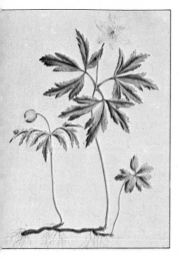

Hazel

The wands of priest and magician are as ancient as mythology itself; there are references to them in Chaldean and Egyptian records. Hazel *(Corylus avellana)* was one of the main plants to be used for wands, and also for royal sceptres. It is to be found as such in Hebrew, classical and Nordic mythology; in Scandinavia it was sacred to Thor, and a protection against lightning. The Romans believed that Mercury was given a hazel rod by Apollo, which he used to calm human passions and improve their virtues. This ancient heraldic staff, or *caduceus*, was imagined as intertwined with serpents and bearing a pair of wings at the top, and was taken over by Asclepius to become the symbol of the medical profession.

Hebrew tradition traces the rod of Moses from one originally cut by Adam in the Garden of Eden, taken by Noah into the Ark, passed down to Shem, Abraham, Isaac and Jacob, given to Joseph and to Moses. Unfortunately, modern translators often turn these hazel wands into almond rods.

The making of a magic wand was inevitably attended by ritual. An old Hebrew tradition stipulates the use of a 'virgin branch' – a young growth with no sideshoots upon it.

Divining rods were also to be cut under very special conditions. They had to be made at night on holy days such as Good Friday, St John's Day, Epiphany or Shrove Tuesday. They could also be made on the first night of a new moon or on the previous night. The cutter had to face east, the rod had to be cut from the eastern side of the tree, and the freshly cut rod had then to be presented to the rays of the rising sun.

There are many lesser beliefs connected with hazel. It was anciently held in Germany to be symbolic of immortality, perhaps because of its end-of-winter flowering. More recently it was linked with happiness in marriage, a belief arising from the paired nuts; at Black Forest weddings the leader of the procession would carry a hazel wand. In medieval England the hazel nut symbolized fertility.

Ireland's lack of poisonous snakes is attributed to St Patrick who, holding a hazel rod, caused all the snakes to come together in one place and then cast them into the sea.

Herbs

The wood anemone has an antique mythology through its more colourful Mediterranean relations. The scarlet anemone is often connected with the death of Adonis, representing his spilling blood after he was mortally wounded by a boar; and red flowers were strewn at the ritual celebrating his death and rebirth dating back to perhaps 3000 BC. Greek legends suggest that Anemos, the Wind, sent his plants – the anemones – as heralds of spring.

Angelica, a stately plant related to cow parsley, is widespread in Europe and was highly valued for medicinal purposes; indeed the root was still listed recently in some European pharmacopoeias. In Eastern Europe there are records of ancient customs in which the plant was carried into towns to the accompaniment of chanting before being offered for sale, which suggests a ritual origin. More recently angelica became associated with the festival of the Annunciation, whence came its Latin specific name – *Angelica archangelica*. It was sometimes linked with St Michael the Archangel and was even called 'The Root of the Holy Ghost'. As such it protected against witchcraft, evil spirits, spells and enchantment.

The main mythological interest in the group of plants named after Asclepius, the founder of medicine, is in that of the soma plant, an Indian native which was personified as Soma, one of the Vedic gods. The ninth book of the *Rig Veda* is devoted to his praise, and here the soma plant is described as the king of the plants. The juice was prepared at a sacred ceremony, by crushing the plant between two millstones, and it was supposed to be a drink of the gods, conferring health, long life and immortality. Under its influence Indra created the universe. In later writings soma became identified with the moon.

Sweet basil is believed by some to have derived its name from the basilisk, the fabulous dragon-like creature that was deadly to anyone who looked at it. This may well be based on an old belief that basil attracted or even begot scorpions. Parkinson (1629) wrote that 'being gently handed it gave a pleasant smell, but being hardly wrung and bruised would breed scorpions'. Culpeper quotes the experience of 'Hilarius,

Above *Anemones, which according to a Greek myth sprang from the blood of Adonis after he was mortally wounded by a boar, were used to cure colds, gout and leprosy; betony, named after Beronice, a woman healed by Christ, was believed to cure almost all ills, both of the body and of the soul, and it was a powerful protection against witchcraft and evil spirits; blackberry brambles were legendarily used by Christ to drive out the money-changers from the temple, and children were at one time passed through a bramble arch as a cure for rickets; bryony, used by witches in spells was taken as a purgative and is still considered a potent aphrodisiac.*

a French physician, who affirms upon his own knowledge, that an acquaintance of his, by common smelling of it (basil), had a scorpion breed in his brain'. Culpeper goes on to assure us that basil, connected with scorpions as it is, will draw the poison out of an insect sting or snake-bite. In India, it was sacred to Vishnu and Krishna, and was regarded as a protective plant – even more than that, as a benificent spirit. A basil leaf on the body of a dead Hindu was his assurance of reaching Paradise. Bush basil, a smaller species, was used in Italy and Moldavia as a love token and in Crete represented 'love washed with tears'. To the Greeks it symbolized hate and misfortune.

Parsley was not regarded by the ancients as a herb; it had connections both noble and funereal. Thus it was made into wreaths at games – dried parsley at the Isthmian games, fresh at the Nemean. The Greeks also strewed it on graves, and the phrase 'to be in need of parsley' meant to be near death.

There is a legend that, because it often takes so long to germinate, it goes nine times to the Devil before appearing above ground. In some places one had to sow it on Good Friday to counteract the Devil's influence, and it was unlucky to sow it at any other time. In some quarters it was thought unlucky to grow parsley at all, and there is still a widespread belief that parsley should never be transplanted. Other sayings suggest, according to locality, that parsley grows best where the wife 'wears the trousers', or for an honest man, or alternatively, only for the wicked. To plant parsley might, if you were a young woman in Lincolnshire, result in your bearing a child.

Mary Evans Picture Library

Holly and Ivy

Two evergreen trees, the holly and the ivy, are regularly linked together. Both are inseparably associated with Christmas. Ivy is the more ancient plant, mythologically speaking, first of all in connection with the god Dionysus, who was born after Zeus had bedded Semele, daughter of Cadmus, King of Thebes. Zeus's wife Hera, in the guise of a nurse, suggested to Semele that she should ask Zeus to unveil himself to her. But when he did the divine flames consumed her, and would have killed the unborn child but for a sudden growth of ivy. Zeus placed the infant in his own thigh until it was ready for birth. Another version of this legend makes Semele abandon the infant under an ivy bush. *Kissos* or *cissos*, the ancient name for ivy, was supposed to have been Dionysus's earliest name. Kissos in another legend is the name of a nymph who danced with such abandon at a Dionysian feast that she collapsed and died of exhaustion before the god; he, grieving at this untimely death, changed her into ivy.

Dionysus (also called Bacchus) was often portrayed with an ivy wreath on his head, and the plant is mentioned in many of the legends associated with him. There was a Dionysus ivy in the Attic town of Acharnae (as there were other trees elsewhere linked with Dionysus as god of trees). Plutarch records that the Bacchae ate ivy and that the resulting intoxication gave rise to their 'inspired fury' (although ivy was later supposed to diminish drunkenness). If the priests of Jupiter even touched ivy this was thought to put them into a prophetic trance.

From its association with Bacchus, god of wine – a reputed source of inspiration – ivy became a suitable plant for a poet's crown; Virgil thought it should be accorded to woodland or bucolic poets rather than urban ones. At one time ivy was the recognized wreath-plant for victors in the Isthmian games held at Corinth, and ivy crowns were also presented at a Spartan festival honouring Hyacinthus. At Greek wedding ceremonies, a wreath of ivy was given by the priest to the newly married couple since – presumably because of its twining propensities – ivy is an ancient symbol of fidelity.

Laurel

The bay, *Laurus nobilis*, is the laurel of mythology, not the cherry laurel, *Prunus laurocerasus*, nor the Alexandrian laurel, *Ruscus racemosus*, with which Paris was once crowned. The Greeks, however, call it Daphne in colloquial speech (although botanically the genus *Daphne* is entirely distinct), recalling the myth in which the unwilling nymph of that name, daughter of the river god Peneus, was amorously pursued by Apollo; she called for help and was transformed into a laurel tree. Apollo, his ardour cooled, crowned his head with the leaves and decreed that the tree should be evergreen and be held sacred to him from that time on.

Apollo's prophetess at Delphi probably chewed laurel leaves and inhaled their smoke from a fire in order to reach a state of inspiration.

Many other oracles, including the one at Dodona, made use of this stimulant. The prophetess was concealed from sight by a barrier of laurel, and those asking her advice were supposed to wear a laurel wreath. Later it was considered sufficient for a prophet to hold a laurel bough to foretell the future; another belief was that a laurel leaf under the pillow would enable the sleeper to foretell the future in dreams. Sprays might be burnt during incantations, and omens could be established from the way the leaves crackled in the flames.

The diarist John Evelyn (1620–1706), repeating these beliefs, added that laurel would also inspire 'poetical fury'.

The Greeks used the laurel wreath to honour poets, military heroes, priests, the victors in the Pythian and Olympian Games and certain high officials. Greek military heralds carried a branch of either laurel or olive, while the Athenian heralds used the Harvest Wreath or *eiresione*, a similar branch bound with wool to which fruits in season would be attached. This wreath was carried in the Harvest Festival procession and was eventually fixed over the farm door for the coming year as an augur of prosperity and success on the land.

The sanctity of laurel was very important to the Romans. As J. G. Frazer tells us, records from Imperial times indicate that magistrates presiding over the games at the Circus, and generals celebrating victory, wore the costume of Jupiter as he appeared enshrined in his Capitol temple. Apart from the special robes and crown, the eagle-topped sceptre and the reddened face attributed to the god, they carried a laurel branch in one hand and a laurel wreath on the head, while the four horses pulling the chariot were likewise crowned with laurel.

Generals not only wore a laurel wreath on returning in triumph but would send their despatches announcing victory in laurel.

Lily

The trumpet-shaped Madonna lily (*Lilium candidum*) is the lily which is usually represented in mythology. Its common name indicates its later importance as a symbol dedicated to the Virgin. Long before the birth of Christ, however, the lily was significant. In early civilizations this flower was a symbol of motherhood and fruitfulness: there are references to it in the mythology of Sumeria, Babylon, Assyria and Egypt. In Crete, where representations of the lily are frequent on pottery, it was sacred to Britomartis, the 'sweet virgin', who was pursued by Minos. After leaping to her apparent doom she was saved in the nets of a fisherman and afterwards became Dictynna, 'mother of the nets' and mother goddess. Both Greeks and Romans placed wreaths of lily and corn – symbols of virginity and fertility – on the heads of brides. To the Greeks the lily was the flower of Hera, who was goddess – among other things – of marriage and childbirth, while the emblem was readily transferred by the Romans to Juno, who had similar responsibilities. One Jewish legend suggested that the lily grew where Eve had shed tears on discovering, after her expulsion from the Garden of Eden, that she was pregnant.

Most of the many references to the lily found in the Bible – the 'lilies of the field' is a well-known example – are probably mis-translations. It seems possible that *Lilium candidum* was once widespread in Palestine; and there is also a red lily, *L. chalcedonicum*, which may once have been abundant. The only passages which appear to refer specifically to these plants occur in the Song of Solomon: the white lily in the verse, 'My beloved has gone to his garden, to the beds of spices, to pasture his flock in the gardens and to gather lilies'; and the red in the verse, 'His cheeks are like beds of spices, yielding fragrance. His lips are lilies, distilling liquid myrrh.' Even in biblical times the lily represented power against evil; when Judith killed the Assyrian general Holofernes, she wore a crown or wreath of lilies.

The sacred associations of the lily led to its use against witches and their spells; it was one of the flowers used in protective magic on the Eve and Feast of St John and lilies were always prominent on that occasion in the city of London.

According to an old superstition, if a man treads upon a lily, he endangers the purity of his wife and daughters.

In the language of flowers the white lily stands for purity or sweetness, but a yellow one for falsehood or gaiety. To dream of lilies means good luck.

Above *Holly, associated with Christmas since the time of the Roman Saturnalia, forms a fitting crown and sceptre for Father Christmas himself.* **Facing page** *The white water-lily of Africa was the sacred lotus of ancient Egypt, a symbol of fertility and resurrection because of its connection with the life-giving river Nile. It was used in funeral rites and offered to the gods, here to the lion-headed Sekhmet.*

Lotus

Osiris, god of the underworld, is usually represented as wearing a crown of lotus blooms, while Horus, in his aspect of god of silence, sits on a flower, Buddha-like, his fingers to his lips. In Egyptian mythology the water-lily represented the newly-created earth, seen in the form of the flower floating on the water, enshrining the mysterious secrets of the gods.

In Hindu mythology the lotus represents the female life principle, and is the symbol of the *yoni* or female generative organs. When the lingam or sacred phallus is depicted, it is often shown resting on or surrounded by lotus petals. The earliest representation of the lotus in art is found among the flowers adorning the head of a statue of an Earth Mother figure (c 3000 BC) discovered at Mohenjo-Daro in the Indus valley. Such a fertility goddess appears later as Lakshmi, the consort of Vishnu, who emerged out of a lotus which sprang from his forehead: she is known also as Padma (lotus). In the form of Kali, she holds the lotus symbol of regeneration in one hand.

In Hindu creation mythology the spirit of the Supreme Being was personified by a golden lotus on a great sea. From Vishnu, the 'lotus-navelled', issued a lotus on which sat Brahma, the 'lotus-born' Creator. The lotus expanded into the universe, and from its petals arose the mountains, hills, valleys and rivers.

Buddha was associated with this flower at his birth, and it was his symbol, topped by a trident representing the sun. From this mythology of creation is obtained the familiar prayer and incantation, inscribed millions of times on prayer-flags and prayer-wheels, 'O, the Jewel in the Lotus'.

The lotus which brought forgetfulness to the Lotus-eaters of Greek legend is a small tree of the buckthorn family, *Zizyphus lotus*, found all round the Mediterranean. The fruits of this tree were, and still are, used for food and can be made into a kind of bread. It was once an important item in the diet of the poor and the word *lotophagi*, lotus-eaters, became synonymous with poverty – a reality considerably less attractive than the myth which grew up around it.

British Museum

British Museum

Mandrake

The main mythology of mandrake concerned its forking roots, which were supposed to resemble the human body in form. The Greeks and Romans had noticed this, calling the plant *Anthropomorphon* and *Semi-homo* respectively. In the old herbals the plant is typically pictured with leaves, flowers and fruits emerging from the head of a bearded man or a long-haired woman; for there were supposed to be both male and female forms, depending on the plant's colouring and girth, sometimes called mandrake and womandrake. Even the later, more accurate botanical drawings, such as those of Pierandrea Mattioli, drew attention to the two forms, and although not literally depicting a human body, made the roots of the plant resemble the trunk and legs of a man or woman.

This resemblance to the human body naturally had sexual connotations. The earliest reflection of the belief in the value of mandrake as an aphrodisiac and an aid to conception is in the biblical passage (Genesis, chapter 30) where 'in the days of wheat harvest Reuben went and found mandrakes in the field, and brought them to his mother Leah.

Then Rachel went and said to Leah, "Give me, I pray, some of your son's mandrakes." But she said to her, "Is it a small matter that you have taken away my husband? Would you take away my son's mandrakes also?" Rachel said, "Then he may lie with you tonight for your son's mandrakes." When Jacob came from the field in the evening,

Left Most of the superstitions about the mandrake had their origin in the supposed resemblance of the forked roots to the human body. If dug up, the plant was believed to utter a shriek fatal to the hearer; it was therefore recommended that it should be pulled up by a dog.

Leah went out to meet him, and said "You must come in to me; for I have hired you with my son's mandrakes." So he lay with her that night. And God hearkened to Leah, and she conceived and bore Jacob a fifth son.'

The Arabs refer to mandrake's supposed aphrodisiac properties by calling it 'apples of jan' or 'devil's apples' because of its supposed power to excite voluptuousness, and they also believe it to help the infertile. In England, it was known as 'love-apple', a name later transferred to the tomato.

It is clear that by Shakespeare's day the mandrake's aphrodisiac attributes had brought the plant into some disrepute. Falstaff refers to Justice Shallow in *Henry IV* Part 2 as 'lecherous as a monkey, and the whores call'd him mandrake'.

Even in Pliny's time, when the root's valuable properties were already known, the collecting of mandrake was accompanied by special ceremony. The herbalist had to stand with his back to the wind, draw three concentric circles around the plant with his sword, pour a libation and then, turning to the west, dig it up with his sword. The plant would otherwise flee away.

In Germany the word *alruna* referred, in the time of the Goths, to both witch and mandrake, and it was the Germans who probably started the practice of making amulets or mannikins of the roots with millet grains as eyes, called alrunes and also puppets or mammets. These were carefully tended, being regularly bathed, dressed and undressed, and were consulted as oracles. Sometimes they were kept in a coffin or a secret cupboard. French peasants believed these amulet figures to be the home of an elf, called *main-de-gloire* or *magloire*. In other countries the spirit had a more monstrous form, such as half chick and half man. If the elf or monster was fed and respected, it gave advice, multiplied riches and so on, but if it were neglected its owner would surely die.

In Italy a mannikin might be worth 30 golden ducats. Mandrake amulets were certainly imported into Britain in large numbers in the reign of Henry VIII. It was probably then that the practice began, only discontinued perhaps a century ago, of cutting fake mandrakes from the massive roots of white bryony, an English plant.

Mandrake was one of the plants reputed to be able to open locks. Another myth about it, recorded by Josephus, is that the plant's leaves shine in the dark and, if one tries to pick them, they fly away. To this day Arabs call the plant 'devil's candles', and Thomas Moore, in *Lalla Rookh*, wrote:

> Such rank and deadly lustre dwells
> As in the hellish fires that light
> The Mandrake's charnel leaves at night.

In the language of flowers, mandrake not surprisingly represents horror – but where would a nice Victorian maiden get one?

Mistletoe

The importance of the mistletoe to Frazer's study was based on the Norse legend of Balder, as recorded in the *Prose Edda*. Balder was the son of Odin, wise, gentle and much loved. He told his fellow gods of dreams which seemed to foretell his death. They gathered together and agreed that the goddess Frigg should extract an oath from every conceivable creature, plant and substance, promising not to harm Balder. This was done and the oaths were tested by striking the god and throwing at him everything possible, and he remained unscathed. However, the resentful god Loki was angry and jealous of Balder.

Disguised as an old woman, he managed to trick Frigg into admitting that she had not troubled to gain an assurance from the mistletoe, because it seemed too young to take an oath. Loki went away, gathered mistletoe, and rejoined the gods, who were still amusing themselves proving Balder's invulnerability. He spoke to blind Hoder and asked if he would not like to join in and, in effect, do honour to Balder. He gave Hoder the mistletoe branch and directed his aim: the branch struck home and the helpless Balder fell dead.

The god was ceremonially cremated at sea, amid universal mourning.

Frazer wrote that the tale 'suggests that it belongs to that class of myths that have been dramatized in ritual'. He sets out to illustrate that the main incidents – the cutting of the mistletoe, followed by the death and burning of the god – had many counterparts in primitive rites.

In certain parts of Scandinavia, mistletoe was until very recently, and perhaps still is, gathered for the Midsummer festival, when bonfires called *Balder's Balar* (Balder's balefires) are lit. Almost certainly an effigy of Balder was burned on these fires in former times.

It seems likely that burning an effigy was a more civilized version of an older custom of burning a human representative of the god, the end – according to Frazer – of 'the sacred drama which was acted year by year as a magical rite to cause the sun to shine, trees to grow, crops to thrive, and to guard man and beast from the baleful arts of fairies and trolls, of witches and warlocks.' The victims died 'as living embodiments of tree-spirits or deities of vegetation'. Such a sacrifice was, the historian Strabo recounted carried out in remote ages in Italy at a Midsummer fire festival in the Arician Grove or Glade of Diana, where the one-year King of the Wood was burned on a perpetual fire that was doubtless fed with oak-wood as would be most fitting.

Frazer argued that Balder must have been a tree deity, the personification of the oak. And the sacred oak had to be burned, just as the god had to die, for the good of man. The evergreen mistletoe represented the life-spring of the oak-tree, so before burning the tree the mistletoe had to be ceremonially removed to preserve its virtues; in any case if the mistletoe were not cut off, the oak would remain invulnerable.

Mushroom

The mushroom which is named *A. muscaria* – popularly 'Fly agaric' – has now been proved by Gordon Wasson's detailed examination of the Vedic hymns to have been the food of the gods. It is there named 'soma'. That it is also 'ambrosia' and 'nectar' (both these words mean 'immortal'), famous as food and drink of the Greek Olympian gods, had been shown some 12 years previously.

Two early Greek poets, Sappho and Alcman, had preserved the ancient tradition of ambrosia as a drink, not a food. This was because the juice of the mushroom – which lost its virtue when cooked – was squeezed out of it between boards, then mixed with milk or curds, and the pulp was thrown away. According to the Vedic hymns, Agni the Hindu god of mystic illumination and holy fire, who was also expressly identified with the sacred drink soma, had been created when the father god Indra threw a lightning bolt at the earth.

Dionysus, the Greek god of mystic illumination among other things, was also born when his father the god Zeus threw a lightning bolt at the earth goddess Semele; the bolt killed Semele but her child was saved and sewn up in his father's thigh, whence he was later granted a second birth. Dionysus is said to have eventually conducted his mother to heaven where she changed her name to Thyone, meaning 'queen of the maenads' (or raging women) and presided over Dionysus' ecstatic October festival, called 'the Ambrosia'. October was the mushroom season. The effect of the *A. muscaria* taken without other intoxicants is to give the taker the most delightful hallucinations, if he is in a state of grace, but horrible nightmares otherwise. Fortified, however, with beer and the juice of yellow ivy it would send Greek men and women mad.

Mansell Collection

National Museum, Guatemala

Above *Sculptural representation of the hallucinogenic mushroom of the Mexicans.* **Right** *The juice of 'Fly agaric'*, Amanita muscaria, *may have been the principal ingredient in soma, the drink of the ancient Indian gods, and in the ambrosia of the Greeks.* **Left** *Victorian modesty under the mistletoe; but the ancient symbolism of this custom was that to be kissed under the mistletoe ensured fertility.*

The pre-classical priests of Dionysus, a god now known to have been active in Mycenean times, seem to have claimed sole rights in this scarlet mushroom, the memory of which they had brought from their original homes in central Asia and which is not found growing further south towards the Equator, except at a great height and always in birch groves. The Vedic priests of Agni seem to have imported their supply from the groves of the high Himalayas. Throughout the world mushrooms were believed to be begotten only by lightning.

That Dionysus was ambrosia, as his Indian counterpart Agni was soma, is proved by the legend of his birth from Zeus's thigh. The Vedic hymns make it clear that the priests of Indra and Agni used the two different ways of taking soma still found among the paleo-Siberians called Koryaks, and also in a small Mongol enclave of Afghanistan.

When, according to the Greek myth, the corn goddess Demeter visited Eleusis, the Attic city where the famous Mysteries were to be celebrated for another 2000 years, she is reputed to have ordered Triptolemus, son of the local king, to drive around the civilized world in a chariot drawn by snakes, spreading the arts of agriculture as he went. This myth is clearly deceptive. Corn had been sown and harvested in Palestine for several thousands of years before Demeter's arrival at Eleusis. What may have happened is that the local priestess sent a message about the newly-discovered mushroom to priests and priestesses throughout the civilized world – hence the explanation of the snakes in Triptolemus's chariot.

Why mushrooms were called 'toad's bread' or 'toadstools' by mycophobes can readily be explained. When the toad is attacked or scared the warts on its back exude *bufonenin*, the same poison that is secreted in the white hallucinogenic warts of the *A. muscaria*. In ancient Greece the toad was the emblem of Argolis, the leading state of the Peloponnese. The capital city was Mycene ('mushroom city') said to have been built by the legendary king Phoroneus's successor Perseus ('the destroyer') who had found a mushroom growing on the site beside a spring of water. The toad was also the emblem of Tlaloc, the Mexican god of inspiration, and appears surrounded by mushrooms in an Aztec mural painting of Tlalocan, his paradise.

The Slavs are not mycophobic probably because their remote ancestors were nomadic on the treeless steppes and unacquainted with the *A. muscaria*. Their fermented mare's milk satisfied their need for occasional intoxication.

Hodder & Stoughton/Colourcel

Oak

From primitive times to those of the Druids the oak, strong, durable and very long lived, was undoubtedly the chief sacred tree all over Europe and Scandinavia. The oak was associated with the myth of Balder because the sacred mistletoe, the mysterious 'golden bough' by which the Scandinavian god was slain, grew on its branches. Balder was perhaps a later version of a tree deity, who had to be sacrificed in order to ensure fertility of crops and men. In later times this ritual was worked into a kind of mummers' play associated with May Day, in which the tree spirit, enveloped in leafy oak boughs, was executed.

Several references in the Bible indicate that oaks were important to the earliest worshippers of Yahweh, as when Jacob buries the 'foreign gods' and the ear-rings of his household under the oak of Shechem (Genesis 35.4).

The much despised followers of Baal sacrificed below an oak tree or in an oak grove – 'under every leafy oak, wherever they offered pleasing odour to all their idols' (Ezekiel 6.13).

One of the most famous oracles of ancient Greece, that of Zeus at Dodona in the northeast, was in an oak wood, and the priestess had her temple under an enormous oak, the rustling of whose leaves she interpreted in answer to questions. The Argonauts' ship, Argo, was built of oaks from this grove, and one timber could speak and advise the voyagers. Socrates swore by the oak, as the sacred oracle tree; Homer describes how people made solemn agreements under an oak because it was a place of security; and oak wreaths were worn by those taking part in the Mysteries of Eleusis at the temple of Demeter.

A possible parallel with the Balder myth may be seen in ancient Italy, where in the Arician Grove there lived the King of the Wood. The same grove was also the home of the water nymph Egeria, described by Plutarch as one of the oak nymphs who lived in every oak grove. Egeria married King Numa in the sacred grove. J.G. Frazer considered this 'a reminiscence of a sacred marriage which the old Roman kings regularly contracted with a goddess of vegetation and water for the purpose of enabling him to discharge his divine or magical functions', and pointed out 'how very often in early society the king is held responsible for the fall of rain and the fruitfulness of the earth'. In Roman times oak boughs were carried at weddings to ensure a fruitful marriage.

Later on, the oak became the sacred tree of the Romans, and Jupiter was reputedly sheltered by an oak at his birth. Acorns were widely held to have been the first of man's foods and legend tells how Ceres – the Roman goddess chiefly of agriculture – replaced them with corn; to recognize man's debt to the acorn, oak was worn at festivals in honour of Ceres and by reapers as they harvested. Romans who had saved the life of a fellow citizen were granted an oak leaf crown.

Olive

In Greek legend Athene (Minerva to the Romans and Etruscans) was responsible for having made the olive bear fruit. Virgil referred to her as *Oleae inventrix*. When she and Poseidon were disputing for the possession of Attica, Poseidon caused a saltwater spring to gush from the rock of the Acropolis on striking it with his trident (another legend suggests that he created a horse). Athene, however, caused an olive tree to appear, and this was considered by the gods to be the more valuable gift. So the city of Athens got its name, and the Athenians adopted Athene as their particular goddess. Goats were the special sacrifice to Athene because of the harm they did to olives (as to most vegetation).

The olive on the Acropolis was burnt by Xerxes when he sacked Athens in 480 BC but it reappeared as if by magic. There is still an olive on the Acropolis. Herodotus tells how Xerxes, before his Greek expedition, dreamt that he was crowned with an olive wreath which instantly vanished, and indeed his was a hollow victory. The Athenians revered the sacred olive and severely punished anyone who damaged it. Olive was used for victors' crowns at the Olympic Games, and was equal to the laurel.

Olive was also one of the symbols of the Greek harvest festival, represented in more recent times by a symbolic tree branch known as the Harvest-May. The *eiresione*, a branch of olive or laurel decorated with fruits of the earth and bedecked with ribbons, was carried in procession and finally fixed over the farm door. Here it was left for a year, guaranteeing the successful growth of further crops.

Medieval Christians had many legends about the olive. One of the basic – if very variable – ones was that when Adam died the angel guarding the garden of Eden – the first orchard – gave Seth a seed each of olive, cedar and cypress. These were placed in Adam's mouth and eventually sprouted from his grave, forming a single triple-trunked tree. It was from this tree that Noah's dove plucked the symbolic leaf, beneath this tree that David wept, and it was this tree that Solomon cut down. Too hard to be formed into timber, it was used as a bridge on which the Queen of Sheba crossed a bog. Eventually it formed the basis of the Cross.

Palm

The Bible relates how 'branches of palm trees' (the huge individual branch-like fronds) were carried on special occasions, as in Revelation 7.9, where they become a symbol of martyrdom: 'And after this I looked, and behold, a great multitude...standing before the throne...clothed in white robes, with palm branches in their hands.' It was in the time of Judas Maccabeus, when the Temple was restored, that it first became customary to carry palm fronds in procession. The fronds – known as 'lulab' or 'lulav' – would be interlaced with myrtle on the right side and citron on the left, and after being carried at the Feast of the Tabernacles were preserved at home where they brought luck and protection in the coming year. In an earlier palm festival the Jews had made cabins of the fronds outside their townships, in which they passed a holiday week notable for family reunions, in memory of the 40 years of camp life in the wilderness, before they reached the Promised Land. Among Christians the carrying of fronds – and the English 'palm', which is the pussy willow – on Palm Sunday is a recollection of that day when Jesus entered Jerusalem and the people waved palms and strewed his path with them. Today in many Christian Mediterranean countries the palm frond is represented by a cross of palm pieces carried in the hand or stuck into one's hat.

Early Christian martyrs believed that angels brought palm fronds to carry their souls up to heaven. It later became the custom to make a fire of palm fronds on All Souls' Day; the smoke was supposed to assist souls from purgatory to reach heaven.

Pilgrims would often carry a staff of palm and were consequently known as palmers. This explains Helena's question in Shakespeare's *All's Well That Ends Well* (Act III, Sc. 5) 'Where do the palmers lodge, I do beseech you?' The palm was also a symbol of victory, as is apparent in a number of other Shakespearean quotations. In *Coriolanus* (Act V, Sc. 3) Volumnia says in scorn:

And bear the palm for having bravely shed wife and children's blood...

Below *As an emblem of peace and reconciliation, the olive was adopted as a Christian symbol: early Christian sign of a bird with an olive branch in its beak, from a Roman catacomb.*

incontra ueneno alfo fegnoze
ige fan logrande honoze
icom in la fcripuira fe troua fcripto
in ge fen quel honoz ku uedito.

British Museum

Rowan

The mountain ash or rowan, *Sorbus aucuparia*, is among the plants most positively protective against witchcraft and evil, especially in the temperate countries of the North, where it is most abundant. It is reputed to have been one of the sacred trees of the Druids, because it is so often found in and near ancient stone circles. It appears earliest in Scandinavian myth, where it was called Thor's Helper, since it once assisted him to cross a difficult river. The wood of this tree was used in the construction of Viking ships, to protect them from Ran, the enemy of seamen. A similar belief in the protective power of the rowan was held in Britain, and there is a reference in the ballad of 'The Laidley Worm of Spindleston Heughs' to the Child of Wynd's ship having a mast of rowan so that the evil queen's witch hags could not harm it.

In Wales, it was believed that the mountain ash had furnished the Holy Cross, and for this reason it was widely planted in cemeteries. The 17th-century diarist John Evelyn wrote, 'this tree is reputed so sacred that there is not a churchyard without one of them planted in it...on a certain day in the year, everyone religiously wears a cross of the wood'. Apart from restraining evil, rowan planted among the graves kept the dead from rising prematurely.

In general, a rowan tree near a house was thought lucky and protective; to cut it down brought misfortune.

In some areas a day known as Rowan-Tree Day, or Rowan-Tree Witch Day was celebrated at the beginning of May, at the time of the old Beltane festival. On that day the branches of rowan needed for protective purposes were brought home. To be really effective, they had to be taken from a mountain ash which the person concerned had neither seen nor heard of previously, and had to be brought home by a different route from the outward one. It was worth the trouble, however, because the rowan so gathered afforded every building and its inmates protection for a year. After fastening the twigs in all the appropriate places, bonfires would be lit.

Rowan was often used instead of hazel for water divining and tracing hidden treasure. In folk medicine whooping cough and other ailments could be cured by pushing some of the sufferer's hair into a cut in a mountain ash trunk, and the berries were prized to ease childbirth.

Among the many alternative names of this tree are Quick Beam and Quicken, similar names occurring in some Germanic languages. 'Quick' is used in the sense of living, and we can therefore presume it was originally a tree deity. This is shown in Irish folklore, and in the story of Diarmaid and Grania the tree's fairy guardian is described – with crooked teeth, large nose, black face and one red eye. Although he has sought the guardian's permission to shelter in the wood, Diarmaid kills him in order to acquire the magic berries which had the power of restoring anyone who ate them to the age of 30.

Above *Christ's entry into Jerusalem, from a 14th-century manuscript: the palm was also traditionally one of the four woods from which the cross was made, and was said to have formed the piece to which Christ's hands were nailed.* **Below** *'This tree is reputed so sacred that there is not a churchyard without one of them planted in it': rowan, or mountain ash, which later produces orange berries.*

Royal Botanical Gardens

Willow

A traditional emblem of grief and melancholy, the willow is also a symbol of forsaken love, and it was once customary for the jilted to wear a willow garland. In *The Merchant of Venice* Shakespeare describes the forsaken Queen of Carthage:

> In such a night
> Stood Dido, with a willow in her hand,
> Upon the wild sea-banks. . . .

Ophelia hangs her symbolic bunch of wild flowers upon a willow that 'grows aslant a brook', and Desdemona sings 'a song of "willow"' about a jilted girl.

It was not only the jilted but the bereaved who should wear the willow. In *Henry IV* (Part 3) when Bona, sister of the Queen of France, hears of Edward IV's marriage with Elizabeth Grey, she says: 'Tell him, in hope he'll prove a widower shortly, I'll wear the willow-garland for his sake.'

The association with grief dates only from the late Middle Ages; there is little doubt that the biblical 'willows' upon which the exiled Jews hung their harps as they wept by the rivers of Babylon were the Euphrates aspen, a kind of poplar. Even the 18th-century Swedish botanist Linnaeus was misled by the Bible into christening the weeping willow, which actually comes from China, *Salix babylonica*.

There is, however, an ancient association between the willow and death. In the 2nd century AD Pausanias, the Greek historian, wrote of a grove sacred to Persephone, queen of the underworld, where willow and poplars grew, and also describes Orpheus holding a willow branch in the underworld. On the island of the enchantress Circe there was said to be a grove of willows, from which corpses hung. In China coffins were covered with willow boughs, and the trees were planted in cemeteries to suggest immortality. The Chinese also considered the tree to be magical and capable of averting harm and illness, a belief that is also found in Ireland, where the pussy willow, one of the 'seven noble trees of the land', was a charm against enchantment.

Because of its ancient sacredness the willow is one of the trees that should be invoked when a person 'touches wood'. The pussy willow provided the English substitute for palm branches in churches on Palm Sunday. It is sometimes thought to be unlucky to take the catkins or 'pussies' indoors, but more often this is said to bring good luck, especially if they are brought into the house on May Day.

Yew

The evergreen yew lives to an immense age for it can continue to grow with a completely hollow centre. It has been claimed that the tree can survive for over 3000 years, but this seems unlikely. However, like other conifers, it has an ancient reputation for immortality and became a symbol of life after death. Mourners carried yew branches at funerals, which were placed in the grave; and shoots of yew were sometimes put in a dead person's shroud.

As a symbol of the Resurrection, yew was often incorporated in Eastertide church decorations and used on Palm Sunday. However, it was considered unlucky to bring it into a house, and for this reason it is not used for Christmas decorations. Because of its sacred associations, in Ireland yew wood was made into croziers and shrines. While a common yew was valued at 15 pence in the Middle Ages, a consecrated yew was worth a pound.

It was most unlucky to cut down or damage a growing yew tree; this is not surprising for the yew was among the most potent of trees for protection against evil, and was therefore often planted alongside a house or where it might form a windbreak against the invisible wind as well as against the unknown powers of evil. Doubtless its planting in churchyards was largely to prevent witchcraft and to restrain the spirits of the buried dead.

However, Robert Turner, writing in 1664, suggested that its main function in churchyards was that it 'attracts and imbibes putrefaction and gross oleaginous vapours exhaled out of the Graves by the setting Sun, and sometimes drawn into those Meteors called *Ignes Fatui*'. Its protectiveness presumably arose from its longevity, its very tough timber, and its red 'berries'. It was, of course, also prized for making bows, although most English bows were made from imported yew, for the native variety was often too brittle and too full of knots. The most antique wooden weapons known are early Paleolithic spears made from yew.

The yew cannot be called a cheerful tree, although its autumn display of what Wordsworth called 'unrejoicing berries' is spectacular. Its churchyard affinities have given it funereal associations, and it was also considered a malign tree, perhaps because its foliage is poisonous. Because of this, and because weapons were made from it, Shakespeare referred to it as 'double-fatal' (*Richard II*). It seems likely that the 'cursed ebenon' referred to by the ghost in *Hamlet* is of yew; Marlowe also mentions 'juice of hebon' in *The Jew of Malta*.

Associated with death by the ancient Greeks, the willow is traditionally an emblem of forsaken love; in Hamlet *Ophelia hangs her wild flowers on a 'willow . . . aslant a brook' before drowning herself: painting by Millais.*

Appendix

Cypress

A graveyard tree, symbolic of death and, because it is evergreen, of resurrection; associated with powers of the underworld by the Greeks and Romans. According to various stories, the cross on which Christ was crucified, the pillars of Solomon's Temple, the club of Hercules and the arrows of Cupid were made of cypress wood.

Maize

Or corn, staple food plant of many American Indian peoples, and so an important focus of lore and ritual; often personified as Corn Mother or Corn Maiden, with a myth about her seasonal disappearance and return.

Beech

The 16th-century herbalist Gerard says, 'the wood is hard and firm, which being brought into the house there follows hard travail of child and miserable deaths'; in ancient Greece the sacred grove of Zeus at Dodona was of beeches and oaks.

Birch

Sacred to the Scandinavian god Thor and a symbol of spring; a branch of birch on a house was thought to protect the family.

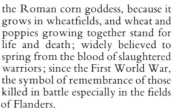

Myrtle

As an evergreen, connected with death and resurrection; Greek emigrants carried myrtle boughs to the founding of a new colony as a symbol of the end of one life and the beginning of another; said to have been the principal scented tree of Eden; sacred to love goddesses in the Mediterranean area, and generally considered lucky in Europe and connected with fertility, love and marriage.

Poppy

Symbol of sleep, death and the soothing of pain, because it yields opium; it was connected with Ceres,

the Roman corn goddess, because it grows in wheatfields, and wheat and poppies growing together stand for life and death; widely believed to spring from the blood of slaughtered warriors; since the First World War, the symbol of remembrance of those killed in battle especially in the fields of Flanders.

Rice

The staple diet of many oriental communities, its cultivation, from sowing to threshing, is often accompanied by elaborate ceremony; in Japan plays are performed and prayers are said, to propitiate the spirits and ensure a good harvest; and among certain tribes in Southeast Asia rice is said to have a soul to which sacrifices must be offered; in the West an ancient symbol of fertility, it is still thrown over newly married couples to bring them good luck and prosperity.

Rosemary

A holy and magical plant in folklore, protecting against evil spirits, fairies, witches and storms; symbol of remembrance, it used to be carried by mourners at a funeral and dropped on the coffin to show that the dead

person would not be forgotten; sprigs of it were dropped in the wine at a wedding feast before the bride and groom drank, as a token of faithfulness and lasting devotion in love.

Tree of Life

The concept of the universe as a tree is best known in its Scandinavian form, where the ash, Yggdrasil, is the world tree, but also appears in other traditions, in some of which the cosmic tree bears fruits which the gods eat to ensure their immortality; the Garden of Eden contained the tree of life (Genesis, chapter 2); in the Cabala, the Tree of Life is a diagram of God, man and the universe.

Vine

Through its connection with intoxicating wine, often linked with life-energy and a state of closeness to the divine; plant of Dionysus as god of wine. In the Old Testament God's people are the vine which he brought out of Egypt and tended (Psalm 80, Isaiah, chapter 5); Jesus said, 'I am the true vine, and my Father is the vinedresser ... I am the vine, you are the branches' (John, chapter 15).

Wand

As symbols of authority, the wand and the rod can be traced back to the staffs of the priest kings and magician healers of antiquity. The sceptre is an old symbol of kingship. A herald, the inviolable emissary of a king, carried a staff of office, and the caduceus of the Greek god Hermes was his herald's wand.

Index

ACKNOWLEDGMENTS

Jacket front:
Tutankhamen in the guise of Osiris, Egyptian god of the dead; he was thus depicted in the hope that he would live again. Painting on the wall of Tutankhamen's tomb at Luxor, mid 14th century BC (William MacQuitty).

Jacket back:
Horse and rider worked in silver on a helmet found in the tomb of a Thracian chief, 4th century (Bucharest National Museum of Antiquities; C.M. Dixon).

Case:
Chinese 18th century embroidery pattern showing heavenly spirit with flowers (Pearl Binder).

Endpapers:
Chinese 16th century tapestry hanging showing a pair of phoenixes among peonies and rocks; the Chinese phoenix was a heavenly emissary. (Victoria and Albert Museum; Michael Holford).

Page 5:
Gawain taking leave of Arthur and Guinivere before setting out on a quest, 15th century (Bodleian Library Colour Filmstrip).

Pages 6–7:
Giant columns of mythical warrior figures at Quetzalcoatl's temple at Tula, the ancient capital of the Toltecs, 9th century (Werner Forman).

Pages 8–9:
Rama, with bow and arrows, attempting to retrieve his consort from a rival; from a wall painting of the *Ramayana* painting in the Raja's Palace at Cochin, 17th century (Werner Forman).